1학기 전과정

적중"100plus

영어 기출문제집

중2

천재 | 정사열

Best Collection

구성과 특징

교과서의 주요 학습 내용을 중심으로 학습 영역별 특성에 맞춰 단계별로 다양한 학습 기회를 제공하여
단원별 학습능력 평가는 물론 중간 및 기말고사 시험 등에 완벽하게 대비할 수 있도록 내용을 구성

Words & Expressions

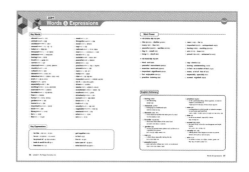

Step1	Key Words 단원별 핵심 단어 설명 및 풀이
	Key Expression 단원별 핵심 숙어 및 관용어 설명
	Word Power 반대 또는 비슷한 뜻 단어 배우기
	English Dictionary 영어로 배우는 영어 단어
Step2	실력평가 단원별 수시평가 대비 주관식, 객관식 문제풀이
Step3	서술형 대비 학업성취도 및 수행능력평가 대비 서술형 문제풀이

Conversation

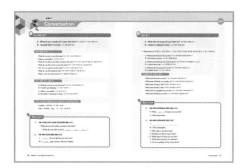

Step1	핵심 의사소통 소통에 필요한 주요 표현 방법 요약
	핵심 Check 기본적인 표현 방법 및 활용능력 확인
Step2	대화문 익히기 교과서 대화문 심층 분석 및 확인
Step3	교과서 확인학습 빈칸 채우기를 통한 문장 완성 능력 확인
Step4	기본평가 시험대비 기초 학습 능력 평가
Step5	실력평가 단원별 수시평가 대비 주관식, 객관식 문제풀이
Step6	서술형 대비 학업성취도 및 수행능력평가 대비 서술형 문제풀이

Grammar

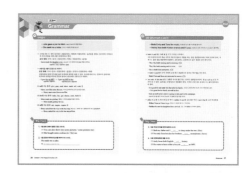

Step1	주요 문법 단원별 주요 문법 사항과 예문을 알기 쉽게 설명
	핵심 Check 기본 문법사항에 대한 이해 여부 확인
Step2	기본평가 시험대비 기초 학습 능력 평가
Step3	실력평가 단원별 수시평가 대비 주관식, 객관식 문제풀이
Step4	서술형 대비 학업성취도 및 수행능력평가 대비 서술형 문제풀이

Reading

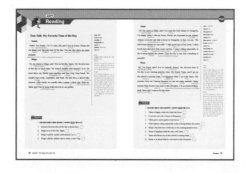

Step1	구문 분석 단원별로 제시된 문장에 대한 구문별 분석과 내용 설명
	확인문제 문장에 대한 기본적인 이해와 인지능력 확인
Step2	확인학습A 빈칸 채우기를 통한 문장 완성 능력 확인
Step3	확인학습B 제시된 우리말을 영어로 완성하여 작문 능력 키우기
Step4	실력평가 단원별 수시평가 대비 주관식, 객관식 문제풀이
Step5	서술형 대비 학업성취도 및 수행능력평가 대비 서술형 문제풀이
	교과서 구석구석 교과서에 나오는 기타 문장까지 완벽 학습

Composition

|영역별 핵심문제|

단어 및 어휘, 대화문, 문법, 독해 등 각 영역별 기출문제의 출제 유형을 분석하여 실전에 대비하고 연습할 수 있도록 문제를 배열

|단원별 예상문제|

기출문제를 분석한 후 새로운 시험 출제 경향을 더하여 새롭게 출제될 수 있는 문제를 포함하여 시험에 완벽하게 대비할 수 있도록 준비

|서술형 실전 및 창의사고력 문제|

학교 시험에서 점차 늘어나는 서술형 시험에 집중 대비하고 고득점을 취득하는데 만전을 기하기 위한 학습 코너

|단원별 모의고사|

영역별, 단계별 학습을 모두 마친 후 실전 연습을 위한 모의고사

on the textbook

교과서 파헤치기

- 단어Test1~3 영어 단어 우리말 쓰기, 우리말을 영어 단어로 쓰기, 영영풀이에 해당하는 단어와 우리말 쓰기
- 대화문Test1~2 대화문 빈칸 완성 및 전체 대화문 쓰기
- 본문Test1~5 빈칸 완성, 우리말 쓰기, 문장 배열연습, 영어 작문하기 복습 등 단계별 반복 학습을 통해 교과서 지문에 대한 완벽한 습득
- 구석구석지문Test1~2 지문 빈칸 완성 및 전문 영어로 쓰기

이책의 차례

Contents

Lesson ①	Time to Start Again	05~56
Lesson ②	I Love My Town!	57~108
Lesson ③	Be Active, Be Safe!	109~160
Lesson ④	Memories in Your Heart	161~212
Special Lesson	Little Red Writing Hood	213~228

〈Insight on the textbook〉 교과서 파헤치기   01~95

〈책 속의 책〉 정답 및 해설   01~56

Time to Start Again

 의사소통 기능

- 의견 묻기
  What do you think of this diary?

- 희망 · 기대 표현하기
  I can't wait for his birthday party!

 언어 형식

- to부정사의 형용사적 용법
  Do you have something **to say**?

- 접속사 that
  I think **(that)** I lost it.

Words & Expressions

교과서

Key Words

- **activity** [æktívəti] 명 활동
- **always** [ɔ́:lweiz] 부 항상
- **anyway** [éniwèi] 부 어쨌든
- **bell** [bel] 명 종
- **boring** [bɔ́:riŋ] 형 지루한 (↔ interesting)
- **busy** [bízi] 형 바쁜
- **cafeteria** [kæfətíəriə] 명 카페테리아, 구내식당
- **class** [klæs] 명 수업
- **continue** [kəntínju:] 동 계속하다 (↔ stop)
- **cool** [ku:l] 형 멋진, 시원한
- **corner** [kɔ́:rnər] 명 구석
- **cover** [kʌ́vər] 명 표지
- **delicious** [dilíʃəs] 형 맛있는 (= tasty, yummy)
- **diary** [dáiəri] 명 수첩, 일기
- **dish** [diʃ] 명 접시, 요리
- **excited** [iksáitid] 형 흥분한, 신이 난
- **exciting** [iksáitiŋ] 형 신나는, 흥미진진한
- **fan** [fæn] 명 팬, 부채
- **final** [fáinl] 명 결승전
- **floor** [flɔ:r] 명 바닥 (↔ ceiling)
- **fresh** [freʃ] 형 신선한
- **grow** [grou] 동 기르다, 재배하다
- **hard** [ha:rd] 부 열심히, 어려운
- **health** [helθ] 명 건강
- **homeroom teacher** 담임선생님
- **hurry** [hə́:ri] 동 서둘러 가다, 서두르다
- **interesting** [íntərəstiŋ] 형 재미있는 (↔ boring 지루한)
- **join** [dʒɔin] 동 가입하다
- **judge** [dʒʌdʒ] 동 판단하다
- **kind** [kaind] 형 친절한 (= friendly)
- **magic** [mǽdʒik] 명 마법, 마술
- **math** [mæθ] 명 수학
- **mean** [mi:n] 동 의미하다
- **note** [nout] 명 메모
- **pleased** [pli:zd] 형 기쁜 (= glad)
- **post** [poust] 동 게시[공고]하다
- **practice** [prǽktis] 동 연습하다
- **present** [préznt] 명 선물 (= gift)
- **problem** [prábləm] 명 문제
- **realize** [rí:əlàiz] 동 깨닫다
- **really** [rí:əli] 부 정말
- **remember** [rimémbər] 동 기억하다 (↔ forget 잊다)
- **reply** [riplái] 동 대답하다
- **right** [rait] 형 맞는 (↔ wrong), 알맞은
- **saying** [séiiŋ] 명 속담 (= proverb)
- **serious** [síəriəs] 형 진지한
- **serve** [sə:rv] 동 제공하다
- **shout** [ʃaut] 동 외치다
- **solve** [salv] 동 풀다, 해결하다
- **strict** [strikt] 형 엄격한
- **take** [teik] 동 데리고 가다, 가져가다
- **ticket** [tíkit] 명 표, 입장권
- **together** [təgéðər] 부 함께
- **trick** [trik] 명 마술, 속임수
- **trust** [trʌst] 동 믿다
- **word** [wə:rd] 명 말, 단어

Key Expressions

- **after school** 방과 후에
- **be good for** ~에 좋다
- **bump into** ~에 부딪히다
- **can't wait for** ~이 몹시 기다려지다
- **come over** 오다
- **cut in on** (말·대화에) 끼어들다
- **find out** ~을 알게 되다
- **happen to+동사원형** 우연히 ~하게 되다
- **look for** ~을 찾다
- **lots of** 많은
- **on one's way to** ~으로 가는 길에[도중에]
- **pay someone back** ~에게 신세를 갚다
- **play the ukulele** 우쿨렐레를 연주하다
- **right now** 당장
- **think of** ~에 대해 생각하다
- **think to oneself** 마음속으로 생각하다
- **this way** 이런 식으로
- **this year** 올해

Word Power

※ 현재분사(-ing)와 과거분사(-ed)형 형용사

□ **amazing** (놀라운, 굉장한) – **amazed** (대단히 놀란)

□ **boring** (지루한) – **bored** (지루해하는)

□ **disappointing** (실망시키는) – **disappointed** (실망한)

□ **exciting** (흥미진진한) – **excited** (들뜬, 흥분한)

□ **interesting** (흥미로운) – **interested** (흥미 있어 하는)

□ **satisfying** (만족하게 하는) – **satisfied** (만족하는)

□ **surprising** (놀라운) – **surprised** (놀란)

□ **tiring** (피곤하게 만드는) – **tired** (피곤한, 지친)

English Dictionary

□ **cafeteria** 구내식당
→ a restaurant where you choose and pay for your meal at a counter and carry it to a table
카운터에서 선택하고 식사비를 지불하고 그것을 테이블로 가지고 가는 식당

□ **cover** 표지
→ the outer part of a book or magazine
책이나 잡지의 바깥 부분

□ **dish** 접시
→ a shallow container that you cook or serve food in
요리하거나 음식을 제공하는 데 쓰는 얕은 그릇

□ **fan** 팬
→ a person who admires someone or something or enjoys watching or listening to someone or something very much
누군가 또는 무언가를 동경하거나 누군가 또는 무언가를 보거나 듣는 것을 즐기는 사람

□ **final** 결승전
→ the last and most important game or race in a competition
시합에서 마지막이자 가장 중요한 경기 또는 경주

□ **grow** 재배하다
→ to make plants grow
식물을 자라게 하다

□ **hurry** 서두르다, 서둘러 가다
→ to move, act, or go quickly
급히 움직이거나 행동하거나 가다

□ **judge** 판단하다
→ to form an opinion about something or someone after careful thought
주의 깊이 생각한 후에 무언가 또는 누군가에 대한 견해를 형성하다

□ **magic** 마술
→ the art of doing tricks that seem impossible in order to entertain people
사람들을 즐겁게 하기 위해 불가능해 보이는 재주를 부리는 기술

□ **post** 게시[공고]하다
→ to put up a sign, notice, etc. so that it can be seen by many people
많은 사람이 볼 수 있도록 표지판, 게시문 등을 붙이다

□ **realize** 깨닫다
→ to understand or become aware of something
어떤 것을 이해하거나 알게 되다

□ **reply** 대답하다
→ to say or write something as an answer to someone or something
누군가 또는 무언가에 대한 대답으로 무언가를 말하거나 쓰다

□ **saying** 속담
→ an old and well-known phrase that expresses an idea that most people believe is true
대부분의 사람이 옳다고 믿고 있는 생각을 표현하는 오래되고 유명한 어구

□ **serve** 제공하다
→ to give food or drink to someone at a meal, in a restaurant, etc.
음식점 따위에서 식사할 때 음식이나 음료수를 사람에게 주다

□ **strict** 엄격한
→ demanding that rules, especially rules about behavior, should be obeyed
규칙, 특히 행동에 대한 규칙을 따라야 한다고 요구하는

□ **trust** 믿다
→ to believe that someone is honest or will not do anything bad or wrong
누군가가 정직하거나 또는 나쁘거나 잘못된 일을 하지 않을 것이라고 믿다

01 다음 중 짝지어진 단어의 관계가 나머지 넷과 <u>다른</u> 것은?

① present : gift ② right : wrong

③ kind : friendly ④ pleased : glad

⑤ delicious : tasty

02 다음 우리말에 맞도록 빈칸에 알맞은 것은?

> 너는 10분 후에 알게 될 거야.
> ➡ You'll find _____ in 10 minutes.

① up ② out

③ with ④ into

⑤ over

03 다음 영영풀이에 해당하는 단어로 알맞은 것은?

> to put up a sign, notice, etc. so that it can be seen by many people

① throw ② join

③ mean ④ post

⑤ carry

04 다음 빈칸에 알맞은 말이 바르게 짝지어진 것은?

> • I can't wait _____ this weekend.
> • I saw him bump _____ the wall.

① on – to ② for – up

③ with – in ④ on – over

⑤ for – into

05 다음 짝지어진 두 단어의 관계가 같도록 빈칸에 알맞은 말을 쓰시오.

> strong : weak = _____ : boring

06 다음 빈칸에 들어갈 말로 적절하지 <u>않은</u> 것은?

> • They _____ food to poor people.
> • What does this sentence _____?
> • I have math problems to _____ today.
> • I'm going to _____ Dami with me.

① take ② mean

③ solve ④ serve

⑤ find

07 다음 영영풀이에 해당하는 단어를 쓰시오.

> to move, act, or go quickly

➡ _____

08 다음 우리말에 맞게 빈칸에 알맞은 말을 쓰시오.

> 그는 숲 속에서 단서들을 찾고 있다.
> ➡ He is _____ _____ clues in the woods.

01 다음 짝지어진 두 단어의 관계가 같도록 빈칸에 알맞은 말을 쓰시오.

(1) interesting : boring = _____ : stop

(2) easy : difficult = _____ : remember

(3) glad : sad = right : _____

(4) kind : friendly = proverb : _____

02 다음 우리말에 맞게 빈칸에 알맞은 말을 쓰시오.

(1) 여기에 빨리 좀 와!

➡ Please _____ _____ here quickly!

(2) 나는 방과 후에 축구하는 것을 즐긴다.

➡ I enjoy playing soccer _____ _____.

(3) 나는 올해 호주를 방문할 계획이다.

➡ I plan to visit Australia _____ _____.

03 다음 빈칸에 공통으로 들어갈 말을 〈보기〉에서 골라 쓰시오.

┌─ 보기 ─┐
right   dish   hard
└────────┘

(1) • This test was _____.

• I studied _____ yesterday because of my English test.

(2) • The _____ really tastes good.

• She got honey and put it into a _____.

(3) • He's the _____ man for the job.

• The woman is bending her _____ arm.

04 다음 빈칸에 들어갈 알맞은 말을 〈보기〉에서 골라 쓰시오.

┌─ 보기 ─┐
fresh   boring   strict
└────────┘

(1) He looks very _____ and serious.

(2) The film was _____, so I fell asleep.

(3) He eats _____ vegetables and fruit every day.

05 다음 빈칸에 알맞은 말을 〈보기〉에서 골라 쓰시오.

┌─ 보기 ─┐
bump into   be good for   cut in on
└────────┘

(1) He _____ our talk.

(2) This will also _____ my health.

(3) You can _____ other people while using your phone.

06 다음 영영풀이에 해당하는 단어를 주어진 철자로 시작하여 쓰시오.

(1) f_____ : the last and most important game or race in a competition

(2) c_____ : the outer part of a book or magazine

(3) r_____ : to understand or become aware of something

Conversation

① 의견 묻기

A What do you think of this diary? 이 수첩에 대해 어떻게 생각하니?
B Its cover is cool. I think it's good for Minjun. 표지가 멋져. 민준에게 좋을 것 같아.

■ 상대방에게 의견을 물어볼 때에는 What do you think of ~?를 이용하고, 그에 대한 응답으로 자신의 의견을 표현할 때에는 I think ~. 표현을 이용한다.

• A: What do you think of my new brush? 너는 내 새 붓에 어떻게 생각하니?
  B: I think it's cool. 멋지다고 생각해.

의견 묻기 표현

• What do you think of[about] James? James에 대해 어떻게 생각해?
• What's your opinion on this matter? 이 문제에 관한 너의 의견은 무엇이니?
  (= Can I have your opinion of this matter?)
• What's your view on school uniforms? 교복에 대해 어떻게 생각하니?
• How do you like my new coat? 내 새 코트 어때?

의견 말하기 표현

• I think it's interesting. 나는 재미있다고 생각해.
• In my opinion, it's too expensive. 내 생각에 그것은 너무 비싸.
• In my view, it is great. 내 생각에 그것은 좋아.
• I have no idea. 잘 모르겠어.

핵심 Check

1. 다음 우리말과 일치하도록 빈칸에 알맞은 말을 쓰시오.

(1) **A:** _____ do you _____ _____ today's lunch? (오늘의 점심에 대해 어떻게 생각하니?)
   B: _____ _____ it's okay. (괜찮다고 생각해.)

(2) **A:** _____ is your _____ _____ the novel? (그 소설에 대한 너의 의견은 무엇이니?)
   B: _____ my _____, it's very interesting. (내 의견으로는, 그것은 매우 재미있어.)

② 희망 · 기대 표현하기

A What do you think of my new dress? 내 새 드레스에 대해 어떻게 생각하니?
B I think it's cool. 멋진 것 같아.
A I can't wait for the party. 파티가 너무 기다려져.

■ I can't wait for ~.는 '나는 ~이 매우 기다려져. / 나는 ~이 무척 기대돼.'라는 뜻으로 희망이나 기대를 나타내는 표현이다.

> • A: What do you think of my new ukulele? 내 새 우쿨렐레 어때?
> B: I think it's cool. 멋진 것 같아.
> A: I can't wait for the concert. 콘서트가 너무 기다려져.

희망 · 기대를 나타내는 표현

> • I can't wait for+명사(구) ~. 나는 ~이[하는 것이] 매우 기다려진다.
> • I can't wait to+동사원형 ~. 나는 빨리 ~하고 싶어.
> • I'm looking forward to+(동)명사 ~. 나는 ~을 고대하고 있다.
> • I'm expecting + 명사(구) / to+동사원형 ~. 나는 ~을 기대하고 있다.
> • I hope[want] to+동사원형 ~. 나는 ~하기를 바란다[원한다].
> • I would like to+동사원형 ~. 나는 ~하고 싶다.

> • I can't wait for the art contest. 나는 미술 대회가 매우 기다려져.
> = I'm looking forward to the art contest.

핵심 Check

2. 다음 우리말과 일치하도록 빈칸에 알맞은 말을 쓰시오.

(1) **A:** When are you going to leave? (언제 떠날 예정이니?)

B: Next Tuesday. I can't _____ _____ the trip. (다음 주 화요일. 여행이 무척 기다려져.)

(2) **A:** When is Chuseok _____ _____? (올해 추석이 언제니?)

B: It's on October 1. I'm _____ _____ to it. (10월 1일이야. 나는 그것을 아주 고대하고 있어.)

A. Start Off - Listen & Talk B

> **B:** Let's join the Green Garden club together. ❶What do you think of it?
>
> **G:** Okay. I like growing vegetables.
>
> **B:** ❷You know what? I like eating vegetables.
>
> **G:** Let's join the club right now. We can have a party with fresh vegetables every month.
>
> **B:** Great. ❸The first party is on April 30.
>
> **G:** ❹I can't wait for the party.

> **B:** 초록 정원 동아리에 함께 가 입하자. 그것에 대해 어떻게 생각하니?
>
> **G:** 좋아. 나는 채소를 기르는 것 을 좋아해.
>
> **B:** 그거 알아?(있잖아.) 나는 채 소를 먹는 것을 좋아해.
>
> **G:** 지금 당장 그 동아리에 가입 하자. 매달 신선한 채소가 있 는 파티를 열 수 있어.
>
> **B:** 좋아. 첫 번째 파티는 4월 30 일이야.
>
> **G:** 나는 파티가 너무 기다려져.

❶ What do you think of ~?: ~에 대해 어떻게 생각하니?=What's your opinion about[of, on] ~? / How do you like ~? / How do you feel about ~?(의견을 묻는 표현)

❷ You know what?: 너 그거 알아?, 있잖아.

❸ on April 30: on + 날짜

❹ I can't wait for the party.: 나는 파티가 너무 기다려져. = I'm looking forward to the party.

Check(√) True or False

(1) The girl likes to grow vegetables.　　　　　　　　　　　　T ☐ F ☐

(2) They can have a party with fresh vegetables every week.　　T ☐ F ☐

 B. Step Up - Real-life Scene

> **I Can't Wait for His Class**
>
> **Seho:** Miso, what do you think of Mr. Park?
>
> **Miso:** The new math teacher? ❶He looks very strict and serious.
>
> **Seho:** ❷Don't judge a book by its cover.
>
> **Miso:** What do you mean, Seho?
>
> **Seho:** My first class with Mr. Park was great. ❸He was very kind, and his class was so exciting.
>
> **Miso:** Really?
>
> **Seho:** Yes. ❹During the first class, we did interesting math activities with our cell phones.
>
> **Miso:** Wow! I can't wait for his class tomorrow. ❺It's my first math class this year.

> **나는 그의 수업이 너무 기다려져.**
>
> **세호:** 미소야, 박 선생님에 대해 어떻게 생각하니?
>
> **미소:** 새로 오신 수학 선생님? 그는 매우 엄격하고 진지 해 보이셔.
>
> **세호:** 겉모습만으로 판단하지 마.
>
> **미소:** 무슨 뜻이야, 세호?
>
> **세호:** 박 선생님과의 첫 수업은 훌륭했어. 그는 매우 친절 하셨고, 그의 수업은 매우 흥미로웠어.
>
> **미소:** 정말?
>
> **세호:** 응. 첫 수업 동안, 우리는 휴대 전화로 흥미로운 수 학 활동을 했어.
>
> **미소:** 와! 내일 그 선생님의 수업 이 너무 기다려진다. 올해 첫 번째 수학 수업이야.

❶ look+형용사: ~하게 보이다 / strict: 엄격한 / serious: 진지한

❷ Don't judge a book by its cover.: 겉모습만으로 판단하지 마라.

❸ 주어가 그 감정을 느끼게 하는 것이므로 현재분사형 형용사 exciting이 알맞다.

❹ During the first class: during + 특정한 기간: ~ 동안

❺ It=his class

Check(√) True or False

(3) Mr. Park is very strict and serious.　　　　　　　　　　T ☐ F ☐

(4) Miso is looking forward to Mr. Park's class.　　　　　　T ☐ F ☐

Get Ready -2

1. G: ❶Hey, what do you think of this notebook?
   B: ❷It looks great! Is it for science?
   G: Yes. This year I'm going to study science harder with this notebook.
2. B: ❸Look at the teachers. Who's going to be our new homeroom teacher?
   G: ❹We'll find out in 10 minutes.
   B: I'm very excited. ❺I can't wait!
3. M: Hello, everyone! My name is Yun Kihun. I'm your English teacher.
   G&B: Glad to meet you, Mr. Yun.
   M: What do you think of English?
   G: It's interesting. I like English a lot.

❶ think of: ~에 대해 생각하다
❷ look+형용사: ~하게 보이다
❸ look at: ~을 보다
❹ find out: 알게 되다
❺ I can't wait.: 너무 기대된다.

 Start Off - Listen & Talk A

1. B: This club looks good for you. What do you think of it?
   G: The health club? ❶I think it's boring.
   B: ❷Then which club do you want to join?
   G: I'll join the soccer club. I like playing soccer.
2. G: What do you think of the magic club?
   B: ❸I think it's the right club for me. I want to learn many interesting tricks.
   G: ❹I'll join it, too. When is the first meeting?
   B: Next Wednesday. ❺I can't wait for the first meeting!

❶ I think ~: 나는 ~라고 생각해. / boring: 지루한
❷ which+명사: 어느 ~
❸ right: 맞는, 알맞은
❹ it = the magic club
❺ I can't wait for the first meeting!=I'm looking forward to the first meeting!

 Start Off - Speak Up

A: Look! What do you think of this diary?
B: ❶Its cover is cool. ❷I think it's good for Minjun.
A: ❸Yes, he'll like it a lot.
B: ❹I can't wait for his birthday party!

❶ Its = This diary's
❷ be good for: ~에 좋다
❸ it = this diary / a lot: 매우
❹ I can't wait for his birthday party! = I'm looking forward to his birthday party!

Express Yourself A

1. B: What do you think of today's lunch?
   G: I think it's okay. What's on tomorrow's menu?
   B: Wow! We can eat spaghetti tomorrow.
   G: ❶I can't wait for lunchtime tomorrow.
2. G: Look! ❷Two dishes of vegetables! What do you think of today's menu?
   B: ❸It's not bad. I like vegetables.
   G: I don't eat vegetables.
   B: Try some. ❹They are good for our health.

❶ I can't wait for lunchtime. = I'm looking forward to lunchtime.
❷ dish: 접시
❸ It = today's menu
❹ be good for: ~에 좋다 / health: 건강

Check Yourself - Listen & Speak

B: Let's join the School Band club together. What do you think of it?
G: Okay. ❶I like playing the flute.
B: I like playing the ukulele.
G: ❷Let's join the club right now. They practice after school every Tuesday and Thursday.
B: ❸They're going to have the first concert on July 15.
G: Great. ❹I hope to play in the concert.
B: Me, too. I can't wait for the concert.

❶ play the flute: 플루트를 연주하다
❷ Let's + 동사원형 ~: ~하자 / right now: 당장
❸ be going to+동사원형: ~할 예정이다
❹ I hope to+동사원형 ~: 나는 ~하고 싶다

다음 우리말과 일치하도록 빈칸에 알맞은 말을 쓰시오.

Get Ready - 2

1. **G:** Hey, what do you _____ of this notebook?

   B: It _____ great! Is it _____ science?

   G: Yes. _____ _____ I'm _____ to study science harder _____ this notebook.

2. **B:** _____ _____ the teachers. Who's _____ _____ be our new homeroom teacher?

   G: We'll _____ _____ in 10 minutes.

   B: I'm very _____. I can't _____!

3. **M:** Hello, everyone! My name is Yun Kihun. I'm _____ English teacher.

   G&B: Glad _____ meet you, Mr. Yun.

   M: _____ do you _____ of English?

   G: It's interesting. I like English _____ _____.

Start Off - Listen & Talk A

1. **B:** This club looks _____ _____ you. _____ do you think of it?

   G: The health club? I _____ it's _____.

   B: Then _____ club do you want _____ _____?

   G: I'll join the soccer club. I like _____ soccer.

2. **G:** What do you _____ _____ the magic club?

   B: I think it's the _____ club for me. I want _____ _____ many interesting tricks.

   G: I'll join it, _____. When is the _____ meeting?

   B: Next Wednesday. I can't _____ _____ the first meeting!

Start Off - Listen & Talk B

B: _____ join the Green Garden club together. What do you think of it?

G: Okay. I like _____ vegetables.

B: You know _____? I like eating vegetables.

G: _____ join the club _____ _____. We can have a party _____ fresh vegetables every month.

B: Great. The first party is _____ April 30.

G: I can't wait _____ the party.

해석

1. G: 이 봐, 이 공책 어떻게 생각하니?
   B: 멋져 보여! 과학용이니?
   G: 응. 올해에는 이 공책을 가지고 과학을 더 열심히 공부할 거야.

2. B: 선생님들을 좀 봐. 누가 우리 새 담임선생님이 될까?
   G: 우리는 10분 후에 알게 될 거야.
   B: 너무 흥분돼. 너무 기대돼!

3. M: 안녕하세요, 여러분! 제 이름은 윤기훈입니다. 저는 여러분의 영어 선생님입니다.
   G&B: 만나서 반갑습니다, 윤 선생님.
   M: 여러분은 영어에 대해 어떻게 생각하세요?
   G: 재미있어요. 저는 영어를 매우 좋아해요.

1. B: 이 동아리는 너에게 맞는 것 같아. 그것에 대해 어떻게 생각하니?
   G: 헬스 동아리? 지루하다고 생각해.
   B: 그럼 넌 어떤 동아리에 가입하고 싶니?
   G: 난 축구 동아리에 가입할 거야. 나는 축구를 좋아해.

2. G: 마술 동아리에 대해 어떻게 생각하니?
   B: 나한테 맞는 동아리인 것 같아. 나는 재미있는 마술을 많이 배우고 싶어.
   G: 나도 가입할게. 첫 모임은 언제니?
   B: 다음 주 수요일이야. 나는 첫 모임이 너무 기다려져!

B: 초록 정원 동아리에 함께 가입하자. 그것에 대해 어떻게 생각하니?
G: 좋아, 나는 채소를 기르는 것을 좋아해.
B: 그거 알아?(있잖아.) 나는 채소를 먹는 것을 좋아해.
G: 지금 당장 그 동아리에 가입하자. 매달 신선한 채소가 있는 파티를 열 수 있어.
B: 좋아. 첫 번째 파티는 4월 30일이야.
G: 나는 파티가 너무 기다려져.

Step Up - Real-life Scene

I Can't Wait for His Class

Seho: Miso, _____ do you _____ _____ Mr. Park?

Miso: The new math teacher? He _____ very _____ and serious.

Seho: _____ _____ a book _____ its cover.

Miso: What do you _____, Seho?

Seho: My first class _____ Mr. Park was great. He was very kind, and his class was so _____.

Miso: Really?

Seho: Yes. _____ the first _____, we did interesting math activities _____ our cell phones.

Miso: Wow! I _____ _____ _____ his class tomorrow. It's my first math class _____ _____.

Express Yourself A

1. **B:** _____ do you think of today's lunch?

   G: _____ _____ it's okay. What's _____ tomorrow's menu?

   B: Wow! We _____ _____ spaghetti tomorrow.

   G: I _____ _____ _____ lunchtime tomorrow.

2. **G:** Look! Two _____ of vegetables! What do you _____ _____ today's menu?

   B: It's not _____. I like vegetables.

   G: I _____ _____ vegetables.

   B: _____ some. They are _____ for our health.

Check Yourself - Listen & Speak

B: _____ _____ the School Band club together. _____ do you think _____ it?

G: Okay. I like _____ the flute.

B: I like _____ the ukulele.

G: Let's join the club _____ _____. They practice _____ _____ every Tuesday and Thursday.

B: They're _____ _____ have the first concert _____ July 15.

G: Great. I hope _____ _____ in the concert.

B: Me, _____. I can't _____ _____ the concert.

해석

나는 그의 수업이 너무 기다려져.

세호: 미소야, 박 선생님에 대해 어떻게 생각하니?

미소: 새로 오신 수학 선생님? 그는 매우 엄격하고 진지해 보이셔.

세호: 겉모습만으로 판단하지 마.

미소: 무슨 뜻이야, 세호?

세호: 박 선생님과의 첫 수업은 훌륭했어. 그는 매우 친절하셨고, 그의 수업은 매우 흥미로웠어.

미소: 정말?

세호: 응. 첫 수업 동안, 우리는 휴대 전화로 흥미로운 수학 활동을 했어.

미소: 와! 내일 수업이 너무 기다려진다. 올해 첫 번째 수학 수업이야.

1. B: 오늘 점심에 대해 어떻게 생각하니?

   G: 괜찮은 것 같아. 내일 메뉴는 뭐니?

   B: 와! 내일 우리는 스파게티를 먹을 수 있어.

   G: 내일 점심시간이 몹시 기다려진다.

2. G: 봐! 야채 두 접시! 오늘 메뉴 어때?

   B: 나쁘지 않아. 나는 야채를 좋아해.

   G: 나는 야채를 안 먹어.

   B: 조금 먹어 봐. 그것들은 우리 건강에 좋아.

B: 우리 학교 밴드 동아리에 같이 가입하자. 그것에 대해서 어떻게 생각하니?

G: 좋아. 나는 플루트 연주하는 것을 좋아해.

B: 난 우쿨렐레 연주하는 걸 좋아해.

G: 지금 당장 그 동아리에 가입하자. 그들은 매주 화요일과 목요일 방과 후에 연습을 해.

B: 그들은 7월 15일에 첫 번째 음악회를 열 거야.

G: 좋아. 나는 음악회에서 연주를 하고 싶어.

B: 나도. 나는 음악회가 너무 기다려져.

01 다음 대화의 빈칸에 공통으로 알맞은 것은?

> A: What do you _____ of having a pet?
> B: I _____ it is exciting.

① take   ② think
③ introduce   ④ see
⑤ thought

02 다음 대화의 빈칸에 들어갈 말로 알맞은 것은?

> A: What do you think of my new trick?
> B: I think it's cool.
> A: I can't wait for the _____.

① game   ② concert
③ art contest   ④ party
⑤ magic show

03 다음 대화의 빈칸에 올 수 없는 것은?

> A: What do you think of Emily?
> B: _____

① She is nice.   ② I like her, too.
③ I think she's pretty.   ④ I think she is a liar.
⑤ In my opinion, she is the best student in our class.

04 다음 주어진 표현과 의미가 같은 것은?

> I can't wait for the trip.

① What a nice trip!   ② How was the trip?
③ I don't like the trip.   ④ I can't go on the trip.
⑤ I'm looking forward to the trip.

[01~04] 다음 대화를 읽고, 물음에 답하시오.

B: Let's join the Green Garden club together. ____ⓐ____ do you think of it?

G: ____ⓑ____ I like growing vegetables.

B: You know what? I like eating vegetables.

G: Let's join the club right now. We can have a party with fresh vegetables every month.

B: Great. The first party is ____ⓒ____ April 30.

G: ⓓ나는 파티가 너무 기다려져.

01 위 대화의 빈칸 ⓐ에 알맞은 것은?

① How
② What
③ Why
④ When
⑤ Which

02 위 대화의 빈칸 ⓑ에 알맞은 것은?

① I don't think so.
② Don't mention it.
③ I think it's great.
④ I'm not so sure about it.
⑤ The Green Garden club isn't that good.

03 위 대화의 빈칸 ⓒ에 알맞은 것은?

① at
② in
③ on
④ of
⑤ by

04 위 대화의 밑줄 친 ⓓ의 우리말을 바르게 옮긴 것은?

① I'm waiting for the party.
② I must wait for the party.
③ I can't wait for the party.
④ I'm going to attend the party.
⑤ I'm thinking of attending the party.

[05~06] 다음 대화를 읽고, 물음에 답하시오.

G: Look! Two dishes of vegetables! ⓐWhat do you think of today's menu?

B: It's not bad. I like vegetables.

G: I don't eat vegetables.

B: Try some. They are good ____ⓑ____ our health.

05 위 대화의 밑줄 친 ⓐ와 바꿔 쓸 수 있는 것은?

① What is on today's menu?
② What's your opinion on today's menu?
③ What makes you think of today's menu?
④ Why don't you think of today's menu?
⑤ How about thinking of today's menu?

06 위 대화의 빈칸 ⓑ에 알맞은 것은?

① at
② of
③ for
④ with
⑤ from

[07~10] 다음 대화를 읽고, 물음에 답하시오.

I Can't Wait for His Class

Seho: Miso, ⓐwhat do you think of Mr. Park?

Miso: The new math teacher? He looks very strict and serious.

Seho: Don't judge a book ___ⓑ___ its cover.

Miso: What do you mean, Seho?

Seho: My first class ___ⓒ___ Mr. Park was great. He was very kind, and his class was so exciting.

Miso: Really?

Seho: Yes. During the first class, we did interesting math activities ___ⓓ___ our cell phones.

Miso: Wow! I can't wait for his class tomorrow. It's my first math class this year.

07 위 대화의 밑줄 친 ⓐ의 의도로 알맞은 것은?

① 의견 묻기　　　　② 의견 동의하기
③ 능력 여부 묻기　　④ 선호에 대해 묻기
⑤ 제안이나 권유하기

08 위 대화의 빈칸 ⓑ에 알맞은 것은?

① of　　　　　② by
③ with　　　　④ from
⑤ about

서답형
09 위 대화의 빈칸 ⓒ와 ⓓ에 공통으로 알맞은 말을 쓰시오.

➡ _____

10 위 대화의 내용과 일치하지 <u>않는</u> 것은?

① Miso thinks Mr. Park looks very strict and serious.
② Seho liked his first class with Mr. Park.
③ Seho thinks that Mr. Park's class was boring.
④ Seho and his classmates did interesting math activities during the first class.
⑤ Miso is looking forward to Mr. Park's class tomorrow.

[11~13] 다음 대화를 읽고, 물음에 답하시오.

A: Look! What do you think ___ⓐ___ this diary?

B: Its ___ⓑ___ is cool. I think it's good for Minjun.

A: Yes, he'll like it a lot.

B: ⓒ<u>나는 그의 생일 파티가 너무 기다려져.</u>

11 위 대화의 빈칸 ⓐ에 알맞은 것을 <u>모두</u> 고르면?

① of　　　　　② for
③ about　　　　④ on
⑤ over

서답형
12 위 대화의 빈칸 ⓑ에 다음 영영풀이에 해당하는 단어를 쓰시오.

| the outer part of a book or magazine |

➡ _____

서답형
13 위 대화의 밑줄 친 ⓒ의 우리말에 맞게 주어진 단어를 이용하여 영작하시오.

| (wait) |

➡ _____

[01~03] 다음 대화를 읽고, 물음에 답하시오.

B: This club looks (A)[good / well] for you.
ⓐ너는 그것에 대해 어떻게 생각하니?
G: The health club? I think it's (B)[bored / boring].
B: Then which club do you want to join?
G: I'll join the soccer club. I like playing soccer.

01 위 대화의 괄호 (A)와 (B)에서 어법상 알맞은 것을 골라 쓰시오.

(A) _____ (B) _____

02 위 대화의 밑줄 친 ⓐ의 우리말을 주어진 단어를 이용하여 영어로 옮기시오.

(what / think)

➡ _____

03 What does the girl think of the health club? Answer in English.

➡ _____

04 다음 대화의 순서를 바르게 배열하시오.

(A) I can't wait for his birthday party!
(B) Look! What do you think of this diary?
(C) Yes, he'll like it a lot.
(D) Its cover is cool. I think it's good for Minjun.

➡ _____

[05~08] 다음 대화를 읽고, 물음에 답하시오.

B: Let's join the Green Garden club together. ____ⓐ____ do you think of it?
G: Okay. I like growing vegetables.
B: You know ____ⓑ____? I like eating vegetables.
G: Let's join the club right now. We can have a party with fresh vegetables every month.
B: Great. The first party is on April 30.
G: ⓒ(can't / I / the party / for / wait)

05 위 대화의 빈칸 ⓐ와 ⓑ에 공통으로 알맞은 말을 쓰시오. (대·소문자 무시)

➡ _____

06 When can they have a party with fresh vegetables? Answer in English.

➡ _____
_____

07 When is the first party? Answer in English.

➡ _____

08 위 대화의 괄호 ⓒ 안의 단어를 바르게 배열하시오.

➡ _____

① to부정사의 형용사적 용법

- Do you have something **to say**? 너는 할 말이 있니?
- I have no time **to play**. 나는 놀 시간이 없다.
- A: Are you busy? 너 바쁘니?
  B: Yes. I have lots of homework **to do**. 응. 나는 해야 할 숙제가 많아.

■ to부정사가 명사나 부정대명사를 뒤에서 꾸며주는 형용사의 역할을 할 때는 '~할', '~해야 할'로 해석한다.

- Dami needs some water **to drink**. 다미는 마실 물이 좀 필요하다.
- He had no friends **to help** him. 그는 자기를 도와줄 친구가 하나도 없었다.
- You feel that you have nothing **to wear**. 너는 입을 것이 아무것도 없다고 느낀다.

■ 명사+to부정사+전치사: 수식받는 명사가 전치사의 목적어인 경우는 to부정사 뒤에 반드시 전치사를 쓴다.

- I need a pen **to write with**. 나는 쓸 펜이 한 자루 없다.
- She's looking for a chair **to sit on**. 그녀는 앉을 의자를 찾고 있다.
- We have no house **to live in**. 우리는 살 집이 필요하다.
- He needs a friend **to talk to**. 그는 말할 친구가 필요하다.
- She bought some paper **to write on**. 그녀는 쓸 종이를 좀 샀다.

cf. -thing+형용사+to부정사: -thing으로 끝나는 부정대명사는 형용사가 뒤에서 수식하며, 이를 다시 to부정사가 뒤에서 수식한다.

- I want something cold **to drink**. 나는 차가운 마실 것을 원한다.

핵심 Check

1. 다음 괄호 안에서 알맞은 것을 고르시오.

(1) It's time (go / to go) to school.

(2) Give me a pen (to write / to write with).

(3) Seho has a lot of friends (helping / to help).

(4) Would you like something (to drink cold / cold to drink)?

2. 다음 주어진 단어를 빈칸에 알맞은 형태로 바꾸어 쓰시오.

(1) Is there nobody _____ _____ to my story? (listen)

(2) I have something important _____ _____ you. (tell)

(3) There are so many places _____ _____ in my town. (visit)

② 접속사 that

> • I think **(that)** I lost it. 나는 그것을 잃어버린 것 같아.
>
> • A: Look! There's a schoolbag. 봐! 책가방이 있어.
>
> B: I think **that** it's a boy's bag. 내 생각에는 소년의 가방인 것 같아.

■ 접속사는 절과 절을 연결하는 역할을 하므로 접속사 that은 「주어+동사+that+주어+동사 ~」의 형태로 쓰인다.

  • I think **that** he is a genius. 나는 그가 천재라고 생각해.

  • I believe **that** she will come to the party. 나는 그녀가 파티에 올 것이라고 믿는다.

■ 접속사 that이 이끄는 절은 문장 안에서 주어, 목적어, 보어의 역할을 하므로 이때의 that을 명사절 접속사라 한다. 목적어 역할을 하는 명사절을 이끄는 that은 생략 가능하다.

  • **That** he plays soccer well is true. [주어 역할] 그가 축구를 잘한다는 것은 사실이다.

  • I think **(that)** he is American. [목적어 역할] 나는 그가 미국인이라고 생각한다

  • The truth is **that** she is a liar. [보어 역할] 사실은 그녀가 거짓말쟁이라는 것이다.

cf. that은 '저것'을 뜻하는 지시대명사나 지시형용사로 사용될 수도 있으므로, 문장 안에서 명사 역할을 하는 접속사 용법과 구분하도록 한다.

  • I need **that** pen. 나는 저 펜이 필요해.

  • I want **that** blue shirt. 나는 저 파란색 셔츠를 원해.

핵심 Check

3. 다음 괄호 안에서 알맞은 것을 고르시오.

  (1) I think (what / that) he is honest.

  (2) I know (that / when) she was a teacher.

4. 다음 문장에서 that이 들어갈 수 있는 곳에 V표를 하시오.

  (1) I hope you get better.

  (2) Miss. Susan says the Han River is beautiful.

  (3) He thinks his dog went away.

01 다음 우리말과 일치하도록 빈칸에 알맞은 말을 쓰시오.

(1) 그녀는 내가 숙제를 했다고 믿는다.
➡ She _____ _____ I did my homework.

(2) 그는 내가 공연을 잘했다고 생각한다.
➡ He _____ _____ I performed well.

perform 공연하다

02 다음 괄호 안에 주어진 단어를 바르게 배열하시오.

(1) He is the only person _____ _____ _____. (help / to / us)

(2) There are _____ _____ _____ _____. (do / things / to / many)

only 유일한
person 사람

03 다음 우리말과 같도록 괄호 안의 단어를 바르게 배열하여 문장을 완성하시오.

(1) 나는 Jenny가 집에 있다고 생각한다.
(at / is / home / Jenny / that / think)
➡ I _____.

(2) 나는 우리 부모님이 건강하길 바란다.
(that / hope / are / healthy / my parents)
➡ I _____.

(3) 그녀는 그가 돌아올 거라고 믿었다.
(he / back / believed / come / that / would)
➡ She _____.

04 다음 우리말과 일치하도록 빈칸에 알맞은 말을 쓰시오.

(1) 여기는 덥다. 나는 마실 것을 원한다.
➡ It's hot in here! I want something _____ _____.

(2) Vicky는 이번 주말에 읽을 흥미로운 책이 필요하다.
➡ Vicky needs an interesting book _____ _____ this weekend.

(1) 나는 매우 바쁘다. 나는 오늘 해야 할 일이 많다.
➡ I'm so busy. I have a lot of work _____ _____ today.

busy 바쁜
a lot of 많은
work 일

01 다음 우리말과 같도록 빈칸에 알맞은 것은?

> 나는 학교 다닐 때 탈 자전거를 사고 싶다.
> ➡ I want to buy a bike _____ to school.

① ride   ② rides   ③ to ride
④ riding   ⑤ to riding

02 다음 중 접속사 that이 들어갈 알맞은 곳은?

> I (①) hope (②) I have (③) a lot of (④) money (⑤).

①   ②   ③   ④   ⑤

03 다음 중 밑줄 친 부분의 쓰임이 나머지 넷과 다른 것은?

① We have no time to waste.
② I need a friend to talk to.
③ I have a lot of books to read.
④ They decided to leave home.
⑤ We cannot find a place to park our car.

04 다음 문장의 빈칸에 알맞지 않은 것은?

> I _____ that he is sick today.

① know   ② believe
③ heard   ④ think
⑤ made

서답형

05 다음 우리말을 참고하여 빈칸에 알맞은 말을 쓰시오.

> 나는 내 숙제를 도와 줄 누군가가 필요하다.
> ➡ I need somebody _____ _____ me with my homework.

중요

06 다음 중 밑줄 친 that의 쓰임이 나머지 넷과 다른 하나는?

① I think that honesty is the most important thing.
② I think that Jinny has a dog.
③ Ann believes that man is my husband.
④ Susan thinks that he is very smart.
⑤ Runa believes that her hometown is New York.

중요

09 다음 빈칸에 공통으로 알맞은 것은?

> • Would you like something _____ drink?
> • Jenny has some money _____ spend on everyday things.

① on   ② to   ③ as
④ for   ⑤ with

서답형

08 다음 문장에서 어법상 틀린 부분을 찾아 바르게 고쳐 쓰시오.

> She thinks what the English teacher is handsome.

_____ ➡ _____

서답형

09 다음 문장에서 어법상 어색한 부분을 찾아 고쳐 쓰시오.

> I need some medicine taking right away.

_____ ➡ _____

중요

10 다음 밑줄 친 that 중 생략할 수 없는 것은?

① I think that you are so beautiful.
② I hope that I will get good grades.
③ I believe that Jenny is a kind girl.
④ I believe that he will be an engineer.
⑤ I know that man is Ann's math teacher.

11 다음 중 밑줄 친 부분의 쓰임이 나머지 넷과 다른 하나는?

① I have something to eat.
② My brothers have books to read.
③ Sarah let her son go to the park.
④ Joe has a lot of homework to do.
⑤ Ken has many friends to help him.

서답형

12 다음 두 문장의 빈칸에 공통으로 알맞은 말을 쓰시오.

> • I believe _____ I can fly in the air.
> • We don't hope _____ you will like it.

서답형

13 다음 문장에서 어법상 어색한 부분을 찾아 고쳐 쓰시오.

> They found a nice house to live.

_____ ➡ _____

14 다음 밑줄 친 부분 중 어법상 어색한 것은?

① Jane has a lot of things to do.
② There's nothing to worry about.
③ Check prices for clothes to buy.
④ I had a lot of work to complete.
⑤ Let me get you a chair to sit.

서답형

15 다음 우리말과 같도록 주어진 어휘를 바르게 배열하시오.

> 나는 진우가 훌륭한 리더가 될 것이라고 생각한다.
> (Jinwoo / great / be / will / that / think / I / a / leader).

➡ _____

중요

16 다음 문장의 빈칸에 공통으로 알맞은 것은?

> • I don't have any friends to play _____.
> • Kelly is looking for a pencil to write _____.

① of
② to
③ for
④ with
⑤ 필요 없음

17 다음 중 〈보기〉의 밑줄 친 that과 쓰임이 같은 것은?

> ┤ 보기 ├
>
> He thinks <u>that</u> science is a useful subject.

① Look at <u>that</u> old temple.

② Where did you find <u>that</u> pencil?

③ He walked this way and <u>that</u> way.

④ I know <u>that</u> man sings very well.

⑤ I believe <u>that</u> everything will be fine.

18 다음 밑줄 친 부분 중 용법이 <u>다른</u> 하나는?

① I went to the cafeteria <u>to have</u> lunch.

② I'm glad <u>to meet</u> you.

③ I need some medicine <u>to take</u>.

④ She grew up <u>to become</u> a doctor.

⑤ He must be rich <u>to buy</u> that car.

서답형

19 다음 문장에서 어법상 어색한 부분을 찾아 고쳐 쓰시오.

> I don't know that he will come to the meeting.

_____ ➡ _____

20 다음 중 어법상 어색한 것은?

① He has no friends to talk to.

② I bought some books to read.

③ She's looking for something reading.

④ I got up early to see her.

⑤ I have a lot of homework to do.

21 다음 중 밑줄 친 부분의 쓰임이 나머지 넷과 <u>다른</u> 것은?

① I need some money <u>to buy</u> a bicycle.

② I don't have anything <u>to drink</u>.

③ You have to study hard <u>to get</u> good grades.

④ He is buying a bike <u>to ride</u> in the race.

⑤ She wants a pair of shoes <u>to wear</u> during the tour.

서답형

22 다음 괄호 안에 주어진 단어를 이용하여 우리말에 맞도록 문장을 완성하시오.

> 그녀는 앉을 의자가 필요하다. (sit)
>
> ➡ She needs _____.

23 다음 중 문장의 빈칸에 들어갈 말이 <u>다른</u> 하나는? (대 · 소 문자 무시)

① Do you know _____ man?

② I think _____ she is pretty.

③ Do you know _____ he is sick?

④ _____ you finish it, let me know.

⑤ _____ he never came back is true.

24 다음 중 밑줄 친 부분의 쓰임이 같은 것끼리 묶인 것은?

> ⓐ I need something <u>to drink</u>.
>
> ⓑ She wants <u>to become</u> a teacher.
>
> ⓒ The girl had nothing <u>to wear</u>.
>
> ⓓ She went out <u>to meet</u> her boyfriend.

① ⓐ, ⓑ   ② ⓑ, ⓓ

③ ⓑ, ⓒ   ④ ⓐ, ⓒ

⑤ ⓒ, ⓓ

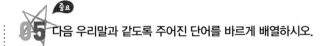

01 다음 빈칸에 공통으로 알맞은 말을 쓰시오.

- Mike had no time _____ do his homework.
- We are going to buy a house _____ live in.

02 다음 두 문장을 한 문장으로 만드시오.

(1) They believe. + There is an alien here.

➡ _____

(2) I know. + You came back home late.

➡ _____

03 다음 〈보기〉에서 알맞은 단어를 골라 문장을 완성하시오.

┌─── 보기 ───┐
sit buy eat drink talk wear
└──────────────┘

(1) I'm hungry. I need some food _____ _____.

(2) I'm very thirsty. I need something _____ _____.

(3) There's no chair here. I need a chair to _____ _____.

(4) Tony feels lonely. He needs friends to _____ _____.

04 다음 빈칸에 공통으로 알맞은 말을 쓰시오.

- I believe _____ the story is true.
- Does your mother know _____ boy in the room?

05 다음 우리말과 같도록 주어진 단어를 바르게 배열하시오.

그녀는 입을 뭔가가 필요하다.
(put / something / on / she / needs / to)

➡ _____

06 다음 괄호 안에 주어진 단어와 that을 이용하여 바르게 배열하시오.

(1) (Chinese / I / is / think / he)

➡ _____ that _____.

(2) (is / wife / know / I / a / wise / she)

➡ _____ that _____.

07 다음 두 문장을 to부정사를 이용하여 한 문장으로 고쳐 쓰시오.

(1) I want some snacks. I will eat them in the afternoon.

➡ _____

(2) They need four chairs. They'll sit on the chair.

➡ _____

08 다음 주어진 문장에서 어법상 <u>어색한</u> 부분을 바르게 고쳐 다시 쓰시오.

Do you have warm something to wear?

➡ _____

09 다음 문장에서 어법상 <u>어색한</u> 부분을 찾아 바르게 고쳐 쓰시오.

(1) He needs a chair to sit.

_____ ➡ _____

(2) There are many places visiting in Paris.

_____ ➡ _____

10 다음 주어진 우리말을 영작하시오.

> 나는 나의 영어 선생님이 예쁘다고 생각한다.

➡ _____

11 다음 우리말과 일치하도록 주어진 어구를 이용하여 영작하시오.

(1) 그녀는 자신을 도울 힘센 누군가가 필요하다.
(someone / help)

➡ _____

(2) 그는 같이 놀 친구들이 없다. (no / play)

➡ _____

12 다음 우리말과 같도록 괄호 안의 단어를 바르게 배열하시오.

(1) 나는 네가 모든 것을 할 수 있다고 생각한다.
(everything / do / you / can / that)
➡ I think _____.

(2) 너는 그녀가 예쁘다고 생각하니?
(is / think / she / pretty / that / you)
➡ Do _____?

13 다음 〈보기〉와 같이 두 문장을 한 문장으로 바꿔 쓰시오.

> ─┤ 보기 ├─
> Brian has a lot of books. + He will read a lot of books.
> ➡ Brian has a lot of books to read.

(1) We cannot find a place. + We will park our car.

➡ _____

(2) Dave wants to buy a bike. + He will ride a bike to school.

➡ _____

(3) Kate has a lot of homework. + She will do a lot of homework.

➡ _____

14 다음 우리말에 맞게 빈칸에 알맞은 말을 쓰시오.

> 그녀는 쓸 펜이 필요하다.
> ➡ She needs _____ _____ _____
> _____ _____.

15 다음 괄호 안에 주어진 단어를 이용하여 우리말을 영어로 옮기시오.

(1) 그는 그녀가 부자라는 것을 안다.
(know / that)

➡ _____

(2) 나는 그가 미국인이라고 생각하지 않는다.
(think / that)

➡ _____

16 다음 주어진 어구를 바르게 배열하시오.

(1) (anything / don't have / they / about / to talk).

➡ _____

(2) (we / in Paris / are looking for / stay at / to / a hotel)

➡ _____

The Tickets

Seho and Jihun were talking in the hallway when Dami came over.
과거진행형: be동사의 과거형+-ing(~하고 있었다)   접 ~할 때   come over: 오다

"Happy birthday!" she said to Seho. "Here. They're from my dad."
= two KBL tickets

"Wow, two KBL tickets! Thanks!"

"Who are you going to take with you?" Dami asked.
be going to: ~할 것이다

"Minjun. He took me to a soccer game before. So, it's time to pay him
take A to B: A를 B로 데려가다   pay someone back: ~에게 신세를 갚다
back."

"You know what?" Jihun cut in. "Minjun isn't a fan of basketball. But
(말·대화에) 끼어들다
I am!"

"Well, I'll ask him first anyway," replied Seho.
= Minjun

"He won't go with you. Trust me," said Jihun.
will not의 줄임말

"Who is this guy?" Dami thought to herself, "He wants Minjun's
think to oneself: 마음속으로 생각하다
ticket."

"Oh! There's the bell. See you later," said Dami. She hurried to class.
종이 울린다.

"Come on, Jihun," said Seho, and he started to run.
start to+동사원형: ~하기 시작하다

---

hallway 복도
ticket 표, 입장권
take 데려가다
before 전에
fan 팬
anyway 어쨌든
reply 대답하다
trust 믿다
later 나중에
class 수업

확인문제

● 다음 문장이 본문의 내용과 일치하면 T, 일치하지 않으면 F를 쓰시오.

1 Dami said to Seho, "Happy birthday!" ☐

2 Dami gave Jihun two KBL tickets. ☐

3 Minjun took Jihun to a soccer game before. ☐

4 Jihun said Minjun is not a fan of basketball. ☐

5 Dami thought to herself, "Jihun wants Minjun's ticket." ☐

6 Dami hurried to class when the bell rang. ☐

At the corner, Seho bumped into someone. "Sorry!" he said and
bump into: ~에 부딪히다
continued to run. Just then, Jihun saw something on the floor.
continue+to부정사: 계속해서 ~하다   바로 그때

"Wait, Seho!" he said, but Seho was not there.

After class, Seho went to Dami and said, "I can't find one of my
수업이 끝난 후에   one of: ~ 중 하나
tickets. Did you happen to see it?"
우연히 ~하다   = a ticket
"No," she answered. "Isn't it in your bag?"

"No, it's not there. I think I lost it," said Seho.

On her way home, Dami saw Jihun. He had the ticket in his hand.
집으로 오는 도중에
Dami got angry and said, "Hey! Why do you ...?"
get+형용사 = become+형용사
Just then, Jihun saw Seho and shouted, "Seho! I found a ticket in the

hallway. I think it's yours."
=your ticket
"Thanks! I was looking for that!" said Seho.
look for: ~을 찾다
"He's not so bad," Dami thought.

"So, what were you saying? Do you have something to say, Dami?"
to부정사의 형용사적 용법
asked Jihun.

"Um, how about going to the school basketball game with me this
How about -ing ~?: ~하는 게 어때?   ~와 함께
Friday? It's the finals."
= the school basketball game
Jihun looked really pleased. "I'd love to!"
look+형용사: ~하게 보이다   = I would

| floor 바닥 |
| find 발견하다 |
| answer 대답하다 |
| sad 슬픈 |
| shout 외치다 |
| hallway 복도 |
| final 결승전 |
| pleased 기쁜 |

📎 확인문제

● 다음 문장이 본문의 내용과 일치하면 T, 일치하지 않으면 F를 쓰시오.

1 Seho bumped into someone at the corner. ☐

2 Jihun saw something on the ground. ☐

3 After school, when Dami saw one of Seho's tickets in Jihun's hand, she got angry. ☐

4 Dami and Jihun are going to the school basketball game together this Friday. ☐

● 우리말을 참고하여 빈칸에 알맞은 말을 쓰시오.

1 Seho and Jihun _____ _____ in the hallway _____ Dami came _____.

2 "Happy birthday!" she _____ _____ Seho.

3 "Here. They're _____ my dad."

4 "Wow, two KBL _____! Thanks!"

5 "Who are you _____ to take _____ you?" Dami asked.

6 "Minjun. He _____ me _____ a soccer game before.

7 So, it's time to _____ him _____."

8 "You know _____?" Jihun cut _____.

9 "Minjun _____ a _____ of basketball. _____ I am!"

10 "Well, I'll ask him first _____," _____ Seho.

11 "He _____ go with you. _____ me," said Jihun.

12 "Who is this guy?" Dami _____ _____ _____, "He wants Minjun's ticket."

13 "Oh! _____ the bell. See you _____," said Dami.

14 She _____ to class.

15 "Come _____, Jihun," said Seho, and he started _____ _____.

16 _____ the corner, Seho _____ _____ someone.

17 "Sorry!" he said and _____ _____ run.

18 _____ then, Jihun saw something _____ the floor.

1 세호와 지훈이는 다미가 왔을 때 복도에서 이야기를 나누고 있었다.

2 "생일 축하해!" 다미가 세호에게 말했다.

3 "이거 받아. 우리 아빠가 주신 거야."

4 "와, KBL 입장권 두 장! 고마워!"

5 "넌 누구를 데려갈 거니?" 다미가 물었다.

6 "민준이. 그가 전에 나를 축구 경기에 데려갔어.

7 그래서 그에게 신세를 갚아야 할 때야."

8 "그거 알아?" 지훈이가 끼어들었다.

9 "민준이는 농구 팬이 아니야. 하지만 난 농구 팬이야!"

10 "음, 어쨌든 먼저 민준이에게 물어볼 거야." 세호가 대답했다.

11 "그는 너와 함께 가지 않을 거야. 날 믿어." 지훈이가 말했다.

12 "이 녀석은 누구지?" 다미는 "그는 민준이의 입장권을 원하는구나." 라고 마음속으로 생각했다.

13 "아, 종이 울린다. 나중에 보자," 다미가 말했다.

14 그녀는 서둘러 수업에 들어갔다.

15 "어서, 지훈아," 세호는 말하고 달리기 시작했다.

16 모퉁이에서, 세호는 누군가와 부딪혔다.

17 그는 "미안해!"라고 말하고는 계속 달렸다.

18 바로 그때, 지훈이가 바닥에 있는 무언가를 보았다.

19 "Wait, Seho!" he said, _____ Seho _____ _____ there.

20 _____ class, Seho went _____ Dami and said, "I can't find _____ _____ my tickets.

21 Did you _____ _____ see it?"

22 "No," she _____.

23 "_____ it _____ your bag?"

24 "No, it's _____ there. I think I _____ it," said Seho.

25 _____ her way home, Dami _____ Jihun.

26 He _____ the ticket _____ his hand.

27 Dami got _____ and said, "Hey! _____ do you ...?"

28 _____ _____, Jihun saw Seho and _____, "Seho! I found a ticket _____ the hallway.

29 I think it's _____."

30 "Thanks! I was _____ _____ that!" said Seho.

31 "He's _____ so bad," Dami _____.

32 "So, what _____ you _____?

33 Do you have something _____ _____, Dami?" _____ Jihun.

34 "Um, how _____ going _____ the school basketball game _____ me this Friday?

35 It's the _____."

36 Jihun _____ really _____. "I'd _____ _____!"

19 "기다려, 세호야!"라고 그가 말했지만 세호는 거기에 없었다.

20 수업이 끝난 후, 세호는 다미에게 가서 말했다. "내 입장권 한 장을 찾을 수 없어.

21 너 혹시 입장권을 봤니?"

22 "아니," 그녀가 대답했다.

23 "네 가방 안에 있지 않니?"

24 "아니, 거기에 없어. 내 생각에 그것을 잃어버린 것 같아." 세호가 말했다.

25 집으로 돌아오는 길에 다미는 지훈을 보았다.

26 그는 손에 입장권을 가지고 있었다.

27 다미는 화가 나서 "이봐! 너가 왜 ...?"라고 말했다.

28 바로 그때, 지훈이는 세호를 보고 소리쳤다. "세호야! 내가 복도에서 입장권을 찾았어.

29 네 것 같아."

30 "고마워! 나는 그것을 찾고 있었어!" 세호가 말했다.

31 "그는 그렇게 나쁘진 않아."라고 다미는 생각했다.

32 "그래서, 무슨 말을 하고 있었던 거야?

33 너 할 말이 있니, 다미야?" 지훈이가 물었다.

34 "음, 이번 금요일에 나랑 학교 농구 경기에 같이 가는 게 어때?

35 그것은 결승전이야."

36 지훈은 정말 기뻐 보였다. "가고 싶어!"

● 우리말을 참고하여 본문을 영작하시오.

1 세호와 지훈이는 다미가 왔을 때 복도에서 이야기를 나누고 있었다.

➡ _____

2 "생일 축하해!" 다미가 세호에게 말했다.

➡ _____

3 "이거 받아. 우리 아빠가 주신 거야."

➡ _____

4 "와, KBL 입장권 두 장! 고마워!"

➡ _____

5 "넌 누구를 데려갈 거니?" 다미가 물었다.

➡ _____

6 "민준이. 그가 전에 나를 축구 경기에 데려갔어.

➡ _____

7 그래서 그에게 신세를 갚아야 할 때야."

➡ _____

8 "그거 알아?" 지훈이가 끼어들었다.

➡ _____

9 "민준이는 농구 팬이 아니야. 하지만 난 농구 팬이야!"

➡ _____

10 "음, 어쨌든 먼저 민준이에게 물어볼 거야." 세호가 대답했다.

➡ _____

11 "그는 너와 함께 가지 않을 거야. 날 믿어." 지훈이가 말했다.

➡ _____

12 "이 녀석은 누구지?" 다미는 "그는 민준이의 입장권을 원하는구나."라고 마음속으로 생각했다.

➡ _____

13 "아, 종이 울린다. 나중에 보자,"라고 다미가 말했다.

➡ _____

14 그녀는 서둘러 수업에 들어갔다.

➡ _____

15 "어서, 지훈아." 세호는 말하고 달리기 시작했다.

➡ _____

16 모퉁이에서, 세호는 누군가와 부딪혔다.

➡ _____

17 그는 "미안해!"라고 말하고는 계속 달렸다.

➡ _____

18 바로 그때, 지훈이가 바닥에 있는 무언가를 보았다.

➡ _____

19 "기다려, 세호야!" 그가 말했지만 세호는 거기에 없었다.

➡ _____

20 수업이 끝난 후, 세호는 다미에게 가서 말했다. "내 입장권 한 장을 찾을 수 없어.

➡ _____

21 너 혹시 입장권을 봤니?"

➡ _____

22 "아니," 그녀가 대답했다.

➡ _____

23 "네 가방 안에 있지 않니?"

➡ _____

24 "아니, 거기에 없어. 내 생각에 그것을 잃어버린 것 같아." 세호가 말했다.

➡ _____

25 집으로 돌아오는 길에 다미는 지훈을 보았다.

➡ _____

26 그는 손에 입장권을 가지고 있었다.

➡ _____

27 다미는 화가 나서 "이봐! 너가 왜 ...?"라고 말했다.

➡ _____

28 바로 그때, 지훈이는 세호를 보고 소리쳤다. "세호야! 내가 복도에서 입장권을 찾았어.

➡ _____

29 네 것 같아."

➡ _____

30 "고마워! 나는 그것을 찾고 있었어!" 세호가 말했다.

➡ _____

31 "그는 그렇게 나쁘진 않아." 다미는 생각했다.

➡ _____

32 "그래서, 무슨 말을 하고 있었던 거야?

➡ _____

33 너 할 말이 있니, 다미야?" 지훈이가 물었다.

➡ _____

34 "음, 이번 금요일에 나랑 학교 농구 경기에 같이 가는 게 어때?

➡ _____

35 그것은 결승전이야."

➡ _____

36 지훈은 정말 기뻐 보였다. "가고 싶어!"

➡ _____

[01~05] 다음 글을 읽고, 물음에 답하시오.

At the corner, Seho bumped ⓐ someone. "Sorry!" he said and continued to run. Just then, Jihun saw something on the floor.

"Wait, Seho!" he said, ⓑ Seho was not there.

After class, Seho went to Dami and said, "I can't find one of my tickets. Did you happen to see ⓒit?"

"No," she answered.

"Isn't it in your bag?"

"No, it's not there. I think I lost it," said Seho.

⭐ 중요

01 위 글의 빈칸 ⓐ에 알맞은 것은?

① up   ② to
③ at   ④ into
⑤ over

02 위 글의 빈칸 ⓑ에 알맞은 것은?

① so   ② but
③ for   ④ or
⑤ and

서답형

03 위 글의 밑줄 친 ⓒ가 가리키는 것을 영어로 쓰시오.

➡ _____

서답형

04 위 글에서 다음 영영풀이에 해당하는 단어를 찾아 쓰시오.

> the flat surface that you stand on inside a building

➡ _____

서답형

05 위 글을 읽고, 다음 질문에 완전한 문장으로 답하시오.

> **Q:** What did Seho drop on the floor?
> **A:** _____

[06~10] 다음 글을 읽고, 물음에 답하시오.

Seho and Jihun were talking in the hallway when Dami came ⓐ .

"Happy birthday!" she said to Seho. "Here. ⓑThey're from my dad."

"Wow, two KBL tickets! Thanks!"

"Who are you going to take with you?" Dami asked.

"Minjun. He took me ⓒ a soccer game before. ⓓ , it's time to pay him back."

06 위 글의 빈칸 ⓐ에 알맞은 것은?

① off   ② out
③ at   ④ over
⑤ across

서답형

07 위 글의 밑줄 친 ⓑ가 의미하는 것을 영어로 쓰시오.

➡ _____

서답형

08 위 글의 빈칸 ⓒ에 알맞은 전치사를 쓰시오.

➡ _____

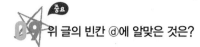

09 위 글의 빈칸 ⓓ에 알맞은 것은?

① But ② Also
③ Then ④ However
⑤ So

10 위 글의 내용과 일치하지 <u>않는</u> 것은?

① 세호와 지훈이는 복도에서 이야기하고 있었다.
② 농구 입장권은 다미의 아빠가 다미에게 주신 것이다.
③ 다미가 농구 입장권 두 장을 세호에게 주었다.
④ 세호는 민준이와 함께 농구를 보러 갈 거라고 말했다.
⑤ 세호는 민준이에게 돈을 빌린 적이 있다.

[11~15] 다음 글을 읽고, 물음에 답하시오.

　　　ⓐ　　 her way home, Dami saw Jihun. He had the ticket in his hand. Dami got angry and said, "Hey! Why do ①you ...?"
Just then, Jihun saw Seho and shouted, "Seho! ②I found a ticket in the hallway. I think it's yours."
"Thanks! I was looking for that!" said Seho.
"③He's not so bad," Dami thought.
"So, what were you saying? Do you have something ⓑto say, Dami?" asked Jihun.
"Um, how about going to the school basketball game with ④me this Friday? ⓒIt's the finals."
Jihun looked really pleased. "⑤I'd love to!"

11 위 글의 빈칸 ⓐ에 알맞은 것은?

① At ② In
③ On ④ To
⑤ Over

12 위 글의 밑줄 친 ①~⑤ 중 지칭하는 대상이 <u>다른</u> 하나는?

① ② ③ ④ ⑤

13 위 글의 밑줄 친 ⓑ와 쓰임이 같은 것은?

① I got up early to see her.
② He has many friends to help him.
③ He did his best to solve the problem.
④ To play the guitar is not easy.
⑤ He studies hard to pass the exam.

서답형

14 위 글의 밑줄 친 ⓒIt이 가리키는 것을 찾아 쓰시오.

➡ _____

15 위 글을 읽고, 답할 수 <u>없는</u> 질문은?

① When did Dami see Jihun?
② Why did Dami get angry?
③ Where did Jihun find a ticket?
④ What time is the school basketball game?
⑤ Who will Dami go to see the school basketball game with?

[16~20] 다음 글을 읽고, 물음에 답하시오.

"You know what?" Jihun cut ___ⓐ___ . "Minjun isn't a fan of basketball. But ①I am!"

"Well, I'll ask him first anyway," replied Seho.

"②He won't go with you. ___ⓑ___ me," said Jihun.

"Who is ③this guy?" Dami thought ___ⓒ___ herself, "④He wants Minjun's ticket."

"Oh! There's the bell. See you later," said Dami. She hurried to class.

"Come on, ⑤Jihun," said Seho, and he started to run.

중요

16 위 글의 빈칸 ⓐ에 알맞은 것은?

① in ② off
③ out ④ on
⑤ down

17 위 글의 밑줄 친 ①~⑤ 중 지칭하는 대상이 <u>다른</u> 하나는?

① ② ③ ④ ⑤

서답형

18 위 글의 빈칸 ⓑ에 다음 영영풀이에 해당하는 단어를 주어진 철자로 시작하여 쓰시오.

to believe that someone is honest or will not do anything bad or wrong

➡ T_____

서답형

19 위 글의 빈칸 ⓒ에 알맞은 전치사를 쓰시오.

➡ _____

서답형

20 위 글을 읽고, 다음 질문에 대한 답을 완성하시오.

Q: Why did Dami hurry to class?
A: Because _____ .

[21~26] 다음 글을 읽고, 물음에 답하시오.

①On her way to home, Dami saw Jihun. He had the ticket in his hand. Dami got angry and said, "Hey! ___ⓐ___ do you ...?"

Just then, Jihun saw Seho and shouted, "Seho! I found a ticket in the ___ⓑ___ . ⓒI think it's yours."

"Thanks! I ②was looking for that!" said Seho.

"He's not so bad," Dami thought.

"So, what were you ③saying? Do you have something ④to say, Dami?" asked Jihun.

"Um, ⓓhow about going to the school basketball game with me this Friday? It's the finals."

Jihun looked really ⑤pleased. "I'd love to!"

중요

21 위 글의 밑줄 친 ①~⑤ 중 어법상 <u>틀린</u> 것은?

① ② ③ ④ ⑤

22 위 글의 빈칸 ⓐ에 알맞은 것은?

① What ② How
③ Why ④ Where
⑤ When

서답형

23 위 글의 빈칸 ⓑ에 다음 영영풀이에 해당하는 단어를 주어진 철자로 시작하여 쓰시오.

> a passage in a building or house that leads to many of the rooms

➡ h_____

서답형

24 위 글의 밑줄 친 ⓒ에서 생략된 말을 추가하여 문장을 다시 쓰시오.

➡ _____

서답형

25 위 글의 밑줄 친 ⓓ를 다음과 같이 바꿔 쓸 때 빈칸에 알맞은 말을 쓰시오.

> _____ _____ _____ go to the school basketball game with me this Friday?

26 위 글의 내용과 일치하지 <u>않는</u> 것은?

① 다미는 집에 가는 도중에 지훈이를 만났다.
② 다미는 지훈이가 입장권을 가지고 있는 것을 보고 화가 났다.
③ 지훈이는 복도에서 입장권을 발견했다.
④ 다미는 지훈이가 나쁜 소년이라는 생각이 바뀌지 않았다.
⑤ 다미와 지훈이는 이번 주 금요일에 학교 농구 경기에 갈 것이다.

[27~29] 다음 글을 읽고, 물음에 답하시오.

At the corner, Seho bumped into someone. (①) "Sorry!" ⓐhe said and continued to run. Just then, Jihun saw something ___(A)___ the floor. (②)
"Wait, Seho!" ⓑhe said, but Seho was not there. (③)
After class, Seho went to Dami and said, "ⓒI can't find one ___(B)___ my tickets. (④)"
"No," she answered.
"Isn't it in "ⓓyour bag?"
"No, it's not there. (⑤) I think ⓔI lost it," said Seho.

27 위 글의 빈칸 (A)와 (B)에 알맞은 말이 바르게 짝지어진 것은?

① in – from
② at – for
③ from – in
④ over – about
⑤ on – of

28 위 글의 ①~⑤ 중 주어진 문장이 들어갈 알맞은 곳은?

> Did you happen to see it?

①   ②   ③   ④   ⑤

29 위 글의 밑줄 친 ⓐ~ⓔ 중 지칭하는 대상이 <u>다른</u> 하나는?

① ⓐ   ② ⓑ   ③ ⓒ   ④ ⓓ   ⑤ ⓔ

[01~04] 다음 글을 읽고, 물음에 답하시오.

　　Seho and Jihun were talking in the hallway when Dami came (A)[out / over].

　　"Happy birthday!" she said to Seho. "Here. They're from my dad."

　　"Wow, two KBL tickets! Thanks!"

　　"Who are you going to take with you?" Dami asked.

　　"Minjun. He took me to a soccer game before. So, ⓐ그에게 신세를 갚아야 할 때야."

　　"You know what?" Jihun cut (B)[in / out]. "Minjun isn't a fan of basketball. But I am!"

　　"Well, I'll ask him first anyway," replied Seho.

01 위 글의 괄호 (A)와 (B)에서 알맞은 것을 골라 쓰시오.

(A) _____　　(B) _____

02 Who did Dami give two basketball tickets to? Answer in English.

➡ _____

03 Who does Seho want to go to a basketball game with? Answer in English.

➡ _____

04 위 글의 밑줄 친 ⓐ의 우리말에 맞도록 주어진 어구를 순서대로 배열하시오.

(him / back / to / it's / pay / time)

➡ _____

[05~08] 다음 글을 읽고, 물음에 답하시오.

　　At the corner, Seho bumped into someone. "Sorry!" he said and continued to run. Just then, Jihun saw something on the floor.

　　"Wait, Seho!" he said, but Seho was not there.

　　After class, Seho went to Dami and said, "I can't find one of my tickets. Did you happen to see it?"

　　"No," she answered.

　　"Isn't it in your bag?"

　　"No, it's not ⓐthere. ⓑ나는 그것을 잃어버린 것 같아," said Seho.

05 Where did Seho bump into someone? Answer in English.

➡ _____

06 What did Seho say to Dami when he went to her? Answer in Korean.

➡ _____
_____

07 위 글의 밑줄 친 ⓐ가 의미하는 것을 영어로 쓰시오.

➡ _____

08 위 글의 밑줄 친 ⓑ의 우리말을 주어진 단어와 필요한 단어를 추가하여 영어로 옮기시오.

(think / it)

➡ _____

[09~12] 다음 글을 읽고, 물음에 답하시오.

"You know what?" ⓐ민준이가 끼어들었다. "Minjun isn't a fan of basketball. But ⓑI am!"

"Well, I'll ask him first anyway," replied Seho.

"He won't go with you. Trust me," said Jihun.

"Who is this guy?" ⓒ다미는 마음속으로 생각했다, "He wants Minjun's ticket."

"Oh! There's the bell. See you later," said Dami. She hurried to _____ⓓ_____.

"Come on, Jihun," said Seho, and he started to run.

09 위 글의 밑줄 친 ⓐ의 우리말에 맞게 빈칸에 알맞은 말을 쓰시오.

Minjun cut _____.

10 위 글의 밑줄 친 ⓑ 다음에 생략된 말을 보충하여 다시 쓰시오.

➡ _____

11 위 글의 밑줄 친 ⓒ의 우리말에 맞게 주어진 단어를 이용하여 영어로 옮기시오. (필요하면 어형을 바꿀 것)

(think / her)

➡ _____

12 위 글의 빈칸 ⓓ에 다음 영영풀이에 해당하는 단어를 쓰시오.

a series of meetings in which students are taught a particular subject or activity

➡ _____

[13~16] 다음 글을 읽고, 물음에 답하시오.

ⓐ집으로 오는 도중에, Dami saw Jihun. He had the ticket in his hand. Dami got angry and sad, "Hey! Why do you ...?"

Just then, Jihun saw Seho and shouted, "Seho! I found a ticket in the hallway. I think it's yours."

"Thanks! I was looking for that!" said Seho.

"He's not so bad," Dami thought.

"So, what were you saying? Do you have something to say, Dami?" asked Jihun.

"Um, how about going to the school basketball game with me this Friday? It's the _____ⓑ_____."

13 위 글의 밑줄 친 ⓐ의 우리말에 맞게 빈칸에 알맞은 말을 쓰시오.

_____ _____ _____ home

14 Why did Dami get angry? Answer in English.

➡ _____

15 Where did Jihun find the ticket? Answer in English.

➡ _____

16 위 글의 빈칸 ⓑ에 다음 영영풀이에 해당하는 단어를 쓰시오. (복수형으로 쓸 것)

the last and most important game in a competition

➡ _____

Express Yourself - C

Do you have something to say about the school cafeteria? Then post your

to부정사의 형용사적 용법(~할)

notes here!

• I think the line is too long. Are there any ways to solve this problem?

명사절을 이끄는 접속사 that 생략

• I think the chairs are too high. Do you have any plans to change them?

= the chairs

• I think the chicken was really delicious. Do you have any plans to serve it

= the chicken

more often?

구문해설 • cafeteria: 구내식당 • post: 게시[공고]하다 • note: 메모 • problem: 문제
• delicious: 맛있는 • serve: 제공하다

해석

학교 구내식당에 대해 할 말이 있니? 그럼 여기 네 메모를 게시해!

• 줄이 너무 긴 것 같아. 이 문제를 해결할 방법이 있을까?

• 의자가 너무 높다고 생각해. 의자를 바꿀 계획이 있는가?

• 닭고기가 정말 맛있었다고 생각해. 닭고기를 더 자주 제공할 계획이 있는가?

Project - Link to the World

가는 말이 고와야 오는 말이 곱다.

This saying means "Nice words for nice words" in English. I will say nice

영어로

words to others first. Then they will say nice words to me, too. I believe

= a lot of, many

that I can make lots of good friends this way. This year, I will always try to

명사절을 이끄는 접속사 that(목적어 역할)   이런 식으로   빈도부사는 일반동사 앞이나 be동사, 조동사 뒤에 위치한다.

remember this saying and say nice words to others.

구문해설 • saying: 속담 • mean: 의미하다 • word: 말 • this way: 이런 식으로 • always: 항상
• remember: 기억하다(↔ forget 잊다)

가는 말이 고와야 오는 말이 곱다

이 속담은 영어로 '좋은 말에는 좋은 말로'를 뜻한다. 나는 먼저 다른 사람들에게 좋은 말을 할 것이다. 그러면 그들도 나에게 좋은 말을 할 것이다. 나는 이런 식으로 좋은 친구들을 많이 사귈 수 있다고 믿어. 올해, 나는 항상 이 속담을 기억하고 다른 사람들에게 좋은 말을 하려고 노력할 것이다.

Learning Diary - Read & Write

Dami gave Seho two basketball tickets. Jihun wanted to go to the basketball

= Dami gave two basketball tickets to Seho.

game with Seho. Seho dropped one of the tickets on his way to class. Jihun

~ 중 하나   on one's way to: ~로 가는 도중에

found Seho's ticket in the hallway. Dami saw Seho's ticket in Jihun's hand, and

she thought, "He's a bad boy." Jihun gave the ticket back to Seho, and Dami

give A back to B: A를 B에게 돌려주다

realized that she was wrong. Dami wanted to go to the school basketball game

명사절을 이끄는 접속사 that(목적어 역할)

with Jihun. Jihun was really pleased.

구문해설 • drop: 떨어뜨리다 • class: 수업 • hallway: 복도 • realize: 깨닫다 • pleased: 기쁜

다미가 세호에게 농구 입장권 두 장을 주었다. 지훈이는 세호와 농구 경기에 가고 싶어했다. 세호는 수업에 가는 길에 입장권 하나를 떨어뜨렸다. 지훈이는 복도에서 세호의 입장권을 발견했다. 다미는 지훈이의 손에 있는 세호의 입장권을 보았고 그녀는 "그는 나쁜 소년이야."라고 생각했다. 지훈이는 세호에게 입장권을 돌려주었고 다미는 그녀가 틀렸다는 것을 깨달았다. 다미는 지훈이와 함께 학교 농구 경기에 가고 싶었다. 지훈이는 정말 기뻐했다.

영역별 핵심문제

01 다음 영영풀이에 해당하는 단어로 알맞은 것은?

> to form an opinion about something or someone after careful thought

① reply   ② expect
③ promise   ④ realize
⑤ judge

02 다음 빈칸에 알맞은 것은?

> I met her _____ my way to school.

① on   ② at
③ from   ④ in
⑤ over

03 다음 중 짝지어진 두 단어의 관계가 <u>다른</u> 것은?

① right : wrong   ② floor : ceiling
③ tasty : delicious   ④ ask : answer
⑤ remember : forget

04 다음 우리말과 같도록 빈칸에 알맞은 말을 주어진 철자로 시작하여 쓰시오.

> 우리 선생님은 엄격하시고 진지하시다.
> ➡ My teacher is strict and s_____.

05 다음 빈칸에 공통으로 알맞은 말을 주어진 철자로 시작하여 쓰시오.

> • They _____ traditional French food.
> • Their job is to _____ and protect people.

➡ s_____

06 다음 빈칸에 우리말에 맞도록 알맞은 말을 쓰시오.

> 올해 우리는 화이트 크리스마스를 기대하고 있다.
> ➡ We are expecting a white Christmas _____ _____.

07 다음 대화의 빈칸에 알맞은 것은?

> A: What did you think of the musical, Kelly?
> B: _____
> A: I agree with you. I enjoyed it a lot.

① You're right.
② I thought so, too.
③ Sounds great. Let's go.
④ I think it was great.
⑤ I don't think you're right.

08 다음 대화의 빈칸에 들어갈 말로 적절하지 <u>않은</u> 것은?

> A: What are you going to do this Sunday?
> B: I'm going to watch a *Harry Potter* movie. _____

① I'm looking forward it.
② I'm expecting it.
③ I can't wait to watch it.
④ I'm worried about it.
⑤ It will be nice to watch it.

09 다음 대화의 순서를 바르게 배열하시오.

> (A) I can't wait for lunchtime tomorrow.
> (B) What do you think of today's lunch?
> (C) Wow! We can eat spaghetti tomorrow.
> (D) I think it's okay. What's on tomorrow's menu?

➡ _____

[10~14] 다음 대화를 읽고, 물음에 답하시오.

> B: Let's join the Green Garden club together. ⓐ<u>너는 그것에 대해 어떻게 생각하니?</u>
> G: Okay. I like growing vegetables.
> B: You know what? I like eating vegetables.
> G: Let's join the club right ___ ⓑ ___. We can have a party with fresh vegetables every month.
> B: Great. The first party is ___ ⓒ ___ April 30.
> G: ⓓ<u>I can't wait for the party.</u>

10 위 대화의 밑줄 친 ⓐ를 영어로 옮길 때 빈칸에 알맞은 말을 쓰시오.

> _____ do you _____ _____ it?

11 위 대화의 빈칸 ⓑ에 알맞은 것은?

① on   ② at
③ in   ④ from
⑤ now

12 위 대화의 빈칸 ⓒ에 알맞은 전치사를 쓰시오.

➡ _____

13 위 대화의 밑줄 친 ⓓ와 바꿔 쓸 수 있는 것은?

① I can't attend the party.
② I don't expect the party.
③ I don't want to have the party.
④ I'm not going to go to the party.
⑤ I'm looking forward to the party.

14 위 대화를 읽고, 답할 수 <u>없는</u> 질문은?

① Does the girl want to join the Green Garden club?
② Does the girl like growing vegetables?
③ Does the boy like eating vegetables?
④ How often do they have a party with fresh vegetables?
⑤ What day does the first party take place?

Grammar

15 다음 우리말과 일치하도록 빈칸에 알맞은 말을 쓰시오.

> 나는 이 아이스크림이 맛있다고 생각한다.
> ➡ I _____ _____ this ice cream is delicious.

16 다음 문장의 빈칸에 알맞은 것은?

> The doctor has a lot of patients _____.

① taken care
② to take care
③ take care of
④ taking care of
⑤ to take care of

17 다음 밑줄 친 that 중 쓰임이 다른 하나는?

① I think <u>that</u> the movie was terrible.
② I know <u>that</u> Sally doesn't have a job.
③ I think <u>that</u> bag is yours.
④ I hope <u>that</u> he will be my boyfriend.
⑤ I know <u>that</u> she will go abroad to study.

18 다음 중 밑줄 친 부분의 쓰임이 나머지 넷과 다른 것은?

① I need a skirt <u>to wear</u> tomorrow.
② I decided <u>to write</u> a letter to her.
③ I have a lot of homework <u>to do</u>.
④ New York is a great city <u>to visit</u>.
⑤ I am looking for a chair <u>to sit</u> on.

19 다음 우리말과 일치하도록 주어진 단어를 바르게 배열하시오.

> 우리는 그녀가 파티에 올 것이라고 믿지 않는다.
> (party / the / she / come / to / that / will / don't / believe / we)

➡ _____

20 다음 문장에서 어법상 어색한 부분을 찾아 고치시오.

> I have no friends to talk.

_____ ➡ _____

21 다음 중 어법상 어색한 문장은?

① That sounds good.
② That would be great.
③ I'm going to have a party.
④ I think that the girl pretty.
⑤ I hope that you enjoy your trip.

22 다음 중 밑줄 친 that의 쓰임이 〈보기〉와 같은 것은?

> ┤ 보기 ├
> I think <u>that</u> you already did your homework.

① Look at <u>that</u>!
② I'm sorry to hear <u>that</u>.
③ <u>That</u> cat is drinking water.
④ <u>That</u> he has a cold is true.
⑤ I want to make movie like <u>that</u>.

23 다음 〈보기〉의 우리말을 영어로 바르게 옮긴 것은?

┌─ 보기 ├─
그는 살 좋은 집을 갖기를 원한다.
└─────────────┘

① He wants to have a good house live.
② He wants to have a good house live in.
③ He wants to have live in a good house.
④ He wants to have to live in a good house.
⑤ He wants to have a good house to live in.

24 다음 우리말과 같도록 주어진 단어를 바르게 배열하시오.

┌─────────────────────┐
그녀는 그가 잘생겼다고 생각하지 않았다.
(he / handsome / think / that / was / didn't)
➡ She _____.
└─────────────────────┘

25 다음 중 어법상 어색한 문장은?

① I want something to drink.
② I need a house to live.
③ There is a bench to sit on.
④ He went to the store to buy a toy.
⑤ She grew up to be a pianist.

26 다음 주어진 단어를 이용하여 우리말을 영어로 옮기시오.

┌─────────────────────┐
나는 읽을 책이 한 권 필요하다. (need / read)
└─────────────────────┘

➡ _____

[27~33] 다음 글을 읽고, 물음에 답하시오.

Seho and Jihun were talking in the hallway ___ⓐ___ Dami came over. "Happy birthday!" she said to Seho. "Here. They're from my dad."

"Wow, two KBL tickets! Thanks!"

"Who are you going to take ___ⓑ___ you?" Dami asked.

"Minjun. He took me to a soccer game before. ___ⓒ___, it's time ⓓto pay him back."

"You know ___ⓔ___?" Jihun cut in. "Minjun isn't a fan of basketball. ___ⓕ___ I am!"

"Well, I'll ask him first anyway," replied Seho.

"He won't go with you. Trust me," said Jihun.

"Who is this guy?" Dami thought ___ⓖ___ herself, "He wants Minjun's ticket."

"Oh! There's the bell. See you later," said Dami. She hurried to class.

27 위 글의 빈칸 ⓐ와 ⓔ에 알맞은 말이 바르게 짝지어진 것은?

① if – how   ② that – when
③ where – what   ④ when – what
⑤ because – how

28 위 글의 빈칸 ⓑ에 알맞은 전치사를 쓰시오.

➡ _____

29 위 글의 빈칸 ⓒ와 ⓕ에 알맞은 말이 바르게 짝지어진 것은?

① But – Or   ② So – But
③ Then – For   ④ Also – And
⑤ However – So

30 위 글의 밑줄 친 ⓓ와 쓰임이 같은 것은?

① His dream was to draw pictures.

② It's easy to memorize English words.

③ I have a lot of work to do today.

④ He wants to play tennis after school.

⑤ She studied very hard to pass the exam.

31 위 글의 빈칸 ⑨에 알맞은 것은?

① at   ② on

③ to   ④ in

⑤ of

32 위 글에서 다음 영영풀이에 해당하는 단어를 찾아 쓰시오.

> at a time in the future

➡ _____

33 위 글을 읽고, 답할 수 없는 질문은?

① Where were Seho and Jihun talking?

② Who did Dami's dad get the basketball tickets from?

③ Who did Dami give two basketball tickets to?

④ Why does Seho want to go to the basketball game with Minjun?

⑤ Why did Dami hurry to class?

[34~37] 다음 글을 읽고, 물음에 답하시오.

(①) This saying means "Nice words for nice words"   ⓐ   English. (②) I will say nice words to others first. (③) I believe that I can make ⓑlots of good friends this way. (④) This year, I will always try to remember this saying and say nice words to others. (⑤)

34 위 글의 ①~⑤ 중 다음 문장이 들어갈 알맞은 곳은?

> Then they will say nice words to me, too.

①   ②   ③   ④   ⑤

35 위 글의 빈칸 ⓐ에 알맞은 전치사를 쓰시오.

➡ _____

36 위 글의 밑줄 친 ⓑ를 한 단어로 바꿔 쓰시오.

➡ _____

37 위 글의 제목으로 알맞은 것은?

① 농담 속에 진실이 많다.

② 행하기보다는 말하기가 쉽다.

③ 쉽게 얻은 것은 쉽게 나간다.

④ 가는 말이 고와야 오는 말이 곱다.

⑤ 낮말은 새가 듣고 밤 말은 쥐가 듣는다.

01 출제율 90%

다음 짝지어진 두 단어의 관계가 같도록 빈칸에 알맞은 말을 쓰시오.

> dangerous : safe = remember : _____

02 출제율 95%

다음 빈칸에 공통으로 알맞은 것을 쓰시오.

> • Sam is looking _____ his teddy bear.
> • Vegetables are good _____ our health.

➡ _____

03 출제율 90%

다음 중 영영풀이가 잘못된 것은?

① grow: to make plants grow
② boring: dull and uninteresting
③ floor: the inside surface at the top of a room
④ join: to become a member of a group or organization
⑤ cover: the outer part of a book or magazine

04 출제율 100%

다음 우리말에 맞도록 빈칸에 알맞은 말을 쓰시오.

> 수지는 마음속으로 생각했다.
> ➡ Suji _____ _____ _____.

05 출제율 95%

다음 빈칸에 알맞은 말이 바르게 짝지어진 것은?

> • I bumped _____ a basketball post yesterday.
> • My dad promised to buy a cake _____ his way home.

① at – in
② in – for
③ with – at
④ into – on
⑤ from – on

06 출제율 85%

다음 빈칸에 공통으로 들어갈 알맞은 말을 주어진 철자로 시작하여 쓰시오.

> • The referee blew the _____ whistle.
> • At the _____ game, Korea beat Japan 3-0.

➡ f_____

07 출제율 90%

다음 대화의 빈칸에 알맞은 것은?

> A: _____
> B: I think he works hard.
> A: He always tries to do his best. That's why students like him.

① What does Mr. Kim do on weekends?
② Who does Mr. Kim live with?
③ Who does Mr. Kim work with?
④ Why does Mr. Kim work hard?
⑤ What do you think about Mr. Kim?

[08~11] 다음 대화를 읽고, 물음에 답하시오.

> G: What do you think of the magic club?
> B: ⓐ그것은 나에게 맞는 동아리인 것 같아. I want to learn many interesting ⓑ .
> G: I'll join ⓒit, too. When is the first meeting?
> B: Next Wednesday. ⓓI can't wait for the first meeting!

출제율 90%

08 위 대화의 밑줄 친 ⓐ의 우리말에 맞도록 주어진 단어를 이용하여 영어로 옮기시오. (8단어)

(right / for / think)

➡ _____

출제율 85%

09 위 대화의 빈칸 ⓑ에 다음 영영풀이에 해당하는 단어를 주어진 철자로 시작하여 쓰시오. (복수형으로 쓸 것)

a clever and skillful action that someone performs to entertain or amuse people

➡ t_____

출제율 100%

10 위 대화의 밑줄 친 ⓒ가 가리키는 것을 찾아 쓰시오.

➡ _____

출제율 95%

11 위 대화의 밑줄 친 ⓓ의 의도로 알맞은 것은?

① 금지하기   ② 이의 제기하기
③ 기대 표현하기   ④ 놀람 표현하기
⑤ 상기시켜 주기

출제율 90%

12 다음 빈칸에 들어갈 말로 알맞은 것은?

My father says _____ I should study more.

① when   ② that
③ if   ④ while
⑤ before

출제율 85%

13 다음 문장의 빈칸에 알맞은 것은?

We want to introduce _____ water.

① saving a way   ② to save a way
③ a way save   ④ a way saving
⑤ a way to save

출제율 90%

14 다음 괄호 안에 주어진 단어를 이용하여 우리말을 영어로 옮기시오.

(1) 그녀는 딸이 아프다고 생각한다.
   (think / that / sick)
   ➡ _____

(2) 나는 Nick이 파티에 올 것이라고 믿지 않는다.
   (believe / that)
   ➡ _____

출제율 95%

15 다음 중 밑줄 친 부분의 용법이 나머지 넷과 다른 것은?

① She met Mike to play table tennis.
② I have no house to live in.
③ He saved money to buy a new bike.
④ I turned on the TV to watch the news.
⑤ Amy went to London to meet her friend.

16 다음 두 문장을 한 문장으로 쓸 때 빈칸에 알맞은 말을 쓰시오.

> I need a friend. + I play with the friend.
> ➡ I need a friend _____ .

17 다음 중 밑줄 친 부분의 쓰임이 다른 하나는?

① I think that he is American.
② He knows that she is rich.
③ We don't hope that you will like it.
④ I can't believe that you made this.
⑤ The news that he would not recover worried me.

18 다음 밑줄 친 부분의 쓰임이 〈보기〉와 같은 것은? (2개)

> I had a lot of work to complete.

① To see is to believe.
② She grew up to become a doctor.
③ Do you have time to play basketball?
④ I went to a mall to buy new shoes.
⑤ Give me a chair to sit on.

19 다음 우리말과 같도록 주어진 단어를 이용하여 빈칸에 알맞은 말을 쓰시오.

> 우리는 케이크를 구울 더 많은 밀가루가 필요하다.
> (flour / bake)

➡ _____

[20~25] 다음 글을 읽고, 물음에 답하시오.

> ⓐDami gave Seho two basketball tickets. Jihun wanted to go to the basketball game with Seho. Seho dropped one of the tickets ⓑ his way to class. Jihun found Seho's ticket in the hallway. Dami saw Seho's ticket in Jihun's hand, and she thought, "He's a bad boy." ⓒJihun gave the ticket back to Seho, and Dami realized ⓓ she was ⓔ. Dami wanted to go to the school basketball game with Jihun. Jihun was really pleased.

20 위 글의 밑줄 친 ⓐ를 3형식 문장으로 바꿔 쓰시오.

➡ _____

21 위 글의 빈칸 ⓑ에 알맞은 것은?

① at   ② in
③ to   ④ on
⑤ by

22 위 글의 밑줄 친 ⓒ를 우리말로 쓰시오.

➡ _____

23 위 글의 빈칸 ⓓ에 알맞은 것을 쓰시오.

➡ _____

24 위 글의 빈칸 ⓔ에 다음 영영풀이에 해당하는 단어를 쓰시오. *출제율95%*

> speaking, acting, or judging in a way that does not agree with the facts or truth

➡ _____

25 위 글을 읽고, 답할 수 <u>없는</u> 질문은? *출제율90%*

① Who did Jihun want to go to the basketball game with?

② What did Seho drop on his way to class?

③ Where did Jihun find Seho's ticket?

④ Why did Dami think Jihun was a bad boy?

⑤ What time is the school basketball game?

[26~30] 다음 글을 읽고, 물음에 답하시오.

> _ⓐ_ her way home, Dami saw Jihun. He had the ticket in his hand. Dami got angry and said, "Hey! Why do ①<u>you</u> ...?"
>
> Just then, Jihun saw Seho and shouted, "Seho! ②<u>I</u> found a ticket in the hallway. I think it's ⓑ<u>you</u>."
>
> "Thanks! I was looking _ⓒ_ that!" said Seho.
>
> "③<u>He's</u> not so bad," Dami thought.
>
> "So, what were you saying? Do you have something ⓓ<u>say</u>, Dami?" asked Jihun.
>
> "Um, how about ⓔ<u>go</u> to the school basketball game with ④<u>me</u> this Friday? It's the finals."
>
> Jihun looked really pleased. "⑤<u>I'd</u> love to!"

26 위 글의 밑줄 친 ①~⑤ 중 지칭하는 대상이 <u>다른</u> 하나는? *출제율90%*

①　　②　　③　　④　　⑤

27 위 글의 빈칸 ⓐ와 ⓒ에 알맞은 말이 바르게 짝지어진 것은? *출제율85%*

① On – at　　② In – for

③ At – at　　④ On – for

⑤ In – about

28 위 글의 밑줄 친 ⓑ를 알맞은 형태로 고쳐 쓰시오. (한 단어로 쓸 것) *출제율90%*

➡ _____

29 위 글의 밑줄 친 ⓓ와 ⓔ를 알맞은 형태로 고쳐 쓰시오. *출제율100%*

ⓓ _____　ⓔ _____

30 Why did Dami think Jihun was not so bad? Answer in Korean. *출제율85%*

➡ _____

단원별 예상문제 **49**

서술형 실전문제

01 다음 우리말과 같은 뜻이 되도록 빈칸에 알맞은 말을 쓰시오.

> 나는 그 여행이 매우 기대돼.
> ➡ I _____ _____ for the trip.

02 다음 대화의 빈칸에 주어진 말을 이용하여 영어로 쓰시오.

> A: _____ (what / think)
>   (너의 영어 선생님에 대해서 어떻게 생각하니?)
> B: She is kind.

➡ _____

03 다음 대화의 괄호 안의 단어들을 바르게 배열하여 대화를 완성하시오.

> A: When does your summer vacation start?
> B: This Friday. (to / forward / it / looking / I'm).

➡ _____

04 자연스러운 대화가 되도록 (A)~(D)의 순서를 바르게 배열하시오.

> (A) I'll join the soccer club. I like playing soccer.
> (B) The health club? I think it's boring.
> (C) This club looks good for you. What do you think of it?
> (D) Then which club do you want to join?

➡ _____

05 다음 문장에서 어법상 <u>어색한</u> 부분을 찾아 바르게 고쳐 쓰시오.

> I need a pen to write.

_____ ➡ _____

[06~07] 다음 괄호 안에 주어진 어구를 이용하여 우리말을 영어로 옮기시오.

06 (1) 나는 그녀가 선생님이었다는 것을 안다.
   (know / that / teacher)
   ➡ _____

   (2) 나는 그가 정직하다고 생각한다.
   (think / that / honest)
   ➡ _____

   (3) 그는 그것이 매우 재미있을 것이라고 믿는다.
   (believe / that / a lot of fun)
   ➡ _____

07 (1) 그녀는 가수가 되려는 강한 욕망을 갖고 있다.
   (strong desire, be, singer)
   ➡ _____

   (2) 우리는 이야기할 것이 있었다.
   (something, talk about)
   ➡ _____

   (3) 나는 쓸 종이를 한 장 원한다.
   (want, write)
   ➡ _____

   (4) 제게 뜨거운 마실 것을 좀 주십시오.
   (please, something, drink)
   ➡ _____

ⓐOn her way to home, Dami saw Jihun. He had the ticket in his hand. Dami got angry and said, "Hey! Why do you ...?"

Just then, Jihun saw Seho and shouted, "Seho! I found a ticket in the hallway. ⓑ(I / it's / yours / think / that)."

"Thanks! I was looking for that!" said Seho.

"He's not so bad," Dami thought.

"So, what were you saying? Do you have something to say, Dami?" asked Jihun.

"Um, how about going to the school basketball game with me this Friday? It's the finals."

Jihun looked really ___ⓒ___. "I'd love to!"

08 위 글의 밑줄 친 ⓐ에서 어법상 어색한 부분을 바르게 고쳐 문장을 다시 쓰시오.

➡ _____

09 위 글의 ⓑ 안의 단어들을 순서대로 바르게 배열하시오.

➡ _____

10 When is the school basketball game? Answer in English.

➡ _____

11 위 글의 빈칸 ⓒ에 다음 영영풀이에 해당하는 단어를 주어진 철자로 시작하여 쓰시오.

> feeling happy about something

➡ p_____

_____

This ___ⓐ___ means "Nice words for nice words" in English. I will say nice words to others first. Then they will say nice words to me, (A)[too / either]. I believe that I can make lots of good friends ⓑthis way. This year, I will always try (B)[remembering / to remember] this ___ⓒ___ and say nice words to others.

12 위 글의 빈칸 ⓐ와 ⓒ에 공통으로 알맞은 것을 다음 영영풀이를 참조하여 주어진 철자로 시작하여 쓰시오.

> an old and well-known phrase that expresses an idea that most people believe is true

➡ s_____

13 위 글의 괄호 (A)와 (B)에서 알맞은 것을 골라 쓰시오.

(A) _____ (B) _____

14 위 글의 밑줄 친 ⓑ가 의미하는 것을 우리말로 쓰시오.

➡ _____

_____

15 위 글의 빈칸에 알맞은 제목을 우리말 속담으로 쓰시오.

➡ _____

창의사고력 서술형 문제

01 다음 질문에 각자의 답을 to부정사를 이용하여 〈보기〉와 같이 쓰시오.

> ⊢ 보기 ⊨
>
> I want a pair of short pants to wear during the summer.

> **Q:** What do you want for your birthday present? You should mention at least two items.

(1) _____

(2) _____

02 다음 (A), (B), (C)에 주어진 어구를 이용하여 〈보기〉와 같이 문장을 4개 쓰시오. (필요하면 어형을 바꿀 것)

(A)	(B)	(C)
I	know that	Jenny is kind
He	hope that	they need help
She	say that	it's delicious
Tony	think that	many children are hungry
They	hear that	everyone will be happy

> ⊢ 보기 ⊨
>
> I hope that everyone will be happy.

(1) _____

(2) _____

(3) _____

(4) _____

03 자신의 경우에 맞게 to부정사를 이용하여 〈보기〉와 같이 지금 필요한 것에 대해 써 보시오.(3 문장 이상)

> ⊢ 보기 ⊨
>
> I need something to drink.

(1) _____

(2) _____

(3) _____

(4) _____

단원별 모의고사

01 다음 영영풀이에 해당하는 단어로 알맞은 것은?

> to give food or drink to someone at a meal, in a restaurant, etc.

① wait   ② reply
③ hurry   ④ serve
⑤ practice

02 다음 중 밑줄 친 우리말 뜻이 잘못된 것은?

① She cut in on our talk.
    끼어들었다
② It will snow a lot this year.
            올해
③ I happened to hear the news.
    우연히 들었다
④ After school, I was walking home alone.
    방과 후에
⑤ I found out about it yesterday.
    발견했다

03 다음 빈칸에 들어갈 말로 적절하지 않은 것은? (대・소문자 무시)

> • _____ your notes here.
> • Can you tell me how to _____ this problem?
> • I will _____ back the money within three days.
> • Spend time with people that you _____.

① trust   ② mean
③ pay   ④ solve
⑤ post

04 다음 빈칸에 알맞은 말이 바르게 짝지어진 것은?

> • Look _____ the price tag.
> • Walking in the morning is good _____ the health.

① in – to   ② at – for
③ of – for   ④ to – at
⑤ for – at

05 다음 빈칸에 공통으로 알맞은 말을 주어진 철자로 시작하여 쓰시오.

> • He is a big baseball f_____.
> • He turned on the f_____ because it was too hot.

06 다음 우리말에 맞도록 빈칸에 알맞은 말을 쓰시오.

> 남의 이야기 중에 끼어드는 것은 무례한 짓이다.
> ➡ It is rude to _____ _____ while others are talking.

07 다음 중 그 의미가 나머지 넷과 다른 하나는?

① I'm looking forward to the game.
② I'm expecting the game.
③ I can't wait to see the game.
④ I'm worried about the game.
⑤ I want to see the game.

[08~12] 다음 대화를 읽고, 물음에 답하시오.

> B: Let's join the School Band club together. ⓐWhat do you think of it?
> G: Okay. I like playing the flute. (①)
> B: I like playing the ukulele.
> G: Let's join the club right now. (②) They practice after school every Tuesday and Thursday. (③)
> B: They're going to have the first concert ___ⓑ___ July 15. (④)
> G: Great. (⑤)
> B: Me, too. ⓒ나는 콘서트가 매우 기다려져.

08 위 대화의 밑줄 친 ⓐ와 바꿔 쓸 수 없는 것은?

① How do you like it?
② Why don't you think of it?
③ What's your opinion on it?
④ How do you feel about it?
⑤ What do you think about it?

09 위 대화의 ①~⑤ 중 다음 문장이 들어갈 알맞은 곳은?

> I hope to play in the concert.

①　　　②　　　③　　　④　　　⑤

10 위 대화의 빈칸 ⓑ에 알맞은 것은?

① at　　　② in　　　③ on
④ for　　　⑤ over

11 위 대화의 밑줄 친 ⓒ의 우리말을 주어진 단어를 이용하여 영작하시오.

> (wait)

➡ _____

12 위 대화의 내용을 다음과 같이 포스터로 만들 때 빈칸에 알맞은 말을 쓰시오.

School Band
• Practice: after school on _____ and _____
• First Concert: _____ _____

13 다음 빈칸에 알맞은 것은?

> This is a good story _____.

① read　　　　② reads
③ to read　　　④ reading
⑤ to reading

14 다음 중 밑줄 친 부분의 쓰임이 나머지와 다른 하나는?

① I think that he is handsome.
② He believes that he can be a good doctor.
③ She hopes that there will be no more exams.
④ Do you know that handsome guy over there?
⑤ Professor Kim says that we should save energy.

15 다음 괄호 안에 주어진 단어를 이용하여 우리말에 맞도록 문장을 완성하시오.

> 차가운 마실 것 좀 주세요.
> (something / cold)
> ➡ Give me _____.

16 다음 빈칸에 들어갈 말로 알맞지 <u>않은</u> 것은?

> I think _____.

① it is easy
② she is pretty
③ is she busy
④ that he likes you
⑤ that she is taller than you

17 다음 문장의 괄호 안의 말을 바르게 배열한 것은?

> She needs (paper, on, to write).

① on paper to write
② paper on to write
③ to write paper on
④ paper to write on
⑤ on write to paper

18 다음 〈보기〉의 밑줄 친 부분과 쓰임이 같은 것은?

> ┤ 보기 ├
> This is a question <u>to solve</u> now.

① <u>To study</u> English is interesting.
② I need something <u>to write</u> on.
③ I want <u>to do</u> well this semester.
④ My plan is <u>to travel</u> around the world.
⑤ Where do you plan <u>to spend</u> your holiday?

19 다음 우리말에 맞도록 빈칸에 알맞은 말을 쓰시오.

> Ann은 그 없이는 살 수 없을 것이라는 사실을 몰랐다.
> ➡ Ann _____ _____ _____ she wouldn't be able to live without him.

[20~24] 다음 글을 읽고, 물음에 답하시오.

ⓐOn her way home, Dami saw Jihun. (①) He had the ticket in his hand. (②) Dami got angry and said, "Hey! (A)<u>Why do you ...?</u>"

Just then, Jihun saw Seho and ⓑ<u>shouted</u>, "Seho! I found a ticket in the hallway. I think (B)<u>it</u>'s yours. (③)"

"Thanks! (④)" said Seho.

"He's not so bad," Dami thought.

"So, what were you saying? Do you have something ⓒ<u>saying</u>, Dami?" asked Jihun.

"Um, how about ⓓ<u>going</u> to the school basketball game with me this Friday? (C)<u>It</u>'s the finals. (⑤)"

Jihun looked really ⓔ<u>pleased</u>. "I'd love to!"

20 위 글의 ①~⑤ 중 다음 문장이 들어갈 알맞은 곳은?

> I was looking for that!

①　　　②　　　③　　　④　　　⑤

21 위 글의 밑줄 친 (A)에서 생략된 말을 넣어 완전한 문장으로 다시 쓰시오.

➡ _____

22 위 글의 밑줄 친 ⓐ~ⓔ 중 어법상 <u>틀린</u> 것은?

① ⓐ　② ⓑ　③ ⓒ　④ ⓓ　⑤ ⓔ

23 위 글의 밑줄 친 (B)it와 (C)It가 가리키는 것을 각각 쓰시오.

(B) _____
(C) _____

24 위 글의 내용과 일치하면 T, 일치하지 않으면 F를 쓰시오.

(1) When Dami saw one of Seho's tickets in Jihun's hand, she was pleased. (　)

(2) Jihun gave the ticket back to Seho, and Dami realized that she was wrong. (　)

[25~27] 다음 글을 읽고, 물음에 답하시오.

> At the corner, Seho bumped ⓐ someone. "Sorry!" he said and continued to run. Just then, Jihun saw something ⓑ the floor.
> "Wait, Seho!" he said, but Seho was not there.
> After class, Seho went to Dami and said, "ⓒ(find / of / I / my tickets / can't / one). ⓓDid you happen to see it?"
> "No," she answered.
> "Isn't it in your bag?"
> "No, it's not there. I think I lost it," said Seho.

25 위 글의 빈칸 ⓐ와 ⓑ에 알맞은 말이 바르게 짝지어진 것은?

① up – over
② to – in
③ into – on
④ with – from
⑤ over – under

26 위 글의 괄호 ⓒ 안의 단어들을 바르게 배열하시오.

➡ _____

27 위 글의 밑줄 친 ⓓ를 우리말로 옮기시오.

➡ _____

[28~30] 다음 글을 읽고, 물음에 답하시오.

> "You know what?" Jihun cut in. "Minjun isn't a ⓐ of basketball. But ①I am!"
> "Well, I'll ask him first anyway," replied Seho.
> "②He won't go with you. Trust ③me," said Jihun.
> "Who is ④this guy?" Dami thought ⓑ herself, "⑤He wants Minjun's ticket."
> "Oh! There's the bell. See you later," said Dami. She hurried ⓒ class.
> "Come on, Jihun," said Seho, and he started to run.

28 위 글의 빈칸 ⓐ에 다음 영영풀이에 해당하는 단어를 쓰시오.

> a person who admires someone or something or enjoys watching or listening to someone or something very much

➡ _____

29 위 글의 ①~⑤ 중 지칭하는 대상이 다른 하나는?

①　　②　　③　　④　　⑤

30 위 글의 빈칸 ⓑ와 ⓒ에 공통으로 알맞은 것을 쓰시오.

➡ _____

Lesson 2

I Love My Town!

🐦 의사소통 기능

- 계획 말하기
  I'm planning to volunteer at the library.

- 약속 정하기
  Can you make it at 3 p.m.?

🐦 언어 형식

- 조건을 나타내는 접속사 if
  He will get better **if** he gets enough rest.

- 지각동사
  Ryan **heard** the doorbell **ring**.

Words & Expressions
교과서

Key Words

- **address** [ədrés] 몡 주소
- **around** [əráund] 쩐 ~ 주위에
- **away** [əwéi] 뿐 떨어진 곳에
- **block** [blak] 몡 구역, 블록
- **borrow** [bárou] 통 빌리다(↔ lend)
- **brown** [braun] 몡 갈색의
- **build** [bild] 통 짓다, 건축하다
- **butterfly** [bʌtərflài] 몡 나비
- **care** [kɛər] 몡 돌봄, 보살핌
- **chat** [tʃæt] 통 수다를 떨다
- **check** [tʃek] 통 살피다, 확인하다
- **closely** [klóusli] 뿐 자세히, 면밀히
- **clothes** [klouz] 몡 옷, 의복
- **cry** [krai] 통 울다(↔ laugh)
- **cut** [kʌt] 몡 상처 통 자르다, 베다
- **cute** [kjuːt] 몡 귀여운
- **director** [diréktər] 몡 감독
- **doorbell** [dɔrbel] 몡 초인종
- **elderly** [éldərli] 몡 연세가 드신
- **enough** [inʌf] 몡 충분한
- **exactly** [igzæktli] 뿐 꼭, 정확히
- **feed** [fiːd] 통 먹이를 주다
- **follow** [fálou] 통 따라가다
- **free** [friː] 몡 무료의, 한가한
- **gate** [ɡeit] 몡 문
- **green** [ɡriːn] 몡 초록색의
- **guess** [ɡes] 통 알아맞히다
- **hard** [haːrd] 뿐 열심히

- **hope** [houp] 몡 희망 통 바라다
- **hurry** [hə́ːri] 통 급히[서둘러] 가다
- **inside** [ìnsáid] 뿐 안에(↔ outside)
- **leave** [liːv] 통 ~을 두고 오다[가다]
- **lonely** [lóunli] 몡 외로운
- **lost** [lɔːst] 몡 잃어버린
- **miss** [mis] 통 놓치다, 그리워하다
- **move** [muːv] 통 이사하다, 옮기다
- **neighbor** [néibər] 몡 이웃
- **nervous** [nə́ːrvəs] 몡 긴장되는
- **nod** [nɑd] 통 (고개를) 끄덕이다
- **outside** [áutsáid] 뿐 밖에, 밖에서
- **pass** [pæs] 통 지나가다, 통과하다
- **perfect** [pə́ːrfikt] 몡 완벽한
- **practice** [præktis] 통 연습하다
- **rest** [rest] 몡 휴식(= break)
- **return** [ritə́ːrn] 통 돌아오다[가다]
- **sell** [sel] 통 팔다(↔ buy)
- **shape** [ʃeip] 몡 모양
- **special** [spéʃəl] 몡 특별한(↔ general)
- **spot** [spot] 몡 점, 반점
- **stage** [steidʒ] 몡 무대
- **still** [stil] 뿐 여전히
- **strange** [streindʒ] 몡 이상한
- **used** [juːst] 몡 중고의
- **volunteer** [vùləntíər] 몡 자원봉사자 통 자원봉사하다
- **wash** [waʃ] 통 씻다

Key Expressions

- **a pair of** 한 켤레[벌]의
- **be good at** ~을 잘하다
- **be late for** ~에 늦다
- **clean up** 청소하다
- **get better** (병·상황 따위가) 좋아지다, 호전되다
- **get enough rest**: 충분한 휴식을 취하다
- **in front of** ~의 앞쪽에[앞에]
- **in need** 어려움에 처한, 도움이 필요한
- **last month** 지난달
- **look around** 둘러보다

- **look at** ~을 보다
- **look like** ~처럼 보이다
- **over there** 저쪽에
- **prepare for** ~을 준비하다
- **put up** ~을 붙이다
- **run after** ~을 쫓아다니다, ~을 뒤쫓다
- **take A to B** A를 B로 데려가다
- **take a break** 휴식을 취하다
- **take care of** ~을 돌보다
- **thanks to** ~ 덕분에

Word Power

※ 명사에 -ly를 붙여 형용사가 되는 단어

□ **cost** (비용) → **costly** (비용이 많이 드는)

□ **coward** (겁쟁이) → **cowardly** (겁 많은)

□ **friend** (친구) → **friendly** (친한)

□ **leisure** (여가) → **leisurely** (한가한)

□ **love** (사랑) → **lovely** (사랑스러운)

□ **time** (시간) → **timely** (시기적절한)

※ 형용사에 -ly를 붙여 부사가 되는 단어

□ **easy** (쉬운) → **easily** (쉽게)

□ **careful** (주의 깊은) → **carefully** (주의 깊게)

□ **kind** (친절한) → **kindly** (친절하게)

□ **loud** (소리가 큰) → **loudly** (큰 소리로)

□ **special** (특별한) → **specially** (특별히)

□ **sudden** (갑작스러운) → **suddenly** (갑자기)

English Dictionary

□ **address** 주소
→ details of where someone lives or works and where letters, etc. can be sent
누군가가 살거나 일하는 곳과 편지 등을 보낼 수 있는 곳에 대한 세부 사항

□ **block** 구역, 블록
→ a group of buildings with streets on all sides
사방에 거리가 있는 건물의 그룹

□ **borrow** 빌리다
→ to take and use something that belongs to someone else, and return it to them at a later time
다른 사람의 것을 가져와서 사용하고, 나중에 그들에게 돌려주다

□ **build** 짓다
→ to make something by putting together parts or materials
여러 가지 부품과 재료를 결합하여 어떤 것을 만들다

□ **butterfly** 나비
→ a flying insect with a long thin body and four large, usually brightly colored wings
길고 얇은 몸과 네 개의 큰 보통은 밝은 색상의 날개들을 가진 날아다니는 곤충

□ **cut** 상처
→ a wound on a person's body that is made by something sharp
날카로운 것에 의해 사람의 몸에 생긴 상처

□ **doorbell** 초인종
→ a bell on the outside of a house which you can ring so that the people inside know that you want to see them
당신이 안에 있는 사람들을 보기를 원한다는 것을 알 수 있도록 울릴 수 있는 집 바깥에 있는 종

□ **feed** 먹이를 주다
→ to give food to a person or an animal
사람이나 동물에게 음식을 주다

□ **lonely** 외로운
→ unhappy because you have no friends or people to talk to
친구나 대화할 사람이 없기 때문에 불행한

□ **neighbor** 이웃
→ someone who lives next to you or near you
당신 옆이나 당신 근처에 사는 사람

□ **nod** (고개를) 끄덕이다
→ to move your head up and down, especially in order to show agreement or understanding
특히 동의나 이해를 보여주기 위해 머리를 위아래로 움직이다

□ **perfect** 완벽한
→ complete and without faults or weaknesses
완전하고 결점이나 약점이 없는

□ **rest** 휴식
→ a period of time in which you relax, sleep, or do nothing after you have been active or doing work
활동하거나 일을 한 후에 쉬거나 잠을 자거나 아무 일도 하지 않는 기간

□ **return** 돌아오다[가다]
→ to come or go to a place again
어떤 장소로 다시 오거나 가다

□ **volunteer** 자원봉사자
→ a person who does a job without being paid for it
그 일에 대한 대가를 받지 않고 일을 하는 사람

01 다음 중 단어의 성격이 다른 것은?

① lonely ② friendly
③ lovely ④ loudly
⑤ cowardly

02 다음 우리말에 맞도록 빈칸에 알맞은 것은?

나는 아빠와 함께 공원을 청소할 계획이다.
➡ I'm planning to clean _____ the park with my dad.

① up ② with
③ out ④ over
⑤ into

03 다음 영영풀이에 해당하는 단어로 알맞은 것은?

to move your head up and down, especially in order to show agreement or understanding

① feed ② bend
③ build ④ nod
⑤ catch

서답형
04 다음 짝지어진 두 단어의 관계가 같도록 빈칸에 알맞은 말을 쓰시오.

hungry : full = lend : _____

서답형
05 다음 우리말과 일치하도록 빈칸에 알맞은 말을 쓰시오.

나는 네 덕분에 좋은 이웃을 만났다.
➡ I met a good _____ thanks to you.

06 다음 빈칸에 알맞은 말이 바르게 짝지어진 것은?

• Look _____ the pictures on page 229.
• She is putting _____ a poster on the wall.

① in – about ② up – over
③ for – with ④ at – up
⑤ over – on

07 다음 중 짝지어진 단어의 관계가 다른 것은?

① cry : laugh ② far : near
③ inside : outside ④ rest : break
⑤ special : general

서답형
08 다음 영영풀이에 해당하는 단어를 쓰시오.

details of where someone lives or works and where letters, etc. can be sent

➡ _____

01 다음 짝지어진 두 단어의 관계가 같도록 빈칸에 알맞은 말을 쓰시오.

(1) delicious : tasty = _____ : break

(2) easy : difficult = borrow : _____

(3) right : wrong = buy : _____

(4) remember : forget = cry : _____

02 다음 우리말에 맞게 빈칸에 알맞은 말을 쓰시오.

(1) 장갑 한 켤레와 커다란 비닐봉지를 가져와라.
➡ Please bring _____ _____ _____ gloves and a big plastic bag.

(2) 오후 2시에 시계탑 앞에서 만나자.
➡ Let's meet at 2 p.m. _____ _____ _____ the clock tower.

03 다음 빈칸에 공통으로 들어갈 말을 〈보기〉에서 골라 쓰시오.

┌─ 보기 ─┐
miss   cut   pass
└────────┘

(1) • She studied hard to _____ the exam.
  • We will _____ through the village.

(2) • He had a small _____ above her left eye.
  • She _____ her finger on a piece of glass.

(3) • I _____ my mom and dad a lot.
  • If she is late, he will _____ the train.

04 다음 빈칸에 들어갈 알맞은 말을 〈보기〉에서 골라 쓰시오.

┌─ 보기 ─┐
lonely   elderly   enough
└────────┘

(1) He needs to take _____ rest.

(2) The girl is very polite to the _____.

(3) He has no friend, so he feels _____.

05 다음 빈칸에 알맞은 말을 〈보기〉에서 골라 쓰시오.

┌─ 보기 ─┐
prepare for   be good at   take care of
└────────┘

(1) I want to _____ math.

(2) They need volunteers to _____ the animals.

(3) He's planning to go to the library to _____ the exam.

06 다음 영영풀이에 해당하는 단어를 주어진 철자로 시작하여 쓰시오.

(1) b_____ : a group of buildings with streets on all sides

(2) p_____ : complete and without faults or weaknesses

(3) v_____ : a person who does a job without being paid for it

Conversation

A What are you planning to do this Saturday? 너는 이번 토요일에 무엇을 할 계획이니?

B I'm planning to clean up the park with my dad. 나는 우리 아빠와 함께 공원을 청소할 계획이야.

■ What are you planning to do ~?는 상대방에게 미래의 계획에 대해 물을 때 쓰는 표현이다.

• A: What are you planning to do this weekend? 너는 이번 주말에 뭐 할 계획이니?
  B: I'm planning to go to the movies. 영화 보러 갈 계획이야.

계획을 묻는 표현

• What are you planning[going] to do this weekend? 너는 이번 주말에 무엇을 할 거니?
• What are your plans for this weekend? 이번 주말에 너의 계획은 뭐니?
• What will you do this Sunday? 너는 이번 일요일에 무엇을 할 거니?
• Do you have any plans for this weekend? 너는 이번 주말에 무슨 계획이 있니?

■ 자신의 계획을 말할 때는 be planning to를 사용하여 말할 수 있다.

• A: Do you have any plans for the weekend? 너는 주말에 어떤 계획이라도 있니?
  B: Yes. I'm planning to practice dancing at the youth center.
    응. 나는 청소년 센터에서 춤을 연습할 계획이야.

계획을 말하는 표현

• I'm planning[going] to go hiking. 나는 하이킹을 갈 계획이야.
• I will play baseball with my brothers. 나는 내 동생들과 야구를 할 거야.
• I plan to visit my grandparents. 나는 조부모님을 방문할 계획이야.
• I have a plan to go to the library. 나는 도서관에 갈 계획이야.

핵심 Check

1. 다음 우리말과 일치하도록 빈칸에 알맞은 말을 쓰시오.

(1) **A:** _____ are you _____ to do this evening? (너는 오늘 저녁에 무엇을 할 거니?)

  B: _____ _____ _____ go shopping with my parents.
    (나는 부모님과 쇼핑하러 갈 거야.)

(2) **A:** _____ are your _____ for this weekend? (이번 주말에 너의 계획은 뭐니?)

  B: I _____ _____ play soccer with my brother. (남동생과 축구를 할 계획이야.)

② 약속 정하기

A Can you make it at 3 p.m.? 오후 3시에 올 수 있니?

B Sure. Let's meet in front of the library. 물론. 도서관 앞에서 만나자.

■ Can you make it at three?는 '3시에 만날 수 있니?'라는 뜻으로 약속을 정할 때 쓰는 표현이다. make it은 '해내다, 성공하다'라는 의미를 갖고 있지만, 시간이나 장소의 표현과 함께 쓰여 '시간에 맞춰 가다' 또는 '도착하다'라는 의미를 갖는다.

약속 정하기 표현

- Can we meet at six? 6시에 만날까?
- Why don't we meet at six?
- How[What] about meeting at six?
- Shall we meet at six?
- Let's meet at six.

약속 정하기에 답하는 표현

(승낙하기)

It's fine with me. / No problem. / Why not? / Sure, I'd love to. / That's a good idea. / (That) Sounds great.

(거절하기)

I'm sorry, I can't. / I'm afraid not. / I'd love to, but I can't. / Not this time, thanks. / Maybe next time.

핵심 Check

2. 다음 우리말과 일치하도록 빈칸에 알맞은 말을 쓰시오.

(1) **A:** Can you _____ _____ at five at the bus stop? (5시에 버스 정류장에서 만날까?)

　　B: _____. See you _____. (물론이지. 그때 보자.)

(2) **A:** _____ _____ _____ to the movie theater tomorrow?

　　(우리 내일 영화관에 가는 게 어때?)

　　B: No _____. (문제없어.)

(3) **A:** _____ _____ soccer this Saturday. (이번 토요일에 농구하자.)

　　B: _____, _____ _____. (미안하지만, 못하겠어.)

 A. Start Off - Listen & Talk B

B: ❶What are you going to do this Saturday?

G: ❷I'm planning to clean up the park with my dad.

B: ❸Sounds like a wonderful plan. Can I join you?

G: Sure. ❹Can you make it at the bus stop at 1 p.m.?

B: ❺I'm afraid not. How about 2?

G: Fine with me. ❻Please bring a pair of gloves and a big plastic bag.

B: Okay. See you on Saturday.

B: 이번 토요일에 뭐 할 거니?
G: 아빠와 함께 공원을 청소할 계획이야.
B: 멋진 계획인 것 같구나. 같이 가도 될까?
G: 물론이지. 버스 정류장에서 오후 1시에 만날 수 있니?
B: 안 될 것 같아. 2시는 어때?
G: 난 괜찮아. 장갑 한 켤레와 커다란 비닐봉지를 가져와.
B: 알았어. 토요일에 보자.

❶ What are you going to do ~?: 너는 ~에 무엇을 할 예정이니?(= What are you planning to do ~?
❷ I'm planning to+동사원형 ~: 나는 ~할 계획이야.(= I'm going to + 동사원형 ~) / clean up: ~을 청소하다
❸ sound like + 명사(구): ~처럼 들리다
❹ Can you make it ~?: ~에 만날 수 있니? (약속 시간을 제안하는 표현)
❺ I'm afraid not.: 안 될 것 같아.(제안에 거절하는 표현)
❻ a pair of: 한 켤레의

Check(√) True or False

(1) The boy and the girl will meet at the bus stop at 1 p.m.   T ☐ F ☐

(2) The boy should bring a pair of gloves and a big plastic bag.   T ☐ F ☐

 B. Step Up - Real-life Scene

Let's Volunteer for a Better Town!

Jina: ❶I'm planning to volunteer at the animal care center this Sunday morning.

Alex: You mean the one near Grand Park, Jina?

Jina: Right. ❷Will you come with me, Alex? ❸They need volunteers to take care of the animals.

Alex: I'd love to join. I like feeding and walking animals. ❹I'm also good at washing them.

Jina: Great. You can bring other friends with you, too.

Alex: Okay. I'll ask my neighbor Nancy. She loves animals, too. ❺What time shall we meet?

Jina: Can you make it at 8 a.m. at the Grand Park bus stop?

Alex: Sure. I'll see you on Sunday.

더 나은 마을을 위해 자원 봉사합시다!
지나: 이번 일요일 아침에 동물 보호 센터에서 자원봉사를 할 계획이야.
Alex: Grand Park 근처에 있는 거 말하는 거니, 지나야?
지나: 맞아. 나랑 같이 갈래, Alex? 그들은 동물들을 돌볼 자원 봉사자들이 필요해.
Alex: 나도 함께하고 싶어. 나는 동물들에게 먹이를 주고 산책시키는 것을 좋아해. 그리고 그들을 씻기는 것도 잘해.
지나: 좋아. 다른 친구들도 데려와도 돼.
Alex: 알았어. 내 이웃인 Nancy에게 물어볼게. 그녀도 동물들을 아주 좋아해. 몇 시에 만날까?
지나: Grand Park 버스 정류장에서 오전 8시에 만날까?
Alex: 알았어. 일요일에 보자.

❶ I'm planning to+동사원형 ~: 나는 ~할 계획이야.(= I'm going to+동사원형 ~)
❷ Will you ~?: ~할래?(= Can you ~?= Would you ~?= Could you ~?)
❸ take care of: ~을 돌보다
❹ be good at: ~을 잘하다 / them = animals
❺ What time shall we meet?: 우리 몇 시에 만날까?(약속 정하기 표현)

Check(√) True or False

(3) The animal care center is near Grand Park.   T ☐ F ☐

(4) Jina and Alex will meet at Grand Park on Saturday.   T ☐ F ☐

Get Ready -2

1. B: ❶I'm going to take some pictures in front of the flower gate.

   G: ❷Sounds good. It's over there.

2. B: Hello. It's me, Jamie. I think I'll get there in 20 minutes.

   G: Okay. ❸Let's meet at 2 p.m. in front of the clock tower.

3. B: ❹I'm planning to buy some clothes for a school picnic.

   G: Look. They're selling old books and clothes over there.

   B: Great. ❺Let's go and look around.

❶ in front of: ~ 앞에서
❷ sound+형용사: ~하게 들리다 / over there: 저쪽에
❸ Let's meet at ~: ~에서 만나자.
❹ I'm planning to+동사원형 ~: 나는 ~할 계획이야.(= I'm going to+동사원형 ~)
❺ look around: 둘러보다

Start Off - Listen & Talk A

1. G: ❶Do you have any plans for the weekend?

   B: Yes. I'm planning to practice dancing at the youth center.

   G: ❷Sounds great. ❸Can I join you?

   B: ❹Why not?

2. G: I'm planning to go to the library to prepare for the exam.

   B: You mean City Library? I want to study with you.

   G: Great. ❺Can you make it at 3 p.m. tomorrow?

   B: Sure. See you then.

❶ Do you have any plans for~?: ~에 어떤 계획이라도 있니?
❷ sound + 형용사: ~하게 들리다
❸ Can I ~?: 내가 ~해도 될까?(= May I ~?)
❹ Why not?: 왜 안 되겠니?, 그거 좋지.(Okay. = Sure. = Of course. = No problem.)
❺ Can you make it at ~?: ~에 만날 수 있을까?

Start Off - Speak Up - Look and talk.

A: ❶I'm planning to volunteer at the library this Tuesday.

B: Great. ❷Can I come with you?

A: ❸Why not? Can you make it at 3 p.m.?

B: Sure. ❹Let's meet in front of the library.

❶ I'm planning to+동사원형 ~: 나는 ~할 계획이야.(= I'm going to + 동사원형 ~)
❷ Can I ~?: 내가 ~해도 될까?(= May I ~?)
❸ Why not?: 왜 안 되겠니?, 그거 좋지.(Okay. = Sure. = Of course. = No problem.)
❹ Let's+동사원형 ~.: ~하자. / in front of: ~ 앞에서

Express Yourself A

1. M: ❶I'm planning to go to the town festival to watch a dance show.

   W: Sounds interesting. Can I come with you?

   M: Of course. Can you make it at the school gate at 6 p.m.?

   W: ❷No problem. See you then.

2. W: I'm planning to enter a singing contest in my town, but I'm nervous.

   M: Don't worry. ❸If you practice hard, you can win the contest.

   W: Thank you.

❶ I'm planning to+동사원형 ~: 나는 ~할 계획이다. / to watch: to부정사의 부사적 용법(목적)
❷ No problem.: 물론. (=Okay.=Sure.=Of course.=Why not?)
❸ If+주어+현재시제 ~, 주어+will[can/may]+동사원형 ~.

Check Yourself - Listen & Speak

B: ❶What are you going to do this Friday, Aria?

G: I'm planning to volunteer at the post office.

B: Sounds great!

G: ❷Will you come with me, Eric?

B: Sure. ❸When shall we meet?

G: Can you make it at 3 p.m.?

B: I'm afraid not. ❹How about 4 p.m.?

G: Good. See you then.

❶ What are you going to+동사원형 ~?: 너는 ~에 무엇을 할 예정이니?
❷ Will you ~?: ~할래?(= Can you ~? = Would you ~? = Could you ~?)
❸ When shall we meet?: 우리 언제 만날까?(약속 정하기 표현)
❹ How about ~?: ~는 어때?(=What about ~?)

● 다음 우리말과 일치하도록 빈칸에 알맞은 말을 쓰시오.

Get Ready - 2

1. **B:** I'm _____ _____ _____ some pictures in _____ _____ the flower gate.

   G: _____ good. It's _____ there.

2. **B:** Hello. _____ me, Jamie. I think I'll _____ there in 20 minutes.

   G: Okay. _____ meet _____ 2 p.m. _____ front of the clock tower.

3. **B:** I'm _____ to buy some clothes _____ a school picnic.

   G: Look. They're _____ old books and clothes _____ _____.

   B: Great. _____ go and look _____.

Start Off - Listen & Talk A

1. **G:** Do you have _____ plans _____ the weekend?

   B: Yes. I'm _____ _____ practice _____ at the youth center.

   G: _____ great. _____ I _____ you?

   B: Why _____?

2. **G:** I'm _____ _____ go to the library _____ _____ for the exam.

   B: You _____ City Library? I want to study _____ you.

   G: Great. Can you _____ _____ at 3 p.m. tomorrow?

   B: Sure. See you _____.

Start Off - Listen & Talk B

B: What _____ you _____ _____ do this Saturday?

G: I'm planning to _____ _____ the park _____ my dad.

B: Sounds _____ a wonderful plan. _____ I _____ you?

G: Sure. Can you _____ _____ at the bus stop _____ 1 p.m.?

B: I'm afraid _____. How _____ 2?

G: Fine _____ me. Please bring _____ _____ _____ gloves and a big plastic bag.

B: Okay. _____ you _____ Saturday.

Start Off - Speak Up - Look and talk.

A: I'm _____ _____ volunteer _____ the library this Tuseday.

B: Great. _____ I come _____ you?

A: _____ _____? Can you _____ it at 3 p.m.?

B: Sure. _____ meet in _____ _____ the library.

Step Up - Real-life Scene

Let's Volunteer for a Better Town!

Jina: I'm planning _____ _____ at the animal _____ center this Sunday morning.

Alex: You _____ the one _____ Grand Park, Jina?

Jina: Right. _____ you come _____ me, Alex? They need volunteers to _____ _____ _____ the animals.

Alex: I'd _____ to join. I like feeding and _____ animals. I'm also _____ _____ washing them.

Jina: Great. You can _____ other friends _____ you, _____.

Alex: Okay. I'll ask my _____ Nancy. She loves animals, _____. What time _____ we _____?

Jina: Can you _____ it _____ 8 a.m. _____ the Grand Park bus stop?

Alex: Sure. I'll see you _____ Sunday.

Express Yourself A

1. **M:** _____ _____ _____ go to the town festival _____ _____ a dance show.

   W: Sounds _____. Can I come _____ you?

   M: _____ course. _____ you _____ it at the school gate _____ 6 p.m.?

   W: _____ problem. See you _____.

2. **W:** I'm planning _____ _____ a singing contest in my town, but I'm nervous.

   M: _____ worry. If you practice hard, you _____ _____ the contest.

   W: _____ you.

Learning Diary - Listen & Speak

B: What _____ you _____ _____ do this Friday, Aria?

G: I'm _____ to volunteer _____ the post office.

B: Sounds _____!

G: _____ you come _____ me, Eric?

B: Sure. When _____ we _____?

G: Can you _____ _____ at 3 p.m.?

B: I'm _____ not. How _____ 4 p.m.?

G: Good. _____ you _____.

해석

더 나은 마을을 위해 자원 봉사합시다!

지나: 이번 일요일 아침에 동물 보호 센터에서 자원봉사를 할 계획이야.

Alex: Grand Park 근처에 있는 거 말하는 거니, 지나야?

지나: 맞아. 나랑 같이 갈래, Alex? 그들은 동물들을 돌볼 자원 봉사자들이 필요해.

Alex: 나도 함께하고 싶어. 나는 동물들에게 먹이를 주고 산책시키는 것을 좋아해. 그리고 그들을 씻기는 것도 잘해.

지나: 좋아. 다른 친구들도 데려와도 돼.

Alex: 알았어. 내 이웃인 Nancy에게 물어볼게. 그녀도 동물들을 아주 좋아해. 몇 시에 만날까?

지나: Grand Park 버스 정류장에서 오전 8시에 만날까?

Alex: 물론. 일요일에 보자.

1. **M:** 나는 춤 공연을 보기 위해 마을 축제에 갈 계획이야.
   W: 재미있겠다. 같이 가도 될까?
   M: 물론이지. 오후 6시에 학교 정문에서 만날까?
   W: 그래. 그럼 그때 보자.

2. **W:** 나는 우리 동네 노래 경연 대회에 나갈 계획인데, 긴장돼.
   M: 걱정하지 마. 열심히 연습하면 너는 대회에서 우승할 수 있어.
   W: 고마워.

B: 이번 금요일에 뭐 할 거니, Aria?
G: 우체국에서 자원봉사를 할 계획이야.
B: 멋지다!
G: 나랑 같이 갈래, Eric?
B: 물론이지. 우리 언제 만날까?
G: 오후 3시에 만날 수 있을까?
B: 안 될 것 같아. 오후 4시는 어때?
G: 좋아. 그때 보자.

[01~02] 다음 대화의 밑줄 친 부분과 바꿔 쓸 수 있는 것을 고르시오.

01

A: <u>What are you going to do this evening?</u>
B: I'm going to the park.

① Will you go to the park this evening?
② Do you go to the park this evening?
③ What's your plan for this evening?
④ Can you go to the park this evening?
⑤ Would you like to go to the park this evening?

02

A: What time should we meet tomorrow?
B: <u>Can you make it at five?</u>

① Let's go there at five.　　② Let's meet tomorrow.
③ Let's meet at five.　　④ I can't make it at five.
⑤ How about meeting together?

[03~04] 다음 대화의 빈칸에 알맞은 것을 고르시오.

03

A: _____
B: I'm planning to go travelling.

① What are you doing now?
② What did you do last winter?
③ Are you planning to go travelling?
④ When are you planning to go travelling?
⑤ What are you planning to do this winter?

> travel 여행하다

04

A: Let's go see a movie tomorrow.
B: Good idea!
A: _____
B: Okay. Let's meet at 5 o'clock.

① Where can we meet?　　② When can you come?
③ How would you like it?　　④ Can you make it at 5?
⑤ What time shall we meet?

[01~04] 다음 대화를 읽고, 물음에 답하시오.

> B: ⓐ<u>What are you going to do</u> this Saturday? (①)
> G: I'm planning to clean up the park with my dad. (②)
> B: Sounds like a wonderful plan. (③)
> G: Sure. Can you make it at the bus stop at 1 p.m.? (④)
> B: _____ⓑ_____ How about 2?
> G: Fine with me. (⑤) Please bring a pair of gloves and a big plastic bag.
> B: Okay. See you on Saturday.

01 위 대화의 ①~⑤ 중 다음 문장이 들어갈 알맞은 곳은?

> Can I join you?

① ② ③ ④ ⑤

 02 위 대화의 밑줄 친 ⓐ와 바꿔 쓸 수 있는 것은?

① What did you do
② Where are you going
③ Where will you go
④ What will you do
⑤ What will you buy

03 위 대화의 빈칸 ⓑ에 알맞은 것은?

① Of course.　　② No problem.
③ Good idea.　　④ I'm afraid not.
⑤ Sure, why not?

04 위 대화를 읽고, 답할 수 <u>없는</u> 질문은?

① What is the girl planning to do this Saturday?
② Who is the girl planning to clean up the park with?
③ Why can't the boy meet the girl at 1 p.m.?
④ What time will the boy and the girl meet?
⑤ What should the boy bring?

[05~07] 다음 대화를 읽고, 물음에 답하시오.

> G: Do you have any plans for the weekend?
> B: Yes. ⓐ<u>I'm planning to</u> practice ⓑ<u>dance</u> at the youth center.
> G: Sounds great. Can I join you?
> B: ⓒ<u>Why not?</u>

05 위 대화의 밑줄 친 ⓐ와 바꿔 쓸 수 있는 것은?

① I went to　　② I will going to
③ I'm going to　　④ I go to
⑤ I was going to

서답형

06 위 대화의 밑줄 친 ⓑ를 알맞은 형태로 고쳐 쓰시오.

➡ _____

07 위 대화의 밑줄 친 ⓒ와 바꿔 쓸 수 <u>없는</u> 것은?

① Okay.　　② Sure.
③ Of course.　　④ Not at all.
⑤ No problem.

[08~14] 다음 대화를 읽고, 물음에 답하시오.

> Jina: I'm planning to volunteer at the animal care center this Sunday morning. (①)
>
> Alex: You mean @the one near Grand Park, Jina?
>
> Jina: Right. Will you come with me, Alex? They need volunteers to take care ____ⓑ____ the animals. (②)
>
> Alex: I'd love to join. I like feeding and walking animals. (③)
>
> Jina: Great. You ©can bring other friends with you, too. (④)
>
> Alex: Okay. I'll ask my neighbor Nancy. (⑤) She loves animals, too. ____ⓓ____
>
> Jina: ⓔCan you make it at 8 a.m. at the Grand Park bus stop?
>
> Alex: Sure. I'll see you on Sunday.

08 위 대화의 ①~⑤ 중 다음 문장이 들어갈 알맞은 곳은?

> I'm also good at washing them.

①   ②   ③   ④   ⑤

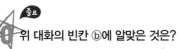

09 위 대화의 밑줄 친 @가 가리키는 것을 찾아 쓰시오.

➡ _____

10 위 대화의 빈칸 ⓑ에 알맞은 것은?

① for   ② of
③ in   ④ with
⑤ about

11 위 대화의 밑줄 친 ©와 쓰임이 같은 것은?

① Can the rumor be true?
② The child can not walk yet.
③ He can speak German very well.
④ You can go out and play outdoors.
⑤ Can you speak any foreign languages?

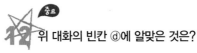

12 위 대화의 빈칸 ⓓ에 알맞은 것은?

① When can you come?
② Where should we meet?
③ How would you like it?
④ Can you make it at ten?
⑤ What time shall we meet?

13 위 대화의 밑줄 친 ⓔ를 다음과 같이 바꿔 쓸 때 빈칸에 알맞은 말을 쓰시오.

> _____ _____ meeting at 8 a.m. at the Grand Park bus stop?

14 위 대화를 읽고, 답할 수 없는 질문은?

① What is Jina planning to do this Sunday morning?
② Where is the animal care center?
③ Why does the animal care center need volunteers?
④ How many animals does Alex have?
⑤ Where will Jina and Alex meet?

Conversation 서술형 시험대비

[01~03] 다음 대화를 읽고, 물음에 답하시오.

> B: I'm planning to volunteer at the library this Tuesday.
> G: Great. Can I come with you?
> B: Why not? ⓐCan you make it at 3 p.m.?
> G: Sure. ⓑ도서관 앞에서 만나자.

01 위 대화의 밑줄 친 ⓐ를 다음과 같이 바꿔 쓸 때 빈칸에 알맞은 말을 쓰시오.

How about _____ at 3 p.m.?

02 위 대화의 밑줄 친 ⓑ의 우리말을 주어진 단어를 이용하여 영작하시오.

(front / the library / let's)

➡ _____

03 What is the boy planning to do this Tuesday? Answer in Korean.

➡ _____

04 다음 대화의 순서를 바르게 배열하시오.

(A) Why not?
(B) Yes. I'm planning to practice dancing at the youth center.
(C) Do you have any plans for the weekend?
(D) Sounds great. Can I join you?

➡ _____

[05~08] 다음 대화를 읽고, 물음에 답하시오.

> B: ⓐ너는 이번 토요일에 무엇을 할 거니?
> G: I'm planning to clean up the park with my dad.
> B: Sounds like a wonderful plan. Can I join you?
> G: Sure. ⓑ오후 1시에 버스 정류장에서 만날까?
> B: I'm afraid not. How about 2?
> G: Fine with me. Please bring a pair of gloves and a big plastic bag.
> B: Okay. See you ⓒ ____ Saturday.

05 위 대화의 밑줄 친 ⓐ의 우리말을 주어진 단어들을 이용하여 영작하시오.

(going / this)

➡ _____

06 위 대화의 밑줄 친 ⓑ의 우리말과 같도록 할 때, 빈칸에 알맞은 말을 쓰시오.

Can you _____ _____ at the bus stop at 1 p.m.?

07 What time and where will the boy and the girl meet? Answer in English.

➡ _____

08 위 대화의 빈칸 ⓒ에 알맞은 전치사를 쓰시오.

➡ _____

Grammar

① 조건을 나타내는 접속사 if

- He will get better **if** he gets enough rest. 충분한 휴식을 취하면, 그는 더 좋아질 것이다.
- **If** I hurry, I will catch the bus. 서두르면, 나는 버스를 탈 것이다.

■ 접속사 if는 두 개의 절을 연결하는 접속사이며, '만약 ~하면'이라는 의미로 조건을 나타낸다. if가 이끄는 종속절은 주절의 앞이나 뒤에 올 수 있다.

- **If** it's rainy, I will read a book. 비가 내리면, 나는 책을 읽을 것이다.

- You can win the contest **if** you practice hard. 열심히 연습한다면, 너는 대회에서 우승을 할 수 있다.

■ 조건을 나타내는 접속사 if가 이끄는 절에서는 미래의 일을 나타내는 경우에도 동사는 현재형을 쓴다.

- **If** it will be sunny tomorrow, I will go swimming. (X)

- **If** it is sunny tomorrow, I will go swimming. (○)
  내일 날씨가 맑으면, 나는 수영하러 갈 것이다.

■ '만약 ~하지 않는다면'이라는 의미의 「if+주어+don't[doesn't]+동사원형 ~」은 「unless+주어+동사의 현재형 ~」으로 바꿔 쓸 수 있다.

- **If** you do **not** read the book, you can't do your homework.
  = **Unless** you read the book, you can't do your homework.

  네가 그 책을 읽지 않으면, 너는 숙제를 할 수 없다.

핵심 Check

1. 다음 괄호 안에서 알맞은 것을 고르시오.

(1) If I am late, I (miss / will miss) the train.

(2) (If / Because) I get there on time, I will catch the train.

(3) If she (takes / will take) the subway, she will be there on time.

(4) Unless he (studies / doesn't study) hard, he can't get a high score.

② 지각동사

> • Ryan **heard** the doorbell **ring**. Ryan은 초인종이 울리는 소리를 들었다.
>
> • I **saw** Amy **read** a book to the children. 나는 Amy가 아이들에게 책을 읽어주는 것을 보았다.

- 지각동사란 눈으로 보고 귀로 듣는 것과 같이 감각기관을 통하여 우리가 느끼는 것을 표현하는 동사로 see, watch, hear, listen to, feel 등이 있다.

- 지각동사가 쓰인 5형식 문장은 '주어+지각동사+목적어+목적격 보어(동사원형[분사])' 형태로 나타내며, '목적어가 ~하는 것을 보다[듣다/느끼다]'의 의미를 나타낸다. 이때 목적격 보어 자리에 현재분사(동사 -ing)를 쓰면, '동작이 진행되는 순간'의 의미가 더 강조된다.

  - I **watched** Jane **swim** in the pool. 나는 Jane이 수영장에서 수영하는 것을 보았다.

  - I **felt** the ground **shake**. 나는 땅이 흔들리는 것을 느꼈다.

  - I **saw** her **crossing** the street. 나는 그녀가 길을 건너고 있는 것을 보았다.

  - Peter **heard** Susan **ringing** the bell. Peter는 Susan이 벨을 울리는 것을 들었다.

- 지각동사의 목적어와 목적격 보어의 관계가 능동일 때는 목적격 보어로 동사원형을, 수동일 때는 과거분사를 사용한다.

  - I **felt** someone **touch** my bag. 나는 누군가가 내 가방을 만지는 것을 느꼈다.

  - I **heard** my name **called** by her. 나는 내 이름이 그녀에 의해서 불리는 것을 들었다.

핵심 Check

2. 다음 괄호 안에서 알맞은 것을 고르시오.

(1) They saw a monkey (play / played) on a branch.

(2) He heard someone (knocked / knocking) on his door.

(3) They felt the building (shook / shaking).

(4) She saw the window (broken / breaking) by somebody.

01 다음 우리말에 맞게 〈보기〉에서 골라 빈칸에 알맞은 형태로 고쳐 쓰시오.

> ┤ 보기 ├
>
> touch   hear   arrive   see   feel   run

(1) Tom은 누군가가 그의 등을 만지는 것을 느꼈다.

➡ Tom _____ somebody _____ his back.

(2) 그는 기차가 역에 도착하는 소리를 들었다.

➡ He _____ the train _____ at the station.

(3) 그녀는 소년이 공원에서 달리는 것을 보았다.

➡ She _____ a boy _____ in the park.

02 다음 두 문장을 if를 써서 한 문장으로 나타내시오. (단, 종속절이 주절의 앞에 오는 문장으로 바꿀 것.)

hurry up 서두르다
go on a picnic 소풍가다

(1) Hurry up. You will catch the bus.

➡ _____.

(2) It will be fine tomorrow. We will go on a picnic.

➡ _____.

(3) You are tired. You can sit here.

➡ _____.

03 다음 괄호 안에 주어진 어구를 적당한 위치에 알맞은 형태로 넣어서 문장을 다시 쓰시오.

(1) She watched her husband the wall. (paint)

➡ _____.

(2) The dog heard the baby. (cry)

➡ _____.

(3) The police officer sees a girl a bottle. (pick up)

➡ _____.

04 다음 우리말과 일치하도록 빈칸에 알맞은 말을 넣어 문장을 완성하시오.

(1) 네가 만일 열심히 공부한다면, 너는 그 시험에 합격할 거야.

➡ _____ _____ _____ _____, you'll pass the exam.

(2) 만일 내일 비가 오면, 우리는 집에 있을 것이다.

➡ _____ _____ _____ tomorrow, we'll stay home.

01 다음 우리말에 맞도록 빈칸에 알맞은 것은?

> 선생님은 그들이 열심히 공부하고 있는 것을 보았다.
> ➡ The teacher saw them _____ hard.

① to study ② studied
③ studying ④ to studying
⑤ are studying

02 다음 문장의 빈칸에 들어갈 말로 알맞은 것은?

> If we don't start now, we _____ the bus.

① take ② will miss
③ will take ④ don't miss
⑤ don't take

03 다음 문장의 빈칸에 올 수 <u>없는</u> 것은?

> He watched a lot of people _____.

① sit on the grass
② dancing to the music
③ walk along the street
④ sing along with the band
⑤ to walk toward the park

04 다음 빈칸에 들어갈 말이 바르게 짝지어진 것은?

> If she _____ her cell phone, she _____ her mother.

① found – calls ② finds – will call
③ found – will call ④ finds – would call
⑤ will find – will call

서답형
05 다음 우리말과 같도록 빈칸에 알맞은 말을 써서 문장을 완성하시오.

> 만약 이번 일요일에 날씨가 맑으면, 우리는 소풍을 갈 것이다.
> ➡ _____ _____ _____ sunny this Sunday, we _____ _____ on a picnic.

06 다음 빈칸에 알맞은 것을 <u>모두</u> 고르면? (정답 2개)

> Have you ever seen him _____?

① dance ② dancing
③ danced ④ to dance
⑤ to dancing

07 다음 밑줄 친 ①~⑤ 중 어법상 <u>어색한</u> 것은?

> ①If ②it ③will snow ④tomorrow, we ⑤will go out.

①　　②　　③　　④　　⑤

08 다음 빈칸에 알맞은 말이 바르게 짝지어진 것은?

> • Did you see him _____ his room?
> • I heard Ann _____ with her sister.

① cleaning – to talk ② to clean – talking
③ to clean – to talk ④ cleaning – talking
⑤ to clean – to talking

중요

09 다음 빈칸에 들어갈 말이 바르게 짝지어진 것은?

> • _____ you get up early, you'll be late for school.
> • I am happy _____ you are always with me.

① When – as   ② Since – as
③ If – because   ④ Unless – because
⑤ Although – as

서답형

10 다음 문장에서 어법상 틀린 부분을 찾아 고쳐 쓰시오.

> David felt someone touched his head.

_____ ➡ _____

11 다음 중 어법상 틀린 것은?

① Did you hear the girl sang?
② I saw the boy run in the park.
③ I felt somebody touch my back.
④ I heard someone call my name.
⑤ We saw him cleaning the classroom.

중요

12 다음 중 밑줄 친 if의 쓰임이 나머지 넷과 다른 것은?

① If I have enough time, I'll visit my uncle.
② If the weather is fine tomorrow, we'll go on a picnic.
③ He asked me if I needed a pen.
④ If I am rich, I'll help poor people.
⑤ I'll go alone if you are busy.

서답형

13 다음 두 문장이 같은 뜻이 되도록 한 문장으로 다시 쓰시오.

> We heard the rain. The rain was falling on the roof.

➡ _____

중요

14 다음 빈칸에 공통으로 알맞은 것은?

> • He _____ the car move.
> • I _____ a bird singing yesterday.
> • I've _____ him laughing loudly with others.

① had   ② got   ③ made
④ heard   ⑤ wanted

서답형

15 다음 우리말과 의미가 같도록 두 문장의 빈칸에 알맞은 말을 쓰시오.

> 만일 네가 너무 많이 먹는 것을 멈추지 않으면, 너는 살찌게 될 것이다.
> ➡ _____ you _____ stop eating too much, you'll get fat.
> ➡ _____ you stop eating too much, you'll get fat.

16 다음 문장의 빈칸에 공통으로 알맞은 것은?

> 너는 Paul이 노래하는 것을 들어본 적이 있니?

① Do you hear Paul sing a song?
② Were you hear Paul singing a song?
③ Have you heard Paul sing a song?
④ Have you heard Paul has sung a song?
⑤ Have you heard Paul is singing a song?

17 다음 문장에서 어법상 어색한 부분을 찾아 바르게 고쳐 쓰시오.

If it will rain tomorrow, I will not go there, either.

_____ ➡ _____

18 다음 중 밑줄 친 부분의 의미가 〈보기〉와 다른 하나는?

┤ 보기 ├

<u>If</u> you want to go there, you have to finish your homework first.

① <u>If</u> she can't, I'll do it instead.
② I can't tell <u>if</u> it will rain or not.
③ <u>If</u> the rumor is true, I'll be very sad.
④ Add more hot water <u>if</u> the soup is too thick.
⑤ I'll go home <u>if</u> he doesn't come out in two minutes.

19 다음 우리말과 같도록 주어진 단어를 배열하여 문장을 완성하시오.

그녀는 누군가가 그녀를 치는 것을 느꼈다.
(hit / her / somebody / felt)

➡ She _____.

20 다음 중 어법상 틀린 문장은?

① You'll be able to swim if I teach you.
② If I have a garden, I will make it beautiful.
③ If you don't take this pill, you'll be sick.
④ If he is sick, I'll take him to the hospital.
⑤ They'll go to the zoo if it will be sunny this Sunday.

21 다음 주어진 어구를 이용하여 우리말을 영어로 옮기시오.

만약에 네가 티켓을 구한다면, 우리는 콘서트에 갈 수 있다. (get / go to the concert)

➡ _____

22 다음 중 어법상 알맞은 것은?

① Chris felt someone touched his shoulder.
② Rachel heard me called her name.
③ I saw the boy throwing stones at the dog.
④ I felt the ground shook several times.
⑤ Did you see the man stole the wallet?

23 다음 중 빈칸에 If[if]가 올 수 <u>없는</u> 것은?

① _____ you practice hard, you can win the contest.
② You may go out _____ you finish your homework.
③ _____ you hurry, you can catch the last bus.
④ Subong likes Sumi _____ she is very kind.
⑤ _____ I go shopping, I'll buy some vegetables.

24 다음 주어진 단어들을 사용하여 우리말 의미에 맞도록 영작하시오.

그가 계단을 내려가는 소리가 들리니?
(you / down / the / him / go / can / stairs / hear)?

➡ _____

01 다음 두 문장을 한 문장으로 연결하시오.

(1) I saw a strange man. + The man entered my house.

➡ _____

(2) I saw my brother. + He was meeting a lady in the bakery.

➡ _____

(3) I felt something. + It crawled up my arm.

➡ _____

(4) I heard the church bells.+They rang out in the distance.

➡ _____

02 다음 괄호 안에 주어진 단어와 접속사 if를 이용하여 문장을 완성하시오.

(1) (sunny / tomorrow)

➡ _____, I will play badminton.

(2) (not / stop / rain)

➡ _____, we won't take a walk in the park.

03 다음 문장에서 어법상 틀린 부분을 찾아 바르게 고쳐 쓰시오.

(1) I saw him to read books in the library.

_____ ➡ _____

(2) Tom heard his brother sang a song.

_____ ➡ _____

04 접속사 if를 사용하여 다음 두 문장을 한 문장으로 고쳐 쓰시오. (단, 종속절이 주절 앞에 오는 문장으로 바꿀 것)

(1) The weather is nice. I always walk to school.

➡ _____

(2) It rains on weekends. We watch TV.

➡ _____

(3) I am late for class. My teacher gets very angry.

➡ _____

05 다음 주어진 어구를 배열하여 문장을 완성하시오.

(1) (baseball / playing / the boys / saw)

➡ I _____ .

(2) (hit / felt / her / somebody)

➡ She _____ .

06 다음 빈칸에 알맞은 말을 〈보기〉에서 골라 쓰시오. (문장의 앞에 오는 경우 대문자로 쓰시오.)

┌─ 보기 ─┐
when   if   unless
└────────┘

(1) _____ you don't leave now, you will miss the last train.

(2) We had a big party _____ Sarah came home.

(3) _____ you start now, you'll be late for the meeting.

07 다음 주어진 어구를 이용하여 우리말을 영어로 옮기시오.

> 나는 어제 한 유명한 가수가 무대 위에서 노래하는 것을 들었다. (hear / on the stage)

➡ _____

_____

08 다음 두 문장이 같은 뜻이 되도록 빈칸에 알맞은 말을 쓰시오

(1) If you don't leave now, you will miss the school bus.

➡ _____ _____ _____ now, you will miss the school bus.

(2) Unless it rains tomorrow, I will go camping.

➡ _____ _____ _____ rain tomorrow, I will go camping.

09 다음 주어진 단어들을 이용하여 우리말을 영작하시오.

(1) 나는 아빠가 세차하시는 것을 지켜보았다.
(watch / wash)

➡ _____

(2) 지수는 Tom이 자전거를 타는 것을 보았다.
(see / ride)

➡ _____

(3) 그는 따뜻한 손이 자신의 등에 닿는 것을 느꼈다.
(feel / touch)

➡ _____

10 다음 문장에서 어법상 틀린 부분을 찾아 바르게 고쳐 쓰시오.

(1) If you will have a cold, you had better take a rest.

_____ ➡ _____

(2) If I have gone to France, I will visit the Louvre Museum.

_____ ➡ _____

(2) If I won't send an e-mail tomorrow, call me.

_____ ➡ _____

11 다음 주어진 단어를 바르게 배열하여 문장을 다시 쓰시오.

(1) If you (hurry / you'll / late / don't / up / be)

➡ _____

(2) If you (find / three / supermarket / straight / you / blocks / a / go / will)

➡ _____

12 다음 주어진 어구를 바르게 배열하여 문장을 완성하시오.

(1) (the / I / shake / felt / building)

➡ _____

(2) (never / play / I / piano / my sister / have / heard / the)

➡ _____

Bear and Max

Bear was a black and brown cat with green eyes. He lived with a boy,
~을 가진   ~와 함께
Ryan. Ryan always thought that "Bear" was a perfect name for the cat
a boy = Ryan   빈도부사는 일반동사 앞이나 be동사와 조동사 뒤에 위치
because he had a black spot in the shape of a bear. Bear liked to go
접 ~ 때문에   like to+동사원형: ~하는 것을 좋아하다
outside every morning and run after butterflies. He always came home
                                    ~를 쫓아다니다
just in time for dinner.
          저녁 식사 시간에 맞춰
 Five blocks away, Max the cat lived with a girl, Sheila. When Sheila
                                            a girl=Sheila   접 ~할 때
moved to this town last month, she was lonely. She had no friends
                      지난달   친구가 없었다
there. But, after Max followed her home, he became a good friend to
= in this town   접 ~한 후에   = Max
her.
 One day, Sheila saw Max sitting under the desk. He was making
   어느 날   지각동사 see+목적어+현재분사   과거진행형
a strange sound. "What's wrong?" asked Sheila. She looked at him
                                                              ~을 보다
closely and found a bad cut on his leg. She took him to the animal
                                                take A to B: A를 B로 데려가다
hospital. The doctor said, "He will get better if he gets enough rest.
                                  (병·상황 따위가) 좋아지다   충분한 휴식을 취하다
Keep him inside for a week."
                일주일 동안
 That night, at Ryan's house, there was no Bear. Ryan checked outside,
                              ~이 없었다
but he couldn't find him. He made posters and put them up around
                                                    put up: ~을 붙이다
town. A third night passed. Still no Bear.

brown 갈색의
perfect 완벽한
spot 점. 반점
shape 모양
outside 밖에, 밖으로
block 구역, 블록
away 떨어진 곳에
move 이사하다
lonely 외로운
follow 따라가다
strange 이상한
closely 자세히, 면밀히
cut 상처
inside 안에
around ~ 주위에
pass 지나가다
still 여전히

📎 **확인문제**

● 다음 문장이 본문의 내용과 일치하면 T, 일치하지 않으면 F를 쓰시오.

1 Bear had a brown spot in the shape of a bear. ☐

2 Bear went outside every morning and came home late in the evening. ☐

3 Max followed Sheila home and became her friend. ☐

4 Max had a bad cut on his leg. ☐

5 Ryan could find Max after three days. ☐

When Sheila was walking near her house, she saw a poster about
접 ~할 때)   과거진행형

the lost cat. She read it closely, and her eyes got big. "This cat looks
= a poster

exactly like Max. It's so strange." She hurried home. "Come on, Max!
look like: ~처럼 보이다

Let's go!" She took him to the address on the poster. "Ding-Dong."
take A to B: A를 B로 데려가다

When Ryan heard the doorbell ring, he ran to the door and opened it.
지각동사 hear+목적어+동사원형   = the door

"Bear, you're back!" Ryan cried. Max jumped up into Ryan's arms.
be back: 돌아오다   뛰어오르다

"Let me guess," said Sheila. "Your cat comes home only in the
사역동사 let+목적어+동사원형

evenings, doesn't he?" Ryan nodded. "And you lost him last Friday,
부가의문문

didn't you?" Sheila said. "Yes! How did you know?" said Ryan.

"Because this is my cat, too, and he usually comes to my home only
접 ~ 때문에   빈도부사는 일반동사 앞. be동사나 조동사 뒤에 위치   낮 동안에만

during the day."

"Our cat has two families!" said Ryan. "Hey, if you have time, please
조건을 나타내는 접속사 if(~하면)

come in and have some cookies." "Sure," said Sheila. "Thank you,
먹다 (= eat)

Max," she thought. "I met a good neighbor thanks to you!"
~ 덕분에

near ~가까이에(서)
exactly 꼭, 정확히
lost 잃어버린
strange 이상한
hurry 급히[서둘러] 가다
address 주소
hear 듣다
doorbell 초인종
cry 울다, 외치다
guess 알아맞히다
nod (고개를) 끄덕이다
lose 잃어버리다
neighbor 이웃

 확인문제

● 다음 문장이 본문의 내용과 일치하면 T, 일치하지 않으면 F를 쓰시오.

1   Sheila saw a poster about the lost cat near her house. ☐

2   Sheila took Max to the address on the poster. ☐

3   The cat usually comes to Sheila's home only in the evenings. ☐

4   Ryan lost Max last Thursday. ☐

● 우리말을 참고하여 빈칸에 알맞은 말을 쓰시오.

1 Bear was a black and brown cat _____ green eyes.

2 He lived _____ a boy, Ryan.

3 Ryan _____ _____ that "Bear" was a _____ name for the cat _____ he had a black _____ in the shape of a bear.

4 Bear liked to go _____ every morning and _____ _____ butterflies.

5 He always came home just _____ time _____ dinner.

6 Five blocks _____, Max the cat _____ _____ a girl, Sheila.

7 When Sheila moved _____ this town last month, she was _____.

8 She had _____ friends there.

9 But, _____ Max _____ her home, he became a good friend to her.

10 _____ _____, Sheila saw Max _____ under the desk.

11 He _____ _____ a strange sound.

12 "What's _____?" asked Sheila.

13 She looked _____ him _____ and found a bad _____ on his leg.

14 She _____ him _____ the animal hospital.

15 The doctor said, "He will _____ _____ if he gets _____ rest. Keep him _____ for a week."

16 That night, _____ Ryan's house, there _____ no Bear.

17 Ryan checked _____, but he _____ find him.

18 He made posters and _____ them _____ around town.

19 A _____ night passed. _____ no Bear.

20 _____ Sheila was _____ near her house, she saw a poster about the _____ cat.

<table>
<tr><td>1</td><td>Bear는 초록색 눈을 가진 검은색과 갈색의 고양이였다.</td></tr>
<tr><td>2</td><td>그는 소년 Ryan과 함께 살았다.</td></tr>
<tr><td>3</td><td>Ryan은 항상 "Bear"가 곰 모양의 검은 반점이 있기 때문에 그 고양이에게 딱 맞는 이름이라고 생각했다.</td></tr>
<tr><td>4</td><td>Bear는 매일 아침 밖으로 나가 나비를 쫓아다니는 것을 좋아했다.</td></tr>
<tr><td>5</td><td>그는 항상 저녁 식사 시간에 맞춰 집에 왔다.</td></tr>
<tr><td>6</td><td>다섯 블록 떨어진 곳에, 고양이 Max는 Sheila라는 소녀와 함께 살았다.</td></tr>
<tr><td>7</td><td>지난달에 Sheila가 이 마을로 이사 왔을 때, 그녀는 외로웠다.</td></tr>
<tr><td>8</td><td>그녀는 그곳에 친구가 없었다.</td></tr>
<tr><td>9</td><td>하지만 Max가 그녀를 따라 집으로 온 후, 그는 그녀에게 좋은 친구가 되었다.</td></tr>
<tr><td>10</td><td>어느 날, Sheila는 책상 밑에 앉아 있는 Max를 보았다.</td></tr>
<tr><td>11</td><td>그는 이상한 소리를 내고 있었다.</td></tr>
<tr><td>12</td><td>"무슨 일 있니?" Sheila가 물었다.</td></tr>
<tr><td>13</td><td>그녀는 그를 자세히 살펴보고 그의 다리에 심한 상처가 난 것을 발견했다.</td></tr>
<tr><td>14</td><td>그녀는 그를 동물 병원으로 데려갔다.</td></tr>
<tr><td>15</td><td>의사는 "충분한 휴식을 취하면 좋아질 거야. 그를 일주일 동안 안에 있도록 해라."라고 말했다.</td></tr>
<tr><td>16</td><td>그날 밤, Ryan의 집에는 Bear가 없었다.</td></tr>
<tr><td>17</td><td>Ryan은 바깥을 살폈지만 그는 그를 찾을 수 없었다.</td></tr>
<tr><td>18</td><td>그는 포스터를 만들어서 마을을 다니며 그것을 붙였다.</td></tr>
<tr><td>19</td><td>세 번째 밤이 지났다. 여전히 Bear는 나타나지 않았다.</td></tr>
<tr><td>20</td><td>Sheila가 그녀의 집 근처를 걷고 있었을 때, 그녀는 잃어버린 고양이에 대한 포스터를 보았다.</td></tr>
</table>

21 She _____ it closely, and her eyes got _____ .

22 "This cat _____ exactly _____ Max. It's so _____ ."

23 She _____ home.

24 "Come _____ , Max! _____ go!"

25 She took him _____ the address _____ the poster.

26 "_____ ." When Ryan _____ the doorbell _____ , he _____ to the door and _____ it.

27 "Bear, you're _____ !" Ryan _____ .

28 Max _____ _____ into Ryan's arms.

29 "_____ me _____ ," said Sheila.

30 "Your cat comes home only _____ the evenings, _____ he?"

31 Ryan _____ .

32 "And you lost him _____ Friday, _____ _____ ?" Sheila said.

33 "Yes! _____ did you _____ ?" said Ryan.

34 "_____ this is my cat, _____ , and he usually comes to my home only _____ the day."

35 "_____ cat _____ two families!" said Ryan.

36 "Hey, _____ you have time, please _____ _____ and _____ some cookies."

37 "_____ ," said Sheila.

38 "_____ you, Max," she _____ .

39 "I _____ a good neighbor _____ _____ you!"

21 그녀는 그것을 자세히 읽고, 그녀의 눈은 커졌다.

22 "이 고양이는 꼭 Max 같아 보여. 너무 이상해."

23 그녀는 서둘러 집으로 돌아갔다.

24 "자, Max! 가자!"

25 그녀는 그를 포스터에 적힌 주소로 데려갔다.

26 "딩동." Ryan은 초인종이 울리는 소리를 듣고 문으로 달려가 문을 열었다.

27 "Bear야, 돌아왔구나!" Ryan이 외쳤다.

28 Max가 Ryan의 팔 안으로 뛰어올랐다.

29 "내가 맞춰 볼게," Sheila가 말했다.

30 "너의 고양이는 저녁에만 집에 오지, 그렇지?"

31 Ryan은 고개를 끄덕였다.

32 "그리고 너는 지난 금요일에 그를 잃어버렸지, 그렇지 않니?" Sheila가 말했다.

33 "응! 어떻게 알았니?"라고 Ryan은 말했다.

34 "이것은 또한 내 고양이이기 때문이야, 보통 낮에만 우리 집에 오거든."

35 "우리 고양이는 가족이 둘이야!" Ryan이 말했다.

36 이봐, 시간이 있으면 들어와서 쿠키 좀 먹어."

37 "그래," Sheila가 말했다.

38 "고마워, Max." 그녀는 생각했다.

39 "나는 네 덕분에 좋은 이웃을 만났어!"

● 우리말을 참고하여 본문을 영작하시오.

1 Bear는 초록색 눈을 가진 검은색과 갈색의 고양이였다.
➡ _____

2 그는 소년 Ryan과 함께 살았다.
➡ _____

3 Ryan은 항상 "Bear"가 곰 모양의 검은 반점이 있기 때문에 그 고양이에게 딱 맞는 이름이라고 생각했다.
➡ _____

4 Bear는 매일 아침 밖으로 나가 나비를 쫓아다니는 것을 좋아했다.
➡ _____

5 그는 항상 저녁 식사 시간에 맞춰 집에 왔다.
➡ _____

6 다섯 블록 떨어진 곳에, 고양이 Max는 Sheila라는 소녀와 함께 살았다.
➡ _____

7 지난달에 Sheila가 이 마을로 이사 왔을 때, 그녀는 외로웠다.
➡ _____

8 그녀는 그곳에 친구가 없었다.
➡ _____

9 하지만 Max가 그녀를 따라 집으로 온 후, 그는 그녀에게 좋은 친구가 되었다.
➡ _____

10 어느 날, Sheila는 책상 밑에 앉아 있는 Max를 보았다.
➡ _____

11 그는 이상한 소리를 내고 있었다.
➡ _____

12 "무슨 일 있니?" Sheila가 물었다.
➡ _____

13 그녀는 그를 자세히 살펴보고 그의 다리에 심한 상처가 난 것을 발견했다.
➡ _____

14 그녀는 그를 동물 병원으로 데려갔다.
➡ _____

15 의사는 "충분한 휴식을 취하면 좋아질 거야. 그를 일주일 동안 안에 있도록 해라."라고 말했다.
➡ _____

16 그날 밤, Ryan의 집에는 Bear가 없었다.
➡ _____

17 Ryan은 바깥을 살폈지만 그는 그를 찾을 수 없었다.
➡ _____

18 그는 포스터를 만들어서 마을을 다니며 그것을 붙였다.
➡ _____

19 세 번째 밤이 지났다. 여전히 Bear는 나타나지 않았다.
➡ _____

20 Sheila가 그녀의 집 근처를 걷고 있었을 때, 그녀는 잃어버린 고양이에 대한 포스터를 보았다.
➡ _____

21 그녀는 그것을 자세히 읽고, 그녀의 눈은 커졌다.

➡ _____

22 "이 고양이는 꼭 Max 같아 보여. 너무 이상해."

➡ _____

23 그녀는 서둘러 집으로 돌아갔다.

➡ _____

24 "자, Max! 가자!"

➡ _____

25 그녀는 그를 포스터에 적힌 주소로 데려갔다.

➡ _____

26 "딩동." Ryan은 초인종이 울리는 소리를 듣고 문으로 달려가 문을 열었다.

➡ _____

27 "Bear야, 돌아왔구나!" Ryan이 외쳤다.

➡ _____

28 Max가 Ryan의 팔 안으로 뛰어올랐다.

➡ _____

29 "내가 맞춰 볼게," Sheila가 말했다.

➡ _____

30 "너의 고양이는 저녁에만 집에 오지, 그렇지?"

➡ _____

31 Ryan은 고개를 끄덕였다.

➡ _____

32 "그리고 너는 지난 금요일에 그를 잃어버렸지, 그렇지 않니?" Sheila가 말했다.

➡ _____

33 "응! "어떻게 알았니?"라고 Ryan은 말했다.

➡ _____

34 "이것은 또한 내 고양이이기 때문이야, 보통 낮에만 우리 집에 오거든."

➡ _____

35 "우리 고양이는 가족이 둘이야!" Ryan이 말했다.

➡ _____

36 이봐, 시간이 있으면 들어와서 쿠키 좀 먹어."

➡ _____

37 "그래," Sheila가 말했다.

➡ _____

38 "고마워, Max." 그녀는 생각했다.

➡ _____

39 "나는 네 덕분에 좋은 이웃을 만났어!"

➡ _____

[01~05] 다음 글을 읽고, 물음에 답하시오.

Bear was a black and brown cat with green eyes. He lived ___ⓐ___ a boy, Ryan. Ryan always thought that "Bear" was a perfect name for the cat ___ⓑ___ he had a black spot in the shape of a bear. Bear liked to go outside every morning and run after butterflies. He always came home just ___ⓒ___ time for dinner.

서답형

01 위 글의 빈칸 ⓐ에 알맞은 전치사를 쓰시오.

➡ _____

중요

02 위 글의 빈칸 ⓑ에 알맞은 것은?

① when   ② until
③ while   ④ before
⑤ because

03 위 글의 빈칸 ⓒ에 알맞은 것은?

① at   ② in
③ for   ④ of
⑤ across

서답형

04 위 글에서 다음 영영풀이에 해당하는 단어를 찾아 쓰시오.

> a small area of a surface that is different from other areas

➡ _____

05 위 글을 읽고, 답할 수 없는 질문은?

① What is Bear?
② What color are Bear's eyes?
③ Who did Bear live with?
④ Why did Bear run after butterflies?
⑤ When did Bear always come home?

[06~10] 다음 글을 읽고, 물음에 답하시오.

Five blocks away, Max the cat lived with a girl, Sheila. When Sheila moved to this town last month, she was ___ⓐ___ . She had no friends there. ___ⓑ___ , after Max followed her home, he became a good friend to her.

One day, ⓒSheila saw Max to sit under the desk. He was making a strange sound. "What's wrong?" asked Sheila. She looked ___ⓓ___ him closely and found a bad cut on his leg. She took him ___ⓔ___ the animal hospital. The doctor said, "He will get better if he gets enough rest. Keep him inside for a week."

중요

06 위 글의 빈칸 ⓐ에 알맞은 것은?

① bored   ② pleased
③ excited   ④ lonely
⑤ disappointed

07 위 글의 빈칸 ⓑ에 알맞은 것은?

① So   ② But
③ Also   ④ Or
⑤ Then

서답형

08 위 글의 밑줄 친 ⓒ에서 어법상 틀린 부분을 찾아 바르게 고쳐 쓰시오.

_____ ➡ _____

중요

09 위 글의 빈칸 ⓓ와 ⓔ에 알맞은 말이 바르게 짝지어진 것은?

① up – in ② into – on
③ at – to ④ for – from
⑤ after – in

10 위 글을 읽고, 답할 수 없는 질문은?

① Who did Max live with?
② When did Sheila move to this town?
③ Did Sheila have friends in this town?
④ What did Sheila find on Max's leg?
⑤ Why did Max get hurt?

[11~15] 다음 글을 읽고, 물음에 답하시오.

That night, at Ryan's house, there was no Bear. Ryan checked outside, ___ⓐ___ he couldn't find him. He made posters and put them ___ⓑ___ around town. A third night passed. Still no Bear.

When Sheila was walking near her house, she saw a poster about the lost cat. She read ⓒit closely, and her eyes got big. "This cat looks exactly ___ⓓ___ Max. It's so strange." She hurried home. "Come on, Max! Let's go!" She took him to the address ___ⓔ___ the poster.

11 위 글의 빈칸 ⓐ에 알맞은 것은?

① or ② and
③ so ④ but
⑤ for

중요

12 위 글의 빈칸 ⓑ와 ⓔ에 알맞은 말이 바르게 짝지어진 것은?

① up – on ② on – in
③ out – at ④ down – of
⑤ away – for

서답형

13 위 글의 밑줄 친 ⓒit이 가리키는 것을 영어로 쓰시오.

➡ _____

서답형

14 위 글의 빈칸 ⓓ에 알맞은 전치사를 쓰시오.

➡ _____

중요

15 위 글을 읽고, 답할 수 없는 질문은?

① Was Bear at Ryan's house that night?
② Where did Ryan put up the posters?
③ Why did Ryan lose Bear?
④ When did Sheila see a poster about the lost cat?
⑤ Why did Sheila's eyes get big when she saw the poster?

[16~20] 다음 글을 읽고, 물음에 답하시오.

"Ding-Dong." ⓐWhen Ryan heard the doorbell to ring, he ran to the door and opened it. "Bear, you're back!" Ryan cried. Max jumped __ⓑ__ into Ryan's arms.

"Let me guess," said Sheila. "Your cat comes home only __ⓒ__ the evenings, __ⓓ__ he?" Ryan nodded. "And you lost him last Friday, didn't you?" Sheila said. "Yes! How did you know?" said Ryan. "Because this is my cat, too, and ⓔhe comes usually to my home only during the day."

서답형

16 위 글의 밑줄 친 ⓐ에서 어법상 틀린 부분을 찾아 바르게 고쳐 쓰시오.

_____ ➡ _____

중요

17 위 글의 빈칸 ⓑ와 ⓒ에 알맞은 말이 바르게 짝지어진 것은?

① in – at   ② up – in
③ on – for   ④ at – on
⑤ off – over

서답형

18 위 글의 빈칸 ⓓ에 알맞은 것을 쓰시오.

➡ _____

서답형

19 위 글의 밑줄 친 ⓔ에서 어법상 어색한 부분을 찾아 바르게 고쳐 쓰시오.

_____ ➡ _____

20 위 글을 읽고, 답할 수 없는 질문은?

① Why did Ryan run to the door?
② When does Bear come to Ryan's house?
③ When did Ryan lose Bear?
④ When does Sheila's cat come to her house?
⑤ How did Sheila know Max was Ryan's cat?

[21~22] 다음 글을 읽고, 물음에 답하시오.

Bear was a black and brown cat with green eyes. He lived with a boy, Ryan. Ryan always thought __ⓐ__ "Bear" was a perfect name for the cat because he had a black spot in the shape of a bear. Bear liked to go outside every morning and run after butterflies. He always came home just in time for dinner.

중요

21 위 글의 빈칸 ⓐ에 알맞은 것은?

① if   ② that
③ though   ④ whether
⑤ because

22 위 글의 Bear에 대한 내용으로 옳지 않은 것은?

① 검은색과 갈색의 고양이이다.
② 초록색 눈을 가지고 있다.
③ 곰 모양의 검은 반점이 있다.
④ 나비를 쫓아다니는 것을 좋아했다.
⑤ 항상 저녁 식사 시간보다 늦게 집에 왔다.

[23~26] 다음 글을 읽고, 물음에 답하시오.

One day, Sheila saw Max sitting under the desk. (①) He was making a strange sound. (②) "What's wrong?" asked Sheila. (③) She looked at him closely and found a bad cut ____ⓐ____ his leg. (④) The doctor said, "He will ⓑget better if he gets enough rest. Keep him inside ____ⓒ____ a week." (⑤)

23 위 글의 ①~⑤ 중 다음 문장이 들어갈 알맞은 곳은?

> She took him to the animal hospital.

①   ②   ③   ④   ⑤

24 위 글의 빈칸 ⓐ와 ⓒ에 알맞은 말이 바르게 짝지어진 것은?

① in – until
② on – for
③ at – in
④ from – by
⑤ over – during

25 위 글의 밑줄 친 ⓑ와 의미가 같은 것은?

① wake
② suffer
③ develop
④ improve
⑤ recover

서답형

26 위 글에서 다음 영영풀이에 해당하는 단어를 찾아 쓰시오.

> a wound on a person's body that is made by something sharp

➡ _____

[27~29] 다음 글을 읽고, 물음에 답하시오.

ⓐThat night, at Ryan's house, there were no Bear. Ryan checked outside, but he couldn't find him. He made posters and put them up around town. A third night passed. Still no Bear.

When Sheila was walking near her house, she saw a poster about the lost cat. She read it closely, and her eyes got big. "This cat looks exactly like Max. ⓑIt's so strange." She hurried home. "Come on, Max! Let's go!" She took him to the address on the poster.

서답형

27 위 글의 밑줄 친 ⓐ에서 어법상 틀린 부분을 찾아 바르게 고쳐 쓰시오.

_____ ➡ _____

서답형

28 위 글의 밑줄 친 ⓑ가 의미하는 것을 우리말로 쓰시오.

➡ _____

29 위 글의 내용과 일치하지 않는 것은?

① Ryan은 Bear를 찾기 위해 포스터를 마을 주위에 붙였다.
② 사흘이 지났지만 여전히 Bear는 나타나지 않았다.
③ Sheila는 마을 입구에서 잃어버린 고양이에 대한 포스터를 보았다.
④ Sheila는 포스터에 있는 고양이가 Max와 꼭 닮은 것을 보고 이상하게 여겼다.
⑤ Sheila는 포스터에 적힌 주소로 Max를 데리고 갔다.

[01~04] 다음 글을 읽고, 물음에 답하시오.

Bear was a black and brown cat ⓐ green eyes. He lived with a boy, Ryan. Ryan always thought that "Bear" was a ____ⓑ____ name for the cat because he had a black spot in the shape of a bear. Bear liked to go outside every morning and run after butterflies. He always came home just in time for dinner.

01 위 글의 빈칸 ⓐ에 알맞은 전치사를 쓰시오.

➡ _____

02 What color are Bear's eyes? Answer in English.

➡ _____

03 위 글의 빈칸 ⓑ에 다음 영영풀이에 해당하는 단어를 주어진 철자로 시작하여 쓰시오.

complete and without faults or weaknesses

➡ p_____

04 Why did Ryan think that "Bear" was a perfect name for the cat? Answer in English.

➡ _____

_____

[05~08] 다음 글을 읽고, 물음에 답하시오.

"Ding-Dong." ⓐ(the doorbell / when / ring / heard / Ryan), he ran to the door and opened it. "Bear, you're back!" Ryan cried. Max jumped up into Ryan's arms.

"Let me guess," said Sheila. "Your cat comes home only in the evenings, doesn't he?" Ryan nodded. "And you lost him last Friday, ____ⓑ____?" Sheila said. "Yes! How did you know?" said Ryan. "Because this is my cat, too, and he usually comes to my home only during the day."

05 위 글의 괄호 ⓐ 안의 단어들을 순서대로 배열하시오.

➡ _____

06 When did Ryan lose Bear? Answer in English.

➡ _____

07 위 글의 빈칸 ⓑ에 알맞은 부가의문문을 쓰시오.

➡ _____

08 When does Sheila's cat come to her home? Answer in English.

➡ _____

[09~12] 다음 글을 읽고, 물음에 답하시오.

Five blocks away, Max the cat lived with a girl, Sheila. When Sheila moved to this town last month, she was lonely. She had no friends there. But, (A)[before / after] Max followed her home, he became a good friend to her.

One day, Sheila saw Max (B)[sitting / to sit] under the desk. He was making a strange sound. "What's wrong?" asked Sheila. She looked at him closely and found a bad cut on his leg. She took him to the animal hospital. The doctor said, "He will get better if he (C)[gets / will get] enough rest. Keep him inside for a week."

09 When did Sheila move to this town? Answer in English.

➡ _____

10 위 글에서 다음 영영풀이에 해당하는 단어를 찾아 쓰시오.

> unhappy because you have no friends or people to talk to

➡ _____

11 위 글의 괄호 (A)~(C)에서 문맥상 또는 어법상 알맞은 것을 골라 쓰시오.

(A) _____ (B) _____ (C) _____

12 Why did Sheila take Max to the animal hospital? Complete the blank.

> Because _____.

[13~16] 다음 글을 읽고, 물음에 답하시오.

That night, at Ryan's house, there was no Bear. Ryan checked outside, but he couldn't find him. He made posters and put them up around town. A third night passed. Still no Bear.

When Sheila was walking near her house, she saw a poster about the lost cat. She read it ⓐ(close / closely), and her eyes got big. "This cat looks exactly ⓑ(like / alike) Max. It's so strange." She hurried home. "Come on, Max! Let's go!" She took him to the ___ⓒ___ on the poster.

13 What did Ryan do to find Bear? Answer in English.

➡ _____

14 위 글의 괄호 ⓐ와 ⓑ에서 알맞은 것을 골라 쓰시오.

ⓐ _____ ⓑ _____

15 When did Sheila see a poster about the lost cat? Answer in English.

➡ _____

16 위 글의 빈칸 ⓒ에 다음 영영풀이에 해당하는 단어를 쓰시오.

> details of where someone lives or works and where letters, etc. can be sent

➡ _____

Express Yourself C1~C2

C1: Do you want to watch a magic show? If you visit the town festival <u>on</u>
조건을 나타내는 접속사 if(~하면)

<u>Monday</u>, you will see <u>Harry do magic tricks</u>. Have fun at the festival!
on + 요일   지각동사 see+목적어+동사원형

C2: Do you want to watch an outdoor movie? If you visit the town festival on

Friday, you will <u>hear Mr. Jackson, a director talk</u> about his new movie. It
지각동사 hear + 목적어 + 동사원형

will be fun!

구문해설 · magic: 마술의   · magic trick: 마술 묘기   · festival: 축제   · outdoor: 야외의
· director: 영화감독

C1: 마술쇼를 보고 싶니? 월요일에 마을 축제에 가면, Harry가 마술 묘기를 부리는 것을 볼 수 있을 거야. 축제 잘 보내!

C2: 야외 영화 보고 싶니? 금요일에 마을 축제에 가면, 너는 영화감독 Jackson 씨가 그의 새 영화에 대해 이야기하는 것을 들을 거야. 그것은 재미있을 거야!

Project - Step 2

This is my favorite *tteokbokki* restaurant in my town. If you go there, you will
조건을 나타내는 접속사 if(~하면)

<u>see many students eating</u> *tteokbokki* and chatting.
지각동사 see + 목적어 + 현재분사

This is a small but beautiful park near the school. If you want to <u>take a nice</u>
take a break 휴식을 취하다

<u>break</u>, please visit it. You can <u>hear birds singing</u> in the trees.
지각동사 hear + 목적어 + 현재분사

구문해설 · favorite: 가장 좋아하는   · chat: 수다를 떨다   · near: ~에서 가까이

이곳은 우리 동네에서 내가 제일 좋아하는 떡볶이 식당이다. 그곳에 가면, 너는 많은 학생들이 떡볶이를 먹으면서 수다를 떨고 있는 것을 볼 수 있을 것이다.

이곳은 학교 근처에 있는 작지만 아름다운 공원이다. 편안한 휴식을 취하고 싶다면, 꼭 이곳을 방문해라. 너는 나무에서 새들이 지저귀는 소리를 들을 수 있다.

Link to the World

Let's make a better town!

In the U.S., <u>there is</u> a volunteer project to build houses for families <u>in need</u>.
There is + 단수 명사 ~: ~이 있다   도움이 필요한

Many people <u>are joining</u> the project to <u>give them hope</u>.
현재진행형   수여동사 give + 간접목적어 + 직접목적어

It's a <u>little</u> <u>free</u> library <u>in Canada</u>. If you want to read books together <u>with</u>
작은   무료의   in + 국가 명   조건을 나타내는 접속사 if(~하면)   ~와 함께

your neighbors, make one <u>in front of</u> your house!
~ 앞에

It's a special refrigerator in Germany. People can leave food in this

refrigerator for people <u>in need</u>.
도움이 필요한

구문해설 · build: 짓다   · hope: 희망   · free: 무료의   · special: 특별한   · refrigerator: 냉장고
· leave: ~을 두고 오다[가다]

더 나은 마을을 만들자!

미국에서는 도움이 필요한 가정을 위해 집을 짓는 자원봉사 프로젝트가 있다. 많은 사람들이 그들에게 희망을 주기 위해 이 프로젝트에 참여하고 있다.

이것은 캐나다에 있는 작은 무료 도서관이다. 만약 여러분이 여러분의 이웃과 함께 책을 읽고 싶다면, 여러분의 집 앞에 그것을 만들어라!

이것은 독일에 있는 특별한 냉장고다. 사람들은 도움이 필요한 사람들을 위해 이 냉장고 안에 음식을 두고 갈 수 있다.

01 다음 영영풀이에 해당하는 단어로 알맞은 것은?

> a small round area that has a different color or feels different from the surface it is on

① cut ② care
③ block ④ spot
⑤ shape

02 다음 중 짝지어진 단어의 관계가 <u>다른</u> 것은?

① sell : buy ② inside : outside
③ lost : missing ④ ask : reply
⑤ remember : forget

03 다음 빈칸에 공통으로 알맞은 것은?

> • Let's _____ a break for ten minutes.
> • He loves to _____ care of animals.

① make ② get
③ have ④ take
⑤ keep

04 다음 우리말과 같도록 빈칸에 알맞은 말을 주어진 철자로 시작하여 쓰시오.

> 이상한 소리에 그는 잠을 깼다.
> ➡ A s_____ noise broke his sleep.

05 다음 빈칸에 공통으로 알맞은 것을 쓰시오.

> • She always sends money to children _____ need.
> • There is a young boy _____ front of the door.

06 다음 영영풀이에 해당하는 단어를 쓰시오.

> a flying insect with a long thin body and four large, usually brightly colored, wings

➡ _____

07 다음 대화의 빈칸에 알맞은 것은?

> A: What are you planning to do this vacation?
> B: _____

① I visited my grandmother.
② I went to America.
③ Yes. I have a plan to go to America.
④ I have a plan to go to Australia.
⑤ No. I'm not going to America.

08 다음 대화의 빈칸에 알맞은 것은?

> A: Can you make it at two?
>
> B: _____ Let's meet at the school gym.

① You're welcome.　② No problem.

③ I don't know.　④ You're right.

⑤ I'm afraid not.

09 다음 대화의 순서를 바르게 배열하시오.

> (A) No problem. See you then.
>
> (B) Sounds interesting. Can I come with you?
>
> (C) Of course. Can you make it at the school gate at 6 p.m.?
>
> (D) I'm planning to go to the town festival to watch a dance show.

➡ _____

10 다음 짝지어진 대화 중 <u>어색한</u> 것은?

① A: What time should we meet?
　 B: Let's meet at 5.

② A: Can you make it at 6?
　 B: Sure. See you then.

③ A: How about meeting in front of the museum?
　 B: That museum was great.

④ A: Where should we meet?
　 B: Can we meet at the bus stop?

⑤ A: Do you want to go skateboarding?
　 B: Sure. That sounds like fun.

[11~14] 다음 대화를 읽고, 물음에 답하시오.

> B: ⓐ너는 이번 토요일에 무엇을 할 계획이니?
>
> G: I'm planning to clean up the park with my dad.
>
> B: Sounds like a wonderful plan. ____ⓑ____
>
> G: Sure. Can you ____ⓒ____ it at the bus stop at 1 p.m.?
>
> B: I'm afraid not. How about 2?
>
> G: Fine with me. Please bring a pair of gloves and a big plastic bag.
>
> B: Okay. See you on Saturday.

11 위 대화의 밑줄 친 ⓐ의 우리말에 맞도록 주어진 단어를 이용하여 영작하시오. (필요하면 어형을 바꿀 것)

> (plan / this Saturday)

➡ _____

12 위 대화의 빈칸 ⓑ에 알맞은 것은?

① Can I help you?

② Can I join you?

③ Where do you play?

④ What sport do you like?

⑤ What time shall we meet?

13 위 대화의 빈칸 ⓒ에 알맞은 단어를 쓰시오.

➡ _____

14 위 대화를 읽고, 다음 질문에 완전한 문장으로 답하시오.

> Q: What time and where will the boy and the girl meet?
>
> A: _____

Grammar

15 다음 문장의 빈칸에 알맞은 것은?

She _____ at the station.

① arrive heard the train
② the train heard arrive
③ heard the train arrives
④ heard the train arrive
⑤ heard arriving the train

16 다음 우리말에 맞게 빈칸에 알맞은 것은?

만일 그가 내일 여기에 도착하면, 내가 너에게 전화할게.

➡ _____, I'll call you.

① If he arrives here tomorrow
② If he doesn't arrive here tomorrow
③ If he will arrive here tomorrow
④ Unless he will arrive here tomorrow
⑤ Unless he arrives here tomorrow

17 다음 문장에서 어법상 틀린 부분을 찾아 바르게 고쳐 쓰시오.

I saw a boy to get on the train.

_____ ➡ _____

18 다음 빈칸에 공통으로 알맞은 것은?

• You will get one free _____ you buy this.
• I wonder _____ she is really a middle school student.

① as   ② if
③ that   ④ since
⑤ whether

19 다음 문장에서 어법상 어색한 부분을 찾아 바르게 고쳐 쓰시오.

If you won't clean your room, I won't let you go out.

_____ ➡ _____

20 다음 중 어법상 어색한 문장은?

① I felt the ground move under me.
② She saw Daniel cleaning the window.
③ I heard someone calling my name.
④ We see Jenny shopping at the mart.
⑤ I heard a cat cried in the park.

21 다음 중 밑줄 친 if의 쓰임이 〈보기〉와 다른 것은?

┌─ 보기 ─┐
Don't wait for me if I'm late this evening.

① I can help you if you want.
② You will miss the train if you don't hurry up.
③ If it snows tomorrow, I will go out.
④ I don't know if he will leave for Busan tomorrow.
⑤ If you read the book again, you can understand it.

22 다음 우리말에 맞게 주어진 단어들을 바르게 배열하시오.

나는 어떤 노인이 기차에서 내리는 것을 보았다.
(get off / saw / the train / I / an old man)

➡ _____

23 다음 두 문장을 한 문장으로 바꿔 쓰시오.

> Susan does not get up now. She will miss the train.

➡ _____

_____

_____

24 다음 문장의 밑줄 친 ①~⑤ 중 어법상 어색한 것은?

> ①The boy ②watched ③a man ④to turn off ⑤the faucet.

①   ②   ③   ④   ⑤

25 다음 빈칸에 들어갈 말이 나머지 넷과 다른 것은?

① Mike will stay at home _____ it is cold.

② You can stay at home _____ you're tired.

③ She'll watch TV _____ she finishes her work early.

④ He'll buy a necktie for his dad _____ he goes shopping.

⑤ I think _____ Anderson won't come back.

26 다음 주어진 단어를 이용하여 우리말을 영어로 옮기시오.

> Kate는 누군가가 그녀를 향해 소리치는 것을 들었다. (heard / someone)

➡ _____

Reading

[27~32] 다음 글을 읽고, 물음에 답하시오.

Bear was a black and brown cat ⓐ green eyes. He lived with a boy, Ryan. Ryan always thought ⓑthat "Bear" was a perfect name for the cat ⓒ he had a black spot in the shape of a bear. Bear liked to go outside every morning and run after butterflies. He always came home just in time for dinner.

Five ⓓ away, Max the cat lived with a girl, Sheila. When Sheila moved to this town last month, she was lonely. She had no friends there. But, ⓔ Max followed her home, he became a good friend to her.

27 위 글의 빈칸 ⓐ에 알맞은 것은?

① of   ② on

③ into   ④ with

⑤ from

28 위 글의 밑줄 친 ⓑ와 쓰임이 다른 하나는?

① I think that the movie was terrible.

② I know that Sally doesn't have a job.

③ I think that bag is yours.

④ I hope that he will be my boyfriend.

⑤ I know that she will go abroad to study.

29 위 글의 빈칸 ⓒ에 알맞은 것은?

① if   ② so

③ when   ④ because

⑤ though

30 위 글의 빈칸 ⓓ에 다음 영영풀이를 참조하여 알맞은 단어를 쓰시오.

> a group of buildings with streets on all sides

➡ _____

31 위 글의 빈칸 ⓔ에 알맞은 것은?

① while　　　　② before

③ after　　　　④ until

⑤ although

32 위 글을 읽고, 답할 수 <u>없는</u> 질문은?

① What color was Bear?

② Did Bear like to go outside?

③ When did Bear always come home?

④ Why did Sheila move to this town?

⑤ Why was Sheila lonely?

[33~37] 다음 글을 읽고, 물음에 답하시오.

One day, Sheila saw Max ___ⓐ___ under the desk. He was making a strange sound. "What's wrong?" asked Sheila. She looked at him ⓑ <u>close</u> and found a bad cut ___ⓒ___ his leg. She took him to the animal hospital. The doctor said, "He will get better if he will get enough rest. Keep him inside for a week."

That night, at Ryan's house, there was no Bear. Ryan checked outside, but he couldn't find him. He made posters and put them ___ⓓ___ around town. A third night passed. Still no Bear.

33 위 글의 빈칸 ⓐ에 알맞은 것은?

① sat　　　　　② to sit

③ sitting　　　④ to sitting

⑤ is sitting

34 위 글의 밑줄 친 ⓑ를 올바른 형태로 고쳐 쓰시오.

➡ _____

35 위 글의 빈칸 ⓒ와 ⓓ에 알맞은 말이 바르게 짝지어진 것은?

① in – off　　　② at – over

③ for – in　　　④ from – on

⑤ on – up

36 위 글에서 다음 영영풀이에 해당하는 단어를 찾아 쓰시오.

> a period of time in which you relax, sleep, or do nothing after you have been active or doing work

➡ _____

37 위 글을 읽고, 답할 수 <u>없는</u> 질문은?

① Where was Max sitting?

② What did Sheila find on his leg after looking at Max closely?

③ Was the animal hospital near Sheila's house?

④ Was Bear at Lyan's house that night?

⑤ Why did Lyan put up posters around town?

✏️ 출제율 90%

01 다음 영영풀이에 해당하는 것은?

> a wound on a person's body that is made by something sharp

① hit   ② cut
③ hide   ④ hurt
⑤ lose

✏️ 출제율 100%

02 다음 빈칸에 공통으로 알맞은 것을 쓰시오.

> • She put _____ a notice on a board.
> • After cleaning _____ his room, he sat at his desk.

➡ _____

✏️ 출제율 95%

03 다음 빈칸에 공통으로 알맞은 것은?

> • I hope you'll _____ better soon.
> • I didn't _____ enough rest during the weekend.

① do   ② get
③ take   ④ have
⑤ become

✏️ 출제율 85%

04 다음 우리말에 맞도록 빈칸에 알맞은 말을 쓰시오.

> 밖으로 나가서 도시를 둘러보아라.
> ➡ Go outside and _____ _____ the city.

✏️ 출제율 95%

05 다음 빈칸에 들어갈 말로 적절하지 <u>않은</u> 것은?

> • I'll ask my _____ Nancy.
> • He was making a _____ sound.
> • He felt really _____ before the interview.
> • She has such beautiful _____ eyes.

① strange   ② brown
③ neighbor   ④ used
⑤ nervous

✏️ 출제율 85%

06 다음 우리말에 맞도록 빈칸에 알맞은 단어를 주어진 철자로 시작하여 쓰시오.

> 영화감독 Jackson 씨는 그의 새 영화에 대해 이야기할 것이다.
> ➡ Mr. Jackson, a movie d_____, will talk about his new movie.

✏️ 출제율 90%

07 다음 대화의 빈칸에 알맞은 것은?

> A: Let's go to the concert this Saturday.
> B: Sounds good. _____
> A: Fine with me.

① Can I join you?
② May I go to the concert?
③ How about going to the concert?
④ Do you like the concert?
⑤ Can you make it at 3?

08 다음 대화의 빈칸에 <u>어색한</u> 것은?

> A: What are you going to do this Sunday?
> B: _____

① I'm planning to go to the zoo.
② I can go to the zoo.
③ I'm going to go to the zoo.
④ I plan to go to the zoo.
⑤ I have a plan to go to the zoo.

[09~12] 다음 대화를 읽고, 물음에 답하시오.

> B: What are you going to do this Friday, Aria? (①)
> G: I'm planning to ___ⓐ___ at the post office. (②)
> B: Sounds great! (③)
> G: Will you come with me, Eric? (④)
> B: Sure. When shall we meet?
> G: ⓑ(it / you / 3 p.m. / can / make / at / ?)
> B: I'm afraid not. (⑤)
> G: Good. See you then.

출제율 90%

09 위 대화의 ①~⑤ 중 다음 문장이 들어갈 알맞은 곳은?

> How about 4 p.m.?

①　　②　　③　　④　　⑤

출제율 95%

10 위 대화의 빈칸 ⓐ에 다음 영영풀이에 해당하는 단어를 쓰시오.

> to offer to do something without expecting any reward

➡ _____

출제율 85%

11 위 대화의 괄호 ⓑ 안의 단어들을 바르게 배열하여 완성하시오.

➡ _____

출제율 90%

12 위 대화를 읽고, 다음 질문에 완전한 문장으로 답하시오.

> Q: What time will Aria and Eric meet?
> A: _____

출제율 100%

13 다음 우리말과 같도록 할 때, 빈칸에 알맞은 것은?

> 만약 내일 그가 오지 않으면, 나는 매우 슬플 것이다.
> ➡ _____, I will feel very sad.

① If he comes tomorrow
② If he won't come tomorrow
③ If he doesn't come tomorrow
④ Unless he won't come tomorrow
⑤ Unless he doesn't come tomorrow

출제율 90%

14 다음 빈칸에 알맞은 것을 <u>모두</u> 고르면? (정답 2개)

> Susan saw Chris _____ down the street.

① run　　② runs
③ ran　　④ has run
⑤ running

15 다음 문장에서 어법상 어색한 부분을 바르게 고쳐 쓰시오. `출제율 95%`

> I heard a cat to cry in the park.

_____ ➡ _____

[16~17] 다음 중 어법상 어색한 문장을 고르시오.

16 `출제율 90%`
① If you eat too much, you'll get fat.
② If you're thirsty, have some water.
③ If I will pass the test, I'll be very happy.
④ If it rains outside, I usually stay at home.
⑤ If school finishes early today, I'll go shopping.

17 `출제율 95%`
① I watched my mother cooking.
② She heard the birds sing.
③ He saw his brother hit the ball.
④ We can hear his father shouting.
⑤ I felt the ground to move under me.

18 다음 두 문장의 의미가 같도록 빈칸에 알맞은 말을 쓰시오. `출제율 85%`

> If you don't like the food, you don't have to pay.
> ➡ _____, you don't have to pay.

[19~24] 다음 글을 읽고, 물음에 답하시오.

> "Ding-Dong." When Ryan heard the doorbell ①ring, he ran to the door and opened it. "Bear, you're back!" Ryan cried. Max jumped up into Ryan's arms.
> "Let me ②guess," said Sheila. "Your cat comes home only in the evenings, ③did he?" Ryan nodded. "And you lost him last Friday, didn't you?" Sheila said. "Yes! How did you know?" said Ryan. "___ⓐ___ this is my cat, ④too, and he usually comes to my home only ___ⓑ___ the day."
> "Our cat has two families!" said Ryan. "Hey, ___ⓒ___ you have time, please come in and ⑤have some cookies." "Sure," said Sheila. "Thank you, Max," she thought. "I met a good neighbor thanks ___ⓓ___ you!"

19 위 글의 밑줄 친 ①~⑤ 중 어법상 틀린 것은? `출제율 85%`

①   ②   ③   ④   ⑤

20 위 글의 빈칸 ⓐ에 알맞은 것은? `출제율 90%`

① If   ② That
③ Though   ④ Because
⑤ Whether

21 위 글의 빈칸 ⓑ와 ⓓ에 알맞은 말이 바르게 짝지어진 것은? `출제율 100%`

① for – of   ② for – by
③ during – to   ④ during – for
⑤ for – from

22 위 글의 빈칸 ⓒ에 알맞은 것은?

① as
② if
③ that
④ while
⑤ when

23 위 글에서 다음 영영풀이에 해당하는 단어를 찾아 쓰시오. (원형으로 쓸 것)

to move your head up and down, especially in order to show agreement or understanding

➡ _____

24 위 글을 읽고, 다음 질문에 완전한 문장으로 답하시오.

Q: When does Max come to Ryan's home?
A: _____

[25~29] 다음 글을 읽고, 물음에 답하시오.

Bear was a black and brown cat with green eyes. He lived with a boy, Ryan. Ryan always thought ___ⓐ___ "Bear" was a perfect name for the cat (A)[because / because of] he had a black spot in the ___ⓑ___ of a bear. Bear liked to go outside every morning and run ___ⓒ___ butterflies. He always came home just in time for dinner.

Five blocks away, Max the cat lived with a girl, Sheila. When Sheila moved to this town last month, she was lonely. She had no friends there. But, (B)[before / after] Max followed her home, he became a good friend to her.

25 위 글의 빈칸 ⓐ에 알맞은 것은?

① as
② if
③ that
④ while
⑤ when

26 위 글의 빈칸 ⓑ에 다음 영영풀이에 해당하는 단어를 쓰시오.

the form or outline of an object

➡ _____

27 위 글의 괄호 (A)와 (B)에서 알맞은 것을 골라 쓰시오.

(A) _____ (B) _____

28 위 글의 빈칸 ⓒ에 알맞은 것은?

① off
② over
③ down
④ after
⑤ into

29 위 글의 내용과 일치하지 않는 것은?

① Bear는 초록색 눈을 가진 검은색과 갈색의 고양이었다.
② Bear는 곰 모양의 검은색 반점이 있다.
③ Bear는 가끔 저녁 시간에 맞춰 Ryan의 집에 왔다.
④ Sheila는 Ryan의 집에서 다섯 블록 떨어진 곳에 살았다.
⑤ Sheila는 지난달에 Ryan의 마을로 이사 왔다.

01 다음 주어진 단어를 이용하여 대화를 완성하시오.

> G: What are your plans for the weekend?
> B: _____
>
> (plan / visit / my grandparents)

02 다음 주어진 문장과 같은 의미가 되도록 빈칸에 알맞은 말을 쓰시오.

> What will you do on New Year's day?
> ➡ What _____ on New Year's day?
> ➡ What _____ on New Year's day?

[03~04] 다음 대화를 읽고, 물음에 답하시오.

> B: I'm planning to see a movie this Sunday. Do you want to come with me?
> G: Sure. ⓐ우리 몇 시에 만날까?
> B: ⓑCan you make it at the bus stop at 9 a.m.?
> G: Okay. See you then.

03 위 대화의 밑줄 친 ⓐ의 우리말을 주어진 단어를 이용하여 영작하시오.

> (shall)
>
> ➡ _____

04 위 대화의 밑줄 친 ⓑ를 다음과 같이 바꿔 쓸 때 빈칸에 알맞은 말을 쓰시오.

> Can we _____ at the bus stop at 9 a.m.?

05 다음 문장에서 어법상 어색한 부분을 찾아 고쳐 쓰시오. (한 군데)

(1) I heard someone to play the trumpet last night.

_____ ➡ _____

(2) If she will go tomorrow, I will go, too.

_____ ➡ _____

(3) I watched my sister drew a picture.

_____ ➡ _____

06 다음 두 문장의 뜻이 같도록 빈칸에 알맞은 말을 쓰시오.

> If you don't hurry up, you will miss the bus.
> ➡ _____ you hurry up, you will miss the bus.

07 다음 우리말과 같도록 주어진 어휘들을 바르게 배열하시오.

> Hana는 그녀의 고양이가 벽을 올라가는 것을 보았다.
> (saw / cat / her / the / climbing / wall / Hana).
>
> ➡ _____

08 다음 괄호 안에 주어진 표현을 이용하여 우리말과 같은 뜻이 되도록 영작하시오.

> 만약 네가 시간을 어기지 않고 도착한다면, 네 친구가 너를 기다릴 필요가 없을 것이다.
> (on time, have to)
>
> ➡ _____
> _____

That night, at Ryan's house, there was no Bear. Ryan checked outside, but he couldn't find him. ⓐHe made posters and put up them around town. A third night passed. Still no Bear.

When Sheila was walking near her house, she saw a poster about the lost cat. She read it closely, and her eyes got big. "ⓑ이 고양이는 꼭 Max처럼 보인다. It's so strange." She hurried home. "Come on, Max! Let's go!" She took him to the address on the poster.

09 위 글의 밑줄 친 ⓐ에서 어법상 어색한 부분을 고쳐 문장을 다시 쓰시오.

➡ _____

10 위 글에서 다음 영영풀이에 해당하는 단어를 찾아 쓰시오.

> happening or existing before now and continuing into the present

➡ _____

11 위 글의 밑줄 친 ⓑ의 우리말에 맞게 주어진 단어들을 바르게 배열하시오.

> (like / this / Max / exactly / looks / cat)

➡ _____

12 Where did Sheila take Max? Answer in English.

➡ _____

One day, ⓐSheila는 Max가 책상 밑에 앉아 있는 것을 보았다. He was making a strange sound. "What's wrong?" asked Sheila. She looked at him closely and found a bad ___ⓑ___ on his leg. She took him to the animal hospital. The doctor said, "ⓒHe will get better if he gets enough rest. Keep him inside for a week."

13 위 글의 밑줄 친 ⓐ의 우리말에 맞게 주어진 단어를 바르게 배열하시오.

> (the desk / sitting / Sheila / under / Max / saw)

➡ _____

14 위 글의 빈칸 ⓑ에 다음 영영풀이에 해당하는 단어를 주어진 철자로 쓰시오.

> a wound on a body that is made by something sharp

➡ c_____

15 Where did Sheila take Max? Answer in English.

➡ _____

16 위 글의 밑줄 친 ⓒ를 우리말로 쓰시오.

➡ _____

창의사고력 서술형 문제

01 다음 〈보기〉와 같이 주어진 단어를 이용하여 문장을 만드시오. (3문장)

보기
I saw Mom wash[washing] the dishes.

(A)	(B)	(C)
heard	somebody	touch my leg
saw	a man	ring
felt	a phone	plant trees

(1) _____

(2) _____

(3) _____

02 다음과 같은 상황이 벌어진다면 어떨지 상상하여 〈보기〉와 같이 쓰시오.

• go to China
• get an A on the math test
• it is sunny tomorrow
• find an abandoned dog on the street

보기
If I go to China, I can see the Great Wall.

(1) _____

(2) _____

(3) _____

03 다음 〈보기〉의 지각동사를 이용하여 문장을 4개 쓰시오. (필요시 어형을 바꿀 것)

보기
feel   watch   hear   see

(1) _____

(2) _____

(3) _____

(4) _____

단원별 모의고사

01 다음 중 짝지어진 단어의 관계가 나머지 넷과 <u>다른</u> 것은?

① ask : answer
② laugh : cry
③ lend : borrow
④ gate : door
⑤ forget : remember

02 다음 빈칸에 알맞은 말이 바르게 짝지어진 것은?

> • I'll take care _____ the dog.
> • Thanks _____ your help, I was able to do it.

① in – to
② at – for
③ of – for
④ of – to
⑤ for – at

03 다음 빈칸에 공통으로 알맞은 것을 주어진 철자로 시작하여 쓰시오.

> • Hurry up, or we'll m_____ the train.
> • They m_____ their homes, their friends, and family.

04 다음 중 영영풀이가 <u>잘못된</u> 것은?

① sell: to exchange something for money
② move: to go to a different place to live
③ feed : to give food to a person or an animal
④ return: to come or go to a place again
⑤ borrow: to give something to someone to be used for a period of time and then returned

05 다음 빈칸에 알맞은 말이 바르게 짝지어진 것은?

> • Let's _____ a break under this tree.
> • He _____ up pictures of his favorite flowers.

① have – turn
② take – put
③ keep – pick
④ get – set
⑤ make – post

06 다음 빈칸에 우리말에 맞도록 알맞은 말을 쓰시오.

(1) 그들은 저쪽에서 헌 책과 옷을 팔고 있다.
➡ They're selling old books and clothes _____ there.

(2) 그는 또한 어려움에 처한 사람들을 돕는 것을 좋아한다.
➡ He also likes to help people _____ need.

07 다음 대화의 빈칸에 알맞은 말을 <u>모두</u> 고르면? (2개)

> A: What are you going to do this Sunday?
> B: _____

① I will be busy this Saturday.
② I'm planning to go camping.
③ I visited my uncle yesterday.
④ I'm going to the museum now.
⑤ I'm going to play basketball with my friends.

[08~12] 다음 대화를 읽고, 물음에 답하시오.

Jina: I'm planning to volunteer at the animal care center this Sunday morning. (①)

Alex: You mean the one near Grand Park, Jina?

Jina: Right. (②) Will you come with me, Alex? ⓐThey need volunteers to take care ⓑ ___ the animals.

Alex: I'd love to join. I like feeding and walking animals. I'm also good ⓒ ___ washing them.

Jina: Great. (③)

Alex: Okay. I'll ask my neighbor Nancy. She loves animals, too. What time shall we meet? (④)

Jina: ⓓGrand Park 버스 정류장에서 오전 8시에 만날 수 있을까?

Alex: Sure. I'll see you on Sunday. (⑤)

08 위 대화의 ①~⑤ 중 다음 문장이 들어갈 알맞은 곳은?

> You can bring other friends with you, too.

①   ②   ③   ④   ⑤

09 위 대화의 밑줄 친 ⓐ가 가리키는 것을 우리말로 쓰시오.

➡ _____

10 위 대화의 빈칸 ⓑ와 ⓒ에 알맞은 말이 바르게 짝지어진 것은?

① in – for   ② about – in
③ for – up   ④ of – at
⑤ of – about

11 위 대화의 밑줄 친 ⓓ의 우리말과 같도록 빈칸에 알맞은 말을 쓰시오.

> Can you _____ _____ _____ 8 a.m. at the Grand Park bus stop?

12 위 대화를 읽고, 답할 수 없는 질문은?

① When is Jina planning to volunteer at the animal care center?
② What kind of animal does Jina have?
③ Is Alex good at washing animals?
④ Whose neighbor is Nancy?
⑤ What day will Jina and Alex meet?

13 다음 대화의 빈칸에 알맞은 것은?

> A: John is sick, so he can't come.
> B: No way! I saw him _____ tennis yesterday.

① plays   ② play
③ to play   ④ played
⑤ to playing

14 다음 중 어법상 어색한 문장은?

① If I get an A on the exam, I will be happy.
② If you will go by bus, it will be cheaper.
③ If she comes back to Korea, her husband will be pleased.
④ If my brother comes home early, my dad won't be angry.
⑤ If you speak too fast, Mike will not understand you.

15 다음 문장에서 어법상 어색한 부분을 찾아 바르게 고쳐 문장을 다시 쓰시오.

> If Mary will sleep early, we will go to the theater at night.

➡ _____

_____

16 다음 중 어법상 틀린 것은?

① Did you feel the train stopping?

② I heard this song sung on TV.

③ I saw a horse run on the road.

④ Nobody noticed you leave the classroom.

⑤ I heard your number calling out a few minutes ago.

17 다음 문장에서 어법상 어색한 곳을 찾아 바르게 쓰시오.

(1) I watched the tree cutting down.

_____ ➡ _____

(2) I saw something to burn.

_____ ➡ _____

18 다음 중 밑줄 친 부분의 쓰임이 다른 하나는?

① I don't know if he will come soon.

② Can you tell me if the test is on Friday?

③ He wanted to know if she had a broken bone.

④ Do you know if he will have dinner with us?

⑤ I will go out if it is fine tomorrow.

[19~22] 다음 글을 읽고, 물음에 답하시오.

> (①) One day, Sheila saw Max sitting under the desk. (②) "ⓐWhat's wrong?" asked Sheila. She looked at him closely and found a bad cut on his leg. (③) She took him to the animal hospital. (④) The doctor said, "ⓑHe will get better if he will get enough rest. Keep him inside for a week." (⑤)

19 위 글의 ①~⑤ 중 다음 문장이 들어갈 알맞은 곳은?

> He was making a strange sound.

①　　　②　　　③　　　④　　　⑤

20 위 글의 밑줄 친 ⓐ와 바꿔 쓸 수 없는 것은?

① What's the matter?

② Is anything wrong?

③ What's wrong with you?

④ What happened?

⑤ Why are you so scared?

21 위 글의 밑줄 친 ⓑ에서 어법상 틀린 부분을 고쳐 문장을 다시 쓰시오.

➡ _____

22 위 글에서 다음 영영풀이에 해당하는 단어를 찾아 쓰시오.

> as many or as much as is needed or wanted

➡ _____

[23~26] 다음 글을 읽고, 물음에 답하시오.

"Ding-Dong." _____ⓐ_____ Ryan heard the doorbell ring, he ran to the door and opened it. "Bear, you're back!" Ryan cried. Max jumped up into Ryan's arms.

"_____ⓑ_____ me guess," said Sheila. "Your cat comes home only in the evenings, doesn't he?" Ryan nodded. "And you lost him last Friday, _____ⓒ_____?" Sheila said. "Yes! How did you know?" said Ryan. "Because this is my cat, _____ⓓ_____, and he usually comes to my home only during the day."

23 위 글의 빈칸 ⓐ에 들어갈 알맞은 것은?

① If   ② Since
③ Though   ④ When
⑤ Because

24 위 글의 빈칸 ⓑ에 들어갈 알맞은 것은?

① Be   ② Don't
③ Have   ④ Let
⑤ Let's

25 위 글의 빈칸 ⓒ에 알맞은 부가의문문을 쓰시오.

➡ _____

26 위 글의 빈칸 ⓓ에 알맞은 것은?

① also   ② too
③ then   ④ either
⑤ neither

[27~30] 다음 글을 읽고, 물음에 답하시오.

That night, at Ryan's house, there was no Bear. Ryan checked outside, _____ⓐ_____ he couldn't find him. He made posters and put ⓑ them up around town. A third night passed. Still no Bear.

When Sheila was walking near her house, she saw a poster _____ⓒ_____ the lost cat. She read it closely, and her eyes got big. "This cat looks exactly like Max. It's so strange." She hurried home. "Come on, Max! Let's go!" She took him to the address _____ⓓ_____ the poster.

27 위 글의 빈칸 ⓐ에 알맞은 것은?

① but   ② so   ③ and
④ for   ⑤ when

28 위 글의 밑줄 친 ⓑ가 가리키는 것을 찾아 영어로 쓰시오.

➡ _____

29 위 글의 빈칸 ⓒ와 ⓓ에 알맞은 말이 바르게 짝지어진 것은?

① of – in   ② for – from
③ at – with   ④ about – on
⑤ on – over

30 위 글의 내용과 일치하지 <u>않는</u> 것은?

① Ryan put up posters around town to find Bear.
② The third night passed, but Bear still did not show up.
③ Sheila saw a poster about a lost cat on her way to school.
④ Sheila was surprised to see that the cat on the poster looked like Max.
⑤ Sheila took Max to the address on the poster.

Be Active, Be Safe!

🐟 의사소통 기능

- 경험 묻고 답하기
  A: Have you ever heard of beach safety rules?
  B: Yes, I have.

- 금지하기
  You shouldn't swim too far.

🐟 언어 형식

- 현재완료
  I **have visited** a selfie museum before.

- 접속사 though
  Though the boys are not really riding horses, it looks like they are.

Words & Expressions

Key Words

- **active** [ǽktiv] 형 활동적인, 활발한
- **actually** [ǽktʃuəli] 부 실제로, 정말로
- **advice** [ædváis] 명 조언(= tip), 충고
- **alone** [əlóun] 부 혼자
- **back** [bæk] 명 등 부 뒤로, 다시
- **balance** [bǽləns] 명 균형, 평형
- **beach** [bi:tʃ] 명 해변, 바닷가
- **before** [bifɔ́:r] 전 ~하기 전에 부 전에, 앞에
- **behind** [biháind] 전 ~ 뒤에 부 뒤에
- **bite** [bait] 동 (이빨로) 물다, 베어 물다
- **careful** [kέərfəl] 형 조심하는, 주의 깊은(↔ careless)
- **chat** [tʃæt] 명 담소, 이야기 동 담소하다, 채팅하다
- **climb** [klaim] 동 오르다, 올라가다
- **climber** [kláimər] 명 등반가
- **close** [klouz] 형 가까운, 친한
- **clothes** [klouz] 명 옷, 의복
- **create** [kriéit] 동 창조하다, 만들다
- **dangerous** [déindʒərəs] 형 위험한(↔ safe)
- **direction** [dirékʃən] 명 방향, (주로 복수로) 지시
- **during** [djúəriŋ] 전 ~ 동안[내내], (~하는) 중에
- **else** [els] 부 또[그 밖의] 다른, 다른
- **even** [í:vən] 부 ~도[조차], 심지어
- **exist** [igzíst] 동 ~에 있다, 존재하다
- **far** [fa:r] 형 먼(↔ near) 부 멀리
- **festival** [féstəvəl] 명 축제
- **figure** [fígjər] 명 인물, 모습
- **following** [fálouiŋ] 형 다음에 나오는, 그 다음의
- **fun** [fʌn] 명 재미 형 재미있는
- **grass** [græs] 명 풀, 잔디
- **harmony** [há:rməni] 명 조화, 화합
- **helmet** [hélmit] 명 헬멧
- **information** [ìnfərméiʃən] 명 정보
- **join** [dʒɔin] 동 함께하다, 가입하다

- **kind** [kaind] 명 종류
- **later** [léitər] 부 나중에, 후에
- **loose** [lu:s] 형 헐거워진, 풀린, 헐렁한(↔ tight)
- **mirror** [mírə] 명 거울
- **museum** [mju:zí:əm] 명 박물관, 미술관
- **painter** [péintər] 명 화가, 칠장이
- **past** [pæst] 명 과거, 지난날
- **place** [pleis] 명 곳, 장소
- **pose** [pouz] 명 포즈[자세] 동 포즈[자세]를 취하다
- **practice** [prǽktis] 동 연습하다
- **princess** [prínsis] 명 공주(↔ prince)
- **probably** [prábəbli] 부 아마
- **push** [puʃ] 동 밀다(↔ pull)
- **real** [rí:əl] 형 진짜의, 현실적인
- **remember** [rimémbər] 동 기억하다(↔ forget)
- **ride** [raid] 동 타다
- **rock** [rak] 명 바위, 암석
- **rule** [ru:l] 명 규칙
- **safe** [seif] 형 안전한
- **safety** [séifti] 명 안전, 안전성
- **scenery** [sí:nəri] 명 경치, 풍경
- **search** [sə:rtʃ] 동 찾다, 수색하다
- **selfie** [selfi:] 명 셀피(스마트폰으로 찍은 자신의 사진)
- **sign** [sain] 명 표지판, 간판
- **skill** [skil] 명 기술, 기량
- **someday** [sʌmdei] 부 언젠가, 훗날
- **special** [spéʃəl] 형 특별한, 특수한(↔ general)
- **street** [stri:t] 명 길, 거리, 도로
- **teenage** [tineidʒ] 형 십대의
- **touch** [tʌtʃ] 동 만지다, 건드리다
- **trick** [trik] 명 비결, 요령, 속임수
- **without** [wiðáut] 전 ~ 없이, ~하지 않고
- **yet** [jet] 부 아직

Key Expressions

- **be good for** ~에 좋다
- **for example** 예를 들면, 예를 들어
- **for the first time** 처음으로
- **go up** 오르다
- **hang up** 전화를 끊다
- **hear of** ~에 대해 듣다

- **in front of** ~ 앞에
- **keep ~ in mind** ~을 명심하다, ~을 잊지 않다
- **look at** ~을 보다
- **lots of** 수많은
- **make noise** 떠들다, 소란 피우다
- **over there** 저쪽에, 저기에서

Word Power

※ 명사에 형용사 어미 -ful 이 붙으면 형용사가 되는 단어들이 있다. 이때 철자가 변하는 것도 있으므로 주의해야 한다.

- □ **care**(주의) – **careful**(주의 깊은)
- □ **help**(도움) – **helpful**(도움이 되는)
- □ **color**(색) – **colorful**(다채로운)

- □ **sorrow**(슬픔) – **sorrowful**(슬픈)
- □ **beauty**(아름다움) – **beautiful**(아름다운)
- □ **harm**(해) – **harmful**(해로운)

English Dictionary

- □ **active** 활동적인, 활발한
  → moving around a lot or doing a lot of things
  많이 움직이거나 많은 일을 하는

- □ **advice** 조언, 충고
  → what you think someone should do in a particular situation
  당신이 생각하기에 누군가가 특정한 상황에서 해야 하는 것

- □ **beach** 해변, 바닷가
  → an area of sand or stones beside the sea
  바다 옆의 모래나 돌이 있는 지역

- □ **careful** 조심하는, 주의 깊은
  → giving serious attention to what you are doing, in order to avoid harm, damage, or mistakes
  해나 손상 또는 실수를 피하기 위해 당신이 하고 있는 일에 심각한 주의를 기울이는

- □ **chat** 담소[이야기]하다
  → to talk to each other in an informal and friendly way
  비형식적이고 친근한 태도로 서로 이야기하다

- □ **climb** 오르다, 올라가다
  → to move towards the top of something such as a tree, mountain, or ladder
  나무, 산, 사다리 같은 것의 꼭대기 쪽으로 움직이다

- □ **clothes** 옷, 의복
  → the things that people wear, such as shirts, coats, trousers, and dresses
  셔츠, 코트, 바지, 드레스와 같은 사람들이 입는 옷들

- □ **dangerous** 위험한
  → able or likely to hurt or harm you
  당신을 다치게 하거나 해를 끼칠 수 있는

- □ **helmet** 헬멧
  → a hat made of a strong material which you wear to protect your head
  당신의 머리를 보호하기 위해 당신이 착용하는 튼튼한 재료로 만들어진 모자

- □ **mirror** 거울
  → a flat piece of glass which reflects light, so that when you look at it you can see yourself reflected in it
  빛을 반사하는 납작한 유리조각으로, 그것을 볼 때 당신은 그 안에 반사된 자신을 볼 수 있다

- □ **painter** 화가
  → an artist who paints pictures
  그림을 그리는 화가

- □ **past** 과거
  → the time before the present, and the things that have happened
  현재 이전의 시간과 현재까지 일어난 일들

- □ **princess** 공주
  → a female member of a royal family, usually the daughter of a king or queen
  왕가의 여성 일원으로 왕이나 왕비의 딸

- □ **push** 밀다
  → to use force to make something move away from you or away from its previous position
  어떤 것을 당신에게서 멀어지게 하거나 이전의 위치에서 멀어지게 하기 위해 힘을 사용하다

- □ **ride** 타다
  → sit on a horse or bike and control its movements
  말이나 자전거에 앉아 그 움직임을 통제하다

- □ **rock** 바위, 암석
  → the hard substance which the Earth is made of
  지구가 구성되어 있는 단단한 물질

- □ **street** 길, 도로
  → a road in a city, town, or village, usually with houses along it
  대개 그것을 따라 집들이 있는, 도시나 읍 또는 마을의 도로

- □ **teenage** 십대의
  → aged between thirteen and nineteen years old
  열세 살에서 열아홉 살 사이의 나이인

01 다음 중 나머지 넷을 대표할 수 있는 단어는?

① coats   ② shirts
③ trousers   ④ dresses
⑤ clothes

중요

02 다음 빈칸에 알맞은 말이 바르게 짝지어진 것은?

• We met _____ the first time five years ago.
• What are you looking _____?

① of – at   ② for – at
③ on – for   ④ at – for
⑤ to – over

03 다음 영영풀이에 해당하는 단어로 알맞은 것은?

a road in a city, town, or village, usually with houses along it

① yard   ② ground
③ stadium   ④ street
⑤ garden

서답형

04 다음 짝지어진 두 단어의 관계가 같도록 빈칸에 알맞은 말을 쓰시오.

remember : forget = careful : _____

05 다음 우리말에 맞게 빈칸에 알맞은 것은?

저기에 주유소가 있네요.
➡ There's a gas station _____ there.

① up   ② on
③ over   ④ from
⑤ along

서답형

06 다음 영영풀이에 해당하는 단어를 쓰시오.

aged between thirteen and nineteen years old

➡ _____

서답형

07 다음 우리말에 맞게 빈칸에 알맞은 말을 쓰시오.

교실 안에서 소란 피우지 말아요.
➡ Don't _____ noise in the classroom.

중요

08 다음 빈칸에 공통으로 알맞은 것은?

• He took some coins out _____ his pocket.
• We had lots _____ fun at the party.

① in   ② of
③ up   ④ about
⑤ at

01 다음 짝지어진 두 단어의 관계가 같도록 빈칸에 알맞은 말을 쓰시오.

(1) care : careful = color : _____

(2) actor : actress = prince : _____

(3) dangerous : _____ = strong : weak

02 다음 우리말에 맞게 빈칸에 알맞은 말을 쓰시오.

(1) 예를 들면, 인도에서는 어떤 동전은 사각형이다.
➡ In India, _____ _____, some coins have square sides.

(2) 우리는 Sarah의 파티에서 아주 재미있게 보냈다.
➡ We _____ a lot of _____ at Sarah's party.

(3) 너의 앨범을 보아도 좋으니?
➡ May I _____ _____ your album?

03 다음 빈칸에 들어갈 알맞은 말을 〈보기〉에서 골라 쓰시오.

— 보기 —
even someday during following

(1) My grandfather died _____ the war.

(2) _____ a child can understand it.

(3) Answer the _____ questions.

(4) I hope you will visit here _____.

04 다음 괄호 안의 단어를 문맥에 맞게 고쳐 쓰시오.

(1) It's not _____ raining now. (actual)

(2) Follow your doctor's _____. (advise)

(3) The traffic here is very _____ for children. (danger)

05 다음 빈칸에 알맞은 말을 〈보기〉에서 골라 쓰시오.

— 보기 —
keep in mind look for
hear of good at

(1) Nancy is _____ dancing.

(2) I was surprised to _____ his failure.

(3) You had better _____ your dog at the park.

(4) Please _____ what I said.

06 다음 영영풀이에 해당하는 단어를 주어진 철자로 시작하여 쓰시오.

(1) r_____ : sit on a horse or bike and control its movements

(2) c_____ : to move towards the top of something such as a tree, mountain, or ladder

(3) p_____ : the time before the present, and the things that have happened

Conruation 교과서

1 경험 묻고 답하기

> **A** Have you heard of beach safety rules? 넌 해변 안전 규칙에 대해 들어본 적 있니?
> **B** Yes, I have. 응, 있어.

■ **경험 묻기**

'~해 본 적이 있나요?'라고 과거부터 현재까지의 상대방의 경험을 물을 때는 「Have you (ever)+과거분사 ~?」 형태인 현재완료 의문문으로 물을 수 있다.

경험에 대한 물음에 대답하기

- 경험이 있으면 Yes, I have. / Yes, I have+과거분사. 등으로 한다.
- 경험이 없으면 No, I haven't. / No, I have never+과거분사. / Not yet. 등으로 한다.

- A: Have you ever seen a bear? 너는 곰을 본 적이 있니?
  B: Yes, I have. / No, I haven't. 응, 본 적이 있어. / 아니, 본 적이 없어.

cf. '~에 가본 적 있니?'라고 묻는 표현은 Have you ever gone to ~?가 아니라 Have you ever been to ~?임에 주의한다.

- have been to: ~에 가본 적이 있다(경험) / ~에 다녀 왔다(완료)
- have gone to: ~에 가버렸다(결과)

■ 경험을 나타낼 때는 다음과 같은 부사(구)를 함께 쓰는 경우가 많다. ever(지금까지), never(~한 적 없는), before(이전에), once(한 번), twice(두 번), 「숫자+times(~번, ~차례)」, many times(여러 번), often(자주)

- She has made fried rice many times. 그녀는 볶음밥을 여러 번 만든 적이 있다.

핵심 Check

1. 다음 우리말과 일치하도록 빈칸에 알맞은 말을 쓰시오.

(1) A: _____ you ever _____ *Les Miserables*? (너 '레미제라블' 읽어 봤니?)

   B: Yes, I _____. (응, 있어.)

(2) A: _____ you _____ of Rock Boys? (너는 Rock Boys에 대해 들어 봤니?)

   B: No, I _____. (아니, 나는 못 들어 봤어.)

2 금지하기

A May I swim in this lake? 이 호수에서 수영해도 돼요?

B Okay, Mike, but you shouldn't swim too far. 그래, Mike야, 하지만 너무 멀리까지 수영하면 안 된다.

■ You should not ~은 '~하면 안 돼.'라는 뜻으로 어떤 일을 하지 말아야 함을 이야기할 때 사용하는 금지의 표현이다.

· A: Tony, you should not run when you cross the street. Tony, 길을 건널 때 뛰면 안 돼.
  B: Okay, I see. 응, 알겠어.

■ You should ~는 '~해야 한다.'라는 뜻으로 상대방에게 제안이나 충고를 할 때 사용한다.

· You should have breakfast every day. 너는 매일 아침식사를 해야 한다.

금지를 나타내는 표현

· You should not take pictures at the museum. 박물관에서는 사진을 찍으면 안 돼.

= You must not take pictures at the museum.

= Don't[Do not] take pictures at the museum.

= You can't take pictures at the museum.

= You'd better not take pictures at the museum.

= You're not supposed[allowed/permitted] to take pictures at the museum.

핵심 Check

2. 다음 우리말과 일치하도록 빈칸에 알맞은 말을 쓰시오.

(1) **A:** Excuse me. You _____ _____ your cell phone here.

（실례합니다. 이곳에서 휴대 전화를 사용하시면 안 됩니다.）

B: Oh, I'm _____. (오, 죄송합니다.)

(2) **G:** Wait. _____ jump into the water yet. (잠깐만. 아직 물속으로 뛰어들지 마.)

B: Why _____? (왜 안 돼?)

G: You _____ swim without a life jacket. (구명조끼 없이 수영하면 안 돼.)

(3) **A:** I _____ I've got a _____. (나 감기에 걸린 것 같아.)

B: You'd _____ _____ _____ cold water. (너는 차가운 물을 마시지 않는 게 좋겠어.)

A. Start Off - Listen & Talk B

B: ❶Have you heard of bird watching?

M: Sure. I tried it when I was a child.

B: That's nice. ❷Actually, I'm doing it for the first time this Saturday.

M: Are you? You should bring warm clothes and something to eat.

B: Okay. What else should I keep in mind?

M: ❸You shouldn't make any noise when you watch the birds.

B: I'll keep that in mind. Thanks, Dad.

B: 새 관찰에 대해 들어보셨어요?
M: 물론이지. 어렸을 때 해 봤어.
B: 그거 멋지네요. 사실, 전 이번 주 토요일에 처음으로 그것을 할 거예요.
M: 그래? 넌 따뜻한 옷과 먹을 것을 가져가야 해.
B: 알았어요. 그 밖에 또 무엇을 명심해야 하나요?
M: 너는 새들을 관찰할 때 아무 소리도 내지 말아야 해.
B: 그것을 명심할게요. 고마워요, 아빠.

❶ Have you heard of ~?: ~에 대해 들어본 적이 있나요?(경험을 묻는 표현)
❷ I'm doing ~: 현재진행형이 미래의 일을 나타내는 경우 / it=bird watching
❸ You shouldn't ~: 너는 ~해서는 안 된다(금지를 나타내는 표현)

Check(√) True or False

(1) The boy's father tried bird watching when he was a child. T☐ F☐

(2) The boy may make some noise when he watches the birds. T☐ F☐

B. Step Up - Real-life Scene

Video Chat with Minjun from Jeju

A: Hello, Somin! It's me! Can you see me?

B: Oh, hi, Minjun! What's up?

A: ❶This is so cool, isn't it? We can video chat on the phone! Have you heard of Jeju *Olle*?

B: Yes, I have. I really want to go there someday.

A: ❷Guess what? I'm on it now. Actually, I'm going to go up Seongsan Ilchulbong now.

B: That's great!

A: ❸Don't hang up. Enjoy the beautiful scenery with me.

B: Be careful! ❹You shouldn't use your cell phone while you're walking.

A: Oh, right. Thank you. I'll send you photos later.

제주에서 걸려 온 민준과의 화상 채팅
A: 여보세요, 소민아! 나야! 나를 볼 수 있니?
B: 오, 안녕, 민준아! 무슨 일이니?
A: 이거 정말 멋지지 않니? 전화로 화상 채팅도 할 수 있어! 너 제주 올레에 대해 들어 본 적이 있니?
B: 응, 있어. 나는 언젠가 꼭 가 보고 싶어.
A: 그거 알아? 나 지금 올레에 있어. 사실은, 지금 성산 일출봉에 올라가려고 해.
B: 멋지다!
A: 끊지 마. 나와 함께 아름다운 경치를 즐겨.
B: 조심해! 걸을 때는 휴대폰을 사용해서는 안 돼.
A: 아, 맞다. 고마워. 나중에 사진 보여 줄게.

❶ This is so cool, isn't it?: 부가의문문에서 This는 it으로 받는다.
❷ Guess what?: 있잖아., 그거 알아?(어떤 것에 대해 말을 꺼낼 때 쓰는 관용적인 표현)
❸ hang up: 전화를 끊다
❹ while: ~하는 동안

Check(√) True or False

(3) Minjun is going to go up Seongsan Ilchulbong. T☐ F☐

(4) Somin wants to enjoy the beautiful scenery with Minjun. T☐ F☐

Get Ready -2

1. **G:** Look at that boy. He's great.
   B: ❶He's riding an MTB. Do you know about it?
   G: No. What is it?
   B: ❷It's a special bike for riding on a mountain.
2. **G:** Wait. Don't jump into the water yet.
   B: ❸Why not?
   G: You shouldn't swim without a life jacket.
3. **G:** Look at the beautiful flowers over there! ❹ I'd like to take a selfie in front of them.
   B You shouldn't go over there.
   G: Oh, okay.
4. **B:** ❺I want to watch the birds in the trees.
   G: You shouldn't go up too close to the birds.
   B: All right, thanks.

❶ MTB: mountain bike
❷ for riding a mountain: 산을 오르기 위한
❸ Why not?=Why can't I jump into the water?
❹ I'd like to: ~하고 싶다 / in front of: ~ 앞에서
❺ in the trees: 나무에 있는(the birds를 수식하는 형용사구)

 Start Off - Listen & Talk A

1. **G:** ❶Dad, have you ever heard of Kim Soyun, the rock climber?
   M: Yes, I've seen her on TV.
   G: ❷She's teaching rock climbing at a camp this Saturday. I want to join the camp.
   M: Okay, Miso, but you shouldn't climb up too high.
   G: ❸All right. Thanks, Dad.
2. **G:** Have you heard of Rock Boys?
   M: No, I haven't.
   G: ❹It's my favorite band. There's a concert this Saturday. Can I go?
   M: Okay, Minju, but you shouldn't come home too late.
   G: All right. Thanks, Dad.

❶ Kim Soyun과 the rock climber는 동격 관계이다.
❷ She's teaching=She will teach
❸ All right.: 알았어요., 좋아요.
❹ It = Rock Boys

 Start Off - Speak Up - Look and talk.

A: Have you heard of safety rules for mountain hiking?
B: Yes. But I don't know much about them.
A: ❶Let me tell you one. You shouldn't walk too fast.
B: ❷Oh, I see.

❶ Let me ~: 내가 ~할게 / one=a safety rule for mountain hiking
❷ I see.: 알겠어.

 Express Yourself A

1. **G:** Have you heard of Elvis Presley?
   B: No, I haven't. Who is he?
   G: He was a famous American singer and actor. ❶We can see a figure of Elvis here.
   B: ❷Sounds interesting. I want to take pictures with it.
   G: Okay. Let's go.
2. **W:** You shouldn't take selfies here. Van Gogh's painting is behind you.
   B: Don't worry, Mom. It's not his real painting. ❸So I can take selfies in front of it.
   W: Really? Sounds interesting. Can I take selfies here, too?
   B: ❹Why not?

❶ a figure of Elvis: Elvis의 모형
❷ Sounds interesting.: 흥미롭게 들린다.
❸ so: 그래서 / in front of: ~의 앞에
❹ Why not?: 물론 되고말고.

Check Yourself - Listen & Speak

1. **B:** Wait, Jimin.
   G: Why?
   B: Look at that sign. ❶You shouldn't take a photo here.
   G: Oh, okay.
2. **B:** ❷This place is good for bike riding.
   G: Look, there's a sign. You shouldn't ride a bike here.

❶ You shouldn't ~.: 너는 ~ 해서는 안 된다.
❷ be good for: ~에 좋다

● 다음 우리말과 일치하도록 빈칸에 알맞은 말을 쓰시오.

Get Ready - 2

1. **G:** Look _____ that boy. He's _____.

   B: He's _____ an MTB. Do you _____ about it?

   G: No. _____ is it?

   B: It's a _____ bike for _____ on a mountain.

2. **G:** Wait. _____ jump _____ the water yet.

   B: _____ not?

   G: You _____ swim _____ a life jacket. _____ it _____.

3. **G:** _____ at the beautiful flowers _____ there! I'd _____ to _____ a selfie in _____ of them.

   B: You shouldn't go _____ there.

   G: Oh, _____.

4. **B:** I want to _____ the birds _____ the trees.

   G: You shouldn't go _____ too close to the _____.

   B: All _____, thanks.

해석

1. G: 저 소년을 봐. 그는 대단하다.
   B: 그는 MTB를 타고 있어. 넌 그것에 대해 알고 있니?
   G: 아니. 그게 뭐지?
   B: 그것은 산에서 타는 특별한 자전거야.

2. G: 기다려. 아직 물속으로 뛰어들지 마.
   B: 왜 안 돼?
   G: 구명조끼 없이 수영하면 안 돼. 이것을 입어.

3. G: 저기 있는 아름다운 꽃들을 봐! 그 꽃들 앞에서 셀피를 찍고 싶어.
   B: 거기 가면 안 돼.
   G: 아, 알았어.

4. B: 나는 나무에 있는 새들을 보고 싶어.
   G: 새들에게 너무 가까이 가지 마.
   B: 알았어, 고마워.

Start Off - Listen & Talk A

1. **G:** Dad, have you _____ heard of Kim Soyun, the rock _____?

   M: Yes, I've _____ her _____ TV.

   G: She's teaching rock _____ at a _____ this Saturday. I want to _____ the camp.

   M: Okay, Miso, _____ you shouldn't _____ up too high.

   G: All _____. Thanks, Dad.

2. **G:** _____ you _____ of Rock Boys?

   M: No, I _____.

   G: It's my _____ band. There's a _____ this Saturday. _____ I go?

   M: Okay, Minju, but you _____ come home _____ late.

   G: All _____. Thanks, Dad.

1. G: 아빠, 암벽 등반가인 김소윤에 대해 들어 본 적 있으세요?
   M: 응, TV에서 봤어.
   G: 그녀가 이번 토요일에 캠프에서 암벽 등반을 가르쳐요. 저는 캠프에 참가하고 싶어요.
   M: 알았어, 미소야. 하지만 너무 높이 올라가면 안 돼.
   G: 알았어요. 고마워요, 아빠.

2. G: Rock Boys에 대해 들어보셨어요?
   M: 아니, 듣지 못했다.
   G: 그건 제가 제일 좋아하는 밴드에요. 이번 토요일에 콘서트가 있어요. 가도 돼요?
   M: 좋아, 민주야. 하지만 너무 늦게 집에 오면 안 돼.
   G: 알았어요. 고마워요, 아빠.

Start Off - Listen & Talk B

B: Have you _____ _____ bird watching?

M: Sure. I tried it _____ I was a child.

B: That's nice. Actually, I'm _____ it _____ the first time this Saturday.

M: Are you? You _____ _____ warm clothes and something to eat.

B: Okay. What else _____ I _____ in mind?

M: You _____ make any noise _____ you watch the birds.

B: I'll keep that _____ _____. Thanks, Dad.

Step Up - Real-life Scene

Video Chat with Minjun from Jeju

A: Hello, Somin! _____ me! Can you _____ me?

B: Oh, _____, Minjun! What's _____?

A: This is so cool, _____ it? We can video _____ on the phone! Have you _____ of Jeju *Olle*?

B: Yes, I have. I really _____ to go there someday.

A: _____ what? I'm on it now. Actually, I'm _____ to go up Seongsan Ilchulbong now.

B: That's _____!

A: Don't hang _____. Enjoy the beautiful _____ with me.

B: _____ careful! You shouldn't _____ your cell phone _____ you're walking.

A: Oh, _____. _____ you. I'll _____ you photos _____.

Express Yourself A

1. **G:** Have you _____ of Elvis Presley?

   B: No, I _____. _____ is he?

   G: He was a famous American _____ and _____. We can see a _____ of Elvis here.

   B: _____ interesting. I want to _____ pictures with it.

   G: Okay. _____ go.

2. **W:** You shouldn't _____ selfies here. Van Gogh's _____ is behind you.

   B: Don't _____, Mom. It's not his _____ painting. _____ I can take selfies in _____ of it.

   W: Really? Sounds interesting. _____ I take _____ here, too?

   B: Why _____?

해석

B: 새 관찰에 대해 들어보셨어요?

M: 물론이지. 어렸을 때 해 봤어.

B: 그거 멋지네요. 사실, 전 이번 주 토요일에 처음으로 그것을 할 거예요.

M: 그래? 넌 따뜻한 옷과 먹을 것을 가져가야 해.

B: 알았어요. 그 밖에 또 무엇을 명심해야 하나요?

M: 너는 새들을 관찰할 때 아무 소리도 내지 말아야 해.

B: 그것을 명심할게요. 고마워요, 아빠.

제주에서 걸려온 민준과의 화상 채팅

A: 여보세요, 소민아! 나야! 나를 볼 수 있니?

B: 오, 안녕, 민준! 무슨 일이니?

A: 이거 정말 멋지지 않니? 전화로 화상 채팅도 할 수 있어! 너 제주 올레에 대해 들어 본 적이 있니?

B: 응, 있어. 나는 언젠가 꼭 가 보고 싶어.

A: 그거 알아? 나 지금 올레에 있어. 사실은, 지금 성산 일출봉에 올라가려고 해.

B: 멋지다!

A: 끊지 마. 나와 함께 아름다운 경치를 즐겨.

B: 조심해! 걸을 때는 휴대폰을 사용해서는 안 돼.

A: 아, 맞다. 고마워. 나중에 사진 보내 줄게.

1. **G:** 엘비스 프레슬리에 대해 들어 본 적 있니?

   B: 아니, 없어. 그는 누구인데?

   G: 그는 유명한 미국 가수이자 배우였어. 우리는 여기서 엘비스의 모형을 볼 수 있어.

   B: 재미있을 것 같다. 그것과 함께 사진을 찍고 싶어.

   G: 좋아. 가자.

2. **W:** 넌 여기서 셀피를 찍으면 안 돼. 반 고흐의 그림이 네 뒤에 있어.

   B: 엄마, 걱정하지 마세요. 그건 그의 진짜 그림이 아니에요. 그래서 그 앞에서 셀피를 찍을 수 있어요.

   W: 정말이지? 재미있겠다. 나도 여기서 셀피를 찍을 수 있을까?

   B: 물론이죠.

01 다음 두 문장의 의미가 같은 뜻이 되도록 빈칸에 알맞은 말을 쓰시오.

> You shouldn't swim too far.
> = You had _____ _____ swim too far.

02 다음 대화의 밑줄 친 우리말에 해당하는 것은?

> A: Jina, I'm going to Vietnam with my family this winter.
> B: Wow. That sounds like fun.
> A: 너 전에 그곳에 가 본 적 있니?
> B: No, I haven't.

① Were you there before?
② Had you been there before?
③ Have you been there before?
④ Have you gone there before?
⑤ When did you go there before?

03 다음 대화의 빈칸에 알맞은 것은?

> A: It's going to rain. _____
> B: Okay. If it rains, I'll stay inside.

① You will go outside.　② You shouldn't go outside.
③ You would go outside.　④ You might not go outside.
⑤ You can go outside.

stay 머물다
inside 안에

04 다음 대화의 빈칸에 알맞은 것은?

> A: Have you eaten this food?
> B: No, _____.

① I don't　② I didn't
③ I haven't　④ I hadn't
⑤ I have eaten it

01 다음 대화의 밑줄 친 부분과 바꿔 쓸 수 있는 것은?

> **A:** Is it okay to eat chocolate?
> **B:** Sure, but don't eat too much.

① you can eat too much
② you don't have to eat too much
③ you won't eat too much
④ you should eat too much
⑤ you'd better not eat too much

서답형
02 다음 대화의 빈칸에 알맞은 말을 쓰시오.

> **A:** _____ you _____ tried kimchi, Ann?
> **B:** Yes, I _____. It was very tasty.

03 다음 대화를 의미가 통하도록 알맞게 배열한 것은?

> (A) Why not?
> (B) Really? Sounds interesting. Can I take selfies here, too?
> (C) You shouldn't take selfies here. Van Gogh's painting is behind you.
> (D) Don't worry, Mom. It's not his real painting. So I can take selfies in front of it.

① (A) – (D) – (B) – (C)
② (B) – (C) – (D) – (A)
③ (C) – (D) – (B) – (A)
④ (D) – (B) – (C) – (A)
⑤ (D) – (C) – (B) – (A)

04 다음 대화의 빈칸에 가장 알맞은 것은?

> **A:** Have you seen the movie, *Avatar*, Sue?
> **B:** No, I haven't. _____
> **A:** Yes, it's my favorite movie.

① Do you?
② Will you?
③ Had you?
④ Have you?
⑤ What do you want to see?

중요
05 다음 대화의 빈칸에 들어갈 말로 알맞은 것은?

> **A:** You should not _____.
> **B:** Oh, I'm sorry. I won't do that again.

① walk to school
② recycle plastics
③ reuse gift boxes
④ leave computers on
⑤ take a short shower

[06~09] 다음 대화를 읽고, 물음에 답하시오.

> **G:** Dad, have you ever ⓐhear of Kim Soyun, the rock climber?
> **M:** Yes, I've seen her ⓑ ____ TV.
> **G:** She's teaching rock climbing at a camp this Saturday. I want to join the camp.
> **M:** Okay, Miso, but you ⓒ ____ climb up too high.
> **G:** All right. Thanks, Dad.

서답형
06 위 대화의 밑줄 친 ⓐ를 알맞은 형으로 고치시오.

➡ _____

07 위 대화의 빈칸 ⓑ에 알맞은 것은?

① in　　　② on　　　③ by

④ with　　⑤ from

08 위 대화의 빈칸 ⓒ에 들어갈 수 없는 것은? (2개)

① don't　　　　② must not

③ need not　　　④ shouldn't

⑤ had better not

09 위 대화의 내용과 일치하지 않는 것은?

① 미소의 아버지는 김소윤을 알고 있다.

② 김소윤은 암벽 등반가이다.

③ 김소윤은 캠프에서 이번 토요일에 암벽 등반을 강의할 것이다.

④ 미소는 캠프에 참여하기를 원한다.

⑤ 미소의 아버지는 미소가 암벽 등반하는 것을 반대했다.

[10~14] 다음 대화를 읽고, 물음에 답하시오.

A: Hello, Somin! It's me! Can you see me?

B: Oh, hi, Minjun! What's ____ⓐ____ ?

A: This is so cool, ____ⓑ____ ? We can video chat on the phone! Have you heard of Jeju *Olle*?

B: Yes, I have. I really want to go there someday.

A: Guess what? I'm on it now. ⓒActual, I'm going to go up Seongsan Ilchulbong now.

B: That's great!

A: Don't hang up. Enjoy the beautiful ____ⓓ____ with me.

B: Be careful! You shouldn't use your cell phone while you're walking.

A: Oh, right. Thank you. I'll send you photos later.

10 위 대화의 빈칸 ⓐ에 알맞은 것은?

① on　　　　② to

③ at　　　　④ up

⑤ for

11 위 대화의 빈칸 ⓑ에 알맞은 것은?

① is this　　　　② does it

③ isn't this　　　④ doesn't it

⑤ isn't it

서답형
12 위 대화의 밑줄 친 ⓒ를 알맞은 어형으로 고치시오.

➡ _____

서답형
13 위 대화의 빈칸 ⓓ에 다음 영영풀이에 해당하는 단어를 쓰시오.

> the land, water, or plants that you can see around you

➡ _____

14 위 대화를 읽고, 답할 수 없는 질문은?

① Can Somin see Minjun?

② Where is Minjun now?

③ Where does Somin want to go someday?

④ Is Minjun going to go up Seongsan Ilchulbong?

⑤ How many photos will Minjun send to Somin?

[01~02] 다음 대화의 빈칸에 알맞은 말을 쓰시오.

01
> G: Wait. Don't jump into the water yet.
> B: Why not?
> G: You _____ swim without a life jacket.

02
> G: _____ you ever slept in a tent?
> B: No, I _____.

03 다음 대화를 의미가 통하도록 알맞게 배열하시오.

> (A) It's a special bike for riding on a mountain.
> (B) Look at that boy. He's great.
> (C) He's riding an MTB. Do you know about it?
> (D) No. What is it?

➡ _____

[04~06] 다음 대화를 읽고, 물음에 답하시오.

> G: Have you heard of Rock Boys?
> M: ⓐNo, I have.
> G: ⓑIt's my favorite band. There's a concert this Saturday. Can I go?
> M: Okay, Minju, ___ⓒ___ you shouldn't come home too late.
> G: All right. Thanks, Dad.

04 위 대화의 밑줄 친 ⓐ에서 어법상 어색한 것을 고치시오.

_____ ➡ _____

05 위 대화의 밑줄 친 ⓑ가 가리키는 것을 영어로 쓰시오.

➡ _____

06 위 대화의 빈칸 ⓒ에 알맞은 접속사를 쓰시오.

➡ _____

[07~08] 다음 대화를 읽고, 물음에 답하시오.

> G: Have you heard of Elvis Presley?
> B: No, I haven't. Who is he?
> G: He was a famous American singer and ___ⓐ___ . We can see a figure of Elvis here.
> B: Sounds interesting. I want to take pictures with ⓑit.
> G: Okay. Let's go.

07 위 대화의 빈칸 ⓐ에 다음 정의에 해당하는 단어를 쓰시오.

> someone whose job is acting in plays or films

➡ _____

08 위 대화의 밑줄 친 ⓑ가 가리키는 것을 우리말로 쓰시오.

➡ _____

Grammar

① 현재완료

> • I **have visited** a selfie museum before. 나는 전에 셀피 박물관을 방문한 적이 있다.
> • **Have** you ever **heard** of beach safety rules? 너는 해변 안전 규칙에 대해 들어본 적이 있니?

■ **현재완료의 형태**
'have[has]+과거분사'의 형태를 취한다.
  • It **has been** such a long time. 정말 오랜만이다.
  • I **have had** many different jobs. 나는 많은 다양한 직업을 가져왔다.

cf. yesterday, two days ago, last Sunday 등과 같이 특정한 과거 시점을 나타내는 표현이 오면 현재
  완료시제로 쓰지 않고 과거시제로 써야 한다.
  • I read the book yesterday.   (○) 나는 어제 그 책을 읽었다.
  • I have read the book yesterday. (X)

■ **현재완료의 용법**
현재완료는 경험, 계속, 완료, 결과의 용법이 있다.

분류	용법	예문
경험	과거부터 현재까지의 경험 before, ever, never, often 등과 쓰임	I **have** never **been** to Rome. (나는 로마에 가 본 적이 없다.)
계속	과거의 일이 지금까지 계속됨 'since+특정 시점', 'for+기간' 등과 쓰임	I **have known** him since I was a little child. (나는 어릴 때부터 그를 알아 왔다.)
완료	과거에 시작된 일이 이제 막 완료됨 just, already, yet 등과 쓰임	He **has** just **finished** his homework. (그는 방금 숙제를 끝냈다.)
결과	과거의 일이 현재의 결과를 가져옴 '~해서 (지금) …하다'의 의미임	They **have gone** to Madrid. (그들은 마드리드에 가고 없다.)

■ **현재완료의 부정문**
'have[has]와 과거분사 사이에 not을 넣는다.
  • He **has not written** the letter yet. 그는 아직 그 편지를 쓰지 않았다.

■ **현재완료의 의문문**
'Have[Has]+주어+과거분사 ~?'의 형태를 취한다.
  • **Have** you ever **seen** a lion? 너는 사자를 본 적이 있니?

핵심 Check

1. 다음 괄호 안에서 알맞은 것을 고르시오.

   (1) Ann has just (did / done) her homework.
   (2) They (have / do) not (ate / eaten) the pizza.
   (3) He (lived / has lived) in this town since he was seven.
   (4) I have known her (for / since) three years.

② 접속사 though

> • **Though** there's a fire, you can be safe. 비록 화재가 나도 너는 안전할 수 있다.
>
> • **Though** the boys are not riding horses, it looks like they are.
>   비록 그 소년들은 말을 타고 있지 않지만, 말을 타고 있는 것처럼 보인다.
>
> • **Though** it was raining, the children played outside.
>   비록 비가 오고 있었지만 아이들은 밖에서 놀았다.

■ 접속사 though는 '비록 ~이지만'의 의미로 사용되며 양보의 부사절을 이끄는 접속사이다.
  • **Though** it was cold, she wasn't wearing a coat. 비록 날씨가 추웠지만, 그녀는 코트를 입고 있지 않았다.
  • **Though** I'm on a diet, I'll eat every hamburger here.
    비록 나는 다이어트를 하고 있지만, 여기에 있는 모든 햄버거를 먹겠다.

■ though 대신 although나 even though를 써도 같은 의미가 된다.
  • **Though** they are so poor, they seem happy. 그들은 아주 가난하지만, 행복해 보인다.
    = **Alhough** they are so poor, they seem happy.
    = **Even though** they are so poor, they seem happy.
  • **Though** you do not like it, you must do it. 너는 그것을 좋아하지 않아도 해야 한다.
    = **Alhough** you do not like it, you must do it.
    = **Even though** you do not like it, you must do it.

■ 종속접속사 though 대신 등위접속사 but을 써서 같은 뜻의 문장으로 바꿔 쓸 수 있다.
  • **Though** I like tennis, I'm not very good at it. 나는 테니스를 좋아하지만, 그것을 별로 잘하지 못한다.
    = I like tennis, **but** I'm not very good at it. 나는 테니스를 좋아한다. 그러나 그것을 별로 잘하지 못한다.

핵심 Check

2. 다음 괄호 안에서 알맞은 것을 고르시오.
  (1) (Though / Because) they were rich, they weren't very happy.
  (2) (As / Though) the man was very old, he was strong.
  (3) (If / Though) I like baseball, I am not a good player.
  (4) (Although / While) it was cold, Frank didn't wear a coat.

Grammar 시험대비 기본평가

01 다음 괄호 안에서 알맞은 것을 고르시오.

> reach 도착하다

(1) Jane (was / has been) busy since last week.

(2) How often have you (gone / been) to the United States?

(3) He (has finished / finished) reading a book two hours ago.

(4) He (has just finished / just finishes) his homework.

(5) We (arrived / have arrived) here yesterday.

(6) When (have you reached / did you reach) here?

02 다음 문장에서 어법상 어색한 것을 찾아 고쳐 쓰시오.

> thin 마른

(1) Because Jenny is so thin, she is strong.

_____ ➡ _____

(2) We lost the game since everyone played well.

_____ ➡ _____

(3) As the sun was shining, it wasn't very warm.

_____ ➡ _____

03 다음 괄호 안에 주어진 단어를 어법상 알맞은 형태로 바꾸어 문장을 다시 쓰시오.

> sick 아픈
> newspaper 신문

(1) He (be) sick in bed since last Friday.

➡ _____

(2) How long (you know) Miss Smith?

➡ _____

(3) (you ever read) the Christmas Carol?

➡ _____

(4) My father (not read) the newspaper yet.

➡ _____ .

01 다음 두 문장을 한 문장으로 만들 때 빈칸에 알맞은 것은?

> I moved here two years ago. I still live here.
> ➡ I _____ here for two years.

① live
② lived
③ will live
④ am living
⑤ have lived

[02~03] 다음 문장의 빈칸에 알맞은 것을 고르시오.

02
> _____ the car is old, it still runs well.

① As
② If
③ Unless
④ Because
⑤ Though

03
> Ted is hungry because he _____ nothing since this morning.

① eat
② eats
③ ate
④ has eaten
⑤ had eaten

서답형
04 다음 빈칸에 공통으로 알맞은 말을 쓰시오.

> • _____ the service was slow, the waiters were kind.
> • His speech was very good. It was a little too long, _____.

서답형
05 다음 빈칸에 공통으로 알맞은 말을 쓰시오.

> • Sorry to _____ kept you waiting. I _____ been to the station.
> • We _____ known each other since our childhood.

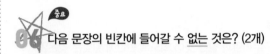
06 다음 문장의 빈칸에 들어갈 수 없는 것은? (2개)

> _____ I met the girl once, I can't remember her name.

① Whether
② Though
③ Although
④ As though
⑤ Even though

07 다음 문장의 빈칸에 알맞지 않은 것은?

> They have been to England _____.

① once
② twice
③ before
④ never
⑤ many times

서답형
08 다음 우리말과 일치하도록 주어진 단어를 바르게 배열하시오.

> 비록 교통체증이 심했지만 우리는 제시간에 도착했다.
> (we, was, the, on, traffic, time, though, heavy, arrived).

> ➡ _____
> _____

09 다음 괄호 안에 주어진 단어를 어법상 바르게 쓴 것은?

> I know some good restaurants here because I (live) in this town for five years.

① live　　　　② lived

③ is living　　④ have lived

⑤ had lived

10 다음 우리말과 같은 뜻이 되도록 빈칸에 알맞은 것은?

> 내일 비가 올지라도, 나는 집에 있지 않을 것이다.
> ➡ _____ it rains tomorrow, I won't stay home.

① As　　　　② Since

③ While　　　④ Although

⑤ Because

서답형

11 다음 빈칸에 알맞은 말을 쓰시오.

> My mother has gone shopping. She is _____ here.

12 다음 두 문장의 뜻이 같도록 할 때 빈칸에 알맞은 것은?

> Though Mike likes dogs, his wife doesn't.
> ➡ Mike likes dogs, _____ his wife doesn't.

① and　　　　② so

③ but　　　　④ for

⑤ because

서답형

13 다음 두 문장의 의미가 같도록 빈칸에 알맞은 말을 쓰시오.

> We have been married for ten years.
> ➡ Ten years have passed _____ we got married.

14 다음 문장의 빈칸에 가장 알맞은 것은?

> _____, I tried not to fall asleep.

① Although I was sleepy

② Though I tried my best

③ Even though we played well

④ Although my family was poor

⑤ Even though my sister was young

15 다음 대화의 빈칸에 알맞은 것은?

> A: Have you ever heard the news?
> B: No, I _____ the news.

① heard　　　　　　② have not heard

③ was not heard　　④ did not hear

⑤ had not heard

서답형

16 다음 문장의 밑줄 친 부분을 어법에 맞도록 고쳐 문장을 다시 쓰시오.

> <u>While</u> he played well, he lost the soccer game.

➡ _____

_____

17 다음 두 문장의 뜻이 같도록 할 때 빈칸에 알맞은 것은?

> Though the boy was sick, he went to school.
>
> ➡ _____ the boy was sick, he went to school.

① So   ② Such

③ Although   ④ Therefore

⑤ Whatever

18 다음 중 어법상 어색한 문장은?

① I have had a fever since last Friday.

② Two years have passed since I came here.

③ We have known each other for many years.

④ He has been seventy years old when he died.

⑤ It has been a long time since I saw you.

19 다음 중 문맥상 어색한 문장은?

① I waited until he came.

② He couldn't buy the camera though he had no money.

③ He has played soccer since he was a boy.

④ Although he was tired, he studied hard.

⑤ Though I was tired, I had to do my homework.

20 다음 대화의 빈칸에 알맞은 말을 쓰시오.

> **A:** How long has she been absent from school?
>
> **B:** She _____ _____ _____ from school since this Wednesday.

21 다음 빈칸에 공통으로 알맞은 말을 쓰시오.

> • Have you done your homework _____?
>
> • She hasn't come home _____.

22 다음 빈칸에 알맞은 것을 순서대로 바르게 짝지은 것은?

> • _____ they were poor, they were very happy.
>
> • _____ you are late, you must hurry up.

① If – Because

② Though – As

③ When – Even though

④ Unless – Since

⑤ Because – Although

23 다음 밑줄 친 부분의 쓰임이 나머지 넷과 다른 하나는?

① I <u>have seen</u> the movie before.

② My uncle <u>has</u> never <u>lived</u> in China before.

③ How many times <u>have</u> they <u>been</u> to England?

④ Mr. Smith <u>has gone</u> to Berlin on business.

⑤ Sora and Minjun <u>have been</u> to America once.

01 다음 우리말과 같도록 문장을 완성하시오.

(1) 그들은 이미 프로젝트를 끝마쳤다.
➡ They _____ already _____ the project.

(2) 그는 아직 런던에서 돌아오지 않았다.
➡ He _____ _____ _____ from London yet.

(3) 죄송하지만, 그녀는 회의에 가고 없습니다.
➡ I'm sorry, but she _____ _____ _____ a meeting.

02 다음 두 문장의 뜻이 같도록 빈칸에 알맞은 말을 쓰시오.

(1) Even though Kathy couldn't concentrate well, she did her homework.
➡ _____ Kathy couldn't concentrate well, she did her homework.

(2) She doesn't come, but I will finish the work.
➡ I will finish the work _____ she doesn't come.

03 다음 문장에서 어법상 어색한 것을 찾아 바르게 고쳐 쓰시오.

(1) She has gone to Bangladesh last Friday.
_____ ➡ _____

(2) My father hasn't left Seoul already.
_____ ➡ _____

04 다음 빈칸에 공통으로 알맞은 말을 쓰시오.

- _____ he is rich, he has few friends.
- I didn't buy that cap; I liked it, _____.

05 다음 문장에서 어법상 어색한 것을 찾아 바르게 고쳐 쓰시오.

(1) Jack has seen the koala last year.
_____ ➡ _____

(2) The weather is good for ten days.
_____ ➡ _____

06 다음 주어진 단어를 바르게 배열하여 문장을 완성하시오.

(1) (Italy / many / he / to / been / times / has)
➡ _____

(2) (very / days / I / busy / these / been / have)
➡ _____

(3) (have / Paris / before / I / visited / never)
➡ _____

07 다음 보기에서 알맞은 말을 골라 빈칸에 쓰시오.

┌─ 보기 ─┐
since / if / that / though /
because / before
└─────┘

(1) Take a bath _____ you go to bed.

(2) He was so tired _____ he went to bed early.

(3) Mike has known Mary _____ he was a baby.

(4) Tim couldn't finish the project _____ he was very busy.

(5) I won't go on a picnic _____ it rains tomorrow.

(6) Ann isn't good at swimming _____ she lives near the river.

08 다음 문장에서 어법상 어색한 부분을 바르게 고쳐 문장을 다시 쓰시오.

(1) I have been to London four years ago.

➡ _____

(2) When have you seen a white lion?

➡ _____

(3) I have often played with her when I was a child.

➡ _____

(4) He has been ill in bed last month.

➡ _____

09 다음 문장에서 어법상 어색한 부분을 고치시오.

(1) Because the boy is so young, he is very wise.

_____ ➡ _____

(2) I failed the exam as I studied hard.

_____ ➡ _____

10 다음 주어진 단어를 이용하여 우리말을 영어로 옮기시오.

(1) 그는 1970년 이래로 뉴욕에서 살았다.
(live, since)

➡ _____

(2) 너는 이 이야기를 벌써 다 읽었니?
(finish, this, story, yet)

➡ _____

(3) 나는 그 영화를 한 번 본 적이 있다.
(see, once)

➡ _____

11 다음 우리말과 뜻이 같도록 빈칸에 주어진 철자로 시작하는 알맞은 말을 쓰시오.

┌──────────────────────┐
│ 비록 과일이 건강에 좋다고 해도, 그는 과일을 좋 │
│ 아하지 않는다.   │
│ ➡ A_____ fruit is good for his health, │
│   he doesn't like it.   │
└──────────────────────┘

Reading

A Selfie Show

Have you ever heard of a "selfie"? When you take a photograph
of yourself, it's a selfie. The students from Minji's photo club have
searched for information about selfies for one month. Here are some of
their presentations about selfies.

Selfies in the Past – Minji

Did people in the past take selfies? Though it wasn't easy at that
time, the answer is yes. Look at this photo of Princess Anastasia. She
used a mirror to take a picture of herself. She looks nervous. Can you
guess why? Well, I think it was her first selfie. And it was probably the
world's first teenage selfie ever.

Fun Places for Selfies – Yunho

You can take selfies at world-famous places like Big Ben and the
Leaning Tower of Pisa. To take great pictures, just do fun poses and
use camera tricks.

You can also visit special museums to take fun selfies. For example,
there is a famous selfie museum in the Philippines. It has special spots
to take selfies. You can touch the paintings and even step inside them.
Look at the following pictures. Though the boys are not really riding
horses, it looks like they are. Though the man is just holding a big
brush, it looks like he is painting the Mona Lisa. Selfie museums exist
in Korea, too.

selfie 셀피
search 찾다
presentation 프레젠테이션, 발표
past 과거
nervous 초조한
mirror 거울
probably 아마
teenage 10대의
fun 재미; 재미있는
pose 포즈, 자세
for example 예를 들면
touch 손을 대다
exist 있다, 존재하다

 확인문제

● 다음 문장이 본문의 내용과 일치하면 T, 일치하지 <u>않으면</u> F를 쓰시오.

1 Minji belongs to the photo club. ☐

2 People in the past didn't take selfies. ☐

3 Princess Anastasia took pictures of herself several times. ☐

4 There is a famous selfie museum in the Philippines. ☐

5 There aren't any selfie museums in Korea. ☐

I have visited one in Chuncheon before. Why don't you go there
경험을 나타내는 현재완료 / ~하지 그래요?

yourself?
주어를 강조하는 재귀대명사

Selfie Safety – Jihun

These selfies look great, but were they a good idea? I don't think
look+형용사: ~해 보이다 / = these selfies

so. They don't look safe. You should take special care when you take
= they were a good idea / ~ 해야 한다 / ~할 때 - 때를 나타내는 접속사

selfies in the wild or at high places like these. A monkey could bite you
야생에서 / ~와 같은 / ~할 수 있다: 가능성

at any time, or you could fall. Here are some safety tips:
some+복수 명사

1. Don't take selfies while you're walking.
부정명령문 / ~하는 동안 -때를 나타내는 접속사

2. Do not pose with or near wild animals.
= Don't: 부정명령문 / ~ 가까이에서: 전치사

3. Never take selfies in dangerous places.
결코 ~하지 마라: 부정명령문

Selfies for a Better School Life – Soyun

I think we can use selfies to make a better school life. We can do good
앞에 접속사 that이 생략 / good의 비교급

things at school and take selfies. Then we can post the photos on our
do와 함께 can에 연결됨

school website. I've watered the plants and flowers at school for one
= have watered: 계속을 나타내는 현재완료

month. I've also helped the teacher at the school library many times.
경험을 나타내는 현재완료 / 여러 번

Look at my selfies of those things. How about joining me to create a
How about -ing?: ~하는 게 어때?

better school life?

before 전에	
safety 안전	
safe 안전한	
special 특별한	
care 관심	
wild 야생; 야생의	
place 장소, 곳	
bite 물다	
at any time 언제고	
while: ~하는 동안	
dangerous 위험한	
post 올리다, 게재하다	
plant 식물	
create 창조하다, 만들어 내다	

📎 **확인문제**

● 다음 문장이 본문의 내용과 일치하면 T, 일치하지 않으면 F를 쓰시오.

1 There is a selfie museum in Chuncheon. ☐

2 You should take special care when you take selfies in dangerous places. ☐

3 A monkey doesn't bite you. ☐

4 Selfies can be used to make a better school life. ☐

5 Soyun has watered the plants and flowers at school for a year. ☐

● 우리말을 참고하여 빈칸에 알맞은 말을 쓰시오.

1 _____ you ever _____ of a "selfie"?

2 When you _____ a photograph of _____, it's a selfie.

3 The students from Minji's photo _____ have searched _____ information about selfies _____ one month.

4 _____ are some of their presentations _____ selfies.

5 Did _____ in the past _____ selfies?

6 _____ it wasn't easy at that time, the _____ is yes.

7 _____ at this photo of Princess Anastasia.

8 She _____ a mirror to take a picture of _____.

9 She looks _____.

10 Can you guess _____?

11 Well, I _____ it was her _____ selfie.

12 And it was _____ the world's first _____ selfie ever.

13 You can _____ selfies at world-famous places _____ Big Ben and the Leaning Tower of Pisa.

14 To _____ great pictures, just do fun poses and use camera _____.

15 You can _____ visit special museums to take _____ selfies.

16 For _____, there is a _____ selfie museum in the Philippines.

17 It has _____ spots to _____ selfies.

18 You can _____ the paintings and _____ step inside them.

19 Look at the _____ pictures.

20 _____ the boys are not really _____ horses, it looks _____ they are.

1 여러분은 "셀피"에 대해 들어본 적이 있나요?

2 여러분 자신의 사진을 찍을 때 그것이 셀피에요.

3 민지의 사진 동아리 학생들은 한 달 동안 셀피에 대한 정보를 찾았습니다.

4 여기 셀피에 대한 그들의 발표 내용이 있습니다.

5 과거의 사람들은 셀피를 찍었나요?

6 그 때는 셀피를 찍는 것이 쉽지는 않았지만. 답은 '그렇다'입니다.

7 아나스타샤 공주의 이 사진을 보세요.

8 그녀는 거울을 사용하여 자신의 사진을 찍었습니다.

9 그녀는 긴장되어 보입니다.

10 왜인지 추측할 수 있나요?

11 글쎄. 나는 그것이 그녀의 첫 번째 셀피였다고 생각해요.

12 그리고 그것은 아마도 세계 최초의 10대 소녀의 셀피였을 거예요.

13 여러분은 빅벤과 피사의 사탑과 같은 세계적으로 유명한 장소에서 셀피를 찍을 수 있습니다.

14 멋진 사진을 찍기 위해서, 단지 재미있는 포즈를 취하고 카메라 기술을 이용하세요.

15 여러분은 또한 재미있는 셀피를 찍기 위해 특별한 박물관을 방문할 수 있습니다.

16 예를 들어, 필리핀에는 유명한 셀피 박물관이 있습니다.

17 그곳은 셀피를 찍기 위한 특별한 장소들이 있습니다.

18 여러분은 그림들을 만질 수 있고 심지어 그림들 안으로 들어갈 수도 있어요.

19 다음 사진들을 보세요.

20 비록 그 소년들은 말을 타고 있는 것은 아니지만, 말을 타고 있는 것처럼 보입니다.

21 Though the man is _____ holding a big _____, it looks like he is _____ the Mona Lisa.

22 Selfie museums _____ in Korea, too.

23 I have _____ one in Chuncheon _____.

24 Why _____ you go there _____?

25 These selfies _____ great, _____ were they a good idea?

26 I don't think _____.

27 They don't look _____.

28 You _____ take special care _____ you take selfies in the wild or at high _____ like these.

29 A monkey _____ bite you at any _____, or you could _____.

30 Here are some _____ tips:

31 1. Don't _____ selfies _____ you're walking.

32 2. Do not _____ with or near _____ animals.

33 3. _____ take selfies in dangerous _____.

34 I think we can _____ selfies to make a _____ school life.

35 We can do good _____ at school and _____ selfies.

36 Then we can _____ the photos on our school _____.

37 I've _____ the plants and flowers at _____ for one month.

38 I've _____ helped the teacher _____ the school library many _____.

39 Look _____ my selfies of _____ things.

40 How _____ joining me to _____ a better school life?

21 비록 그 남자는 단지 커다란 붓을 잡고 있지만, 모나리자를 그리고 있는 것처럼 보입니다.

22 한국에도 셀피 박물관이 있습니다.

23 나는 전에 춘천에 있는 한 박물관을 방문한 적이 있습니다.

24 여러분도 직접 그곳에 가는 게 어때요?

25 이 셀피들은 멋져 보이지만, 그것들은 좋은 생각이었나요?

26 난 그렇게 생각하지 않아요.

27 그것들은 안전해 보이지 않습니다.

28 여러분은 야생이나 이와 같이 높은 곳에서 셀피를 찍을 때 특별한 주의를 기울여야 합니다.

29 원숭이가 언제든지 당신을 물거나 또는 당신은 떨어질 수 있습니다.

30 여기 몇 가지 안전 수칙이 있습니다.

31 1. 걸으면서 셀피를 찍지 마세요.

32 2. 야생 동물들과 함께 또는 가까이에서 포즈를 취하지 마세요.

33 3. 위험한 곳에서는 절대 셀피를 찍지 마세요.

34 나는 우리가 더 나은 학교생활을 만들기 위해 셀피를 이용할 수 있다고 생각해요.

35 우리는 학교에서 좋은 일을 할 수 있고 셀피를 찍을 수도 있습니다.

36 그리고 나서 우리는 학교 웹사이트에 사진을 올릴 수 있어요.

37 나는 한 달 동안 학교에서 식물과 꽃에 물을 주었습니다.

38 나는 또한 학교 도서관에서 선생님을 여러 번 도왔습니다.

39 그런 것들에 대한 내 셀피를 보세요.

40 저와 함께 더 나은 학교생활을 만들어 보는 건 어떨까요?

● 우리말을 참고하여 본문을 영작하시오.

1 여러분은 "셀피"에 대해 들어 본 적이 있나요? 여러분 자신의 사진을 찍을 때 그것이 셀피에요.
➡ _____

2 민지의 사진 동아리 학생들은 한 달 동안 셀피에 대한 정보를 찾았습니다.
➡ _____

3 여기 셀피에 대한 그들의 발표 내용이 있습니다.
➡ _____

4 과거의 사람들은 셀피를 찍었나요?
➡ _____

5 그 때는 셀피를 찍는 것이 쉽지는 않았지만. 답은 '그렇다'입니다.
➡ _____

6 아나스타샤 공주의 이 사진을 보세요. 그녀는 거울을 사용하여 자신의 사진을 찍었습니다.
➡ _____

7 그녀는 긴장되어 보입니다. 왜인지 추측할 수 있나요?
➡ _____

8 글쎄, 나는 그것이 그녀의 첫 번째 셀피였다고 생각해요.
➡ _____

9 그리고 그것은 아마도 세계 최초의 10대 소녀의 셀피였을 거예요.
➡ _____

10 여러분은 빅벤과 피사의 사탑과 같은 세계적으로 유명한 장소에서 셀피를 찍을 수 있습니다.
➡ _____

11 멋진 사진을 찍기 위해서, 단지 재미있는 포즈를 취하고 카메라 기술을 이용하세요.
➡ _____

12 여러분은 또한 재미있는 셀피를 찍기 위해 특별한 박물관을 방문할 수 있습니다.
➡ _____

13 예를 들어, 필리핀에는 유명한 셀피 박물관이 있습니다.
➡ _____

14 그곳은 셀피를 찍기 위한 특별한 장소들이 있습니다.
➡ _____

15 여러분은 그림들을 만질 수 있고 심지어 그림들 안으로 들어갈 수도 있어요.
➡ _____

16 다음 사진들을 보세요.
➡ _____

17 비록 그 소년들은 말을 타고 있는 것은 아니지만, 말을 타고 있는 것처럼 보입니다.

➡ _____

18 비록 그 남자는 단지 커다란 붓을 잡고 있지만, 모나리자를 그리고 있는 것처럼 보입니다.

➡ _____

19 한국에도 셀피 박물관이 있습니다. 나는 전에 춘천에 있는 한 박물관을 방문한 적이 있습니다.

➡ _____

20 여러분도 직접 그곳에 가는 게 어때요? 이 셀피들은 멋져 보이지만, 그것들은 좋은 생각이었나요?

➡ _____

21 난 그렇게 생각하지 않아요. 그것들은 안전해 보이지 않습니다.

➡ _____

22 여러분은 야생이나 이와 같이 높은 곳에서 셀피를 찍을 때 특별한 주의를 기울여야 합니다.

➡ _____

23 원숭이가 언제든지 당신을 물거나 또는 당신은 떨어질 수 있습니다.

➡ _____

24 여기 몇 가지 안전 수칙이 있습니다.

➡ _____

25 걸으면서 셀피를 찍지 마세요.

➡ _____

26 야생 동물들과 함께 또는 가까이에서 포즈를 취하지 마세요.

➡ _____

27 위험한 곳에서는 절대 셀피를 찍지 마세요.

➡ _____

28 나는 우리가 더 나은 학교생활을 만들기 위해 셀피를 이용할 수 있다고 생각해요.

➡ _____

29 우리는 학교에서 좋은 일을 할 수 있고 셀피를 찍을 수도 있습니다.

➡ _____

30 그리고 나서 우리는 학교 웹사이트에 사진을 올릴 수 있어요.

➡ _____

31 나는 한 달 동안 학교에서 식물과 꽃에 물을 주었습니다.

➡ _____

32 나는 또한 학교 도서관에서 선생님을 여러 번 도왔습니다.

➡ _____

33 그런 것들에 대한 내 셀피를 보세요.

➡ _____

34 저와 함께 더 나은 학교생활을 만들어 보는 건 어떨까요?

➡ _____

[01~04] 다음 글을 읽고, 물음에 답하시오.

A Selfie Show

Have you ever heard of a "selfie"? ⓐ you take a photograph of yourself, it's a selfie. The students from Minji's photo club have searched ⓑ information about selfies ⓒ one month. ⓓHere are some of their presentations about selfies.

01 위 글의 빈칸 ⓐ에 알맞은 것은?

① What　　② How
③ When　　④ Because
⑤ While

02 위 글의 빈칸 ⓑ와 ⓒ에 공통으로 알맞은 것은?

① of　　② to
③ with　　④ for
⑤ along

03 위 글의 밑줄 친 ⓓ와 문형이 같은 것은?

① Mike likes music very much.
② The man is strong.
③ Birds fly in the sky.
④ The news made her glad.
⑤ Jane sent me a birthday card.

04 위 글의 뒤에 이어질 내용으로 가장 알맞은 것은?

① 셀피의 의미
② 셀피의 유래
③ 셀피를 찍는 이유
④ 민지의 사진 동아리 학생들이 찍은 여러 가지 셀피들
⑤ 민지의 사진 동아리 학생들이 모은 셀피에 대한 여러 가지 정보

[05~07] 다음 글을 읽고, 물음에 답하시오.

Selfies in the Past – Minji

Did people in the past take selfies? (①) Though it wasn't easy at that time, the answer is yes. (②) ⓐShe used a mirror to take a picture of her. (③) She looks nervous. (④) ⓑCan you guess why? (⑤) Well, I think it was her first selfie. And it was probably the world's first teenage selfie ever.

05 위 글의 ①~⑤ 중 다음 주어진 문장이 들어갈 알맞은 곳은?

Look at this photo of Princess Anastasia.

①　　②　　③　　④　　⑤

06 위 글의 밑줄 친 ⓐ에서 어법상 어색한 것을 고치시오.

➡ ＿＿＿＿＿ ➡ ＿＿＿＿＿

07 위 글의 밑줄 친 ⓑ를 why의 의미가 구체적으로 드러나도록 우리말로 옮기시오.

➡ ＿＿＿＿＿＿＿＿＿＿＿

[08~11] 다음 글을 읽고, 물음에 답하시오.

(①) You can take selfies at world-famous places ⓐlike Big Ben and the Leaning Tower of Pisa. (②) To take great pictures, just do fun poses and use camera tricks. (③)

You can also visit special museums to take fun selfies. (④) _____ⓑ_____, there is a famous selfie museum in the Philippines. (⑤)

08 위 글의 ①~⑤ 중 다음 주어진 문장이 들어갈 알맞은 곳은?

It has special spots to take selfies.

①   ②   ③   ④   ⑤

09 위 글의 밑줄 친 ⓐ와 같은 용법으로 쓰인 것은?

① Do you <u>like</u> apples?
② I <u>like</u> to watch baseball on TV.
③ How do you <u>like</u> this movie?
④ I <u>like</u> to walk in the park on Sundays.
⑤ I want to buy a hat <u>like</u> yours.

10 위 글의 빈칸 ⓑ에 알맞은 것은?

① However   ② For example
③ Therefore   ④ At last
⑤ As a result

11 위 글의 주제로 가장 알맞은 것은?

① 세계적으로 유명한 장소들
② 셀피를 찍는 요령
③ 셀피를 찍기 위한 재미있는 장소
④ 세계의 유명한 박물관들
⑤ 필리핀의 관광 명소

[12~15] 다음 글을 읽고, 물음에 답하시오.

You can touch the paintings and even step inside them. Look at the following pictures. __ⓐ__ the boys are not really riding horses, it looks like they are. __ⓑ__ the man is just holding a big brush, it looks like he is painting the Mona Lisa. Selfie museums ⓒare in Korea, too. I have visited one in Chuncheon before. __ⓓ__ don't you go there yourself?

12 위 글의 빈칸 ⓐ와 ⓑ에 공통으로 알맞은 것은? (2개)

① Though   ② If
③ When   ④ Although
⑤ Since

13 위 글의 밑줄 친 ⓒ와 바꿔 쓸 수 있는 것은?

① fix   ② join
③ exist   ④ stay
⑤ belong

서답형

14 위 글의 빈칸 ⓓ에 알맞은 말을 쓰시오.

➡ _____

15 위 글의 내용과 일치하지 <u>않는</u> 것은?

① 여러분은 그림들을 만질 수 있다.
② 소년들은 실제로 말을 타고 있다.
③ 남자는 모나리자를 그리고 있는 것처럼 보인다.
④ 셀피 박물관은 한국에도 있다.
⑤ 글쓴이는 춘천에 있는 셀피 박물관을 방문한 적이 있다.

[16~19] 다음 글을 읽고, 물음에 답하시오.

Selfie Safety - Jihun
(①) These selfies look great, ___ⓐ___ were they a good idea? (②) I don't think so. (③) ⓑYou should take special care when you take selfies in the wild or at high places like these. (④) A monkey could bite you at any time, or you could fall. (⑤) Here are some safety tips:
1. Don't take selfies ___ⓒ___ you're walking.
2. Do not pose with or near wild animals.
3. Never take selfies in dangerous places.

16 위 글의 ①~⑤ 중 다음 주어진 문장이 들어갈 알맞은 곳은?

> They don't look safe.

① ② ③ ④ ⑤

17 위 글의 빈칸 ⓐ에 알맞은 것은?

① and ② but
③ or ④ so
⑤ for

18 위 글의 밑줄 친 ⓑ를 우리말로 옮기시오.

➡ _____

_____

19 위 글의 빈칸 ⓒ에 알맞은 것은?

① if ② though
③ because ④ since
⑤ while

[20~24] 다음 글을 읽고, 물음에 답하시오.

Selfies for a Better School Life - Soyun
I think we can use selfies ⓐto make a better school life. We can do good things at school and take selfies. ⓑThen we can post the photos on our school website. I've watered the plants and flowers at school ___ⓒ___ one month. I've also helped the teacher at the school library many times. Look at my selfies of those things. ⓓHow about joining me to create a better school life?

20 위 글의 밑줄 친 ⓐ와 같은 용법으로 쓰인 것은?

① My hope is to work as a doctor in Africa.
② It's time to go to bed now.
③ My job is to report the news.
④ The boys hoped to find the hidden treasure.
⑤ Kate went to a shopping mall to buy clothes.

서답형
21 위 글의 밑줄 친 ⓑ를 우리말로 옮기시오.

➡ _____

22 위 글의 빈칸 ⓒ에 알맞은 것은?

① for ② during
③ from ④ since
⑤ while

서답형
23 위 글의 밑줄 친 ⓓ 대신 쓸 수 있는 것을 쓰시오.

➡ _____

24 위 글의 내용으로 보아 대답할 수 없는 질문은?

① What can Soyun use to make a better school life?

② Does Soyun take selfies at school?

③ Where can Soyun post the photos?

④ How long has Soyun watered the plants at school?

⑤ Why did Soyun help the teacher at the school library?

[25~26] 다음 글을 읽고, 물음에 답하시오.

A Selfie Show

Have you ever heard ____ⓐ____ a "selfie"? When you take a photograph ____ⓑ____ yourself, it's a selfie. The students from Minji's photo club ⓒhave searched for information about selfies for one month. Here are some of their presentations about selfies.

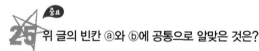 위 글의 빈칸 ⓐ와 ⓑ에 공통으로 알맞은 것은?

① of ② for

③ about ④ into

⑤ from

26 위 글의 밑줄 친 ⓒ와 용법이 같은 것은? (2개)

① I <u>have been</u> in this country since last month.

② Yumi <u>has seen</u> this movie many times.

③ Mike <u>has</u> just <u>cleaned</u> his room.

④ Lisa <u>has had</u> this cat for ten years.

⑤ She <u>has gone</u> out and this room is cold.

[27~30] 다음 글을 읽고, 물음에 답하시오.

Selfies in the Past - Minji

Did people in the past take selfies? ____ⓐ____ it wasn't easy at that time, the answer is yes. Look ____ⓑ____ this photo of Princess Anastasia. ⓒ그녀는 자신의 사진을 찍기 위해 거울을 사용했다. She looks nervous. Can you guess why? Well, I think it was her first selfie. And it was probably the world's first teenage selfie ever.

27 위 글의 빈칸 ⓐ에 알맞은 것은?

① If ② For

③ Though ④ When

⑤ Since

28 위 글의 빈칸 ⓑ에 알맞은 것은?

① at ② in

③ to ④ for

⑤ on

서답형

29 위 글의 밑줄 친 ⓒ를 주어진 단어를 이용하여 영어로 옮기시오.

(use, mirror, take, picture, herself)

➡ _____

30 위 글의 내용과 일치하지 <u>않는</u> 것은?

① 옛날 사람도 셀피를 찍었다.

② Anastasia 공주는 자신의 셀피를 찍었다.

③ Anastasia 공주는 종종 셀피를 찍었다.

④ Anastasia 공주는 초조해 보인다.

⑤ 민지는 Anastasia 공주가 찍은 이 셀피가 세계에서 십대의 첫 번째 셀피라고 생각한다.

[01~05] 다음 글을 읽고, 물음에 답하시오.

Fun Places for Selfies - Yunho

ⓐYou can take selfies at world-famous places like Big Ben and the Leaning Tower of Pisa. To take great pictures, just do fun ___ⓑ___ and use camera tricks.

You can also visit special museums to take fun selfies. ___ⓒ___ example, there is a famous selfie museum in the Philippines. ⓓIt has special spots to take selfies. You can touch the paintings and even step inside them.

01 위 글의 밑줄 친 ⓐ를 우리말로 옮기시오.

➡ _____

_____

02 위 글의 빈칸 ⓑ에 다음 정의에 해당하는 단어를 쓰시오. 필요하면 어형 변화를 할 것.

> a particular way that you stand, sit, or lie, for example when you are being photographed or painted

➡ _____

03 위 글의 빈칸 ⓒ에 알맞은 전치사를 쓰시오.

➡ _____

04 위 글의 밑줄 친 ⓓ가 가리키는 것을 우리말로 쓰시오.

➡ _____

05 Where can you go to take fun selfies? Answer in English.

➡ _____

[06~09] 다음 글을 읽고, 물음에 답하시오.

Look ___ⓐ___ the following pictures. ⓑThough the boys are not really riding horses, it looks like they are. Though the man is just holding a big brush, it looks like he is painting the Mona Lisa. Selfie museums exist in Korea, too. I have visited ⓒone in Chuncheon before. Why don't you go there ⓓyou?

06 위 글의 빈칸 ⓐ에 알맞은 전치사를 쓰시오.

➡ _____

07 위 글의 밑줄 친 ⓑ를 우리말로 옮기시오.

➡ _____

_____

08 위 글의 밑줄 친 ⓒ가 가리키는 것을 영어로 쓰시오.

➡ _____

09 위 글의 밑줄 친 ⓓ를 알맞은 어형으로 고치시오.

➡ _____

[10~14] 다음 글을 읽고, 물음에 답하시오.

Selfie Safety - Jihun

These selfies look great, but were they a good idea? I don't think ⓐso. ⓑThey don't look safely. You should take special care when you take selfies in the wild or at high places like these. A monkey could bite you ____ⓒ____ any time, or you could fall. Here are some safety tips:

1. Don't take selfies while you're walking.
2. Do not pose with or near wild animals.
3. Never take selfies in ⓓdanger places.

10 위 글의 밑줄 친 ⓐ가 가리키는 것을 영어로 쓰시오.

➡ _____

11 위 글의 밑줄 친 ⓑ에서 어법상 어색한 것을 고치시오.

_____ ➡ _____

12 위 글의 빈칸 ⓒ에 알맞은 전치사를 쓰시오.

➡ _____

13 위 글의 밑줄 친 ⓓ를 알맞은 어형으로 고치시오.

➡ _____

14 Why should you take special care when you take selfies in the wild or at high places? Answer in Korean.

➡ _____

[15~18] 다음 글을 읽고, 물음에 답하시오.

Selfie for a Better School Life - Soyun

ⓐI think we can use selfies to make a better school life. We can do good things at school and take selfies. Then we can post the photos on our school website. I've ⓑwater the plants and flowers at school ____ⓒ____ one month. I've also helped the teacher at the school library many times. Look at my selfies of those things. How ____ⓓ____ joining me to create a better school life?

15 위 글의 밑줄 친 ⓐ를 우리말로 옮기시오.

➡ _____

_____

16 위 글의 밑줄 친 ⓑ를 알맞은 어형으로 고치시오.

➡ _____

17 위 글의 빈칸 ⓒ에 알맞은 단어를 쓰시오.

➡ _____

18 위 글의 빈칸 ⓓ에 알맞은 단어를 쓰시오.

➡ _____

해석

Fun Time

A: You shouldn't push others when you go swimming.
~해서는 안 된다   = other people

B: Okay. Thank you for your advice.
thank A for B: A에 대해서 B에게 감사하다

구문해설 • push: 밀다   • advice: 충고

A: 수영하러 갈 때 다른 사람들을 밀면 안 돼.
B: 알았어. 충고 고마워.

Express Yourself - C

Have you heard of the pyramids in Egypt? Though I have never been to
= Although: 비록 ~이지만   ~에 다녀오다. ~에 가 본 적이 있다

Egypt before, I'm standing in front of a pyramid in this picture. I took it at the
현재진행형

selfie museum.

구문해설 • before: 전에   • in front of: ~ 앞에

여러분은 이집트의 피라미드에 대해 들어 본 적이 있나요? 나는 전에 이집트에 가 본 적이 없지만, 이 사진에서 나는 피라미드 앞에 서 있어요. 나는 이 사진을 셀피 박물관에서 찍었어요.

Project - Step 2

Fire Safety Rules

Have you heard of fire safety rules? Though there's a fire, you can be safe.

You shouldn't take the elevator. You should follow the teacher's directions.
should not의 축약형: 금지의 표현   = must: ~해야 한다

구문해설 • safety: 안전   • rule: 규칙, 수칙   • safe:: 안전한   • follow: 따르다   • direction: 지시

화재 안전 수칙

당신은 화재 안전 수칙에 대해 들어 본 적이 있습니까? 불이 났지만, 당신은 안전할 수 있어요. 엘리베이터를 타지 마세요. 선생님의 지시에 따라야 해요.

Link to the World

BMX Bike Riding

Riding a BMX bike is very exciting. You can try lots of skills. You can turn
동명사 주어   동명사 주어는 단수 취급 excited(X)   많은(=many = a lot of)

the bike freely and even jump with the bike. Though it's not easy, it's very
접 비록 ~이지만

exciting. You can start with standing skills. When you try standing skills,
접 ~할 때

balancing is very important. But be careful! You should wear a helmet and
명령문: 동사원형 ~

gloves. Also, you shouldn't go too fast when you're riding.
shouldn't+동사원형: ~해서는 안 된다

구문해설 • exciting: 흥미진진한, 신나는   • try: 시도하다   • freely: 자유롭게   • even: ~도[조차]
• easy: 쉬운   • skill: 기술   • balancing: 균형(잡기)   • important: 중요한
• careful: 조심하는, 주의 깊은

BMX 자전거 타기

BMX 자전거를 타는 것은 매우 흥미롭다. 여러분은 많은 기술을 시도할 수 있다. 여러분은 자전거를 자유롭게 돌릴 수 있고 심지어 자전거와 함께 점프할 수도 있다. 쉽지는 않지만, 매우 흥미롭다. 여러분은 서 있는 기술과 함께 시작하면 된다. 서 있는 기술을 시도할 때, 균형을 잡는 것이 매우 중요하다. 하지만 조심해라! 헬멧과 장갑을 착용해야 한다. 또한, 자전거를 탈 때는 너무 빨리 가지 말아야 한다.

영역별 핵심문제

01 다음 중 짝지어진 단어의 관계가 나머지와 다른 것은?

① loose – tight
② advice – tip
③ kind – unkind
④ birth – death
⑤ remember – forget

02 다음 빈칸에 들어갈 말로 적절하지 않은 것은?

> • Kate didn't receive a letter from him _____.
> • He turned and looked _____.
> • He found the place _____ difficulty.
> • What _____ did he say?

① else
② without
③ other
④ yet
⑤ back

03 다음 빈칸에 알맞은 단어를 쓰시오.

> _____ : present : future

04 다음 문장의 빈칸에 알맞은 것은?

> Vegetables are good _____ health.

① in
② on
③ to
④ for
⑤ with

05 다음 영영풀이에 해당하는 단어는?

> an action that is intended to deceive someone

① object
② joke
③ humor
④ plan
⑤ trick

06 다음 문장의 빈칸에 공통으로 들어갈 말을 쓰시오.

> • I went to London _____ the first time.
> • I like juicy fruits, _____ example, watermelons.

07 다음 우리말에 맞게 빈칸에 알맞은 말을 쓰시오.

> 전화 끊기 전에 나도 그녀에게 말하게 해 줘.
> ➡ Let me speak to her before you _____ _____.

08 다음 대화의 빈칸에 알맞은 말을 쓰시오.

> A: _____ you visited a selfie museum before?
> B: Yes, I _____. It was very interesting.

09 다음 대화에서 밑줄 친 부분의 의도로 알맞은 것은?

> A: Can you take a picture of me?
> B: Sure.
> A: You'd better not use the flash here, David. The baby animals will wake up.
> B: I see.

① 질문하기　　② 요청하기
③ 금지하기　　④ 허락하기
⑤ 칭찬하기

[10~15] 다음 대화를 읽고, 물음에 답하시오.

> A: Hello, Somin! It's me! Can you see me?
> B: Oh, hi, Minjun! What's ⓐ ?
> A: ⓑThis is so cool, isn't this? We can video chat on the phone! Have you heard of Jeju *Olle*?
> B: Yes, I have. I really want to go there someday.
> A: Guess ⓒ ? I'm on it now. Actually, I'm going to go up Seongsan Ilchulbong now.
> B: That's great!
> A: Don't hang ⓓ . Enjoy the beautiful scenery with me.
> B: Be ⓔcare! You shouldn't use your cell phone ⓕ you're walking.
> A: Oh, right. Thank you. I'll send you photos later.

10 위 대화의 빈칸 ⓐ와 ⓓ에 공통으로 들어갈 것은?

① on　　② to
③ with　　④ up
⑤ for

11 위 대화의 밑줄 친 ⓑ에서 어법상 어색한 것을 고치시오.

_____ ➡ _____

12 위 대화의 빈칸 ⓒ에 알맞은 말을 쓰시오.

➡ _____

13 위 대화의 밑줄 친 ⓔ를 알맞은 어형으로 고치시오.

➡ _____

14 위 대화의 빈칸 ⓕ에 알맞은 것은?

① if　　② that
③ though　　④ because
⑤ while

15 위 대화의 내용과 일치하지 <u>않는</u> 것은?

① 소민과 민준은 화상 채팅을 하고 있다.
② 소민은 제주 올레에 관해 들은 적이 있다.
③ 민준은 지금 성산 일출봉을 오르려고 한다.
④ 소민은 민준과 아름다운 경치를 즐길 것이다.
⑤ 민준은 나중에 소민에게 사진들을 보낼 것이다.

Grammar

16 다음 문장의 빈칸에 알맞은 것은?

> I _____ never seen such a beautiful mountain.

① be　　　　　② did
③ have　　　　④ was
⑤ must

17 다음 문장의 빈칸에 알맞은 것은?

> _____ I live near the sea, I'm not good at swimming.

① As　　　　　② Since
③ Unless　　　④ Though
⑤ Because

18 다음 괄호 안에 주어진 단어를 어법상 바르게 쓴 것은?

> Jack (want) this video game since last year.

① wants　　　　② want
③ wanted　　　④ has wanted
⑤ is wanting

19 다음 우리말과 일치하도록 주어진 단어를 바르게 배열하시오.

> 날씨가 추웠지만, 공원에는 사람들이 많이 있었다.
> (was, a lot of, cold, although, were, in the park, people, there, it).

➡ _____

_____

20 다음 중 어법상 어색한 것은?

① He has been sick in bed for a week.
② How long have you stayed in America?
③ I have climbed that mountain last week.
④ You have already walked 100 kilometers.
⑤ I have never been to America.

21 다음 우리말을 영어로 바르게 옮긴 것은?

> 그녀는 비록 돈이 많지만, 행복하지 않다.

① Since she has plenty of money, she is not happy.
② So she has plenty of money, she is not happy.
③ While she has plenty of money, she is not happy.
④ Although she has plenty of money, she is not happy.
⑤ Even although she has plenty of money, she is not happy.

22 다음 문장과 뜻이 가장 가까운 것은?

> Jack's father has gone to Rome.

① Jack's father is going to Rome.
② Jack's father went to Rome.
③ Jack's father went to Rome but he is here now.
④ Jack's father went to Rome and he isn't here now.
⑤ Jack's father went to Rome and he has just come back.

23 다음 〈보기〉의 밑줄 친 부분과 같은 용법으로 사용된 것은?

> **보기**
>
> Nancy <u>has read</u> the novel three times.

① I <u>have lived</u> here since last year.

② Ted <u>has seen</u> a panda before.

③ My mother <u>has finished</u> washing the dishes.

④ Jack <u>has wanted</u> to have a cat for a long time.

⑤ Mrs. Brown <u>has lost</u> her purse somewhere.

24 다음 중 문맥상 어색한 문장은?

① My mother often sings as she works.

② As it started to rain, we stopped playing baseball.

③ I went home early though I felt sick.

④ My camera can take good pictures though it is very old.

⑤ Though it was very warm, she didn't take off her coat.

25 다음 중 밑줄 친 부분의 쓰임이 올바르지 않은 것은?

① I've <u>been</u> to Madrid ten years ago.

② Kate <u>has lived</u> in Seoul for five years.

③ Mike <u>has been</u> sick in hospital since last Monday.

④ She <u>has never seen</u> such a beautiful lake.

⑤ How often <u>have</u> you <u>been</u> to Paris?

26 다음 두 문장의 의미가 같도록 빈칸에 알맞은 말을 쓰시오.

> Though you fall from a high tree, I will catch you.
>
> ➡ _____ _____ you fall from a high tree, I will catch you.

Reading

[27~30] 다음 글을 읽고, 물음에 답하시오.

> **BMX Bike Riding**
>
> Riding a BMX bike is very ⓐ<u>excite</u>. You can try ⓑ<u>lots of</u> skills. You can turn the bike freely and even jump with the bike. Though it's not easy, it's very exciting. You can start with standing skills. When you try standing skills, balancing is very important. But be careful. You should wear a helmet and gloves. Also, you shouldn't go too fast ___ⓒ___ you're riding.

27 위 글의 밑줄 친 ⓐ를 알맞은 어형으로 고치시오.

➡ _____

28 위 글의 밑줄 친 ⓑ 대신 쓸 수 있는 것은?

① much   ② little

③ enough   ④ many

⑤ several

29 위 글의 빈칸 ⓒ에 알맞은 것은?

① if   ② because

③ when   ④ although

⑤ since

30 위 글의 내용으로 보아 알 수 <u>없는</u> 것은?

① BMX 자전거 타는 것은 재미있다.
② BMX 자전거는 값이 비싸다.
③ BMX 자전거를 타려면 많은 기술이 필요하다.
④ BMX 자전거를 타고 점프할 수 있다.
⑤ BMX 자전거를 탈 때는 안전에 주의해야 한다.

[31~35] 다음 글을 읽고, 물음에 답하시오.

You can also visit special museums to take fun selfies. ___ⓐ___ example, there is a famous selfie museum in the Philippines. ⓑIt has special spots to take selfies. You can touch the paintings and even step inside them. Look at the following pictures. Though the boys are not really riding horses, it looks like they are. ⓒThough the man is just holding a big brush, it looks like he is painting the Mona Lisa. Selfie museums exist in Korea, too. I have visited one in Chuncheon before. ___ⓓ___ don't you go there yourself?

31 위 글의 빈칸 ⓐ에 알맞은 것은?

① To   ② In
③ As   ④ For
⑤ With

32 위 글의 밑줄 친 ⓑ가 가리키는 것을 영어로 쓰시오.

➡ _____

33 위 글의 밑줄 친 ⓒ를 우리말로 옮기시오.

➡ _____
_____

34 위 글의 빈칸 ⓓ에 알맞은 것은?

① Why   ② How
③ What   ④ When
⑤ Where

35 위 글의 내용과 일치하지 <u>않는</u> 것은?

① 재미있는 셀피를 찍기 위해 특별한 박물관을 방문할 수 있다.
② 필리핀에는 유명한 셀피 박물관이 있다.
③ 필리핀의 셀피 박물관에서는 그림에 손을 댈 수 없다.
④ 한국에도 셀피 박물관이 있다.
⑤ 글쓴이는 춘천에 있는 셀피 박물관을 다녀온 적이 있다.

[36~37] 다음 글을 읽고, 물음에 답하시오.

Have you heard of fire ⓐsafe rules? ___ⓑ___ there's a fire, you can be safe. You shouldn't take the elevator. You should follow the teacher's directions.

36 위 글의 밑줄 친 ⓐ를 알맞은 형으로 고치시오.

➡ _____

37 위 글의 빈칸 ⓑ에 알맞지 <u>않은</u> 것은? (2개)

① Though   ② Since
③ Although   ④ As though
⑤ Even though

01 다음 중 짝지어진 단어의 관계가 <u>다른</u> 것은?

① king : queen   ② husband : wife

③ uncle : aunt   ④ child : kid

⑤ prince : princess

02 다음 빈칸에 공통으로 알맞은 것은?

> • I was fond _____ sports when I was young.
>
> • The bus stops right in front _____ our house.

① in   ② of

③ from   ④ with

⑤ onto

03 다음 짝지어진 두 단어의 관계가 같도록 빈칸에 알맞은 말을 쓰시오.

> advise : advice = arrive : _____

04 다음 중 영영풀이가 <u>잘못된</u> 것은?

① alone: without any other people

② clothes: the things that people wear, such as shirts, coats, trousers, and dresses

③ painter: an artist who paints pictures

④ pull: to use force to make something move away from you or away from its previous position

⑤ mirror: a flat piece of glass which reflects light, so that when you look at it you can see yourself reflected in it

05 다음 우리말에 맞게 빈칸에 알맞은 말을 쓰시오.

> 그는 이제 더 이상 네 친구가 아니란 걸 명심해.
>
> ➡ Keep _____ _____ that he is not your friend anymore.

06 다음 대화의 밑줄 친 부분의 의도로 알맞은 것은?

> B: I want to watch the birds in the trees.
>
> G: <u>You shouldn't go up too close to the birds.</u>
>
> B: All right, thanks.

① 요청하기   ② 비난하기

③ 제안하기   ④ 금지하기

⑤ 칭찬하기

07 다음 대화의 빈칸에 알맞은 것은?

> A: _____
>
> B: No, I haven't, but I've heard of it many times.

① How often have you been to Haeundae?

② Did you go to Haeundae?

③ When did you go to Haeundae?

④ Have you ever been to Haeundae?

⑤ How many times did you visit Haeundae?

B: Have you heard of bird watching?
M: Sure. I tried ⓐit when I was a child. (①)
B: That's nice. Actually, I'm doing it ___ⓑ___ the first time this Saturday. (②)
M: Are you? You should bring warm clothes and something to eat. (③)
B: Okay. (④)
M: You shouldn't ___ⓒ___ any noise when you watch the birds. (⑤)
B: I'll keep ⓓthat in mind. Thanks, Dad.

08 위 대화의 ①~⑤ 중 다음 주어진 문장이 들어갈 알맞은 곳은?

> What else should I keep in mind?

①   ②   ③   ④   ⑤

09 위 대화의 밑줄 친 ⓐ가 가리키는 것을 영어로 쓰시오.

➡ _____

10 위 대화의 빈칸 ⓑ에 알맞은 것은?

① on   ② to
③ for   ④ in
⑤ with

11 위 대화의 빈칸 ⓒ에 알맞은 것은?

① get   ② make
③ do   ④ bring
⑤ take

12 위 대화의 밑줄 친 ⓓ가 가리키는 것을 우리말로 쓰시오.

➡ _____

13 위 글의 내용과 일치하지 <u>않는</u> 것은?

① 소년의 아버지는 들새 관찰을 해 본 적이 있다.
② 소년은 이번 토요일에 들새 관찰을 할 예정이다.
③ 소년은 따뜻한 옷과 먹을 것을 가져가야 한다.
④ 들새 관찰을 할 때에는 조용해야 한다.
⑤ 소년의 취미는 들새 관찰이다.

14 다음 문장의 빈칸에 알맞지 <u>않은</u> 것은?

> Jenny has seen the movie _____.

① once   ② twice
③ never   ④ before
⑤ many times

15 다음 문장의 빈칸에 알맞은 것은?

> _____ Tom's family is poor, they are always happy.

① If   ② As
③ Since   ④ Unless
⑤ Although

16 다음 밑줄 친 단어의 올바른 형태를 쓰시오. [출제율 85%]

> Jane <u>lived</u> in England since she was ten years old.

➡ _____

17 다음 문장에서 어법상 어색한 부분을 바르게 고쳐 문장을 다시 쓰시오. [출제율 95%]

> I didn't see him since I was eleven.

➡ _____

18 다음 두 문장의 뜻이 같도록 할 때 빈칸에 알맞은 것은? [출제율 85%]

> Though I looked for your pencil, I couldn't find it.
> = I looked for your pencil, _____ I couldn't find it.

① so   ② but

③ and   ④ for

⑤ because

19 다음 〈보기〉 문장과 뜻이 가장 가까운 것은? [출제율 85%]

> ┤ 보기 ├
> Tom has lost his watch.

① Tom lost his watch.

② Tom lost his watch and he forgot it.

③ Tom lost his watch, but he found it.

④ Tom lost his watch, and he hasn't found it yet.

⑤ Tom lost his watch, so he is going to buy a new one.

20 다음 문장 중 밑줄 친 부분이 어색한 것은? [출제율 100%]

① I think <u>that</u> your answer is right.

② It was snowing <u>when</u> I got up.

③ I often sing <u>while</u> I'm taking a shower.

④ <u>Although</u> the boy was sick, he went to school.

⑤ <u>Because</u> Mozart's life was short, he changed music history.

21 다음 밑줄 친 부분의 쓰임이 나머지 넷과 <u>다른</u> 하나는? [출제율 90%]

① Jenny <u>has seen</u> the actor before.

② My grandfather <u>has</u> never <u>visited</u> Seoul.

③ Mr. Lincoln <u>has gone</u> to Berlin on business.

④ How many times <u>have</u> they <u>been</u> to China?

⑤ They <u>have been</u> to Italy three times.

[22~25] 다음 글을 읽고, 물음에 답하시오.

> **Selfies in the Past - Minji**
>
> Did people in the past take selfies? Though ⓐit wasn't easy at that time, the answer is yes. (①) Look at this photo of Princess Anastasia. (②) She used a mirror ⓑto take a picture of herself. (③) She looks nervous. (④) Well, I think it was her first selfie. (⑤) And it was probably the world's first teenage selfie ever.

22 위 글의 ①~⑤ 중 다음 주어진 문장이 들어갈 알맞은 곳은? [출제율 90%]

> Can you guess why?

①   ②   ③   ④   ⑤

23 위 글의 밑줄 친 ⓐ가 가리키는 것을 우리말로 쓰시오.

➡ _____

24 위 글의 밑줄 친 ⓑ와 용법이 같은 것은?

① We decided to visit the house.
② He has no friends to play with.
③ Do you want to go skating now?
④ I had no house to live in.
⑤ He worked hard to support his family.

25 민지는 Anastasia가 왜 긴장하고 있다고 생각하는지 우리말로 간단히 쓰시오.

➡ _____
_____

[26~31] 다음 글을 읽고, 물음에 답하시오.

ⓐRiding a BMX bike is very excited. You can try ⓑ많은 skills. You can turn the bike freely and even jump with the bike. ⓒThough it's not easy, it's very exciting. (①) You can start with standing skills. (②) ⓓ_____ you try standing skills, balancing is very important. (③) But be ⓔcare. (④) Also, you shouldn't go too fast when you're riding. (⑤)

26 위 글의 ①~⑤ 중 다음 주어진 문장이 들어갈 알맞은 곳은?

You should wear a helmet and gloves.

①   ②   ③   ④   ⑤

27 위 글의 밑줄 친 ⓐ에서 어법상 어색한 것을 고치시오.

_____ ➡ _____

28 위 글의 밑줄 친 ⓑ를 영어로 바꿔 쓸 때 알맞지 않은 것은? (2개)

① many   ② much
③ a few   ④ lots of
⑤ a lot of

29 위 글의 밑줄 친 ⓒ와 같은 뜻이 되도록 다음 문장의 빈칸에 알맞은 말을 쓰시오.

It's not easy, _____ it's very exciting.

30 위 글의 빈칸 ⓓ에 알맞은 것은?

① When   ② If
③ After   ④ Because
⑤ Though

31 위 글의 밑줄 친 ⓔ를 알맞은 어형으로 고치시오.

➡ _____

[01~03] 다음 대화를 읽고, 물음에 답하시오.

> G: Dad, have you ever heard of Kim Soyun, the rock ___ⓐ___?
>
> M: Yes, I've ⓑsee her on TV.
>
> G: She's teaching rock climbing at a camp this Saturday. I want to join the camp.
>
> M: Okay, Miso, but you shouldn't climb up too high.
>
> G: All right. Thanks, Dad.

01 위 대화의 빈칸 ⓐ에 다음 정의에 해당하는 단어를 쓰시오.

> someone who climbs rocks or mountains as a sport or a hobby

➡ _____

 02 위 대화의 밑줄 친 ⓑ를 알맞은 형으로 고치시오.

➡ _____

03 What will Kim Soyun do this Saturday? Answer in English.

➡ _____

 04 다음 대화의 순서를 바르게 배열하시오.

> (A) Oh, okay.
> (B) Wait, Jimin.
> (C) Why?
> (D) Look at that sign. You shouldn't take a photo here.

➡ _____

05 다음 〈보기〉와 같이 현재완료 시제를 이용해 두 문장을 한 문장으로 쓰시오.

> ┤ 보기 ├
> Jane moved to Tokyo ten years ago. She still lives there.
> ➡ Jane has lived in Tokyo for ten years.

(1) Peter moved to Peking in 2010. He still lives in Peking.

➡ _____

(2) Tom went to hospital a week ago. He is still in hospital.

➡ _____

(3) My mother went shopping. She is not here.

➡ _____

06 다음 〈조건〉에 맞게 괄호 안의 단어를 이용하여 우리말을 영어로 옮기시오.

> ┤ 조건 ├
> 1. 필요시 관사를 붙이거나 단어를 추가하고 동사의 어형 변화를 할 것.
> 2. 대·소문자 및 구두점에 유의할 것.
> 3. (1), (2)는 접속사로 시작하는 부사절이 주절의 앞에 오고 (3)은 주절의 뒤에 올 것.

(1) 비록 바람이 불기는 했지만, 날씨가 별로 춥지 않았다. (though, it, windy, very, cold)

➡ _____

(2) Tim은 종종 Anne을 짜증스럽게 했지만, 그녀는 그를 좋아했다. (although, often, annoy, fond, of)

➡ _____
_____

(3) 너는 비록 그것이 마음에 들지 않는다고 해도 해야 한다. (though, must, do, it, like)

➡ _____

07 다음 문장에서 어법상 어색한 것을 찾아 바르게 고치시오.

(1) He has gone to Spain last year.

_____ ➡ _____

(2) When have you seen Kathy's little brother?

_____ ➡ _____

(3) I have often played the piano when I was a child.

_____ ➡ _____

[08~11] 다음 글을 읽고, 물음에 답하시오.

Have you ever ⓐhear of a "selfie"? ⓑWhen you take a photograph of you, it's a selfie. The students from Minji's photo club have searched ___ⓒ___ information about selfies ___ⓓ___ one month. Here are some of their presentations about selfies.

08 위 글의 밑줄 친 ⓐ를 알맞은 형으로 고치시오.

➡ _____

09 위 글의 밑줄 친 ⓑ에서 어법상 어색한 것을 고치시오.

_____ ➡ _____

10 위 글의 빈칸 ⓒ와 ⓓ에 공통으로 알맞은 전치사를 쓰시오.

➡ _____

11 What is a selfie? Answer in Korean.

➡ _____

[12~15] 다음 글을 읽고, 물음에 답하시오.

Selfies for a Better School Life - Soyun

I think we can use selfies ⓐ(making, to make) a better school life. We can do good things at school and ___ⓑ___ selfies. Then we can post the photos on our school website. I've watered the ___ⓒ___ and flowers at school for one month. I've also helped the teacher at the school library many times. Look at my selfies of those things. How about ⓓjoin me to create a better school life?

12 위 글의 괄호 ⓐ에서 알맞은 것을 고르시오.

➡ _____

13 위 글의 빈칸 ⓑ에 알맞은 단어를 쓰시오.

➡ _____

14 위 글의 빈칸 ⓒ에 다음 정의에 해당하는 단어를 쓰시오. 필요하면 어형 변화를 하시오.

a living thing that grows in the earth and has a stem, leaves, and roots, especially one that is smaller than a tree or bush

➡ _____

15 위 글의 밑줄 친 ⓓ를 알맞은 형으로 고치시오.

➡ _____

01 다음 주어진 말을 이용하여 현재완료형의 문장을 만드시오.

(1) I, just, send, e-mail

➡ _____

(2) Kate, just, clean, room

➡ _____

(3) Mike, already, finish, job

➡ _____

(4) you, take, medicine, yet

➡ _____

(5) Mary, sing, yet

➡ _____

(6) you, study, yet

➡ _____

(7) Tom, do, homework, yet

➡ _____

02 다음 괄호 안에 주어진 어구를 이용하여 자유롭게 문장을 만드시오. (A)는 접속사로 시작하는 부사절이 주절의 앞에 오고, (B)는 주절의 뒤에 올 것.

(1) (though)

➡ (A) _____

(B) _____

(2) (although)

➡ (A) _____

(B) _____

(3) (even though)

➡ (A) _____

(B) _____

단원별 모의고사

01 다음 중 우리말 뜻이 <u>잘못된</u> 것은?

① go up: 오르다
② for example: 예를 들면
③ over there: 저쪽에
④ be good for: ~을 잘하다
⑤ hang up: 전화를 끊다

02 다음 영영풀이에 해당하는 단어로 알맞은 것은?

> better or more important than other people or things

① real
② special
③ popular
④ common
⑤ strange

03 다음 빈칸에 알맞은 것으로 짝지어진 것은?

> • Will you call me _____ your lunch time?
> • Ask somebody _____ to help you.

① for – else
② for – other
③ during – other
④ during – else
⑤ while – other

04 다음 짝지어진 두 단어의 관계가 같도록 빈칸에 알맞은 말을 쓰시오.

> safe : dangerous = push : _____

05 다음 빈칸에 공통으로 들어갈 말을 쓰시오.

> • We were very sorry to hear _____ your father's death.
> • There are lots _____ nice parks in San Francisco.

06 다음 대화를 의미가 통하도록 알맞게 배열한 것은?

> (A) No, I haven't. How was it?
> (B) Have you ever ridden a horse?
> (C) Yes, I have. How about you?
> (D) It was fun, but it was a little scary, too.

① (A) – (D) – (B) – (C)
② (B) – (C) – (A) – (D)
③ (C) – (D) – (B) – (A)
④ (D) – (B) – (C) – (A)
⑤ (D) – (C) – (A) – (B)

07 다음 대화의 빈칸에 알맞은 것은?

> A: Have you ever caught a big fish?
> B: _____ I wish to catch one someday.

① Yes, I have.
② No, I haven't.
③ I caught a big fish.
④ Yes, my uncle caught a big fish.
⑤ I caught it and put it back.

08 다음 대화의 밑줄 친 부분과 바꾸어 쓸 수 있는 것은?

> A: Peter, you'd better not run when you cross the street.
> B: Okay, I will.

① you may run when you cross the street
② you must run when you cross the street
③ you need to run when you cross the street
④ you have to run when you cross the street
⑤ you shouldn't run when you cross the street

[09~13] 다음 대화를 읽고, 물음에 답하시오.

> B: Have you heard ___ⓐ___ bird watching?
> M: Sure. I tried it when I was a child.
> B: That's nice. Actually, I'm doing it ___ⓑ___ the first time this Saturday.
> M: Are you? You should bring warm clothes and something ⓒto eat.
> B: Okay. ⓓ(in / else / I / keep / what / mind / should)?
> M: You shouldn't make any noise ___ⓔ___ you watch the birds.
> B: I'll keep that in mind. Thanks, Dad.

09 위 대화의 빈칸 ⓐ와 ⓑ에 알맞은 것으로 짝지어진 것은?

① of – to
② of – at
③ of – for
④ at – for
⑤ from – at

10 위 대화의 밑줄 친 ⓒ와 용법이 같은 것은?

① We wished to reach the North Pole.
② Kathy was very sad to hear the song.
③ Please give me something to drink.
④ Do you want to go on a picnic now?
⑤ He must study hard to pass the math exam.

11 위 대화의 괄호 ⓓ를 알맞은 어순으로 배열하시오.

➡ _____

12 위 대화의 빈칸 ⓔ에 알맞은 것은?

① when
② if
③ before
④ after
⑤ although

13 위 대화의 내용으로 보아 알 수 없는 것은?

① The boy's father has tried bird watching.
② The boy is fond of bird watching.
③ The boy will do bird watching this Saturday.
④ The boy should bring warm clothes.
⑤ The boy will need food when he watches the birds.

14 다음 괄호 안에 주어진 단어를 어법상 바르게 쓴 것은?

> He left home at six and (not return) yet.

① doesn't return
② wasn't returned
③ didn't return
④ hasn't returned
⑤ hadn't returned

15 다음 두 문장의 뜻이 같도록 빈칸에 알맞은 것은?

> Even though we were hungry, we didn't eat the food.
> = _____ we were hungry, we didn't eat the food.

① Since ② Before
③ Though ④ Therefore
⑤ Because

16 다음 중 밑줄 친 부분의 쓰임이 바르지 <u>않은</u> 것은?

① I've <u>been</u> to Paris five years ago.
② Jack <u>has practiced</u> the piano since last year.
③ Ann <u>has been</u> sick in bed for two weeks.
④ I <u>have</u> never <u>seen</u> such a wonderful movie.
⑤ <u>Has</u> your teacher ever <u>been</u> to Europe?

17 다음 우리말과 같은 뜻이 되도록 빈칸에 알맞은 것은?

> 비록 어제 아팠지만, 나는 학교에 갔다.
> ➡ _____ I was sick yesterday, I went to school.

① If ② As
③ Besides ④ Though
⑤ While

18 다음 두 문장의 뜻이 같도록 빈칸에 알맞은 말을 쓰시오.

> I _____ _____ my car key.
> = I lost my car key. I don't have the key now.

19 다음 우리말을 영작한 것으로 <u>어색한</u> 것을 <u>모두</u> 고르면?

> 네가 비록 부자일지라도 내 마음을 살 수는 없다.

① Though you're rich, you can't buy my heart.
② Since if you're rich, you can't buy my heart.
③ Although you're rich, you can't buy my heart.
④ Unless you're rich, you can't buy my heart.
⑤ Even though you're rich, you can't buy my heart.

20 다음 문장의 빈칸에 알맞은 것은?

> Frank _____ never seen such a cute cat.

① be ② did ③ has
④ was ⑤ must

[21~23] 다음 글을 읽고, 물음에 답하시오.

> Have you heard ⓐ_____ the pyramids in Egypt? Though I ⓑ<u>have</u> never <u>been</u> to Egypt before, I'm standing in front ⓒ_____ a pyramid in this picture. I took it at the selfie museum.

21 위 글의 빈칸 ⓐ와 ⓒ에 공통으로 알맞은 것은?

① to ② at ③ of
④ on ⑤ about

22 위 글의 밑줄 친 ⓑ와 같은 용법으로 쓰인 것은?

① I <u>have been</u> in Japan since last month.
② I <u>have seen</u> a koala before.
③ My father <u>has</u> already <u>eaten</u> breakfast.
④ He <u>has wanted</u> to be a painter for a long time.
⑤ My grandmother <u>has lost</u> her smartphone somewhere.

23 Where did the writer take the picture? Answer in English.

➡ _____

[24~27] 다음 글을 읽고, 물음에 답하시오.

Selfie Safety – Jihun

These selfies look great, but were they a good idea? ⓐI don't think so. They don't look _____ⓑ_____ . You should take special care when you take selfies in the wild or at high places like these. A monkey could bite you at any time, _____ⓒ_____ you could fall. Here are some safety tips:

1. Don't take selfies while you're walking.
2. Do not pose with or near wild animals.
3. Never take selfies in dangerous places.

24 위 글의 밑줄 친 ⓐ를 so의 의미가 구체적으로 드러나도록 우리말로 옮기시오.

➡ _____

25 위 글의 빈칸 ⓑ에 들어갈 알맞은 것은?

① safe　　　　　② exciting
③ easy　　　　　④ dangerous
⑤ difficult

26 위 글의 빈칸 ⓒ에 알맞은 것은?

① so　　　　　② then
③ or　　　　　④ but
⑤ for

27 위 글의 내용으로 보아 알 수 없는 것은?

① 이 글은 셀피를 찍을 때의 안전 수칙이다.
② 야생에서 사진을 찍을 때는 주의해야 한다.
③ 원숭이는 사람을 잘 따른다.
④ 걸을 때는 셀피를 찍으면 안 된다.
⑤ 야생 동물 근처에서 포즈를 취하면 위험하다.

[28~30] 다음 글을 읽고, 물음에 답하시오.

Have you heard of fire safety _____ⓐ_____ ? _____ⓑ_____ there's a fire, you can be safe. You shouldn't take the elevator. You should follow the teacher's directions.

28 위 글의 빈칸 ⓐ에 다음 정의에 해당하는 단어를 쓰시오.

> instructions that tell you what you are allowed to do and what you are not allowed to do

➡ _____

29 위 글의 빈칸 ⓑ에 알맞은 것은?

① If　　　　　② When
③ As　　　　　④ Though
⑤ Because

30 위 글의 내용과 일치하도록 다음 문장의 빈칸에 알맞은 말을 쓰시오.

> When there is a _____, you shouldn't take the _____.

Lesson 4

Memories in Your Heart

🎤 의사소통 기능

- 기억 여부 묻기
  Do you remember Mr. Kim, our 6th grade teacher?

- 생각할 시간 요청하기
  Let me see.

🎤 언어 형식

- 주격 관계대명사
  Wilfrid was a little boy **who** lived next to a nursing home.

- 목적격 관계대명사의 생략
  It is something (**that**) you remember.

Words & Expressions

Key Words

- **again**[əgén] 🕛 다시, 한 번 더
- **ago**[əɡóu] 🕛 전에
- **album**[ǽlbum] 🕛 앨범
- **alone**[əlóun] 🕛 혼자, 홀로
- **airplane**[ɛ́ərplein] 🕛 비행기
- **aunt**[ænt] 🕛 숙모, 이모, 아주머니
- **board**[bɔːrd] 🕛 판자, 널빤지
- **bounce**[bauns] 🕛 ~을 튀기다
- **bring**[briŋ] 🕛 가져다주다, 가지고 오다
- **cartoon**[kɑːrtúːn] 🕛 만화
- **clean**[kliːn] 🕛 닦다, 청소하다
- **competition**[kàmpətíʃən] 🕛 대회, 시합, 경쟁
- **cook**[kuk] 🕛 요리하다
- **delicious**[dilíʃəs] 🕛 맛있는
- **each other** 서로
- **enjoy**[indʒɔ́i] 🕛 즐기다
- **far**[fɑːr] 🕛 멀리
- **favorite**[féivərit] 🕛 가장 좋아하는
- **February**[fébruèri] 🕛 2월
- **fly**(–**flew**–**flown**)[flai] 🕛 날다, 비행하다
- **field trip** 현장 학습
- **fresh**[freʃ] 🕛 갓 낳은, 신선한
- **fun**[fʌn] 🕛 재미있는
- **funny**[fʌ́ni] 🕛 우스운, 웃기는, 재미있는
- **grade**[greid] 🕛 학년, 성적
- **hairpin**[hɛ́ərpìn] 🕛 머리핀
- **hen**[hen] 🕛 암탉
- **hot air balloon** 열기구
- **laughter**[lǽftər] 🕛 웃음

- **lose**(–**lost**–**lost**)[luːz] 🕛 잃다
- **medal**[médl] 🕛 메달
- **memory**[méməri] 🕛 기억, 추억
- **move**[muːv] 🕛 옮기다, 이사[이동]하다
- **neighbor**[néibər] 🕛 이웃(사람)
- **next to** ~ 옆에
- **nursing home** 양로원
- **perform**[pərfɔ́ːrm] 🕛 공연하다
- **person**[pə́ːrsn] 🕛 사람
- **practice**[prǽktis] 🕛 연습하다
- **precious**[préʃəs] 🕛 귀중한
- **puppet**[pʌ́pit] 🕛 꼭두각시, 인형
- **remember**[rimémbər] 🕛 기억하다
- **round**[raund] 🕛 (경기의) 판, 라운드, 회
- **school nurse** 양호 선생님
- **science**[sáiəns] 🕛 과학
- **secret**[síːkrit] 🕛 비밀
- **sock**[sɑk] 🕛 양말
- **special**[spéʃəl] 🕛 특별한
- **sunlight**[sʌ́nlait] 🕛 햇빛
- **super**[súːpər] 🕛 매우 🕛 굉장히 좋은
- **teach**[tiːtʃ] 🕛 가르치다
- **tear**[tiər] 🕛 눈물
- **thick**[θik] 🕛 두꺼운
- **together**[təɡéðər] 🕛 함께, 같이
- **traditional**[trədíʃənl] 🕛 전통적인, 전통의
- **visit**[vízit] 🕛 방문하다
- **wear**(–**wore**–**worn**)[wɛər] 🕛 입다, 신다, 쓰다, 착용하다
- **whisper**[hwíspər] 🕛 속삭이다

Key Expressions

- **cut holes** 구멍을 내다
- **get married** 결혼하다
- **go into** ~으로 들어가다
- **Guess what?** 있잖아
- **have a great time** 즐거운 시간을 보내다
- **Let's see**(= **Let me see**)
  어디 보자 (생각을 하거나 무엇을 기억하려고 하면서 하는 말)
- **look for** ~을 찾다
- **look like** + 명사 ~처럼 보이다

- **one by one** 하나씩, 차례차례
- **remember + -ing** ~한 것을 기억하다
- **smile at** ~을 보고 미소 짓다
- **thank A for B** B 때문에 A에게 감사하다
- **thanks to** ~ 덕분에
- **the same as** ~ ~와 똑같은, 동종의, 동일한
- **throw a party** 파티를 열다
- **wait for** ~을 기다리다
- **What[How] about + -ing** ~? ~하는 게 어때?

Word Power

※ 서로 반대되는 뜻을 가진 단어

- □ **together** (같이, 함께) ↔ **apart** (따로, 떨어져)
- □ **thick** (두꺼운) ↔ **thin** (얇은, 가는)
- □ **fun** (재미있는) ↔ **boring** (지루한)
- □ **bring** (가져오다) ↔ **take** (가져가다)
- □ **hen** (암탉) ↔ **rooster**, **cock** (수탉)

- □ **remember** (기억하다) ↔ **forget** (잊다)
- □ **special** (특별한) ↔ **general** (일반적인)
- □ **far** (멀리; 먼) ↔ **near** (가까이; 가까운)
- □ **precious** (귀중한) ↔ **worthless** (가치 없는)
- □ **whisper** (속삭이다) ↔ **shout** (소리치다)

※ 서로 비슷한 뜻을 가진 단어

- □ **wear** : **put on** (입다, 쓰다, 신다, 착용하다)
- □ **next to** : **beside** (~ 옆에)
- □ **special** : **particular** (특별한)
- □ **whisper** : **murmur** (속삭이다)

- □ **super** : **extremely** (매우)
- □ **delicious** : **tasty** (맛있는)
- □ **alone** : **solely** (혼자, 홀로)
- □ **go into** : **enter** (들어가다)

English Dictionary

- □ **bounce** 튀기다
  → to move up or away after hitting a surface
  표면을 치고 나서 위로 또는 멀리 이동하다

- □ **favorite** 가장 좋아하는
  → best liked or most enjoyed
  가장 좋아하거나 가장 즐겨 하는

- □ **hole** 구멍
  → an empty space in an object, usually with an opening to the object's surface
  물체의 빈 공간, 대개 물체의 표면에 있는 틈[구멍]

- □ **laughter** 웃음
  → the act or sound of laughing
  웃는 행동 또는 소리

- □ **memory** 기억
  → someone's ability to remember things, places, experiences, etc.
  물건, 장소, 경험 등을 기억하는 사람의 능력

- □ **neighbor** 이웃
  → someone who lives near you
  당신 근처에 사는 사람

- □ **perform** 공연하다
  → to do something to entertain people by acting a play or playing a piece of music
  연기를 하거나 음악을 연주함으로써 사람을 즐겁게 하는 일을 하다

- □ **precious** 귀중한
  → of great value because of being rare, expensive, or important
  희귀하거나 비싸거나 중요하기 때문에 매우 소중한

- □ **puppet** 인형, 꼭두각시
  → a toy in the shape of a person or animal that you can move with strings or by putting your hand inside
  끈으로 또는 안에 손을 넣음으로써 움직일 수 있는 사람 또는 동물 모양의 장난감

- □ **secret** 비밀
  → something that is kept hidden or that is known about by only a few people
  숨겨져 있거나 극소수의 사람들에 의해 알려져 있는 것

- □ **special** 특별한
  → not ordinary or usual
  평범하거나 일반적이지 않은

- □ **tear** 눈물
  → a drop of salty liquid that flows from the eye
  눈에서 흐르는 짠 액체 방울

- □ **whisper** 속삭이다
  → to speak very quietly
  매우 조용히 말하다

서답형

01 다음 짝지어진 두 단어의 관계가 같도록 빈칸에 알맞은 단어를 쓰시오.

thick : thin – general : _____

서답형

02 다음 글의 빈칸에 주어진 영영 풀이에 맞는 알맞은 형태의 단어를 쓰시오.

• Wilfrid told her all his _____.
something that is kept hidden or that is known about by only a few people

➡ _____

중요

03 다음 중, 밑줄 친 단어의 우리말 뜻이 잘못된 것은?

① We watched TV together last weekend.
　　　　　　　　　　　　　같이, 함께
② Mr. Hunter was cleaning his medal.
　　　　　　　　　　　닦고 있었다
③ She has lost her memory.
　　　　　　　　기억
④ His sock puppet always brought laughter
　 to his parents.　　　　　　웃다
⑤ The two girls smiled at each other.
　　　　　　　　　　　서로

[04~05] 다음 영영풀이에 해당하는 단어를 고르시오.

04

a drop of salty liquid that flows from the eye

① hole　　　　　② tear
③ puppet　　　　④ egg
⑤ water

05

of great value because of being rare, expensive or important

① fresh　　　　　② favorite
③ thick　　　　　④ special
⑤ precious

서답형

06 다음 우리말에 맞게 주어진 철자로 시작하는 단어를 쓰시오.

우리는 매우 열심히 연습했어.
We practiced s_____ hard.

➡ _____

07 다음 빈칸에 들어갈 말로 알맞은 것은?

She _____ the football to him.

① whispered　　　② remembered
③ bounced　　　　④ started
⑤ practiced

중요

08 다음 빈칸에 들어갈 단어가 알맞게 짝지어진 것은?

• His football was as _____ as gold to him.
• Ms. Cooper got her memory back thanks _____ the little boy.

① fun – of　　　　② productive – as
③ fresh – to　　　④ precious – to
⑤ special – for

01 다음 빈칸에 들어갈 말을 〈보기〉에서 찾아 쓰시오. (필요하면 변형하여 쓰시오.)

┌─ 보기 ─┐
laugh   one by one   lose   jump

(1) Wilfrid went to Ms. Cooper and gave her the things _____.
(2) His sock puppet always brought _____ to his parents.
(3) She is a poor old lady because she's _____ her memory.

02 다음 우리말과 같은 표현이 되도록 문장의 빈칸을 채우시오.

(1) 그녀는 자신의 과거를 기억해 내기 시작했다.
  ➡ She started to _____ her _____.
(2) 그는 암탉이 품고 있던 따뜻한 달걀을 꺼냈다.
  ➡ He took a warm egg from _____ a _____.
(3) 우리는 열기구를 탔어. 그것은 코끼리처럼 생겼어.
  ➡ We rode a _____ _____ balloon. It _____ _____ an elephant.

03 다음 문장의 밑줄 친 단어의 반의어를 쓰시오.

(1) Don't forget to <u>bring</u> your books with you.
(2) I never <u>forget</u> your face.
➡ (1) _____ (2) _____

04 다음 문장에 들어갈 알맞은 단어를 〈보기〉의 영영 풀이를 보고 쓰시오.

┌─ 보기 ─┐
(1) to speak very quietly
(2) someone who lives near you
(3) to move up or away after hitting a surface
(4) not ordinary or usual

(1) She _____ed to him, "Long ago, I found a small blue egg."
(2) He wanted to know more, so he went to his _____.
(3) The ball _____d twice before he could reach it.
(4) She's a very _____ student.

05 다음 그림에 해당하는 단어를 주어진 철자로 시작하여 쓰시오.

(1)   (2)

➡ c_____ a hole   ➡ g_____ _____

(3)   (4)

➡ t_____ a party   ➡ s_____ _____

Conversation

① 기억 여부 묻기

Do you remember Mr. Kim, our 6th grade teacher?
우리 6학년 때 선생님이셨던 김 선생님 기억하니?

- Do you remember ~?는 '~를 기억하니?'라는 뜻으로, 특정한 사람이나 사물, 사건에 대한 기억 여부를 묻는 표현이다.
- remember 앞에 '여전히'라는 의미의 still을 넣어 Do you still remember ~?라고 묻기도 한다.

기억 여부를 묻는 표현들

- Don't you remember it? 너는 그것이 기억나지 않니?
- Can[Can't] you remember it? 너는 그것을 기억할 수 있니[없니]?
- Have you forgotten it? 너는 그것을 잊어버렸니?

핵심 Check

1. 다음 대화의 빈칸에 알맞은 말을 쓰시오.

   A: Minji, _____

   B: Sure. I met her last year.

   ① long time no see.
   ② do you remember my aunt?
   ③ how have you been doing?
   ④ what does that mean?
   ⑤ would you like to meet my aunt?

2. 다음 대화의 밑줄 친 부분의 의도로 알맞은 것은?

   A: We had a good time last month. <u>Do you remember that, Sujin?</u>

   B: Sure, Jieun.

   ① 기억 묻기   ② 강조하기
   ③ 허락 구하기   ④ 안부 묻기
   ⑤ 설명하기

❷ 생각할 시간 요청하기

Let me see. 어디 보자.

■ 상대방에게 생각할 시간을 요청할 때는 'Let me think.(생각 좀 해 볼게.)', 'Let me see.(어디 보자.)', 'Just a moment, please.(잠깐만요.)', 'Can[May] I think about it for a moment[while]?'(잠시 생각해 봐도 될까요?) 등으로 말할 수 있다.

또한 '아직 생각 중이에요.'라는 뜻의 'I'm still thinking.'이라는 말을 덧붙이기도 한다. 앞에 'well', 'hmm'과 같이 주저할 때 쓰는 표현을 붙여 더 자연스럽게 말할 수도 있다.

생각할 시간 요청을 수락할 때는 'OK.' 혹은 'Sure.'와 같은 표현을 쓰거나 'Take your time.(천천히 하세요.)'과 같은 말을 덧붙이기도 한다.

- A: What do you see in this picture? 이 사진에서 무엇이 보이니?
  B: Let me see. 생각 좀 해 볼게.
    = Let's see.
    = Let me think.
    = Let me think about it.

■ let은 동사원형을 목적격보어로 취하는 점에 유의한다.

- Let me think about it. (○)
- Let me thinking about it. (×)
- Let me to think about it. (×)

핵심 Check

3. 다음 대화의 밑줄 친 부분과 바꾸어 쓸 수 <u>없는</u> 것은?

A: May I take your order?

B: <u>Let me see.</u>... What's today's special?

A: Tomato spaghetti with green salad.

① Let me think.　　　　　　② Just a moment.
③ Take your time.　　　　　④ Can I think about it for a while?
⑤ May I think about it for a moment?

4. 다음 우리말에 맞도록 괄호 안에서 알맞은 것을 고르시오.

• 그에 대해 생각해 볼게.

➡ Let me (think / to think) about him.

 Get Ready

(1) **G:** How are you, Ms. Hwang? We watched TV together last weekend. ❶Do you remember that?

W: Sure, Jieun. I ❷had a great time with you.

(2) **M:** Hi, Minjun. So, you learned to ❸cut holes in the board last time. ❹Let's practice again now.

B: Okay. Let's see. Is this right?

M: Yes. You remember everything.

(3) **G:** Hello, Mr. Yang. ❺This is Minji. Do you remember me?

M: Sure, Minji. ❻Thank you for calling.

(1) **G:** 황 여사님, 안녕하세요? 우리 지난 주말에 함께 TV 를 봤어요. 기억하세요?

W: 물론이지, 지은아. 너랑 즐 거운 시간을 보냈지.

(2) **M:** 안녕, 민준아. 자, 지난번 에 판자에 구멍 뚫는 걸 배웠지. 지금 다시 연습해 보자.

B: 네. 어디 보자. 이렇게 하 는 게 맞나요?

M: 그래, 모두 기억하고 있구 나.

(3) **G:** 안녕하세요, 양 선생님. 저 민지예요. 저 기억하세요?

M: 물론이지, 민지야. 전화 줘 서 고맙다.

❶ '그것을 기억하니?'라는 의미로 상대방의 기억을 묻는 표현이다.
❷ have a great time: 즐거운 시간을 보내다.
❸ cut holes는 '구멍을 뚫다'는 의미다.
❹ 'Let's + 동사원형'은 '~하자' '~하는 게 어때?'라는 의미로 상대방에게 권유할 때 사용하는 표현이다.
❺ This is ~.는 전화 통화를 할 때 '저는 ~입니다.'라는 표현이다.
❻ 'Thank you for+ing/명사' 형태로 '~해 주어서 고마워'라는 표현이다.

Check(√) True or False

(1) Ms. Hwang remembers watching TV with Jieun last weekend.   T ☐ F ☐

(2) Minjun learned to cut holes in the board.   T ☐ F ☐

Start Off Listen & Talk A-1

G: Do you remember Mr. Kim, our 6th grade teacher?

B: Of course. He wore ❶super thick glasses.

G: ❷Guess what? He moved to a new school in February this year.

B: I didn't know that. ❸Let's visit him together.

G: Okay. Good idea.

G: 6학년 때 선생님이셨던 김 선 생님 기억나니?

B: 물론이지. 그분은 엄청나게 두꺼운 안경을 쓰고 계셨는 데.

G: 있지. 그분이 올해 2월에 새 학교로 옮기셨대.

B: 몰랐어. 함께 찾아뵙자.

G: 응. 좋은 생각이야.

❶ super는 부사로 '매우'란 의미로 사용된다.
❷ 'Guess what?'은 대화를 시작할 때나 대화의 화제를 바꿀 때 사용하는 표현으로 '있잖아'라는 뜻이다.
❸ 'Let's+동사원형'은 '~하자', '~하는 게 어때?'라는 의미로 상대방에게 권유할 때 사용하는 표현이다.

Check(√) True or False

(3) Mr. Kim wore very thick glasses.   T ☐ F ☐

(4) The boy knows that Mr. Kim moved to a new school.   T ☐ F ☐

Start Off Listen & Talk A-2

B: ❶Do you remember Ms. Lee?

G: Ms. Lee? Who is she?

B: She was our 4th grade English teacher.

G: Now I remember. She taught a lot of pop songs in her class.

B: ❷She was a good dancer, too.

❶ '～을 기억하니?'라는 의미로 상대방의 기억을 묻는 표현이다.
❷ She danced well, too.와 같은 의미다.

Start Off Listen & Talk B

B: Do you remember ❶Ms. Kang, the school nurse?

G: Sure. She was nice to everyone.

B: ❷Guess what? She's getting married next month.

G: Wow! ❸What shall we do for her?

B: ❹Let me see. ❺What about making a special album?

G: That's a good idea.

❶ Ms. Kang, the school nurse의 콤마는 동격을 나타낸다.
❷ 'Guess what?'은 대화를 시작할 때나 대화의 화제를 바꿀 때 사용하는 표현으로 '있잖아'라는 뜻이다.
❸ 'What shall we do～?'는 '우리 무엇을 할까?'라는 제안의 표현이다.
❹ 상대방에게 생각할 시간을 요청할 때 사용하는 표현이다.
❺ 'What about -ing?'는 '～하는 게 어때?'라고 제안하는 표현이다.

Speak Up Look and talk.

A: ❶Do you remember the field trip last year?

B: Of course. We played fun games.

A: I have some funny pictures from ❷it on my phone.

B: That's great!

❶ '～을 기억하니?'라는 의미로 상대방의 기억을 묻는 표현이다.
❷ it은 the field trip을 가리키는 대명사이다.

Speak Up Mission

A: Do you remember my birthday?

B: ❶Let me see. ❷It's June 3. Right?

A: That's right. / That's not right. It's June 13.

❶ 상대방에게 생각할 시간을 요청할 때 사용하는 표현이다.
❷ it은 날짜를 나타내는 비인칭 주어다.

Real-life Scene

G: Do you remember Ms. Park, the old lady ❶who lives alone?

B: Of course. We ❷threw her a birthday party last year.

G: And she cooked *japchae* for us. She put some chicken in it.

B: Right. It was delicious. And we played card games together. Do you remember ❸that?

G: Yes. She won all the rounds. She's really good at games.

B: When are we going to see her next, Mina?

G: ❹Let me see. Next Saturday.

B: Let's take some pictures with her this time.

G: Great idea, Junsu.

❶ who는 주격 관계대명사로 선행사 lady를 수식하는 형용사절을 이끈다.
❷ '파티를 열다'는 의미로 throw 또는 give, have, hold 등의 동사를 사용할 수 있다.
❸ that은 앞 문장의 'we played card games together'를 가리키는 지시대명사다.
❹ 상대방에게 생각할 시간을 요청할 때 사용하는 표현이다.

Express Yourself

1. G: Do you remember the hot air balloon? We rode ❶it in Turkey.

   M: Of course. ❷It looked like an elephant.

2. G: Do you remember the rock?

   M: Is it ❸the one in Taiwan?

   G: Right.

   M: I remember it. It looked like a queen's head.

❶ it은 the hot air balloon을 가리키는 인칭대명사다.
❷ look like + 명사: ～처럼 보이다
❸ the one은 the rock을 가리키는 부정대명사다.

Learning Diary Check Yourself

B: Do you remember the singing competition last year?

G: Of course. We practiced ❶super hard.

B: I have some funny pictures from ❷it on my phone.

G: That's great!

❶ super는 부사로 '매우'의 의미로 사용된다.
❷ it은 the singing competition을 가리킨다.

● 다음 우리말과 일치하도록 빈칸에 알맞은 말을 쓰시오.

Get Ready

1. **G:** _____ are you, Ms. Hwang? We watched TV together last weekend. Do you _____ that?

   W: Sure, Jieun. I _____ _____ _____ _____ with you.

2. **M:** Hi, Minjun. So, you learned to_____ holes in the board last time. Let's _____ again now.

   B: Okay. _____ _____. Is this right?

   M: Yes. You remember everything.

3. **G:** Hello, Mr. Yang. _____ _____ Minji. Do you remember me?

   M: Sure, Minji. Thank you _____ _____.

Start Off Listen & Talk A

1. **G:** Do you remember Mr. Kim, our 6th grade teacher?

   B: Of course. He _____ _____ thick glasses.

   G: _____ _____? He _____ to a new school in February this year.

   B: I didn't know that. _____ visit him together.

   G: Okay. Good idea.

2. **B:** Do you _____ Ms. Lee?

   G: Ms. Lee? _____ is she?

   B: She was our 4th _____ English teacher.

   G: Now I _____. She _____ a lot of pop songs in her class.

   B: She was a _____ dancer, too.

Start Off Listen & Talk B

B: Do you remember Ms. Kang, the _____ _____?

G: Sure. She was nice to everyone.

B: _____ _____? She's _____ _____ next month.

G: Wow! What _____ do for her?

B: _____ _____ _____. What about _____ a special album?

G: That's a good idea.

해석

1. **G:** 황 여사님, 안녕하세요? 우리 지난 주말에 함께 TV를 봤어요. 기억하세요?
   W: 물론이지, 지은아. 너랑 즐거운 시간을 보냈지.

2. **M:** 안녕, 민준아. 자, 지난번에 판자에 구멍 뚫는 걸 배웠지. 지금 다시 연습해 보자.
   B: 네. 어디 보자. 이렇게 하는 게 맞나요?
   M: 그래, 모두 기억하고 있구나.

3. **G:** 안녕하세요, 양 선생님. 저 민지예요. 저 기억하세요.
   M: 물론이지, 민지야. 전화 줘서 고맙다.

1. **G:** 6학년 때 선생님이셨던 김 선생님 기억나니?
   B: 물론이지. 그분은 엄청나게 두꺼운 안경을 쓰고 계셨는데.
   G: 있지. 그분이 올해 2월에 새 학교로 옮기셨대.
   B: 몰랐어. 함께 찾아뵙자.
   G: 응. 좋은 생각이야.

2. **B:** 너 이 선생님 기억나니?
   G: 이 선생님? 누구신데?
   B: 4학년 때 영어 선생님이셨어.
   G: 이제 기억난다. 그분은 수업시간에 팝송을 많이 가르쳐 주셨지.
   B: 춤도 잘 추셨어.

B: 학교 보건 선생님이셨던 강 선생님 기억하니?
G: 물론이지. 그분은 우리 모두에게 친절하셨잖아.
B: 있지. 그분이 다음 달에 결혼하신대.
G: 와. 그분에게 우리 뭘 해드릴까?
B: 어디 보자. 특별한 앨범을 만들어 드리는 게 어떨까?
G: 좋은 생각이야.

Speak Up Look and talk.

A: Do you remember the _____ _____ last year?

B: Of course. We _____ fun games.

A: I have some _____ pictures from it _____ my phone.

B: That's great!

Speak Up Mission

A: Do you remember my birthday?

B: _____ _____ _____. It's June 3. Right?

A: That's right. / That's not right. It's June 13.

Real-life Scene

G: Do you remember Ms. Park, the old lady _____ lives _____?

B: Of course. We _____ her a birthday party last year.

G: And she cooked *japchae* _____ us. She _____ some chicken _____ it.

B: Right. It was delicious. And we _____ card games _____. Do you remember that?

G: Yes. She _____ all the _____. She's really _____ at games.

B: When _____ we _____ _____ see her next, Mina?

G: _____ _____ _____. Next Saturday.

B: _____ _____ some pictures with her this time.

G: Great idea, Junsu.

Express Yourself

1. G: Do you remember the hot air balloon? We _____ it in Turkey.

   M: Of course. It _____ _____ an elephant.

2. G: Do you remember the rock?

   M: Is it the _____ in Taiwan?

   G: Right.

   M: I remember it. It _____ _____ a queen's head.

Learning Diary Check Yourself

B: Do you remember the _____ _____ last year?

G: Of course. We practiced _____ hard.

B: I have some _____ pictures from it on my phone.

G: That's great!

01 다음 우리말에 맞도록 빈칸에 들어갈 알맞은 말을 쓰시오.

> G: Hello, Mr. Yang. This is Minji. Do you remember me?
>
> M: Sure, Minji. 전화 줘서 고맙다.

➡ Thank you _____ _____.

02 다음 대화의 빈칸에 들어갈 말로 알맞지 <u>않은</u> 것은?

> M: Hi, Minjun. So, you learned to cut holes in the board last time. Let's practice again now.
>
> B: Okay. _____. Is this right?

① Let me see　　　　　　② Just a moment
③ Take your time　　　　④ Let me think
⑤ Let's see

03 다음 대화의 빈칸에 들어갈 말로 가장 적절한 것은?

> B: Do you remember Ms. Lee?
>
> G: Ms. Lee? Who is she?
>
> B: She was our 4th grade English teacher.
>
> G: _____ She taught a lot of pop songs in her class.
>
> B: She was a good dancer, too.

① I don't know her.　　　② Now I remember.
③ Do I know her?　　　　④ No. She is a math teacher.
⑤ What do you say?

04 다음 대화의 밑줄 친 우리말에 맞게 주어진 어구를 알맞은 순서로 배열하시오.

> A: <u>작년에 간 체험학습 기억하니?</u>
>
> B: Of course. We played fun games.

(remember, the, last year, do, field trip, you, ?)

➡ _____

[01~02] 다음 대화를 읽고 물음에 답하시오.

B: Do you remember Ms. Kang, the school nurse?

G: Sure. She was nice to everyone.

B: _____(A)_____ She's getting married next month.

G: Wow! What shall we do for her?

B: Let me see. (B)특별한 앨범을 만들어 드리는 게 어떨까?

G: That's a good idea.

01 위 대화의 빈칸 (A)에 들어갈 말로 알맞은 것은?

① Do you think so?

⑤ That sounds great.

③ Guess what?

④ I don't think so.

② Do you know when she is getting married?

02 위 대화의 밑줄 친 (B)의 우리말에 맞게 주어진 말로 문장을 시작하여 쓰시오.

➡ What about _____?

[03~04] 다음 대화를 읽고 물음에 답하시오.

Jenny: Do you remember Mr. Kim, our 6th grade teacher?

Ben: Of course. He wore ⓐsuper thick glasses.

Jenny: Guess what? He moved to a new school in February this year.

Ben: I didn't know that. Let's visit him together.

Jenny: Okay. Good idea.

03 위 대화의 밑줄 친 ⓐsuper의 뜻과 같은 것은?

① We had a super time in Italy.

② She was super when I was having problems.

③ Shakespeare is a super old English poet, playwright, and actor.

④ What a super idea!

⑤ You got the job? That's super!

04 위 대화의 내용과 일치하지 않는 것은?

① Mr. Kim was Jenny's teacher.

② Ben remembers Mr. Kim, too.

③ Mr. Kim wore glasses.

④ Mr. Kim moved to another school.

⑤ Ben can't visit Mr. Kim with Jenny.

[05~06] 다음 대화를 읽고 물음에 답하시오.

G: Do you ____(A)____ the rock?

M: Is it the one in Taiwan?

G: Right.

M: I ____(B)____ it. It ____(C)____ a queen's head.

05 위 대화의 빈칸 (A)와 (B)에 공통으로 들어갈 말로 알맞은 것은?

① remember ② think

③ win ④ play

⑤ practice

06 위 대화의 빈칸 (C)에 들어갈 말을 주어진 단어를 이용하여 과거형으로 쓰시오.

look

➡ _____

[07~09] 다음 대화를 읽고 물음에 답하시오.

G: Do you remember Ms. Park, the old lady ___(A)___ lives alone?

B: (①) Of course. We ___(B)___ her a birthday party last year.

G: And she cooked *japchae* ___(C)___ us. She put some chicken in it. (②)

B: Right. It was delicious. And we played card games together. (③) Do you remember that?

G: Yes. She won all the rounds. She's really good at games. (④)

B: When are we going to see her next, Mina?

G: (⑤) Next Saturday.

B: Let's take some pictures with her this time.

G: Great idea, Junsu.

07 위 대화의 빈칸 (A)에 들어갈 말로 알맞은 것은?

① what ② who
③ whose ④ which
⑤ whom

08 위 대화의 빈칸 (B)와 (C)에 들어갈 말로 알맞은 것은?

① gave – of ② held – on
③ threw – for ④ have – for
⑤ had – off

09 위 대화의 (①)~(⑤)에서 다음 주어진 문장이 들어갈 위치로 알맞은 것은?

Let me see.

① ② ③ ④ ⑤

10 다음 중 짝지어진 대화가 <u>어색한</u> 것을 고르시오.

① A: Do you remember Anne?
   B: Of course. She had red hair.

② A: What do you remember about her?
   B: Let me see. Ah, she loved flowers.

③ A: Do you remember my birthday?
   B: That's not right. It's July 26.

④ A: Why is she a poor old lady?
   B: Because she's lost her memory.

⑤ A: Do you know the girl who is singing?
   B: Sure. That is Mira.

[11~12] 다음 대화를 읽고 물음에 답하시오.

(1)
G: How are you, Ms. Hwang? We watched TV together last weekend. Do you ___(A)___ that?

W: Sure, Jieun. I had a great time with you.

(2)
G: Hello, Mr. Yang. This is Minji. Do you ___(B)___ me?

M: Sure, Minji. Thank you for ___(C)___.

서답형

11 위 대화의 빈칸 (A)와 (B)에 공통으로 들어갈 단어에 대한 영어 설명을 읽고 알맞은 단어를 쓰시오.

to be able to bring back a piece of information into your mind, or to keep a piece of information in your memory

➡ _____

서답형

12 위 대화의 빈칸 (C)에 주어진 단어를 이용하여 알맞은 형태로 쓰시오.

call

➡ _____

01 다음 대화의 밑줄 친 (A)의 우리말에 맞게 주어진 단어를 이용하여 영어로 쓰시오.

remember, Ms. Lee

B: (A)너 이 선생님 기억하니?
G: Ms. Lee? Who is she?
B: She was our 4th grade English teacher.
G: Now I remember. She taught a lot of pop songs in her class.
B: She was a good dancer, too.

➡ _____

[02~03] 다음 대화를 읽고 물음에 답하시오.

G: Do you ①remember Ms. Park, the old lady who lives alone?
B: Of course. We ②threw her a birthday party last year.
G: And she cooked *japchae* for us. She ③put some chicken in it.
B: Right. It was delicious. And we played card games together. Do you remember that?
G: Yes. She won all the rounds. She's really ④bad at games.
B: When are we going to see her next, Mina?
G: _____(A)_____ Next Saturday.
B: Let's ⑤take some pictures with her his time.
G: Great idea, Junsu.

02 위 대화의 밑줄 친 ①~⑤ 중 어휘의 쓰임이 어색한 것을 찾아 바르게 고치시오.

➡ 틀린 번호: _____
➡ 고쳐 쓰기: _____ → _____

03 위 대화의 빈칸 (A)에 들어갈 표현을 주어진 영영 풀이를 참고하여 세 단어로 쓰시오.

used when you want to think carefully about something or are trying to remember

➡ _____

[04~05] 다음 대화를 읽고 물음에 답하시오.

B: Do you remember Ms. Kang, the school nurse?
G: Sure. She was nice to everyone.
B: _____(A)_____ She's getting married next month.
G: Wow! What shall we do for her?
B: Let me see. _____(B)_____
G: That's a good idea.

04 위 대화의 빈칸 (A)에 들어갈 표현을 주어진 영영 풀이를 참고하여 쓰시오.

used before telling someone something interesting or surprising

➡ _____

05 위 대화의 빈칸 (B)에 두 사람이 선생님을 위해 해줄 일을 그림을 참고해서 주어진 단어를 이용하여 쓰시오.

what, make, a, special

➡ _____

Grammar

① 주격 관계대명사

> • Wilfrid was a little boy **who** lived next to a nursing home.
> Wilfrid는 요양원 옆에 사는 어린 소년이었다.
>
> • I bought a book **that** has many pretty pictures. 나는 많은 예쁜 그림이 있는 책을 샀다.

■ 관계대명사는 접속사와 대명사의 역할을 한다. 관계대명사가 이끄는 절은 명사를 수식해 주는 형용사절의 한 종류로 관계대명사절이 꾸며 주는 말을 선행사라고 하고 관계대명사는 앞의 선행사와 같은 대상을 가리킨다. 관계대명사절에서 주어의 역할을 대신하는 관계대명사를 주격 관계대명사라고 하며, 그 다음에는 동사가 온다. 관계대명사 that은 who와 which 대신 사용할 수 있으며 소유격은 없다.

• Einstein was a scientist. He was born in Germany.

= Einstein was a scientist **who[that]** was born in Germany. Einstein은 독일에서 태어난 과학자였다.

• The dog is very cute. It has a long tail.

= The dog **which[that]** has a long tail is very cute. 긴 꼬리를 가진 그 개는 매우 귀엽다.

• I know the boy and his dog **that** are running together. 나는 함께 뛰고 있는 소년과 그의 개를 안다.

■ 주격 관계대명사는 선행사에 따라 다음과 같이 사용된다.

선행사	주격 관계대명사
사람	who/that
동물, 사물	which/that
사람 + 동물[사물]	that

■ 주격 관계대명사는 생략할 수 없으나 뒤에 분사가 오는 경우 '주격 관계대명사 + be동사'를 생략할 수 있다.

• The boy **(who is)** playing the piano on the stage is my son.
무대에서 피아노를 연주하고 있는 소년이 내 아들이다.

핵심 Check

1. 다음 우리말에 맞게 빈칸에 알맞은 말을 쓰시오.

(1) 그는 지난달에 우리 학교에 온 영어 선생님이다.

➡ He's the English teacher _____ came to our school last month.

(2) 나는 설거지를 할 수 있는 로봇을 가지고 싶다.

➡ I want to have a robot _____ can do the dishes.

② 목적격 관계대명사

> • It is something **that** you remember. 그것은 네가 기억하는 것이란다.
> • The girl **whom** I met was Susan. 내가 만났던 소녀는 Susan이었다.

■ 관계대명사절에서 동사 또는 전치사의 목적어의 역할을 대신하는 관계대명사를 말하며 그 다음에는 '주어+동사 ~'가 온다. 목적격 관계대명사의 선행사가 사람일 경우 who(m), 사물일 경우에는 which가 쓰이며 선행사에 상관없이 that을 쓸 수도 있다.

■ 목적격 관계대명사는 선행사에 따라 다음과 같이 사용된다.

선행사	목적격 관계대명사
사람	whom[who]/that
동물, 사물	which/that
사람 + 동물[사물]	that

  • Do you know that lady **whom[that]** he is talking with? 그가 함께 이야기하고 있는 저 여자를 아니?

  • I like the dog **which[that]** I adopted last year. 나는 내가 작년에 입양한 개를 좋아한다.

■ 주격 관계대명사와 달리 목적격 관계대명사는 흔히 생략되지만 목적격 관계대명사 바로 앞에 전치사가 오는 경우에는 생략할 수 없다.

  • The man **(who/whom/that)** Audrey loves is Jack. Audrey가 사랑하는 남자는 Jack이다.

  • The man with **whom** Audrey falls in love is Jack. Audrey가 사랑에 빠진 남자는 Jack이다.

■ 관계대명사절 내에서 관계대명사가 전치사의 목적어 역할을 할 때, 전치사는 관계대명사절 끝이나 관계대명사 바로 앞에 올 수 있다. 전치사가 관계대명사 바로 앞에 올 경우 관계대명사 that은 쓸 수 없다.

  • This is the house in **which** she lives. = This is the house **which** she lives in. 이것이 그녀가 사는 집이다.

  • This is the house in that she lives. (×)

■ 소유격 관계대명사는 관계대명사절이 되기 전의 문장에서 소유격으로 쓰였던 대명사와 접속사의 역할을 하며 다음에는 명사가 나오고 다른 관계대명사와 달리 완전한 절이 이어진다. 소유격 관계대명사는 whose이며 선행사가 사물일 경우 whose나 of which를 쓴다.

  • I saw a house **whose** roof is red. 나는 지붕이 빨간색인 집을 보았다.

핵심 Check

2. 다음 우리말에 맞게 빈칸에 알맞은 말을 쓰시오.

(1) 그는 그가 타려고 하는 기차를 놓쳤다.

➡ He missed the train _____ he wanted to take.

(2) 그는 그가 사랑하는 여자를 그리워했다.

➡ He missed the woman _____ he loved.

01 다음 빈칸에 들어갈 알맞은 것은?

> Do you know the girl _____ is singing?

① whom　　　② whose　　　③ what
④ which　　　⑤ that

02 다음 문장에서 어법상 어색한 부분을 바르게 고쳐 쓰시오.

(1) We met a girl which wore a beautiful dress.

_____ ➡ _____

(2) Do you like that dog who is running around?

_____ ➡ _____

(3) Jiwon is reading a letter whom Mike wrote to her.

_____ ➡ _____

(4) The man with that she is talking is my math teacher.

_____ ➡ _____

03 다음 우리말에 맞게 괄호 안에 주어진 단어를 바르게 배열하시오. (필요하면 어형을 바꿀 것)

(1) Kate는 예쁜 정원이 있는 집에서 살고 싶어 한다.

(garden, have, pretty, that, a)

➡ Kate wants to live in a house _____.

(2) Brian은 그가 갖고 싶어 하는 책을 샀다.

(he, have, want, that, to)

➡ Brian bought the book _____.

04 다음 문장에서 생략할 수 있는 것을 찾아 쓰시오.

(1) She is the girl whom I met yesterday.
(2) Peter gave me a wallet which was made of leather.

➡ (1) _____ (2) _____

01 다음 빈칸에 들어갈 수 있는 말이 나머지와 <u>다른</u> 하나는?

① Do you know the lady _____ is dancing?

② I like the rabbit _____ ears are long.

③ He is the boy _____ I met at the shop yesterday.

④ I like my history teacher _____ is very kind to students.

⑤ The pictures _____ Steve took are very nice.

02 주어진 어휘를 이용하여 다음 우리말을 영어로 쓰시오.

> 이것이 내가 찾고 있는 책이다. (looking, for)

➡ _____

03 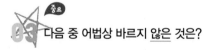 다음 중 어법상 바르지 <u>않은</u> 것은?

① A dictionary is a book which we use to find the meaning of words.

② Do you know the man who is clapping his hands?

③ This is the watch that I bought yesterday.

④ Marianne has a cousin which lives in San Francisco.

⑤ Jiwon is eating the cookies her dad baked for her.

04 다음 괄호 안에서 알맞은 말을 고르시오.

(1) Where is the picture (which / who) was on my desk?

(2) The doctor (who / which) works in this office is very kind.

(3) We had Korean dishes (that / who) was very delicious last night.

(4) It's the key for (that / which) I am looking.

(5) Mariel met the actor (whom / which) she always wanted to meet.

(6) This is the girl (who / whom) came to see you yesterday.

(7) There were an old man and his dog (that / which) used to take a walk together in the afternoon.

05 다음 밑줄 친 that의 성격이 나머지 넷과 <u>다른</u> 것은?

① Someone <u>that</u> I don't know gave me some flowers yesterday.

② I know the man <u>that</u> is playing baduk with his friends.

③ Do you know the girl <u>that</u> is wearing sunglasses?

④ The cap <u>that</u> Mom bought for me is very nice.

⑤ People believed <u>that</u> the earth was flat.

06 다음 빈칸에 알맞은 말이 순서대로 짝지어진 것은?

> • Do you know the girl _____ is playing the piano?
> • She ran a restaurant _____ sold Korean food.

① who – who   ② who – which
③ which – who   ④ which – that
⑤ that – who

07 다음 중 생략할 수 있는 것을 찾아 쓰시오.

(1) This is the card which I got from Miso.
(2) Do you know the man who is standing just behind a tall woman?

➡ (1) _____ (2) _____

08 다음 중 어법상 어색한 문장을 고르시오.

① Is this the novel you were talking about it yesterday?
② How do you like the cake that I cooked for you?
③ The cat which has yellow eyes belongs to Ms. Han.
④ She is the girl whom I talked to about the problem.
⑤ This is the boy who showed me the way to the library.

09 다음 빈칸에 들어갈 수 있는 것을 <u>모두</u> 고르면?

> Christine is a kind girl _____ everyone loves.

① who   ② whom   ③ what
④ that   ⑤ which

10 다음 두 문장을 한 문장으로 바르게 바꾸면?

> • This is a gold medal.
> • We won at the race.

① This is that a gold medal we won at the race.
② This is a gold medal which we won it at the race.
③ This is a gold medal that we won at the race.
④ This is a gold medal that won at the race.
⑤ This is a gold medal who we won at the race.

11 다음 빈칸에 들어갈 알맞은 것은?

> Who broke the vase _____?

① that I made
② which it is very expensive
③ who looks really good
④ that my dad gave it to me
⑤ that I bought it at the shop

12 다음 중 어법상 옳은 문장을 고르시오.

① I hope there is a robot who can do my homework.
② The man which is writing a letter is Mick.
③ Melina likes to take pictures of friends with that she hangs around.
④ Van Gogh painted *Starry Night* who is very famous.
⑤ The girl who I met yesterday was very kind.

서답형

13 〈보기〉에서 알맞은 표현을 골라 문장을 완성하시오.

보기

- which I took a rest
- that looked like an elephant
- whom I can trust

(1) We rode a hot air balloon _____ _____.

(2) The sofa on _____ was too hard.

(3) He is the only man _____.

14 다음 밑줄 친 부분의 쓰임이 <u>어색한</u> 것은?

① This is my favorite book <u>which</u> has many beautiful pictures.

② Children <u>who</u> are too young shouldn't use it.

③ Mom bought me a chair on <u>that</u> I take a rest.

④ Alexander <u>who</u> came from Greece made friends with Sandra.

⑤ Frank Jones is the singer <u>who</u> Michelle likes most.

중요

15 주어진 문장의 밑줄 친 부분과 동일한 역할을 하는 것을 <u>두 개</u> 고르시오.

Laura <u>who</u> is my best friend is kind.

① Try to make friends with someone <u>who</u> you can depend on.

② I know a girl <u>who</u> is very honest.

③ <u>Who</u> is the letter from?

④ Sam has a friend <u>who</u> lives in Jeju.

⑤ Kim likes Richard <u>who</u> Amalia loves.

서답형

16 관계대명사를 이용하여 주어진 두 문장을 한 문장으로 연결하시오.

(1) • I met a man yesterday.
   • This is the man.
   ➡ _____

(2) • I don't know the girl.
   • She is singing.
   ➡ _____

(3) • Julie bought a computer yesterday.
   • She likes it very much.
   ➡ _____

(4) • He completed drawing two pictures.
   • They look very similar.
   ➡ _____

(5) • Mary took a picture of a man and his dog.
   • They were crossing the road.
   ➡ _____

(6) • Mike needs a friend.
   • He wants to play with the friend.
   ➡ _____

서답형

17 우리말에 맞게 괄호 안의 어휘를 바르게 배열하시오.

Amanda는 Steve가 지난주에 그녀에게 말했던 영화를 봤다. (Steve, movie, her, week, watched, talked, that, last, the, to, about) Amanda _____.

➡ _____

01 다음 두 문장을 관계대명사를 이용하여 한 문장으로 연결하여 쓰시오.

(1) • Sejong was a great King.
   • He invented Hangeul.
   ➡ _____
   _____

(2) • An elephant is an animal.
   • It has a long nose.
   ➡ _____
   _____

(3) • Sharon met a man.
   • She loved him very much.
   ➡ _____
   _____

(4) • Tony bought a nice bag.
   • He gave it to Karen.
   ➡ _____
   _____

(5) • There are Ms. Han and her cats.
   • They are playing together.
   ➡ _____
   _____

02 다음 두 문장을 관계대명사를 써서 한 문장으로 쓰시오.

> This is the bank. Melanie works at the bank.

= (1) This is the bank _____ at.
= (2) This is the bank at _____.
= (3) This is the bank _____ at.
= (4) This is the bank _____.

03 다음 그림을 보고 괄호 안에 주어진 어휘를 이용하여 질문을 완성하시오.

(1) Q: Do you know the man _____
   _____ _____ _____ _____
   _____? (sitting, wheelchair)
   A: Yes, I do. He is Mr. Kim.
(2) Q: Do you know the girl _____
   _____ _____ _____?
   (playing, cards)
   A: Yes, I do. She is Jieun.
(3) Q: Do you know the dog _____
   _____ _____ _____ _____
   _____? (sleeping, on, chair)
   A: Yes, I do. It is my pet dog.

04 다음 문장의 잘못된 부분을 바르게 고치시오.

(1) This is the book who was on the table.
   _____ ➡ _____

(2) The man which is singing on the stage is the most famous entertainer.
   _____ ➡ _____

(3) Abigail will meet the boy whom loves her.
   _____ ➡ _____

(4) She bought a scarf which were nice and cheap.
   _____ ➡ _____

(5) John wrote a letter which he sent it to his parents.
   _____

05 다음 두 문장을 관계대명사를 사용하여 한 문장으로 썼을 때, 빈칸에 해당하는 문장을 쓰시오.

(1) • _____

• It shows your brand and products.

➡ You can create a scene that shows your brand and products.

(2) • Jack sent some flowers to Michelle.

• _____

➡ Jack sent some flowers which he bought at the shop to Michelle.

(3) • The photos show the outside of the building well.

_____

➡ The photos that I took yesterday show the outside of the building well.

(4) • I want to adopt a dog.

• _____

➡ I want to adopt a dog which can be my friend.

06 아래 〈보기〉 (A)와 (B)에서 각각 서로 관계있는 문장을 선택한 후 관계대명사 who, whom, which 중 하나를 사용하여 한 문장으로 연결하시오.

┤ 보기A ├

• She has a son.

• Do you like the dog?

• This is the hospital.

┤ 보기B ├

• I was born in the hospital.

• She is very proud of him.

• It is jumping near the piano.

(1) _____

_____

(2) _____

(3) _____

_____

07 다음 문장에서 어법상 어색한 것을 바르게 고쳐 다시 쓰시오.

(1) There are a lot of active seniors which share their knowledge and talents.

➡ _____

_____

(2) What is the title of the film whom you saw yesterday?

➡ _____

_____

(3) Emma bought a dress who looked very expensive.

➡ _____

_____

(4) The woman who is wearing nice glasses are talking on the phone.

➡ _____

_____

(5) The computer which Mom bought it for me last week is really cool.

➡ _____

_____

08 괄호 안에 주어진 어휘를 이용하여 영작하시오.

(1) Adelene은 원하는 컴퓨터를 사려고 돈을 저축한다. (save, that, 10 단어)

➡ _____

_____

(2) 나는 나를 많이 도와주는 친구가 한 명 있다. (have, who, a lot, 9 단어)

➡ _____

(3) Sam은 2년 전에 함께 일했던 사람을 만났다. (a man, that, work with, 11 단어)

➡ _____

_____

Reading

What's a Memory?

Wilfrid Gordon Parker was a little boy <u>who lived next to a nursing</u>
> who 이하의 절은 앞의 'a little boy'를 수식하는 주격 관계대명사절이다.

<u>home</u>. He liked all the people who lived there. But his favorite person
> 'all the people'을 주격 관계대명사절인 'who lived there'가 수식하고 있다. 흔히 선행사에
> 'all'이 오면 관계대명사는 'that'을 쓰는데, 선행사가 사람을 지칭할 때는 'who'를 쓰는 경향이 있다.

was Ms. Nancy Gordon Cooper because her middle name was <u>the</u>

<u>same as his</u>. He told her all his secrets.
> ···와 같은, ···와 동일한 '그의 것'이라는 뜻의 소유대명사 = his middle name

One day, Wilfrid's parents were talking about Ms. Cooper.

"Poor old lady," said his mother. "Why is she a poor old lady?" asked

Wilfrid. "Because <u>she's lost</u> her memory," said his father.
> 'she has lost'를 줄인말(현재완료의 결과 용법)

"What's a memory?" asked Wilfrid.
> Wilfrid는 '기억력'의 의미를 이해하지 못하는 어린아이이므로 할머니가 기억이라는 셀 수 있는 물건을 잃어버렸다고 생각하여, 'a memory'

"It is <u>something you remember</u>," said his father. 라고 표현하였다. 즉, Wilfrid는 셀 수 있는 '기
> something과 you 사이에 목적격 관계대명사 that[which]이 생략되어 있음. 억'이라는 물건이 무엇인지 묻고 있다.

Wilfrid wanted <u>to know</u> more, so he went to his neighbors.
> to부정사의 명사적 용법(목적어)

Ms. Jordan <u>was enjoying</u> the sunlight.
> 과거 진행형

"What's a memory?" he asked.

"Something warm, my child," she said.
> 문장 앞에 'It is'가 생략되었다. 'something, anything' 등 '-thing'으로 끝나는 부정대명사는 형용사가
> 뒤에 오는 후치 수식이 적용된다.

Ms. Mitchell was reading a cartoon.

"What's a memory?" he asked.

"Something that brings you laughter," she said.
> 문장 앞에 'It is'가 생략되었다. 'that' 이하의 절은 앞의 'something'을 꾸며 주는 관계사절로, 'that'은 주격 관계대명사로 쓰였다. 선행사

Mr. Hunter was cleaning his medal.
> 가 'something, everything, anything, nothing'일
> 때는 관계대명사로 보통 'that'을 쓴다.

"It's something <u>as precious as</u> gold, young man," he said.
> 'as+형용사/부사의 원급+as'는 '~만큼 ···한/하게'를 의미하는 비교 표현이다.

---

memory 기억, 기억력, 추억
next to ···의 옆에(= beside)
nursing home 요양원, 양로원
person 사람, 개인
the same as ···와 같은, 동종의, 동일한
secret 비밀
sunlight 햇볕, 햇빛
laughter 웃음, 웃음소리
medal 메달, 훈장
precious 귀중한, 값비싼
gold 금

확인문제

● 다음 문장이 본문의 내용과 일치하면 T, 일치하지 않으면 F를 쓰시오.

1 Wilfrid Gordon Parker lived next to a nursing home. ☐

2 Wilfrid didn't like all the people living in a nursing home. ☐

3 Wilfrid's father said Ms. Cooper was a poor old lady. ☐

4 Wilfrid's father said a memory is something you remember. ☐

5 Ms. Jordan was reading a cartoon. ☐

So Wilfrid went back home to **look for** memories for Ms. Cooper. He

<small>'to look for'는 목적을 나타내는 to부정사의 부사적 용법으로, '…하기 위해'로 해석한다.</small>

went into the hen house and took a fresh, warm egg **from under** a hen.

<small>'memories'는 복수형으로 쓰여, '추억, 기억 내용'을 뜻하는데, 어린 소년 Wilfrid의 입장에서의 'memories'는 요양원에 있는 어르신들이 알려 준 '특성을 가진 여러 가지 물건'이라고 생각하고, 해당 물건을 찾고 있음이 뒤에서 밝혀진다.</small>

<small>'from under'는 이중전치사(double prepositions)로 두 개의 전치사가 한 개의 전치사 역할을 한다. 'from behind, from among, since before, till after' 등이 이에 해당한다.</small>

Next, he looked for his sock puppet. It always brought laughter to his

parents. Finally, he found his football in his toy box. It was **as precious**

<small>동등비교</small>

as gold to him.

Wilfrid went to Ms. Cooper and **gave** her the things one by one. "What

<small>'gave' 이하는 '동사+간접목적어(…에게)+직접목적어(~을/를)'의 4형식 문형으로 쓰였으며, 3형식 문형인 'gave the things to her one by one'으로 바꿔 쓸 수 있다.</small>

a strange, sweet child!" thought Ms. Cooper, "**He's brought** all these

<small>'He's brought'는 'He has brought'가 축약된 현재완료 시제의 문장이다. Wilfrid가 과거에 물건을 가져온 행위가 현재에까지 영향을 미치고 있음을 나타내고 있다.</small>

wonderful things." Then she started **to remember** her past.

<small>명사적 용법의 to부정사</small>

She held the warm egg and whispered to Wilfrid, "Long ago, I found

a small blue egg in my aunt's garden." She **smiled at** the sock puppet

<small>~에게 미소를 지었다</small>

and **remembered** performing a puppet show for her sister. "My sister

<small>'remember+동명사(동사 -ing)'는 과거에 한 일을 기억해 내는 것을 나타내고, 'remember+to부정사'는 앞으로 할 일을 기억하고 있다는 것을 나타낸다.</small>

laughed **a lot**," said Ms. Cooper. She bounced the football to Wilfrid

<small>많이</small>

and remembered him. "Wilfrid? Wilfrid Gordon Parker! My friend!"

She also remembered their secrets one by one.

The two smiled **at each other**. Ms. Cooper got her memory back

<small>서로에게</small>

thanks to the little boy with the same middle name as **hers**.

<small>… 덕분에</small>　　　　　　　　　　　　　　　　　　<small>= her middle name</small>

---

hen 암탉

sock 양말(보통 복수형으로 씀)

puppet 인형, 꼭두각시

football 축구공, 축구(미국에서는 미식축구, 영국에서는 축구 또는 럭비)

one by one 하나씩

share 함께 나누다, 공유하다

whisper 속삭이다

ago … 전에 (과거시제와 함께 쓰이며, 현재완료 시제와는 함께 쓰지 않음)

aunt 이모, 고모, (외)숙모

perform 공연하다, 연주하다, 수행하다

bounce (공이) 튀다, 튀기다

📎 확인문제

● 다음 문장이 본문의 내용과 일치하면 T, 일치하지 <u>않으면</u> F를 쓰시오.

1　Wilfrid looked for memories for Ms. Cooper.　☐

2　A warm egg brought laughter to Wilfrid's parents.　☐

3　Wilfrid's football was as precious as gold to him.　☐

4　Ms. Cooper thought Wilfrid was a very strange, unkind child.　☐

5　Ms. Cooper smiled at the sock puppet.　☐

6　Ms. Cooper's sister performed a puppet show for her.　☐

7　Ms. Cooper got her memory back thanks to Wilfrid.　☐

● 우리말을 참고하여 빈칸에 알맞은 말을 쓰시오.

1 _____ a Memory?

2 Wilfrid Gordon Parker was a little boy _____ lived _____ _____ a nursing home.

3 He liked all the people _____ _____ _____ .

4 But _____ _____ _____ was Ms. Nancy Gordon Cooper because her middle name was _____ _____ _____ .

5 He told her _____ _____ _____ .

6 One day, Wilfrid's parents _____ _____ _____ Ms. Cooper.

7 "_____ _____ _____ ," said his mother.

8 "_____ is she a poor old lady?" _____ Wilfrid.

9 "_____ _____ _____ her memory," said his father.

10 "_____ a memory?" asked Wilfrid.

11 "It is _____ _____ _____ ," said his father.

12 Wilfrid wanted _____ _____ _____ , so he went to his neighbors.

13 Ms. Jordan _____ _____ the sunlight.

14 "What's a memory?" _____ _____ .

15 "_____ _____ , my child," she said.

16 Ms. Mitchell _____ _____ a cartoon.

17 "_____ _____ _____ ?" he asked.

18 "Something that _____ _____ _____ ," she said.

1	추억이란 무엇일까?
2	Wilfrid Gordon Parker는 요양원 옆에 사는 어린 소년이었다.
3	그는 그곳에 사는 모든 사람들을 좋아했다.
4	하지만 그가 가장 좋아하는 사람은 Nancy Gordon Cooper 할머니였는데, 그 이유는 그녀의 가운데 이름이 그의 것과 같았기 때문이었다.
5	그는 자기의 모든 비밀을 그녀에게 말했다.
6	어느 날, Wilfrid의 부모님은 Cooper 할머니에 관해 이야기를 하고 있었다.
7	"불쌍한 분." 그의 어머니가 말했다.
8	"왜 불쌍한 분이세요?"라고 Wilfrid가 물었다.
9	"왜냐하면 그분은 기억을 잃으셨거든." 그의 아버지가 말했다.
10	"기억이 뭐예요?" Wilfrid가 물었다.
11	"그것은 네가 기억하는 것이란다."라고 그의 아버지가 말했다.
12	Wilfrid는 더 알고 싶어서, 그의 이웃들에게 갔다.
13	Jordan 할머니는 햇볕을 즐기고 있었다.
14	"기억이 뭐예요?" 그가 물었다.
15	"따뜻한 거란다, 아가야." 그녀가 말했다.
16	Mitchell 할머니는 만화책을 읽고 있었다.
17	"기억이 뭐예요?" 그가 물었다.
18	"너에게 웃음을 가져다주는 것이란다." 그녀가 말했다.

19 Mr. Hunter was _____ _____ _____ .

20 "It's something _____ _____ _____ _____, young man," he said.

21 So Wilfrid went back home _____ _____ _____ for Ms. Cooper.

22 He _____ _____ the hen house and took a fresh, warm egg _____ _____ a hen.

23 _____, he _____ _____ his sock puppet.

24 It always _____ laughter _____ his parents.

25 _____, he found his football in his toy box.

26 It was _____ _____ _____ _____ to him.

27 Wilfrid went to Ms. Cooper and gave her the things _____ _____ _____ .

28 "What a strange, sweet child!" thought Ms. Cooper, "He's brought _____ _____ _____ _____ ."

29 Then she started _____ _____ her past.

30 She _____ the warm egg and _____ _____ Wilfrid, "Long ago, I found a small blue egg in my aunt's garden."

31 She _____ _____ the sock puppet and remembered _____ a puppet show _____ her sister.

32 "My sister laughed _____ _____," said Ms. Cooper.

33 She _____ _____ _____ to Wilfrid and remembered him.

34 "Wilfrid? Wilfrid Gordon Parker! _____ _____ !"

35 She also remembered their secrets _____ _____ _____ .

36 The two smiled at _____ _____ .

37 Ms. Cooper _____ her memory _____ thanks to the little boy _____ the same middle name _____ _____ .

19 Hunter 할아버지는 자신의 메달을 닦고 있었다.

20 "그건 금처럼 소중한 거지, 어린 친구."라고 그가 말했다.

21 그래서 Wilfrid는 Cooper 할머니께 드릴 기억들을 찾으러 집으로 돌아갔다.

22 그는 닭장 안으로 들어가서 암탉이 품고 있던 신선하고 따뜻한 달걀을 꺼냈다.

23 다음으로, 그는 자신의 양말 인형을 찾았다.

24 그것은 항상 그의 부모님께 큰 웃음을 안겨 주었다.

25 마지막으로, 그는 자신의 장난감 상자 속에서 축구공을 찾아냈다.

26 그것은 그에게는 금만큼이나 소중했다.

27 Wilfrid는 Cooper 할머니께 가서 그녀에게 그 물건들을 하나씩 드렸다.

28 "이상하면서도 귀여운 아이구나! 이 멋진 물건들을 다 가져오다니 말이야."라고 Cooper 할머니는 생각했다.

29 그러다가 그녀는 자신의 과거를 기억해 내기 시작했다.

30 그녀는 따뜻한 달걀을 쥐고 Wilfrid에게, "오래 전에, 나는 나의 이모님 댁 정원에서 작고 푸른 알을 찾았단다."라고 속삭였다.

31 그녀는 양말 인형을 보며 미소를 짓다가 자기 여동생에게 인형극을 공연해 주었던 것을 기억해 냈다.

32 "내 여동생이 엄청나게 웃었지."라고 Cooper 할머니가 말했다.

33 그녀는 축구공을 바닥에 튀게 해서 Wilfrid에게 던져 주다가 그를 기억해 냈다.

34 "Wilfrid? Wilfrid Gordon Parker! 내 친구!"

35 그녀는 또한 그들만의 비밀을 하나씩 기억해 냈다.

36 두 사람은 서로 바라보며 미소 지었다.

37 Cooper 할머니는 가운데 이름이 자신의 것과 같은 어린 소년 덕분에 기억을 다시 찾게 되었다.

● 우리말을 참고하여 본문을 영작하시오.

1 추억이란 무엇일까?

➡ _____

2 Wilfrid Gordon Parker는 요양원 옆에 사는 어린 소년이었다.

➡ _____

3 그는 그곳에 사는 모든 사람들을 좋아했다

➡ _____

4 하지만 그가 가장 좋아하는 사람은 Nancy Gordon Cooper 할머니였는데, 그 이유는 그녀의 가운데 이름이 그의 것과 같았기 때문이었다..

➡ _____

5 그는 자기의 모든 비밀을 그녀에게 말했다.

➡ _____

6 어느 날, Wilfrid의 부모님은 Cooper 할머니에 관해 이야기를 하고 있었다.

➡ _____

7 "불쌍한 분." 그의 어머니가 말했다.

➡ _____

8 "왜 불쌍한 분이세요?"라고 Wilfrid가 물었다.

➡ _____

9 "왜냐하면 그분은 기억을 잃으셨거든." 그의 아버지가 말했다.

➡ _____

10 "기억이 뭐예요?" Wilfrid가 물었다

➡ _____

11 "그것은 네가 기억하는 것이란다."라고 그의 아버지가 말했다.

➡ _____

12 Wilfrid는 더 알고 싶어서, 그의 이웃들에게 갔다.

➡ _____

13 Jordan 할머니는 햇볕을 즐기고 있었다.

➡ _____

14 "기억이 뭐예요?" 그가 물었다.

➡ _____

15 "따뜻한 거란다, 아가야." 그녀가 말했다.

➡ _____

16 Mitchell 할머니는 만화책을 읽고 있었다.

➡ _____

17 "기억이 뭐예요?" 그가 물었다.

➡ _____

18 "너에게 웃음을 가져다주는 것이란다." 그녀가 말했다.

➡ _____

19 Hunter 할아버지는 자신의 메달을 닦고 있었다.
➡ _____

20 "그건 금처럼 소중한 거지, 어린 친구."라고 그가 말했다.
➡ _____

21 그래서 Wilfrid는 Cooper 할머니께 드릴 기억들을 찾으러 집으로 돌아갔다.
➡ _____

22 그는 닭장 안으로 들어가서 암탉이 품고 있던 신선하고 따뜻한 달걀을 꺼냈다.
➡ _____

23 다음으로, 그는 자신의 양말 인형을 찾았다.
➡ _____

24 그것은 항상 그의 부모님께 큰 웃음을 안겨 주었다.
➡ _____

25 마지막으로, 그는 자신의 장난감 상자 속에서 축구공을 찾아냈다.
➡ _____

26 그것은 그에게는 금만큼이나 소중했다.
➡ _____

27 Wilfrid는 Cooper 할머니께 가서 그녀에게 그 물건들을 하나씩 드렸다.
➡ _____

28 "이상하면서도 귀여운 아이구나! 이 멋진 물건들을 다 가져오다니 말이야."라고 Cooper 할머니는 생각했다.
➡ _____

29 그러다가 그녀는 자신의 과거를 기억해 내기 시작했다.
➡ _____

30 그녀는 따뜻한 달걀을 쥐고 Wilfrid에게, "오래 전에, 나는 나의 이모님 댁 정원에서 작고 푸른 알을 찾았단다."라고 속삭였다.
➡ _____

31 그녀는 양말 인형을 보며 미소를 짓다가 자기 여동생에게 인형극을 공연해 주었던 것을 기억해 냈다.
➡ _____

32 "내 여동생이 엄청나게 웃었지."라고 Cooper 할머니가 말했다.
➡ _____

33 그녀는 축구공을 바닥에 튀게 해서 Wilfrid에게 던져 주다가 그를 기억해 냈다.
➡ _____

34 "Wilfrid? Wilfrid Gordon Parker! 내 친구!"
➡ _____

35 그녀는 또한 그들만의 비밀을 하나씩 기억해 냈다.
➡ _____

36 두 사람은 서로 바라보며 미소 지었다.
➡ _____

37 Cooper 할머니는 가운데 이름이 자신의 것과 같은 어린 소년 덕분에 기억을 다시 찾게 되었다.
➡ _____

[01~03] 다음 글을 읽고 물음에 답하시오.

Wilfrid Gordon Parker was a little boy _____ⓐ_____ lived next to a nursing home. He liked all the people _____ⓑ_____ lived there. But his favorite person was Ms. Nancy Gordon Cooper because her middle name was the same as ⓒhis. He told her all his secrets.

01 위 글의 빈칸 ⓐ와 ⓑ에 공통으로 들어갈 알맞은 말을 모두 고르시오.

① that   ② whom   ③ what
④ who   ⑤ which

서답형
02 다음 질문에 대한 알맞은 대답을 주어진 단어로 시작하여 쓰시오. (8 단어)

Q: Why did Wilfrid like Ms. Cooper most?
A: Because _____.

➡ _____

서답형
03 위 글의 밑줄 친 ⓒhis가 가리키는 것을 영어로 쓰시오.

➡ _____

[04~06] 다음 글을 읽고 물음에 답하시오.

ⓐWilfrid wanted knowing more, so he went to his neighbors.
Ms. Jordan was enjoying the sunlight.
"What's a memory?" he asked.
"Something warm, my child," she said.
Ms. Mitchell was reading a cartoon.
"What's a memory?" he asked.
"ⓑ너에게 웃음을 가져다주는 것이란다," she said.
Mr. Hunter was cleaning his medal.
"It's something as precious as gold, young man," he said.

서답형
04 위 글의 밑줄 친 ⓐ에서 어법상 틀린 부분을 찾아 고치시오.

_____ ➡ _____

중요
05 위 글의 제목으로 알맞은 것을 고르시오.

① How to Enjoy the Sunlight
② What's a Memory?
③ Memory Is Something Warm
④ Memory Brings Smile to You
⑤ What Is As Precious As Gold?

서답형
06 위 글의 밑줄 친 ⓑ의 우리말에 맞게 한 단어를 보충하여, 주어진 어휘를 바르게 배열하시오.

laughter / you / brings / something

➡ _____

[07~09] 다음 글을 읽고 물음에 답하시오.

So Wilfrid went back home ⓐto look for memories _____ⓑ_____ Ms. Cooper. He went into the hen house and took a fresh, warm egg from under a hen. Next, he looked for his sock puppet. It always brought laughter to his parents. Finally, he found his football in his toy box. It was as precious as gold _____ⓒ_____ him.

07 위 글의 밑줄 친 ⓐto look과 to부정사의 용법이 다른 것을 모두 고르시오.

① It's not easy to be a math teacher.
② He must be smart to solve it.
③ Give me a pen to write with.
④ I stopped to listen to music.
⑤ She was surprised to see him there.

08 위 글의 빈칸 ⓑ와 ⓒ에 들어갈 전치사가 바르게 짝지어진 것은?

① for – from
② at – by
③ on – to
④ for – to
⑤ on – for

서답형

09 다음 질문에 대한 알맞은 대답을 주어진 단어로 시작하여 쓰시오. (4 단어)

> Q: After Wilfrid went into the hen house, where did he take a fresh, warm egg?
> A: He took it _____.

➡ _____

[10~12] 다음 글을 읽고 물음에 답하시오.

Wilfrid went to Ms. Cooper and ⓐgave her the things one by one. "ⓑWhat a strange, sweet child!" thought Ms. Cooper, "ⓒHe's brought all this wonderful things." Then she started to remember her past.

중요

10 위 글의 밑줄 친 ⓐ를 3형식으로 고칠 때 필요한 전치사를 고르시오.

① for
② by
③ of
④ on
⑤ to

서답형

11 위 글의 밑줄 친 ⓑ를 다음과 같이 바꿔 쓸 때 빈칸에 들어갈 알맞은 말을 쓰시오.

➡ He is a _____ strange, sweet child!

서답형

12 위 글의 밑줄 친 ⓒ에서 어법상 틀린 부분을 찾아 고치시오.

_____ ➡ _____

[13~15] 다음 글을 읽고 물음에 답하시오.

Wilfrid Gordon Parker was a little boy who lived next to a nursing home. He liked all the people who lived there. But his favorite person was Ms. Nancy Gordon Cooper because her ____ⓐ____ name was the same as his. He told her all his secrets.

One day, Wilfrid's parents were talking about Ms. Cooper.

"Poor old lady," said his mother.

"Why is she a poor old lady?" asked Wilfrid.

"Because ⓑshe's lost her memory," said his father.

"ⓒWhat's a memory?" asked Wilfrid.

"It is something you remember," said his father.

서답형

13 위 글의 빈칸 ⓐ에 들어갈 알맞은 말을 쓰시오.

➡ _____

서답형

14 위 글의 밑줄 친 ⓑshe's와 ⓒWhat's가 각각 무엇의 줄임말인지 쓰시오.

➡ ⓑ_____ ⓒ_____

15 위 글의 내용과 일치하지 않는 것은?

① Wilfrid는 요양원 옆에 살았다.
② Wilfrid는 Cooper 할머니를 가장 좋아했다.
③ Cooper 할머니는 Wilfrid에게 자신의 모든 비밀을 말했다.
④ Wilfrid의 어머니는 Cooper 할머니가 불쌍하다고 말했다.
⑤ Cooper 할머니는 기억을 잃어버렸다.

[16~18] 다음 글을 읽고 물음에 답하시오.

Wilfrid wanted to know more, so he went to his neighbors.

Ms. Jordan was ⓐenjoying the sunlight.

"What's a memory?" he asked.

"Something warm, my child," she said.

Ms. Mitchell was reading a cartoon.

"What's a memory?" he asked.

"Something that brings you laughter," she said.

Mr. Hunter was cleaning his medal.

"It's something as precious as gold, young man," he said.

16 위 글의 밑줄 친 ⓐenjoying과 문법적 쓰임이 다른 것을 모두 고르시오.

① Playing soccer is good for your health.

② I saw her crying in her room.

③ He is a walking dictionary.

④ Do you mind opening the window?

⑤ She came home running from school.

서답형

17 다음 문장에서 위 글의 내용과 다른 부분을 찾아서 고치시오.

> When Wilfrid went to his neighbors, Ms. Jordan was reading a cartoon and said that a memory is something that brings you laughter.

_____ ➡ _____

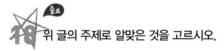

18 위 글의 주제로 알맞은 것을 고르시오.

① the way to find something warm

② the value of a memory

③ the meaning of a memory

④ the thing which is as precious as gold

⑤ how to get back your memory

[19~21] 다음 글을 읽고 물음에 답하시오.

She held the warm egg and whispered to Wilfrid, "Long ago, I found a small blue egg in my aunt's garden." She smiled at the sock puppet and remembered performing a puppet show for her sister. "My sister laughed a lot," said Ms. Cooper. She bounced the football to Wilfrid and remembered him. "Wilfrid? Wilfrid Gordon Parker! My friend!" She also remembered their secrets one by one.

The two smiled at each other. Ms. Cooper got her memory back ⓐ덕분에 the little boy with the same middle name as ___ⓑ___.

서답형

19 위 글의 밑줄 친 ⓐ의 우리말을 두 단어로 쓰시오.

➡ _____

서답형

20 위 글의 빈칸 ⓑ에 she를 알맞은 형태로 쓰시오.

➡ _____

21 위 글의 요지로 알맞은 것을 고르시오.

① 따뜻한 달걀은 기억력 회복에 좋다.

② Cooper 할머니는 여동생에게 인형극을 공연해 주었다.

③ Cooper 할머니의 제일 친한 친구는 Wilfrid이다.

④ Cooper 할머니는 Wilfrid와 공놀이 하는 것을 좋아했다.

⑤ Cooper 할머니는 Wilfrid 덕분에 기억을 다시 찾게 되었다.

[22~24] 다음 글을 읽고 물음에 답하시오.

So Wilfrid went back home to look for memories for Ms. Cooper. He went into the hen house and took a fresh, warm egg ⓐ암탉이 품고 있던. Next, he looked for his sock puppet. It always brought laughter to his parents. Finally, he found his football in his toy box. It was as precious as gold to him.

서답형

22 Wilfrid가 Ms. Cooper에게 주려고 찾은 물건들을 다음 (A)~(C)로 분류하여 각각 우리말로 쓰시오.

➡ (A) 따뜻한 것: _____

(B) 웃음을 가져다주는 것: _____

(C) 소중한 것: _____

서답형

23 위 글의 밑줄 친 ⓐ의 우리말을 네 단어로 쓰시오.

➡ _____

24 위 글을 읽고 알 수 <u>없는</u> 것을 고르시오.

① the reason Wilfrid went back home

② the reason Wilfrid went into the hen house

③ the thing which always brought laughter to Wilfrid's parents

④ the reason the football was as precious as gold to Wilfrid

⑤ the things which Wilfrid found for Ms. Cooper.

[25~27] 다음 글을 읽고 물음에 답하시오.

(①) Wilfrid Gordon Parker is a little boy and he is friends with the old people at the nursing home. (②) His favorite person is Ms. Nancy Gordon Cooper because she has the same middle name as Wilfrid.

(③) He asks everyone he knows about the meaning of a memory. (④) Wilfrid finds a fresh egg for warmth, a sock puppet for laughter, and his precious football. (⑤) When he gives ⓐthem to Ms. Cooper, she gets her memory back.

25 위 글의 흐름으로 보아, 주어진 문장이 들어가기에 가장 적절한 곳은?

One day, Wilfrid hears from his parents that Ms. Cooper has lost her memory.

① 　　② 　　③ 　　④ 　　⑤

서답형

26 위 글의 밑줄 친 ⓐthem이 가리키는 것을 본문에서 찾아 쓰시오.

➡ _____

_____

27 위 글을 읽고 대답할 수 <u>없는</u> 질문은?

① Does Wilfrid get along well with the old people at the nursing home?

② Who is Wilfrid's favorite person in the nursing home?

③ What do Wilfrid's parents say?

④ Does Wilfrid know the meaning of a memory?

⑤ Why is the football precious to Wilfrid?

[01~03] 다음 글을 읽고 물음에 답하시오.

Wilfrid Gordon Parker was a little boy ① who lived next to a nursing home. He liked all the people ②who lived there. But his favorite person was Ms. Nancy Gordon Cooper because her middle name was the same as ③him. He told her all his secrets.

One day, Wilfrid's parents were talking about Ms. Cooper.

"Poor old lady," said his mother.

"Why is she a poor old lady?" asked Wilfrid.

"Because ④she's lost her memory," said his father.

"⑤What's a memory?" asked Wilfrid.

"ⓐIt is something you remember," said his father.

01 위 글의 밑줄 친 ①~⑤ 중 어법상 틀린 것을 찾아 고치시오.

_____ ➡ _____

02 위 글의 밑줄 친 문장 ⓐ에 생략된 단어를 넣어 문장을 다시 쓰시오.

➡ _____

03 본문의 내용과 일치하도록 다음 빈칸에 알맞은 단어를 쓰시오.

Wilfrid liked Ms. Cooper most because she had _____ _____ _____ _____ as he did.

[04~06] 다음 글을 읽고, 물음에 답하시오.

One day, Wilfrid's parents were talking about Ms. Cooper.

"Poor old lady," said his mother.

"Why is she a poor old lady?" asked Wilfrid.

"Because ⓐshe's lost her memory," said his father.

"What's a memory?" asked Wilfrid.

"ⓑIt is something you remember," said his father.

04 다음 질문에 대한 알맞은 대답을 주어진 단어로 시작하여 쓰시오. (4 단어)

Q: Why does Wilfrid's mother say that Ms. Cooper is a poor old lady?

A: Because _____ .

➡ _____

05 위 글의 밑줄 친 ⓐ를 다음과 같이 바꿔 쓸 때 빈칸에 들어 갈 알맞은 말을 쓰시오.

➡ she lost her memory and she _____ it now.

06 위 글의 밑줄 친 ⓑIt이 가리키는 것을 본문에서 찾아 쓰시오.

➡ _____

[07~09] 다음 글을 읽고 물음에 답하시오.

Wilfrid wanted to know more, so he went to his neighbors.

Ms. Jordan was enjoying the sunlight.

"What's a memory?" he asked.

ⓐ"Something warm, my child," she said.

Ms. Mitchell was reading a cartoon.

"What's a memory?" he asked.

ⓑ"Something that brings you laughter," she said.

Mr. Hunter was cleaning his medal.

ⓒ"It's something as precious as gold, young man," he said.

So Wilfrid went back (A)[to home / home] to look (B)[at / for] memories for Ms. Cooper. He went into the hen house and took a fresh, warm egg from under a hen. Next, he looked for his sock puppet. It always (C)[brought / took] laughter to his parents. Finally, he found his football in his toy box. It was as precious as gold to him.

07 다음 빈칸 (a)~(d)에 알맞은 단어를 넣어, 위 글의 ⓐ~ⓒ를 듣고 Wilfrid가 한 행동과 그 이유를 완성하시오.

ⓐ He went into the hen house and took a fresh, _____(a)_____ because it was warm.

ⓑ He looked for his sock puppet because it always brought his parents _____(b)_____.

ⓒ He found his _____(c)_____ in his toy box because it was as _____(d)_____ as gold to him.

➡ (a) _____ (b) _____
   (c) _____ (d) _____

08 위 글의 괄호 (A)~(C)에서 문맥이나 어법상 알맞은 낱말을 골라 쓰시오.

➡ (A) _____ (B) _____ (C) _____

09 본문의 내용과 일치하도록 다음 빈칸에 알맞은 단어를 쓰시오.

Wilfrid's parents always laughed when they saw _____ _____ _____.

[10~12] 다음 글을 읽고, 물음에 답하시오.

She held the warm egg and _____ⓐ_____ to Wilfrid, "Long ago, I found a small blue egg in my aunt's garden." She smiled at the sock puppet and ⓑ자기 여동생에게 인형극을 공연해 주었던 것을 기억해 냈다. "My sister laughed a lot," said Ms. Cooper. She bounced the football to Wilfrid and remembered him. "Wilfrid? Wilfrid Gordon Parker! My friend!" She also remembered their secrets one by one.

The two smiled at each other. Ms. Cooper got her memory back thanks to the little boy with the same middle name as hers.

10 주어진 영영풀이를 참고하여 빈칸 ⓐ에 철자 w로 시작하는 단어를 알맞은 형태로 쓰시오.

to say something very quietly, using your breath rather than your throat, so that only one person can hear you

➡ _____

11 위 글의 밑줄 친 ⓑ의 우리말에 맞게 한 단어를 보충하여, 주어진 어휘를 알맞게 배열하시오.

for / a puppet show / her sister / remembered

➡ _____

12 다음 문장에서 위 글의 내용과 다른 부분을 찾아서 고치시오.

Ms. Cooper got her memory back thanks to the little boy who had the same first name as hers.

_____ ➡ _____

구석구석

Express Yourself

- On May 29, 2017, we went to India. This is a painting that we bought in the
  날짜 앞에 on   목적격 관계대명사
  market. I'll never forget the experience.

- We took pictures of Korean traditional dancers. We saw them at the town
  take a picture: 사진을 찍다   Korean traditional dancers
  festival.

- On June 7, 2017, we arrived in Laos. We met a girl who was wearing a
  날짜 앞에 on   주격 관계대명사
  beautiful dress. I'll never forget the experience.
                              라오스에서 아름다운 옷을 입고 있는 소녀를 만난 것

- We saw a rock. It looked like a queen's head.
                       look like+명사: ~처럼 보이다

구문해설 • **bought**: buy의 과거 • **experience**: 경험 • **traditional** 전통적인 • **festival**: 축제
• **arrive in**: ~에 도착하다

Do It Yourself

I'd like to tell you about a student teacher I can't forget.
                            목적격 관계대명사 who[whom. that] 생략
That person is Ms. Jeon.
지시형용사
Don't forget that you're great, Miso! Just go for it.
            명사절을 이끄는 접속사   명령문
This is the bookmark that she gave to me on the last day. When I feel stressed,
                    목적격 관계대명사   스트레스를 받는 것이므로 과거분사를 사용
I always look at this.

구문해설 • **go for it**: 단호히 목적을 추구하다, 한 번 해보다

Link to the World

- There are a lot of active seniors who share their knowledge and talents.
                                   주격 관계대명사절로 선행사 active seniors를 수식한다.
- Mr. Kim in Busan is a smart farmer and teaches people about farming.
                              동사 is와 병렬 형태로 단수 동사 teaches를 사용한다.
- Ms. Lee was a science teacher in the past. Now she works in a park to teach
                              to teach는 부사적 용법의 부정사로 '~하기 위해'의 의미를 가지고 있다.
  children about plants and birds.

- In Ms. Choi's cooking class, young people learn to make *gimchi* and Korean
                                            learn의 목적어 자리에 사용된 명사적 용법의 부정사다.
  hot pepper sauce.

구문해설 • **a lot of** 많은 • **active** 활동적인, 활발한 • **senior** 노인 • **knowledge** 지식
• **talent** 재능 • **farming** 농사 • **past** 과거

해석

2017년 5월 29일에 우리는 인도에 갔다. 이것은 우리가 시장에서 산 그림이다. 나는 그 경험을 결코 잊지 못할 것이다.
우리는 한국 전통 무용수들의 사진을 찍었다. 우리는 그들을 마을 축제에서 보았다.
2017년 6월 7일에 우리는 라오스에 도착했다. 우리는 아름다운 옷을 입고 있는 한 소녀를 만났다. 나는 그 경험을 결코 잊지 못할 것이다.
우리는 바위를 보았다. 그것은 여왕의 머리처럼 생겼다.

나는 잊을 수 없는 교생 선생님에 대해서 너희들에게 말하고 싶다.
그분은 전 선생님이시다.
"네가 훌륭하다는 걸 잊지 마. 미소야! 목적하는 것을 해보렴."
이건 그분이 마지막 날 내게 주신 책갈피다. 나는 스트레스를 받을 때면, 언제나 이것을 본다.

자신의 지식과 재능을 나누는 활동적인 어르신들이 많이 계시다.
부산의 김 선생님은 스마트 농부이신데 사람들에게 농사에 관한 것을 가르치신다.
이 선생님은 이전에 과학 선생님이셨다. 지금은 공원에서 일하시며 아이들에게 식물과 새에 관해서 가르치신다.
최 여사님의 요리 교실에서는 젊은이들이 김치와 한국의 고추장을 만드는 것을 배운다.

Words & Expressions

01 다음 주어진 두 단어의 관계가 같도록 빈칸에 알맞은 단어를 쓰시오.

> together : apart = general : _____

02 다음 대화의 빈칸 ⓐ와 ⓑ에 들어갈 단어로 바르게 짝지어진 것은?

> G: Do you remember Mr. Kim, our 6th grade teacher?
> B: Of course. He wore ___ⓐ___ thick glasses.
> G: Guess ___ⓑ___? He moved to a new school in February this year.
> B: I didn't know that. Let's visit him together.
> G: Okay. Good idea.

① super – how
② always – how
③ always – what
④ superly – what
⑤ super – what

03 다음 밑줄 친 부분의 뜻이 잘못된 것은?

① Let's <u>take some pictures</u> with her.
　　　　사진을 몇 장 찍다
② <u>What else</u> do you remember about her?
　다른 무엇
③ Something that brings you <u>laughter</u> is memory.
　　　　　　　　　　　　　웃음
④ He went back home to <u>look for</u> memories for her.
　　　　　　　　　　보다
⑤ She started to remember her <u>past</u>.
　　　　　　　　　　　　과거

04 다음 영영 풀이에 해당하는 것을 고르시오.

> to do something to entertain people by acting a play or playing a piece of music

① cut
② throw
③ perform
④ laugh
⑤ remember

05 다음 문장의 빈칸에 들어갈 알맞은 단어를 쓰시오.

> We sat _____ to each other.

➡ _____

06 빈칸에 들어갈 말로 알맞은 것은?

> Nancy Gordon Cooper's middle name was _____ as Wilfrid Gordon Parker's.

① so
② the same
③ like
④ different
⑤ strange

Conversation

07 다음 대화의 빈칸에 들어갈 말로 어색한 것은?

> M: Hi, Minjun. So, you learned to cut holes in the board last time. Let's practice again now.
> B: Okay. _____. Is this right?

① Let me think
② Let's see
③ Just a moment
④ Take your time
⑤ Let's see

08 다음 대화를 알맞은 순서로 배열한 것은?

> (A) Of course. We practiced super hard.
> (B) I have some funny pictures from it on my phone.
> (C) Do you remember the singing competition last year?
> (D) That's great!

① (A) – (B) – (C) – (D)
② (B) – (A) – (C) – (D)
③ (B) – (C) – (A) – (D)
④ (C) – (A) – (B) – (D)
⑤ (C) – (B) – (A) – (D)

[09~10] 다음 대화를 읽고 물음에 답하시오.

> (1)
> G: Do you remember the hot air balloon? We rode ⓐit in Turkey.
> M: Of course. It ____(A)____ an elephant.
> (2)
> G: Do you remember the rock?
> M: Is it the one in Taiwan?
> G: Right.
> M: I remember ⓑit. It ____(B)____ a queen's head.

09 대화의 흐름상 빈칸 (A)와 (B)에 공통으로 들어갈 알맞은 어구를 쓰시오.

➡ _____

10 위 대화의 밑줄 친 ⓐ와 ⓑ가 각각 가리키는 것을 찾아 쓰시오.

➡ ⓐ _____
  ⓑ _____

[11~12] 다음 대화를 읽고 물음에 답하시오.

> G: Do you remember Ms. Park, (A)혼자 사는 할머니?
> B: Of course. We ⓐthrew her a birthday party last year.
> G: And she cooked *japchae* ⓑfor us. She put some chicken ⓒin them.
> B: Right. It was delicious. And we played card games together. Do you remember that?
> G: Yes. She won all the rounds. She's really good at games.
> B: When are we ⓓgoing to see her next, Mina?
> G: Let me see. Next Saturday.
> B: ⓔLet's take some pictures with her this time.
> G: Great idea, Junsu.

11 위 대화의 밑줄 (A)의 우리말에 맞게 주어진 단어를 알맞은 순서로 배열하시오.

> lives, the, old, who, lady, alone

➡ _____

12 위 대화의 밑줄 친 ⓐ~ⓔ 중 어법상 어색한 것은?

① ⓐ ② ⓑ ③ ⓒ ④ ⓓ ⑤ ⓔ

Grammar

13 다음 빈칸에 알맞은 말을 모두 고르시오.

> My grandfather remembers all the people _____ he met in Gyeongju National Park last year.

① who   ② whose   ③ whom
④ which   ⑤ that

14 다음 밑줄 친 부분의 쓰임이 나머지 넷과 다른 것은?

① Wilfrid was a little boy <u>who</u> lived next to a nursing home.

② This is my favorite painting <u>which</u> was painted by Klimt.

③ Kim is satisfied with her cell phone <u>that</u> she bought the previous day.

④ The cute baby <u>who</u> has golden hair is sleeping on the bed.

⑤ I stayed at a hotel in Kuala Lumpur <u>which</u> had big rooms.

15 관계대명사를 이용하여 만든 다음 문장을 원래의 두 문장으로 쓰시오.

> This is the bookmark that she gave to me on the last day.

➡ _____

_____

16 두 문장을 관계대명사를 사용하여 한 문장으로 쓰시오.

(1) • Jiwon is wearing the ribbon.

    • Mira bought it for her.

    ➡ _____

_____

(2) • Harry chats with the man.

    • Harry made friends with him on line.

    ➡ _____

_____

(3) • Ginseng is a food.

    • It can make you stay healthy.

    ➡ _____

_____

(4) • We saw many children.

    • They were playing soccer together.

    ➡ _____

_____

17 다음 빈칸에 들어갈 수 있는 말이 나머지와 다른 하나는?

① Did you meet the girl _____ came to meet you?

② There lived a princess _____ name was Snow White.

③ Alexander sang the song _____ he liked most.

④ Nancy looked for the medal _____ she won at the race.

⑤ The girl _____ is taking a walk is my daughter.

18 다음 중 어법상 바르지 <u>않은</u> 것은?

① I want to marry someone whom trusts me.

② Take a look at the birds that are flying high in the sky.

③ Diana has two puppies which are brown and white.

④ I know a lady who has the same middle name as mine.

⑤ I know the girl whom you had lunch with at school today.

19 다음 중 어법상 옳은 것은?

① I like Christine from that I got a letter.

② A mentor is a person whom we meet for advice.

③ Dan has two dogs which has brown hair.

④ We saw a rock who looked like a queen's head.

⑤ A computer is a thing whom we do many things with.

20 다음 중 두 문장을 한 문장으로 만들 때 의미가 <u>다른</u> 하나는?

① I want to be a hiphop dancer. A hiphop dancer is loved by many people.
➡ I want to be a hiphop dancer who is loved by many people.

② I will catch the train. It leaves for San Francisco.
➡ I will catch the train that leaves for San Francisco.

③ Mom bought me a present. I liked it very much.
➡ Mom liked a present that bought for me.

④ Mariel is a You-tuber. She is Estonian.
➡ Mariel who is Estonian is a You-tuber.

⑤ Jack lives with Julia. He loves her a lot.
➡ Jack lives with Julia whom he loves a lot.

Reading

[21~23] 다음 글을 읽고 물음에 답하시오.

Wilfrid wanted ⓐ<u>to know</u> more, so he went to ①<u>his</u> neighbors.
Ms. Jordan was enjoying the sunlight.
"What's a memory?" he asked.
"Something warm, ②<u>my child</u>," she said.
Ms. Mitchell was reading a cartoon.
"What's a memory?" ③<u>he</u> asked.
"Something that brings you laughter," she said.
Mr. Hunter was cleaning his medal.
"ⓑ그건 금처럼 소중한 거지, ④<u>young man</u>," ⑤<u>he</u> said.

---

21 위 글의 밑줄 친 ⓐ<u>to know</u>와 to부정사의 용법이 같은 것을 모두 고르시오.

① He wished <u>to go</u> to Italy someday.
② She grew up <u>to be</u> a great pianist.
③ I tried <u>to make</u> the dinner in an hour.
④ Do you know the time <u>to meet</u> them?
⑤ I felt very sad <u>to see</u> the sight.

---

22 밑줄 친 ①~⑤ 중에서 가리키는 대상이 나머지 넷과 <u>다른</u> 것은?

①　　　　②　　　　③　　　　④　　　　⑤

---

23 위 글의 밑줄 친 ⓑ의 우리말에 맞게 주어진 어휘를 이용하여 6 단어로 영작하시오.

something, precious

➡ _____

[24~26] 다음 글을 읽고 물음에 답하시오.

Wilfrid Gordon Parker was a little boy who lived next to a nursing home. He liked all the people who lived there. But ⓐ<u>his</u> favorite person was Ms. Nancy Gordon Cooper because her middle name was the same as ⓑ <u>his</u>. He told her all ⓒ<u>his</u> secrets.
(①) One day, Wilfrid's parents were talking about Ms. Cooper.
(②) "Poor old lady," said ⓓ<u>his</u> mother.
(③) "Why is she a poor old lady?" asked Wilfrid.
(④) "Because Ⓐ<u>she's lost</u> her memory," said his father.
(⑤) "It is something you remember," said ⓔ <u>his</u> father.

24 위 글의 밑줄 친 ⓐ~ⓔ 중에서 문법적 쓰임이 나머지 넷과 다른 것은?

① ⓐ   ② ⓑ   ③ ⓒ   ④ ⓓ   ⑤ ⓔ

25 위 글의 흐름으로 보아, 주어진 문장이 들어가기에 가장 적절한 곳은?

> "What's a memory?" asked Wilfrid.

①   ②   ③   ④   ⑤

26 위 글의 밑줄 친 ⒜와 현재완료의 용법이 같은 것을 고르시오.

① I have never seen it before.
② She has been here since last year.
③ Tom has gone to New York.
④ How long have you known him?
⑤ He has already finished the work.

[27~28] 다음 글을 읽고 물음에 답하시오.

So Wilfrid went back home to look for memories for Ms. Cooper. He went into the hen house and took a fresh, warm egg from under a hen. (A)[To begin with / Next], he looked for his sock puppet. It always brought laughter to his parents. Finally, he found his football in his toy box. ⓐIt was as precious as gold to him.

Wilfrid went to Ms. Cooper and gave her the things one by one. "(B)[How / What] a strange, sweet child!" thought Ms. Cooper, "He's brought all these wonderful things." Then she started to remember her (C)[future / past].

27 위 글의 괄호 (A)~(C)에서 문맥이나 어법상 알맞은 낱말을 골라 쓰시오.

➡ (A) _____ (B) _____ (C) _____

28 위 글의 밑줄 친 ⓐIt이 가리키는 것을 본문에서 찾아 쓰시오.

➡ _____

[29~30] 다음 글을 읽고 물음에 답하시오.

She held the warm egg and whispered to Wilfrid, "Long ago, I found a small blue egg in my aunt's garden." She smiled at the sock puppet and remembered performing a puppet show for her sister. "My sister laughed a lot," said Ms. Cooper. She bounced the football to Wilfrid and remembered him. "Wilfrid? Wilfrid Gordon Parker! My friend!" She also remembered their secrets one by one.

The two smiled at each other. Ms. Cooper got her memory back thanks to the little boy with _____ⓐ_____ middle name __ⓑ__ her.

29 위 글의 빈칸 ⓐ와 ⓑ에 들어갈 알맞은 말을 고르시오.

① the usual – with
② the same – as
③ the exact – to
④ the same – for
⑤ the similar – as

30 위 글의 내용과 일치하지 <u>않는</u> 것은?

① 오래 전에 Cooper 할머니는 이모님 댁 정원에서 작고 푸른 알을 찾았다.
② Cooper 할머니는 작은 양말 인형을 보고 자기 여동생에게 인형극을 공연해 주었던 것을 기억해 냈다
③ Wilfrid가 축구공을 바닥에 튀게 해서 Cooper 할머니에게 던져 주었다.
④ Cooper 할머니는 Wilfrid와의 비밀들을 하나씩 기억했다.
⑤ Cooper 할머니는 Wilfrid 덕분에 기억을 되찾았다.

01 출제율 90%

다음 짝지어진 단어의 관계가 같도록 빈칸에 알맞은 말을 쓰시오.

> delicious : tasty = _____ : particular

02 출제율 100%

우리말에 맞게 빈칸에 알맞은 단어를 쓰시오.

> • 이것은 금메달이야. 우리가 경주에 참가해서 그것을 땄지.
> (A) This is a gold medal. We _____ it at the race.
> • 그는 요양원 옆에 사는 어린 소년이었다.
> (B) He was a little boy _____ lived _____ _____ a nursing home.

03 출제율 90%

다음은 활동적인 노후 생활에 관한 글이다. 알맞은 단어를 고르시오.

> • There are a lot of active seniors who (A)[share / lack] their knowledge and talents.
> • Ms. Lee was a science teacher in the past. Now she works in a park to (B) [learn / teach] children about plants and birds.
> • Mr. Kim in Busan is a smart (C) [businessman / farmer] and teaches people about farming.

	(A)	(B)	(C)
①	lack	learn	businessman
②	lack	teach	businessman
③	share	learn	farmer
④	share	teach	farmer
⑤	share	teach	businessman

04 출제율 95%

다음 영영 풀이에 해당하는 단어는?

> an empty space in an object, usually with an opening to the object's surface

① plant   ② system
③ hole   ④ space
⑤ bottle

05 출제율 90%

다음 대화의 내용과 일치하지 <u>않는</u> 것은?

> Ariel: Do you remember Ms. Park, the old lady who lives alone?
> Ben: Of course. We threw her a birthday party last year.
> Ariel: And she cooked *japchae* for us. She put some chicken in it.
> Ben: Right. It was delicious. And we played card games together. Do you remember that?
> Ariel: Yes. She won all the rounds. She's really good at games.
> Ben: When are we going to see her next, Ariel?
> Ariel: Let me see. Next Saturday.
> Ben: Let's take some pictures with her this time.
> Ariel: Great idea, Ben.

① Ariel and Ben threw a party for Ms. Park.
② Ms. Park lives alone.
③ The food that Ms. Park cooked was delicious.
④ Ariel and Ben played card games with Ms. Park.
⑤ Ben hopes to take pictures with Ariel.

[06~07] 다음 대화를 읽고 물음에 답하시오.

> **B:** Do you remember Ms. Kang, @the school nurse? (①)
> **G:** Sure. (②) She was nice ⓑto everyone.
> **B:** Guess what? She's ⓒgetting married next month. (③)
> **G:** Wow! (④)
> **B:** ⓓLet me to see. (⑤) What about ⓔmaking a special album?
> **G:** That's a good idea.

06 다음 주어진 문장이 들어갈 위치로 알맞은 것은?

> What shall we do for her?

① ② ③ ④ ⑤

07 위 대화의 밑줄 친 @~ⓔ 중 어법상 어색한 것은?

① @ ② ⓑ ③ ⓒ ④ ⓓ ⑤ ⓔ

08 다음 대화의 빈칸에 들어갈 말로 알맞은 것은?

> **A:** _____
> **B:** Of course. We played fun games.
> **A:** I have some funny pictures from it on my phone.
> **B:** That's great!

① Let me see.
② Do you remember the field trip last year?
③ Do you remember my aunt?
④ Long time no see! How have you been?
⑤ Do you still play the game?

09 다음 대화의 빈칸에 들어갈 말로 알맞은 것은?

> **G:** Do you remember Mr. Kim, our 6th grade teacher?
> **B:** Of course. He wore super thick glasses.
> **G:** Guess what? He moved to a new school in February this year.
> **B:** _____ Let's visit him together.
> **G:** Okay. Good idea.

① I didn't know that.
② How do you know that?
③ That sounds great.
④ I'm happy to hear that.
⑤ Where is he now?

10 다음 대화의 빈칸 (A)와 (B)에 들어갈 말로 알맞은 것은?

> **G:** Do you ___(A)___ Mr. Kim, our 6th grade teacher?
> **B:** Of course. He wore super thick glasses.
> **G:** Guess what? He moved to a new school in February this year.
> **B:** I didn't know that. ___(B)___ visit him together.
> **G:** Okay. Good idea.

① remember – Let's
② forget – Let me see
③ remember – How about
④ remember – What about
⑤ forget – Let's

11 밑줄 친 who의 용법이 나머지와 다른 하나는?

① He had a son who became a teacher.
② The boy who went out was Josh.
③ I know the boy who Tim met yesterday.
④ The lady who visited Italy is Cindy.
⑤ Rick is my friend who lives in Seoul.

12 밑줄 친 부분 중 어법상 어색한 것은?

> I ①took ②some photos ③of a man and his car ④which ⑤were in the park.

13 빈칸에 공통으로 들어갈 단어는?

> • Charlotte is the B-boy dancer _____ appeared on TV.
> • The dress _____ Anne is wearing is pretty.

① whose ② who ③ that
④ which ⑤ what

14 잘못된 부분을 바르게 고쳐 문장을 다시 쓰시오

(1) Jieun is the girl whose I like the best.

➡ _____

(2) These are the pictures who were taken by my brother.

➡ _____

_____

[15~17] 다음 글을 읽고 물음에 답하시오.

Wilfrid wanted to know more, so he went to his neighbors.
Ms. Jordan was enjoying the sunlight.
"What's a memory?" he asked.
"(A)[Warm something / Something warm], my child," she said.
Ms. Mitchell was reading a cartoon.
"What's a memory?" he asked.
"Something @that brings (B)[you / to you] laughter," she said.
Mr. Hunter was cleaning his medal.
"It's something (C)[as / so] precious as gold, young man," he said.

15 위 글의 괄호 (A)~(C)에서 어법상 알맞은 것을 골라 쓰시오.

➡ (A) _____ (B) _____
(C) _____

16 위 글의 밑줄 친 @that과 문법적 쓰임이 같은 것을 모두 고르시오.

① What's that over there?
② I like the bag that is on the floor.
③ He said that the story was true.
④ Can you see that dog over there?
⑤ It's the best novel that I've ever read.

17 위 글의 내용과 일치하지 않는 것은?

① Jordan 할머니는 햇볕을 즐기고 있었다.
② Jordan 할머니는 기억이란 따뜻한 것이라고 말했다.
③ Mitchell 할머니는 기억이란 너에게 웃음을 가져다주는 것이라고 말했다.
④ Hunter 할아버지가 그의 메달을 닦고 있었다.
⑤ Hunter 할아버지는 금이 기억보다 더 소중하다고 말했다.

[18~19] 다음 글을 읽고 물음에 답하시오.

So Wilfrid went back home to look for memories for Ms. Cooper. He went into the hen house and took a fresh, warm egg from under a hen. Next, he looked for his sock puppet. It always brought laughter to his parents. @Finally, he found his football in his toy box. It was as precious as gold to him.

18 📝 출제율 100%

위 글의 밑줄 친 ⓐFinally와 바꿔 쓸 수 있는 고르시오.

① At first   ② In addition
③ At last   ④ Therefore
⑤ Above all

19 📝 출제율 90%

다음 질문에 대한 알맞은 대답을 영어로 쓰시오. (7 단어)

> **Q**: Where did Wilfrid find his football?
> **A**: _____

➡ _____

[20~22] 다음 글을 읽고 물음에 답하시오.

So Wilfrid went back home to look for memories for Ms. Cooper. He went into the hen house and took a fresh, warm egg from under a hen. Next, he looked for his sock puppet. It always brought laughter to his parents. Finally, he found his football in his toy box. It was as precious as gold to him.

Wilfrid went to Ms. Cooper and gave her the things ⓐ하나하나씩. "ⓑWhat a strange, sweet child!" thought Ms. Cooper, "He's brought ⓒall these wonderful things." Then she started to remember her past.

20 📝 출제율 95%

위 글의 밑줄 친 ⓐ의 우리말을 세 단어로 쓰시오.

➡ _____

21 📝 출제율 85%

위 글의 밑줄 친 ⓑ를 How로 시작하여 바꿔 쓰시오.

➡ _____

22 📝 출제율 95%

다음 중 위 글의 밑줄 친 ⓒ에 해당하지 않는 것을 모두 고르시오.

① the hen house   ② a fresh, warm egg
③ his sock puppet   ④ his football
⑤ his toy box

[23~25] 다음 글을 읽고 물음에 답하시오.

She held the warm egg and whispered to Wilfrid, "Long ago, I found a small blue egg in my aunt's garden." She smiled ___ⓐ___ the sock puppet and remembered performing a puppet show for her sister. (①) "My sister laughed a lot," said Ms. Cooper. (②) "Wilfrid? Wilfrid Gordon Parker! My friend!" (③) She also remembered ⓑtheir secrets one by one.
(④) The two smiled ___ⓐ___ each other. (⑤) Ms. Cooper got her memory back thanks to the little boy ___ⓒ___ the same middle name as hers.

23 📝 출제율 85%

위 글의 흐름으로 보아, 주어진 문장이 들어가기에 가장 적절한 곳은?

> She bounced the football to Wilfrid and remembered him.

①   ②   ③   ④   ⑤

24 📝 출제율 100%

위 글의 빈칸 ⓐ와 ⓒ에 들어갈 전치사가 바르게 짝지어진 것은?

① for – with   ② in – by
③ in – for   ④ at – with
⑤ at – to

25 📝 출제율 95%

위 글의 밑줄 친 ⓑtheir가 가리키는 것을 영어로 쓰시오.
(소유격으로 쓸 것)

➡ _____

01 다음은 노래 경연대회 추억에 관한 대화다. 대화의 흐름상 알맞은 말을 빈칸에 쓰시오.

> B: _____ last year?
>
> G: Of course. We practiced super hard.
>
> B: I have some funny pictures from it on my phone.
>
> G: That's great!

➡ _____

02 다음은 Mina와 Junsu가 작년에 갔던 봉사활동과 올해 갈 예정인 봉사활동에 관한 대화다. 대화를 읽고 아래 문장을 완성하시오.

> G: Do you remember Ms. Park, the old lady who lives alone?
>
> B: Of course. We threw her a birthday party last year.
>
> G: And she cooked *japchae* for us. She put some chicken in it.
>
> B: Right. It was delicious. And we played card games together. Do you remember that?
>
> G: Yes. She won all the rounds. She's really good at games.
>
> B: When are we going to see her next, Mina?
>
> G: Let me see. Next Saturday.
>
> B: Let's take some pictures with her this time.
>
> G: Great idea, Junsu.

> Last Year
> Mina and Junsu _____ _____
> _____ for Ms. Park. And she _____
> *japchae* for them. It was _____. After
> that, they played _____ _____
> together.

> This Year
> They are going to visit Ms. Park _____
> _____. They are going to _____
> _____ with her.

03 다음 대화의 밑줄 친 우리말에 맞게 주어진 어휘를 이용하여 영어로 쓰시오.

> B: Do you remember Ms. Kang, the school nurse?
>
> G: Sure. She was nice to everyone.
>
> B: Guess what? (A)그분이 다음 달에 결혼하셔. (is, get)
>
> G: Wow! What shall we do for her?
>
> B: Let me see. (B)특별한 앨범을 만들어 드리는 게 어떨까? (what about, a special)
>
> G: That's a good idea.

➡ (A) _____
   (B) _____

04 다음 두 문장을 관계대명사를 이용하여 한 문장으로 바꿔 쓰시오.

(1) • This is a picture.
    • We bought it at the market.
    ➡ _____
      _____

(2) • That is the house.
    • Tom was born in the house.
    ➡ _____
      _____

(3) • Marilyn is talking with a man.
    • He is wearing a thick coat.
    ➡ _____
      _____

ⓐWilfrid wanted to know more, so he went to his neighbors.

Ms. Jordan was enjoying the sunlight.

"What's a memory?" he asked.

"Something warm, my child," she said.

Ms. Mitchell was reading a cartoon.

"What's a memory?" he asked.

"Something that brings you laughter," she said.

Mr. Hunter was cleaning his medal.

"It's something as precious as gold, young man," he said.

05 위 글의 밑줄 친 문장 ⓐ를 as로 시작하여 바꿔 쓰시오.

➡ _____

_____

06 다음 질문에 대한 알맞은 대답을 주어진 단어로 시작하여 쓰시오.

> Q: What did Wilfrid's neighbors say about memory?

➡ • Ms. Jordan: It's _____.

• Ms. Mitchell: It's _____

_____.

• Mr. Hunter: It's _____

_____.

07 위 글의 내용을 다음과 같이 정리하고자 한다. 빈칸에 들어갈 알맞은 단어를 쓰시오.

> Wilfrid asked his three neighbors about the _____ of a memory because he wanted to know more about it.

She held the warm egg and whispered to Wilfrid, "Long ago, I found a small blue egg in my aunt's garden." ⓐShe smiled at the sock puppet and remembered to perform a puppet show for her sister. "My sister laughed a lot," said Ms. Cooper. She bounced the football to Wilfrid and remembered him. "Wilfrid? Wilfrid Gordon Parker! My friend!" She also remembered their secrets one by one.

ⓑThe two smiled at each other. Ms. Cooper got her memory back ⓒ자신의 것과 같은 가운데 이름을 가진 어린 소년 덕분으로.

08 위 글의 밑줄 친 ⓐ에서 어법상 틀린 부분을 찾아 고치시오.

_____ ➡ _____

09 위 글의 밑줄 친 ⓑThe two가 구체적으로 가리키는 것을 영어로 쓰시오.

➡ _____

10 위 글의 밑줄 친 ⓒ의 우리말에 맞게 주어진 어휘를 이용하여 12 단어로 영작하시오.

> with, as

➡ _____

_____

01 다음은 여행에 관한 두 사람의 기억에 관한 글이다. 〈보기〉처럼 여행지에서 한 일과 그에 관한 기억을 묻고 답하는 대화문을 완성하시오.

> 보기
>
> **A:** We won a gold medal in London. Do you remember that?
> **B:** Sure. / Of course. We won it at the race.

> 〈여행지〉
> London - This is a gold medal. / Turkey – We rode a hot air balloon.
> Taiwan – We saw a rock. / Korea – We took pictures of Korean traditional dancers.
> 〈기억〉
> We won it at the race. / It looked like an elephant.
> It looked like a queen's head. / We saw them at the town festival.

(1) _____

_____

(2) _____

_____

(3) _____

_____

02 관계대명사를 이용하여 자신이 하고 싶은 일을 설명하는 문장을 쓰시오.

> (1) I want to do something _____.
> (2) I want to do something _____.
> (3) I want to do something _____.
> (4) I want to do something _____.
> (5) I want to do something _____.

03 어린 시절의 추억에 관한 이야기를 바탕으로 추억이 담긴 미니북에 쓸 내용을 완성하시오.

> I'd like to tell you about a student teacher I can't forget. That person is Ms. Jeon.

> Don't forget (A)_____ you're great, Miso! Just go for it.
>
> This is the bookmark (B)_____ she gave to me on the last day. When I feel (C)_____,
> I always look (D)_____ this.

단원별 모의고사

01 다음 단어에 대한 영어 설명이 <u>어색한</u> 것은?

① alone: without other people
② hen: an adult female chicken
③ super: a main meal eaten in the evening
④ favorite: best liked or most enjoyed
⑤ puppet: a toy in the shape of a person or animal that you can move with strings or by putting your hand inside

02 다음 짝지어진 단어의 관계가 같도록 빈칸에 알맞은 말을 쓰시오.

> answer : reply = go into : _____

03 다음 영영풀이에 해당하는 단어를 고르시오.

> the name some people have between their first name and their last name

① middle name   ② surname
③ family name   ④ nickname
⑤ given name

04 다음 대화의 밑줄 친 ⓐ가 가리키는 대상을 찾아 영어로 쓰시오.

> A: Do you remember the field trip last year?
> B: Of course. We played fun games.
> A: I have some funny pictures from ⓐit on my phone.
> B: That's great!

➡ _____

05 빈칸 (A)와 (B)에 들어갈 알맞은 단어는?

> She smiled ___(A)___ the sock puppet and remembered ___(B)___ a puppet show for her sister.

   (A)   (B)
① on – to show
② at – showing
③ on – performing
④ for – to perform
⑤ at – performing

06 다음 대화의 빈칸에 들어갈 말로 알맞은 것은?

> B: Do you remember Ms. Lee?
> G: Ms. Lee? Who is she?
> B: She was our 4th grade English teacher.
> G: _____ She taught a lot of pop songs in her class.
> B: She was a good dancer, too.

① Do I know her?
② You're right. I forgot.
③ Now I remember.
④ I don't think she was my English teacher.
⑤ Sorry, I can't remember her.

07 다음 대화의 빈칸에 들어갈 말을 주어진 단어를 이용하여 두 단어의 영어로 쓰시오.

> A: Do you remember my birthday?
> B: _____ (let) It's June 3. Right?
> A: That's not right. It's June 13.

➡ _____

[08~09] 다음 대화를 읽고 물음에 답하시오.

G: Do you remember Ms. Park, the old lady who lives alone? (①)

B: Of course. We threw her a birthday party last year.

G: And she cooked *japchae* for us. She put some chicken in it. (②)

B: Right. It was delicious. And we played card games together. (③)

G: Yes. She won all the rounds. She's really good at games. (④)

B: When are we going to see her next, Mina?

G: Let me see. (⑤) Next Saturday.

B: Let's take some pictures with her this time.

G: Great idea, Junsu.

08 다음 주어진 문장이 들어갈 위치로 알맞은 것은?

> Do you remember that?

①   ②   ③   ④   ⑤

09 위 대화의 내용과 일치하는 것은?

① Mina visited her grandmother with Junsu.

② The old lady cooked chicken soup.

③ Mina as well as Ms. Park is good at games.

④ Mina and Junsu are going to visit Ms. Park.

⑤ Mina took many pictures with Ms. Park last year.

10 다음 두 사람의 대화가 어색한 것은?

① A: Do you remember the singing competition last year?
   B: Of course. We practiced super hard.

② A: Do you remember my birthday?
   B: Let me see.

③ A: Do you remember the field trip last year?
   B: Of course. I can't remember that.

④ A: Guess what? She's getting married next month.
   B: Wow! What shall we do for her?

⑤ A: Hello, Mr. Yang. This is Minji. Do you remember me?
   B: Sure, Minji. Thank you for calling.

11 다음 대화를 읽고 답할 수 없는 질문은?

> B: Do you remember Ms. Kang, the school nurse?
>
> G: Sure. She was nice to everyone.
>
> B: Guess what? She's getting married next month.
>
> G: Wow! What shall we do for her?
>
> B: Let me see. What about making a special album?
>
> G: That's a good idea.

① What is Ms. Kang?

② How was Ms. Kang to the students?

③ When is Ms. Kang going to get married?

④ What will they do for Ms. Kang?

⑤ When will they make a special album?

12 대화의 빈칸 (A)와 (B)에 들어갈 말로 자연스러운 것은?

> B: Do you remember Ms. Kang, the school nurse?
>
> G: Sure. She was nice to everyone.
>
> B: _____(A)_____ She's getting married next month.
>
> G: Wow! What shall we do for her?
>
> B: _____(B)_____ What about making a special album?
>
> G: That's a good idea.

① Let's see. – I don't know.

② Let's visit her – I don't know.

③ Guess what? – Let me see.

④ Really? – Guess what?

⑤ Just a moment. – Do you think so?

13 다음 중 밑줄 친 that이 관계대명사로 쓰인 것을 모두 고르시오.

① The trouble is that we are short of money.

② Jacky Rose is the pop singer that Jiwon likes.

③ She warned me that I should be more careful.

④ Paul gave me a purse that was made of leather.

⑤ No one can deny the fact that you are wrong.

14 다음 빈칸에 들어갈 알맞은 말을 모두 고르시오.

> Oliver whispered to his aunt _____ was sitting next to him.

① who   ② whose   ③ whom

④ which   ⑤ that

15 다음 주어진 글의 밑줄 친 부분의 쓰임이 어색한 것은?

① Do you remember Ms. Park, the old lady who lives alone?

② Do you like the dog that is chasing the cat?

③ The police are looking for the man and his car which caused the accident.

④ Bella is the smartest girl that I have ever met.

⑤ This is the ring which I bought for her.

[16~18] 다음 글을 읽고 물음에 답하시오.

> Wilfrid wanted to know more, so he went to his neighbors.
> Ms. Jordan was enjoying the sunlight.
> "What's a memory?" he asked.
> "Something warm, my child," she said.
> Ms. Mitchell was ⓐreading a cartoon.
> "What's a memory?" he asked.
> "ⓑSomething that bring you laughter," she said.
> Mr. Hunter was cleaning his medal.
> "It's something as precious as gold, young man," he said.

16 아래 〈보기〉에서 위 글의 밑줄 친 ⓐ와 문법적 쓰임이 같은 것의 개수를 고르시오.

> ┤ 보기 ├
> ① My hobby is reading a cartoon.
> ② Were you reading a cartoon during class?
> ③ Do you enjoy reading a cartoon?
> ④ The boy reading a cartoon is my friend.
> ⑤ She is fond of reading a cartoon.

① 1개   ② 2개   ③ 3개   ④ 4개   ⑤ 5개

17 위 글의 밑줄 친 ⓑ에서 어법상 틀린 부분을 찾아 고치시오.

_____ ➡ _____

18 위 글을 읽고 대답할 수 <u>없는</u> 질문은?

① Why did Wilfrid go to his neighbors?
② Who said that a memory is something warm?
③ What was Ms. Mitchell doing?
④ Why did Mr. Hunter get a medal?
⑤ What did Mr. Hunter say about a memory?

[19~21] 다음 글을 읽고 물음에 답하시오.

So Wilfrid went back home to look for memories for Ms. Cooper. He went into the hen house and took a fresh, warm egg from under a hen. Next, he looked for his sock puppet. ⓐIt always brought laughter to his parents. Finally, he found his football in his toy box. It was as precious as gold to him.

Wilfrid went to Ms. Cooper and gave her the things one by one. "What a strange, sweet child!" thought Ms. Cooper, "He's brought all these wonderful things." ⓑThen she started to remember her past.

19 위 글의 밑줄 친 ⓐ를 4형식으로 고치시오.

➡ _____

20 위 글의 밑줄 친 ⓑ를 다음과 같이 바꿔 쓸 때 빈칸에 들어갈 알맞은 말을 쓰시오.

➡ Then she started _____ her past.

21 위 글의 내용과 일치하지 <u>않는</u> 것은?

① Wilfrid는 닭장 안으로 들어가서 신선하고 따뜻한 달걀을 꺼냈다.
② Wilfrid의 양말 인형은 그의 부모님께 항상 큰 웃음을 안겨 주었다.
③ Wilfrid에게 장난감 상자는 축구공만큼이나 소중했다.
④ Cooper 할머니는 Wilfrid가 이상하면서도 귀여운 아이라고 생각했다.
⑤ Cooper 할머니는 자신의 과거를 기억해 내기 시작했다.

[22~23] 다음 글을 읽고 물음에 답하시오.

She held the warm egg and whispered to Wilfrid, "Long ago, I found a small blue egg in my aunt's garden." She smiled at the sock puppet and remembered performing a puppet show for her sister. "My sister laughed a lot," said Ms. Cooper. She bounced the football to Wilfrid and remembered him. "Wilfrid? Wilfrid Gordon Parker! My friend!" She also remembered their secrets ⓐone by one.

The two smiled at each other. Ms. Cooper got her memory back thanks to the little boy with the same middle name as ⓑhers.

22 위 글의 밑줄 친 ⓐone by one과 바꿔 쓸 수 있는 말을 고르시오.

① side by side   ② one another
③ one after another   ④ time after time
⑤ more and more

23 위 글의 밑줄 친 ⓑhers가 구체적으로 가리키는 것을 영어로 쓰시오.

➡ _____

Special

Little Red Writing Hood

Words & Expressions

Key Words

- **basket** [bǽskit] 몡 바구니
- **blow** [blou] 동 (입으로) 불다, (바람이) 불다
- **check** [tʃek] 동 점검하다
- **dangerous** [déindʒərəs] 혭 위험한
- **end** [end] 몡 끝, 마지막
- **excited** [iksáitid] 혭 신난
- **famous** [féiməs] 혭 유명한
- **follow** [fɑ́lou] 동 따라가다, 뒤따르다
- **front** [frʌnt] 몡 정면, 앞
- **hood** [hud] 몡 (외투 등에 달린) 모자
- **knock** [nɑk] 동 두드리다
- **laugh** [læf] 동 웃다
- **leave** [liːv] 동 떠나다

- **lose** [luːz] 동 잃어버리다, 지다
- **need** [niːd] 동 ~을 필요로 하다
- **piggy** [pígi] 몡 **pig**의 애칭 (*pl.* **piggies**)
- **please** [pliːz] 동 ~을 기쁘게 하다
- **road** [roud] 몡 길, 도로
- **safe** [seif] 혭 안전한
- **scene** [siːn] 몡 장면, 광경
- **shake** [ʃeik] 동 흔들리다
- **stop** [stɑp] 동 (~하는 것을) 막다, 그만두게 하다
- **together** [təɡéðər] 뭔 함께
- **under** [ʌ́ndər] 젼 ~ 아래에
- **writer** [ráitər] 몡 작가

Key Expressions

- **be good for** ~에 좋다
- **blow one's nose** 코를 풀다
- **by the way** 그런데, 그건 그렇고
- **get + 형용사** ~해지다
- **go away** 가 버리다, 사라지다
- **Have you ever heard of** ~?
  ~에 대해 들어 본 적 있니?
- **Let me see.** 어디 보자., 글쎄.
- **look at** ~을 보다
- **look into** …을 들여다보다

- **No problem.** 그럼요., 전혀 문제되지 않아요.
- **out of** ~의 밖으로
- **should not + 동사원형** ~해선 안 된다
- **take a break** 휴식을 취하다
- **take out** ~을 꺼내다
- **talk to oneself** 혼잣말하다
- **thank A for B** B에 대해 A에게 감사하다
- **watch + 목적어 + 목적격보어(동사원형/-ing)**
  목적어가 ~하는 것을 보다
- **What do you mean by that**? 그게 무슨 말이야?

Word Power

※ 서로 반대되는 뜻을 가진 단어

□ **safe**(안전한) ↔ **dangerous**(위험한)

□ **front**(정면, 앞) ↔ **back**(뒤)

□ **kind**(친절한) ↔ **unkind**(불친절한)

□ **famous**(유명한) ↔ **unknown**(알려지지 않은)

□ **end**(끝, 마지막) ↔ **beginning**, **start**(시작)

□ **together**(함께) ↔ **alone**(혼자), **separately**(따로따로)

※ 서로 비슷한 뜻을 가진 단어

□ **check**(점검하다) : **inspect**(점검[검사]하다)

□ **famous**(유명한) : **well-known**(잘 알려진)

□ **follow**(따라가다, 뒤따르다) : **go after**(~를 뒤쫓다, 따라가다)

□ **please**(~을 기쁘게 하다) : **entertain**, **delight**(즐겁게 하다)

□ **end**(끝, 마지막) : **finish**(마지막 부분, 끝)

□ **writer**(작가) : **author**(저자, 작가)

□ **need**(~을 필요로 하다) : **require**(필요로 하다)

□ **dangerous**(위험한) : **harmful**(해로운, 유해한)

English Dictionary

□ **blow** (입으로) 불다
→ to send air out from your mouth
입 밖으로 공기를 내보내다

□ **end** 끝, 마지막
→ the last part of a period of time, event, activity, or story
시간, 사건, 활동 또는 이야기의 마지막 부분

□ **famous** 유명한
→ known about by many people in many places
많은 장소에서 많은 사람들에 의해 알려진

□ **follow** 따라가다, 뒤따르다
→ to go, walk, drive, etc behind or after someone else
다른 어떤 사람의 뒤에서 또는 다른 어떤 사람을 따라서 가거나 걷거나 운전하다

□ **front** 앞, 정면
→ the part of something that faces you
당신과 마주보고 있는 어떤 것의 부분

□ **hood** (외투 등에 달린) 모자
→ a part of a coat, jacket, etc that you can pull up to cover your head
머리를 덮을 수 있게 당겨 쓸 수 있는 코트나 재킷의 부분

□ **knock** 두드리다
→ to hit a door or window with your closed hand to attract the attention of the people inside
안에 있는 사람들의 주의를 끌기 위해 주먹 쥔 손으로 문이나 창문을 치다

□ **leave** 떠나다
→ to go away from a place or a person
한 장소나 안 사람으로부터 떠나가나

□ **please** ~을 기쁘게 하다
→ to make someone happy or satisfied
누군가를 행복하거나 만족스럽게 만들다

□ **safe** 안전한
→ not likely to cause any physical injury or harm
신체적인 손상이나 피해를 유발할 것 같지 않은

□ **stop** (~하는 것을) 막다, 그만두게 하다
→ to not continue, or to make someone or something not continue
계속하지 않거나 또는 다른 사람이나 어떤 것이 계속 이어지지 않도록 만들다

□ **writer** 작가
→ someone who writes books, stories, etc especially as a job
특히 직업으로 책이나 이야기를 쓰는 사람

Reading

Little Red Writing Hood

Scene 1: In front of the three little piggies' house
(*Red comes in with a basket of cakes and cookies.*)
Red: Now I can see the three little piggies' house. I'll take a break here under the tree.
(*Wolf walks in and looks into the house.*)
Wolf: Baby piggies! They look delicious. I'll eat them for lunch.
(*Wolf blows the house hard and it is shaking.*)
Red: Oh, that bad Wolf! What can I do to stop him? Let me see. ... That's it! (*To Wolf*) Hey, you! I'll change the story!
Wolf: What do you mean by that?
Red: (*Taking out a pen and writing something*) "There lived three big strong piggies in the house."
There is 구문의 변형: ~이 살았다
Wolf: You shouldn't do that!
'should not+동사원형': '···해선 안 된다'

(*Wolf blows again, but the three big strong piggies come out of the house.*)
Three Piggies: Hey there! Why did you blow our house?
Wolf: Um ... I didn't. I just blew my nose.
Three Piggies: Don't do that again here. Go away!
Wolf: Okay. I'm so sorry.
(*The piggies go back into the house.*)
Wolf: I can't believe this happened. I'm so hungry! (*Looking at Red's basket*) What are those?
'this' 앞에 접속사 'that'이 생략. '(that) this happened'는 'believe'의 목적어
Red: These are cookies for Grandma.
Wolf: Where does she live?
Red: She lives at the end of this road.
Wolf: (*To himself*) Grandma is good for lunch, too. (*To Red*) See you later. (*Wolf leaves.*)
Red: Bye. (*Talking to herself*) Hmm .... He's going to Grandma's. I think I should change the story again. (*Taking out the pen and writing something*) Okay. If my story works, Grandma will be safe. I'll follow
'if'절에서는 현재시제로 미래를 나타내므로 'will work'가 아니라 'works'
him. (*Red leaves.*)

piggy pig의 애칭 (*pl.* piggies)

blow (입으로) 불다, (바람이) 불다

shake 흔들거리다

go away 가 버리다, 사라지다

end 끝, 마지막

talk to oneself 혼잣말하다

📎 확인문제

● 다음 문장이 본문의 내용과 일치하면 T, 일치하지 <u>않으면</u> F를 쓰시오.

1 Red says she'll take a break under the tree. ☐

2 Wolf ate three baby piggies for lunch. ☐

3 Wolf thinks that Grandma is good for lunch, too. ☐

4 Red tells Wolf to go to Grandma's. ☐

5 Red thinks she should change the story again. ☐

Scene 2: Grandma's house
(*Wolf dances around Grandma. She looks very happy and excited.*)
Red: (*Knocking on the door*) Grandma, it's me. Are you okay?
Grandma: (*Laughing happily and opening the door*) Sure, Red. Come on in. I was watching Wolf dance for me. 과거진행형: '보고 있었다', 'watch + 목적어 + 동사원형'
Red: Hey, Wolf. Thank you for pleasing my grandmother.
Wolf: Well, that's ....
Prince: (*Opening the door and running in*) Hey, you bad Wolf! (*Prince jumps over Wolf.*)
Red: No, no! Stop. He's not dangerous.
Grandma: Right. Look. He is dancing for us. 'you're' 앞에 접속사 'that'이 생략된 구문
Prince: Really? Wolf, I'm sorry. I'm glad you're kind to Grandma.
Wolf: Well, ... I'm glad, too. By the way, do you have anything to eat?
Red: (*Taking some cookies out the basket*) Would you like some cookies?
Wolf: No, thanks. I don't eat cookies. I like chicken.
Red: Don't worry. I'll change the story again. Then you will like eating cookies. (*Checking the basket*) Oh, I lost my pen. What should I do?
Wolf: (*Dancing and crying*) Oh, no! I'm so tired and hungry now.
(*Andersen comes in.*)
Andersen: I think you need my help, right?
Red: Oh, Mr. Andersen. I'm so glad you're here.
Grandma: (*To Red*) Who's that?
Red: He is Mr. Andersen, the famous writer. Have you ever heard of "The Red Shoes"? 앞 문장에서 쓰인 'Have you ...?'에 대해 조동사 'have'를 이용하여 답한 것 경험을 묻는 현재완료 구문
Grandma: Yes, I have. Is he the one who wrote that story?
Red: Right. (*To Andersen*) I changed the story, and the poor Wolf got tired and hungry. get+형용사: '···해지다'
Andersen: You can change the story again. 'you' 앞에 목적격 관계대명사 'which[that]'가 생략된 구문
Red: I'm sorry, but I lost the pen you gave to me. Please help me.
Andersen: No problem. I'll write a happy ending for everyone. Is that okay?
Red: That'll be great!
Andersen: All right. I'll use my pen here. "The kind Wolf stops dancing. He can enjoy cakes and cookies."
Wolf: (*Stopping dancing*) I can stop dancing! (*Eating cookies*) And I can eat cookies! Thank you very much. 'stop'은 목적어로 동명사를 취하는 동사
(*Everybody laughs and enjoys cookies together.*)

knock 두드리다

by the way 그런데, 그건 그렇고

확인문제

● 다음 문장이 본문의 내용과 일치하면 T, 일치하지 않으면 F를 쓰시오.

1 Grandma looks very happy and excited. ☐

2 Wolf thanks Red for pleasing Grandma. ☐

3 Wolf likes cookies but doesn't eat chicken. ☐

4 Wolf is so tired and hungry. ☐

5 Red can change the story again. ☐

6 Mr. Andersen wrote "The Red Shoes." ☐

● 우리말을 참고하여 빈칸에 알맞은 말을 쓰시오.

1 _____ Red Writing Hood

2 _____ 1: _____ _____ _____ the three little piggies' house

3 (Red _____ _____ _____ a basket of cakes and cookies.)

4 Red: Now I can see the three little piggies' house. I'll _____ _____ _____ here under the tree.

5 (Wolf walks in and _____ _____ the house.)

6 Wolf: Baby piggies! They look delicious. I'll eat them _____ _____.

7 (Wolf blows the house hard and it _____ _____.)

8 Red: Oh, that bad Wolf! What can I do _____ _____ him? Let me see. ... That's it! (To Wolf) Hey, you! I'll _____ _____ _____!

9 Wolf: What do you mean _____ _____?

10 Red: (_____ out a pen and _____ something) "There lived three big strong piggies in the house."

11 Wolf: You _____ _____ that!

12 (Wolf blows again, but the three big strong piggies _____ _____ _____ the house.)

13 Three Piggies: _____ _____! Why did you blow our house?

14 Wolf: Um ... I didn't. I just _____ _____ _____ _____.

15 Three Piggies: Don't do that again here. _____ _____!

16 Wolf: Okay. I'm _____ _____.

17 (The piggies _____ _____ _____ the house.)

18 Wolf: I can't believe _____ _____. I'm so hungry! (Looking at Red's basket) What are those?

19 Red: These are cookies _____ Grandma.

20 Wolf: _____ does she live?

21 Red: She lives _____ _____ _____ _____ this road.

22 Wolf: (_____ _____) Grandma is good _____ lunch, too. (To Red) See you later. (Wolf leaves.)

23 Red: Bye. (Talking _____ _____) Hmm .... He's going to Grandma's. I think I should change the story again. (Taking out the pen and writing something) Okay. If my story _____, Grandma will be safe. I'll follow him. (Red leaves.)

24 _____ 2: Grandma's house

25 (Wolf dances around Grandma. She looks very _____ and _____.)

26 Red: (Knocking on the door) Grandma, _____ _____. Are you okay?

27 Grandma: (Laughing _____ and opening the door) Sure, Red. Come on in. I was watching Wolf _____ for me.

28 Red: Hey, Wolf. Thank you _____ _____ my grandmother.

29 Wolf: Well, _____ ....

30 Prince: (Opening the door and running in) Hey, you bad Wolf! (Prince _____ _____ Wolf.)

31 Red: No, no! Stop. He's not _____.

32 Grandma: Right. Look. He is dancing _____ us.

33 Prince: Really? Wolf, I'm sorry. I'm glad you're kind _____ Grandma.

34 Wolf: Well, ... I'm glad, too. _____ _____ _____, do you have anything to eat?

35 Red: (Taking some cookies out the basket) _____ _____ _____ some cookies?

36 Wolf: _____, _____. I don't eat cookies. I like chicken.

37 Red: _____ _____. I'll change the story again. Then you will like eating cookies. (Checking the basket) Oh, I lost my pen. _____ _____ _____ _____?

38 Wolf: (Dancing and crying) Oh, no! I'm so _____ and hungry now.

39 (Andersen comes in.)

40 Andersen: I _____ you need my help, right?

41 Red: Oh, Mr. Andersen. I'm _____ _____ you're here.

42 Grandma: (To Red) _____ that?

43 Red: He is Mr. Andersen, the famous writer. Have you ever _____ _____ "The Red Shoes"?

44 Grandma: Yes, I _____. Is he the one who wrote that story?

45 Red: Right. (To Andersen) I _____ the story, and the poor Wolf _____ _____ and hungry.

46 Andersen: You can _____ _____ _____ again.

47 Red: I'm sorry, but I lost the pen _____ _____ _____ _____. Please help me.

48 Andersen: _____ _____. I'll write a happy ending for everyone. Is that okay?

49 Red: _____ be great!

50 Andersen: All right. I'll use my pen here. "The kind Wolf stops _____. He can enjoy cakes and cookies."

51 Wolf: (Stopping dancing) I can _____ _____! (Eating cookies) And I can eat cookies! Thank you very much.

52 (Everybody laughs and _____ _____ _____.)

26 Red: (문을 두드리며) 할머니, 저예요. 괜찮으세요?

27 할머니: (행복하게 웃으며 문을 열면서) 물론이지, Red야. 어서 들어와. 늑대가 나를 위해 춤추는 걸 보고 있었단다.

28 Red: 이봐, 늑대야. 우리 할머니를 기쁘게 해드려서 고마워.

29 늑대: 음, 그게 ….

30 왕자: (문을 열고 뛰어 들어오며) 이봐, 이 나쁜 늑대야! (왕자가 늑대에게 달려든다.)

31 Red: 아니, 아니에요! 멈춰요. 그는 위험하지 않아요.

32 할머니: 맞아. 보세요. 그가 우리를 위해 춤추고 있잖아요.

33 왕자: 정말요? 늑대야, 미안해. 네가 할머니께 잘해 드린다니 기쁘다.

34 늑대: 음… 나도 기뻐. 그런데, 먹을 것 좀 있어?

35 Red: (바구니에서 과자를 좀 꺼내며) 과자 좀 먹을래?

36 늑대: 고맙지만 됐어. 난 과자를 먹지 않아. 나는 닭고기가 좋아.

37 Red: 걱정하지 마. 내가 이야기를 다시 바꿔야겠네. 그러면 넌 과자 먹는 걸 좋아하게 될 거야. (바구니를 뒤지며) 오, 펜을 잃어버렸어. 어떻게 하지?

38 늑대: (춤을 추며 울부짖으며) 오, 안 돼! 난 지금 너무 피곤하고 배고파.

39 (Andersen이 들어온다.)

40 Andersen: 내 도움이 필요한 것 같은데, 맞지?

41 Red: 오, Andersen 씨. 여기 오셔서 너무 기뻐요.

42 할머니: (Red에게) 저 사람이 누구니?

43 Red: 저분은 유명한 작가 Andersen 씨예요. "빨간 구두"에 대해 들어 보신 적이 있죠?

44 할머니: 그래, 들어 봤지. 그 이야기를 쓴 사람이란 말이지?

45 Red: 맞아요. (Andersen에게) 제가 이야기를 바꿔서 저 불쌍한 늑대가 피곤하고 배고파졌어요.

46 Andersen: 너는 다시 이야기를 바꿀 수 있잖아.

47 Red: 죄송하지만, 제가 작가님이 주신 펜을 잃어버렸어요. 저 좀 도와주세요.

48 Andersen: 문제없지. 내가 모두에게 행복한 결말을 쓸게. 괜찮지?

49 Red: 아주 좋아요!

50 Andersen: 좋아. 여기 내 펜을 써야지. "그 친절한 늑대는 춤추기를 멈춘다. 그는 케이크와 과자를 즐겨 먹을 수 있다."

51 늑대: (춤을 멈추며) 춤을 멈출 수가 있다! (과자를 먹으며) 그리고 과자를 먹을 수 있어! 정말 고마워요.

52 (모두 웃으며 함께 과자를 맛있게 먹는다.)

● 우리말을 참고하여 본문을 영작하시오.

1 빨간 모자
➡

2 장면 1: 아기 돼지 삼 형제의 집 앞에서
➡

3 (Red가 케이크와 과자가 든 바구니를 들고 등장한다.)
➡

4 Red: 이제 아기 돼지 삼 형제의 집이 보인다. 여기 나무 아래에서 좀 쉬어야지.
➡

5 (늑대가 걸어 들어와 집 안을 들여다본다.)
➡

6 늑대: 새끼 돼지들이네! 맛있어 보인다. 점심으로 그들을 먹어야겠어.
➡

7 (늑대가 집을 세게 불자 집이 흔들리고 있다.)
➡

8 Red: 오, 저런 나쁜 늑대 같으니라고! 그를 멈추게 하려면 내가 뭘 할 수 있을까? 어디 보자. … 바로 그거야! (늑대에게) 이봐! 내가 이야기를 바꾸겠어!
➡

9 늑대: 그게 무슨 말이야?
➡

10 Red: (펜을 꺼내 뭔가를 쓰면서) "크고 힘센 아기 돼지 삼 형제가 그 집에 살고 있었다."
➡

11 늑대: 그렇게 하면 안 돼!
➡

12 (늑대가 다시 집을 분다. 그러나 크고 힘센 돼지 삼 형제가 집에서 나온다.)
➡

13 돼지 삼 형제: 이봐, 거기! 왜 우리 집을 불고 있어?
➡

14 늑대: 음… 그러지 않았어. 나는 그냥 코를 풀었을 뿐이야.
➡

15 돼지 삼 형제: 여기서 다시는 그러지 마. 가 버려!
➡

16 늑대: 알았어. 정말 미안해.
➡

17 (돼지들은 집 안으로 다시 들어간다.)
➡

18 늑대: 이런 일이 일어나다니 믿을 수가 없어. 나는 너무 배가 고파! (Red의 바구니를 보며) 그건 뭐야?
➡

19 Red: 할머니께 드릴 과자들이야.
➡

20 늑대: 어디 사시는데?
➡

21 Red: 이 길의 끝에 사셔.
➡

22 늑대: (혼잣말로) 할머니도 점심으로 좋지. (Red에게) 나중에 보자. (늑대가 떠난다.)
➡

23 Red: 안녕. (혼잣말로) 흠…. 그는 할머니 댁으로 갈 거야. 이야기를 다시 바꿔야겠어. (펜을 꺼내서 뭔가를 쓰며) 좋아. 내 이야기가 제대로 돌아가면 할머니는 안전하실 거야. 그를 따라가 봐야지. (Red가 떠난다.)
➡

24 장면 2: 할머니의 집
➡

25 (늑대가 할머니 주변을 맴돌며 춤을 춘다. 할머니는 아주 행복하고 신나 보인다.)
➡

26 Red: (문을 두드리며) 할머니, 저예요. 괜찮으세요?

27 할머니: (행복하게 웃으며 문을 열면서) 물론이지, Red야. 어서 들어와. 늑대가 나를 위해 춤추는 걸 보고 있었단다.

28 Red: 이봐, 늑대야. 우리 할머니를 기쁘게 해드려서 고마워.

29 늑대: 음, 그게 ….

30 왕자: (문을 열고 뛰어 들어오며) 이봐, 이 나쁜 늑대야! (왕자가 늑대에게 달려든다.)

31 Red: 아니, 아니에요! 멈춰요. 그는 위험하지 않아요.

32 할머니: 맞아. 보세요. 그가 우리를 위해 춤추고 있잖아요.

33 왕자: 정말요? 늑대야, 미안해. 네가 할머니께 잘해 드린다니 기쁘다.

34 늑대: 음 … 나도 기뻐. 그런데, 먹을 것 좀 있어?

35 Red: (바구니에서 과자를 좀 꺼내며) 과자 좀 먹을래?

36 늑대: 고맙지만 됐어. 난 과자를 먹지 않아. 나는 닭고기가 좋아.

37 Red: 걱정하지 마. 내가 이야기를 다시 바꿔야겠네. 그러면 넌 과자 먹는 걸 좋아하게 될 거야. (바구니를 뒤지며) 오, 펜을 잃어버렸어. 어떻게 하지?

38 늑대: (춤을 추며 울부짖으며) 오, 안 돼! 난 지금 너무 피곤하고 배고파.

39 (Andersen이 들어온다.)

40 Andersen: 내 도움이 필요한 것 같은데, 맞지?

41 Red: 오, Andersen 씨. 여기 오셔서 너무 기뻐요.

42 할머니: (Red에게) 저 사람이 누구니?

43 Red: 저분은 유명한 작가 Andersen 씨예요. "빨간 구두"에 대해 들어 보신 적이 있죠?

44 할머니: 그래, 들어 봤지. 그 이야기를 쓴 사람이란 말이지?

45 Red: 맞아요. (Andersen에게) 제가 이야기를 바꿔서 저 불쌍한 늑대가 피곤하고 배고파졌어요.

46 Andersen: 너는 다시 이야기를 바꿀 수 있잖아.

47 Red: 죄송하지만, 제가 작가님이 주신 펜을 잃어버렸어요. 저 좀 도와주세요.

48 Andersen: 문제없지. 내가 모두에게 행복한 결말을 쓸게. 괜찮지?

49 Red: 아주 좋아요!

50 Andersen: 좋아. 여기 내 펜을 써야지. "그 친절한 늑대는 춤추기를 멈춘다. 그는 케이크와 과자를 즐겨 먹을 수 있다."

51 늑대: (춤을 멈추며) 춤을 멈출 수가 있다! (과자를 먹으며) 그리고 과자를 먹을 수 있어! 정말 고마워요.

52 (모두 웃으며 함께 과자를 맛있게 먹는다.)

01 다음 짝지어진 단어의 관계가 같도록 빈칸에 알맞은 말을 쓰시오.

> thin : thick – d_____ : safe

[02~03] 다음 대화의 빈칸에 알맞은 것을 쓰시오.

02
> A: _____ you ever heard about the garage sale?
> B: No, I haven't. What is it?

03 중요
> A: What time are you free every Sunday?
> B: _____ me see. I'm free after 2 p.m.

04 다음 빈칸에 공통으로 들어갈 말을 쓰시오.

> • Their songs are full of energy and are good _____ dancing.
> • Thank you _____ helping me.

05 다음 주어진 우리말에 맞게 빈칸을 채우시오. (철자가 주어진 것이 있으면 그 철자로 시작할 것)

(1) 나는 그가 혼잣말을 한다고 생각한다.
➡ I think he's talking to _____.

(2) 당신의 사진 아래에 이름을 쓰세요.
➡ Write your name _____ your picture.

(3) 내가 방을 떠나면 내 아기는 화를 낸다.
➡ My baby g_____ upset when I l_____ the room.

06 중요 다음 빈칸에 알맞은 단어를 〈보기〉에서 골라 쓰시오. (필요하면 어형 변화를 할 것.)

> ┤ 보기 ├
> blow   check   knock   need

(1) Plants _____ light in order to survive.
(2) The first rule in solving any mystery is to _____ the facts.
(3) She _____ onto her coffee to cool it down when I saw her.
(4) We _____ at the door.

07 중요 다음 빈칸을 어법에 알맞게 채우시오. (어휘가 주어진 경우 그 어휘를 활용할 것.)

(1) I was watching Wolf _____ for me. (dance)
(2) I have loved her _____ I first met her at the party.
(3) I needed a sheet of paper _____. (write)
(4) I can't believe _____ this happened.

08 다음 두 문장을 관계대명사를 이용하여 한 문장으로 연결하여 쓰시오.

(1) • I like the pen.
   • You gave it to me.
➡ _____
_____

(2) • Mary had dinner with Sam.
   • Sam is her best friend.
➡ _____
_____

(3) • Kate read the book.
   • It was about global warming.
➡ _____
_____

(A)[Scene / Scenery] 1: In front of the three little piggies' house

(*Red comes in with a basket of cakes and cookies.*)

Red: Now I can see the three little piggies' house. I'll take a break here under the tree.

(*Wolf walks in and looks into the house.*)

Wolf: Baby piggies! They look (B)[delicious / deliciously]. I'll eat them ⓐ lunch.

(Wolf blows the house (C)[*hard / hardly*] and it is shaking.)

Red: Oh, that bad Wolf! What can I do to stop him? Let me see. ... That's it! (*To Wolf*) Hey, you! I'll change the story!

Wolf: ⓑ그게 무슨 말이야?

Red: (*Taking out a pen and writing something*) "There lived three big strong piggies in the house."

Wolf: You shouldn't do that!

09 위 글의 괄호 (A)~(C)에서 문맥이나 어법상 알맞은 낱말을 골라 쓰시오.

➡ (A) _____ (B) _____ (C) _____

10 위 글의 다음 빈칸에 알맞은 말을 쓰시오.

➡ _____

11 위 글의 밑줄 친 ⓑ의 우리말에 맞게 주어진 어휘를 이용하여 6 단어로 영작하시오.

by

➡ _____

Red: (①*Taking some cookies out the basket*) Would you like some cookies?

Wolf: No, thanks. I don't eat cookies. I like chicken.

Red: Don't worry. I'll change the story again. ⓐThen you will like ___ⓑ___ cookies. (②*Checking the basket*) Oh, I lost my pen. What should I do?

Wolf: (③*Dancing* and ④*crying*) Oh, no! I'm so ⑤tiring and hungry now.

(*Andersen comes in.*)

Andersen: I think you need my help, right?

Red: Oh, Mr. Andersen. I'm so glad you're here.

Grandma: (*To Red*) Who's that?

Red: He is Mr. Andersen, the famous writer. Have you ever heard of "The Red Shoes"?

12 위 글의 밑줄 친 ①~⑤ 중 어법상 틀린 것을 찾아 고치시오.

➡ _____

13 위 글의 밑줄 친 ⓐThen을 바를 사용하여 고치시오.

➡ _____

14 위 글의 빈칸 ⓑ에 cat을 알맞은 형태로 쓰시오.

➡ _____

15 다음 빈칸에 들어갈 알맞은 단어를 본문에서 찾아 넣어 Andersen에 대한 소개를 완성하시오.

Andersen is a _____ _____ who wrote "The Red Shoes."

단원별 예상문제

[01~02] 다음 빈칸에 들어갈 말로 적절한 것은?

01

I have to _____ my nose all the time when I have a cold.

① fall   ② break   ③ blow

④ draw   ⑤ flow

02

Before _____ the train, make sure you have all your belongings with you.

① starting   ② getting   ③ making

④ finding   ⑤ leaving

03 다음 제시된 단어를 사용하여 자연스러운 문장을 만들 수 없는 것은? (형태 변화 가능)

follow   need   please   shake

① _____ the bottle before you open it.

② It _____ a new battery.

③ She did it to _____ him.

④ I think I will _____ her advice this time.

⑤ What time do you _____ working?

04 다음 대화의 빈칸에 알맞은 것을 쓰시오.

A: She's a busy bee.

B: _____ do you _____ _____ that?

A: She's a busy worker.

05 〈보기〉의 단어를 사용하여 문장을 만드시오.

┤ 보기 ├

away   by   of   to

(1) _____ the way, will you be free tomorrow evening?

(2) He went _____ like a wind last night.

(3) The crazy man talked _____ himself all the time.

(4) Let's get out _____ here, and go to the movies.

(5) Have you ever heard _____ the new teacher?

06 다음 빈칸에 알맞은 말을 〈보기〉에서 골라 쓰시오.

┤ 보기 ├

though   that   if

(1) We'll drive in the country _____ it's warm tomorrow.

(2) He supported his family _____ he was young.

(3) She told me _____ I should be more careful.

07 다음 문장에서 잘못된 부분을 바르게 고치시오.

(1) I didn't get better if I took the medicine.

(2) I heard Lisa opened the window.

(3) Abigail has met Andy in Seoul then.

(4) If you will find a four-leaf clover, you will have good luck.

(5) John is watering the plant which he bought it last week.

➡ (1) _____ (2) _____

(3) _____ (4) _____

(5) _____

출제율 95%

08 다음 빈칸에 알맞은 말을 <u>모두</u> 고르시오.

> He will ask Ann the question _____ nobody answered.

① who   ② whose   ③ whom
④ which   ⑤ that

출제율 90%

09 다음 빈칸에 공통으로 알맞은 말을 쓰시오.

> • I want something _____.
> • We eat to live, not live _____.

➡ _____

출제율 95%

10 괄호 안에 주어진 어휘를 빈칸에 알맞게 쓰시오.

> Sean watched the girl _____ for the contest. (practice sing)

➡ _____

출제율 100%

11 다음 괄호 안에서 알맞은 것을 고르시오.

(1) (Though / Because) he is quite old, he enjoys playing soccer.

(2) I heard my friend (calling / called) my name.

(3) If you (open / will open) your umbrella in the house, you will have bad luck.

(4) I have (been / gone) to London twice.

(5) He is looking for creative ways (who/ which) can solve the problems.

[12~14] 다음 글을 읽고 물음에 답하시오.

Scene 1: In front of the three little piggies' house

(*Red comes in with a basket of cakes and cookies.*)

Red: Now I can see the three little piggies' house. I'll take a break here under the tree.

(*Wolf walks in and looks into the house.*)

Wolf: Baby piggies! They look delicious. I'll eat ①them ⓐ lunch.

(*Wolf blows the house hard and ②it is shaking.*)

Red: Oh, that bad Wolf! What can I do ⓑto stop ③him? Let me see. ... That's it! (*To Wolf*) Hey, you! I'll change the story!

Wolf: What do you mean ⓒ that?

Red: (*Taking out a pen and writing something*) "There lived three big strong piggies in the house."

Wolf: ④You shouldn't ⑤do that!

출제율 85%

12 위 글의 밑줄 친 ①~⑤가 가리키는 것에 대한 설명으로 옳지 <u>않은</u> 것을 고르시오.

① baby piggies를 가리킨다.
② the house를 가리킨다.
③ the wolf를 가리킨다.
④ Red를 가리킨다.
⑤ take out a pen을 가리킨다.

출제율 85%

13 위 글의 빈칸 ⓐ와 ⓒ에 들어갈 전치사가 바르게 짝지어진 것은?

① for – by   ② in – by
③ in – from   ④ for – to
⑤ on – to

14 위 글의 밑줄 친 ⓑto stop과 to부정사의 용법이 **다른** 것을 **모두** 고르시오.

① He works hard to get a good grade.
② It is easy to acquire a bad habit.
③ Ted got up early to go fishing.
④ She was happy to see the show.
⑤ Who was the first person to invent the airplane?

[15~19] 다음 글을 읽고 물음에 답하시오.

(*Wolf blows again, but the three big strong piggies come out of the house.*)
Three Piggies: Hey there! Why did you blow our house?
Wolf: Um ... I didn't. I just blew my nose.
Three Piggies: Don't ⓐdo that again here. Go away!
Wolf: Okay. I'm so sorry.
(The piggies go back into the house.)

Wolf: I can't believe this (A)[happened / was happened]. I'm so hungry! (*Looking at Red's basket*) What are those?
Red: These are cookies for Grandma.
Wolf: Where does she live?
Red: She lives at the end of this road.
Wolf: (*To* (B)[*him / himself*]) Grandma is good for lunch, too. (*To Red*) See you later. (*Wolf leaves.*)
Red: Bye. (*Talking to herself*) Hmm .... He's going to Grandma's. I think I should change the story again. (*Taking out the pen and writing something*) Okay. If my story ⓑworks, Grandma will be (C)[dangerous / safe]. I'll follow him. (*Red leaves.*)

15 위 글의 밑줄 친 ⓐdo that의 내용을 영어로 쓰시오. (3 단어)

➡ _____

16 위 글의 괄호 (A)~(C)에서 문맥이나 어법상 알맞은 낱말을 골라 쓰시오.

➡ (A) _____ (B) _____ (C) _____

17 위 글의 밑줄 친 ⓑworks와 같은 의미로 쓰인 것을 고르시오.

① He works for an engineering company.
② Jim is looking for work.
③ This medicine works on me.
④ I bought the complete works of Scott.
⑤ It was very hard work.

18 위 글의 마지막 부분에 어울리는 속담으로 적절한 것을 고르시오.

① The grass is greener on the other side of the fence.
② It never rains but it pours.
③ Nothing ventured, nothing gained.
④ Hunger is the best sauce.
⑤ There may be blue and better blue.

19 위 글의 내용과 일치하지 <u>않는</u> 것은?

① 늑대가 다시 집을 불고 있는데, 크고 힘센 돼지 삼 형제가 집에서 나온다.

② 늑대는 돼지 삼 형제의 집을 불고 있는 것이 아니라 코를 풀었을 뿐이라고 한다.

③ 늑대는 일어난 일을 믿을 수 없어 한다.

④ 늑대는 너무 배가 고파서 Red가 할머니께 드릴 과자들을 먹는다.

⑤ Red는 할머니가 안전하시도록 이야기를 다시 바꾸려고 한다.

[20~23] 다음 글을 읽고 물음에 답하시오.

Scene2: Grandma's house
(*Wolf dances around Grandma. She looks very* (A)[*happy / happily*] *and* (B)[*exciting / excited*].)
Red: (*Knocking on the door*) Grandma, it's me. Are you okay?
Grandma: (*Laughing* (C)[*happy / happily*] *and opening the door*) Sure, Red. Come on in. I was watching Wolf dance for me.
Red: Hey, Wolf. Thank you for ⓐ<u>pleasing</u> my grandmother.
Wolf: Well, that's ....
Prince: (*Opening the door and running in*) Hey, you bad Wolf! (*Prince jumps over Wolf.*)
Red: No, no! Stop. He's not dangerous.
Grandma: Right. Look. He is dancing for us.
Prince: Really? Wolf, I'm sorry. ⓑ<u>네가 할머니께 잘해 드린다니 기쁘다.</u>
Wolf: Well, ... I'm glad, too. _____ⓒ_____, do you have anything to eat?

20 위 글의 괄호 (A)~(C)에서 어법상 알맞은 낱말을 골라 쓰시오.

➡ (A) _____ (B) _____ (C) _____

21 위 글의 밑줄 친 ⓐpleasing과 문법적 쓰임이 같은 것을 <u>모두</u> 고르시오.

① <u>Growing</u> plants is not easy.
② She finished <u>doing</u> the dishes.
③ Look at the <u>sleeping</u> baby.
④ I heard her <u>singing</u> in her room.
⑤ He came <u>running</u>.

22 위 글의 밑줄 친 ⓑ의 우리말에 맞게 한 단어를 보충하여, 주어진 어휘를 알맞게 배열하시오.

kind / glad / you're / Grandma / I'm

➡ _____

23 위 글의 빈칸 ⓒ에 들어갈 알맞은 말을 고르시오.

① Therefore
② At last
③ As a result
④ By the way
⑤ In other words

[24~26] 다음 글을 읽고 물음에 답하시오.

Red: (*Taking some cookies out the basket*) Would you like some cookies?
Wolf: No, thanks. I don't eat cookies. I like chicken.
Red: Don't worry. I'll change the story again. ⓐ<u>Then you will like eating chicken.</u> (*Checking the basket*) Oh, I lost my pen. ⓑ<u>What should I do?</u>
Wolf: (*Dancing and crying*) Oh, no! I'm so tired and hungry now.
(*Andersen comes in.*)
Andersen: I think you need my help, right?
Red: Oh, Mr. Andersen. I'm so glad you're here.
Grandma: (*To Red*) Who's that?
Red: He is Mr. Andersen, the famous writer. ⓒ Have you ever <u>heard</u> of "The Red Shoes"?

✏️ 출제율 95%

24 위 글의 밑줄 친 ⓐ에서 흐름상 어색한 부분을 찾아 고치시오.

➡️ _____

✏️ 출제율 90%

25 위 글의 밑줄 친 ⓑ에서 알 수 있는 'I'의 심경으로 가장 알맞은 것을 고르시오.

① bored   ② embarrassed

③ satisfied   ④ depressed

⑤ excited

✏️ 출제율 100%

26 위 글의 밑줄 친 ⓒ와 현재완료의 용법이 같은 것을 모두 고르시오.

① He has gone to New York.

② I have never heard the news.

③ She has been sick since yesterday.

④ Have you seen it yet?

⑤ How many times have you read it?

[27~31] 다음 글을 읽고 물음에 답하시오.

> Grandma: (*To Red*) Who's that?
>
> Red: He is Mr. Andersen, the famous writer. Have you ever heard of "The Red Shoes"?
>
> Grandma: Yes, I ____ⓐ____ . Is he the one who wrote that story?
>
> Red: Right. (*To Andersen*) I changed the story, and the poor Wolf got tired and hungry.
>
> Andersen: You can change the story again.
>
> Red: I'm sorry, ____ⓑ____ I lost the pen you gave to me. Please help me.
>
> Andersen: No problem. I'll write a happy ending for everyone. Is that okay?
>
> Red: That'll be great!
>
> Andersen: All right. I'll use my pen here. "ⓒ<u>The kind Wolf stops to dance. He can enjoy cakes and cookies.</u>"

✏️ 출제율 95%

27 위 글의 빈칸 ⓐ에 들어갈 알맞은 말을 쓰시오.

➡️ _____

✏️ 출제율 90%

28 위 글의 빈칸 ⓑ에 알맞은 것은?

① so   ② and

③ but   ④ for

⑤ though

✏️ 출제율 100%

29 위 글의 밑줄 친 ⓒ에서 어법상 틀린 부분을 찾아 고치시오.

➡️ _____

✏️ 출제율 85%

30 위 글을 읽고 대답할 수 <u>없는</u> 질문은?

① What does Mr. Andersen do?

② Who changed the story of "The Red Shoes"?

③ Why did Red ask Mr. Andersen to help her?

④ Where did Red lose the pen Mr. Andersen had given to her?

⑤ How did Mr. Andersen change the story?

✏️ 출제율 95%

31 Who gave a pen to Red? Answer in English. (3 words)

➡️ _____

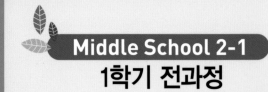

중간 + 기말 plus

적중100 plus

영어 기출문제집

영어 중 2

천재 | 정사열

Best Collection

내용문의 중등영어발전소 적중100 편집부 TEL 070-7707-0457

INSIGHT

on the textbook

교과서 파헤치기

영어 기출 문제집

적중100 plus
1학기 전과정

영어 중 2

천재 | 정사열

INSIGHT
on the textbook

교과서 파헤치기

Lesson **1** **Time to Start Again**

Lesson **2** **I Love My Town!**

Lesson **3** **Be Active, Be Safe!**

Lesson **4** **Memories in Your Heart**

Special
Lesson **Little Red Writing Hood**

※ 다음 영어를 우리말로 쓰시오.

01	post	22	kind
02	realize	23	activity
03	continue	24	note
04	diary	25	math
05	dish	26	right
06	cover	27	together
07	fan	28	word
08	final	29	anyway
09	floor	30	shout
10	really	31	pleased
11	health	32	reply
12	solve	33	grow
13	trust	34	practice
14	ticket	35	cut in
15	strict	36	think of
16	bell	37	bump into
17	fresh	38	can't wait for
18	delicious	39	find out
19	interesting	40	be good for
20	corner	41	on one's way to
21	judge	42	pay someone back
		43	think to oneself

※ 다음 우리말을 영어로 쓰시오.

01 지루한 _____

02 문제 _____

03 연습하다 _____

04 서둘러 가다, 서두르다 _____

05 데리고 가다 _____

06 흥분한, 신이 난 _____

07 마법, 마술 _____

08 구내식당 _____

09 바쁜 _____

10 외치다 _____

11 선물 _____

12 기억하다 _____

13 기르다, 재배하다 _____

14 항상 _____

15 진지한 _____

16 어쨌든 _____

17 열심히, 어려운 _____

18 멋진, 시원한 _____

19 담임선생님 _____

20 가입하다 _____

21 대답하다 _____

22 제공하다 _____

23 신나는, 흥미진진한 _____

24 수업 _____

25 기쁜 _____

26 의미하다 _____

27 속담 _____

28 마술 _____

29 건강 _____

30 바닥 _____

31 엄격한 _____

32 계속하다 _____

33 판단하다 _____

34 표지 _____

35 ~에 좋다 _____

36 ~에 부딪히다 _____

37 (말 · 대화에) 끼어들다 _____

38 방과 후에 _____

39 ~에 대해 생각하다 _____

40 ~을 알게 되다 _____

41 ~을 찾다 _____

42 당장 _____

43 마음속으로 생각하다 _____

※ 다음 영영풀이에 알맞은 단어를 <보기>에서 골라 쓴 후, 우리말 뜻을 쓰시오.

1 _____ : to make plants grow: _____

2 _____ : to move, act, or go quickly: _____

3 _____ : the outer part of a book or magazine: _____

4 _____ : to say or write something as an answer to someone or something: _____

5 _____ : demanding that rules, especially rules about behavior, should be obeyed: _____

6 _____ : a shallow container that you cook or serve food in: _____

7 _____ : the last and most important game or race in a competition: _____

8 _____ : to understand or become aware of something: _____

9 _____ : to give food or drink to someone at a meal, in a restaurant, etc: _____

10 _____ : to form an opinion about something or someone after careful thought: _____

11 _____ : the art of doing tricks that seem impossible in order to entertain people: _____

12 _____ : to put up a sign, notice, etc. so that it can be seen by many people: _____

13 _____ : to believe that someone is honest or will not do anything bad or wrong: _____

14 _____ : an old and well-known phrase that expresses an idea that most people believe is true: _____

15 _____ : a restaurant where you choose and pay for your meal at a counter and carry it to a table: _____

16 _____ : a person who admires someone or something or enjoys watching or listening to someone or something very much: _____

보기			
saying	judge	cover	strict
final	post	reply	cafeteria
hurry	trust	dish	grow
magic	realize	serve	fan

※ 다음 우리말과 일치하도록 빈칸에 알맞은 말을 쓰시오.

Get Ready - 2

1. **G:** Hey, _____ do you _____ this notebook?

   B: It _____ great! Is it _____ science?

   G: Yes. _____ _____ I'm _____ _____ _____ science harder _____ this notebook.

2. **B:** _____ _____ the teachers. Who's _____ _____ be our new _____ _____?

   G: We'll _____ _____ in 10 minutes.

   B: I'm very _____. I _____ _____!

3. **M:** Hello, _____! My name is Yun Kihun. I'm _____ _____ _____.

   G&B: _____ _____ _____ you, Mr. Yun.

   M: _____ do you _____ _____ English?

   G: It's _____. I like English _____ _____.

1. G: 이 봐, 이 공책 어떻게 생각하니?
   B: 멋져 보여! 과학용이니?
   G: 응. 올해에는 이 공책을 가지고 과학을 더 열심히 공부할 거야.

2. B: 선생님들을 좀 봐. 누가 우리 새 담임선생님이 될까?
   G: 우리는 10분 후에 알게 될 거야.
   B: 너무 흥분돼. 너무 기대돼!

3. M: 안녕하세요, 여러분! 제 이름은 윤기훈입니다. 저는 여러분의 영어 선생님입니다.
   G&B: 만나서 반갑습니다, 윤 선생님.
   M: 여러분은 영어에 대해 어떻게 생각하세요?
   G: 재미있어요. 저는 영어를 매우 좋아해요.

Start Off - Listen & Talk A

1. **B:** This club _____ _____ you. _____ do you _____ _____ _____?

   G: The health club? I _____ it's _____.

   B: Then _____ do you want _____ _____?

   G: I'll _____ _____ club. I like _____ soccer.

2. **G:** What do you _____ _____ the magic club?

   B: I _____ it's the _____ club for me. I want _____ _____ _____ _____ _____.

   G: I'll join it, _____. When is the _____ _____?

   B: Next Wednesday. I _____ _____ _____ the first meeting!

1. B: 이 동아리는 너에게 맞는 것 같아. 그것에 대해 어떻게 생각하니?
   G: 헬스 동아리? 지루하다고 생각해.
   B: 그럼 넌 어떤 동아리에 가입하고 싶니?
   G: 난 축구 동아리에 가입할 거야. 나는 축구를 좋아해.

2. G: 마술 동아리에 대해 어떻게 생각하니?
   B: 나한테 맞는 동아리인 것 같아. 나는 재미있는 마술을 많이 배우고 싶어.
   G: 나도 가입할게. 첫 모임은 언제니?
   B: 다음 주 수요일이야. 나는 첫 모임이 너무 기다려져!

Start Off - Listen & Talk B

B: _____ join the Green Garden club together. _____ _____ _____ _____ _____ it?

G: Okay. I like _____ _____.

B: You know _____? I like _____ vegetables.

G: _____ _____ the club _____ _____. We can have a party _____ fresh vegetables _____ _____.

B: Great. The first party is _____ _____ _____.

G: I _____ _____ _____ the party.

B: 초록 정원 동아리에 함께 가입하자. 그것에 대해 어떻게 생각하니?
G: 좋아. 나는 채소를 기르는 것을 좋아해.
B: 그거 알아?(있잖아.) 나는 채소를 먹는 것을 좋아해.
G: 지금 당장 그 동아리에 가입하자. 매달 신선한 채소가 있는 파티를 열 수 있어.
B: 좋아. 첫 번째 파티는 4월 30일이야.
G: 나는 파티가 너무 기다려져.

Step Up - Real-life Scene

I Can't Wait for His Class

Seho: Miso, _____ do you _____ _____ Mr. Park?

Miso: The new math teacher? He _____ very _____ and _____.

Seho: _____ _____ a book _____ its cover.

Miso: _____ do you _____, Seho?

Seho: My first class _____ Mr. Park _____ _____. He was very kind, and his class was so _____.

Miso: Really?

Seho: Yes. _____ the first _____, we did interesting _____ _____ _____ our cell phones.

Miso: Wow! I _____ _____ _____ his class tomorrow. It's my first math class _____ _____.

Express Yourself A

1. **B:** _____ _____ _____ _____ of today's lunch?

   G: _____ _____ it's okay. What's _____ tomorrow's menu?

   B: Wow! We _____ _____ spaghetti tomorrow.

   G: I _____ _____ _____ _____ tomorrow.

2. **G:** Look! Two _____ of vegetables! What do you _____ _____ today's menu?

   B: It's _____ _____. I like _____.

   G: I _____ _____ vegetables.

   B: _____ some. They are _____ _____ _____ _____.

Check Yourself - Listen & Speak

B: _____ _____ the School Band club together. _____ do you think _____ it?

G: Okay. I like _____ _____ _____.

B: I _____ _____ the ukulele.

G: Let's join the club _____ _____. They practice _____ _____ every _____ and _____.

B: They're _____ _____ _____ the first concert _____ July 15.

G: Great. I hope _____ _____ in the concert.

B: Me, _____. I _____ _____ _____ the concert.

나는 그의 수업이 너무 기다려져.

세호: 미소야, 박 선생님에 대해 어떻게 생각하니?

미소: 새로 오신 수학 선생님? 그는 매우 엄격하고 진지해 보이셔.

세호: 겉모습만으로 판단하지 마.

미소: 무슨 뜻이야, 세호?

세호: 박 선생님과의 첫 수업은 훌륭했어. 그는 매우 친절하셨고, 그의 수업은 매우 흥미로웠어.

미소: 정말?

세호: 응. 첫 수업 동안, 우리는 휴대 전화로 흥미로운 수학 활동을 했어.

미소: 와! 내일 수업이 너무 기다려진다. 올해 첫 번째 수학 수업이야.

1. B: 오늘 점심에 대해 어떻게 생각하니?
   G: 괜찮은 것 같아. 내일 메뉴는 뭐니?
   B: 와! 내일 우리는 스파게티를 먹을 수 있어.
   G: 내일 점심시간이 몹시 기다려진다.

2. G: 봐! 야채 두 접시! 오늘 메뉴 어때?
   B: 나쁘지 않아. 나는 야채를 좋아해.
   G: 나는 야채를 안 먹어.
   B: 조금 먹어 봐. 그것들은 우리 건강에 좋아.

B: 우리 학교 밴드 동아리에 같이 가입하자. 그것에 대해서 어떻게 생각하니?
G: 좋아. 나는 플루트 연주하는 것을 좋아해.
B: 난 우쿨렐레 연주하는 걸 좋아해.
G: 지금 당장 그 동아리에 가입하자. 그들은 매주 화요일과 목요일 방과 후에 연습을 해.
B: 그들은 7월 15일에 첫 번째 음악회를 열 거야.
G: 좋아. 나는 음악회에서 연주를 하고 싶어.
B: 나도. 나는 음악회가 너무 기다려져.

※ 다음 우리말에 맞도록 대화를 영어로 쓰시오.

Get Ready - 2

1. G: _____

   B: _____

   G: _____

2. B: _____

   G: _____

   B: _____

3. M: _____

   G&B: _____

   M: _____

   G: _____

Start Off - Listen & Talk A

1. B: _____

   G: _____

   B: _____

   G: _____

2. G: _____

   B: _____

   G: _____

   B: _____

Start Off - Listen & Talk B

B: _____

G: _____

B: _____

G: _____

B: _____

G: _____

해석

1. G: 이 봐, 이 공책 어떻게 생각하니?
   B: 멋져 보여! 과학용이니?
   G: 응. 올해에는 이 공책을 가지고 과학을 더 열심히 공부할 거야.

2. B: 선생님들을 좀 봐. 누가 우리 새 담임선생님이 될까?
   G: 우리는 10분 후에 알게 될 거야.
   B: 너무 흥분돼. 너무 기대돼!

3. M: 안녕하세요, 여러분! 제 이름은 윤기훈입니다. 저는 여러분의 영어 선생님입니다.
   G&B: 만나서 반갑습니다, 윤 선생님.
   M: 여러분은 영어에 대해 어떻게 생각하세요?
   G: 재미있어요. 저는 영어를 매우 좋아해요.

1. B: 이 동아리는 너에게 맞는 것 같아. 그것에 대해 어떻게 생각하니?
   G: 헬스 동아리? 지루하다고 생각해.
   B: 그럼 넌 어떤 동아리에 가입하고 싶니?
   G: 난 축구 동아리에 가입할 거야. 나는 축구를 좋아해.

2. G: 마술 동아리에 대해 어떻게 생각하니?
   B: 나한테 맞는 동아리인 것 같아. 나는 재미있는 마술을 많이 배우고 싶어.
   G: 나도 가입할게. 첫 모임은 언제니?
   B: 다음 주 수요일이야. 나는 첫 모임이 너무 기다려져!

B: 초록 정원 동아리에 함께 가입하자. 그것에 대해 어떻게 생각하니?
G: 좋아, 나는 채소를 기르는 것을 좋아해.
B: 그거 알아?(있잖아.) 나는 채소를 먹는 것을 좋아해.
G: 지금 당장 그 동아리에 가입하자. 매달 신선한 채소가 있는 파티를 열 수 있어.
B: 좋아. 첫 번째 파티는 4월 30일이야.
G: 나는 파티가 너무 기다려져.

Step Up - Real-life Scene

I Can't Wait for His Class

Seho: _____

Miso: _____

Seho: _____

Miso: _____

Seho: _____

Miso: _____

Seho: _____

Miso: _____

나는 그의 수업이 너무 기다려져.

세호: 미소야, 박 선생님에 대해 어떻게 생각하니?

미소: 새로 오신 수학 선생님? 그는 매우 엄격하고 진지해 보이셔.

세호: 겉모습만으로 판단하지 마.

미소: 무슨 뜻이야, 세호?

세호: 박 선생님과의 첫 수업은 훌륭했어. 그는 매우 친절하셨고, 그의 수업은 매우 흥미로웠어.

미소: 정말?

세호: 응. 첫 수업 동안, 우리는 휴대 전화로 흥미로운 수학 활동을 했어.

미소: 와! 내일 수업이 너무 기다려진다. 올해 첫 번째 수학 수업이야.

Express Yourself A

1. B: _____

 G: _____

 B: _____

 G: _____

2. G: _____

 B: _____

 G: _____

 B: _____

1. B: 오늘 점심에 대해 어떻게 생각하니?
 G: 괜찮은 것 같아. 내일 메뉴는 뭐니?
 B: 와! 내일 우리는 스파게티를 먹을 수 있어.
 G: 내일 점심시간이 몹시 기다려진다.

2. G: 봐! 야채 두 접시! 오늘 메뉴 어때?
 B: 나쁘지 않아. 나는 야채를 좋아해.
 G: 나는 야채를 안 먹어.
 B: 조금 먹어 봐. 그것들은 우리 건강에 좋아.

Check Yourself - Listen & Speak

B: _____

G: _____

B: _____

G: _____

B: _____

G: _____

B: _____

B: 우리 학교 밴드 동아리에 같이 가입하자. 그것에 대해서 어떻게 생각하니?

G: 좋아. 나는 플루트 연주하는 것을 좋아해.

B: 난 우쿨렐레 연주하는 걸 좋아해.

G: 지금 당장 그 동아리에 가입하자. 그들은 매주 화요일과 목요일 방과 후에 연습을 해.

B: 그들은 7월 15일에 첫 번째 음악회를 열 거야.

G: 좋아. 나는 음악회에서 연주를 하고 싶어.

B: 나도. 나는 음악회가 너무 기다려져.

※ 다음 우리말과 일치하도록 빈칸에 알맞은 것을 골라 쓰시오.

1 Seho and Jihun were _____ in the hallway _____ Dami _____ over.

A. came   B. when   C. talking

2 "_____ birthday!" she _____ _____ Seho.

A. to   B. said   C. happy

3 "Here. They're _____ _____ dad."

A. my   B. from

4 "Wow, _____ KBL _____! Thanks!"

A. tickets   B. two

5 "Who are you _____ to _____ with you?" Dami _____.

A. asked   B. take   C. going

6 "Minjun. He _____ me _____ a soccer game _____.

A. before   B. to   C. took

7 So, it's _____ to pay him _____."

A. back   B. time

8 "You know _____?" Jihun _____ in.

A. cut   B. what

9 "Minjun _____ a _____ of basketball. But I _____!"

A. am   B. fan   C. isn't

10 "Well, I'll _____ him first _____," _____ Seho.

A. replied   B. anyway   C. ask

11 "He _____ go _____ you. _____ me," said Jihun.

A. with   B. won't   C. trust

12 "Who is this guy?" Dami _____ to _____, "He _____ Minjun's ticket."

A. wants   B. herself   C. thought

13 "Oh! There's the _____. _____ you _____," said Dami.

A. later   B. see   C. bell

14 She _____ to _____.

A. class   B. hurried

15 "Come _____, Jihun," said Seho, and he _____ _____ run.

A. to   B. started   C. on

16 _____ the corner, Seho _____ _____ someone.

A. into   B. bumped   C. at

17 "Sorry!" he _____ and _____ _____ run.

A. to   B. continued   C. said

18 Just _____, Jihun _____ something _____ the floor.

A. saw   B. then   C. on

---

1 세호와 지훈이는 다미가 왔을 때 복도에서 이야기를 나누고 있었다.

2 "생일 축하해!" 다미가 세호에게 말했다.

3 "이거 받아. 우리 아빠가 주신 거야."

4 "와, KBL 입장권 두 장! 고마워!"

5 "넌 누구를 데려갈 거니?" 다미가 물었다.

6 "민준이. 그가 전에 나를 축구 경기에 데려갔어.

7 그래서 그에게 신세를 갚아야 할 때야."

8 "그거 알아?" 지훈이가 끼어들었다.

9 "민준이는 농구 팬이 아니야. 하지만 난 농구 팬이야!"

10 "음, 어쨌든 먼저 민준이에게 물어볼 거야." 세호가 대답했다.

11 "그는 너와 함께 가지 않을 거야. 날 믿어." 지훈이가 말했다.

12 "이 녀석은 누구지?" 다미는 "그는 민준이의 입장권을 원하는구나." 라고 마음속으로 생각했다.

13 "아, 종이 울린다. 나중에 보자," 다미가 말했다.

14 그녀는 서둘러 수업에 들어갔다.

15 "어서, 지훈아." 세호는 말하고 달리기 시작했다.

16 모퉁이에서, 세호는 누군가와 부딪혔다.

17 그는 "미안해!"라고 말하고는 계속 달렸다.

18 바로 그때, 지훈이가 바닥에 있는 무언가를 보았다.

19 "_____, Seho!" he said, _____ Seho was _____ there.

    A. not   B. but   C. wait

20 _____ class, Seho _____ to Dami and said, "I _____ _____ one of my tickets.

    A. find   B. went   C. after   D. can't

21 Did you _____ to _____ it?"

    A. see   B. happen

22 "No," _____ _____.

    A. answered   B. she

23 "_____ it in _____ bag?"

    A. your   B. isn't

24 "No, it's _____ there. I _____ I _____ it," said Seho.

    A. lost   B. think   C. not

25 _____ her _____ home, Dami _____ Jihun.

    A. saw   B. way   C. on

26 He _____ the ticket _____ his hand.

    A. in   B. had

27 Dami _____ _____ and said, "Hey! _____ do you ...?"

    A. why   B. angry   C. got

28 Just then, Jihun _____ Seho and _____, "Seho! I _____ a ticket in the hallway.

    A. found   B. shouted   C. saw

29 I _____ it's _____."

    A. yours   B. think

30 "Thanks! I was _____ _____ that!" _____ Seho.

    A. said   B. for   C. looking

31 "He's _____ so bad," Dami _____.

    A. thought   B. not

32 "So, what _____ you _____?

    A. saying   B. were

33 Do you have _____ to _____, Dami?" _____ Jihun.

    A. asked   B. say   C. something

34 "Um, how _____ _____ the school basketball game with me this Friday?

    A. to   B. about   C. going

35 _____ the _____."

    A. finals   B. it's

36 Jihun _____ really _____. "I'd love _____!"

    A. to   B. pleased   C. looked

---

19 "기다려, 세호야!"라고 그가 말했지만 세호는 거기에 없었다.

20 수업이 끝난 후, 세호는 다미에게 가서 말했다. "내 입장권 한 장을 찾을 수 없어.

21 너 혹시 입장권을 봤니?"

22 "아니," 그녀가 대답했다.

23 "네 가방 안에 있지 않니?"

24 "아니, 거기에 없어. 내 생각에 그것을 잃어버린 것 같아." 세호가 말했다.

25 집으로 돌아오는 길에 다미는 지훈을 보았다.

26 그는 손에 입장권을 가지고 있었다.

27 다미는 화가 나서 "이봐! 너가 왜 ...?"라고 말했다

28 바로 그때, 지훈이는 세호를 보고 소리쳤다. "세호야! 내가 복도에서 입장권을 찾았어.

29 네 것 같아."

30 "고마워! 나는 그것을 찾고 있었어!" 세호가 말했다.

31 "그는 그렇게 나쁘진 않아."라고 다미는 생각했다.

32 "그래서, 무슨 말을 하고 있었던 거야?

33 너 할 말이 있니, 다미야?" 지훈이가 물었다.

34 "음, 이번 금요일에 나랑 학교 농구 경기에 같이 가는 게 어때?

35 그것은 결승전이야."

36 지훈은 정말 기뻐 보였다. "가고 싶어!"

※ 다음 우리말과 일치하도록 빈칸에 알맞은 말을 쓰시오.

1 Seho and Jihun _____ _____ in the hallway _____ Dami _____ _____.

2 "_____ _____!" she _____ _____ Seho.

3 "Here. They're _____."

4 "Wow, _____ _____ _____! Thanks!"

5 "Who are you _____ _____ _____ with you?" Dami asked.

6 "Minjun. He _____ _____ _____ a soccer game before.

7 So, it's _____ _____ _____ _____ _____ _____."

8 "You _____ _____?" Jihun _____ _____.

9 "Minjun _____ a _____ of basketball. _____ I am!"

10 "Well, I'll _____ him first _____," _____ Seho.

11 "He _____ _____ _____ you. _____ me," said Jihun.

12 "Who is this guy?" Dami _____ _____ _____, "He _____ Minjun's _____."

13 "Oh! _____ the bell. _____ _____ _____," said Dami.

14 She _____ _____ _____.

15 "Come _____, Jihun," said Seho, and he _____ _____ _____.

16 _____ the corner, Seho _____ _____ _____.

17 "Sorry!" he said and _____ _____ _____.

18 _____ _____, Jihun saw something _____ the floor.

1 세호와 지훈이는 다미가 왔을 때 복도에서 이야기를 나누고 있었다.

2 "생일 축하해!" 다미가 세호에게 말했다.

3 "이거 받아. 우리 아빠가 주신 거야."

4 "와, KBL 입장권 두 장! 고마워!"

5 "넌 누구를 데려갈 거니?" 다미가 물었다.

6 "민준이. 그가 전에 나를 축구 경기에 데려갔어.

7 그래서 그에게 신세를 갚아야 할 때야."

8 "그거 알아?" 지훈이가 끼어들었다.

9 "민준이는 농구 팬이 아니야. 하지만 난 농구 팬이야!"

10 "음, 어쨌든 먼저 민준이에게 물어볼 거야." 세호가 대답했다.

11 "그는 너와 함께 가지 않을 거야. 날 믿어." 지훈이가 말했다.

12 "이 녀석은 누구지?" 다미는 "그는 민준이의 입장권을 원하는구나." 라고 마음속으로 생각했다.

13 "아, 종이 울린다. 나중에 보자," 다미가 말했다.

14 그녀는 서둘러 수업에 들어갔다.

15 "어서, 지훈아," 세호는 말하고 달리기 시작했다.

16 모퉁이에서, 세호는 누군가와 부딪혔다.

17 그는 "미안해!"라고 말하고는 계속 달렸다.

18 바로 그때, 지훈이가 바닥에 있는 무언가를 보았다.

19 "Wait, Seho!" he said, _____ Seho _____ _____ there.

20 _____ _____, Seho _____ _____ Dami and said, "I can't find _____ _____ _____ _____.

21 Did you _____ _____ see it?"

22 "No," she _____.

23 "_____ it _____ _____ _____ _____?"

24 "No, it's _____ there. I _____ I _____ it," said Seho.

25 _____ _____ _____ _____ _____, Dami saw Jihun.

26 He _____ the ticket _____ _____ _____.

27 Dami _____ _____ and said, "Hey! _____ do you ...?"

28 _____ _____, Jihun saw Seho and _____, "Seho! I _____ _____ _____ _____ the hallway.

29 I _____ it's _____."

30 "Thanks! I _____ _____ _____ that!" said Seho.

31 "He's _____ _____ _____," Dami _____.

32 "So, what _____ you _____?

33 Do you _____ something _____ _____, Dami?" _____ Jihun.

34 "Um, how _____ _____ _____ the school basketball game _____ _____ this Friday?

35 It's the _____."

36 Jihun _____ really _____. "I'd _____ _____!"

19 "기다려, 세호야!"라고 그가 말했지만 세호는 거기에 없었다.

20 수업이 끝난 후, 세호는 다미에게 가서 말했다. "내 입장권 한 장을 찾을 수 없어.

21 너 혹시 입장권을 봤니?"

22 "아니," 그녀가 대답했다.

23 "네 가방 안에 있지 않니?"

24 "아니, 거기에 없어. 내 생각에 그것을 잃어버린 것 같아," 세호가 말했다.

25 집으로 돌아오는 길에 다미는 지훈을 보았다.

26 그는 손에 입장권을 가지고 있었다.

27 다미는 화가 나서 "이봐! 너가 왜 ...?"라고 말했다

28 바로 그때, 지훈이는 세호를 보고 소리쳤다. "세호야! 내가 복도에서 입장권을 찾았어.

29 네 것 같아."

30 "고마워! 나는 그것을 찾고 있었어!" 세호가 말했다.

31 "그는 그렇게 나쁘진 않아."라고 다미는 생각했다.

32 "그래서, 무슨 말을 하고 있었던 거야?

33 너 할 말이 있니, 다미야?" 지훈이가 물었다.

34 "음, 이번 금요일에 나랑 학교 농구 경기에 같이 가는 게 어때?

35 그것은 결승전이야."

36 지훈은 정말 기뻐 보였다. "가고 싶어!"

Step3

※ 다음 문장을 우리말로 쓰시오.

1 Seho and Jihun were talking in the hallway when Dami came over.

➡ _____

2 "Happy birthday!" she said to Seho.

➡ _____

3 "Here. They're from my dad."

➡ _____

4 "Wow, two KBL tickets! Thanks!"

➡ _____

5 "Who are you going to take with you?" Dami asked.

➡ _____

6 "Minjun. He took me to a soccer game before.

➡ _____

7 So, it's time to pay him back."

➡ _____

8 "You know what?" Jihun cut in.

➡ _____

9 "Minjun isn't a fan of basketball. But I am!"

➡ _____

10 "Well, I'll ask him first anyway," replied Seho.

➡ _____

11 "He won't go with you. Trust me," said Jihun.

➡ _____

12 "Who is this guy?" Dami thought to herself, "He wants Minjun's ticket."

➡ _____

13 "Oh! There's the bell. See you later," said Dami.

➡ _____

14 She hurried to class.

➡ _____

15 "Come on, Jihun," said Seho, and he started to run.

➡ _____

16 At the corner, Seho bumped into someone.

➡ _____

17 "Sorry!" he said and continued to run.

➡ _____

18 Just then, Jihun saw something on the floor.

➡ _____

19 "Wait, Seho!" he said, but Seho was not there.

➡ _____

20 After class, Seho went to Dami and said, "I can't find one of my tickets.

➡ _____

21 Did you happen to see it?"

➡ _____

22 "No," she answered.

➡ _____

23 "Isn't it in your bag?"

➡ _____

24 "No, it's not there. I think I lost it," said Seho.

➡ _____

25 On her way home, Dami saw Jihun.

➡ _____

26 He had the ticket in his hand.

➡ _____

27 Dami got angry and said, "Hey! Why do you ...?"

➡ _____

28 Just then, Jihun saw Seho and shouted, "Seho! I found a ticket in the hallway.

➡ _____

29 I think it's yours."

➡ _____

30 "Thanks! I was looking for that!" said Seho.

➡ _____

31 "He's not so bad," Dami thought.

➡ _____

32 "So, what were you saying?

➡ _____

33 Do you have something to say, Dami?" asked Jihun.

➡ _____

34 "Um, how about going to the school basketball game with me this Friday?

➡ _____

35 It's the finals."

➡ _____

36 Jihun looked really pleased. "I'd love to!"

➡ _____

※ 다음 괄호 안의 단어들을 우리말에 맞도록 바르게 배열하시오.

1 (Jihun / and / Seho / talking / were / the / in / hallway / Dami / when / over. / came)
➡ _____

2 (birthday!" / "happy / to / she / Seho. / said)
➡ _____

3 ("here. // from / they're / dad." / my)
➡ _____

4 ("wow, / KBL / tickets! / two / thanks!")
➡ _____

5 (are / who / going / you / take / to / you?" / with / asked. / Dami)
➡ _____

6 ("Minjun. // took / he / to / me / game / a / before. / soccer)
➡ _____

7 (so, / time / it's / him / to / back." / pay)
➡ _____

8 (what?" / know / "you / in. / Jihun / cut)
➡ _____

9 (isn't / "Minjun / of / fan / a / basketball. // am!" / I / but)
➡ _____

10 ("well, / ask / I'll / him / anyway," / first / Seho. / replied)
➡ _____

11 (won't / "he / with / go / you. / me," / trust / Jihun. / said)
➡ _____

12 (this / is / guy?" / "who / Dami / herself, / to / thought / "he / Minjun's / ticket." / wants)
➡ _____

13 (oh! / the / there's / bell. / you / see / later," / Dami. / said)
➡ _____

14 (hurried / she / class. / to)
➡ _____

15 (on, / "come / Jihun," / Seho, / said / and / started / he / run. / to)
➡ _____

16 (corner, / the / at / Seho / into / someone. / bumped)
➡ _____

17 (he / said / "sorry!" / and / run." / to / continued)
➡ _____

18 (then, / just / Jihun / something / saw / floor. / on / the)
➡ _____

19 (Seho!" / "wait, / said, / he / but / was / Seho / there. / not)
➡ _____

1 세호와 지훈이는 다미가 왔을 때 복도에서 이야기를 나누고 있었다.

2 "생일 축하해!" 다미가 세호에게 말했다.

3 "이거 받아. 우리 아빠가 주신 거야."

4 "와, KBL 입장권 두 장! 고마워!"

5 "넌 누구를 데려갈 거니?" 다미가 물었다.

6 "민준이. 그가 전에 나를 축구 경기에 데려갔어.

7 그래서 그에게 신세를 갚아야 할 때야."

8 "그거 알아?" 지훈이가 끼어들었다.

9 "민준이는 농구 팬이 아니야. 하지만 난 농구 팬이야!"

10 "음, 어쨌든 먼저 민준이에게 물어볼 거야." 세호가 대답했다.

11 "그는 너와 함께 가지 않을 거야. 날 믿어." 지훈이가 말했다.

12 "이 녀석은 누구지?" 다미는 "그는 민준이의 입장권을 원하는구나." 라고 마음속으로 생각했다.

13 "아, 종이 울린다. 나중에 보자." 다미가 말했다.

14 그녀는 서둘러 수업에 들어갔다.

15 "어서, 지훈아." 세호는 말하고 달리기 시작했다.

16 모퉁이에서, 세호는 누군가와 부딪혔다.

17 그는 "미안해!"라고 말하고는 계속 달렸다.

18 바로 그때, 지훈이가 바닥에 있는 무언가를 보았다.

19 "기다려, 세호야!"라고 그가 말했지만 세호는 거기에 없었다.

20 (class, / after / went / Seho / Dami / to / said, / and / "I / find / can't / of / my / tickets. / one)

➡ _____

21 (you / did / happen / see / it?" / to)

➡ _____

22 (she / answered. / "no,")

➡ _____

23 (it / isn't / your / bag?" / in)

➡ _____

24 ("no, / there. / not / it's / I / lost / I / think / it," / Seho. / said)

➡ _____

25 (her / on / home, / way / Jihun. / saw / Dami)

➡ _____

26 (had / he / ticket / the / hand. / in / his)

➡ _____

27 (got / Dami / said, / and / angry / "hey! / you / do / ...?" / why)

➡ _____

28 (then, / just / saw / Jihun / and / Seho / shouted, / "Seho! / found / I / a / ticket / hallway. / the / in)

➡ _____

29 (it's / yours." / think / I)

➡ _____

30 ("thanks! / was / I / looking / that!" / for / Seho. / said)

➡ _____

31 (not / bad," / so / "he's / thought. / Dami)

➡ _____

32 (what / "so, / you / saying? / were)

➡ _____

33 (you / do / something / have / to / say, / Dami?" / Jihun. / asked)

➡ _____

34 ("um, / about / how / going / the / to / basketball / school / game / me / with / Friday? / this)

➡ _____

35 (the / finals." / it's)

➡ _____

36 (looked / Jihun / pleased. // really / "I'd / to!" / love)

➡ _____

20 수업이 끝난 후, 세호는 다미에게 가서 말했다. "내 입장권 한 장을 찾을 수 없어.

21 너 혹시 입장권을 봤니?"

22 "아니." 그녀가 대답했다.

23 "네 가방 안에 있지 않니?"

24 "아니, 거기에 없어. 내 생각에 그것을 잃어버린 것 같아," 세호가 말했다.

25 집으로 돌아오는 길에 다미는 지훈을 보았다.

26 그는 손에 입장권을 가지고 있었다.

27 다미는 화가 나서 "이봐! 너가 왜 ...?"라고 말했다

28 바로 그때, 지훈이는 세호를 보고 소리쳤다. "세호야! 내가 복도에서 입장권을 찾았어.

29 네 것 같아."

30 "고마워! 나는 그것을 찾고 있었어!" 세호가 말했다.

31 "그는 그렇게 나쁘진 않아."라고 다미는 생각했다.

32 "그래서, 무슨 말을 하고 있었던 거야?

33 너 할 말이 있니, 다미야?" 지훈이가 물었다.

34 "음, 이번 금요일에 나랑 학교 농구 경기에 같이 가는 게 어때?

35 그것은 결승전이야."

36 지훈은 정말 기뻐 보였다. "가고 싶어!"

※ **다음 우리말을 영어로 쓰시오.**

1 세호와 지훈이는 다미가 왔을 때 복도에서 이야기를 나누고 있었다.
➡ _____

2 "생일 축하해!" 다미가 세호에게 말했다.
➡ _____

3 "이거 받아. 우리 아빠가 주신 거야."
➡ _____

4 "와, KBL 입장권 두 장! 고마워!"
➡ _____

5 "넌 누구를 데려갈 거니?" 다미가 물었다.
➡ _____

6 "민준이. 그가 전에 나를 축구 경기에 데려갔어.
➡ _____

7 그래서 그에게 신세를 갚아야 할 때야."
➡ _____

8 "그거 알아?" 지훈이가 끼어들었다.
➡ _____

9 "민준이는 농구 팬이 아니야. 하지만 난 농구 팬이야!"
➡ _____

10 "음, 어쨌든 먼저 민준이에게 물어볼 거야." 세호가 대답했다.
➡ _____

11 "그는 너와 함께 가지 않을 거야. 날 믿어." 지훈이가 말했다.
➡ _____

12 "이 녀석은 누구지?" 다미는 "그는 민준이의 입장권을 원하는구나."라고 마음속으로 생각했다.
➡ _____

13 "아, 종이 울린다. 나중에 보자,"라고 다미가 말했다.
➡ _____

14 그녀는 서둘러 수업에 들어갔다.
➡ _____

15 "어서, 지훈아." 세호는 말하고 달리기 시작했다.
➡ _____

16 모퉁이에서, 세호는 누군가와 부딪혔다.
➡ _____

17 그는 "미안해!"라고 말하고는 계속 달렸다.
➡ _____

18 바로 그때, 지훈이가 바닥에 있는 무언가를 보았다.
➡ _____

19 "기다려, 세호야!" 그가 말했지만 세호는 거기에 없었다.

➡ _____

20 수업이 끝난 후, 세호는 다미에게 가서 말했다, "내 입장권 한 장을 찾을 수 없어.

➡ _____

21 너 혹시 입장권을 봤니?"

➡ _____

22 "아니," 그녀가 대답했다.

➡ _____

23 "네 가방 안에 있지 않니?"

➡ _____

24 "아니, 거기에 없어. 내 생각에 그것을 잃어버린 것 같아." 세호가 말했다.

➡ _____

25 집으로 돌아오는 길에 다미는 지훈을 보았다.

➡ _____

26 그는 손에 입장권을 가지고 있었다.

➡ _____

27 다미는 화가 나서 "이봐! 너가 왜 ...?"라고 말했다.

➡ _____

28 바로 그때, 지훈이는 세호를 보고 소리쳤다, "세호야! 내가 복도에서 입장권을 찾았어.

➡ _____

29 네 것 같아."

➡ _____

30 "고마워! 나는 그것을 찾고 있었어!" 세호가 말했다.

➡ _____

31 "그는 그렇게 나쁘진 않아." 다미는 생각했다.

➡ _____

32 "그래서, 무슨 말을 하고 있었던 거야?

➡ _____

33 너 할 말이 있니, 다미야?" 지훈이가 물었다.

➡ _____

34 "음, 이번 금요일에 나랑 학교 농구 경기에 같이 가는 게 어때?

➡ _____

35 그것은 결승전이야."

➡ _____

36 지훈은 정말 기뻐 보였다. "가고 싶어!"

➡ _____

※ 다음 우리말과 일치하도록 빈칸에 알맞은 말을 쓰시오.

Project - Link to the World

가는 말이 고와야 오는 말이 곱다

1. This saying _____ "Nice _____ for nice words" _____ English.

2. I _____ _____ nice words to _____ first.

3. Then they will say _____ _____ to me, _____.

4. I _____ that I can _____ lots of good _____ this way.

5. This year, I will _____ _____ _____ remember this _____ and say nice words to _____.

가는 말이 고와야 오는 말이 곱다

1. 이 속담은 영어로 '좋은 말에는 좋은 말로'를 뜻한다.
2. 나는 먼저 다른 사람들에게 좋은 말을 할 것이다.
3. 그러면 그들도 나에게 좋은 말을 할 것이다.
4. 나는 이런 식으로 좋은 친구들을 많이 사귈 수 있다고 믿어.
5. 올해, 나는 항상 이 속담을 기억하고 다른 사람들에게 좋은 말을 하려고 노력할 것이다.

Check Yourself - Read & Write

1. Dami gave _____ _____ _____ _____.

2. Jihun _____ _____ _____ to the basketball game _____ Seho.

3. Seho _____ one of the tickets _____ _____ _____ _____ go class.

4. Jihun _____ Seho's ticket in the _____.

5. Dami _____ Seho's ticket in Jihun's hand, and she _____, "He's a bad boy."

6. Jihun _____ the ticket _____ _____ Seho, and Dami _____ that she _____ _____.

7. Dami _____ _____ _____ _____ the school basketball game with Jihun.

8. Jihun was really _____.

---

1. 다미가 세호에게 농구 입장권 두 장을 주었다.
2. 지훈이는 세호와 농구 경기에 가고 싶어했다.
3. 세호는 수업에 가는 길에 입장권 하나를 떨어뜨렸다.
4. 지훈이는 복도에서 세호의 입장권을 발견했다.
5. 다미는 지훈이의 손에 있는 세호의 입장권을 보았고 그녀는 "그는 나쁜 소년이야."라고 생각했다.
6. 지훈이는 세호에게 입장권을 돌려주었고 다미는 그녀가 틀렸다는 것을 깨달았다.
7. 다미는 지훈이와 함께 학교 농구 경기에 가고 싶었다.
8. 지훈이는 정말 기뻤다.

※ 다음 우리말을 영어로 쓰시오.

Project - Link to the World

가는 말이 고와야 오는 말이 곱다

1. 이 속담은 영어로 '좋은 말에는 좋은 말로'를 뜻한다.

   ➡ _____

2. 나는 먼저 다른 사람들에게 좋은 말을 할 것이다.

   ➡ _____

3. 그러면 그들도 나에게 좋은 말을 할 것이다.

   ➡ _____

4. 나는 이런 식으로 좋은 친구들을 많이 사귈 수 있다고 믿어.

   ➡ _____

5. 올해, 나는 항상 이 속담을 기억하고 다른 사람들에게 좋은 말을 하려고 노력할 것이다.

   ➡ _____

Check Yourself - Read & Write

1. 다미가 세호에게 농구 입장권 두 장을 주었다.

   ➡ _____

2. 지훈이는 세호와 농구 경기에 가고 싶어했다.

   ➡ _____

3. 세호는 수업에 가는 길에 입장권 하나를 떨어뜨렸다.

   ➡ _____

4. 지훈이는 복도에서 세호의 입장권을 발견했다.

   ➡ _____

5. 다미는 지훈이의 손에 있는 세호의 입장권을 보았고 그녀는 "그는 나쁜 소년이야."라고 생각했다.

   ➡ _____

6. 지훈이는 세호에게 입장권을 돌려주었고 다미는 그녀가 틀렸다는 것을 깨달았다.

   ➡ _____

7. 다미는 지훈이와 함께 학교 농구 경기에 가고 싶었다.

   ➡ _____

8. 지훈이는 정말 기뻐했다.

   ➡ _____

※ 다음 영어를 우리말로 쓰시오.

01	elderly	22	hope
02	closely	23	brown
03	block	24	rest
04	neighbor	25	cry
05	butterfly	26	strange
06	address	27	wash
07	cute	28	borrow
08	director	29	clothes
09	doorbell	30	lonely
10	feed	31	perfect
11	free	32	nervous
12	check	33	exactly
13	gate	34	outside
14	green	35	run after
15	hurry	36	take a break
16	leave	37	look around
17	cut	38	get better
18	lost	39	take A to B
19	build	40	get enough rest
20	chat	41	put up
21	volunteer	42	be good at
		43	take care of

※ 다음 우리말을 영어로 쓰시오.

01	~ 주위에	
02	(고개를) 끄덕이다	
03	모양	
04	완벽한	
05	돌봄, 보살핌	
06	옷, 의복	
07	연습하다	
08	특별한	
09	충분한	
10	따라가다	
11	점, 반점	
12	무대	
13	꼭, 정확히	
14	열심히	
15	안에	
16	돌아오다[가다]	
17	외로운	
18	놓치다, 그리워하다	
19	여전히	
20	이사하다, 옮기다	
21	긴장되는	

22	밖에, 밖에서	
23	지나가다, 통과하다	
24	팔다	
25	알아맞히다	
26	중고의	
27	빌리다	
28	이상한	
29	수다를 떨다	
30	이웃	
31	먹이를 주다	
32	연세가 드신	
33	주소	
34	초인종	
35	~에 늦다	
36	~을 준비하다	
37	A를 B로 데려가다	
38	~의 앞쪽에[앞에]	
39	둘러보다	
40	휴식을 취하다	
41	~을 붙이다	
42	청소하다	
43	~ 덕분에	

※ 다음 영영풀이에 알맞은 단어를 <보기>에서 골라 쓴 후, 우리말 뜻을 쓰시오.

1 _____ : complete and without faults or weaknesses: _____

2 _____ : to make something by putting together parts or materials: _____

3 _____ : to give food to a person or an animal: _____

4 _____ : unhappy because you have no friends or people to talk to: _____

5 _____ : to come or go to a place again: _____

6 _____ : a person who does a job without being paid for it: _____

7 _____ : details of where someone lives or works and where letters, etc. can be

    sent: _____

8 _____ : a group of buildings with streets on all sides: _____

9 _____ : someone who lives next to you or near you: _____

10 _____ : a flying insect with a long thin body and four large, usually brightly

    colored, wings: _____

11 _____ : a wound on a person's body that is made by something sharp:

    _____

12 _____ : to move your head up and down, especially in order to show agreement

    or understanding: _____

13 _____ : a period of time in which you relax, sleep, or do nothing after you have

    been active or doing work: _____

14 _____ : a small round area that has a different color or feels different from the

    surface it is on: _____

15 _____ : to take and use something that belongs to someone else, and return it to

    them at a later time: _____

16 _____ : a bell on the outside of a house which you can ring so that the people

    inside know that you want to see them: _____

보기

spot	feed	volunteer	block
cut	address	borrow	return
butterfly	lonely	perfect	build
doorbell	rest	neighbor	nod

※ 다음 우리말과 일치하도록 빈칸에 알맞은 말을 쓰시오.

Get Ready - 2

1. B: I'm _____ _____ some pictures _____ _____ _____ the flower gate.

   G: _____ good. It's _____ _____.

2. B: Hello. _____ me, Jamie. I _____ I'll _____ there in 20 minutes.

   G: Okay. _____ _____ _____ 2 p.m. _____ _____ _____ the clock tower.

3. B: I'm _____ to buy some clothes _____ a school picnic.

   G: Look. They're _____ old books and clothes _____ _____.

   B: Great. _____ _____ and _____ _____.

Start Off - Listen & Talk A

1. G: Do you have _____ _____ _____ the weekend?

   B: Yes. I'm _____ _____ practice _____ at the youth center.

   G: _____ great. _____ I _____ you?

   B: Why _____?

2. G: I'm _____ _____ _____ to the library _____ _____ _____ the exam.

   B: You _____ City Library? I want _____ _____ with you.

   G: Great. Can you _____ _____ _____ 3 p.m. tomorrow?

   B: Sure. _____ _____ _____ _____.

Start Off - Listen & Talk B

B: What _____ you _____ _____ _____ this Saturday?

G: I'm planning _____ _____ _____ the park _____ my dad.

B: Sounds _____ a wonderful plan. _____ I _____ you?

G: Sure. Can you _____ _____ at the bus stop _____ 1 p.m.?

B: I'm _____ _____. _____ _____ 2?

G: _____ _____ me. Please _____ _____ _____ _____ gloves and a big plastic bag.

B: Okay. _____ you _____ _____.

Start Off - Speak Up - Look and talk.

A: I'm _____ _____ _____ at the library this Tuseday.

B: Great. _____ I _____ _____ _____ _____?

A: _____ _____ _____? _____ you _____ _____ at 3 p.m.?

B: Sure. _____ _____ _____ _____ the library.

해석

1. B: 꽃문 앞에서 사진 몇 장을 찍을 거야.
   G: 좋은 생각이야. 그것은 저쪽에 있어.
2. B: 여보세요. 나야, Jamie. 20분 후에 도착할 것 같아.
   G: 알았어. 오후 2시에 시계탑 앞에서 만나자.
3. B: 학교 소풍을 위해 옷을 살 계획이야.
   G: 봐. 저기서 헌 책과 옷을 팔고 있어.
   B: 잘됐다. 가서 둘러보자.

1. G: 주말에 무슨 계획 있니?
   B: 응. 청소년 센터에서 춤을 연습하려고 해.
   G: 정말 잘 됐다. 같이 가도 될까?
   B: 물론이지.
2. G: 나는 시험을 준비하기 위해 도서관에 갈 계획이야.
   B: 시립 도서관 말하는 거니? 나는 너와 함께 공부하고 싶어.
   G: 좋아. 내일 오후 3시에 만날 수 있니?
   B: 물론. 그럼 그때 봐.

B: 이번 토요일에 뭐 할 거니?
G: 아빠와 함께 공원을 청소할 계획이야.
B: 멋진 계획인 것 같구나. 같이 가도 될까?
G: 물론이지. 버스 정류장에서 오후 1시에 만날 수 있니?
B: 안 될 것 같아. 2시는 어때?
G: 난 괜찮아. 장갑 한 켤레와 커다란 비닐봉지를 가져와.
B: 알았어. 토요일에 보자.

A: 이번 화요일에 도서관에서 자원봉사를 할 계획이야.
B: 멋지다. 같이 가도 될까?
A: 왜 안 되겠니? 오후 3시에 만날 수 있을까?
B: 물론이지. 도서관 앞에서 만나자.

Step Up - Real-life Scene

Let's Volunteer for a Better Town!

Jina: I'm _____ at the _____ _____ _____ this Sunday morning.

Alex: You _____ the one _____ Grand Park, Jina?

Jina: Right. _____ you _____ _____ me, Alex? They need _____ _____ _____ _____ _____ the animals.

Alex: I'd _____ _____ join. I like _____ and _____ animals. I'm also _____ _____ _____ them.

Jina: Great. You can _____ other friends _____ you, _____.

Alex: Okay. I'll _____ _____ _____ Nancy. She loves animals, _____. What time _____ we _____?

Jina: Can you _____ it _____ 8 a.m. _____ the Grand Park bus stop?

Alex: Sure. I'll _____ you _____ _____.

Express Yourself A

1. M: _____ _____ _____ _____ _____ _____ the town festival _____ _____ a dance show.

   W: Sounds _____. Can I _____ _____ you?

   M: _____ _____. _____ _____ _____ _____ at the school gate _____ 6 p.m.?

   W: _____ problem. _____ _____ _____ _____.

2. W: I'm _____ _____ _____ a singing contest in my town, but I'm _____.

   M: _____ _____. _____ you _____ hard, you _____ _____ the contest.

   W: _____ you.

Learning Diary - Listen & Speak

B: What _____ _____ _____ _____ do this Friday, Aria?

G: I'm _____ _____ _____ at the post office.

B: Sounds _____!

G: _____ you _____ _____ me, Eric?

B: Sure. _____ _____ we _____?

G: _____ _____ _____ at 3 p.m.?

B: I'm _____ _____. _____ _____ 4 p.m.?

G: Good. _____ _____ _____.

더 나은 마을을 위해 자원 봉사합시다!

지나: 이번 일요일 아침에 동물 보호 센터에서 자원봉사를 할 계획이야.

Alex: Grand Park 근처에 있는 거 말하는 거니, 지나야?

지나: 맞아. 나랑 같이 갈래, Alex? 그들은 동물들을 돌볼 자원 봉사자들이 필요해.

Alex: 나도 함께하고 싶어. 나는 동물들에게 먹이를 주고 산책시키는 것을 좋아해. 그리고 그들을 씻기는 것도 잘해.

지나: 좋아. 다른 친구들도 데려와도 돼.

Alex: 알았어. 내 이웃인 Nancy에게 물어볼게. 그녀도 동물들을 아주 좋아해. 몇 시에 만날까?

지나: Grand Park 버스 정류장에서 오전 8시에 만날까?

Alex: 물론. 일요일에 보자.

1. M: 나는 춤 공연을 보기 위해 마을 축제에 갈 계획이야.
   W: 재미있겠다. 같이 가도 될까?
   M: 물론이지. 오후 6시에 학교 정문에서 만날까?
   W: 그래. 그럼 그때 보자.

2. W: 나는 우리 동네 노래 경연 대회에 나갈 계획인데, 긴장돼.
   M: 걱정하지 마. 열심히 연습하면 너는 대회에서 우승할 수 있어.
   W: 고마워.

B: 이번 금요일에 뭐 할 거니, Aria?
G: 우체국에서 자원봉사를 할 계획이야.
B: 멋지다!
G: 나랑 같이 갈래, Eric?
B: 물론이지. 우리 언제 만날까?
G: 오후 3시에 만날 수 있을까?
B: 안 될 것 같아. 오후 4시는 어때?
G: 좋아. 그때 보자.

※ 다음 우리말에 맞도록 대화를 영어로 쓰시오.

 해석

Get Ready - 2

1. B: _____
   G: _____

2. B: _____
   G: _____

3. B: _____
   G: _____
   B: _____

1. B: 꽃문 앞에서 사진 몇 장을 찍을 거야.
   G: 좋은 생각이야. 그것은 저쪽에 있어.
2. B: 여보세요. 나야, Jamie. 20분 후에 도착할 것 같아.
   G: 알았어. 오후 2시에 시계탑 앞에서 만나자.
3. B: 학교 소풍을 위해 옷을 살 계획이야.
   G: 봐. 저기서 헌 책과 옷을 팔고 있어.
   B: 잘됐다. 가서 둘러보자.

Start Off - Listen & Talk A

1. G: _____
   B: _____
   G: _____
   B: _____

2. G: _____
   B: _____
   G: _____
   B: _____

1. G: 주말에 무슨 계획 있니?
   B: 응. 청소년 센터에서 춤을 연습하려고 해.
   G: 정말 잘 됐다. 같이 가도 될까?
   B: 물론이지.
2. G: 나는 시험을 준비하기 위해 도서관에 갈 계획이야.
   B: 시립 도서관 말하는 거니? 나는 너와 함께 공부하고 싶어.
   G: 좋아. 내일 오후 3시에 만날 수 있니?
   B: 물론. 그럼 그때 봐.

Start Off - Listen & Talk B

B: _____
G: _____
B: _____
G: _____
B: _____
G: _____
B: _____

B: 이번 토요일에 뭐 할 거니?
G: 아빠와 함께 공원을 청소할 계획이야.
B: 멋진 계획인 것 같구나. 같이 가도 될까?
G: 물론이지. 버스 정류장에서 오후 1시에 만날 수 있니?
B: 안 될 것 같아. 2시는 어때?
G: 난 괜찮아. 장갑 한 켤레와 커다란 비닐봉지를 가져와.
B: 알았어. 토요일에 보자.

Start Off - Speak Up - Look and talk.

A: _____
B: _____
A: _____
B: _____

A: 이번 화요일에 도서관에서 자원봉사를 할 계획이야.
B: 멋지다. 같이 가도 될까?
A: 왜 안 되겠니? 오후 3시에 만날 수 있을까?
B: 물론이지. 도서관 앞에서 만나자.

Step Up - Real-life Scene

Let's Volunteer for a Better Town!

Jina: _____

Alex: _____

Jina: _____

_____

Alex: _____

_____

Jina: _____

Alex: _____

_____

Jina: _____

Alex: _____

더 나은 마을을 위해 자원 봉사합시다!

지나: 이번 일요일 아침에 동물 보호 센터에서 자원봉사를 할 계획이야.

Alex: Grand Park 근처에 있는 거 말하는 거니, 지나야?

지나: 맞아. 나랑 같이 갈래, Alex? 그들은 동물들을 돌볼 자원 봉사자들이 필요해.

Alex: 나도 함께하고 싶어. 나는 동물들에게 먹이를 주고 산책시키는 것을 좋아해. 그리고 그들을 씻기는 것도 잘해.

지나: 좋아. 다른 친구들도 데려와도 돼.

Alex: 알았어. 내 이웃인 Nancy에게 물어볼게. 그녀도 동물들을 아주 좋아해. 몇 시에 만날까?

지나: Grand Park 버스 정류장에서 오전 8시에 만날까?

Alex: 물론. 일요일에 보자.

Express Yourself A

1. M: _____

W: _____

M: _____

W: _____

2. W: _____

M: _____

W: _____

1. M: 나는 춤 공연을 보기 위해 마을 축제에 갈 계획이야.
   W: 재미있겠다. 같이 가도 될까?
   M: 물론이지. 오후 6시에 학교 정문에서 만날까?
   W: 그래. 그럼 그때 보자.

2. W: 나는 우리 동네 노래 경연 대회에 나갈 계획인데, 긴장돼.
   M: 걱정하지 마. 열심히 연습하면 너는 대회에서 우승할 수 있어.
   W: 고마워.

Learning Diary - Listen & Speak

B: _____

G: _____

B: _____

G: _____

B: _____

G: _____

B: _____

G: _____

B: 이번 금요일에 뭐 할 거니, Aria?

G: 우체국에서 자원봉사를 할 계획이야.

B: 멋지다!

G: 나랑 같이 갈래, Eric?

B: 물론이지. 우리 언제 만날까?

G: 오후 3시에 만날 수 있을까?

B: 안 될 것 같아. 오후 4시는 어때?

G: 좋아. 그때 보자.

※ 다음 우리말과 일치하도록 빈칸에 알맞은 것을 골라 쓰시오.

1 Bear was a _____ and _____ cat _____ green eyes.
   A. with   B. brown   C. black

2 He _____ a boy, Ryan.
   A. with   B. lived

3 Ryan always thought that "Bear" was a _____ name for the cat _____ he had a black _____ in the _____ of a bear.
   A. shape   B. spot   C. because   D. perfect

4 Bear liked to go _____ every morning and _____ butterflies.
   A. after   B. run   C. outside

5 He _____ home just _____ time for dinner.
   A. in   B. came   C. always

6 Five blocks _____, Max the cat _____ _____ a girl, Sheila.
   A. with   B. lived   C. away

7 When Sheila _____ to this town _____ month, she was _____.
   A. lonely   B. last   C. moved

8 She _____ _____ friends there.
   A. no   B. had

9 But, _____ Max _____ her home, he _____ a good friend to her.
   A. became   B. followed   C. after

10 _____ day, Sheila _____ Max sitting _____ the desk.
   A. under   B. saw   C. one

11 He was _____ a strange _____.
   A. sound   B. making

12 "What's _____?" _____ Sheila.
   A. asked   B. wrong

13 She looked _____ him _____ and _____ a bad _____ on his leg.
   A. cut   B. closely   C. found   D. at

14 She _____ him _____ the animal _____.
   A. hospital   B. to   C. took

15 The doctor said, "He will get _____ if he _____ enough _____. _____ him inside for a week."
   A. keep   B. rest   C. gets   D. better

16 That night, _____ Ryan's house, there _____ _____ Bear.
   A. no   B. was   C. at

17 Ryan checked _____, but he _____ _____ him.
   A. outside   B. find   C. couldn't

18 He _____ posters and _____ them _____ around town.
   A. up   B. put   C. made

19 A _____ night _____. Still _____ Bear.
   A. no   B. passed   C. third

20 When Sheila was _____ _____ her house, she _____ a poster about the _____ cat.
   A. lost   B. near   C. saw   D. walking

1 Bear는 초록색 눈을 가진 검은색과 갈색의 고양이였다.

2 그는 소년 Ryan과 함께 살았다.

3 Ryan은 항상 "Bear"가 곰 모양의 검은 반점이 있기 때문에 그 고양이에게 딱 맞는 이름이라고 생각했다.

4 Bear는 매일 아침 밖으로 나가 나비를 쫓아다니는 것을 좋아했다.

5 그는 항상 저녁 식사 시간에 맞춰 집에 왔다.

6 다섯 블록 떨어진 곳에, 고양이 Max는 Sheila라는 소녀와 함께 살았다.

7 지난달에 Sheila가 이 마을로 이사 왔을 때, 그녀는 외로웠다.

8 그녀는 그곳에 친구가 없었다.

9 하지만 Max가 그녀를 따라 집으로 온 후, 그는 그녀에게 좋은 친구가 되었다.

10 어느 날, Sheila는 책상 밑에 앉아 있는 Max를 보았다.

11 그는 이상한 소리를 내고 있었다.

12 "무슨 일 있니?" Sheila가 물었다.

13 그녀는 그를 자세히 살펴보고 그의 다리에 심한 상처가 난 것을 발견했다.

14 그녀는 그를 동물 병원으로 데려갔다.

15 의사는 "충분한 휴식을 취하면 좋아질 거야. 그를 일주일 동안 안에 있도록 해라."라고 말했다.

16 그날 밤, Ryan의 집에는 Bear가 없었다.

17 Ryan은 바깥을 살폈지만 그는 그를 찾을 수 없었다.

18 그는 포스터를 만들어서 마을을 다니며 그것을 붙였다.

19 세 번째 밤이 지났다. 여전히 Bear는 나타나지 않았다.

20 Sheila가 그녀의 집 근처를 걷고 있었을 때, 그녀는 잃어버린 고양이에 대한 포스터를 보았다.

21 She _____ it _____, and her eyes _____ big.
  A. got   B. closely   C. read

22 "This cat _____ exactly _____ Max. It's so _____."
  A. strange   B. like   C. looks

23 She _____ _____.
  A. home   B. hurried

24 "Come _____, Max! _____ go!"
  A. let's   B. on

25 She _____ him _____ the address _____ the poster.
  A. on   B. to   C. took

26 "Ding-Dong." When Ryan _____ the doorbell _____, he _____ to the door and _____ it.
  A. opened   B. ran   C. ring   D. heard

27 "Bear, you're _____!" Ryan _____.
  A. cried   B. back

28 Max _____ up _____ Ryan's _____.
  A. arms   B. into   C. jumped

29 "_____ me _____," said Sheila.
  A. guess   B. let

30 "Your cat _____ home _____ in the evenings, _____ he?"
  A. doesn't   B. only   C. comes

31 _____ _____.
  A. nodded   B. Ryan

32 "And you _____ him _____ Friday, _____ you?" Sheila said.
  A. didn't   B. last   C. lost

33 "Yes! _____ did you _____?" said Ryan.
  A. know   B. how

34 "_____ this is my cat, _____, and he usually comes to my home _____ _____ the day."
  A. during   B. too   C. only   D. because

35 "_____ cat _____ two families!" _____ Ryan.
  A. said   B. has   C. our

36 "Hey, _____ you have time, please come _____ and _____ some cookies."
  A. have   B. in   C. if

37 "_____," _____ Sheila.
  A. said   B. sure

38 "_____ you, Max," she _____.
  A. thought   B. thank

39 "I _____ a good neighbor _____ _____ you!"
  A. thanks   B. to   C. met

---

21 그녀는 그것을 자세히 읽고, 그녀의 눈은 커졌다.

22 "이 고양이는 꼭 Max 같아 보여. 너무 이상해."

23 그녀는 서둘러 집으로 돌아갔다.

24 "자, Max! 가자!"

25 그녀는 그를 포스터에 적힌 주소로 데려갔다.

26 "딩동." Ryan은 초인종이 울리는 소리를 듣고 문으로 달려가 문을 열었다.

27 "Bear야, 돌아왔구나!" Ryan이 외쳤다.

28 Max가 Ryan의 팔 안으로 뛰어올랐다.

29 "내가 맞춰 볼게," Sheila가 말했다.

30 "너의 고양이는 저녁에만 집에 오지, 그렇지?"

31 Ryan은 고개를 끄덕였다.

32 "그리고 너는 지난 금요일에 그를 잃어버렸지, 그렇지 않니?" Sheila가 말했다.

33 "응! "어떻게 알았니?"라고 Ryan은 말했다.

34 "이것은 또한 내 고양이이기 때문이야, 보통 낮에만 우리 집에 오거든."

35 "우리 고양이는 가족이 둘이야!" Ryan이 말했다.

36 이봐, 시간이 있으면 들어와서 쿠키 좀 먹어."

37 "그래," Sheila가 말했다.

38 "고마워, Max." 그녀는 생각했다.

39 "나는 네 덕분에 좋은 이웃을 만났어!"

※ 다음 우리말과 일치하도록 빈칸에 알맞은 말을 쓰시오.

1 Bear was a black and brown cat _____ _____ _____.

2 He _____ _____ a boy, Ryan.

3 Ryan _____ _____ that "Bear" was a _____ name for the cat _____ he had a black _____ in the _____ of a bear.

4 Bear _____ _____ _____ _____ every morning and _____ _____ butterflies.

5 He _____ came home just _____ time _____ dinner.

6 Five blocks _____, Max the cat _____ _____ a girl, Sheila.

7 _____ Sheila _____ _____ this town _____ _____, she was _____.

8 She _____ _____ _____ there.

9 But, _____ Max _____ _____ _____, he _____ a good friend to her.

10 _____ _____, Sheila _____ Max _____ under the desk.

11 He _____ _____ _____ _____ _____ _____.

12 "What's _____?" _____ Sheila.

13 She _____ _____ him _____ and _____ _____ _____ _____ on his leg.

14 She _____ him _____ the _____ _____.

15 The doctor said, "He will _____ _____ if he _____ _____ _____. _____ _____ for a week."

16 That night, _____ Ryan's house, there _____ _____ Bear.

17 Ryan _____ _____, but he _____ _____ him.

18 He _____ posters and _____ them _____ around town.

19 A _____ _____ _____. _____ no Bear.

20 _____ Sheila _____ _____ her house, she _____ a poster about _____ _____ _____.

1 Bear는 초록색 눈을 가진 검은색과 갈색의 고양이였다.

2 그는 소년 Ryan과 함께 살았다.

3 Ryan은 항상 "Bear"가 곰 모양의 검은 반점이 있기 때문에 그 고양이에게 딱 맞는 이름이라고 생각했다.

4 Bear는 매일 아침 밖으로 나가 나비를 쫓아다니는 것을 좋아했다.

5 그는 항상 저녁 식사 시간에 맞춰 집에 왔다.

6 다섯 블록 떨어진 곳에, 고양이 Max는 Sheila라는 소녀와 함께 살았다.

7 지난달에 Sheila가 이 마을로 이사 왔을 때, 그녀는 외로웠다.

8 그녀는 그곳에 친구가 없었다.

9 하지만 Max가 그녀를 따라 집으로 온 후, 그는 그녀에게 좋은 친구가 되었다.

10 어느 날, Sheila는 책상 밑에 앉아 있는 Max를 보았다.

11 그는 이상한 소리를 내고 있었다.

12 "무슨 일 있니?" Sheila가 물었다.

13 그녀는 그를 자세히 살펴보고 그의 다리에 심한 상처가 난 것을 발견했다.

14 그녀는 그를 동물 병원으로 데려갔다.

15 의사는 "충분한 휴식을 취하면 좋아질 거야. 그를 일주일 동안 안에 있도록 해라."라고 말했다.

16 그날 밤, Ryan의 집에는 Bear가 없었다.

17 Ryan은 바깥을 살폈지만 그는 그를 찾을 수 없었다.

18 그는 포스터를 만들어서 마을을 다니며 그것을 붙였다.

19 세 번째 밤이 지났다. 여전히 Bear는 나타나지 않았다.

20 Sheila가 그녀의 집 근처를 걷고 있었을 때, 그녀는 잃어버린 고양이에 대한 포스터를 보았다.

21 She _____ it _____, and her eyes _____ _____.

22 "This cat _____ exactly _____ Max. It's so _____."

23 She _____ _____.

24 "Come _____, Max! _____ _____!"

25 She _____ him _____ the address on the poster.

26 "Ding-Dong." _____ Ryan _____ the doorbell _____, he _____ _____ the door and _____ it.

27 "Bear, you're _____!" Ryan _____.

28 Max _____ _____ _____ Ryan's arms.

29 "_____ _____ _____," said Sheila.

30 "Your cat _____ _____ only _____ the evenings, _____ he?"

31 Ryan _____.

32 "And you _____ him _____ Friday, _____ _____?" Sheila said.

33 "Yes! _____ _____ you _____?" said Ryan.

34 "_____ this is my cat, _____, and he _____ _____ to my home only _____ _____ _____."

35 "Our cat _____ _____ _____!" said Ryan.

36 "Hey, _____ _____ _____ _____, please _____ _____ and _____ some cookies."

37 "_____," said Sheila.

38 "_____ you, Max," she _____.

39 "I _____ a good neighbor _____ _____ _____!"

---

21 그녀는 그것을 자세히 읽고, 그녀의 눈은 커졌다.

22 "이 고양이는 꼭 Max 같아 보여. 너무 이상해."

23 그녀는 서둘러 집으로 돌아갔다.

24 "사, Max! 가자!"

25 그녀는 그를 포스터에 적힌 주소로 데려갔다.

26 "딩동." Ryan은 초인종이 울리는 소리를 듣고 문으로 달려가 문을 열었다.

27 "Bear야, 돌아왔구나!" Ryan이 외쳤다.

28 Max가 Ryan의 팔 안으로 뛰어올랐다.

29 "내가 맞춰 볼게." Sheila가 말했다.

30 "너의 고양이는 저녁에만 집에 오지, 그렇지?"

31 Ryan은 고개를 끄덕였다.

32 "그리고 너는 지난 금요일에 그를 잃어버렸지, 그렇지 않니?" Sheila가 말했다.

33 "응! "어떻게 알았니?"라고 Ryan은 말했다.

34 "이것은 또한 내 고양이이기 때문이야, 보통 낮에만 우리 집에 오거든."

35 "우리 고양이는 가족이 둘이야!" Ryan이 말했다.

36 이봐, 시간이 있으면 들어와서 쿠키 좀 먹어."

37 "그래," Sheila가 말했다.

38 "고마워, Max." 그녀는 생각했다.

39 "나는 네 덕분에 좋은 이웃을 만났어!"

※ 다음 문장을 우리말로 쓰시오.

1 Bear was a black and brown cat with green eyes.
➡ _____

2 He lived with a boy, Ryan.
➡ _____

3 Ryan always thought that "Bear" was a perfect name for the cat because he had a black spot in the shape of a bear.
➡ _____

4 Bear liked to go outside every morning and run after butterflies.
➡ _____

5 He always came home just in time for dinner.
➡ _____

6 Five blocks away, Max the cat lived with a girl, Sheila.
➡ _____

7 When Sheila moved to this town last month, she was lonely.
➡ _____

8 She had no friends there.
➡ _____

9 But, after Max followed her home, he became a good friend to her.
➡ _____

10 One day, Sheila saw Max sitting under the desk.
➡ _____

11 He was making a strange sound.
➡ _____

12 "What's wrong?" asked Sheila.
➡ _____

13 She looked at him closely and found a bad cut on his leg.
➡ _____

14 She took him to the animal hospital.
➡ _____

15 The doctor said, "He will get better if he gets enough rest. Keep him inside for a week."
➡ _____

16 That night, at Ryan's house, there was no Bear.
➡ _____

17 Ryan checked outside, but he couldn't find him.
➡ _____

18 He made posters and put them up around town.
➡ _____

19 A third night passed. Still no Bear.
➡ _____

20 When Sheila was walking near her house, she saw a poster about the lost cat.
➡ _____

21 She read it closely, and her eyes got big.
➡ _____

22 "This cat looks exactly like Max. It's so strange."
➡ _____

23 She hurried home.
➡ _____

24 "Come on, Max! Let's go!"
➡ _____

25 She took him to the address on the poster.
➡ _____

26 "Ding-Dong." When Ryan heard the doorbell ring, he ran to the door and opened it.
➡ _____

27 "Bear, you're back!" Ryan cried.
➡ _____

28 Max jumped up into Ryan's arms.
➡ _____

29 "Let me guess," said Sheila.
➡ _____

30 "Your cat comes home only in the evenings, doesn't he?"
➡ _____

31 Ryan nodded.
➡ _____

32 "And you lost him last Friday, didn't you?" Sheila said.
➡ _____

33 "Yes! How did you know?" said Ryan.
➡ _____

34 "Because this is my cat, too, and he usually comes to my home only during the day."
➡ _____

35 "Our cat has two families!" said Ryan.
➡ _____

36 "Hey, if you have time, please come in and have some cookies."
➡ _____

37 "Sure," said Sheila.
➡ _____

38 "Thank you, Max," she thought.
➡ _____

39 "I met a good neighbor thanks to you!"
➡ _____

※ 다음 괄호 안의 단어들을 우리말에 맞도록 바르게 배열하시오.

1 (was / Bear / black / and / a / brown / with / cat / eyes. / green)
➡ _____

2 (lived / he / a / with / Ryan. / boy,)
➡ _____

3 (always / Ryan / thought / that / was / "Bear" / perfect / a / name / for / cat / the / because / had / he / a / spot / black / in / the / bear. / of / a / shape)
➡ _____

4 (liked / Bear / go / to / outside / morning / every / and / run / butterflies. / after)
➡ _____

5 (always / he / came / just / home / in / dinner. / for / time)
➡ _____

6 (away, / blocks / five / the / Max / cat / with / lived / Sheila. / girl, / a)
➡ _____

7 (Sheila / moved / when / this / to / town / month, / last / lonely. / was / she)
➡ _____

8 (had / no / she / there. / friends)
➡ _____

9 (but, / Max / followed / after / her / home, / he / became / her. / to / a / friend / good)
➡ _____

10 (day, / one / Max / saw / Sheila / under / desk. / the / sitting)
➡ _____

11 (he / making / was / sound. / strange / a)
➡ _____

12 (wrong?" / "what's / Sheila. / asked)
➡ _____

13 (she / at / looked / him / closely / and / found / a / cut / leg. / bad / his / on)
➡ _____

14 (she / him / to / took / the / hospital. / animal)
➡ _____

15 (the / said, / doctor / "he / get / will / better / if / gets / he / rest. / enough // him / keep / for / inside / week." / a)
➡ _____

16 (night, / that / Ryan's / at / house, / was / there / Bear. / no)
➡ _____

17 (Ryan / outside, / checked / but / couldn't / he / him. / find)
➡ _____

18 (he / posters / made / and / them / put / town. / up / around)
➡ _____

19 (a / night / passed. / third / Bear. / no / still)
➡ _____

20 (Sheila / when / walking / was / her / near / house, / she / a / saw / poster / the / cat. / about / lost)
➡ _____

1 Bear는 초록색 눈을 가진 검은 색과 갈색의 고양이였다.

2 그는 소년 Ryan과 함께 살았다.

3 Ryan은 항상 "Bear"가 곰 모양의 검은 반점이 있기 때문에 그 고양이에게 딱 맞는 이름이라고 생각했다.

4 Bear는 매일 아침 밖으로 나가 나비를 쫓아다니는 것을 좋아했다.

5 그는 항상 저녁 식사 시간에 맞춰 집에 왔다.

6 다섯 블록 떨어진 곳에, 고양이 Max는 Sheila라는 소녀와 함께 살았다.

7 지난달에 Sheila가 이 마을로 이사 왔을 때, 그녀는 외로웠다.

8 그녀는 그곳에 친구가 없었다.

9 하지만 Max가 그녀를 따라 집으로 온 후, 그는 그녀에게 좋은 친구가 되었다.

10 어느 날, Sheila는 책상 밑에 앉아 있는 Max를 보았다.

11 그는 이상한 소리를 내고 있었다.

12 "무슨 일 있니?" Sheila가 물었다.

13 그녀는 그를 자세히 살펴보고 그의 다리에 심한 상처가 난 것을 발견했다.

14 그녀는 그를 동물 병원으로 데려갔다.

15 의사는 "충분한 휴식을 취하면 좋아질 거야. 그를 일주일 동안 안에 있도록 해라."라고 말했다.

16 그날 밤, Ryan의 집에는 Bear가 없었다.

17 Ryan은 바깥을 살폈지만 그는 그를 찾을 수 없었다.

18 그는 포스터를 만들어서 마을을 다니며 그것을 붙였다.

19 세 번째 밤이 지났다. 여전히 Bear는 나타나지 않았다.

20 Sheila가 그녀의 집 근처를 걷고 있었을 때, 그녀는 잃어버린 고양이에 대한 포스터를 보았다.

21 (it / read / she / closely, / and / eyes / her / big. / got)
➡ _____

22 (cat / like / looks / this / exactly / Max. / so / strange." / it's)
➡ _____

23 (home. / hurried / she)
➡ _____

24 (on, / Max! / "come / go!" / let's)
➡ _____

25 (took / she / to / him / address / the / on / poster. / the)
➡ _____.

26 ("Dong-Dong." / Ryan / when / the / ring, / doorbell / heard / he / to / ran / door / the / it. / opened / and)
➡ _____

27 (you're / "Bear, / back!" / cried. / Ryan)
➡ _____

28 (jumped / Max / up / arms. / Ryan's / into)
➡ _____

29 (me / "let / guess," / Sheila. / said)
➡ _____

30 ("your / comes / cat / home / only / the / evenings, / in / he?" / doesn't)
➡ _____

31 (nodded. / Ryan)
➡ _____

32 ("and / him / lost / you / Firday, / last / you?" / didn't / said. / Sheila)
➡ _____

33 ("yes! / you / did / know?" / how / Ryan. / said)
➡ _____

34 (this / "because / is / cat, / my / too, / and / he / usually / to / comes / home / my / during / day." / the / only)
➡ _____

35 (cat / "our / two / families!" / has / Ryan. / said)
➡ _____

36 ("hey, / you / if / time, / have / please / in / come / and / cookies." / some / have)
➡ _____

37 ("sure,' / Sheila. / said)
➡ _____

38 (you, / "thank / Max," / thought. / she)
➡ _____

39 ("I / a / met / neighbor / good / to / you!" / thanks)
➡ _____

21 그녀는 그것을 자세히 읽고, 그녀의 눈은 커졌다.

22 "이 고양이는 꼭 Max 같아 보여. 너무 이상해."

23 그녀는 서둘러 집으로 돌아갔다.

24 "자. Max! 가자!"

25 그녀는 그를 포스터에 적힌 주소로 데려갔다.

26 "딩동." Ryan은 초인종이 울리는 소리를 듣고 문으로 달려가 문을 열었다.

27 "Bear야, 돌아왔구나!" Ryan이 외쳤다.

28 Max가 Ryan의 팔 안으로 뛰어올랐다.

29 "내가 맞춰 볼게," Sheila가 말했다.

30 "너의 고양이는 저녁에만 집에 오지, 그렇지?"

31 Ryan은 고개를 끄덕였다.

32 "그리고 너는 지난 금요일에 그를 잃어버렸지, 그렇지 않니?" Sheila가 말했다.

33 "응! "어떻게 알았니?"라고 Ryan은 말했다.

34 "이것은 또한 내 고양이이기 때문이야, 보통 낮에만 우리 집에 오거든."

35 "우리 고양이는 가족이 둘이야!" Ryan이 말했다.

36 이봐, 시간이 있으면 들어와서 쿠키 좀 먹어."

37 "그래," Sheila가 말했다.

38 "고마워, Max." 그녀는 생각했다.

39 "나는 네 덕분에 좋은 이웃을 만났어!"

※ **다음 우리말을 영어로 쓰시오.**

1 Bear는 초록색 눈을 가진 검은색과 갈색의 고양이였다.
　➡ _____

2 그는 소년 Ryan과 함께 살았다.
　➡ _____

3 Ryan은 항상 "Bear"가 곰 모양의 검은 반점이 있기 때문에 그 고양이에게 딱 맞는 이름이라고 생각했다.
　➡ _____
　_____

4 Bear는 매일 아침 밖으로 나가 나비를 쫓아다니는 것을 좋아했다.
　➡ _____

5 그는 항상 저녁 식사 시간에 맞춰 집에 왔다.
　➡ _____

6 다섯 블록 떨어진 곳에, 고양이 Max는 Sheila라는 소녀와 함께 살았다.
　➡ _____

7 지난달에 Sheila가 이 마을로 이사 왔을 때, 그녀는 외로웠다.
　➡ _____

8 그녀는 그곳에 친구가 없었다.
　➡ _____

9 하지만 Max가 그녀를 따라 집으로 온 후, 그는 그녀에게 좋은 친구가 되었다.
　➡ _____

10 어느 날, Sheila는 책상 밑에 앉아 있는 Max를 보았다.
　➡ _____

11 그는 이상한 소리를 내고 있었다.
　➡ _____

12 "무슨 일 있니?" Sheila가 물었다.
　➡ _____

13 그녀는 그를 자세히 살펴보고 그의 다리에 심한 상처가 난 것을 발견했다.
　➡ _____

14 그녀는 그를 동물 병원으로 데려갔다.
　➡ _____

15 의사는 "충분한 휴식을 취하면 좋아질 거야. 그를 일주일 동안 안에 있도록 해라."라고 말했다.
　➡ _____

16 그날 밤, Ryan의 집에는 Bear가 없었다.
　➡ _____

17 Ryan은 바깥을 살폈지만 그는 그를 찾을 수 없었다.
　➡ _____

18 그는 포스터를 만들어서 마을을 다니며 그것을 붙였다.
　➡ _____

19 세 번째 밤이 지났다. 여전히 Bear는 나타나지 않았다.
　➡ _____

20 Sheila가 그녀의 집 근처를 걷고 있었을 때, 그녀는 잃어버린 고양이에 대한 포스터를 보았다.
　➡ _____

21 그녀는 그것을 자세히 읽고, 그녀의 눈은 커졌다.

➡ _____

22 "이 고양이는 꼭 Max 같아 보여. 너무 이상해."

➡ _____

23 그녀는 서둘러 집으로 돌아갔다.

➡ _____

24 "자, Max! 가자!"

➡ _____

25 그녀는 그를 포스터에 적힌 주소로 데려갔다.

➡ _____

26 "딩동." Ryan은 초인종이 울리는 소리를 듣고 문으로 달려가 문을 열었다.

➡ _____

27 "Bear야, 돌아왔구나!" Ryan이 외쳤다.

➡ _____

28 Max가 Ryan의 팔 안으로 뛰어올랐다.

➡ _____

29 "내가 맞춰 볼게," Sheila가 말했다.

➡ _____

30 "너의 고양이는 저녁에만 집에 오지, 그렇지?"

➡ _____

31 Ryan은 고개를 끄덕였다.

➡ _____

32 "그리고 너는 지난 금요일에 그를 잃어버렸지, 그렇지 않니?" Sheila가 말했다.

➡ _____

33 "응! "어떻게 알았니?"라고 Ryan은 말했다.

➡ _____

34 "이것은 또한 내 고양이이기 때문이야, 보통 낮에만 우리 집에 오거든."

➡ _____

35 "우리 고양이는 가족이 둘이야!" Ryan이 말했다.

➡ _____

36 이봐, 시간이 있으면 들어와서 쿠키 좀 먹어."

➡ _____

37 "그래," Sheila가 말했다.

➡ _____

38 "고마워, Max." 그녀는 생각했다.

➡ _____

39 "나는 네 덕분에 좋은 이웃을 만났어!"

➡ _____

※ 다음 우리말과 일치하도록 빈칸에 알맞은 말을 쓰시오.

Express Yourself C1~C2

1. C1: Do you _____ _____ _____ a magic show?

2. _____ you _____ the town festival on Monday, you _____ _____ Harry _____ magic tricks. _____ _____ at the festival!

3. C2: Do you want _____ _____ an _____ movie?

4. If you visit the town festival _____ _____, you _____ _____ Mr. Jackson, a director _____ _____ his new movie. It will _____ _____!

1. C1: 마술쇼를 보고 싶니?
2. 월요일에 마을 축제에 가면, Harry가 마술 묘기를 부리는 것을 볼 수 있을 거야. 축제 잘 보내!
3. C2: 야외 영화 보고 싶니?
4. 금요일에 마을 축제에 가면, 너는 영화감독 Jackson 씨가 그의 새 영화에 대해 이야기하는 것을 들을 거야. 그것은 재미있을 거야!

Project - Step 2

1. This is my _____ tteokbokki restaurant _____ _____ _____.

2. If you go there, you _____ _____ many students _____ tteokbokki and _____.

3. This is a _____ _____ _____ park near the school.

4. If you _____ _____ _____ a nice _____, please visit it.

5. You can _____ _____ _____ in the trees.

1. 이곳은 우리 동네에서 내가 제일 좋아하는 떡볶이 식당이다.
2. 그곳에 가면, 너는 많은 학생들이 떡볶이를 먹으면서 수다를 떨고 있는 것을 볼 수 있을 것이다.
3. 이곳은 학교 근처에 있는 작지만 아름다운 공원이다.
4. 편안한 휴식을 취하고 싶다면, 꼭 이곳을 방문해라.
5. 너는 나무에서 새들이 지저귀는 소리를 들을 수 있다.

Link to the World

1. _____ make a _____ _____!

2. In the U.S., there _____ a volunteer project _____ _____ houses for families _____ _____.

3. Many people _____ _____ the project to _____ _____ _____.

4. It's _____ _____ _____ _____ _____ in Canada.

5. If you want to read books _____ _____ your neighbors, make one _____ _____ _____ your house!

6. It's a _____ refrigerator _____ _____.

7. People _____ _____ _____ in this refrigerator for people _____ _____.

1. 더 나은 마을을 만들자!
2. 미국에서는 도움이 필요한 가정을 위해 집을 짓는 자원봉사 프로젝트가 있다.
3. 많은 사람들이 그들에게 희망을 주기 위해 이 프로젝트에 참여하고 있다.
4. 그것은 캐나다에 있는 작은 무료 도서관이다.
5. 만약 여러분이 여러분의 이웃과 함께 책을 읽고 싶다면, 집 앞에 그것을 만들어라!
6. 그것은 독일에 있는 특별한 냉장고다.
7. 사람들은 도움이 필요한 사람들을 위해 이 냉장고 안에 음식을 두고 갈 수 있다.

※ 다음 우리말을 영어로 쓰시오.

Express Yourself C1~C2

1. C1: 마술쇼를 보고 싶니?
　➡ _____

2. 월요일에 마을 축제에 가면, Harry가 마술 묘기를 부리는 것을 볼 수 있을 거야. 축제 잘 보내!
　➡ _____

3. C2: 야외 영회 보고 싶니?
　➡ _____

4. 금요일에 마을 축제에 가면, 너는 영화감독 Jackson 씨가 그의 새 영화에 대해 이야기하는 것을 들을 거야. 그것은 재미있을 거야.
　➡ _____
　_____

Project - Step 2

1. 이곳은 우리 동네에서 내가 제일 좋아하는 떡볶이 식당이다.
　➡ _____

2. 그곳에 가면, 너는 많은 학생들이 떡볶이를 먹으면서 수다를 떨고 있는 것을 볼 수 있을 것이다.
　➡ _____

3. 이곳은 학교 근처에 있는 작지만 아름다운 공원이다.
　➡ _____

4. 편안한 휴식을 취하고 싶다면, 꼭 이곳을 방문해라.
　➡ _____

5. 너는 나무에서 새들이 지저귀는 소리를 들을 수 있다.
　➡ _____

Link to the World

1. 더 나은 마을을 만들자!
　➡ _____

2. 미국에서는 도움이 필요한 가정을 위해 집을 짓는 자원봉사 프로젝트가 있다.
　➡ _____

3. 많은 사람들이 그들에게 희망을 주기 위해 이 프로젝트에 참여하고 있다.
　➡ _____

4. 그것은 캐나다에 있는 작은 무료 도서관이다.
　➡ _____

5. 만약 여러분이 여러분의 이웃과 함께 책을 읽고 싶다면, 집 앞에 그것을 만들어라!
　➡ _____

6. 그것은 독일에 있는 특별한 냉장고다.
　➡ _____

7. 사람들은 도움이 필요한 사람들을 위해 이 냉장고 안에 음식을 두고 갈 수 있다.
　➡ _____

※ 다음 영어를 우리말로 쓰시오.

01	alone	22	behind
02	bite	23	someday
03	careful	24	join
04	dangerous	25	kind
05	direction	26	create
06	clothes	27	balance
07	exist	28	later
08	past	29	probably
09	far	30	rule
10	figure	31	search
11	climber	32	touch
12	actually	33	skill
13	following	34	yet
14	fun	35	hang up
15	safety	36	keep ~ in mind
16	real	37	over there
17	special	38	make noise
18	remember	39	be good for
19	climb	40	hear of
20	scenery	41	for the first time
21	harmony	42	for example
		43	go up

※ 다음 우리말을 영어로 쓰시오.

01 활동적인, 활발한 _____

02 표지판, 간판 _____

03 축제 _____

04 인물, 모습 _____

05 밀다 _____

06 곳, 장소 _____

07 풀, 잔디 _____

08 연습하다 _____

09 조언, 충고 _____

10 가까운, 친한 _____

11 안전한 _____

12 포즈[자세] _____

13 정보 _____

14 길, 거리, 도로 _____

15 바위, 암석 _____

16 십대의 _____

17 공주 _____

18 헐거워진, 풀린, 헐렁한 _____

19 거울 _____

20 헬멧 _____

21 박물관, 미술관 _____

22 담소하다, 채팅하다 _____

23 과거, 지난날 _____

24 비결, 요령, 속임수 _____

25 ~ 없이, ~하지 않고 _____

26 해변, 바닷가 _____

27 경치, 풍경 _____

28 균형, 평형 _____

29 조화, 화합 _____

30 옷, 의복 _____

31 조심하는, 주의 깊은 _____

32 위험한 _____

33 안전, 안전성 _____

34 특별한, 특수한 _____

35 예를 들면, 예를 들어 _____

36 처음으로 _____

37 ~을 명심하다 _____

38 ~에 좋다 _____

39 ~ 앞에 _____

40 전화를 끊다 _____

41 떠들다 _____

42 ~에 대해 듣다 _____

43 저쪽에, 저기에서 _____

※ 다음 영영풀이에 알맞은 단어를 <보기>에서 골라 쓴 후, 우리말 뜻을 쓰시오.

1 _____ : an artist who paints pictures: _____

2 _____ : able or likely to hurt or harm you: _____

3 _____ : moving around a lot or doing a lot of things: _____

4 _____ : an area of sand or stones beside the sea: _____

5 _____ : sit on a horse or bike and control its movements: _____

6 _____ : to talk to each other in an informal and friendly way: _____

7 _____ : a female member of a royal family, usually the daughter of a king or
            queen: _____

8 _____ : a road in a city, town, or village, usually with houses along it: _____

9 _____ : aged between thirteen and nineteen years old: _____

10 _____ : the things that people wear, such as shirts, coats, trousers, and dresses:
            _____

11 _____ : the hard substance which the Earth is made of: _____

12 _____ : a hat made of a strong material which you wear to protect your head:
            _____

13 _____ : what you think someone should do in a particular situation: _____

14 _____ : to move towards the top of something such as a tree, mountain, or
            ladder: _____

15 _____ : to use force to make something move away from you or away from its
            previous position: _____

16 _____ : a flat piece of glass which reflects light, so that when you look at it you
            can see yourself reflected in it: _____

보기			
beach	dangerous	chat	street
push	mirror	teenage	active
helmet	painter	ride	advice
clothes	climb	rock	princess

※ 다음 우리말과 일치하도록 빈칸에 알맞은 말을 쓰시오.

Get Ready - 2

1. **G:** Look _____ that boy. He's _____.
   B: He's _____ an MTB. Do you _____ _____ it?
   G: No. _____ is it?
   B: It's a _____ bike _____ _____ _____ a mountain.

2. **G:** Wait. _____ jump _____ the water _____.
   B: _____ _____?
   G: You _____ swim _____ a life jacket. _____ it _____.

3. **G:** _____ _____ the beautiful flowers _____ _____! I'd _____ _____ _____ a selfie _____ _____ _____ them.
   B: You _____ go _____ there.
   G: Oh, _____.

4. **B:** I _____ _____ _____ the birds _____ the trees.
   G: You _____ _____ _____ too close to the _____.
   B: All _____, thanks.

Start Off - Listen & Talk A

1. **G:** Dad, _____ you _____ _____ _____ Kim Soyun, the rock _____?
   M: Yes, I've _____ her _____ _____.
   G: She's _____ _____ _____ at a _____ this Saturday. I _____ _____ _____ the camp.
   M: Okay, Miso, _____ you _____ _____ _____ too high.
   G: All _____. Thanks, Dad.

2. **G:** _____ you _____ of Rock Boys?
   M: _____, _____ _____.
   G: It's my _____ band. There's a _____ this Saturday. _____ _____ _____?
   M: Okay, Minju, but you _____ _____ _____ too late.
   G: All _____. Thanks, Dad.

 해석

1. G: 저 소년을 봐. 그는 대단하다.
   B: 그는 MTB를 타고 있어. 넌 그것에 대해 알고 있니?
   G: 아니. 그게 뭐지?
   B: 그것은 산에서 타는 특별한 자전거야.

2. G: 기다려. 아직 물속으로 뛰어들지 마.
   D: 왜 안 돼?
   G: 구명조끼 없이 수영하면 안 돼. 이 것을 입어.

3. G: 저기 있는 아름다운 꽃들을 봐! 그 꽃들 앞에서 셀피를 찍고 싶어.
   B: 거기 가면 안 돼.
   G: 아, 알았어.

4. B: 나는 나무에 있는 새들을 보고 싶어.
   G: 새들에게 너무 가까이 가지 마.
   B: 알았어, 고마워.

1. G: 아빠, 암벽 등반가인 김소윤에 대해 들어본 적 있으세요?
   M: 응, TV에서 봤어.
   G: 그녀가 이번 토요일에 캠프에서 암벽 등반을 가르쳐요. 저는 캠프에 참가하고 싶어요.
   M: 알았어, 미소야, 하지만 너무 높이 올라가면 안 돼.
   G: 알았어요. 고마워요, 아빠.

2. G: Rock Boys에 대해 들어보셨어요?
   M: 아니, 듣지 못했다.
   G: 그건 제가 제일 좋아하는 밴드에 요. 이번 토요일에 콘서트가 있어요. 가도 돼요?
   M: 좋아, 민주야, 하지만 너무 늦게 집에 오면 안 돼.
   G: 알았어요. 고마워요, 아빠.

Start Off - Listen & Talk B

B: _____ you _____ _____ bird watching?

M: Sure. I _____ it _____ I was a child.

B: That's nice. Actually, I'm _____ it _____ _____ _____ _____ this Saturday.

M: Are you? You _____ _____ warm clothes and _____ _____ _____.

B: Okay. What else _____ I _____ _____ _____?

M: You _____ _____ any noise _____ you watch the birds.

B: I'll _____ _____ _____ _____. Thanks, Dad.

Step Up - Real-life Scene

Video Chat with Minjun from Jeju

A: Hello, Somin! _____ me! _____ you _____ _____?

B: Oh, _____, Minjun! What's _____?

A: This is so cool, _____ _____? We can video _____ on the phone! _____ you _____ _____ Jeju *Olle*?

B: _____, _____ _____. I really _____ to go there someday.

A: _____ _____? I'm on it now. Actually, I'm _____ _____ _____ _____ Seongsan Ilchulbong now.

B: That's _____!

A: Don't _____ _____. Enjoy the beautiful _____ with me.

B: _____ careful! You _____ _____ your cell phone _____ _____ _____.

A: Oh, _____. _____ you. I'll _____ you photos _____.

Express Yourself A

1. **G:** _____ _____ _____ _____ _____ Elvis Presley?

   B: _____, _____ _____. _____ is he?

   G: He was a _____ _____ _____ and _____. We can see a _____ of Elvis here.

   B: _____ interesting. I want to _____ _____ with it.

   G: Okay. _____ _____.

2. **W:** You _____ _____ selfies here. Van Gogh's _____ is _____ you.

   B: _____ _____, Mom. It's not his _____ painting. _____ I can take selfies _____ _____ _____ it.

   W: Really? Sounds interesting. _____ I take _____ here, too?

   B: Why _____?

B: 새 관찰에 대해 들어보셨어요?

M: 물론이지. 어렸을 때 해 봤어.

B: 그거 멋지네요. 사실, 전 이번 주 토요일에 처음으로 그것을 할 거예요.

M: 그래? 넌 따뜻한 옷과 먹을 것을 가져가야 해.

B: 알았어요. 그 밖에 또 무엇을 명심해야 하나요?

M: 너는 새들을 관찰할 때 아무 소리도 내지 말아야 해.

B: 그것을 명심할게요. 고마워요, 아빠.

제주에서 걸려온 민준과의 화상 채팅

A: 여보세요, 소민아! 나야! 나를 볼 수 있니?

B: 오, 안녕, 민준아! 무슨 일이니?

A: 이거 정말 멋지지 않니? 전화로 화상 채팅도 할 수 있어! 너 제주 올레에 대해 들어 본 적이 있니?

B: 응, 있어. 나는 언젠가 꼭 가 보고 싶어.

A: 그거 알아? 나 지금 올레에 있어. 사실은, 지금 성산 일출봉에 올라가려고 해.

B: 멋지다!

A: 끊지 마. 나와 함께 아름다운 경치를 즐겨.

B: 조심해! 걸을 때는 휴대폰을 사용해서는 안 돼.

A: 아, 맞다. 고마워. 나중에 사진 보내줄게.

1. **G:** 엘비스 프레슬리에 대해 들어 본 적 있니?

   B: 아니, 없어. 그는 누구인데?

   G: 그는 유명한 미국 가수이자 배우였어. 우리는 여기서 엘비스의 모형을 볼 수 있어.

   B: 재미있을 것 같다. 그것과 함께 사진을 찍고 싶어.

   G: 좋아. 가자.

2. **W:** 넌 여기서 셀피를 찍으면 안 돼. 반 고흐의 그림이 네 뒤에 있어.

   B: 엄마, 걱정하지 마세요. 그건 그의 진짜 그림이 아니에요. 그래서 그 앞에서 셀피를 찍을 수 있어요.

   W: 정말이지? 재미있겠다. 나도 여기서 셀피를 찍을 수 있을까?

   B: 물론이죠.

※ 다음 우리말에 맞도록 대화를 영어로 쓰시오.

Get Ready - 2

1. G: _____
   B: _____
   G: _____
   B: _____

2. G: _____
   B: _____
   G: _____

3. G: _____
   _____
   B: _____
   G: _____

4. B: _____
   G: _____
   B: _____

Start Off - Listen & Talk A

1. G: _____
   M: _____
   G: _____
   _____
   M: _____
   G: _____

2. G: _____
   M: _____
   G: _____
   M: _____
   G: _____

해석

1. G: 저 소년을 봐. 그는 대단하다.
   B: 그는 MTB를 타고 있어. 넌 그것에 대해 알고 있니?
   G: 아니. 그게 뭐지?
   B: 그것은 산에서 타는 특별한 자전거야.

2. G: 기다려. 아직 물속으로 뛰어들지 마.
   B: 왜 안 돼?
   G: 구명조끼 없이 수영하면 안 돼. 이 것을 입어.

3. G: 저기 있는 아름다운 꽃들을 봐! 그 꽃들 앞에서 셀피를 찍고 싶어.
   B: 거기 가면 안 돼.
   G: 아, 알았어.

4. B: 나는 나무에 있는 새들을 보고 싶어.
   G: 새들에게 너무 가까이 가지 마.
   B: 알았어, 고마워.

1. G: 아빠, 암벽 등반가인 김소윤에 대해 들어 본 적 있으세요?
   M: 응, TV에서 봤어.
   G: 그녀가 이번 토요일에 캠프에서 암벽 등반을 가르쳐요. 저는 캠프에 참가하고 싶어요.
   M: 알았어, 미소야, 하지만 너무 높이 올라가면 안 돼.
   G: 알았어요. 고마워요, 아빠.

2. G: Rock Boys에 대해 들어보셨어요?
   M: 아니, 듣지 못했다.
   G: 그건 제가 제일 좋아하는 밴드에요. 이번 토요일에 콘서트가 있어요. 가도 돼요?
   M: 좋아, 민주야, 하지만 너무 늦게 집에 오면 안 돼.
   G: 알았어요. 고마워요, 아빠.

Start Off - Listen & Talk B

B: _____

M: _____

B: _____

M: _____

B: _____

M: _____

B: _____

Step Up - Real-life Scene

Video Chat with Minjun from Jeju

A: _____

B: _____

A: _____
_____

B: _____

A: _____
_____

B: _____

A: _____

B: _____

A: _____

Express Yourself A

1. G: _____

   B: _____

   G: _____
   _____

   B: _____

   G: _____

2. W: _____

   B: _____

   W: _____

   B: _____

B: 새 관찰에 대해 들어보셨어요?

M: 물론이지. 어렸을 때 해 봤어.

B: 그거 멋지네요. 사실, 전 이번 주 토요일에 처음으로 그것을 할 거예요.

M: 그래? 넌 따뜻한 옷과 먹을 것을 가져가야 해.

B: 알았어요. 그 밖에 또 무엇을 명심해야 하나요?

M: 너는 새들을 관찰할 때 아무 소리도 내지 말아야 해.

B: 그것을 명심할게요. 고마워요, 아빠.

제주에서 걸려온 민준과의 화상 채팅

A: 여보세요, 소민아! 나야! 나를 볼 수 있니?

B: 오, 안녕, 민준아! 무슨 일이니?

A: 이거 정말 멋지지 않니? 전화로 화상 채팅도 할 수 있어! 너 제주 올레에 대해 들어 본 적이 있니?

B: 응, 있어. 나는 언젠가 꼭 가 보고 싶어.

A: 그거 알아? 나 지금 올레에 있어. 사실은, 지금 성산 일출봉에 올라가려고 해.

B: 멋지다!

A: 끊지 마. 나와 함께 아름다운 경치를 즐겨.

B: 조심해! 걸을 때는 휴대폰을 사용해서는 안 돼.

A: 아, 맞다. 고마워. 나중에 사진 보내줄게.

1. G: 엘비스 프레슬리에 대해 들어 본 적 있니?

   B: 아니, 없어. 그는 누구인데?

   G: 그는 유명한 미국 가수이자 배우였어. 우리는 여기서 엘비스의 모형을 볼 수 있어.

   B: 재미있을 것 같다. 그것과 함께 사진을 찍고 싶어.

   G: 좋아. 가자.

2. W: 넌 여기서 셀피를 찍으면 안 돼. 반 고흐의 그림이 네 뒤에 있어.

   B: 엄마, 걱정하지 마세요. 그건 그의 진짜 그림이 아니에요. 그래서 그 앞에서 셀피를 찍을 수 있어요.

   W: 정말이지? 재미있겠다. 나도 여기서 셀피를 찍을 수 있을까?

   B: 물론이죠.

※ 다음 우리말과 일치하도록 빈칸에 알맞은 것을 골라 쓰시오.

1 _____ you _____ _____ of a "selfie"?
A. heard   B. ever   C. have

2 _____ you _____ a photograph of _____, it's a selfie.
A. yourself   B. take   C. when

3 The students from Minji's photo club _____ searched _____ information _____ selfies for one month.
A. about   B. for   C. have

4 _____ are some of their _____ about _____.
A. selfies   B. presentations C. here

5 Did _____ in the past _____ selfies?
A. take   B. people

6 _____ it wasn't easy _____ that time, the _____ is yes.
A. answer   B. at   C. though

7 _____ _____ this photo _____ Princess Anastasia.
A. of   B. at   C. look

8 She _____ a mirror to _____ a picture of _____.
A. herself   B. take   C. used

9 She _____ _____.
A. nervous   B. looks

10 Can you _____ _____?
A. why   B. guess

11 Well, I _____ it was her _____ selfie.
A. first   B. think

12 And it was _____ the world's first _____ selfie _____.
A. teenage   B. ever   C. probably

13 You can _____ selfies _____ world-famous places _____ Big Ben and the Leaning Tower of Pisa.
A. like   B. at   C. take

14 To _____ great pictures, just do fun _____ and use camera _____.
A. tricks   B. poses   C. take

15 You can _____ visit _____ museums to take _____ selfies.
A. fun   B. special   C. also

16 For _____, there _____ a _____ selfie museum in the Philippines.
A. is   B. famous   C. example

17 It has special _____ to _____ selfies.
A. take   B. spots

18 You can _____ the paintings and _____ _____ inside them.
A. step   B. touch   C. even

19 Look _____ the _____ pictures.
A. following   B. at

20 _____ the boys are not really _____ horses, it looks _____ they are.
A. like   B. riding   C. though

1 여러분은 "셀피"에 대해 들어 본 적이 있나요?

2 여러분 자신의 사진을 찍을 때 그것이 셀피에요.

3 민지의 사진 동아리 학생들은 한 달 동안 셀피에 대한 정보를 찾았습니다.

4 여기 셀피에 대한 그들의 발표 내용이 있습니다.

5 과거의 사람들은 셀피를 찍었나요?

6 그 때는 셀피를 찍는 것이 쉽지는 않았지만. 답은 '그렇다'입니다.

7 아나스타샤 공주의 이 사진을 보세요.

8 그녀는 거울을 사용하여 자신의 사진을 찍었습니다.

9 그녀는 긴장되어 보입니다.

10 왜인지 추측할 수 있나요?

11 글쎄, 나는 그것이 그녀의 첫 번째 셀피였다고 생각해요.

12 그리고 그것은 아마도 세계 최초의 10대 소녀의 셀피였을 거예요.

13 여러분은 빅벤과 피사의 사탑과 같은 세계적으로 유명한 장소에서 셀피를 찍을 수 있습니다.

14 멋진 사진을 찍기 위해서, 단지 재미있는 포즈를 취하고 카메라 기술을 이용하세요.

15 여러분은 또한 재미있는 셀피를 찍기 위해 특별한 박물관을 방문할 수 있습니다.

16 예를 들어, 필리핀에는 유명한 셀피 박물관이 있습니다.

17 그곳은 셀피를 찍기 위한 특별한 장소들이 있습니다.

18 여러분은 그림들을 만질 수 있고 심지어 그림들 안으로 들어갈 수도 있어요.

19 다음 사진들을 보세요.

20 비록 그 소년들은 말을 타고 있는 것은 아니지만, 말을 타고 있는 것처럼 보입니다.

21 Though the man is just _____ a big _____, it looks like he is _____ the Mona Lisa.
  A. painting   B. brush   C. holding

22 Selfie museums _____ in Korea, _____.
  A. too   B. exist

23 I have _____ one in Chuncheon _____.
  A. before   B. visited

24 Why _____ you go there _____?
  A. yourself   B. don't

25 These selfies _____ great, _____ _____ they a good idea?
  A. were   B. but   C. look

26 I _____ think _____.
  A. so   B. don't

27 They don't _____ _____.
  A. safe   B. look

28 You _____ take special _____ when you take _____ in the wild or at high _____ like these.
  A. places   B. selfies   C. care   D. should

29 A monkey could _____ you at any _____, or you _____ fall.
  A. could   B. time   C. bite

30 Here _____ some _____ tips:
  A. safety   B. are

31 1. _____ take selfies _____ you're _____.
  A. walking   B. while   C. don't

32 2. _____ not _____ with or _____ wild animals.
  A. near   B. pose   C. do

33 3. _____ take selfies _____ dangerous _____.
  A. places   B. in   C. never

34 I think we can _____ selfies to _____ a _____ school life.
  A. better   B. make   C. use

35 We _____ do good _____ at school and _____ selfies.
  A. take   B. things   C. can

36 Then we can _____ the photos _____ our school _____.
  A. website   B. on   C. post

37 I've _____ the _____ and flowers at school _____ one month.
  A. for   B. plants   C. watered

38 I've _____ helped the teacher _____ the school library many _____.
  A. times   B. at   C. also

39 _____ _____ my selfies of _____ things.
  A. those   B. at   C. look

40 How _____ me to _____ a better school life?
  A. create   B. joining   C. about

---

21 비록 그 남자는 단지 커다란 붓을 잡고 있지만, 모나리자를 그리고 있는 것처럼 보입니다.

22 한국에도 셀피 박물관이 있습니다.

23 나는 전에 춘천에 있는 한 박물관을 방문한 적이 있습니다.

24 여러분도 직접 그곳에 가는 게 어때요?

25 이 셀피들은 멋져 보이지만, 그것들은 좋은 생각이었나요?

26 난 그렇게 생각하지 않아요.

27 그것들은 안전해 보이지 않습니다.

28 여러분은 야생이나 이와 같이 높은 곳에서 셀피를 찍을 때 특별한 주의를 기울여야 합니다.

29 원숭이가 언제든지 당신을 물거나 또는 당신은 떨어질 수 있습니다.

30 여기 몇 가지 안전 수칙이 있습니다.

31 1. 걸으면서 셀피를 찍지 마세요.

32 2. 야생 동물들과 함께 또는 가까이에서 포즈를 취하지 마세요.

33 3. 위험한 곳에서는 절대 셀피를 찍지 마세요.

34 나는 우리가 더 나은 학교생활을 만들기 위해 셀피를 이용할 수 있다고 생각해요.

35 우리는 학교에서 좋은 일을 할 수 있고 셀피를 찍을 수도 있습니다.

36 그리고 나서 우리는 학교 웹사이트에 사진을 올릴 수 있어요.

37 나는 한 달 동안 학교에서 식물과 꽃에 물을 주었습니다.

38 나는 또한 학교 도서관에서 선생님을 여러 번 도왔습니다.

39 그런 것들에 대한 내 셀피를 보세요.

40 저와 함께 더 나은 학교생활을 만들어 보는 건 어떨까요?

※ 다음 우리말과 일치하도록 빈칸에 알맞은 말을 쓰시오.

1 _____ you _____ _____ _____ a "selfie"?

2 When you _____ a photograph _____ _____, it's a selfie.

3 The students from Minji's photo _____ have _____ _____ _____ about selfies _____ one month.

4 _____ are some of _____ _____ about selfies.

5 Did _____ in the past _____ _____?

6 _____ it _____ easy at that time, the _____ is yes.

7 _____ _____ this photo of Princess Anastasia.

8 She _____ a mirror _____ _____ a picture of _____.

9 She _____ _____.

10 _____ you _____ _____?

11 Well, I _____ it was _____ _____ _____.

12 And it was _____ the world's first _____ selfie ever.

13 You _____ _____ _____ at world-famous places _____ Big Ben and the Leaning Tower of Pisa.

14 _____ _____ great _____, just do fun _____ and _____ _____ _____.

15 You can _____ visit special museums to take _____ selfies.

16 For _____, there is a _____ selfie museum in the Philippines.

17 It _____ _____ _____ to _____ selfies.

18 You can _____ the paintings and _____ _____ inside them.

19 _____ _____ the _____ pictures.

20 _____ the boys are not really _____ horses, it _____ _____ they are.

1 여러분은 "셀피"에 대해 들어 본 적이 있나요?

2 여러분 자신의 사진을 찍을 때 그것이 셀피예요.

3 민지의 사진 동아리 학생들은 한 달 동안 셀피에 대한 정보를 찾았습니다.

4 여기 셀피에 대한 그들의 발표 내용이 있습니다.

5 과거의 사람들은 셀피를 찍었나요?

6 그 때는 셀피를 찍는 것이 쉽지는 않았지만, 답은 '그렇다'입니다.

7 아나스타샤 공주의 이 사진을 보세요.

8 그녀는 거울을 사용하여 자신의 사진을 찍었습니다.

9 그녀는 긴장되어 보입니다.

10 왜인지 추측할 수 있나요?

11 글쎄, 나는 그것이 그녀의 첫 번째 셀피였다고 생각해요.

12 그리고 그것은 아마도 세계 최초의 10대 소녀의 셀피였을 거예요.

13 여러분은 빅벤과 피사의 사탑과 같은 세계적으로 유명한 장소에서 셀피를 찍을 수 있습니다.

14 멋진 사진을 찍기 위해서, 단지 재미있는 포즈를 취하고 카메라 기술을 이용하세요.

15 여러분은 또한 재미있는 셀피를 찍기 위해 특별한 박물관을 방문할 수 있습니다.

16 예를 들어, 필리핀에는 유명한 셀피 박물관이 있습니다.

17 그곳은 셀피를 찍기 위한 특별한 장소들이 있습니다.

18 여러분은 그림들을 만질 수 있고 심지어 그림들 안으로 들어갈 수도 있어요.

19 다음 사진들을 보세요.

20 비록 그 소년들은 말을 타고 있는 것은 아니지만, 말을 타고 있는 것처럼 보입니다.

21 Though the man is _____ _____ a big _____, it _____ _____ he is _____ the Mona Lisa.

22 Selfie museums _____ in Korea, _____.

23 I _____ _____ one in Chuncheon _____.

24 _____ _____ you go there _____?

25 These selfies _____ great, _____ were they a good idea?

26 I _____ _____ _____.

27 They _____ _____ _____.

28 You _____ _____ _____ _____ when you take selfies in the wild or at high _____ _____ these.

29 A monkey _____ _____ you _____ _____ _____, or you _____ _____.

30 _____ _____ some _____ _____:

31 1. Don't _____ selfies _____ _____ _____.

32 2. Do _____ _____ with or near _____ animals.

33 3. _____ _____ _____ in dangerous _____.

34 I think we can _____ selfies to make a _____ school life.

35 We can do good _____ at school and _____ selfies.

36 Then we _____ _____ the photos on our school _____.

37 I've _____ the plants and flowers at _____ for one month.

38 I've _____ _____ the teacher _____ the school library _____ _____.

39 _____ _____ my selfies of _____ things.

40 _____ _____ joining me to _____ a better school life?

21 비록 그 남자는 단지 커다란 붓을 잡고 있지만, 모나리자를 그리고 있는 것처럼 보입니다.

22 한국에도 셀피 박물관이 있습니다.

23 나는 전에 춘천에 있는 한 박물관을 방문한 적이 있습니다.

24 여러분도 직접 그곳에 가는 게 어때요?

25 이 셀피들은 멋져 보이지만, 그것들은 좋은 생각이었나요?

26 난 그렇게 생각하지 않아요.

27 그것들은 안전해 보이지 않습니다.

28 여러분은 야생이나 이와 같이 높은 곳에서 셀피를 찍을 때 특별한 주의를 기울여야 합니다.

29 원숭이가 언제든지 당신을 물거나 또는 당신은 떨어질 수 있습니다.

30 여기 몇 가지 안전 수칙이 있습니다.

31 1. 걸으면서 셀피를 찍지 마세요.

32 2. 야생 동물들과 함께 또는 가까이에서 포즈를 취하지 마세요.

33 3. 위험한 곳에서는 절대 셀피를 찍지 마세요.

34 나는 우리가 더 나은 학교생활을 만들기 위해 셀피를 이용할 수 있다고 생각해요.

35 우리는 학교에서 좋은 일을 할 수 있고 셀피를 찍을 수도 있습니다.

36 그리고 나서 우리는 학교 웹사이트에 사진을 올릴 수 있어요.

37 나는 한 달 동안 학교에서 식물과 꽃에 물을 주었습니다.

38 나는 또한 학교 도서관에서 선생님을 여러 번 도왔습니다.

39 그런 것들에 대한 내 셀피를 보세요.

40 저와 함께 더 나은 학교생활을 만들어 보는 건 어떨까요?

※ 다음 문장을 우리말로 쓰시오.

1 Have you ever heard of a "selfie"? When you take a photograph of yourself, it's a selfie.

➡ _____

2 The students from Minji's photo club have searched for information about selfies for one month.

➡ _____

3 Here are some of their presentations about selfies.

➡ _____

4 Did people in the past take selfies?

➡ _____

5 Though it wans't easy at that time. the answer is yes.

➡ _____

6 Look at this photo of Princess Anastasia. She used a mirror to take a picture of herself.

➡ _____

7 She looks nervous. Can you guess why?

➡ _____

8 Well, I think it was her first selfie.

➡ _____

9 And it was probably the world's first teenage selfie ever.

➡ _____

10 You can take selfies at world-famous places like Big Ben and the Leaning Tower of Pisa.

➡ _____

11 To take great pictures, just do fun poses and use camera tricks.

➡ _____

12 You can also visit special museums to take fun selfies.

➡ _____

13 For example, there is a famous selfie museum in the Philippines.

➡ _____

14 It has special spots to take selfies.

➡ _____

15 You can touch the paintings and even step inside them.

➡ _____

16 Look at the following pictures.

➡ _____

17 Though the boys are not really riding horses, it looks like they are.
➡ _____

18 Though the man is just holding a big brush, it looks like he is painting the Mona Lisa.
➡ _____

19 Selfie museums exist in Korea, too. I have visited one in Chuncheon before.
➡ _____

20 Why don't you go there yourself? These selfies look great, but were they a good idea?
➡ _____

21 I don't think so. They don't look safe.
➡ _____

22 You should take special care when you take selfies in the wild or at high places like these.
➡ _____

23 A monkey could bite you at any time, or you could fall.
➡ _____

24 Here are some safety tips:
➡ _____

25 Don't take selfies while you're walking.
➡ _____

26 Do not pose with or near wild animals.
➡ _____

27 Never take selfies in dangerous places.
➡ _____

28 I think we can use selfies to make a better school life.
➡ _____

29 We can do good things at school and take selfies.
➡ _____

30 Then we can post the photos on our school website.
➡ _____

31 I've watered the plants and flowers at school for one month.
➡ _____

32 I've also helped the teacher at the school library many times.
➡ _____

33 Look at my selfies of those things.
➡ _____

34 How about joining me to create a better school life?
➡ _____

※ 다음 괄호 안의 단어들을 우리말에 맞도록 바르게 배열하시오.

1 (you / have / ever / of / heard / "selfie"? / a // when / take / you / photograph / of / a / yourself, / a / selfie. / it's)

➡ _____

_____

2 (students / the / from / photo / Minji's / club / searched / have / information / for / about / selfies / month. / one / for)

➡ _____

_____

3 (are / here / of / some / their / presentations / selfies. / about)

➡ _____

4 (people / did / in / past / the / selfies? / take)

➡ _____

5 (it / though / wasn't / easy / that / at / time, / yes. / is / answer / the)

➡ _____

6 (at / look / photo / this / Princess / of / Anastasia. // used / she / mirror / a / take / to / picture / a / herself. / of)

➡ _____

_____

7 (looks / she / nervous. // you / can / guess / why?)

➡ _____

8 (well, / think / I / was / it / selfie. / first / her)

➡ _____

9 (and / was / it / the / probably / world's / teenage / first / ever. / selfie)

➡ _____

10 (you / take / can / selfies / at / places / world-famous / like / Big / Ben / and / Pisa. / of / Tower / the / Leaning)

➡ _____

11 (take / great / to / pictures, / do / just / poses / fun / and / tricks. / camera / use)

➡ _____

12 (you / also / can / visit / museums / special / selfies. / take / to / fun)

➡ _____

13 (example, / for / is / there / famous / a / selfie / in / museum / Philippines. / the)

➡ _____

14 (has / it / spots / special / selfies. / take / to)

➡ _____

15 (can / you / touch / paintings / the / and / step / even / them. / inside)

➡ _____

16 (at / look / the / pictures. / following)

➡ _____

1 여러분은 "셀피"에 대해 들어 본 적이 있나요? 여러분 자신의 사진을 찍을 때 그것이 셀피에요.

2 민지의 사진 동아리 학생들은 한 달 동안 셀피에 대한 정보를 찾았습니다.

3 여기 셀피에 대한 그들의 발표 내용이 있습니다.

4 과거의 사람들은 셀피를 찍었나요?

5 그 때는 셀피를 찍는 것이 쉽지는 않았지만. 답은 '그렇다'입니다.

6 아나스타샤 공주의 이 사진을 보세요. 그녀는 거울을 사용하여 자신의 사진을 찍었습니다.

7 그녀는 긴장되어 보입니다. 왜 인지 추측할 수 있나요?

8 글쎄, 나는 그것이 그녀의 첫 번째 셀피였다고 생각해요.

9 그리고 그것은 아마도 세계 최초의 10대 소녀의 셀피였을 거예요.

10 여러분은 빅벤과 피사의 사탑과 같은 세계적으로 유명한 장소에서 셀피를 찍을 수 있습니다.

11 멋진 사진을 찍기 위해서, 단지 재미있는 포즈를 취하고 카메라 기술을 이용하세요.

12 여러분은 또한 재미있는 셀피를 찍기 위해 특별한 박물관을 방문할 수 있습니다.

13 예를 들어, 필리핀에는 유명한 셀피 박물관이 있습니다.

14 그곳은 셀피를 찍기 위한 특별한 장소들이 있습니다.

15 여러분은 그림들을 만질 수 있고 심지어 그림들 안으로 들어갈 수도 있어요.

16 다음 사진들을 보세요.

17 (the / though / boys / are / really / not / horses, / riding / looks / it / like / are. / they)

➡ _____

18 (the / man / though / is / holding / just / big / a / brush, / it / like / looks / is / he / painting / Lisa. / Mona / the)

➡ _____

19 (museums / selfie / in / exist / too. / Korea, // have / I / visited / in / one / before. / Chuncheon)

➡ _____

20 (you / don't / why / go / yourself? / there // selfies / these / great, / look / but / they / were / idea? / good / a)

➡ _____

21 (don't / so. / I / think // don't / they / safe. / look)

➡ _____ .

22 (you / take / should / care / special / when / take / you / selfies / the / in / wild / or / high / at / these. / places / like)

➡ _____

23 (monkey / a / bite / could / you / at / time, / any / or / fall. / could / you)

➡ _____

24 (are / here / safety / tips: / some)

➡ _____

25 (selfies / don't / take / while / walking. / you're)

➡ _____

26 (pose / not / do / with / or / animals. / near / wild)

➡ _____

27 (take / never / selfies / places. / dangerous / in)

➡ _____

28 (we / think / I / use / can / selfies / make / to / a / school / better / life.)

➡ _____

29 (we / do / can / things / good / school / at / and / selfies. / take)

➡ _____

30 (then / we / post / can / photos / the / on / website. / school / our)

➡ _____

31 (I've / the / plants / watered / and / flowers / school / at / month. / one / for)

➡ _____

32 (I've / helped / also / teacher / the / at / school / the / library / times. / many)

➡ _____

33 (at / my / look / selfies / things. / those / of)

➡ _____

34 (about / how / joining / to / me / create / a / life? / school / better)

➡ _____

17 비록 그 소년들은 말을 타고 있는 것은 아니지만, 말을 타고 있는 것처럼 보입니다.

18 비록 그 남자는 단지 커다란 붓을 잡고 있지만, 모나리자를 그리고 있는 것처럼 보입니다.

19 한국에도 셀피 박물관이 있습니다. 나는 전에 춘천에 있는 한 박물관을 방문한 적이 있습니다.

20 여러분도 직접 그곳에 가는 게 어때요? 이 셀피들은 멋져 보이지만, 그것들은 좋은 생각이었나요?

21 난 그렇게 생각하지 않아요. 그것들은 안전해 보이지 않습니다.

22 여러분은 야생이나 이와 같이 높은 곳에서 셀피를 찍을 때 특별한 주의를 기울여야 합니다.

23 원숭이가 언제든지 당신을 물거나 또는 당신은 떨어질 수 있습니다.

24 여기 몇 가지 안전 수칙이 있습니다.

25 걸으면서 셀피를 찍지 마세요.

26 야생 동물들과 함께 또는 가까이에서 포즈를 취하지 마세요.

27 위험한 곳에서는 절대 셀피를 찍지 마세요.

28 나는 우리가 더 나은 학교생활을 만들기 위해 셀피를 이용할 수 있다고 생각해요.

29 우리는 학교에서 좋은 일을 할 수 있고 셀피를 찍을 수도 있습니다.

30 그리고 나서 우리는 학교 웹사이트에 사진을 올릴 수 있어요.

31 나는 한 달 동안 학교에서 식물과 꽃에 물을 주었습니다.

32 나는 또한 학교 도서관에서 선생님을 여러 번 도왔습니다.

33 그런 것들에 대한 내 셀피를 보세요.

34 저와 함께 더 나은 학교생활을 만들어 보는 건 어떨까요?

※ 다음 우리말을 영어로 쓰시오.

1 여러분은 "셀피"에 대해 들어 본 적이 있나요? 여러분 자신의 사진을 찍을 때 그것이 셀피에요.

➡ _____

2 민지의 사진 동아리 학생들은 한 달 동안 셀피에 대한 정보를 찾았습니다.

➡ _____

3 여기 셀피에 대한 그들의 발표 내용이 있습니다.

➡ _____

4 과거의 사람들은 셀피를 찍었나요?

➡ _____

5 그 때는 셀피를 찍는 것이 쉽지는 않았지만. 답은 '그렇다'입니다.

➡ _____

6 아나스타샤 공주의 이 사진을 보세요. 그녀는 거울을 사용하여 자신의 사진을 찍었습니다.

➡ _____

7 그녀는 긴장되어 보입니다. 왜인지 추측할 수 있나요?

➡ _____

8 글쎄, 나는 그것이 그녀의 첫 번째 셀피였다고 생각해요.

➡ _____

9 그리고 그것은 아마도 세계 최초의 10대 소녀의 셀피였을 거예요.

➡ _____

10 여러분은 빅벤과 피사의 사탑과 같은 세계적으로 유명한 장소에서 셀피를 찍을 수 있습니다.

➡ _____

11 멋진 사진을 찍기 위해서, 단지 재미있는 포즈를 취하고 카메라 기술을 이용하세요.

➡ _____

12 여러분은 또한 재미있는 셀피를 찍기 위해 특별한 박물관을 방문할 수 있습니다.

➡ _____

13 예를 들어, 필리핀에는 유명한 셀피 박물관이 있습니다.

➡ _____

14 그곳은 셀피를 찍기 위한 특별한 장소들이 있습니다.

➡ _____

15 여러분은 그림들을 만질 수 있고 심지어 그림들 안으로 들어갈 수도 있어요.

➡ _____

16 다음 사진들을 보세요.

➡ _____

17 비록 그 소년들은 말을 타고 있는 것은 아니지만, 말을 타고 있는 것처럼 보입니다.

➡ _____

18 비록 그 남자는 단지 커다란 붓을 잡고 있지만, 모나리자를 그리고 있는 것처럼 보입니다.

➡ _____

19 한국에도 셀피 박물관이 있습니다. 나는 전에 춘천에 있는 한 박물관을 방문한 적이 있습니다.

➡ _____

20 여러분도 직접 그곳에 가는 게 어때요? 이 셀피들은 멋져 보이지만, 그것들은 좋은 생각이었나요?

➡ _____

21 난 그렇게 생각하지 않아요. 그것들은 안전해 보이지 않습니다.

➡ _____

22 여러분은 야생이나 이와 같이 높은 곳에서 셀피를 찍을 때 특별한 주의를 기울여야 합니다.

➡ _____

23 원숭이가 언제든지 당신을 물거나 또는 당신은 떨어질 수 있습니다.

➡ _____

24 여기 몇 가지 안전 수칙이 있습니다.

➡ _____

25 걸으면서 셀피를 찍지 마세요.

➡ _____

26 야생 동물들과 함께 또는 가까이에서 포즈를 취하지 마세요.

➡ _____

27 위험한 곳에서는 절대 셀피를 찍지 마세요.

➡ _____

28 나는 우리가 더 나은 학교생활을 만들기 위해 셀피를 이용할 수 있다고 생각해요.

➡ _____

29 우리는 학교에서 좋은 일을 할 수 있고 셀피를 찍을 수도 있습니다.

➡ _____

30 그러고 나서 우리는 학교 웹사이트에 사진을 올릴 수 있어요.

➡ _____

31 나는 한 달 동안 학교에서 식물과 꽃에 물을 주었습니다.

➡ _____

32 나는 또한 학교 도서관에서 선생님을 여러 번 도왔습니다.

➡ _____

33 그런 것들에 대한 내 셀피를 보세요.

➡ _____

34 저와 함께 더 나은 학교생활을 만들어 보는 건 어떨까요?

➡ _____

※ 다음 우리말과 일치하도록 빈칸에 알맞은 말을 쓰시오.

Express Yourself-C

1. _____ you _____ of the pyramids in Egypt?

2. Though I _____ never _____ _____ _____ Egypt before, I'm standing _____ _____ _____ a pyramid in this picture.

3. I _____ it at the selfie _____.

Project-Step 2

1. Fire _____ _____

2. _____ you _____ _____ fire safety rules?

3. _____ there's a fire, you can _____ _____.

4. You _____ _____ the elevator.

5. You should _____ the teacher's _____.

Link to the World

1. BMX Bike _____

2. _____ a BMX bike _____ very _____.

3. You can try _____ _____ _____.

4. You can _____ the bike _____ and _____ _____ with the bike.

5. _____ it's not _____, it's very _____.

6. You _____ _____ _____ standing skills.

7. _____ you try _____ skills, _____ is very important.

8. But _____. You _____ _____ a helmet and gloves.

9. Also, you _____ _____ too fast _____ you're _____.

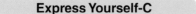

※ 다음 우리말을 영어로 쓰시오.

Express Yourself-C

1. 여러분은 이집트의 피라미드에 대해 들어 본 적이 있나요?
   ➡ _____

2. 나는 전에 이집트에 가 본 적이 없지만, 이 사진에서 나는 피라미드 앞에 서 있어요.
   ➡ _____

3. 나는 이 사진을 셀피 박물관에서 찍었어요.
   ➡ _____

Project - Step 2

1. 화재 안전 수칙
   ➡ _____

2. 당신은 화재 안전 수칙에 대해 들어 본 적이 있습니까?
   ➡ _____

3. 불이 났지만, 당신은 안전할 수 있어요.
   ➡ _____

4. 엘리베이터를 타지 마세요.
   ➡ _____

5. 선생님의 지시에 따라야 해요.
   ➡ _____

Link to the World

1. BMX 자전거 타기
   ➡ _____

2. BMX 자전거를 타는 것은 매우 흥미롭다.
   ➡ _____

3. 여러분은 많은 기술을 시도할 수 있다.
   ➡ _____

4. 여러분은 자전거를 자유롭게 돌릴 수 있고 심지어 자전거와 함께 점프할 수도 있다.
   ➡ _____

5. 쉽지는 않지만, 매우 흥미롭다.
   ➡ _____

6. 여러분은 서 있는 기술과 함께 시작하면 된다.
   ➡ _____

7. 서 있는 기술을 시도할 때, 균형을 잡는 것이 매우 중요하다.
   ➡ _____

8. 하지만 조심해라! 헬멧과 장갑을 착용해야 한다.
   ➡ _____

9. 또한, 자전거를 탈 때는 너무 빨리 가지 말아야 한다.
   ➡ _____

※ 다음 영어를 우리말로 쓰시오.

01 remember

02 practice

03 grade

04 super

05 move

06 February

07 special

08 field trip

09 funny

10 cook

11 far

12 delicious

13 memory

14 medal

15 nursing home

16 secret

17 lose

18 sunlight

19 bring

20 laughter

21 hen

22 whisper

23 aunt

24 bounce

25 hairpin

26 traditional

27 thick

28 competition

29 neighbor

30 perform

31 alone

32 puppet

33 together

34 precious

35 thank A for B

36 What about+-ing ~?

37 the same as ~

38 go into

39 one by one

40 remember+-ing

41 cut holes

42 thanks to

43 look like+명사

※ 다음 우리말을 영어로 쓰시오.

01 함께, 같이	22 전에
02 판자, 널빤지	23 공연하다
03 다시, 한 번 더	24 눈물
04 입다, 쓰다, 착용하다	25 머리핀
05 두꺼운	26 학년, 성적
06 양호 선생님	27 속삭이다
07 앨범	28 기억, 추억
08 재미있는	29 햇빛
09 대회, 경쟁	30 ~을 튀기다
10 날다, 비행하다	31 웃음
11 혼자, 홀로	32 맛있는
12 (경기의) 판, 회	33 연습하다
13 꼭두각시, 인형	34 특별한
14 과학	35 ~한 것을 기억하다
15 가장 좋아하는	36 ~처럼 보이다
16 사람	37 ~으로 들어가다
17 이웃 (사람)	38 ~ 덕분에
18 만화	39 ~와 똑같은
19 닦다, 청소하다	40 결혼하다
20 귀중한	41 B 때문에 A에게 감사하다
21 갓 낳은, 신선한	42 하나씩, 차례차례
	43 ~을 보고 미소 짓다

※ 다음 영영풀이에 알맞은 단어를 <보기>에서 골라 쓴 후, 우리말 뜻을 쓰시오.

1 _____ : to speak very quietly: _____

2 _____ : best liked or most enjoyed: _____

3 _____ : a drop of salty liquid that flows from the eye: _____

4 _____ : not ordinary or usual: _____

5 _____ : a pin that is worn in your hair: _____

6 _____ : the act or sound of laughing: _____

7 _____ : someone who lives near you: _____

8 _____ : the action or sound of laughing: _____

9 _____ : to move up or away after hitting a surface: _____

10 _____ : someone's ability to remember things, places, experiences, etc.:

_____

11 _____ : one of the levels in a school with children of similar age: _____

12 _____ : something that is kept hidden or that is known about by only a few

people: _____

13 _____ : an empty space in an object, usually with an opening to the object's

surface: _____

14 _____ : of great value because of being rare, expensive, or important: _____

15 _____ : to do something to entertain people by acting a play or playing a piece

of music: _____

16 _____ : a toy in the shape of a person or animal that you can move with strings

or by putting your hand inside: _____

보기			
perform	tear	special	precious
whisper	hairpin	puppet	laughter
grade	bounce	hole	hen
favorite	memory	secret	neighbor

대화문 Test

※ 다음 우리말과 일치하도록 빈칸에 알맞은 말을 쓰시오.

Get Ready

1. **G:** _____ are you, Ms. Hwang? We _____ TV together _____ _____. _____ you _____ that?

   M: Sure, Jieun. I _____ a great time _____ you.

2. **M:** Hi, Minjun. So, you _____ _____ _____ _____ in the board _____ _____. _____ _____ again now.

   B: Okay. _____ _____. Is this right?

   M: Yes. You _____ _____.

3. **G:** Hello, Mr. Yang. _____ _____ Minji. Do you _____ _____?

   M: Sure, Minji. Thank you _____ _____.

Start Off Listen & Talk A

1. **G:** Do you _____ Mr. Kim, _____ _____ _____ teacher?

   B: _____ _____. He _____ super _____ _____.

   G: _____ what? He _____ _____ a new school in February _____ _____.

   B: I _____ _____ that. _____ _____ him together.

   G: Okay. _____ _____.

2. **B:** _____ you _____ Ms. Lee?

   G: Ms. Lee? _____ is _____?

   B: She was _____ _____ _____ English teacher.

   G: Now I _____. She _____ _____ _____ _____ pop songs in her class.

   B: She was a _____ _____, _____.

Start Off Listen & Talk B

B: Do you _____ Ms. Kang, the _____ _____?

G: Sure. She was _____ _____ _____.

B: _____ _____? She's _____ _____ next month.

G: Wow! What _____ we _____ for her?

B: _____ _____ _____. What _____ _____ a special album?

G: That's a _____ _____.

1. **G:** 황 여사님, 안녕하세요? 우리 지난 주말에 함께 TV를 봤어요. 기억하세요?

   W: 물론이지, 지은아. 너랑 즐거운 시간을 보냈지.

2. **M:** 안녕, 민준아. 자, 지난번에 판자에 구멍 뚫는 걸 배웠지. 지금 다시 연습해 보자.

   B: 네. 어디 보자. 이렇게 하는 게 맞나요?

   M: 그래, 모두 기억하고 있구나.

3. **G:** 안녕하세요, 양 선생님. 저 민지예요. 저 기억하세요?

   M: 물론이지, 민지야. 전화 줘서 고맙다.

1. **G:** 6학년 때 선생님이셨던 김 선생님 기억나니?

   B: 물론이지. 그분은 엄청나게 두꺼운 안경을 쓰고 계셨는데.

   G: 있지. 그분이 올해 2월에 새 학교로 옮기셨대.

   B: 몰랐어. 함께 찾아뵙자.

   G: 응. 좋은 생각이야.

2. **B:** 너 이 선생님 기억나니?

   G: 이 선생님? 누구신데?

   B: 4학년 때 영어 선생님이셨어.

   G: 이제 기억난다. 그분은 수업시간에 팝송을 많이 가르쳐 주셨지.

   B: 춤도 잘 추셨어.

B: 학교 보건 선생님이셨던 강 선생님 기억하니?

G: 물론이지. 그분은 우리 모두에게 친절하셨잖아.

B: 있지. 그분이 다음 달에 결혼하신대.

G: 와. 그분에게 우리 뭘 해드릴까?

B: 어디 보자. 특별한 앨범을 만들어 드리는 게 어떨까?

G: 좋은 생각이야.

Speak Up Look and talk.

A: Do you remember the field trip _____ _____ ?
B: _____ _____ . We played fun games.
A: I have some _____ _____ from it _____ my phone.
B: That's _____ !

Speak Up Mission

A: Do you _____ _____ _____ ?
B: _____ _____ _____ . It's _____ 3. Right?
A: That's _____ . / That's _____ _____ . It's _____ _____ .

Real-life Scene

G: Do you remember Ms. Park, the old lady _____ _____ _____ ?
B: _____ _____ . We _____ her a birthday party _____ _____ .
G: And she _____ *japchae* for us. She _____ some chicken _____ it.
B: Right. It was _____ . And we _____ card games _____ . Do you _____ _____ ?
G: Yes. She _____ all the _____ . She's really _____ _____ games.
B: When _____ we _____ _____ see her next, Mina?
G: _____ _____ _____ . Next Saturday.
B: _____ _____ some pictures with her _____ _____ .
G: _____ _____ , Junsu.

Express Yourself

1. G: _____ _____ _____ the hot air balloon? We _____ it in Turkey.
   M: Of course. It _____ _____ an elephant.

2. G: Do you remember the rock?
   M: Is it the _____ _____ _____ ?
   G: Right.
   M: I _____ it. It _____ _____ a queen's head.

Learning Diary Check Yourself

B: Do you remember the _____ _____ last year?
G: _____ _____ . We _____ super _____ .
B: I have some _____ _____ from it _____ my phone.
G: That's _____ !

A: 작년에 간 체험학습 기억하니?
B: 물론이지. 우리 신나는 게임을 했잖아.
A: 내 휴대 전화에 그때 찍은 재미있는 사진이 좀 있어.
B: 멋지다!

A: 내 생일 기억하니?
B: 어디 보자. 6월 3일이지. 그렇지?
A: 맞아. / 아니야. 6월 13일이야.

G: 혼자 사시는 할머니, 박 여사님 기억하니?
B: 물론이지. 작년에 우리가 생신 잔치를 해 드렸잖아.
G: 그리고 그분이 우리를 위해 잡채 요리를 해주셨지. 안에 닭고기를 넣으셨어.
B: 맞아. 맛있었어. 그러고 나서 함께 카드 게임도 했는데. 그거 기억나?
G: 응. 그분이 모든 판을 다 이기셨지. 게임을 정말 잘하셔.
B: 미나야, 다음에 언제 그분을 뵈러 갈 거야?
G: 어디 보자. 다음 주 토요일.
B: 이번에는 그분과 같이 사진을 몇 장 찍자.
G: 좋은 생각이다, 준수야.

1. G: 그 열기구 기억나? 터키에서 탔었지.
   M: 물론이지. 그것은 코끼리처럼 생겼었지.

2. G: 그 바위 기억나?
   M: 대만에 있는 거지?
   G: 맞아.
   M: 기억나지. 그것은 여왕의 머리처럼 생겼었지.

B: 작년에 한 노래 경연 대회 기억하니?
G: 물론이지. 우리 엄청나게 연습했잖아.
B: 내 휴대 전화에 그때 찍은 재미있는 사진이 좀 있어.
G: 멋지다!

※ 다음 우리말에 맞도록 대화를 영어로 쓰시오.

Get Ready

1. G: _____

   _____

   W: _____

2. M: _____

   _____

   B: _____

   M: _____

3. G: _____

   M: _____

Start Off Listen & Talk A

1. G: _____

   B: _____

   G: _____

   B: _____

   G: _____

2. B: _____

   G: _____

   B: _____

   G: _____

   B: _____

Start Off Listen & Talk B

B: _____

G: _____

B: _____

G: _____

B: _____

G: _____

해석

1. G: 황 여사님, 안녕하세요? 우리 지난 주말에 함께 TV를 봤어요. 기억하세요?
   W: 물론이지, 지은아. 너랑 즐거운 시간을 보냈지.

2. M: 안녕, 민준아. 자, 지난번에 판자에 구멍 뚫는 걸 배웠지. 지금 다시 연습해 보자.
   B: 네. 어디 보자. 이렇게 하는 게 맞나요?
   M: 그래, 모두 기억하고 있구나.

3. G: 안녕하세요, 양 선생님. 저 민지예요. 저 기억하세요?
   M: 물론이지, 민지야. 전화 줘서 고맙다.

1. G: 6학년 때 선생님이셨던 김 선생님 기억나니?
   B: 물론이지. 그분은 엄청나게 두꺼운 안경을 쓰고 계셨는데.
   G: 있지. 그분이 올해 2월에 새 학교로 옮기셨대.
   B: 몰랐어. 함께 찾아뵙자.
   G: 응. 좋은 생각이야.

2. B: 너 이 선생님 기억나니?
   G: 이 선생님? 누구신데?
   B: 4학년 때 영어 선생님이셨어.
   G: 이제 기억난다. 그분은 수업시간에 팝송을 많이 가르쳐 주셨지.
   B: 춤도 잘 추셨어.

B: 학교 보건 선생님이셨던 강 선생님 기억하니?
G: 물론이지. 그분은 우리 모두에게 친절하셨잖아.
B: 있지. 그분이 다음 달에 결혼하신대.
G: 와. 그분에게 우리 뭘 해드릴까?
B: 어디 보자. 특별한 앨범을 만들어 드리는 게 어떨까?
G: 좋은 생각이야.

Speak Up Look and talk.

A: _____

B: _____

A: _____

B: _____

Speak Up Mission

A: _____

B: _____

A: _____

Real-life Scene

G: _____

B: _____

G: _____

B: _____

G: _____

B: _____

G: _____

B: _____

G: _____

Express Yourself

1. G: _____

   M: _____

2. G: _____

   M: _____

   G: _____

   M: _____

Learning Diary Check Yourself

B: _____

G: _____

B: _____

G: _____

A: 작년에 간 체험학습 기억하니?
B: 물론이지. 우리 신나는 게임을 했잖아.
A: 내 휴대 전화에 그때 찍은 재미있는 사진이 좀 있어.
B: 멋지다!

A: 내 생일 기억하니?
B: 어디 보자. 6월 3일이지. 그렇지?
A: 맞아. / 아니야. 6월 13일이야.

G: 혼자 사시는 할머니, 박 여사님 기억하니?
B: 물론이지. 작년에 우리가 생신 잔치를 해 드렸잖아.
G: 그리고 그분이 우리를 위해 잡채 요리를 해주셨지. 안에 닭고기를 넣으셨어.
B: 맞아. 맛있었어. 그러고 나서 함께 카드 게임도 했는데. 그거 기억나?
G: 응. 그분이 모든 판을 다 이기셨지. 게임을 정말 잘하셔.
B: 미나야, 다음에 언제 그분을 뵈러 갈 거야?
G: 어디 보자. 다음 주 토요일.
B: 이번에는 그분과 같이 사진을 몇 장 찍자.
G: 좋은 생각이다, 준수야.

1. G: 그 열기구 기억나? 터키에서 탔었지.
   M: 물론이지. 그것은 코끼리처럼 생겼었지.

2. G: 그 바위 기억나?
   M: 대만에 있는 거지?
   G: 맞아.
   M: 기억나지. 그것은 여왕의 머리처럼 생겼었지.

B: 작년에 한 노래 경연 대회 기억하니?
G: 물론이지. 우리 엄청나게 연습했잖아.
B: 내 휴대 전화에 그때 찍은 재미있는 사진이 좀 있어.
G: 멋지다!

※ 다음 우리말과 일치하도록 빈칸에 알맞은 것을 골라 쓰시오.

1 _____ a _____?
A. Memory　　　B. What's

2 Wilfrid Gordon Parker was a _____ boy _____ lived _____ to a nursing home.
A. little　　　B. next　　　C. who

3 He liked _____ the people _____ lived _____.
A. there　　　B. who　　　C. all

4 But his _____ person was Ms. Nancy Gordon Cooper because her middle name was the _____ as _____.
A. his　　　B. favorite　　　C. same

5 He told _____ _____ his _____.
A. all　　　B. secrets　　　C. her

6 _____ day, Wilfrid's parents were _____ _____ Ms. Cooper.
A. about　　　B. one　　　C. talking

7 "_____ old _____," said _____ mother.
A. lady　　　B. poor　　　C. his

8 "_____ is she a poor _____ lady?" _____ Wilfrid.
A. asked　　　B. why　　　C. old

9 "_____ she's _____ her _____," said his father.
A. memory　　　B. lost　　　C. because

10 "_____ a memory?" _____ Wilfrid.
A. asked　　　B. what's

11 "It is _____ you _____," said his father.
A. remember　　　B. something

12 Wilfrid wanted to know _____, _____ he went to his _____.
A. so　　　B. more　　　C. neighbors

13 Ms. Jordan was _____ the _____.
A. sunlight　　　B. enjoying

14 "What's a _____?" he _____.
A. asked　　　B. memory

15 "_____ _____, my _____," she said.
A. warm　　　B. child　　　C. something

16 Ms. Mitchell was _____ a _____.
A. reading　　　B. cartoon

17 "What's a _____?" he _____.
A. asked　　　B. memory

18 "_____ that _____ you _____," she said.
A. laughter　　　B. something　　　C. brings

19 Mr. Hunter _____ _____ his _____.
A. was　　　B. medal　　　C. cleaning

1 추억이란 무엇일까?

2 Wilfrid Gordon Parker는 요양원 옆에 사는 어린 소년이었다.

3 그는 그곳에 사는 모든 사람들을 좋아했다.

4 하지만 그가 가장 좋아하는 사람은 Nancy Gordon Cooper 할머니였는데, 그 이유는 그녀의 가운데 이름이 그의 것과 같았기 때문이었다.

5 그는 자기의 모든 비밀을 그녀에게 말했다.

6 어느 날, Wilfrid의 부모님은 Cooper 할머니에 관해 이야기를 하고 있었다.

7 "불쌍한 분." 그의 어머니가 말했다.

8 "왜 불쌍한 분이세요?"라고 Wilfrid가 물었다.

9 "왜냐하면 그분은 기억을 잃으셨거든." 그의 아버지가 말했다.

10 "기억이 뭐예요?" Wilfrid가 물었다.

11 "그것은 네가 기억하는 것이란다."라고 그의 아버지가 말했다.

12 Wilfrid는 더 알고 싶어서, 그의 이웃들에게 갔다.

13 Jordan 할머니는 햇볕을 즐기고 있었다.

14 "기억이 뭐예요?" 그가 물었다.

15 "따뜻한 거란다, 아가야." 그녀가 말했다.

16 Mitchell 할머니는 만화책을 읽고 있었다.

17 "기억이 뭐예요?" 그가 물었다.

18 "너에게 웃음을 가져다주는 것이란다." 그녀가 말했다.

19 Hunter 할아버지는 자신의 메달을 닦고 있었다.

20 "It's _____ as _____ _____ gold, young man," he said.
    A. as   B. precious   C. something

21 So Wilfrid _____ _____ home to _____ _____ memories for Ms. Cooper.
    A. for   B. back   C. went   D. look

22 He _____ _____ the hen house and _____ a fresh, warm egg _____ under a hen.
    A. took   B. from   C. into   D. went

23 _____, he _____ _____ his sock puppet.
    A. for   B. next   C. looked

24 It _____ _____ laughter _____ his parents.
    A. brought   B. to   C. always

25 _____, he _____ his football _____ his toy box.
    A. found   B. finally   C. in

26 It was _____ _____ as _____ to him.
    A. gold   B. precious   C. as

27 Wilfrid _____ to Ms. Cooper and _____ her the things one _____ one.
    A. by   B. gave   C. went

28 "_____ a strange, sweet child!" thought Ms. Cooper, "He's _____ all these wonderful _____."
    A. brought   B. what   C. things

29 Then she started _____ _____ _____ her _____.
    A. past   B. remember   C. to

30 She _____ the warm egg and _____ _____ Wilfrid, "Long _____, I found a small blue egg in my aunt's garden."
    A. whispered   B. held   C. ago   D. to

31 She smiled _____ the sock puppet and _____ _____ a puppet show _____ her sister.
    A. performing   B. at   C. for   D. remembered

32 "My sister _____ _____ _____," said Ms. Cooper.
    A. lot   B. laughed   C. a

33 She _____ the football _____ Wilfrid and _____ him.
    A. remembered   B. bounced   C. to

34 "Wilfrid? Wilfrid Gordon Parker! _____ _____!"
    A. friend   B. my

35 She _____ _____ their secrets _____ by one.
    A. remembered   B. one   C. also

36 The two smiled _____ _____ _____.
    A. at   B. other   C. each

37 Ms. Cooper _____ her memory _____ thanks to the little boy _____ the same middle name _____ hers.
    A. got   B. with   C. back   D. as

---

20 "그건 금처럼 소중한 거지, 어린 친구."라고 그가 말했다.

21 그래서 Wilfrid는 Cooper 할머니께 드릴 기억들을 찾으러 집으로 돌아갔다.

22 그는 닭장 안으로 들어가서 암탉이 품고 있던 신선하고 따뜻한 달걀을 꺼냈다.

23 다음으로, 그는 자신의 양말 인형을 찾았다.

24 그것은 항상 그의 부모님께 큰 웃음을 안겨 드렸다.

25 마지막으로, 그는 자신의 장난감 상자 속에서 축구공을 찾아냈다.

26 그것은 그에게는 금만큼이나 소중했다.

27 Wilfrid는 Cooper 할머니께 가서 그녀에게 물건들을 하나씩 드렸다.

28 "이상하면서도 귀여운 아이구나! 이 멋진 물건들을 다 가져오다니 말이야."라고 Cooper 할머니는 생각했다.

29 그러다가 그녀는 자신의 과거를 기억해 내기 시작했다.

30 그녀는 따뜻한 달걀을 쥐고 Wilfrid에게, "오래 전에, 나는 나의 이모님 댁 정원에서 작고 푸른 알을 찾았단다."라고 속삭였다.

31 그녀는 양말 인형을 보며 미소를 짓다가 자기 여동생에게 인형극을 공연해 주었던 것을 기억해 냈다.

32 "내 여동생이 엄청나게 웃었지."라고 Cooper 할머니가 말했다.

33 그녀는 축구공을 바닥에 튀게 해서 Wilfrid에게 던져 주다가 그를 기억해 냈다.

34 "Wilfrid? Wilfrid Gordon Parker! 내 친구!"

35 그녀는 또한 그들만의 비밀을 하나씩 기억해 냈다.

36 두 사람은 서로 바라보며 미소 지었다.

37 Cooper 할머니는 가운데 이름이 자신의 것과 같은 어린 소년 덕분에 기억을 다시 찾게 되었다.

※ 다음 우리말과 일치하도록 빈칸에 알맞은 말을 쓰시오.

1 _____ a Memory?

2 Wilfrid Gordon Parker was _____ _____ _____ who _____ _____ _____ a nursing home.

3 He liked _____ the people _____ _____ there.

4 But his _____ _____ was Ms. Nancy Gordon Cooper _____ her middle name was _____ _____ _____ _____ .

5 He _____ _____ all his _____ .

6 One day, Wilfrid's parents were _____ _____ Ms. Cooper.

7 "_____ _____ _____ ," _____ his mother.

8 "_____ is she a _____ old lady?" _____ Wilfrid.

9 "_____ she's _____ her memory," _____ his father.

10 "What's a _____ ?" _____ Wilfrid.

11 "It is _____ _____ _____ ," said his father.

12 Wilfrid _____ _____ know more, so he _____ to his neighbors.

13 Ms. Jordan _____ _____ the sunlight.

14 "What's a memory?" _____ _____ .

15 "_____ _____ , my child," she said.

16 Ms. Mitchell _____ _____ a cartoon.

17 "_____ _____ _____ ?" he asked.

18 "Something that _____ _____ _____ ," she said.

1 추억이란 무엇일까?

2 Wilfrid Gordon Parker는 요양원 옆에 사는 어린 소년이었다.

3 그는 그곳에 사는 모든 사람들을 좋아했다.

4 하지만 그가 가장 좋아하는 사람은 Nancy Gordon Cooper 할머니였는데, 그 이유는 그녀의 가운데 이름이 그의 것과 같았기 때문이었다.

5 그는 자기의 모든 비밀을 그녀에게 말했다.

6 어느 날, Wilfrid의 부모님은 Cooper 할머니에 관해 이야기를 하고 있었다.

7 "불쌍한 분." 그의 어머니가 말했다.

8 "왜 불쌍한 분이세요?"라고 Wilfrid가 물었다.

9 "왜냐하면 그분은 기억을 잃으셨거든." 그의 아버지가 말했다.

10 "기억이 뭐예요?" Wilfrid가 물었다.

11 "그것은 네가 기억하는 것이란다."라고 그의 아버지가 말했다.

12 Wilfrid는 더 알고 싶어서, 그의 이웃들에게 갔다.

13 Jordan 할머니는 햇볕을 즐기고 있었다.

14 "기억이 뭐예요?" 그가 물었다.

15 "따뜻한 거란다, 아가야." 그녀가 말했다.

16 Mitchell 할머니는 만화책을 읽고 있었다.

17 "기억이 뭐예요?" 그가 물었다.

18 "너에게 웃음을 가져다주는 것이란다." 그녀가 말했다.

19 Mr. Hunter _____ _____ his medal.

20 "It's something _____ _____ _____ gold, young man," he said.

21 So Wilfrid _____ _____ home _____ _____ _____ memories for Ms. Cooper.

22 He _____ _____ the hen house and took a fresh, warm egg _____ _____ _____ _____ .

23 Next, he _____ _____ his sock puppet.

24 It _____ _____ _____ to his parents.

25 Finally, he _____ his football _____ his toy box.

26 It was _____ precious _____ _____ to him.

27 Wilfrid _____ _____ Ms. Cooper and gave her the things _____ _____ _____ .

28 "_____ a strange, sweet child!" _____ Ms. Cooper, "He's _____ all these wonderful things."

29 Then she _____ _____ _____ her past.

30 She _____ the warm egg and _____ to Wilfrid, "Long ago, I _____ a small blue egg in my aunt's garden."

31 She _____ _____ the sock puppet and _____ _____ a puppet show for her sister.

32 "My sister _____ _____ _____ ," said Ms. Cooper.

33 She _____ the football _____ Wilfrid and remembered him.

34 "Wilfrid? Wilfrid Gordon Parker! _____ _____ !"

35 She also _____ their _____ one by one.

36 The two smiled _____ _____ _____ .

37 Ms. Cooper got her memory back _____ _____ the little boy with _____ _____ middle name _____ hers.

19 Hunter 할아버지는 자신의 메달을 닦고 있었다.

20 "그건 금처럼 소중한 거지, 어린 친구."라고 그가 말했다.

21 그래서 Wilfrid는 Cooper 할머니께 드릴 기억들을 찾으러 집으로 돌아갔다.

22 그는 닭장 안으로 들어가시 암탉이 품고 있던 신선하고 따뜻한 달걀을 꺼냈다.

23 다음으로, 그는 자신의 양말 인형을 찾았다.

24 그것은 항상 그의 부모님께 큰 웃음을 안겨 드렸다.

25 마지막으로, 그는 자신의 장난감 상자 속에서 축구공을 찾아냈다.

26 그것은 그에게는 금만큼이나 소중했다.

27 Wilfrid는 Cooper 할머니께 가서 그녀에게 물건들을 하나씩 드렸다.

28 "이상하면서도 귀여운 아이구나! 이 멋진 물건들을 다 가져오다니 말이야."라고 Cooper 할머니는 생각했다.

29 그러다가 그녀는 자신의 과거를 기억해 내기 시작했다.

30 그녀는 따뜻한 달걀을 쥐고 Wilfrid에게, "오래 전에, 나는 나의 이모님 댁 정원에서 작고 푸른 알을 찾았단다."라고 속삭였다.

31 그녀는 양말 인형을 보며 미소를 짓다가 자기 여동생에게 인형극을 공연해 주었던 것을 기억해 냈다.

32 "내 여동생이 엄청나게 웃었지."라고 Cooper 할머니가 말했다.

33 그녀는 축구공을 바닥에 튀게 해서 Wilfrid에게 던져 주다가 그를 기억해 냈다.

34 "Wilfrid? Wilfrid Gordon Parker! 내 친구!"

35 그녀는 또한 그들만의 비밀을 하나씩 기억해 냈다.

36 두 사람은 서로 바라보며 미소 지었다.

37 Cooper 할머니는 가운데 이름이 자신의 것과 같은 어린 소년 덕분에 기억을 다시 찾게 되었다.

※ 다음 문장을 우리말로 쓰시오.

1 What's a Memory?
➡ _____

2 Wilfrid Gordon Parker was a little boy who lived next to a nursing home.
➡ _____

3 He liked all the people who lived there.
➡ _____

4 But his favorite person was Ms. Nancy Gordon Cooper because her middle name was the same as his.
➡ _____
_____

5 He told her all his secrets.
➡ _____

6 One day, Wilfrid's parents were talking about Ms. Cooper.
➡ _____

7 "Poor old lady," said his mother.
➡ _____

8 "Why is she a poor old lady?" asked Wilfrid.
➡ _____

9 "Because she's lost her memory," said his father.
➡ _____

10 "What's a memory?" asked Wilfrid.
➡ _____

11 "It is something you remember," said his father.
➡ _____

12 Wilfrid wanted to know more, so he went to his neighbors.
➡ _____

13 Ms. Jordan was enjoying the sunlight.
➡ _____

14 "What's a memory?" he asked.
➡ _____

15 "Something warm, my child," she said.
➡ _____

16 Ms. Mitchell was reading a cartoon.
➡ _____

17 "What's a memory?" he asked.
➡ _____

18 "Something that brings you laughter," she said.
➡ _____

19 Mr. Hunter was cleaning his medal.

➡ _____

20 "It's something as precious as gold, young man," he said.

➡ _____

21 So Wilfrid went back home to look for memories for Ms. Cooper.

➡ _____

22 He went into the hen house and took a fresh, warm egg from under a hen.

➡ _____

23 Next, he looked for his sock puppet.

➡ _____

24 It always brought laughter to his parents.

➡ _____

25 Finally, he found his football in his toy box.

➡ _____

26 It was as precious as gold to him.

➡ _____

27 Wilfrid went to Ms. Cooper and gave her the things one by one.

➡ _____

28 "What a strange, sweet child!" thought Ms. Cooper, "He's brought all these wonderful things."

➡ _____

29 Then she started to remember her past.

➡ _____

30 She held the warm egg and whispered to Wilfrid, "Long ago, I found a small blue egg in my aunt's garden."

➡ _____

31 She smiled at the sock puppet and remembered performing a puppet show for her sister.

➡ _____

32 "My sister laughed a lot," said Ms. Cooper.

➡ _____

33 She bounced the football to Wilfrid and remembered him.

➡ _____

34 "Wilfrid? Wilfrid Gordon Parker! My friend!"

➡ _____

35 She also remembered their secrets one by one.

➡ _____

36 The two smiled at each other.

➡ _____

37 Ms. Cooper got her memory back thanks to the little boy with the same middle name as hers.

➡ _____

본문 Test

※ 다음 괄호 안의 단어들을 우리말에 맞도록 바르게 배열하시오.

1 (Memory? / a / What's)
➡ _____

2 (Gordon / Wilfrid / Parker / a / was / boy / little / lived / who / to / next / home. / nursing / a)
➡ _____

3 (liked / he / the / all / who / people / there. / lived)
➡ _____

4 (his / but / person / favorite / was / Nancy / Ms. / Cooper / Gordon / because / middle / her / was / name / the / as / his. / same)
➡ _____
_____

5 (told / he / all / her / secrets. / his)
➡ _____

6 (day, / one / parents / Wilfrid's / talking / were / about / Cooper. / Ms.)
➡ _____

7 (old / "poor / lady," / his / mother. / said)
➡ _____

8 (is / "why / she / a / old / poor / lady?" / Wilfrid. / asked)
➡ _____

9 (she's / "because / her / lost / memory," / father. / his / said)
➡ _____

10 (a / "what's / memory?" / Wilfrid. / asked)
➡ _____

11 (is / "it / something / remember," / you / father. / his / said)
➡ _____

12 (wanted / Wilfrid / know / to / more, / he / so / to / went / neighbors. / his)
➡ _____

13 (Jordan / Ms. / enjoying / was / sunlight. / the)
➡ _____

14 (a / "what's / memory?" / asked. / he)
➡ _____

15 (warm, / "something / child," / my / said. / she)
➡ _____

16 (Mitchell / Ms. / reading / was / cartoon. / a)
➡ _____

17 (a / "what's / memory?" / asked. / he)
➡ _____

18 (that / "something / birngs / laughter," / you / said. / she)
➡ _____

---

1 추억이란 무엇일까?

2 Wilfrid Gordon Parker는 요양원 옆에 사는 어린 소년이었다.

3 그는 그곳에 사는 모든 사람들을 좋아했다.

4 하지만 그가 가장 좋아하는 사람은 Nancy Gordon Cooper 할머니였는데, 그 이유는 그녀의 가운데 이름이 그의 것과 같았기 때문이었다.

5 그는 자기의 모든 비밀을 그녀에게 말했다.

6 어느 날, Wilfrid의 부모님은 Cooper 할머니에 관해 이야기를 하고 있었다.

7 "불쌍한 분." 그의 어머니가 말했다.

8 "왜 불쌍한 분이세요?"라고 Wilfrid가 물었다.

9 "왜냐하면 그분은 기억을 잃으셨거든." 그의 아버지가 말했다.

10 "기억이 뭐예요?" Wilfrid가 물었다.

11 "그것은 네가 기억하는 것이란다."라고 그의 아버지가 말했다.

12 Wilfrid는 더 알고 싶어서, 그의 이웃들에게 갔다.

13 Jordan 할머니는 햇볕을 즐기고 있었다.

14 "기억이 뭐예요?" 그가 물었다.

15 "따뜻한 거란다, 아가야." 그녀가 말했다.

16 Mitchell 할머니는 만화책을 읽고 있었다.

17 "기억이 뭐예요?" 그가 물었다.

18 "너에게 웃음을 가져다주는 것이란다." 그녀가 말했다.

19 (Hunter / Mr. / cleaning / was / medal. / his)
➡ _____

20 (something / "it's / precious / as / gold, / as / man," / young / said. / he)
➡ _____

21 (Wilfrid / so / back / went / home / look / to / memories / for / Cooper. / for / Ms.)
➡ _____

22 (went / he / into / hen / the / house / took / and / fresh, / a / egg / warm / under / hen. / a / from)
➡ _____

23 (next, / looked / he / for / puppet. / sock / his)
➡ _____

24 (always / it / laughter / brought / parents. / his / to)
➡ _____

25 (finally, / found / he / football / his / in / box. / toy / his)
➡ _____

26 (was / it / precious / as / to / gold / him. / as)
➡ _____

27 (Wilfrid / to / went Cooper / Ms. / gave / and / her / things / the / one. / by / one)
➡ _____

28 (a / "what / strange, / child!" / sweet / Ms. / thought / Cooper, / "he's / all / brought / things." / wonderful / these)
➡ _____

29 (she / then / to / started / her / remember / past.)
➡ _____

30 (held / she / warm / the / egg / and / to / whispered / Wilfrid, / ago, / "long / found / I / small / a / egg / blue / in / garden." / aunt's / my)
➡ _____

31 (smiled / she / the / at / puppet / sock / and / performing / remembered / puppet / a / show / her / sister. / for)
➡ _____

32 ("my / laughed / sister / lot," / a / Cooper. / Ms. / said)
➡ _____

33 (bounced / she / football / the / Wilfrid / to / him. / and / remembered)
➡ _____

34 ("Wilfrid? / Gordon / Wilfrid / Parker! / friend!" / my)
➡ _____

35 (also / she / remembered / secrets / their / one. / by / one)
➡ _____

36 (two / the / smiled / at / other. / each)
➡ _____

37 (Cooper / Ms. / her / got / memory / thanks / back / to / little / the / boy / with / same / the / name / middle / hers. / as)
➡ _____

19 Hunter 할아버지는 자신의 메달을 닦고 있었다.
20 "그건 금처럼 소중한 거지, 어린 친구."라고 그가 말했다.
21 그래서 Wilfrid는 Cooper 할머니께 드릴 기억들을 찾으러 집으로 돌아갔다.
22 그는 닭장 안으로 들어가서 암탉이 품고 있던 신선하고 따뜻한 달걀을 꺼냈다.
23 다음으로, 그는 자신의 양말 인형을 찾았다.
24 그것은 항상 그의 부모님께 큰 웃음을 안겨 드렸다.
25 마지막으로, 그는 자신의 장난감 상자 속에서 축구공을 찾아냈다.
26 그것은 그에게는 금만큼이나 소중했다.
27 Wilfrid는 Cooper 할머니께 가서 그녀에게 물건들을 하나씩 드렸다.
28 "이상하면서도 귀여운 아이구나! 이 멋진 물건들을 다 가져오다니 말이야."라고 Cooper 할머니는 생각했다.
29 그러다가 그녀는 자신의 과거를 기억해 내기 시작했다.
30 그녀는 따뜻한 달걀을 쥐고 Wilfrid에게, "오래 전에, 나는 나의 이모님 댁 정원에서 작고 푸른 알을 찾았단다."라고 속삭였다.
31 그녀는 양말 인형을 보며 미소를 짓다가 자기 여동생에게 인형극을 공연해 주었던 것을 기억해 냈다.
32 "내 여동생이 엄청나게 웃었지."라고 Cooper 할머니가 말했다.
33 그녀는 축구공을 바닥에 튀게 해서 Wilfrid에게 던져 주다가 그를 기억해 냈다.
34 "Wilfrid? Wilfrid Gordon Parker! 내 친구!"
35 그녀는 또한 그들만의 비밀을 하나씩 기억해 냈다.
36 두 사람은 서로 바라보며 미소 지었다.
37 Cooper 할머니는 가운데 이름이 자신의 것과 같은 어린 소년 덕분에 기억을 다시 찾게 되었다.

※ 다음 우리말을 영어로 쓰시오.

1 추억이란 무엇일까?

➡ _____

2 Wilfrid Gordon Parker는 요양원 옆에 사는 어린 소년이었다.

➡ _____

3 그는 그곳에 사는 모든 사람들을 좋아했다.

➡ _____

4 하지만 그가 가장 좋아하는 사람은 Nancy Gordon Cooper 할머니였는데, 그 이유는 그녀의 가운데 이름이 그의 것과 같았기 때문이었다.

➡ _____
_____

5 그는 자기의 모든 비밀을 그녀에게 말했다.

➡ _____

6 어느 날, Wilfrid의 부모님은 Cooper 할머니에 관해 이야기를 하고 있었다.

➡ _____

7 "불쌍한 분." 그의 어머니가 말했다.

➡ _____

8 "왜 불쌍한 분이세요?"라고 Wilfrid가 물었다.

➡ _____

9 "왜냐하면 그분은 기억을 잃으셨거든." 그의 아버지가 말했다.

➡ _____

10 "기억이 뭐예요?" Wilfrid가 물었다.

➡ _____

11 "그것은 네가 기억하는 것이란다."라고 그의 아버지가 말했다.

➡ _____

12 Wilfrid는 더 알고 싶어서, 그의 이웃들에게 갔다.

➡ _____

13 Jordan 할머니는 햇볕을 즐기고 있었다.

➡ _____

14 "기억이 뭐예요?" 그가 물었다.

➡ _____

15 "따뜻한 거란다, 아가야." 그녀가 말했다.

➡ _____

16 Mitchell 할머니는 만화책을 읽고 있었다.

➡ _____

17 "기억이 뭐예요?" 그가 물었다.

➡ _____

18 "너에게 웃음을 가져다주는 것이란다." 그녀가 말했다.

➡ _____

19 Hunter 할아버지는 자신의 메달을 닦고 있었다.

➡ _____

20 "그건 금처럼 소중한 거지, 어린 친구."라고 그가 말했다.

➡ _____

21 그래서 Wilfrid는 Cooper 할머니께 드릴 기억들을 찾으러 집으로 돌아갔다.

➡ _____

22 그는 닭장 안으로 들어가서 암탉이 품고 있던 신선하고 따뜻한 달걀을 꺼냈다.

➡ _____

23 다음으로, 그는 자신의 양말 인형을 찾았다.

➡ _____

24 그것은 항상 그의 부모님께 큰 웃음을 안겨 드렸다.

➡ _____

25 마지막으로, 그는 자신의 장난감 상자 속에서 축구공을 찾아냈다.

➡ _____

26 그것은 그에게는 금만큼이나 소중했다.

➡ _____

27 Wilfrid는 Cooper 할머니께 가서 그녀에게 물건들을 하나씩 드렸다.

➡ _____

28 "이상하면서도 귀여운 아이구나! 이 멋진 물건들을 다 가져오다니 말이야."라고 Cooper 할머니는 생각했다.

➡ _____

29 그러다가 그녀는 자신의 과거를 기억해 내기 시작했다.

➡ _____

30 그녀는 따뜻한 달걀을 쥐고 Wilfrid에게, "오래 전에, 나는 나의 이모님 댁 정원에서 작고 푸른 알을 찾았단다."라고 속삭였다.

➡ _____

31 그녀는 양말 인형을 보며 미소를 짓다가 자기 여동생에게 인형극을 공연해 주었던 것을 기억해 냈다.

➡ _____

32 "내 여동생이 엄청나게 웃었지."라고 Cooper 할머니가 말했다.

➡ _____

33 그녀는 축구공을 바닥에 튀게 해서 Wilfrid에게 던져 주다가 그를 기억해 냈다.

➡ _____

34 "Wilfrid? Wilfrid Gordon Parker! 내 친구!"

➡ _____

35 그녀는 또한 그들만의 비밀을 하나씩 기억해 냈다.

➡ _____

36 두 사람은 서로 바라보며 미소 지었다.

➡ _____

37 Cooper 할머니는 가운데 이름이 자신의 것과 같은 어린 소년 덕분에 기억을 다시 찾게 되었다.

➡ _____

※ 다음 우리말과 일치하도록 빈칸에 알맞은 말을 쓰시오.

Express Yourself

1. _____ May 29, 2017, we _____ _____ India.

2. This is a _____ _____ _____ _____ in the market.

3. I'll _____ _____ the experience.

4. We _____ _____ of Korean _____ _____.

5. We _____ them at the _____ festival.

6. _____ June 7, 2017, we _____ _____ Laos.

7. We met a _____ _____ _____ _____ a beautiful dress.

8. I'll _____ _____ the _____.

9. We _____ a rock. It _____ _____ a queen's head.

1. 2017년 5월 29일에 우리는 인도에 갔다.
2. 이것은 우리가 시장에서 산 그림이다.
3. 나는 그 경험을 결코 잊지 못할 것이다.
4. 우리는 한국 전통 무용수들의 사진을 찍었다.
5. 우리는 그들을 마을 축제에서 보았다.
6. 2017년 6월 7일에 우리는 라오스에 도착했다.
7. 우리는 아름다운 옷을 입고 있는 한 소녀를 만났다.
8. 나는 그 경험을 결코 잊지 못할 것이다.
9. 우리는 바위를 보았다. 그것은 여왕의 머리처럼 생겼다.

Do It Yourself

1. I'd _____ _____ _____ you about a student teacher I can't forget.

2. _____ _____ is Ms. Jeon.

3. _____ _____ _____ you're great, Miso! _____ _____ _____ _____.

4. This is the bookmark that she gave to me _____ _____ _____ _____.

5. When I _____ _____, I always _____ _____ this.

1. 나는 잊을 수 없는 교생 선생님에 대해서 너희들에게 말하고 싶다.
2. 그분은 전 선생님이시다.
3. "네가 훌륭하다는 걸 잊지 마. 미소야! 계속 목적하는 것을 해보렴."
4. 이건 그분이 마지막 날 내게 주신 책갈피다.
5. 나는 스트레스를 받을 때면, 언제나 이것을 본다.

Link to the World

1. There are a lot of _____ _____ who _____ _____ _____ _____ and talents.

2. Mr. Kim in Busan is a smart farmer and _____ people _____ _____.

3. Ms. Lee was a science teacher _____ _____ _____.

4. Now she _____ in a park _____ _____ children about plants and birds.

5. In Ms. Choi's _____ _____, young people _____ _____ gimchi and Korean hot pepper sauce.

1. 자신의 지식과 재능을 나누는 활동적인 어르신들이 많이 계시다.
2. 부산의 김 선생님은 스마트 농부이신데 사람들에게 농사에 관한 것을 가르치신다.
3. 이 선생님은 이전에 과학 선생님이셨다.
4. 지금은 공원에서 일하시며 아이들에게 식물과 새에 관해서 가르치신다.
5. 최 여사님의 요리 교실에서는 젊은이들이 김치와 한국의 고추장을 만드는 것을 배운다.

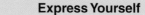

※ 다음 우리말을 영어로 쓰시오.

Express Yourself

1. 2017년 5월 29일에 우리는 인도에 갔다.
   ➡ _____

2. 이것은 우리가 시장에서 산 그림이다.
   ➡ _____

3. 나는 그 경험을 결코 잊지 못할 것이다.
   ➡ _____

4. 우리는 한국 전통 무용수들의 사진을 찍었다.
   ➡ _____

5. 우리는 그들을 마을 축제에서 보았다.
   ➡ _____

6. 2017년 6월 7일에 우리는 라오스에 도착했다.
   ➡ _____

7. 우리는 아름다운 옷을 입고 있는 한 소녀를 만났다.
   ➡ _____

8. 나는 그 경험을 결코 잊지 못할 것이다.
   ➡ _____

9. 우리는 바위를 보았다. 그것은 여왕의 머리처럼 생겼다.
   ➡ _____

Do It Yourself

1. 나는 잊을 수 없는 교생 선생님에 대해서 너희들에게 말하고 싶다.
   ➡ _____

2. 그분은 전 선생님이시다.
   ➡ _____

3. "네가 훌륭하다는 걸 잊지 마. 미소야! 계속 목적하는 것을 해보렴."
   ➡ _____

4. 이건 그분이 마지막 날 내게 주신 책갈피다.
   ➡ _____

5. 나는 스트레스를 받을 때면, 언제나 이것을 본다.
   ➡ _____

Link to the World

1. 자신의 지식과 재능을 나누는 활동적인 어르신들이 많이 계시다.
   ➡ _____

2. 부산의 김 선생님은 스마트 농부이신데 사람들에게 농사에 관한 것을 가르치신다.
   ➡ _____

3. 이 선생님은 이전에 과학 선생님이셨다.
   ➡ _____

4. 지금은 공원에서 일하시며 아이들에게 식물과 새에 관해서 가르치신다.
   ➡ _____

5. 최 여사님의 요리 교실에서는 젊은이들이 김치와 한국의 고추장을 만드는 것을 배운다.
   ➡ _____

※ 다음 영어를 우리말로 쓰시오.

01 lose

02 need

03 please

04 check

05 follow

06 stop

07 dangerous

08 end

09 scene

10 excited

11 front

12 basket

13 safe

14 hood

15 knock

16 laugh

17 blow

18 leave

19 piggy

20 road

21 together

22 under

23 writer

24 famous

25 shake

26 by the way

27 get + 형용사

28 blow one's nose

29 Let me see.

30 be good for

31 take out

32 No problem.

33 out of

34 look into

35 talk to oneself

36 should not+동사원형

37 take a break

38 look at

39 go away

40 thank A for B

※ 다음 우리말을 영어로 쓰시오.

01 웃다 _____

02 함께 _____

03 ~ 아래에 _____

04 작가 _____

05 (입으로) 불다 _____

06 따라가다, 뒤따르다 _____

07 ~을 기쁘게 하다 _____

08 (~하는 것을) 그만두게 하다 _____

09 길, 도로 _____

10 정면, 앞 _____

11 유명한 _____

12 pig의 애칭 _____

13 흔들리다 _____

14 잃어버리다 _____

15 점검하다 _____

16 ~을 필요로 하다 _____

17 위험한 _____

18 바구니 _____

19 안전한 _____

20 (외투 등에 달린) 모자 _____

21 끝, 마지막 _____

22 장면, 광경 _____

23 두드리다 _____

24 신난 _____

25 떠나다 _____

26 ~을 들여다보다 _____

27 ~의 밖으로 _____

28 ~에 좋다 _____

29 그럼요, 전혀 문제되지 않아요 _____

30 ~을 보다 _____

31 ~을 꺼내다 _____

32 가 버리다, 사라지다 _____

33 ~해선 안 된다 _____

34 어디 보자., 글쎄. _____

35 그런데, 그건 그렇고 _____

36 B에 대해 A에게 감사하다 _____

37 휴식을 취하다 _____

38 코를 풀다 _____

39 혼잣말하다 _____

40 ~에 대해 들어 본 적 있니? _____

※ 다음 영영풀이에 알맞은 단어를 <보기>에서 골라 쓴 후, 우리말 뜻을 쓰시오.

1 _____ : to go away from a place or a person: _____

2 _____ : to send air out from your mouth: _____

3 _____ : the last part of a period of time, event, activity, or story: _____

4 _____ : known about by many people in many places: _____

5 _____ : to go, walk, drive, etc behind or after someone else: _____

6 _____ : to make someone happy or satisfied: _____

7 _____ : not likely to cause any physical injury or harm: _____

8 _____ : someone who writes books, stories, etc especially as a job: _____

9 _____ : the part of something that faces you: _____

10 _____ : a hard flat surface for vehicles, people, and animals to travel on:

   _____

11 _____ : to be unable to find something or someone: _____

12 _____ : likely to injure or harm someone, or to damage or destroy something:

   _____

13 _____ : to not continue, or to make someone or something not continue:

   _____

14 _____ : to make the sounds and movements of your face that show you are happy

   or think something is funny: _____

15 _____ : a part of a coat, jacket, etc that you can pull up to cover your head:

   _____

16 _____ : to hit a door or window with your closed hand to attract the attention of

   the people inside: _____

보기	knock	leave	follow	dangerous
	end	hood	stop	front
	laugh	famous	road	writer
	safe	blow	please	lose

※ 다음 우리말과 일치하도록 빈칸에 알맞은 것을 골라 쓰시오.

1 Little ＿＿＿＿＿＿ Writing ＿＿＿＿＿＿
　　A. Hood　　　　　B. Red

2 ＿＿＿＿＿＿ 1: In ＿＿＿＿＿＿ of the three ＿＿＿＿＿＿ piggies' house
　　A. front　　　　B. scene　　　　C. little

3 (Red comes ＿＿＿＿＿＿ a ＿＿＿＿＿＿ of cakes and cookies.)
　　A. basket　　　B. in　　　　　C. with

4 Red: Now I can see the three little piggies' house. I'll ＿＿＿＿＿＿ a ＿＿＿＿＿＿ here ＿＿＿＿＿＿ the tree.
　　A. take　　　　B. under　　　C. break

5 (Wolf ＿＿＿＿＿＿ in and ＿＿＿＿＿＿ the house.)
　　A. looks　　　B. walks　　　C. into

6 Wolf: Baby piggies! They ＿＿＿＿＿＿ delicious. I'll eat them ＿＿＿＿＿＿ ＿＿＿＿＿＿.
　　A. look　　　　B. lunch　　　C. for

7 (Wolf ＿＿＿＿＿＿ the house ＿＿＿＿＿＿ and it is ＿＿＿＿＿＿.)
　　A. shaking　　B. hard　　　C. blows

8 Red: Oh, that bad Wolf! What can I do to ＿＿＿＿＿＿ him? ＿＿＿＿＿＿ me ＿＿＿＿＿＿. ... That's it! (To Wolf) Hey, you! I'll ＿＿＿＿＿＿ the story!
　　A. change　　B. see　　　　C. stop　　　D. let

9 Wolf: ＿＿＿＿＿＿ do you ＿＿＿＿＿＿ ＿＿＿＿＿＿ that?
　　A. by　　　　　B. mean　　　C. what

10 Red: (＿＿＿＿＿＿ out a pen and ＿＿＿＿＿＿ something) "There ＿＿＿＿＿＿ three big strong piggies in the house."
　　A. writing　　B. lived　　　C. taking

11 Wolf: You ＿＿＿＿＿＿ ＿＿＿＿＿＿ that!
　　A. do　　　　　B. shouldn't

12 (Wolf ＿＿＿＿＿＿ again, ＿＿＿＿＿＿ the three big strong piggies come ＿＿＿＿＿＿ ＿＿＿＿＿＿ the house.)
　　A. of　　　　　B. but　　　C. out　　　D. blows

13 Three Piggies: Hey ＿＿＿＿＿＿! ＿＿＿＿＿＿ did you ＿＿＿＿＿＿ our house?
　　A. there　　　B. blow　　　C. why

14 Wolf: Um ... I ＿＿＿＿＿＿. I just ＿＿＿＿＿＿ my ＿＿＿＿＿＿.
　　A. didn't　　　B. nose　　　C. blew

15 Three Piggies: ＿＿＿＿＿＿ do that again here. ＿＿＿＿＿＿ ＿＿＿＿＿＿!
　　A. away　　　B. don't　　　C. go

16 Wolf: Okay. I'm ＿＿＿＿＿＿ ＿＿＿＿＿＿.
　　A. sorry　　　B. so

17 (The piggies ＿＿＿＿＿＿ ＿＿＿＿＿＿ ＿＿＿＿＿＿ the house.)
　　A. into　　　　B. back　　　C. go

1 빨간 모자

2 장면 1: 아기 돼지 삼 형제의 집 앞에서

3 (Red가 케이크와 과자가 든 바구니를 들고 등장한다.)

4 Red: 이제 이기 돼지 삼 형제의 집이 보인다. 여기 나무 아래에서 좀 쉬어야지.

5 (늑대가 걸어 들어와 집 안을 들여다본다.)

6 늑대: 새끼 돼지들이네! 맛있어 보인다. 점심으로 그들을 먹어야겠어.

7 (늑대가 집을 세게 불자 집이 흔들리고 있다.)

8 Red: 오, 저런 나쁜 늑대 같으니라고! 그를 멈추게 하려면 내가 뭘 할 수 있을까? 어디 보자. … 바로 그거야! (늑대에게) 이봐! 내가 이야기를 바꾸겠어!

9 늑대: 그게 무슨 말이야?

10 Red: (펜을 꺼내 뭔가를 쓰면서) "크고 힘센 아기 돼지 삼 형제가 그 집에 살고 있었다."

11 늑대: 그렇게 하면 안 돼!

12 (늑대가 다시 집을 분다. 그러나 크고 힘센 돼지 삼 형제가 집에서 나온다.)

13 돼지 삼 형제: 이봐, 거기! 왜 우리 집을 불고 있어?

14 늑대: 음… 그러지 않았어. 나는 그냥 코를 풀었을 뿐이야.

15 돼지 삼 형제: 여기서 다시는 그러지 마. 가 버려!

16 늑대: 알았어. 정말 미안해.

17 (돼지들은 집 안으로 다시 들어간다.)

18 Wolf: I can't _____ this _____. I'm so hungry! (Looking _____ Red's basket) What are those?

    A. at   B. happened   C. believe

19 Red: _____ are cookies _____ Grandma.

    A. for   B. these

20 Wolf: _____ does she _____?

    A. live   B. where

21 Red: She _____ _____ the _____ of this road.

    A. end   B. at   C. lives

22 Wolf: (To _____) Grandma is good _____ lunch, too. (To Red) See you _____. (Wolf leaves.)

    A. for   B. himself   C. later

23 Red: Bye. (Talking to _____) Hmm .... He's going to Grandma's. I think I should change the story again. (Taking out the pen and writing something) Okay. If my story _____, Grandma will be _____. I'll _____ him. (Red leaves.)

    A. works   B. safe   C. follow   D. herself

24 _____ 2: Grandma's _____

    A. house   B. scene

25 (Wolf dances _____ Grandma. She looks very _____ and _____.)

    A. happy   B. excited   C. around

26 Red: (_____ _____ the door) Grandma, _____ me. Are you okay?

    A. on   B. knocking   C. it's

27 Grandma: (Laughing _____ and _____ the door) Sure, Red. Come on in. I was watching Wolf _____ for me.

    A. dance   B. happily   C. opening

28 Red: Hey, Wolf. _____ you _____ _____ my grandmother.

    A. thank   B. pleasing   C. for

29 Wolf: _____, _____ ....

    A. that's   B. well

30 Prince: (Opening the door and _____ in) Hey, you bad Wolf! (Prince _____ _____ Wolf.)

    A. running   B. over   C. jumps

31 Red: No, no! Stop. He's _____ _____.

    A. dangerous   B. not

32 Grandma: Right. Look. He is _____ _____ us.

    A. for   B. dancing

33 Prince: Really? Wolf, I'm sorry. I'm _____ you're _____ _____ Grandma.

    A. glad   B. to   C. kind

34 Wolf: Well, ... I'm glad, _____. _____ the _____, do you have _____ to eat?

    A. too   B. anything   C. way   D. by

18 늑대: 이런 일이 일어나다니 믿을 수가 없어. 나는 너무 배가 고파! (Red의 바구니를 보며) 그건 뭐야?

19 Red: 할머니께 드릴 과자들이야.

20 늑대: 어디 사시는데?

21 Red: 이 길의 끝에 사셔.

22 늑대: (혼잣말로) 할머니도 점심으로 좋지. (Red에게) 나중에 보자. (늑대가 떠난다.)

23 Red: 안녕. (혼잣말로) 흠···. 그는 할머니 댁으로 갈 거야. 이야기를 다시 바꿔야겠어. (펜을 꺼내서 뭔가를 쓰며) 좋아. 내 이야기가 제대로 돌아가면 할머니는 안전하실 거야. 그를 따라가 봐야지. (Red가 떠난다.)

24 장면 2: 할머니의 집

25 (늑대가 할머니 주변을 맴돌며 춤을 춘다. 할머니는 아주 행복하고 신나 보인다.)

26 Red: (문을 두드리며) 할머니, 저예요. 괜찮으세요?

27 할머니: (행복하게 웃으며 문을 열면서) 물론이지, Red야. 어서 들어와. 늑대가 나를 위해 춤추는 걸 보고 있었단다.

28 Red: 이봐, 늑대야. 우리 할머니를 기쁘게 해드려서 고마워.

29 늑대: 음, 그게 ···.

30 왕자: (문을 열고 뛰어 들어오며) 이봐, 이 나쁜 늑대야! (왕자가 늑대에게 달려든다.)

31 Red: 아니, 아니에요! 멈춰요. 그는 위험하지 않아요.

32 할머니: 맞아. 보세요. 그가 우리를 위해 춤추고 있잖아요.

33 왕자: 정말요? 늑대야, 미안해. 네가 할머니께 잘해 드린다니 기쁘다.

34 늑대: 음··· 나도 기뻐. 그런데, 먹을 것 좀 있어?

35 Red: (Taking some cookies _____ the basket) _____ you _____ some cookies?
A. out   B. like   C. would

36 Wolf: No, _____. I _____ eat cookies. I _____ chicken.
A. don't   B. thanks   C. like

37 Red: _____ worry. I'll change the story again. Then you will like _____ cookies. (Checking the basket) Oh, I _____ my pen. What _____ I do?
A. eating   B. don't   C. should   D. lost

38 Wolf: (Dancing and _____) Oh, no! I'm so _____ and _____ now.
A. tired   B. crying   C. hungry

39 (Andersen _____ _____.)
A. in   B. comes

40 Andersen: I _____ you _____ my help, _____?
A. need   B. right   C. think

41 Red: Oh, Mr. Andersen. I'm _____ _____ you're _____.
A. glad   B. so   C. here

42 Grandma: (_____ Red) Who's _____?
A. that   B. to

43 Red: He is Mr. Andersen, the _____ writer. Have you ever _____ _____ "The Red Shoes"?
A. of   B. famous   C. heard

44 Grandma: Yes, I _____. Is he the _____ who _____ that story?
A. one   B. have   C. wrote

45 Red: Right. (To Andersen) I _____ the story, and the poor Wolf _____ _____ and hungry.
A. changed   B. tired   C. got

46 Andersen: You _____ _____ the story _____.
A. change   B. again   C. can

47 Red: I'm sorry, but I _____ the pen you _____ to me. Please _____ me.
A. help   B. gave   C. lost

48 Andersen: No _____. I'll write a happy _____ for everyone. Is that _____?
A. ending   B. problem   C. okay

49 Red: _____ _____ great!
A. be   B. that'll

50 Andersen: All right. I'll use my pen here. "The kind Wolf _____ _____. He _____ _____ cakes and cookies."
A. can   B. dancing   C. enjoy   D. stops

51 Wolf: (Stopping dancing) I can _____ _____! (Eating cookies) And I _____ _____ cookies! Thank you very much.
A. eat   B. dancing   C. can   D. stop

52 (Everybody _____ and _____ cookies _____.)
A. together   B. enjoys   C. laughs

35 Red: (바구니에서 과자를 좀 꺼내며) 과자 좀 먹을래?

36 늑대: 고맙지만 됐어. 난 과자를 먹지 않아. 나는 닭고기가 좋아.

37 Red: 걱정하지 마. 내가 이야기를 다시 바꿔야겠네. 그러면 넌 과자 먹는 걸 좋아하게 될 거야. (바구니를 뒤지며) 오, 펜을 잃어버렸어. 어떻게 하지?

38 늑대: (춤을 추며 울부짖으며) 오, 안 돼! 난 지금 너무 피곤하고 배고파.

39 (Andersen이 들어온다.)

40 Andersen: 내 도움이 필요한 것 같은데, 맞지?

41 Red: 오, Andersen 씨. 여기 오셔서 너무 기뻐요.

42 할머니: (Red에게) 저 사람이 누구니?

43 Red: 저분은 유명한 작가 Andersen 씨예요. "빨간 구두"에 대해 들어 보신 적이 있죠?

44 할머니: 그래, 들어 봤지. 그 이야기를 쓴 사람이란 말이지?

45 Red: 맞아요. (Andersen에게) 제가 이야기를 바꿔서 저 불쌍한 늑대가 피곤하고 배고파졌어요.

46 Andersen: 너는 다시 이야기를 바꿀 수 있잖아.

47 Red: 죄송하지만, 제가 작가님이 주신 펜을 잃어버렸어요. 저 좀 도와주세요.

48 Andersen: 문제없지. 내가 모두에게 행복한 결말을 쓸게. 괜찮지?

49 Red: 아주 좋아요!

50 Andersen: 좋아. 여기 내 펜을 써야지. "그 친절한 늑대는 춤추기를 멈춘다. 그는 케이크와 과자를 즐겨 먹을 수 있다."

51 늑대: (춤을 멈추며) 춤을 멈출 수가 있다! (과자를 먹으며) 그리고 과자를 먹을 수 있어! 정말 고마워요.

52 (모두 웃으며 함께 과자를 맛있게 먹는다.)

※ 다음 우리말과 일치하도록 빈칸에 알맞은 말을 쓰시오.

1 Little _____ Writing _____

2 _____ 1: _____ _____ _____ the three _____ piggies' house

3 (Red _____ _____ _____ a basket of cakes and cookies.)

4 Red: Now I _____ _____ the three little piggies' house. I'll _____ _____ _____ here _____ the tree.

5 (Wolf _____ _____ and _____ _____ the house.)

6 Wolf: Baby piggies! They _____ _____ . I'll eat them _____ _____ .

7 (Wolf _____ the house _____ and it _____ _____ .)

8 Red: Oh, that bad Wolf! What can I do _____ _____ him? _____ _____ _____ . ... That's it! (To Wolf) Hey, you! I'll _____ _____ _____ !

9 Wolf: _____ do you _____ _____ that?

10 Red: (_____ _____ a pen and _____ _____) "_____ _____ three big strong piggies in the house."

11 Wolf: You _____ _____ that!

12 (Wolf _____ again, but the three big strong piggies _____ _____ _____ the house.)

13 Three Piggies: Hey _____ ! _____ _____ you _____ our house?

14 Wolf: Um ... I _____ . I _____ _____ my _____ .

15 Three Piggies: _____ _____ that again here. _____ _____ !

16 Wolf: Okay. I'm _____ _____ .

17 (The piggies _____ _____ _____ the house.)

1 빨간 모자

2 장면 1: 아기 돼지 삼 형제의 집 앞에서

3 (Red가 케이크와 과자가 든 바구니를 들고 등장한다.)

4 Red: 이제 아기 돼지 삼 형제의 집이 보인다. 여기 나무 아래에서 좀 쉬어야지.

5 (늑대가 걸어 들어와 집 안을 들여다본다.)

6 늑대: 새끼 돼지들이네! 맛있어 보인다. 점심으로 그들을 먹어야겠어.

7 (늑대가 집을 세게 불자 집이 흔들리고 있다.)

8 Red: 오, 저런 나쁜 늑대 같으니라고! 그를 멈추게 하려면 내가 뭘 할 수 있을까? 어디 보자. … 바로 그거야! (늑대에게) 이봐! 내가 이야기를 바꾸겠어!

9 늑대: 그게 무슨 말이야?

10 Red: (펜을 꺼내 뭔가를 쓰면서) "크고 힘센 아기 돼지 삼 형제가 그 집에 살고 있었다."

11 늑대: 그렇게 하면 안 돼!

12 (늑대가 다시 집을 분다. 그러나 크고 힘센 돼지 삼 형제가 집에서 나온다.)

13 돼지 삼 형제: 이봐, 거기! 왜 우리 집을 불고 있어?

14 늑대: 음… 그러지 않았어. 나는 그냥 코를 풀었을 뿐이야.

15 돼지 삼 형제: 여기서 다시는 그러지 마. 가 버려!

16 늑대: 알았어. 정말 미안해.

17 (돼지들은 집 안으로 다시 들어간다.)

18 Wolf: I _____ _____ this _____. I'm so hungry! (_____ _____ Red's basket) What are those?

19 Red: _____ are cookies _____ Grandma.

20 Wolf: _____ _____ she _____?

21 Red: She _____ _____ _____ _____ of this road.

22 Wolf: (To _____) Grandma is good _____ _____, _____. (To Red) See you _____. (Wolf leaves.)

23 Red: Bye. (Talking to _____) Hmm …. He's _____ _____ Grandma's. I think I should change the story again. (Taking out the pen and writing something) Okay. If my story _____, Grandma will be _____. I'll _____ him. (Red leaves.)

24 _____ 2: Grandma's _____

25 (Wolf _____ _____ Grandma. She _____ very _____ and _____.)

26 Red: (_____ _____ the door) Grandma, _____ me. Are you _____?

27 Grandma: (Laughing _____ and _____ the door) Sure, Red. Come on in. I was _____ Wolf _____ for me.

28 Red: Hey, Wolf. _____ you _____ _____ my grandmother.

29 Wolf: _____, _____ ….

30 Prince: (Opening the door and _____ _____) Hey, you bad Wolf! (Prince _____ _____ Wolf.)

31 Red: No, no! Stop. He's _____ _____.

32 Grandma: Right. Look. He _____ _____ _____ us.

33 Prince: Really? Wolf, I'm sorry. I'm _____ you're _____ Grandma.

34 Wolf: Well, … I'm glad, too. _____ _____ _____, do you _____ _____ _____ _____?

---

18 늑대: 이런 일이 일어나다니 믿을 수가 없어. 나는 너무 배가 고파! (Red의 바구니를 보며) 그건 뭐야?

19 Red: 할머니께 드릴 과자들이야.

20 늑대: 어디 사시는데?

21 Red: 이 길의 끝에 사셔.

22 늑대: (혼잣말로) 할머니도 점심으로 좋지. (Red에게) 나중에 보자. (늑대가 떠난다.)

23 Red: 안녕. (혼잣말로) 흠…. 그는 할머니 댁으로 갈 거야. 이야기를 다시 바꿔야겠어. (펜을 꺼내서 뭔가를 쓰며) 좋아. 내 이야기가 제대로 돌아가면 할머니는 안전하실 거야. 그를 따라가 봐야지. (Red가 떠난다.)

24 장면 2: 할머니의 집

25 (늑대가 할머니 주변을 맴돌며 춤을 춘다. 할머니는 아주 행복하고 신나 보인다.)

26 Red: (문을 두드리며) 할머니, 저예요. 괜찮으세요?

27 할머니: (행복하게 웃으며 문을 열면서) 물론이지, Red야. 어서 들어와. 늑대가 나를 위해 춤추는 걸 보고 있었단다.

28 Red: 이봐, 늑대야. 우리 할머니를 기쁘게 해드려서 고마워.

29 늑대: 음, 그게 ….

30 왕자: (문을 열고 뛰어 들어오며) 이봐, 이 나쁜 늑대야! (왕자가 늑대에게 달려든다.)

31 Red: 아니, 아니에요! 멈춰요. 그는 위험하지 않아요.

32 할머니: 맞아. 보세요. 그가 우리를 위해 춤추고 있잖아요.

33 왕자: 정말요? 늑대야, 미안해. 네가 할머니께 잘해 드린다니 기쁘다.

34 늑대: 음… 나도 기뻐. 그런데, 먹을 것 좀 있어?

35 Red: (_____ some cookies _____ _____ _____)
_____ you _____ some cookies?

36 Wolf: _____, _____. I _____ eat cookies. I _____
chicken.

37 Red: _____ _____. I'll change the story again. Then you will
like _____ cookies. (Checking the basket) Oh, I _____ my
pen. _____ _____ _____ _____?

38 Wolf: (Dancing and _____) Oh, no! I'm _____ _____ and
_____ now.

39 (Andersen _____ _____.)

40 Andersen: I _____ you _____ my _____, _____?

41 Red: Oh, Mr. Andersen. I'm _____ _____ you're _____.

42 Grandma: (_____ Red) _____ _____?

43 Red: He is Mr. Andersen, the _____ writer. _____ you
_____ _____ _____ "The Red Shoes"?

44 Grandma: Yes, I _____. Is he the _____ who _____ that
story?

45 Red: Right. (To Andersen) I _____ the story, and the poor Wolf
_____ _____ and _____.

46 Andersen: You _____ _____ the story _____.

47 Red: I'm sorry, but I _____ the pen you _____ to me. Please
_____ _____.

48 Andersen: No _____. I'll write _____ _____ _____
_____ everyone. Is that _____?

49 Red: _____ _____ _____!

50 Andersen: All right. I'll use my pen here. "The kind Wolf _____
_____. He _____ _____ cakes and cookies."

51 Wolf: (Stopping dancing) I can _____ _____! (Eating
cookies) And I _____ _____ cookies! Thank you very much.

52 (Everybody _____ and _____ cookies _____.)

35 Red: (바구니에서 과자를 좀 꺼내며) 과자 좀 먹을래?

36 늑대: 고맙지만 됐어. 난 과자를 먹지 않아. 나는 닭고기가 좋아.

37 Red: 걱정하지 마. 내가 이야기를 다시 바꿔야겠네. 그러면 넌 과자 먹는 걸 좋아하게 될 거야. (바구니를 뒤지며) 오, 펜을 잃어버렸어. 어떻게 하지?

38 늑대: (춤을 추며 울부짖으며) 오, 안 돼! 난 지금 너무 피곤하고 배고파.

39 (Andersen이 들어온다.)

40 Andersen: 내 도움이 필요한 것 같은데, 맞지?

41 Red: 오, Andersen 씨. 여기 오셔서 너무 기뻐요.

42 할머니: (Red에게) 저 사람이 누구니?

43 Red: 저분은 유명한 작가 Andersen 씨예요. "빨간 구두"에 대해 들어 보신 적이 있죠?

44 할머니: 그래, 들어 봤지. 그 이야기를 쓴 사람이란 말이지?

45 Red: 맞아요. (Andersen에게) 제가 이야기를 바꿔서 저 불쌍한 늑대가 피곤하고 배고파졌어요.

46 Andersen: 너는 다시 이야기를 바꿀 수 있잖아.

47 Red: 죄송하지만, 제가 작가님이 주신 펜을 잃어버렸어요. 저 좀 도와주세요.

48 Andersen: 문제없지. 내가 모두에게 행복한 결말을 쓸게. 괜찮지?

49 Red: 아주 좋아요!

50 Andersen: 좋아. 여기 내 펜을 써야지. "그 친절한 늑대는 춤추기를 멈춘다. 그는 케이크와 과자를 즐겨 먹을 수 있다."

51 늑대: (춤을 멈추며) 춤을 멈출 수가 있다! (과자를 먹으며) 그리고 과자를 먹을 수 있어! 정말 고마워요.

52 (모두 웃으며 함께 과자를 맛있게 먹는다.)

※ 다음 문장을 우리말로 쓰시오.

1 ▶ Little Red Writing Hood

➡ _____

2 ▶ Scene 1: In front of the three little piggies' house

➡ _____

3 ▶ (Red comes in with a basket of cakes and cookies.)

➡ _____

4 ▶ Red: Now I can see the three little piggies' house. I'll take a break here under the tree.

➡ _____

5 ▶ (Wolf walks in and looks into the house.)

➡ _____

6 ▶ Wolf: Baby piggies! They look delicious. I'll eat them for lunch.

➡ _____

7 ▶ (Wolf blows the house hard and it is shaking.)

➡ _____

8 ▶ Red: Oh, that bad Wolf! What can I do to stop him? Let me see. ... That's it! (To Wolf) Hey, you! I'll change the story!

➡ _____

➡ _____

9 ▶ Wolf: What do you mean by that?

➡ _____

10 ▶ Red: (Taking out a pen and writing something) "There lived three big strong piggies in the house."

➡ _____

11 ▶ Wolf: You shouldn't do that!

➡ _____

12 ▶ (Wolf blows again, but the three big strong piggies come out of the house.)

➡ _____

13 ▶ Three Piggies: Hey there! Why did you blow our house?

➡ _____

14 ▶ Wolf: Um ... I didn't. I just blew my nose.

➡ _____

15 ▶ Three Piggies: Don't do that again here. Go away!

➡ _____

16 ▶ Wolf: Okay. I'm so sorry.

➡ _____

17 ▶ (The piggies go back into the house.)

➡ _____

18 Wolf: I can't believe this happened. I'm so hungry! (Looking at Red's basket) What are those?

➡ _____

19 Red: These are cookies for Grandma.

➡ _____

20 Wolf: Where does she live?

➡ _____

21 Red: She lives at the end of this road.

➡ _____

22 Wolf: (To himself) Grandma is good for lunch, too. (To Red) See you later. (Wolf leaves.)

➡ _____

23 Red: Bye. (Talking to herself) Hmm .... He's going to Grandma's. I think I should change the story again. (Taking out the pen and writing something) Okay. If my story works, Grandma will be safe. I'll follow him. (Red leaves.)

➡ _____

_____

24 Scene2: Grandma's house

➡ _____

25 (Wolf dances around Grandma. She looks very happy and excited.)

➡ _____

26 Red: (Knocking on the door) Grandma, it's me. Are you okay?

➡ _____

27 Grandma: (Laughing happily and opening the door) Sure, Red. Come on in. I was watching Wolf dance for me.

➡ _____

28 Red: Hey, Wolf. Thank you for pleasing my grandmother.

➡ _____

29 Wolf: Well, that's ....

➡ _____

30 Prince: (Opening the door and running in) Hey, you bad Wolf! (Prince jumps over Wolf.)

➡ _____

31 Red: No, no! Stop. He's not dangerous.

➡ _____

32 Grandma: Right. Look. He is dancing for us.

➡ _____

33 Prince: Really? Wolf, I'm sorry. I'm glad you're kind to Grandma.

➡ _____

34 Wolf: Well, ... I'm glad, too. By the way, do you have anything to eat?

➡ _____

35 Red: (Taking some cookies out the basket) Would you like some cookies?

➡ _____

36 Wolf: No, thanks. I don't eat cookies. I like chicken.

➡ _____

37 Red: Don't worry. I'll change the story again. Then you will like eating cookies. (Checking the basket) Oh, I lost my pen. What should I do?

➡ _____

38 Wolf: (Dancing and crying) Oh, no! I'm so tired and hungry now.

➡ _____

39 (Andersen comes in.)

➡ _____

40 Andersen: I think you need my help, right?

➡ _____

41 Red: Oh, Mr. Andersen. I'm so glad you're here.

➡ _____

42 Grandma: (To Red) Who's that?

➡ _____

43 Red: He is Mr. Andersen, the famous writer. Have you ever heard of "The Red Shoes"?

➡ _____

44 Grandma: Yes, I have. Is he the one who wrote that story?

➡ _____

45 Red: Right. (To Andersen) I changed the story, and the poor Wolf got tired and hungry.

➡ _____

46 Andersen: You can change the story again.

➡ _____

47 Red: I'm sorry, but I lost the pen you gave to me. Please help me.

➡ _____

48 Andersen: No problem. I'll write a happy ending for everyone. Is that okay?

➡ _____

49 Red: That'll be great!

➡ _____

50 Andersen: All right. I'll use my pen here. "The kind Wolf stops dancing. He can enjoy cakes and cookies."

➡ _____

51 Wolf: (Stopping dancing) I can stop dancing! (Eating cookies) And I can eat cookies! Thank you very much.

➡ _____

52 (Everybody laughs and enjoys cookies together.)

➡ _____

※ 다음 괄호 안의 단어들을 우리말에 맞도록 바르게 배열하시오.

1 (Red / Little / Hood / Writing)
➡ _____

2 (scene 1: / of / front / in / three / the / little / house. / piggies')
➡ _____

3 ((comes / Red / with / in / of / basket / a / cookies. / and / cakes))
➡ _____

4 (Red: / I / now / see / can / three / the / house / piggies' / little // take / I'll / break / a / under / tree. / here / the)
➡ _____

5 ((walks / Wolf / and / in / into / house. / the / into / looks)
➡ _____

6 (Wolf: / piggies! / baby // look / they / delicious. // I'll / for / eat / lunch. / them)
➡ _____

7 ((blows / Wolf / house / the / and / hard / shaking. / is / it))
➡ _____

8 (Red: / oh, / bad / that / Wolf! // can / what / do / I / stop / to / him? // me / see. / let / ... // it! / that's / (to / Wolf) / you! / hey, // change / I'll / story! / the)
➡ _____

9 (Wolf: / do / what / mean / you / that? / by)
➡ _____

10 (Red: / (taking / a / out / pen / and / something) / writing // "there / three / lived / strong / big / piggies / house." / the / in)
➡ _____

11 (Wolf: / shouldn't / you / that! / do)
➡ _____

12 ((Wolf / again, / blows / but / three / the / big / piggies / strong / out / come / house. / the / of))
➡ _____

13 (piggies: / three / there! / hey // did / why / blow / house? / our / you)
➡ _____

14 (Wolf: / um / ... / didn't. / I // just / I / nose. / my / blew)
➡ _____

15 (piggies: / three / do / don't / that / here. / again // away! / go)
➡ _____

16 (Wolf: okay. // sorry. / so / I'm)
➡ _____

17 ((piggies / the / back / go / house. / the / into))
➡ _____

1 빨간 모자

2 장면 1: 아기 돼지 삼 형제의 집 앞에서

3 (Red가 케이크와 과자가 든 바구니를 들고 등장한다.)

4 Red: 이제 아기 돼지 삼 형제의 집이 보인다. 여기 나무 아래에서 좀 쉬어야지.

5 (늑대가 걸어 들어와 집 안을 들여다본다.)

6 늑대: 새끼 돼지들이네! 맛있어 보인다. 점심으로 그들을 먹어야겠어.

7 (늑대가 집을 세게 불자 집이 흔들리고 있다.)

8 Red: 오, 저런 나쁜 늑대 같으니라고! 그를 멈추게 하려면 내가 뭘 할 수 있을까? 어디 보자. … 바로 그거야! (늑대에게) 이봐! 내가 이야기를 바꾸겠어!

9 늑대: 그게 무슨 말이야?

10 Red: (펜을 꺼내 뭔가를 쓰면서) "크고 힘센 아기 돼지 삼 형제가 그 집에 살고 있었다."

11 늑대: 그렇게 하면 안 돼!

12 (늑대가 다시 집을 분다. 그러나 크고 힘센 돼지 삼 형제가 집에서 나온다.)

13 돼지 삼 형제: 이봐, 거기! 왜 우리 집을 불고 있어?

14 늑대: 음… 그러지 않았어. 나는 그냥 코를 풀었을 뿐이야.

15 돼지 삼 형제: 여기서 다시는 그러지 마. 가 버려!

16 늑대: 알았어. 정말 미안해.

17 (돼지들은 집 안으로 다시 들어간다.)

18 (Wolf: / can't / I / believe / happened. / this // hungry! / so / I'm // (looking / Red's / at / basket) // those? / are / what)

➡ _____

19 (Red: / are / these / cookies / Grandma. / for)

➡ _____

20 (Wolf: / does / where / live? / she)

➡ _____

21 (Red: / lives / she / the / at / of / end / road. / this)

➡ _____

22 (Wolf: / (to / himself) // is / Grandma / good / is / lunch, / too. / for // (to / red) / you / see / later. // (Wolf / leaves.)

➡ _____

23 (Red: / bye. // (talking / herself) / to // hmm / .... / going / he's / Grandma's. / to // think / I / should / I / change / story / the / again. // (taking / the / out / pen / and / something) / writing // okay. / my / if / story / works, / will / Grandma / safe. / be // him. / follow / I'll // (Red / leaves.)

➡ _____

➡ _____

24 (scene 2: / house / Grandma's)

➡ _____

25 ((dances / Wolf / Grandma. / around // looks / she / very / excited. / and / happy)

➡ _____

26 (Red: / on / (knocking / the / on / door) // Grandma, / me. / it's // okay? / you / are)

➡ _____

27 (Grandma: / (laughing / and / happily / the / opening / door) // Red. / sure, // in. / on / come // was / I / watching / dance / Wolf / me. / for)

➡ _____

28 (Red: Wolf. / hey, // you / thank / pleasing / for / grandmother. / my)

➡ _____

29 (Wolf: / that's / .... / well,)

➡ _____

30 (Prince: / (opening / door / the / running / and / in) // you / hey, / Wolf! / bad // (Prince / over / jumps / Wolf.)

➡ _____

31 (Red: no! / no, // stop. // not / he's / dangerous.)

➡ _____

32 (Grandma: / right. // look. // is / he / dancing / us. / for)

➡ _____

33 (Prince: / really? // I'm / Wolf, / sorry. // glad / I'm / kind / you're / Grandma. / to)

➡ _____

34 (Wolf: / ... / well, / glad, / I'm / too. // the / by / way, / you / have / do / anything / eat? / to)

➡ _____

18 늑대: 이런 일이 일어나다니 믿을 수가 없어. 나는 너무 배가 고파! (Red의 바구니를 보며) 그건 뭐야?

19 Red: 할머니께 드릴 과자들이야.

20 늑대: 어디 사시는데?

21 Red: 이 길의 끝에 사셔.

22 늑대: (혼잣말로) 할머니도 점심으로 좋지. (Red에게) 나중에 보자. (늑대가 떠난다.)

23 Red: 안녕. (혼잣말로) 흠···. 그는 할머니 댁으로 갈 거야. 이야기를 다시 바꿔야겠어. (펜을 꺼내서 뭔가를 쓰며) 좋아. 내 이야기가 제대로 돌아가면 할머니는 안전하실 거야. 그를 따라가 봐야지. (Red가 떠난다.)

24 장면 2: 할머니의 집

25 (늑대가 할머니 주변을 맴돌며 춤을 춘다. 할머니는 아주 행복하고 신나 보인다.)

26 Red: (문을 두드리며) 할머니. 저예요. 괜찮으세요?

27 할머니: (행복하게 웃으며 문을 열면서) 물론이지, Red야. 어서 들어와. 늑대가 나를 위해 춤추는 걸 보고 있었단다.

28 Red: 이봐, 늑대야. 우리 할머니를 기쁘게 해드려서 고마워.

29 늑대: 음, 그게···.

30 왕자: (문을 열고 뛰어 들어오며) 이봐, 이 나쁜 늑대야! (왕자가 늑대에게 달려든다.)

31 Red: 아니, 아니에요! 멈춰요. 그는 위험하지 않아요.

32 할머니: 맞아. 보세요. 그가 우리를 위해 춤추고 있잖아요.

33 왕자: 정말요? 늑대야, 미안해. 네가 할머니께 잘해 드린다니 기쁘다.

34 늑대: 음··· 나도 기뻐. 그런데, 먹을 것 좀 있어?

35 (Red: / (taking / cookies / some / the / out / basket) // you / like / would / cookies? / some)

➡ _____

36 (Wolf: / thanks. / no, // don't / I / cookies. / eat // chicken. / like / I)

➡ _____

37 (Red: / worry. / don't // change / I'll / story / again. / the // you / then / like / will / cookies. / eating // (checking / basket / the) // oh, / lost / my / I / pen. // should / what / do? / I)

➡ _____

38 (Wolf: / (dancing / and / crying) / no! / oh, // so / I'm / hungry / and / now. / tired)

➡ _____

39 ((comes / Andersen / in.))

➡ _____

40 (Andersen: / think / I / need / you / right? / help, / my)

➡ _____

41 (Red: / Mr. / oh, / Andersen. // so / I'm / here. / you're / glad)

➡ _____

42 (Grandma: / (to / red) // that? / who's)

➡ _____

43 (Red: / is / he / Andersen, / Mr. / famous / the / writer. // you / have / heard / ever / of / Shoes"? / Red / "The)

➡ _____

44 (Grandma: / have. / I / yes, // he / is / one / the / who / story? / that / wrote)

➡ _____

45 (Red: / right. // (to / Adnersen) // changed / I / story, / the / and / poor / the / got / Wolf / tired / hungry. / and)

➡ _____

46 (Andersen: / can / you / change / story / again. / the)

➡ _____

47 (Red: / sorry, / I'm / but / lost / I / pen / the / gave / you / me. / to // me. / help / please)

➡ _____

48 (Andersen: / problem. / no // write / I'll / happy / a / ending / everyone. / for // okay? / that / is)

➡ _____

49 (Red: / be / that'll / great!)

➡ _____

50 (Andersen: / right. / all // use / I'll / pen / my / here. // kind / "the / dancing. / stops / Wolf // can / he / cakes / cookies." / and / enjoy)

➡ _____

51 (Wolf: / (stopping / dancing) // can / I / dancing! / stop / (eating / cookies) // and / can / I / cookies! / eat // you / thank / much. / very)

➡ _____

52 ((laughs / everybody / enjoys / and / together. / cookies))

➡ _____

35 Red: (바구니에서 과자를 좀 꺼내며) 과자 좀 먹을래?

36 늑대: 고맙지만 됐어. 난 과자를 먹지 않아. 나는 닭고기가 좋아.

37 Red: 걱정하지 마. 내가 이야기를 다시 바꿔야겠네. 그러면 넌 과자 먹는 걸 좋아하게 될 거야. (바구니를 뒤지며) 오, 펜을 잃어버렸어. 어떻게 하지?

38 늑대: (춤을 추며 울부짖으며) 오, 안 돼! 난 지금 너무 피곤하고 배고파.

39 (Andersen이 들어온다.)

40 Andersen: 내 도움이 필요한 것 같은데, 맞지?

41 Red: 오, Andersen 씨. 여기 오셔서 너무 기뻐요.

42 할머니: (Red에게) 저 사람이 누구니?

43 Red: 저분은 유명한 작가 Andersen 씨예요. "빨간 구두"에 대해 들어 보신 적이 있죠?

44 할머니: 그래, 들어 봤지. 그 이야기를 쓴 사람이란 말이지?

45 Red: 맞아요. (Andersen에게) 제가 이야기를 바꿔서 저 불쌍한 늑대가 피곤하고 배고파졌어요.

46 Andersen: 너는 다시 이야기를 바꿀 수 있잖아.

47 Red: 죄송하지만, 제가 작가님이 주신 펜을 잃어버렸어요. 저 좀 도와주세요.

48 Andersen: 문제없지. 내가 모두에게 행복한 결말을 쓸게. 괜찮지?

49 Red: 아주 좋아요!

50 Andersen: 좋아. 여기 내 펜을 써야지. "그 친절한 늑대는 춤추기를 멈춘다. 그는 케이크와 과자를 즐겨 먹을 수 있다."

51 늑대: (춤을 멈추며) 춤을 멈출 수가 있다! (과자를 먹으며) 그리고 과자를 먹을 수 있어! 정말 고마워요.

52 (모두 웃으며 함께 과자를 맛있게 먹는다.)

※ 다음 우리말을 영어로 쓰시오.

1 빨간 모자

➡ _____

2 장면 1: 아기 돼지 삼 형제의 집 앞에서

➡ _____

3 (Red가 케이크와 과자가 든 바구니를 들고 등장한다.)

➡ _____

4 Red: 이제 아기 돼지 삼 형제의 집이 보인다. 여기 나무 아래에서 좀 쉬어야지.

➡ _____

5 (늑대가 걸어 들어와 집 안을 들여다본다.)

➡ _____

6 늑대: 새끼 돼지들이네! 맛있어 보인다. 점심으로 그들을 먹어야겠어.

➡ _____

7 (늑대가 집을 세게 불자 집이 흔들리고 있다.)

➡ _____

8 Red: 오, 저런 나쁜 늑대 같으니라고! 그를 멈추게 하려면 내가 뭘 할 수 있을까? 어디 보자. … 바로 그거야! (늑대에게) 이봐! 내가 이야기를 바꾸겠어!

➡ _____

_____

9 늑대: 그게 무슨 말이야?

➡ _____

10 Red: (펜을 꺼내 뭔가를 쓰면서) "크고 힘센 아기 돼지 삼 형제가 그 집에 살고 있었다."

➡ _____

11 늑대: 그렇게 하면 안 돼!

➡ _____

12 (늑대가 다시 집을 분다. 그러나 크고 힘센 돼지 삼 형제가 집에서 나온다.)

➡ _____

13 돼지 삼 형제: 이봐, 거기! 왜 우리 집을 불고 있어?

➡ _____

14 늑대: 음… 그러지 않았어. 나는 그냥 코를 풀었을 뿐이야.

➡ _____

15 돼지 삼 형제: 여기서 다시는 그러지 마. 가 버려!

➡ _____

16 늑대: 알았어. 정말 미안해.

➡ _____

17 (돼지들은 집 안으로 다시 들어간다.)

➡ _____

18 늑대: 이런 일이 일어나다니 믿을 수가 없어. 나는 너무 배가 고파! (Red의 바구니를 보며) 그건 뭐야?

➡ _____

19 Red: 할머니께 드릴 과자들이야.

➡ _____

20 늑대: 어디 사시는데?

➡ _____

21 Red: 이 길의 끝에 사셔.

➡ _____

22 늑대: (혼잣말로) 할머니도 점심으로 좋지. (Red에게) 나중에 보자. (늑대가 떠난다.)

➡ _____

23 Red: 안녕. (혼잣말로) 흠…. 그는 할머니 댁으로 갈 거야. 이야기를 다시 바꿔야겠어. (펜을 꺼내서 뭔가를 쓰며) 좋아. 내 이야기가 제대로 돌아가면 할머니는 안전하실 거야. 그를 따라가 봐야지. (Red가 떠난다.)

➡ _____

➡ _____

24 장면 2: 할머니의 집

➡ _____

25 (늑대가 할머니 주변을 맴돌며 춤을 춘다. 할머니는 아주 행복하고 신나 보인다.)

➡ _____

26 Red: (문을 두드리며) 할머니, 저예요. 괜찮으세요?

➡ _____

27 할머니: (행복하게 웃으며 문을 열면서) 물론이지, Red야. 어서 들어와. 늑대가 나를 위해 춤추는 걸 보고 있었단다.

➡ _____

28 Red: 이봐, 늑대야. 우리 할머니를 기쁘게 해드려서 고마워.

➡ _____

29 늑대: 음, 그게 ….

➡ _____

30 왕자: (문을 열고 뛰어 들어오며) 이봐, 이 나쁜 늑대야! (왕자가 늑대에게 달려든다.)

➡ _____

31 Red: 아니, 아니에요! 멈춰요. 그는 위험하지 않아요.

➡ _____

32 할머니: 맞아. 보세요. 그가 우리를 위해 춤추고 있잖아요.

➡ _____

33 왕자: 정말요? 늑대야, 미안해. 네가 할머니께 잘해 드린다니 기쁘다.

➡ _____

34 늑대: 음 … 나도 기뻐. 그런데, 먹을 것 좀 있어?

➡ _____

35 Red: (바구니에서 과자를 좀 꺼내며) 과자 좀 먹을래?

➡ _____

36 늑대: 고맙지만 됐어. 난 과자를 먹지 않아. 나는 닭고기가 좋아.

➡ _____

37 Red: 걱정하지 마. 내가 이야기를 다시 바꿔야겠네. 그러면 넌 과자 먹는 걸 좋아하게 될 거야. (바구니를 뒤지며) 오, 펜을 잃어버렸어. 어떻게 하지?

➡ _____

38 늑대: (춤을 추며 울부짖으며) 오, 안 돼! 난 지금 너무 피곤하고 배고파.

➡ _____

39 (Andersen이 들어온다.)

➡ _____

40 Andersen: 내 도움이 필요한 것 같은데, 맞지?

➡ _____

41 Red: 오, Andersen 씨. 여기 오셔서 너무 기뻐요.

➡ _____

42 할머니: (Red에게) 저 사람이 누구니?

➡ _____

43 Red: 저분은 유명한 작가 Andersen 씨예요. "빨간 구두"에 대해 들어 보신 적이 있죠?

➡ _____

44 할머니: 그래, 들어 봤지. 그 이야기를 쓴 사람이란 말이지?

➡ _____

45 Red: 맞아요. (Andersen에게) 제가 이야기를 바꿔서 저 불쌍한 늑대가 피곤하고 배고파졌어요.

➡ _____

46 Andersen: 너는 다시 이야기를 바꿀 수 있잖아.

➡ _____

47 Red: 죄송하지만, 제가 작가님이 주신 펜을 잃어버렸어요. 저 좀 도와주세요.

➡ _____

48 Andersen: 문제없지. 내가 모두에게 행복한 결말을 쓸게. 괜찮지?

➡ _____

49 Red: 아주 좋아요!

➡ _____

50 Andersen: 좋아. 여기 내 펜을 써야지. "그 친절한 늑대는 춤추기를 멈춘다. 그는 케이크와 과자를 즐겨 먹을 수 있다."

➡ _____

51 늑대: (춤을 멈추며) 춤을 멈출 수가 있다! (과자를 먹으며) 그리고 과자를 먹을 수 있어! 정말 고마워요.

➡ _____

52 (모두 웃으며 함께 과자를 맛있게 먹는다.)

➡ _____

MEMO

영어 기출 문제집

적중100 plus

1학기 전과정

1학기

정답 및 해설

천재 | 정사열

중 2

영어 기출 문제집

적중100

1학기

정답 및 해설

천재 | 정사열

중 2

적중100

Lesson 1

Time to Start Again

01 ②   02 ②   03 ④   04 ⑤
05 interesting   06 ⑤   07 hurry   08 looking
for

01 ②는 반의어 관계이고 나머지는 유의어 관계이다.

02 find out: 알게 되다

03 많은 사람이 볼 수 있도록 표지판, 게시문 등을 붙이다: post(게시하다)

04 can't wait for: ~이 몹시 기다려지다 / bump into: ~에 부딪히다

05 반의어 관계이다. 강한 : 약한 = 흥미로운 : 지루한

06 • 그들은 가난한 사람들에게 음식을 제공한다. serve: 제공하다 • 이 문장은 무엇을 의미하니? mean: 의미하다 • 나는 오늘 풀 수학 문제가 있다. solve: 풀다 • 나는 다미를 데리고 갈 거야. take: 데리고 가다

07 급히 움직이거나 행동하거나 가다: hurry(서두르다)

08 look for: ~을 찾다

01 (1) continue (2) forget (3) wrong (4) saying
02 (1) come over (2) after school (3) this year
03 (1) hard (2) dish (3) right
04 (1) strict (2) boring (3) fresh
05 (1) cut in on (2) be good for (3) bump into
06 (1) (f)inal (2) (c)over (3) (r)ealize

01 (1), (2), (3) 반의어 관계이다. (1) 흥미로운 : 지루한 = 계속하다 : 멈추다 (2) 쉬운 : 어려운 = 잊다 : 기억하다 (3) 기쁜 : 슬픈 = 맞는 : 틀린 (4) 친절한 : 친절함 = 속담 : 속담

02 (1) come over: 오다 (2) after school: 방과 후에 (3) this year: 올해

03 (1) hard: 어려운; 열심히 (2) dish: 요리; 접시 (3) right: 알맞은; 오른쪽의

04 (1) strict: 엄격한 (2) boring: 지루한 (3) fresh: 신선한

05 (1) cut in on: (말·대화에) 끼어들다 (2) be good for: ~에 좋다 (3) bump into: ~에 부딪히다

06 (1) final: 결승전 (2) cover: 표지 (3) realize: 깨닫다

교과서 Conversation

1 (1) What, think of[about] / I think
(2) What, opinion[view] on[about] / In, opinion[view]
2 (1) wait for
(2) this year / looking forward

교과서 대화문 익히기

1 T   2 F   3 F   4 T

교과서 확인학습   p.14~15

Get Ready - 2
1 think / looks, for / This year, going, with
2 Look at, going to / find out / excited, wait
3 your / to / What, think / a lot

Start Off - Listen & Talk A
1 good for, What / think, boring / which, to join / playing
2 think of / right, to learn / too, first / wait for

Start Off - Listen & Talk B
Let's / growing / what / Let's, right now, with / on / for

Step Up - Real-life Scene
what, think of / looks, strict / Don't judge, by / mean / with, exciting / During, class, with / can't wait for, this year

Express Yourself A
1 What / I think, on / can eat / can't wait for
2 dishes, think of / bad / don't eat / Try, good

Check Yourself - Listen & Speak
Let's join, What, of / playing / playing / right now, after school / going to, on / to play / too, wait for

시험대비 기본평가　　　　　　　p.16

01 ②	02 ⑤	03 ②	04 ⑤

01 의견을 물을 때는 What do you think of ~?를 사용하고, 자신의 의견을 말할 때는 I think ~로 나타내므로, 빈칸에는 think가 들어가야 한다.

02 새로운 마술이 멋지다고 했으므로 마술 쇼가 기다려진다는 말이 와야 알맞다.

03 Emily에 대한 의견을 묻는 질문에 '나도 그녀를 좋아해.'라는 대답은 어울리지 않는다.

04 can't wait for와 같은 표현은 ⑤ look forward to이다.

시험대비 실력평가　　　　　　　p.17~18

01 ②	02 ③	03 ③	04 ③
05 ②	06 ③	07 ①	08 ②
09 with	10 ③	11 ①, ③	12 cover
13 I can't wait for his birthday party.			

01 전치사 of의 목적어가 되는 의문대명사 what이 알맞다.

02 빈칸 다음의 말로 보아 의견 묻기에 대한 긍정의 대답이 와야 한다.

03 on+날짜

04 I can't wait for ~: 나는 ~이 매우 기다려진다.

05 의견을 묻는 표현인 What do you think of[about] ~?는 What's your opinion on ~?으로 바꿔 쓸 수 있다.

06 be good for ~에 좋다

07 What do you think of ~?는 상대방의 생각이나 의견을 물을 때 사용한다.

08 by: ~으로, ~에 의해

09 with: ~와 함께, ~을 써서[이용하여]

10 ③ 세호는 박 선생님과의 첫 수업이 매우 흥미로웠다고 생각한다.

11 What do you think of[about] ~?: ~에 대해서 어떻게 생각하니?

12 책이나 잡지의 바깥 부분: 표지(cover)

13 can't wait for: ~이 매우 기다려지다

서술형 시험대비　　　　　　　　p.19

01 (A) good   (B) boring

02 What do you think of[about] it?

03 She thinks it's boring.

04 (B) - (D) - (C) - (A)　　05 what

06 They can have a party with fresh vegetables every month.

07 It's on April 30.

08 I can't wait for the party.

01 (A) look + 형용사: ~하게 보이다 (B) 주어가 지루한 감정을 느끼게 하는 원인이므로 현재분사형 형용사 boring이 알맞다.

02 '~에 대해 어떻게 생각하니?'는 What do you think of[about] ~?으로 표현한다.

03 소녀는 헬스 동아리가 지루하다고 생각한다고 했다.

04 (B) 봐! 이 수첩에 대해 어떻게 생각하니? - (D) 표지가 멋져. 그것은 민준에게 좋은 것 같아. - (C) 그래, 그는 그것을 아주 좋아할 거야. - (A) 나는 그의 생일 파티가 너무 기다려져!

05 ⓐ What do you think of ~?: 너는 ~에 대해 어떻게 생각하니? ⓑ You know what?: 너 그거 알아?(있잖아.)

06 그들은 매달 신선한 야채가 있는 파티를 열 수 있다고 언급되었다.

07 첫 번째 파티는 4월 30일이다.

08 I can't wait for ~: 나는 ~이 무척 기다려진다.

교과서

Grammar

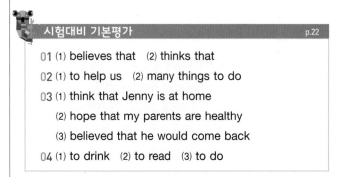

핵심 Check　　　　　　　　　　p.20~21

1 (1) to go　(2) to write with　(3) to help　(4) cold to drink

2 (1) to listen　(2) to tell　(3) to visit

3 (1) that　(2) that

4 (1) hope ✓ you　(2) says ✓ the　(3) thinks ✓ his

시험대비 기본평가　　　　　　　p.22

01 (1) believes that　(2) thinks that

02 (1) to help us　(2) many things to do

03 (1) think that Jenny is at home

　　(2) hope that my parents are healthy

　　(3) believed that he would come back

04 (1) to drink　(2) to read　(3) to do

02 (1) to부정사구(to help us)는 앞에 나온 명사 the only person을 꾸며주는 형용사 역할을 한다. (2) '해야 할 많은 일'이라는 뜻으로 to do가 many things를 뒤에서 수식해 준다.

03 that이 접속사로 동사의 목적어가 되는 명사절을 이끄는 경우이다.

04 to부정사구가 앞에 나온 명사(구)를 꾸며주는 형용사 역할을 한다.

시험대비 실력평가　　　　　　　p.23~25

01 ③	02 ②	03 ④	04 ⑤
05 to help	06 ③	07 ②	08 what →
that	09 taking → to take		10 ⑤

3

11 ③	12 that	13 to live → to live in
14 ⑤	15 I think that Jinwoo will be a great
leader.	16 ④	17 ⑤	18 ③
19 that → if[whether]	20 ③	21 ③
22 a chair to sit on[in]	23 ④	24 ④

01 형용사적 용법의 to부정사가 들어가야 한다.

02 접속사는 절과 절을 연결해 주는 역할을 하므로 I hope 뒤와 I have의 앞인 ②에 오는 것이 적절하다.

03 나머지는 모두 형용사적 용법의 to부정사이고 ④는 명사적 용법의 to부정사이다.

04 ⑤ be동사 made 다음에 that이 이끄는 명사절이 나오는 것은 어색하다.

05 형용사적 용법의 to부정사가 들어가야 한다.

06 ③은 지시형용사이고, 나머지는 모두 명사절을 이끄는 접속사로 쓰였다.

07 to부정사의 형용사적 용법으로 앞의 부정대명사와 명사를 수식하고 있다.

08 접속사 that은 동사의 목적어 역할을 하는 명사절을 이끈다.

09 to부정사의 형태는 'to+동사원형'을 사용한다.

10 ①, ②, ③, ④의 that은 접속사로 쓰여서 생략이 가능하고 ⑤는 지시형용사로 쓰였으므로 생략할 수 없다.

11 to부정사의 형용사적 용법으로 앞의 (대)명사를 수식하고 'to + 동사원형'의 형태로 쓰인다. ③은 방향을 나타내는 전치사로 쓰였다.

12 목적어절을 이끄는 접속사 that이 필요하다.

13 '~에 살다'는 live in이므로 to live 다음에 전치사 in을 넣어야 한다.

14 명사+to부정사의 구문에서 sit이 자동사이고 의미상 의자에 앉는 것이므로 전치사 on이나 in을 sit 뒤에 써야 한다.

15 '나는 ~라고 생각한다'는 I think that을 이용해서 나타낸다.

16 수식을 받는 명사가 전치사의 목적어일 경우에는 to부정사 뒤에 전치사를 써야 한다. play with: ~와 놀다 / write with: ~로 쓰다

17 주어진 문장과 ⑤의 that은 접속사로서 목적어절을 이끄는 역할을 한다.

18 ③은 to부정사의 형용사적 용법이고, 나머지는 모두 부사적 용법이다.

19 I don't know 뒤에 절이 따라올 때는 that 대신 if나 whether를 쓴다.

20 ③ something reading → something to read

21 ③은 to부정사의 부사적 용법이고 나머지는 모두 형용사적 용법으로 쓰였다.

22 to부정사의 수식을 받는 명사가 전치사의 목적어일 경우 to부정사 뒤에 반드시 전치사를 써야 한다.

23 ①, ②, ③, ⑤: that[That] / ④: 접속사 When

24 ⓐ, ⓒ to부정사의 형용사적 용법 ⓑ to부정사의 명사적 용법 ⓓ to부정사의 부사적 용법

01 to

02 (1) They believe (that) there is an alien here.
   (2) I know (that) you came back home late.

03 (1) to eat   (2) to drink   (3) sit on[in]   (4) talk with

04 that

05 She needs something to put on.

06 (1) I think, he is Chinese
   (2) I know, she is a wise wife

07 (1) I want some snacks to eat in the afternoon.
   (2) They need four chairs to sit on.

08 Do you have something warm to wear?

09 (1) a chair to sit → a chair to sit on[in]
   (2) visiting → to visit

10 I think (that) my English teacher is pretty.

11 (1) She needs someone strong to help her.
   (2) He has no friends to play with.

12 (1) that you can do everything
   (2) you think that she is pretty

13 (1) We cannot find a place to park our car.
   (2) Dave wants to buy a bike to ride to school.
   (3) Kate has a lot of homework to do.

14 a pen to write with

15 (1) He knows that she is rich.
   (2) I don't think that he is American.

16 (1) They don't have anything to talk about.
   (2) We are looking for a hotel to stay at in Paris.

01 앞의 명사를 수식하는 형용사적 용법의 to부정사가 필요하다.

02 명사절 접속사 that을 사용하여 연결한다. 이때 that은 생략 가능하다.

03 앞의 명사를 꾸며주는 to부정사의 형용사적 용법을 이용한다.

04 첫 번째 문장의 that은 접속사, 두 번째 문장의 that은 지시형용사이다.

05 형용사 역할의 to부정사는 수식하는 명사나 부정대명사의 뒤에 위치한다.

06 접속사 that은 동사의 목적어절을 이끄는 역할을 한다.

07 (2) 의미상 to부정사구 뒤에 전치사 on이 와야 한다.

08 -thing으로 끝나는 부정대명사의 경우 형용사와 to부정사의 수식을 동시에 받을 때 「-thing+형용사+to부정사」 어순으로 쓰인다.

09 (1) to부정사의 수식을 받는 명사가 전치사의 목적어일 경우 to부정사 뒤에 반드시 전치사를 써야 한다. (to sit → to sit on[in]) (2) '~할'이라는 의미로 명사를 수식하는 to부정사가

와야 한다. (형용사적 용법)

10 I think (that)+주어+동사 ~ : 나는 ~이 …라고 생각한다.

11 (1) -one+형용사+to부정사 (2) 명사+to부정사+전치사

12 that이 목적어가 되는 명사절을 이끄는 문장이다.

13 (1) 우리는 차를 주차할 장소를 찾을 수 없다. (2) Dave는 학교에
    타고 갈 자전거를 사고 싶다. (3) Kate는 해야 할 숙제가 많다.

14 write with a pen의 구조이다.

16 (1) 형용사적 용법의 to부정사가 부정대명사(anything)를 수식
    한다. (2) 명사+to부정사+전치사

Reading

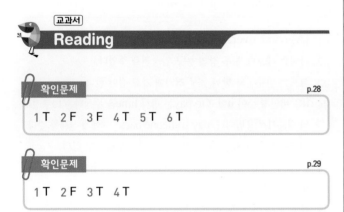

확인문제   p.28

1 T 2 F 3 F 4 T 5 T 6 T

확인문제   p.29

1 T 2 F 3 T 4 T

교과서 확인학습 A   p.30~31

01 were talking, when, over   02 said to
03 from   04 tickets   05 going, with
06 took, to   07 pay, back   08 what, in
09 isn't, fan, But   10 anyway, replied
11 won't, Trust   12 thought to herself
13 There's, later   14 hurried   15 on, to run
16 At, bumped into   17 continued to
18 Just, on   19 but, was not
20 After, to, one of   21 happen to
22 answered   23 Isn't, in   24 not, lost
25 On, saw   26 had, in   27 angry, Why
28 Just then, shouted, in   29 yours
30 looking for   31 not, thought 32 were, saying
33 to say, asked   34 about, to, with 35 finals
36 looked, pleased, love to

교과서 확인학습 B   p.32~33

1 Seho and Jihun were talking in the hallway when
  Dami came over.
2 "Happy birthday!" she said to Seho.

3 "Here. They're from my dad."
4 "Wow, two KBL tickets! Thanks!"
5 "Who are you going to take with you?" Dami
   asked.
6 "Minjun. He took me to a soccer game before.
7 So, it's time to pay him back."
8 "You know what?" Jihun cut in.
9 "Minjun isn't a fan of basketball. But I am!"
10 "Well, I'll ask him first anyway," replied Seho.
11 "He won't go with you. Trust me," said Jihun.
12 "Who is this guy?" Dami thought to herself, "He
   wants Minjun's ticket."
13 "Oh! There's the bell. See you later," said Dami.
14 She hurried to class.
15 "Come on, Jihun," said Seho, and he started to
   run.
16 At the corner, Seho bumped into someone.
17 "Sorry!" he said and continued to run.
18 Just then, Jihun saw something on the floor.
19 "Wait, Seho!" he said, but Seho was not there.
20 After class, Seho went to Dami and said, "I can't
   find one of my tickets.
21 Did you happen to see it?"
22 "No," she answered.
23 "Isn't it in your bag?"
24 "No, it's not there. I think I lost it," said Seho.
25 On her way home, Dami saw Jihun.
26 He had the ticket in his hand.
27 Dami got angry and said, "Hey! Why do you …?"
28 Just then, Jihun saw Seho and shouted, "Seho! I
   found a ticket in the hallway.
29 I think it's yours."
30 "Thanks! I was looking for that!" said Seho.
31 "He's not so bad," Dami thought.
32 "So, what were you saying?
33 Do you have something to say, Dami?" asked
   Jihun.
34 "Um, how about going to the school basketball
   game with me this Friday?
35 It's the finals."
36 Jihun looked really pleased. "I'd love to!"

시험대비 실력평가   p.34~37

01 ④   02 ②   03 one of my tickets
04 floor   05 He dropped one of his tickets.
06 ④   07 two KBL tickets   08 to

5

09 ⑤	10 ⑤	11 ③	12 ④
13 ②	14 the school basketball game		
15 ④	16 ①	17 ②	18 (T)rust
19 to	20 the bell rang		21 ①
22 ③	23 (h)allway	24 I think that it's yours.	
25 why don't you		26 ④	27 ⑤
28 ④	29 ②		

01 bump into: ~에 부딪히다

02 but: 그러나

03 인칭대명사 it은 one of my tickets를 가리킨다.

04 당신이 건물 안에서 서 있는 평평한 표면: 바닥

05 세호는 바닥에 그의 입장권 중 하나를 떨어뜨렸다.

06 come over: 오다

07 They는 two KBL tickets를 의미한다.

08 take A to B: A를 B에 데려가다

09 so는 '그래서, 그 결과'의 의미로, 결과를 나타내는 접속사이다.

10 돈을 빌린 적이 있는 것이 아니라 전에 민준이가 축구 경기에 데려간 적이 있어서 신세를 갚아야 한다고 언급되었다.

11 on one's way home: 집에 오는 길에

12 나머지는 모두 Jihun을 가리키고 ④는 Dami를 가리킨다.

13 ⓑ와 ②는 to부정사의 형용사적 용법, ①③⑤는 부사적 용법, ④는 명사적 용법이다.

14 인칭대명사 it은 앞 문장에 나온 the school basketball game을 가리킨다.

15 위 글을 통해서는 학교 농구 경기를 몇 시에 하는지는 알 수 없다.

16 cut in: (말·대화에) 끼어들다

17 ②는 민준이를 가리키고 나머지는 지훈이를 가리킨다.

18 어떤 사람이 정직하거나 또는 나쁜 일이나 그릇된 일을 하지 않을 것이라고 믿다

19 think to oneself: 마음속으로 생각하다

20 다미가 서둘러 수업에 간 이유는 종이 울렸기 때문이다.

21 on one's way home: 집으로 가는 도중에 (이때의 home은 부사이므로 전치사 to는 붙지 않음)

22 문맥상 입장권을 가지고 있는 이유를 묻는 의문사 why가 알맞다.

23 많은 방들로 이어지는 건물이나 집의 통로: 복도

24 목적어절을 이끄는 접속사 that은 생략할 수 있다.

25 How about -ing ~?는 Why don't you ~?로 바꿔 쓸 수 있다.

26 ④ 다미는 지훈이가 하는 말을 듣고 그가 나쁘지 않다고 생각했다.

27 (A) on: ~ 위에

   (B) one of: ~ 중 하나

28 주어진 문장의 it은 one of my tickets를 가리키므로 ④번이 적절하다.

29 ⓑ의 he는 지훈이를 가리킨다.

---

01 (A) over (B) in	02 She gave them to

01 (A) over (B) in   02 She gave them to Seho.   03 He wants to go to a basketball game with Minjun.   04 it's time to pay him back   05 He bumped into someone at the corner.   06 그는 그의 입장권 중 하나를 찾을 수 없다. 그녀에게 혹시 그것을 보았는지 물었다.   07 in my bag   08 I think (that) I lost it.   09 in   10 I am a fan of basketball! 11 Dami thought to herself.   12 class   13 On her way   14 Because Jihun had the ticket in his hand. 15 He found the ticket in the hallway.   16 finals

01 (A) come over: 오다 (B) cut in: (말·대화에) 끼어들다

02 다미는 세호에게 두 장의 농구 입장권을 주었다.

03 세호는 민준이와 함께 농구 경기에 가고 싶어 한다.

04 it은 비인칭 주어 it이고 to pay는 명사 time을 수식하는 to부정사의 형용사적 용법이다. pay someone back: ~에게 신세를 갚다

05 세호는 모퉁이에서 누군가와 부딪혔다고 언급되어 있다.

06 I can't find one of my tickets. Did you happen to see it?라고 말했다.

07 장소 부사 there는 in my bag을 의미한다.

08 I think (that) + 주어 + 동사 ~의 구문을 쓴다.

09 cut in: (말·대화에) 끼어들다

10 be동사 am 다음에는 a fan of basketball이 생략되었다.

11 think to oneself: 마음속으로 생각하다

12 학생들이 특정한 과목이나 활동을 배우는 일련의 모임: 수업

13 on one's way home: 집으로 오는 도중에

14 다미는 지훈이가 입장권을 그의 손에 갖고 있었기 때문에 화가 났다고 언급되었다.

15 지훈이는 복도에서 입장권을 찾았다고 언급되었다.

16 시합에서 마지막이자 가장 중요한 경기 : finals(결승)

---

01 ⑤	02 ①	03 ③	
04 (s)erious	05 (s)erve	06 this year	07 ④
08 ④	09 (B) – (D) – (C) – (A)		10 What, think of[about]
		11 ⑤	12 on
13 ⑤	14 ⑤	15 think that	16 ⑤
17 ③	18 ②	19 We don't believe that she will come to the party.	
		20 to talk → to talk with[to]	
21 ④	22 ④	23 ⑤	24 didn't think that he was handsome
	25 ②	26 I need a book to read.	
27 ④	28 with	29 ②	
30 ③	31 ③	32 later	33 ②
34 ③	35 in	36 many	37 ④

01 주의 깊이 생각한 후에 무언가 또는 누군가에 대한 견해를 형성하다: 판단하다(judge)

02 on one's way to: ～로 가는 도중에

03 ③은 유의어 관계이고 나머지는 반의어 관계이다.

04 serious: 진지한

05 serve: 제공하다, 봉사하다

06 this year: 올해

07 A가 I agree with you. I enjoyed it a lot.이라고 말했으므로 B도 긍정적인 의견을 말했음을 알 수 있다.

08 영화를 볼 예정이라고 말한 다음에 기대를 표현하는 말이 이어지는 것이 자연스럽다.

09 (B) 오늘 점심에 대해 어떻게 생각하니? - (D) 괜찮은 것 같아. 내일 메뉴는 뭐니? - (C) 와! 내일 우리는 스파게티를 먹을 수 있어. - (A) 내일 점심시간이 기다려진다.

10 '～에 대해 어떻게 생각하니?'라고 상대방의 의견을 묻는 표현으로 What do you think of[about] ～?를 쓸 수 있다.

11 right now: 지금 당장

12 on + 날짜

13 I can't wait for ～는 I'm looking forward to ～.로 바꿔 쓸 수 있다.

14 ⑤ 첫 번째 파티가 무슨 요일에 열리는지는 알 수 없다.

15 I think that ～: ～라고 생각한다

16 to부정사의 형용사적 용법이므로, 'to+동사원형' 형태가 쓰인다. take care of: ～을 돌보다

17 ①, ②, ④, ⑤는 명사절을 이끄는 접속사 that이고 ③은 지시형용사이다.

18 ①, ③, ④, ⑤는 형용사적 용법의 to부정사로 각각 앞의 명사를 수식하고 있다. ②는 decided의 목적어 역할을 하는 명사적 용법의 to부정사이다.

19 접속사 that 이하의 내용이 부정일 때, that 앞에 있는 동사를 부정으로 만든다.

20 명사+to부정사+전치사 구문이다.

21 ④ 명사절 접속사 that 뒤에 주어(the girl)는 있지만 동사가 빠져 있으므로 동사 is를 넣어야 한다.

22 <보기>, ④: 명사절을 이끄는 접속사 ①, ②, ⑤: 지시대명사, ③: 지시형용사

23 to부정사인 to live가 앞의 명사 a good house를 수식한다. 수식을 받는 명사가 전치사의 목적어인 경우 to부정사 뒤에 전치사가 와야 한다.

24 think는 that절을 목적어로 취하는 동사로, 「주어+think+주어+동사 ～」의 어순으로 쓰는데, 과거형 부정문이므로 think 앞에 didn't가 온다.

25 to부정사의 수식을 받는 명사가 전치사의 목적어인 경우 to부정사 뒤에 반드시 전치사를 써야 한다. live → live in

26 to부정사의 형용사적 용법: ～할

27 ⓐ when: ～할 때 ⓔ You know what?: 너 그거 알아?

28 with: ～와 함께

29 ⓒ so: 그래서 ⓕ but: 그러나

30 ⓓ와 ③은 형용사적 용법의 to부정사이고, ①, ②, ④는 명사적 용법, ⑤는 부사적 용법의 to부정사이다.

31 think to oneself: 마음속으로 생각하다

32 미래의 어느 때에: 나중에(later)

33 ② 다미의 아빠가 농구 입장권을 누구에게서 받았는지는 알 수 없다.

34 주어진 문장은 '그러면 그들도 나에게 좋은 말을 할 것이다.'라는 의미로 '내가 먼저 다른 사람들에게 좋은 말을 할 것이다'라는 문장 다음에 오는 것이 적절하다.

35 in English: 영어로

36 lots of: 많은(=many)

37 Nice words for nice words.는 가는 말이 고와야 오는 말이 곱다는 영어 속담이다.

단원별 예상문제 p.46~49

01 forget 　02 for 　03 ③ 　04 thought to herself 　05 ④ 　06 (f)inal 　07 ⑤
08 I think it's the right club for me. 　09 (t)ricks
10 the magic club 　11 ③ 　12 ②
13 ⑤ 　14 (1) She thinks that her daughter is sick. (2) I don't believe that Nick will come to the party. 　15 ② 　16 to play with 17 ⑤
18 ③, ⑤ 　19 We need more flour to bake a cake with. 　20 Dami gave two basketball tickets to Seho. 　21 ④ 　22 지훈이는 입장권을 세호에게 돌려주었다. 　23 that 　24 wrong
25 ⑤ 　26 ④ 　27 ④ 　28 yours
29 ⓓ to say 　ⓔ going 　30 지훈이가 입장권 한 장을 세호에게 주는 것을 보았기 때문이다.

---

01 반의어 관계이다. 위험한 : 안전한 = 기억하다 : 잊다

02 look for: ～을 찾다 / be good for: ～에 좋다

03 ③은 ceiling(천장)의 영영풀이다.

04 think to oneself: 마음속으로 생각하다

05 bump into: ～에 부딪히다 / on one's way home: 집으로 가는 도중에

06 final: 마지막의, 결승전

07 의견을 표현하는 답변이 나오므로 의견을 묻는 질문이 들어가야 자연스럽다.

08 의견 묻기와 자신의 의견을 표현하는 대화이다.

09 사람들을 즐겁거나 재미있게 하려고 하는 기발하고 교묘한 동작: 마술

10 인칭대명사 it은 the magic club을 가리킨다.

7

11 I can't wait for ~는 '나는 ~이 무척 기다려진다'는 뜻으로 기대를 나타내는 표현이다.

12 빈칸 뒤에 이어지는 문장이 says의 목적어 역할을 하므로 빈칸에는 '~하는 것'을 뜻하는 명사절 접속사 that이 적절하다.

13 to부정사인 to save가 앞의 명사 a way를 꾸며주는 형용사 역할을 한다.

14 (2) 접속사 that 이하의 내용이 부정일 때, that 앞에 있는 동사를 부정으로 만든다.

15 ②는 to부정사의 형용사적 용법이고 나머지는 부사적 용법이다.

16 앞의 명사를 수식하는 to부정사를 이용하여 한 문장으로 만들도록 한다. 수식을 받는 명사가 전치사의 목적어인 경우 to부정사 뒤에 전치사가 와야 한다.

17 ①~④는 명사절을 이끄는 접속사 that으로, that 이하가 문장에서 동사의 목적어의 역할을 하며 생략 가능하다. ⑤의 that은 동격의 명사절을 이끄는 접속사로 쓰였다.

18 to부정사의 형용사적 용법을 찾는다. ① 명사적 용법 ② 부사적 용법(결과) ④ 부사적 용법(목적)

19 밀가루를 가지고 케이크를 구워야 하므로 전치사 with를 써야 한다.

20 수여동사 give + 간접목적어 + 직접목적어(4형식) → 수여동사 give + 직접목적어 + to + 간접목적어(3형식)

21 on one's way to: ~로 가는 도중에

22 give someone back something: 누군가에게 어떤 것을 되돌려주다

23 목적어절을 이끄는 접속사 that이 알맞다.

24 사실이나 진실과 일치하지 않는 방식으로 말하거나 행동하거나 판단하는: 틀린, 잘못 알고 있는(wrong)

25 학교 농구 경기가 몇 시에 하는지는 알 수 없다.

26 ④의 me는 Dami를 가리킨다.

27 ⓐ on one's way home: 집으로 가는 도중에 ⓒ look for: ~을 찾다

28 yours: 너의 것

29 ⓓ something을 꾸며 주는 형용사적 용법의 to부정사가 되어야 한다. ⓔ How about + 동명사 ~?: ~하는 게 어때?

서술형 실전문제　　　p.50~51

01 can't wait　02 What do you think of[about] your English teacher?　03 I'm looking forward to it.　04 (C) - (B) - (D) - (A)　05 to write → to write with　06 (1) I know that she was a teacher. (2) I think that he is honest. (3) He believes that it will be a lot of fun.　07 (1) She has a strong desire to be a singer. (2) We had something to talk about. (3) I want a sheet[piece] of

paper to write on.　(4) Please give me something hot to drink.　08 On her way home, Dami saw Jihun.　09 I think that it's yours.　10 It's on this Friday.　11 (p)leased　12 (s)aying　13 (A) too (B) to remember　14 내가 먼저 다른 사람들에게 좋은 말을 하고 그러면 다른 사람들도 나에게 좋은 말을 해서　15 가는 말이 고와야 오는 말이 곱다.

01 I can't wait for ~는 '나는 ~이 무척 기다려져.'라는 의미로 기대를 나타내는 표현이다.

02 '~에 대해 어떻게 생각하니?'는 What do you think of[about] ~?으로 표현한다.

03 I'm looking forward to ~: 나는 ~이 무척 기대돼.

04 (C) 이 동아리는 너에게 맞는 것 같아. 그것에 대해 어떻게 생각하니? - (B) 헬스 동아리? 지루하다고 생각해. - (D) 그럼 넌 어떤 동아리에 가입하고 싶니? - (A) 난 축구 동아리에 가입할 거야. 나는 축구를 좋아해.

05 to부정사인 to write가 앞의 명사 a pen을 수식한다. 이때는 write with a pen이라는 전치사의 목적어 관계이므로 write 다음의 전치사 with를 빠뜨리지 않도록 주의한다.

06 that: 명사절(목적어)을 이끄는 접속사

07 (1), (2) to부정사의 형용사적 용법을 이용해 「명사+to부정사」의 형태로 쓴다. (3) to부정사의 목적어가 있고 to부정사의 동사가 자동사일 때는 전치사가 필요하다. (4) -thing으로 끝나는 부정대명사는 「-thing+형용사+to부정사」의 어순을 따른다.

08 on one's way home: 집으로 가는 도중에

09 I think that + 주어 + 동사 ~: 나는 ~가 ...라고 생각한다.

10 학교 농구 경기는 이번 주 금요일에 있다고 언급되었다.

11 어떤 것에 대해 행복해하는: 기쁜

12 대부분의 사람이 옳다고 믿고 있는 생각을 표현하는 오래되고 유명한 어구: 속담

13 too: (긍정문에서) ~도 (B) try to+동사원형: ~하려고 노력하다

15 Nice words for nice words는 '가는 말이 고와야 오는 말이 곱다'는 영어 속담이다.

창의사고력 서술형 문제　　　p.52

[모범답안]

01 (1) I want a bicycle to ride on weekends.

　(2) I want a hat to wear when I go out.

02 (1) He thinks that Jenny is kind.

　(2) She heard that they need help.

　(3) Tony says that it's delicious.

　(4) They know that many children are hungry.

03 (1) I need a chair to sit on.

　(2) I need a friend to talk with.

　(3) I need some food to eat.

(4) I need ski gloves to put on.

02 동사의 목적어가 되는 명사절을 이끄는 접속사 that을 사용하여 내용상 어울리는 것끼리 연결한다.

03 앞의 명사를 꾸며주는 to부정사의 형용사적 용법을 이용한다.

단원별 모의고사   p.53~56

01 ④	02 ⑤	03 ②	04 ②
05 (f)an	06 cut in	07 ④	08 ②
09 ⑤	10 ③	11 I can't wait for the concert.	
12 Tuesday, Thursday / July 15			
13 ③	14 ④	15 something cold to drink	
16 ③	17 ④	18 ②	
19 didn't know that	20 ④	21 Why do you have the ticket in your hand?	22 ③
23 (B) a ticket (C) the school basketball game			
24 (1) F (2) T	25 ③	26 I can't find one of my tickets.	
27 너 혹시 그것(내 입장권 하나)을 보았니?			
28 fan	29 ②	30 to	

01 식사할 때나 식당 등에서 먹을 것과 마실 것을 사람에게 주다: 제공하다(serve)

02 find out: ~을 알게 되다

03 • 여기에 너의 메모를 게시해라. • 이 문제 푸는 방법을 말해 줄래? • 나는 3일 내에 그 돈을 갚을 것이다. • 네가 믿을 수 있는 사람들과 시간을 보내라.

04 look at: ~을 보다 / be good for: ~에 좋다

05 fan: 팬, 선풍기

06 cut in: (말·대화에) 끼어들다

07 ④는 시합을 걱정한다는 의미이고, 나머지는 모두 '게임을 기대하고 있다'는 의미이다.

08 ②는 '학교 밴드 동아리에 대해 생각해 보는 게 어때?'라는 의미이고, 나머지는 학교 밴드 동아리에 대한 의견을 묻는 표현이다.

09 주어진 문장은 '나는 콘서트에서 연주하기를 희망한다.'라는 의미로, Me, too.(나도 콘서트에서 연주하기를 희망한다) 앞에 와야 한다.

10 on +날짜

11 I can't wait for ~: 나는 ~이 무척 기다려진다

12 매주 화요일과 목요일 방과 후에 연습을 하고, 7월 15일에 첫 번째 콘서트를 열 것이다.

13 명사 뒤에서 to+동사원형은 앞의 명사를 꾸며주며, '~할, ~할 수 있는'으로 해석한다.

14 ①, ②, ③, ⑤: 명사절을 이끄는 접속사 ④: 지시형용사

15 「-thing+형용사+to부정사」의 어순으로 쓴다.

16 think 뒤에 절이 올 경우 접속사 「that+주어+동사」의 어순으로

쓰고, 이때 접속사 that은 생략 가능하다. ③은 의문문의 어순으로 되어 있으므로 that절 뒤에 이어질 수 없다.

17 부정사인 to write가 앞의 명사 paper를 수식한다. 이때 paper는 write on의 목적어이므로 write 다음에 전치사 on을 붙여야 한다.

18 <보기>와 ②는 앞에 나오는 명사나 부정대명사를 꾸며주는 to부정사의 형용사적 용법이다. ① 명사적 용법(주어) ③ 명사적 용법(목적어) ④ 명사적 용법(보어) ⑤ 명사적 용법(목적어)

19 목적어절을 이끄는 접속사 that이 필요하다.

20 주어진 문장은 '나는 그것(입장권 한 장)을 찾고 있었어.'라는 의미로 '고맙다!'는 말 다음에 오는 것이 적절하다.

22 something을 수식하는 to부정사의 형용사적 용법이 되어야 한다.

23 (B)는 a ticket을 가리키고, (C)는 the school basketball game을 가리킨다.

24 (1) 다미는 세호의 손에 있는 입장권을 보고 화가 났다.

25 ⓐ bump into: ~에 부딪히다 ⓑ on: ~위에

26 one of: ~ 중 하나

27 Do you happen to+동사원형 ~?: 너 혹시 ~하니?

28 누군가 또는 무언가를 숭배하거나 누군가 또는 무언가를 보거나 듣는 것을 즐기는 사람: 팬

29 ②는 민준이를 가리키고 나머지는 지훈이를 가리킨다.

30 ⓑ think to oneself: 마음속으로 생각하다 ⓒ to: ~에

9

I Love My Town!

| 01 ④ | 02 ① | 03 ④ | 04 borrow |
| 05 neighbor | 06 ④ | 07 ④ | 08 address |

01 ④는 부사형이고 나머지는 형용사형이다.

02 clean up: 청소하다

03 특히 동의나 이해를 나타내기 위해 머리를 위아래로 움직이다:
(고개를) 끄덕이다(nod)

04 반의어 관계이다. 배고픈 : 배부른 = 빌려주다 : 빌리다

05 neighbor: 이웃

06 look at: ~을 보다 / put up: ~을 붙이다

07 ④는 유의어 관계이고 나머지는 반의어 관계이다.

08 누군가가 살거나 일하는 곳과 편지 등을 보낼 수 있는 곳에 대한
세부사항: 주소

01 (1) rest (2) lend (3) sell (4) laugh   02 (1) a
pair of (2) in front of   03 (1) pass (2) cut (3)
miss   04 (1) enough (2) elderly (3) lonely
05 (1) be good at (2) take care of (3) prepare for
06 (1) (b)lock (2) (p)erfect (3) (v)olunteer

01 (1)은 유의어 관계이다. 맛있는 : 맛있는 = 휴식 : 휴식 (2),
(3), (4)는 반의어 관계이다. (2) 쉬운 : 어려운 = 빌리다 : 빌려
주다 (3) 옳은 : 틀린 = 사다 : 팔다 (4) 기억하다 : 잊다 = 울다
: 웃다

02 (1) a pair of: 한 켤레의 (2) in front of: ~ 앞에서

03 (1) pass: 합격하다; 통과하다 (2) cut: 상처; 베다 (3) miss: 그
리워하다; 놓치다

04 (1) enough: 충분한 (2) elderly: 연세가 드신 (3) lonely: 외
로운

05 (1) be good at: ~을 잘하다 (2) take care of: ~을 돌보다
(3) prepare for: ~을 준비하다

06 (1) block: 블록, 구획 (2) perfect: 완벽한 (3) volunteer: 자
원봉사자

1 (1) What, going[planning] / I'm going[planning] to
(2) What, plans / plan to
2 (1) make it / Sure, then   (2) How about going, problem
(3) Let's play / Sorry, I can't

1 F   2 T   3 T   4 F

Get Ready - 2

1 going to take, front of / Sounds, over
2 It's, get / Let's, at, in
3 planning, for / selling, over there / Let's, around

Start Off - Listen & Talk A

1 any, for / planning to, dancing / Sounds, Can, join
/ not
2 planning to, to prepare / mean, with / make it /
then

Start Off - Listen & Talk B

are, going to / clean up, with / like, Can, join / make
it, at / not, about / with, a pair of / See, on

Start Off - Speak Up - Look and talk.

planning to, at / Can, with / Why not, make / Let's,
front of

Step Up - Real-life Scene

to volunteer, care / mean, near / Will, with, take care
of / love, walking, good at / bring, with, too /
neighbor, too, shall, meet / make, at, at / on

Express Yourself A

1 I'm planning to, to watch / interesting, with / Of,
Can, make, at / No, then
2 to enter / Don't, can win / Thank

Learning Diary - Listen & Speak

are, going to / planning, at / great / Will, with / shall,
meet / make it / afraid, about / See, then

시험대비 기본평가 p.68

01 ③　　　02 ③　　　03 ⑤　　　04 ④

01 계획을 묻는 표현이다.

02 Can you make it at ~?은 약속 시간을 정할 때 쓰는 표현이다.

03 여행을 갈 계획이라는 B의 대답으로 보아 계획을 묻는 질문이 들어가야 한다.

04 B가 동의하고 5시에 만나자고 말했으므로 약속 시간을 정하는 표현인 ④가 알맞다.

시험대비 실력평가 p.69~70

01 ③　　02 ④　　03 ④　　04 ③
05 ③　　06 dancing　07 ④　　08 ③
09 the animal care center　10 ②　　11 ④
12 ⑤　　13 How[What] about　14 ④

01 주어진 문장은 '같이 가도 될까?'라는 의미로, Sure.(물론.)의 질문으로 오는 것이 적절하다.

02 be going to =will: ~할 예정이다

03 빈칸 다음의 문장으로 보아 제안에 거절하는 표현이 알맞다.

04 ③ 소년이 오후 1시에 만날 수 없는 이유는 알 수 없다.

05 be planning to ~: ~할 계획이다(=be going to)

06 practice는 목적어로 동명사를 취한다.

07 Why not?은 요청에 수락하는 표현이다. Not at all.: 천만에.

08 주어진 문장의 them은 animals를 가리킨다.

09 the one은 앞 문장의 the animal care center를 가리킨다.

10 take care of: ~을 돌보다

11 ⓒ와 ④는 '허가', ①은 '추측', ②③⑤는 '가능, 능력'을 나타낸다.

12 지나가 오전 8시에 만나자고 하는 것으로 보아 몇 시에 만날지를 묻는 질문이 알맞다.

13 Can you make it ~?은 How[What] about meeting ~? 으로 바꿔 쓸 수 있다.

14 ④ Alex가 동물을 몇 마리 기르는지는 알 수 없다.

서술형 시험대비 p.71

01 meeting　　02 Let's meet in front of the library.
03 소년은 이번 화요일에 도서관에서 자원봉사를 할 계획이다.
04 (C) – (B) – (D) – (A)　　05 What are you going to do this Saturday?　　06 make it　　07 They will meet at the bus stop at 2 p.m.　　08 on

01 오후 3시에 만날 수 있느냐는 의미이다.

02 Let's+동사원형 ~.: ~하자. / in front of: ~ 앞에서

03 volunteer: 자원봉사를 하다

04 (C) 주말에 무슨 계획 있니? (B) 응. 청소년 센터에서 춤을 연습할 계획이야. (D) 좋은데. 같이 가도 될까? (A) 그거 좋지.

05 What are you going to+동사원형 ~?: 너는 ~에 무엇을 할 거니?

06 make it은 시간이나 장소의 표현과 함께 쓰여 '시간에 맞춰 가다, 도착하다'라는 의미를 갖는다.

07 그들은 오후 2시에 버스 정류장에서 만날 것이다.

08 on + 요일

교과서
Grammar

핵심 Check p.72~73

1 (1) will miss　(2) If　(3) takes　(4) studies
2 (1) play　(2) knocking　(3) shaking　(4) broken

시험대비 기본평가 p.74

01 (1) felt, touch[touching]　(2) heard, arrive[arriving]
　(3) saw, run[running]
02 (1) If you hurry up, you will catch the bus.
　(2) If it is fine tomorrow, we will go on a picnic.
　(3) If you are tired, you can sit here.
03 (1) She watched her husband paint[painting] the wall.
　(2) The dog heard the baby cry[crying].
　(3) The police officer sees a girl pick[picking] up a bottle.
04 (1) If you study hard　(2) If it rains

01 「지각동사+목적어+동사원형[현재분사]」의 형태로 써야 한다.

02 「If+주어+현재시제, 주어+will[can/may]+동사원형 ~.」의 어순이다.

03 「지각동사 + 목적어 + 목적격 보어(동사원형/현재분사)」 어순이다.

04 '만약 ~한다면'이라는 의미로 조건을 나타내는 표현은 「if+주어+동사의 현재형」으로 나타낸다.

시험대비 실력평가 p.75~77

01 ③　　02 ②　　03 ⑤　　04 ②
05 If it is, will go　　06 ①, ②　　07 ③
08 ④　　09 ④　　10 touched → touch
[touching]　　11 ①　　12 ③　　13 We heard the rain falling on the roof.　　14 ④

11

01 지각동사는 목적격 보어로 동사원형과 현재분사를 쓸 수 있는데, 동작의 진행을 강조하는 경우에는 현재분사를 쓴다.

02 조건을 나타내는 if절은 미래의 의미이더라도 현재시제로 나타내지만, 주절은 미래시제로 써야 한다.

03 5형식 문장에서 지각동사는 목적격 보어로 동사원형이나 현재분사를 취한다.

04 현재나 미래에 실현 가능성이 있는 조건의 if 문장이다.

05 조건의 부사절에서는 현재가 미래시제를 대신한다. 날씨를 말할 때는 비인칭 주어 it을 사용한다.

06 지각동사 see는 목적격 보어로 동사원형이나 현재분사를 취한다.

07 조건을 나타내는 접속사 if가 이끄는 절에서는 미래의 일을 나타내는 경우일지라도 동사는 현재형을 쓴다. ③ will snow → snows

08 지각동사 see, hear 등은 목적격 보어로 동사원형 또는 현재분사를 쓸 수 있다.

09 • '~하지 않으면'의 의미인 Unless가 알맞다. • '~이기 때문에'라는 의미의 because나 as가 알맞다.

10 지각동사 feel의 목적격 보어로 동사원형 또는 현재분사를 쓸 수 있다.

11 ① 지각동사 hear는 목적격 보어로 동사원형이나 현재분사를 취한다. (sang → sing[singing])

12 ③은 '~인지 아닌지'의 의미이고 나머지는 '만일 ~이라면'의 뜻이다.

13 비가 떨어지고 있는 것을 들었으므로 진행의 의미를 갖는 현재분사를 쓴다.

14 목적격 보어로 동사원형과 현재분사를 쓸 수 있는 동사는 지각동사이다. / get, want+목적어+to부정사 / make, have+목적어+동사원형 / hear+목적어+동사원형[현재분사]

15 if ~not은 unless(~하지 않으면)로 바꿔 쓸 수 있다.

16 '경험'을 나타내므로 현재완료시제가 적합하고, 지각동사가 쓰였으므로 목적격 보어로 동사원형을 쓴다.

17 조건을 나타내는 if절에서는 현재시제가 미래시제를 대신한다.

18 <보기>와 나머지는 '만약 ~라면'이라는 의미로 조건을 나타내는 접속사로 쓰였고, ②는 '~인지 아닌지'라는 의미로 명사절을 이끄는 접속사로 쓰였다.

19 「지각동사+목적어+동사원형」의 어순으로 써야 한다.

20 조건을 나타내는 if절에서는 현재시제가 미래시제를 대신한다. (⑤ it will be → it is)

21 조건을 나타내는 if절에서는 현재시제가 미래시제를 대신한다.

22 ① touched → touch[touching] ② called → call[calling] ④ shook → shake[shaking] ⑤ stole → steal[stealing]

23 ④는 이유를 나타내는 접속사 because가 와야 한다.

24 'Can you+지각동사(hear)+목적어(him)+목적격 보어(go) ~?'의 어순으로 배열한다. '계단을 내려가다'는 go down the stairs이다.

서술형 시험대비   p.78~79

01 (1) I saw a strange man enter my house.
   (2) I saw my brother meeting a lady in the bakery.
   (3) I felt something crawl up my arm.
   (4) I heard the church bells ring out in the distance.
02 (1) If it is sunny tomorrow
   (2) If it doesn't stop raining
03 (1) to read → read / reading
   (2) sang → sing / singing
04 (1) If the weather is nice, I always walk to school.
   (2) If it rains on weekends, we watch TV.
   (3) If I am late for class, my teacher gets very angry.
05 (1) saw the boys playing baseball
   (2) felt somebody hit her
06 (1) If   (2) when   (3) Unless
07 I heard a famous singer sing[singing] on the stage yesterday.
08 (1) Unless you leave   (2) If it doesn't
09 (1) I watched my dad wash[washing] his car.
   (2) Jisu saw Tom ride[riding] a bike.
   (3) He felt a warm hand touch[touching] his back.
10 (1) will have → have   (2) have gone → go
   (3) won't send → don't send
11 (1) If you don't hurry up, you'll be late.
   (2) If you go straight three blocks, you will find a supermarket.
12 (1) I felt the building shake.
   (2) I have never heard my sister play the piano.

01 지각동사의 목적격 보어로 동사원형이나 현재분사를 써서 두 문장을 한 문장으로 쓸 수 있다.

02 조건을 나타내는 If절에서는 미래의 의미이더라도 현재시제로 써야 한다. stop+-ing: ~하는 것을 멈추다

03 지각동사의 목적격 보어는 동사원형이나 현재분사를 사용한다.

04 if는 종속절을 이끄는 접속사이다.

05 「지각동사+목적어+현재분사/동사원형」 어순으로 써야 한다.

06 when은 때, if는 조건을 나타낸다. unless는 if ~ not의 뜻이다.

07 「지각동사 hear+목적어(a famous singer)+목적격 보어(원형
　　동사/현재분사)」구문으로 만든다.

08 unless는 if ~ not과 같은 뜻이다.

09 watch, see, feel 등은 지각동사로 목적격 보어로 동사원형이
　　나 현재분사 형태를 쓸 수 있다.

10 if 조건절에서는 현재시제가 미래시제를 대신한다.

11 If 조건문 – If+주어+동사(현재형), 주어+will[won't]+동사
　　원형

12 주어+지각동사+목적어+목적보어(동사원형)의 어순이다.

교과서 Reading

확인문제　　　　　　　　　　p.80

1 F　2 F　3 T　4 T　5 F

확인문제　　　　　　　　　　p.81

1 T　2 T　3 F　4 F

교과서 확인학습 A　　　　　　p.82~83

01 with　　　　　　02 with

03 always thought, perfect, because, spot

04 outside, run after　　　05 in, for

06 away, lived with　　　07 to, lonely

08 no　　　　　09 after, followed

10 One day, sitting　　　11 was making

12 wrong　　　13 at, closely, cut 14 took, to

15 get better, enough, inside　　16 at, was

17 outside, couldn't　　　18 put, up

19 third, Still　　20 When, walking, lost

21 read, big　　22 looks, like, strange

23 hurried　　24 on, Let's　　25 to, on

26 Ding-Dong, heard, ring, ran, opened

27 back, cried　　28 jumped up　　29 Let, guess

30 in, doesn't　　31 nodded　　32 last, didn't you

33 How, know　　34 Because, too, during

35 Our, has　　36 if, come in, have

37 Sure　　38 Thank, thought

39 met, thanks to

교과서 확인학습 B　　　　　　p.84~85

1 Bear was a black and brown cat with green eyes.

2 He lived with a boy, Ryan.

3 Ryan always thought that "Bear" was a perfect name for the cat because he had a black spot in the shape of a bear.

4 Bear liked to go outside every morning and run after butterflies.

5 He always came home just in time for dinner.

6 Five blocks away, Max the cat lived with a girl, Sheila.

7 When Sheila moved to this town last month, she was lonely.

8 She had no friends there.

9 But, after Max followed her home, he became a good friend to her.

10 One day, Sheila saw Max sitting under the desk.

11 He was making a strange sound.

12 "What's wrong?" asked Sheila.

13 She looked at him closely and found a bad cut on his leg.

14 She took him to the animal hospital.

15 The doctor said, "He will get better if he gets enough rest. Keep him inside for a week."

16 That night, at Ryan's house, there was no Bear.

17 Ryan checked outside, but he couldn't find him.

18 He made posters and put them up around town.

19 A third night passed. Still no Bear.

20 When Sheila was walking near her house, she saw a poster about the lost cat.

21 She read it closely, and her eyes got big.

22 "This cat looks exactly like Max. It's so strange."

23 She hurried home.

24 "Come on, Max! Let's go!"

25 She took him to the address on the poster.

26 "Ding-Dong." When Ryan heard the doorbell ring, he ran to the door and opened it.

27 "Bear, you're back!" Ryan cried.

28 Max jumped up into Ryan's arms.

29 "Let me guess," said Sheila.

30 "Your cat comes home only in the evenings, doesn't he?"

31 Ryan nodded.

32 "And you lost him last Friday, didn't you?" Sheila said.

33 "Yes! How did you know?" said Ryan.

34 "Because this is my cat, too, and he usually comes to my home only during the day."

35 "Our cat has two families!" said Ryan.

36 "Hey, if you have time, please come in and have some cookies."

37 "Sure," said Sheila.

38 "Thank you, Max," she thought.

39 "I met a good neighbor thanks to you!"

시험대비 실력평가
p.86~89

01 with   02 ⑤   03 ②   04 spot
05 ④   06 ④   07 ②   08 to sit →
sitting[sit]   09 ③   10 ⑤   11 ④
12 ①   13 a poster   14 like   15 ③
16 to ring → ring[ringing]   17 ②   18 doesn't
19 comes usually → usually comes   20 ⑤
21 ②   22 ⑤   23 ④   24 ②
25 ⑤   26 cut   27 were → was
28 포스터에 있는 고양이가 Max와 꼭 닮은 것 29 ③

01 with: ~와 함께

02 이유를 나타내는 접속사 because가 알맞다.

03 in time for: ~에 시간 맞춰

04 다른 부분과 달리 보이는 표면의 작은 부분: 점, 반점(spot)

05 ④ Bear가 왜 나비를 쫓아다녔는지는 알 수 없다.

06 Sheila는 친구가 없었다고 했으므로 외로웠을 것이다. lonely: 외로운

07 but: 그러나

08 지각동사 see는 목적격 보어로 현재분사 또는 동사원형을 쓴다.

09 ⓓ look at: ~을 보다 ⓔ take A to B: A를 B로 데려가다

10 Max가 왜 다쳤는지는 알 수 없다.

11 but: 그러나

12 ⓑ put up: ~을 붙이다 ⓔ on: ~에

13 인칭대명사 it은 앞 문장에 나온 a poster를 가리킨다.

14 look like: ~처럼 보이다

15 ③ 왜 Ryan이 Bear를 잃어버렸는지는 알 수 없다.

16 지각동사 hear는 목적격 보어로 동사원형이나 현재분사를 쓴다.

17 jump up: 뛰어오르다 / in the evenings: 저녁마다

18 평서문의 동사가 일반동사 현재형이고 주어가 3인칭 단수이므로 doesn't가 알맞다.

19 빈도부사는 일반동사 앞에 위치한다.

20 Max가 Ryan의 고양이인 것을 Sheila가 어떻게 알았는지는 알 수 없다.

21 목적어절을 이끄는 접속사 that이 알맞다.

22 저녁 식사 시간에 맞춰 집에 왔다고 언급되었다.

23 주어진 문장은 '그녀는 그를 동물 병원에 데려갔다.'는 의미로 그

의 다리에 심한 상처를 발견했다는 문장 다음에 오는 것이 자연스럽다.

24 ⓐ on: ~에 ⓒ for a week: 일주일 동안

25 get better는 '(병이) 좋아지다, 호전되다'는 뜻으로 recover와 바꿔 쓸 수 있다.

26 날카로운 것에 의해 사람의 몸에 생긴 상처: cut

27 주어가 Bear로 단수이므로 was가 되어야 한다.

28 인칭대명사 It은 앞 문장을 받는다.

29 Sheila는 그녀의 집 근처를 걷고 있을 때 포스터를 보았다고 언급되었다.

서술형 시험대비
p.90~91

01 with   02 His eyes are green.
03 (p)erfect   04 Because "Bear" had a black spot in the shape of a bear.   05 When Ryan heard the doorbell ring   06 He lost him last Friday.   07 didn't you 08 He usually comes to her home only during the day.   09 She moved to this town last month.   10 lonely
11 (A) after   (B) sitting   (C) gets   12 he had a bad cut on his leg   13 He made posters and put them up around town.   14 ⓐ closely ⓑ like   15 She saw it when she was walking near her house.   16 address

01 with: ~을 가진

02 Bear의 눈은 초록색이라고 언급되었다.

03 결점이나 약점이 없고 완전한: 완벽한

04 곰 모양의 검은 반점이 있었기 때문에 "Bear"가 그 고양이에 대한 완벽한 이름이라고 생각했다.

05 when+주어+지각동사 hear+목적어+동사원형

06 Ryan은 그의 고양이를 지난 금요일에 잃어버렸다고 언급되었다.

07 평서문의 주어가 you이고 일반동사 과거형이므로 부가의문문은 didn't you가 알맞다.

08 Sheila의 고양이는 보통 그녀의 집에 낮 동안에만 온다고 언급되었다.

09 Sheila는 지난달에 이 마을로 이사를 왔다고 언급되었다.

10 말할 친구나 사람이 없어서 행복하지 않은: 외로운

11 (A) 문맥상 after가 알맞다. (B) 지각동사 see+목적어+현재분사 (C) if 조건절에서는 미래시제 대신 현재시제를 쓴다.

12 Sheila는 Max가 다리에 심한 상처를 입었기 때문에 Max를 병원에 데려갔다.

13 Ryan은 포스터를 만들어서 그것들을 마을 주위에 붙였다고 언급되었다.

14 ⓐ 동사를 수식하는 부사가 되어야 한다. ⓑ look like: ~처럼

보이다

15 Sheila는 그녀의 집 근처를 걷고 있을 때 잃어버린 고양이에 대한 포스터를 보았다고 언급되었다.

16 누군가가 살거나 일하는 곳과 편지 등을 보낼 수 있는 곳에 대한 세부사항: 주소

영역별 핵심문제   p.93~97

01 ④   02 ③   03 ④
04 (s)trange 05 in   06 butterfly 07 ④
08 ②   09 (D) – (B) – (C) – (A)   10 ③
11 What are you planning to do this Saturday?
12 ②   13 make   14 They will meet at the bus stop at 2 p.m.   15 ④   16 ①
17 to get → get[getting]   18 ②   19 won't
→ don't   20 ⑤   21 ④   22 I saw an old man get off the train.   23 If Susan does not get up now, she will miss the train. 또는 Susan will miss the train if she does not get up now.   24 ④   25 ⑤   26 Kate heard someone shouting[shout] at her.   27 ④
28 ③   29 ④   30 blocks   31 ③
32 ④   33 ③   34 closely   35 ⑤
36 rest   37 ③

01 색이 다르거나 그것이 있는 표면과 다른 느낌이 드는 작고 둥근 부분: 점, 반점(spot)

02 ③은 유의어 관계이고 나머지는 반의어 관계이다.

03 take a break: 휴식을 취하다 / take care of: ~을 돌보다

04 strange: 이상한

05 in need: 어려움에 처한 / in front of: ~ 앞에

06 길고 얇은 몸과 보통 밝은 색상의 날개들을 가진 날아다니는 곤충: 나비(butterfly)

07 A: 너는 이번 방학에 무엇을 할 계획이니? ① 나는 할머니를 방문했어. ② 나는 미국에 갔다. ③ 응. 나는 미국에 갈 계획이야. ④ 나는 오스트레일리아에 갈 계획이야. ⑤ 아니. 나는 미국에 가지 않을 예정이야.

08 9시에 만나자는 제안에 학교 체육관에서 보자고 했으므로 제안에 수락하는 말이 와야 한다.

09 (D) 나는 댄스 쇼를 보기 위해 마을 축제에 갈 계획이야. (B) 흥미롭구나. 같이 가도 될까? (C) 물론이지. 오후 6시에 학교 정문에서 만날까? (A) 그래. 그럼 그때 보자.

10 박물관 앞에서 만나자는 말에 '그 박물관은 좋은 곳이었어.'라고 대답하는 것은 어색하다.

11 '~할 계획이다'는 「be planning to+동사원형」으로 나타낼 수 있다. / this Saturday: 이번 토요일에

12 공원을 청소할 계획이라는 말에 멋진 계획인 것 같다고 답했으

므로 이어질 말로 함께할 수 있는지 묻는 표현이 자연스럽다.

13 make it: 시간에 대다, 만나다

14 소년이 오후 2시에 버스 정류장에서 만나자고 제안하자 소녀는 괜찮다고 했다.

15 「지각동사+목적어+동사원형」 어순이다.

16 '만약 ~한다면'을 의미하는 접속사 if를 이용하며, if절에서는 미래의 일이라도 will을 쓸 수 없고 현재시제를 쓴다.

17 「지각동사+목적어+동사원형/현재분사」 형태이다.

18 '만약 ~하면'의 뜻으로 조건절을 이끄는 접속사와 '~인지 아닌지'의 뜻으로 명사절을 이끄는 접속사 역할을 하는 if가 알맞다.

19 if절에서는 미래의 일을 현재시제로 나타낸다.

20 모두 지각동사가 있는 5형식 문장이다. 목적격 보어로 현재분사, 동사원형이 올 수 있다. ⑤는 cried를 cry 또는 crying으로 고쳐 써야 한다.

21 '만약 ~라면'의 뜻으로 조건을 나타내지 않는 문장을 찾는다. ④ if절은 '~인지 아닌지'의 뜻으로 명사절을 이끄는 접속사로 쓰였다.

22 「주어(I)+지각동사(saw)+목적어(an old man)+동사원형(get off) ~」의 어순으로 쓴다.

23 첫 문장이 두 번째 문장의 조건이 되므로 접속사 if를 이용하여 연결한다.

24 지각동사 watch의 목적격 보어로 동사원형이나 현재분사가 와야 한다.

25 ①~④는 내용상 조건을 나타내는 접속사 if가 와야 하고, ⑤는 동사 think의 목적어 역할을 하는 접속사 that이 적절하다.

26 지각동사+목적어+목적격 보어(목적어와 능동 관계이면 현재분사나 동사원형이 쓰인다.)

27 with: ~을 가진

28 ①, ②, ④, ⑤는 명사절을 이끄는 접속사 that이고 ③은 지시형용사이다.

29 because: ~ 때문에

30 사방에 거리가 있는 건물들의 그룹: 구획, 블록

31 문맥상 after가 알맞다.

32 Sheila가 이 마을로 왜 이사를 왔는지는 알 수 없다.

33 지각동사 + 목적어 + 현재분사

34 동사를 수식하는 부사가 되어야 한다.

35 on: ~에 / put up: ~을 붙이다

36 활동하거나 일을 한 후에 쉬거나 잠을 자거나 아무 일도 하지 않는 기간: 휴식

37 Sheila의 집 근처에 동물 병원이 있었는지는 알 수 없다.

단원별 예상문제   p.98~101

01 ②   02 up   03 ②   04 look around   05 ④   06 (d)irector 07 ⑤
08 ②   09 ⑤   10 volunteer 11 Can

15

you make it at 3 p.m.?   12 They will meet at 4
p.m.   13 ③   14 ①, ⑤   15 to cry
→ cry[crying] 16 ③   17 ⑤   18 Unless
you like the food   19 ③   20 ④
21 ③   22 ②   23 nod   24 He
comes to his home only in the evenings. 25 ③
26 shape   27 (A) because   (B) after   28 ④
29 ③

01 날카로운 것에 의해 사람의 몸에 생긴 상처: cut

02 put up: ~을 붙이다 / clean up: ~을 청소하다

03 get better: (병 따위가) 좋아지다 / get enough rest: 충분한
휴식을 취하다

04 look around: ~을 둘러보다

05 neighbor: 이웃 / strange: 이상한 / nervous: 긴장되는 /
brown: 갈색의

06 director: 감독

07 콘서트에 가자는 A의 제안에 B가 동의를 했으므로, 뒤에는 만
나는 시간 약속을 하는 내용이 이어지는 것이 자연스럽다.

08 미래에 할 계획이나 의도를 묻는 표현에 대한 응답으로 ②의 할
수 있다는 표현은 어색하다.

09 Aria가 오후 3시에 만나자고 제안하자 Eric이 안 된다고 하고,
오후 4시에 만나자는 제안을 하는 흐름이 알맞다.

10 어떤 보상을 기대하지 않고 무언가를 하겠다고 제안하다: 자원봉
사를 하다

11 '시간에 맞춰 가다'는 make it이다. '너는 오후 3시에 올 수 있
니?'라는 뜻의 의문문을 만든다.

12 Eric이 오후 4시에 만나자고 제안하자 Aria가 좋다고 했다.

13 조건을 나타내는 if절에서는 현재시제가 미래의 일을 나타내므로
③이 알맞다.

14 지각동사의 목적격 보어로는 동사원형이나 현재분사가 쓰인다.

15 heard는 지각동사이므로 목적격 보어 자리에 동사원형이나 현
재분사를 사용한다.

16 조건의 부사절에서는 현재시제로 미래를 나타낸다. ③ will
pass → pass

17 지각동사(hear, see, feel, watch) + 목적어 + 목적격 보어: 목
적어와 능동 관계인 경우 동사원형이나 현재분사를 쓴다. ⑤의
to move는 move나 moving으로 고쳐야 바른 문장이 된다.

18 '만약 ~하지 않는다면'이라는 의미의 「If+주어+don't
[doesn't]+동사원형 ~」은 「Unless+주어+동사의 현재형 ~」으
로 바꿔 쓸 수 있다.

19 ③ 평서문의 일반동사가 현재형이고 주어가 3인칭 단수이므로
부가의문은 doesn't he가 되어야 한다.

20 because: ~ 때문에

21 during the day: 낮 동안에 / thanks to: ~ 덕분에

22 '만약 ~하면'의 조건절을 이끄는 접속사 if가 알맞다.

23 특히 동의나 이해를 보여주기 위해 머리를 위아래로 움직이다:
(고개를) 끄덕이다

24 Ryan의 고양이는 저녁에만 집에 온다고 언급되었다.

25 thought 다음에 나오는 내용이 목적어의 역할을 하고 있으므로
명사절을 이끄는 접속사 that이 와야 한다.

26 사물의 형태나 윤곽: 모양

27 (A) because + 주어 + 동사: ~ 때문에 (B) after: ~한 후에

28 run after: ~을 쫓아다니다

29 ③ Bear는 항상 저녁 시간에 맞춰 Ryan의 집에 왔다고 언급되
었다.

🦉 서술형 실전문제   p.102~103

01 I'm planning to visit my grandparents.

02 are you going to do / are you planning to do

03 What time shall we meet?   04 meet

05 (1) to play → play[playing]   (2) will go → goes
    (3) drew → draw[drawing]

06 Unless   07 Hana saw her cat climbing the wall.

08 If you arrive on time, your friend won't have to
wait for you.

09 He made posters and put them up around town.

10 still   11 This cat looks exactly like Max.

12 She took him to the address on the poster.

13 Sheila saw Max sitting under the desk.

14 (c)ut   15 She took him to the animal hospital.

16 그가 충분한 휴식을 취하면 좋아질 거야.

01 be planning to: ~할 계획이다

02 미래의 계획을 묻는 표현은 What will you do ~? = What
are you going to do ~? = What are you planning to do
~? 등이다.

03 What time shall we meet?: 우리 몇 시에 만날까?

04 Can you make it ~?은 Can we meet ~?으로 바꿔 쓸 수
있다.

05 (1), (3) 지각동사+목적어+목적격 보어(동사원형/현재분사) (2)
조건의 부사절에서는 의미가 미래일지라도 미래시제를 쓰지 않고
현재시제를 쓴다.

06 If ~ not은 '~하지 않는다면'이라는 의미로 Unless와 같다.

07 지각동사 saw가 있으므로 목적어와 목적격 보어를 차례로 쓴다.
목적격 보어는 climbing으로 현재분사 형태로 주어져 있다.

08 주절이 먼저 나오고 if절이 뒤로 가도 상관없다.

09 이어동사의 목적어가 인칭대명사일 때 목적어는 동사와 부사 사
이에 위치해야 한다.

10 전에 일어나거나 존재해서 현재도 계속되는: 여전히(still)

11 look exactly like: 꼭 ~처럼 보이다

12 Sheila는 Max를 포스터에 있는 주소로 데려갔다.

13 「지각동사+목적어+현재분사」의 어순으로 써야 한다.

14 날카로운 것에 의해 몸에 생긴 상처

15 Sheila는 Max를 동물 병원으로 데려갔다고 언급되었다.

16 get better: 좋아지다, 나아지다 / get enough rest: 충분한 휴식을 취하다

창의사고력 서술형 문제
p.104

|모범답안|

01 (1) I saw a man plant[planting] trees.
  (2) I heard a phone ring[ringing].
  (3) I felt somebody touch[touching] my leg.

02 (1) If I get an A on the math test, my parents will be happy.
  (2) If it is sunny tomorrow, I will go hiking with my friends.
  (3) If I find an abandoned dog on the street, I will bring it to my house.

03 (1) My mother saw me wash[washing] the dishes.
  (2) I felt the ground move[moving] under me.
  (3) I heard my mom call[calling] my name.
  (4) I watched a girl swim[swimming] in the sea.

01 「지각동사+목적어+동사원형/현재분사」 구문을 이용하여 문장을 만들어 본다.

02 '만약 ~이라면'의 뜻의 if를 활용하여 조건절을 만든다. if가 이끄는 절이 부사절일 때는 미래시제 대신 현재시제를 쓰는 것에 유의한다.

단원별 모의고사
p.105~108

01 ④	02 ④	03 (m)iss	04 ⑤
05 ②	06 (1) over (2) in		07 ②, ⑤
08 ③	09 동물 보호 센터에서 근무하는 사람들		
10 ④	11 make it at	12 ②	13 ②
14 ②	15 If Mary sleeps early, we will go to the theater at night.		
	16 ⑤	17 (1) cutting → cut (2) to burn → burn[burning]	18 ⑤
19 ②	20 ⑤	21 He will get better if he gets enough rest.	
	22 enough	23 ④	
24 ④	25 didn't you	26 ②	27 ①
28 posters	29 ④	30 ③	

01 ④는 유의어 관계이고 나머지는 반의어 관계이다.

02 take care of: ~을 돌보다 / thanks to ~덕분에

03 miss: 놓치다, 그리워하다.

04 ⑤는 lend(빌려주다)의 영영풀이다.

05 take[have] a break: 휴식을 취하다 / put up: ~을 내붙이다, 게시하다

06 (1) over there: 저쪽에서 (2) in need: 어려움에 처한

07 '나는 ~할 예정이다'라는 뜻의 I'm going to ~, I'm planning to ~.로 표현할 수 있다.

08 주어진 문장은 '너는 다른 친구들도 데려와도 돼.'라는 의미로, '알겠어. 내 이웃인 Nancy에게 물어볼게.'라는 문장 앞에 와야 한다.

09 They는 동물 보호 센터에서 근무하는 사람들을 가리킨다.

10 take care of: ~을 돌보다 / be good at: ~을 잘하다

11 make it: 시간에 대다, 만나다 / at + 시각

12 ② 지나가 어떤 동물을 기르는지는 알 수 없다.

13 saw가 지각동사이므로 목적격 보어로 동사원형이나 현재분사가 와야 한다. '테니스 치다'는 play tennis로 한다.

14 조건을 나타내는 if절에서는 현재시제가 미래시제를 대신한다.
  ② will go → go

15 조건을 나타내는 if절에서는 현재시제가 미래시제를 대신한다.

16 ⑤에서 목적어 your number와 목적보어의 관계가 수동이므로 현재분사(calling) 대신 과거분사(called)가 와야 한다.

17 (1) 나무가 베어진 것은 수동의 의미이므로 과거분사형인 cut이 적절하다. (2) 지각동사 saw의 목적격 보어로 원형동사나 -ing형이 온다.

18 ⑤는 '만일 ~라면'의 의미의 접속사이고, 나머지는 '~인지 아닌지'라는 의미의 접속사로 쓰였다.

19 주어진 문장은 '그는 이상한 소리를 내고 있었다.'는 의미로, 무슨 문제가 있는지 묻는 말 앞에 오는 것이 적절하다.

20 상대방의 증상을 묻는 표현이 쓰여야 한다. ⑤는 '너는 왜 그렇게 무서워하는 거야?'라는 뜻이다.

21 if 조건절은 의미상 미래이더라도 현재시제를 쓴다.

22 필요하거나 원하는 만큼 많은: 충분한

23 when: ~할 때

24 Let me ~: 내가 ~하겠다

25 주어가 you이고 동사가 일반동사 과거형이므로 부가의문문은 didn't you가 맞다.

26 too: 또한

27 역접의 접속사 but이 알맞다.

28 인칭대명사 them은 앞에 나온 복수명사를 가리킨다.

29 about: ~에 대한 / on: ~(위)에

30 Sheila는 그녀의 집 근처를 걷고 있을 때, 잃어버린 고양이에 대한 포스터를 보았다고 언급되었다.

Be Active, Be Safe!

핵심 Check
p.114~115

1 (1) Have, read / have (2) Have, heard / haven't

2 (1) shouldn't use, sorry (2) Don't / not / shouldn't

  (3) think, cold / better not drink

시험대비 실력평가
p.112

01 ⑤	02 ②	03 ④	04 careless
05 ③	06 teenage	07 make	08 ②

01 ①, ②, ③, ④는 모두 clothes(옷)에 속한다.

02 for the first time: 처음으로 / look at: ~을 보다

03 대개 그것을 따라 집들이 있는, 도시나 읍 또는 마을의 도로: street(길, 도로)

04 반의어의 관계이다. 기억하다 : 잊다 = 주의 깊은 : 부주의한

05 over there: 저기에

06 열세 살에서 열아홉 살 사이의 나이인: teenage(십대의)

07 make noise: 떠들다, 소란 피우다

08 out of: ~에서 / lots of: 많은

교과서 대화문 익히기

Check(√) True or False
p.116

1 T 2 F 3 T 4 F

서술형 시험대비
p.113

01 (1) colorful (2) princess (3) safe

02 (1) for example (2) had, fun (3) look at

03 (1) during (2) Even (3) following (4) someday

04 (1) actually (2) advice (3) dangerous

05 (1) good at (2) hear of (3) look for (4) keep in mind

06 (1) (r)ide (2) (c)limb (3) (p)ast

01 (1) 명사에 -ful을 붙이면 형용사가 된다. (2) 남성명사에 -ess를 붙이면 여성명사가 된다. (3) 반의어 관계이다. 위험한 : 안전한 = 강한 : 약한

02 (1) for example: 예를 들면 (2) have a lot of fun: 아주 재미있게 지내다 (3) look at: ~을 보다

03 (1) during: ~ 중에 (2) even: ~도, ~조차 (3) following: 다음에 나오는 (4) someday: 언젠가

04 (1) actually: 실제로, 사실 / actual: 실제의 (2) advice: 충고 / advise: 충고하다 (3) dangerous: 위험한 / danger: 위험

05 (1) be good at: ~을 잘하다 (2) hear of: ~에 대해 듣다 (3) look for: ~을 찾다 (4) keep in mind: ~을 명심하다

06 (1) ride: 타다 (2) climb: 오르다 (3) past: 과거

교과서 확인학습
p.118~119

Get Ready - 2

1 at, great / riding, know / What / special, riding

2 Don't, into / Why / shouldn't, without, Put, on

3 Look, over, like, take, front / over / okay

4 watch, in / up, birds / right

Start Off - Listen & Talk A

1 ever, climber / seen, on / climbing, camp, join / but, climb / right

2 Have, heard / haven't / favorite, concert, Can / shouldn't, too / right

Start Off - Listen & Talk B

heard of / when / doing, for / should bring / should, keep / shouldn't, when / in mind

Step Up - Real-life Scene

It's, see / hi, up / isn't, chat, heard / want / Guess, going / great / up, scenery / Be, use, while / right. Thank, send, later

Express Yourself A

1 heard, haven't, Who / singer, actor, figure / Sounds, take / Let's

2 take, painting / worry, real, So, front / Can, selfies, not

시험대비 기본평가
p.120

01 better not	02 ③	03 ②	04 ③

01 금지를 나타낼 때는 should not[shouldn't]이나 had better not
을 쓴다.

02 '~에 가 본 적 있니?'라고 경험을 물을 때는 Have you been ~?
표현을 사용한다. '전에'는 before로 쓴다.

03 B의 답변으로 보아, 빈칸에는 금지를 나타내는 should not을
사용한 문장이 들어가야 한다.

04 현재완료로 경험을 묻는 말에 부정으로 답할 때는 No, I
haven't.라고 한다.

시험대비 실력평가
p.121~122

01 ⑤	02 Have, ever / have	03 ③
04 ④	05 ④	06 heard	07 ②
08 ①, ③	09 ⑤	10 ④	11 ⑤
12 Actually	13 scenery	14 ⑤

01 금지의 표현은 명령문 「Don't+동사원형 ~.」을 쓰거나 You
shouldn't + 동사원형 ~. / You'd better not + 동사원형 ~
을 쓸 수 있다.

02 경험을 묻는 현재완료를 쓴다.

03 넌 여기서 셀피를 찍으면 안 돼. 반 고흐의 그림이 네 뒤에 있어.
- 엄마, 걱정하지 마세요. 그건 그의 진짜 그림이 아니에요. 그래
서 그 앞에서 셀피를 찍을 수 있어요. - 정말이지? 재미있겠다.
나도 여기서 셀피를 찍을 수 있을까? - 물론이죠.

04 영화를 본 경험이 있는지 묻는 말에 본 적이 없다고 답하며 '너는
봤니?'라고 상대방에게 되묻는 표현이다. 대화의 흐름상 현재완
료형으로 물어야 하므로 ④ Have you (seen it)?가 적절하다.

05 B가 자기의 행동을 사과하고 있으므로 잘못된 행동을 금지하는
말이 와야 알맞다. ④ leave computers on: 컴퓨터를 켠 채로
두다

06 현재완료이므로 'have+과거분사'의 형이 알맞다.

07 on TV: 텔레비전으로

08 금지의 표현인 must not, should not, had better not가 들어가
야 한다.

09 ⑤ 암벽 등반을 반대한 것이 아니라 너무 높이 올라가지 말라고
말했다.

10 What is up?: 무슨 일 있니?

11 부가의문문이므로 is의 부정형인 isn't가 오고, this는 인칭대명
사 it으로 바꾼다.

12 문장 전체를 수식하는 부사가 되어야 한다.

13 여러분 주위에서 볼 수 있는 땅, 물, 식물들: scenery(경치, 풍경)

14 ⑤ 민준이가 얼마나 많은 사진을 소민에게 보낼지는 위 대화를
통해 알 수 없다.

서술형 시험대비
p.123

01 shouldn't	02 Have / haven't
03 (B) – (C) – (D) – (A)	
04 have → haven't	05 Rock Boys
06 but	07 actor	08 Elvis의 모습

01 금지를 나타낼 때는 should not[shouldn't]나 must not[mustn't]
등을 쓸 수 있다.

02 경험을 나타내는 현재완료 문장이다.

03 저 소년을 봐. 그는 대단하다. - 그는 MTB를 타고 있어. 넌 그
것에 대해 알고 있니? - 아니. 그게 뭐지? - 산에 오르기 위한 특
별한 자전거야.

04 No로 시작하는 부정문이므로 haven't로 고쳐야 한다.

05 It은 인칭대명사로 앞에 나온 단수명사를 받는다. Rock Boys는
그룹의 명칭이므로 단수 취급한다.

06 앞뒤의 내용이 반대되는 개념이므로 but이 알맞다.

07 연극이나 영화에서 연기하는 것이 직업인 사람: actor(배우)

08 it은 위 문장의 a figure of Elvis를 받는다.

교과서
Grammar

핵심 Check
p.124~125

1 (1) done (2) have / eaten (3) has lived (4) for
2 (1) Though (2) Though (3) Though (4) Although

시험대비 기본평가
p.126

01 (1) has been (2) been (3) finished
   (4) has just finished (5) arrived (6) did you reach
02 (1) Because → Though / Although
   (2) since → though / although
   (3) As → Though / Although
03 (1) He has been sick in bed since last Friday.
   (2) How long have you known Miss Smith?
   (3) Have you ever read the Christmas Carol?
   (4) My father hasn't read the newspaper yet.

01 (1) 부사구 since ~가 있으므로 현재완료가 맞다. (2) '~에 다
녀오다'=have been to (3) two hours ago와 같이 명백한 과
거 시점을 나타내는 부사구가 있으므로 현재완료가 아닌 과거시
제로 써야 한다. (4) just와 함께 '이제 막 마쳤다'라는 의미이므
로 현재완료가 맞다. (5) yesterday와 같이 명백한 과거 시점

을 나타내는 부사가 있으므로 현재완료가 아닌 과거시제로 써야 한다. (6) 의문사 when은 특정 시점에 대해 묻는 의문사이므로 현재완료와 함께 쓸 수 없다.

02 '비록 ~이지만'의 의미를 나타내는 접속사 though나 although 를 사용해야 한다.

03 (1) 계속 용법의 현재완료이다. (2) 계속 용법의 현재완료이다. (3) 경험 용법의 현재완료이다. (4) 완료 용법의 현재완료이다.

시험대비 실력평가

01 ⑤   02 ⑤   03 ④
04 T(t)hough 05 have   06 ①, ④   07 ④
08 Though the traffic was heavy, we arrived on time. / We arrived on time though the traffic was heavy.   09 ④   10 ④   11 not
12 ③   13 since   14 ①   15 ②
16 Although[Even though/Though] he played well, he lost the soccer game.   17 ③   18 ④
19 ②   20 has been absent   21 yet
22 ②   23 ④

01 계속을 나타내는 현재완료이다.
02 though: 비록 ~이지만
03 계속을 나타내는 현재완료이다.
04 though: ~이지만(접속사); 그러나, 하지만(부사)
05 「have+p.p.」로 현재완료 시제로 쓰인 문장이다.
06 whether: ~인지 아닌지 / as though: 마치 ~처럼
07 현재완료의 경험 용법이 사용된 문장에서 빈도부사 never는 have와 been 사이에 위치해야 한다.
08 though로 시작하는 부사절은 주절의 앞이나 뒤에 올 수 있다.
09 계속을 나타내는 현재완료이다.
10 although: 비록 ~이지만
11 앞 문장이 현재완료 결과의 문장이므로 '나의 엄마는 쇼핑에 가고 여기 없다.'의 뜻이 되어야 한다.
12 though는 but을 써서 같은 의미로 바꿔 쓸 수 있다.
13 '~한 이래로'는 since로 나타낸다.
14 빈칸 뒤의 내용이 '나는 잠을 자지 않으려고 노력했다'의 의미이므로 문맥상 졸렸다는 내용이 들어가야 한다.
15 현재완료형으로 물었으므로 현재완료형으로 대답해야 한다.
16 While은 Though[Even though/Although] 등의 양보 접속사로 바꿔 써야 한다.
17 though는 '비록 ~이지만'의 뜻으로 although, even though 등과 같은 의미로 사용된다.
18 ④와 같이 when ~이 명백한 과거의 시점을 나타낼 때는 현재완료 시제는 쓸 수 없다. (has been → was)
19 ② though를 이유를 나타내는 접속사 as나 because로 고쳐야

자연스럽다.
20 결석을 얼마나 오랫동안 했는지 물었으므로 현재완료(have+p.p.) 로 쓴다.
21 yet: 1. 이미, 벌써(의문문) 2. 아직(부정문)
22 첫 번째 빈칸에는 양보의 접속사 though, although, even though 등이 들어가고, 두 번째 빈칸에는 이유의 접속사 as, because 등이 들어간다.
23 ④의 has gone은 '~에 가고 없다'는 의미의 현재완료 결과 용법이다. 나머지는 모두 현재완료 경험의 용법으로 쓰였다.

서술형 시험대비

01 (1) have, finished   (2) has not returned
   (3) has gone to
02 (1) Though[Although]   (2)though[although]
03 (1) has gone → went   (2) already → yet
04 T(t)hough
05 (1) has seen → saw   (2) is → has been
06 (1) He has been to Italy many times.
   (2) I have been very busy these days.
   (3) I have never visited Paris before.
07 (1) before   (2) that   (3) since   (4) because   (5) if
   (6) though
08 (1) I went to London four years ago.
   (2) When did you see a white lion?
   (3) I often played with her when I was a child.
   (4) He was ill in bed last month.
09 (1) Because → Although / Though
   (2) as → although / though
10 (1) He has lived in New York since 1970.
   (2) Have you finished reading this story yet?
   (3) I have seen the movie once.
11 (A)lthough

01 (1) 현재완료 완료 용법 (2) yet은 과거에서 현재까지 아직 완료 되지 않은 상태를 말한다. (3) 현재완료 결과 용법
02 양보의 접속사는 though, although, even though 등이 쓰인다.
03 (1) 과거를 나타내는 부사구가 있으므로 현재완료 시제가 아니라 과거시제를 써야 한다. (2) 부정문에서 '아직'의 뜻으로는 yet을 쓴다.
04 though가 문장 끝에 올 때는 부사로 '그러나, 하지만'의 뜻으로 쓰 인다.
05 (1) 과거를 나타내는 부사구가 있으므로 현재완료 시제가 아니라 과거시제를 써야 한다. (2) 계속을 나타내는 현재완료가 알맞다.
06 (1) 현재완료 경험 용법 (2) 일정한 기간을 나타내는 부사구 (these days)는 현재완료와 함께 쓰일 수 있다. (3) 현재완료 경

20 정답 및 해설

07 (1) before: ~하기 전에 (2) so ~ that ...: 아주 ~해서 …하다 (3) since: ~부터, ~한 이래 (4) because: ~이기 때문에 (5) if: 만일 ~한다면 (6) though: 비록 ~이지만

08 (1) 과거 시점을 나타내는 four years ago가 있으므로 과거시제로 쓴다. (2) when은 과거의 특정 시점을 묻는 표현이므로 과거시제로 써야 한다. (3) when 이하의 절이 과거의 특정 시점을 나타내므로 과거시제로 쓴다. (4) '지난달(last month)'이라는 명백한 과거 시점이 있으므로 과거시제로 나타낸다.

09 '비록 ~이지만'의 의미를 나타내는 접속사 though나 although를 사용해야 한다.

10 (1) 현재완료 계속 용법 (2) 현재완료 완료 용법 (3) 현재완료 경험 용법

11 although: 비록 ~이지만(= though, even though)

[교과서] Reading

확인문제 p.132

1 T 2 F 3 F 4 T 5 F

확인문제 p.133

1 T 2 T 3 F 4 T 5 F

교과서 확인학습 A p.134~135

01 Have, heard
02 take, yourself
03 club, for, for
04 Here, about
05 people, take
06 Though, answer
07 Look
08 used, herself
09 nervous
10 why
11 think, first
12 probably, teenage
13 take, like
14 take, tricks
15 also, fun
16 example, famous
17 special, take
18 touch, even
19 following
20 Though, riding, like
21 just, brush, painting
22 exist
23 visited, before
24 don't, yourself
25 look, but
26 so
27 safe
28 should, when, places
29 could, time, fall
30 safety
31 take, while
32 pose, wild
33 Never, places
34 use, better
35 things, take
36 post, website
37 watered, school
38 also, at, times
39 at, those
40 about, create

교과서 확인학습 B p.136~137

1 Have you ever heard of a "selfie"? When you take a photograph of yourself, it's a selfie.

2 The students from Minji's photo club have searched for information about selfies for one month.

3 Here are some of their presentations about selfies.

4 Did people in the past take selfies?

5 Though it wasn't easy at that time, the answer is yes.

6 Look at this photo of Princess Anastasia. She used a mirror to take a picture of herself.

7 She looks nervous. Can you guess why?

8 Well, I think it was her first selfie.

9 And it was probably the world's first teenage selfie ever.

10 You can take selfies at world-famous places like Big Ben and the Leaning Tower of Pisa.

11 To take great pictures, just do fun poses and use camera tricks.

12 You can also visit special museums to take fun selfies.

13 For example, there is a famous selfie museum in the Philippines.

14 It has special spots to take selfies.

15 You can touch the paintings and even step inside them.

16 Look at the following pictures.

17 Though the boys are not really riding horses, it looks like they are.

18 Though the man is just holding a big brush, it looks like he is painting the Mona Lisa.

19 Selfie museums exist in Korea, too. I have visited one in Chuncheon before.

20 Why don't you go there yourself? These selfies look great, but were they a good idea?

21 I don't think so. They don't look safe.

22 You should take special care when you take selfies in the wild or at high places like these.

23 A monkey could bite you at any time, or you

21

could fall.

24 Here are some safety tips:

25 Don't take selfies while you're walking.

26 Do not pose with or near wild animals.

27 Never take selfies in dangerous places.

28 I think we can use selfies to make a better school life.

29 We can do good things at school and take selfies.

30 Then we can post the photos on our school website.

31 I've watered the plants and flowers at school for one month.

32 I've also helped the teacher at the school library many times.

33 Look at my selfies of those things.

34 How about joining me to create a better school life?

시험대비 실력평가
p.138~141

01 ③	02 ④	03 ③	04 ⑤

05 ② 　06 her → herself 　07 여러분은 그녀가 왜 긴장돼 보이는지 추측할 수 있나요? 08 ⑤

09 ⑤	10 ②	11 ③	12 ①, ④
13 ③	14 Why	15 ②	16 ③

17 ② 　18 여러분은 야생이나 이와 같이 높은 곳에서 셀피를 찍을 때 특별한 주의를 기울여야 합니다. 19 ⑤

20 ⑤ 　21 그리고 나서 우리는 학교 웹사이트에 사진을 올릴 수 있다. 　22 ① 　23 What

24 ⑤	25 ①	26 ①, ④	27 ③

28 ① 　29 She used a mirror to take a picture of herself. 　30 ③

01 '~할 때'의 뜻을 나타내는 접속사 when이 알맞다.

02 search for: ~을 찾다 / for+수사가 붙은 기간

03 ⓓ, ③ 1문형 ① 3문형 ② 2문형 ④ 5문형 ⑤ 4문형

04 마지막 문장에 민지의 사진 동아리 학생들의 셀피에 대해 수집한 정보가 제시될 것이라고 서술하고 있다.

05 거울로 셀피를 찍은 Anastasia 공주의 사진을 보라는 뜻이므로 과거에도 셀피를 찍었다고 서술하는 문장 다음에 와야 한다.

06 전치사 of의 목적어가 주어 자신이므로 재귀대명사를 써야 한다.

07 why 뒤에는 she looks nervous가 생략된 것이다.

08 주어진 문장의 It은 a famous selfie museum을 받는다.

09 ⓐ와 ⑤는 전치사로 쓰였고, 나머지는 모두 동사로 쓰였다.

10 빈칸 뒤에 special museums에 대한 구체적인 예가 나오고 있다.

11 위 글은 셀피를 찍기 위한 재미있는 장소를 소개하고 있다.

12 문맥상 '비록 ~이지만'의 뜻인 양보의 접속사가 알맞다.

13 exist: ~에 있다, 존재하다

14 Why don't you ~?: ~하지 그래?

15 ② 소년들은 말을 타고 있는 것처럼 보인다고 언급되어 있다.

16 위험한 장소에서 셀피를 찍을 때는 주의해야 한다는 문장 앞에 와야 한다.

17 상반되는 절을 연결해 주는 접속사 but이 알맞다.

18 should: ~해야 한다 / like: ~와 같은

19 '~하는 동안'의 뜻인 while이 알맞다.

20 ⓐ, ⑤ 목적을 나타내는 부사적 용법 ①, ③, ④ 명사적 용법 ② 형용사적 용법

21 then: 그 다음에 / post: 올리다

22 for+수사가 붙은 기간

23 How[What] about -ing?: ~하는 게 어때?

24 ⑤ 소윤이가 왜 선생님을 도왔는지는 알 수 없다.

25 hear of: ~에 대해 듣다 / take a photograph of: ~의 사진을 찍다

26 ⓒ, ①, ④ 계속 ② 경험 ③ 완료 ⑤ 결과

27 문맥상 '비록 ~이지만'의 뜻인 though가 알맞다.

28 look at: ~을 보다

29 to take a picture of: ~의 사진을 찍기 위해

30 ③ 민지는 Anastasia 공주가 처음으로 셀피를 찍었다고 생각한다.

서술형 시험대비
p.142~143

01 여러분은 빅벤과 피사의 사탑과 같은 세계적으로 유명한 장소에서 셀피를 찍을 수 있습니다. 　02 poses

03 For 　04 필리핀에 있는 유명한 셀피 박물관

05 I can go to special museums to take fun selfies.

06 at 　07 비록 그 소년들은 말을 타고 있는 것은 아니지만, 말을 타고 있는 것처럼 보입니다. 　08 a selfie museum 　09 yourself 　10 they were a good idea 　11 safely → safe 　12 at

13 dangerous 14 야생 동물이 물거나 높은 데서 떨어질 위험이 있기 때문이다. 　15 나는 우리가 더 나은 학교생활을 만들기 위해 셀피를 이용할 수 있다고 생각해요.

16 watered 　17 for 　18 about

01 like: ~와 같은

02 예를 들면 당신을 사진 찍거나 그릴 때 당신이 서 있거나, 앉거나, 또는 누워 있거나 하는 특별한 방법: pose(자세, 포즈)

03 for example: 예를 들면

06 look at: ~을 보다

07 it looks like (that) ~: ~처럼 보이다

08 부정대명사 one은 앞에 나온 'a+보통명사'를 받는다.

09 주어진 you를 강조하는 재귀대명사로 고쳐야 한다.

10 so는 지시대명사로 앞 문장에 나온 긍정의 내용을 받는다.

11 감각동사 look의 보어로 형용사가 와야 한다.

12 at any time: 어느 때고

13 danger의 형용사형으로 고쳐야 한다.

15 I think 뒤에는 명사절을 이끄는 접속사 that이 생략되었다.

16 현재완료 구문이므로 water의 과거분사형인 watered로 고쳐야 한다.

17 for+수사가 붙은 기간

18 How about -ing?: ~하는 게 어때요?

영역별 핵심문제   p.145~149

01 ②	02 ③	03 past	04 ④
05 ⑤	06 for	07 hang up	08 H(h)ave
09 ③	10 ④	11 this → it	12 what
13 careful	14 ⑤	15 ④	16 ③
17 ④	18 ④	19 Although it was cold,	

there were a lot of people in the park.   20 ③

21 ④	22 ④	23 ②	24 ③
25 ①	26 Even if[though]		27 exciting
28 ④	29 ③	30 ②	31 ④

32 a famous selfie museum (in the Philippines)

33 비록 그 남자는 단지 커다란 붓을 잡고 있지만,
모나리자를 그리고 있는 것처럼 보입니다.   34 ①

| 35 ③ | 36 safety | 37 ②, ④ |

01 ①, ③, ④, ⑤는 반의어의 관계이고, ②는 유의어의 관계이다.

02 • Kate는 그에게서 아직 편지를 받지 못했다. • 그가 몸을 돌려 뒤를 보았다. • 그는 그 장소를 어려움 없이 찾았다. • 그가 또 무슨 다른 말을 했나요?

03 과거 : 현재 : 미래

04 be good for: ~에 좋다

05 어떤 사람을 속이기 위해 의도된 행위: trick(속임수, 장난)

06 for the first time: 처음으로 / for example: 예를 들면

07 hang up: 전화를 끊다

08 경험을 묻고 대답하는 대화이다.

09 You'd better not + 동사원형 ~은 '~하지 않는 게 좋겠다.' 라는 의미로 금지하는 표현이다.

10 What's up?: 무슨 일이니? / hang up: 전화를 끊다

11 this는 부가의문문에서 인칭대명사 it으로 바뀐다.

12 Guess what?: 있잖아., 알겠니?

13 be동사 다음은 보어 자리이므로 형용사가 되어야 한다. care에 -ful을 붙이면 형용사형이 된다.

14 문맥상 '~하는 동안'의 뜻인 while이 알맞다.

15 ④ 소민은 민준에게 걷는 동안은 전화기를 사용하지 말라고 충고했다.

16 과거에서 지금까지의 경험을 나타내는 문장이므로 현재완료

(have+p.p.) 시제로 써야 한다.

17 though: 비록 ~이지만

18 계속을 나타내는 현재완료이다.

19 although: 비록 ~이지만

20 ③ last week라는 특정 과거 시점이 있으므로 현재완료가 아니라 과거시제로 써야 한다. (have climbed → climbed)

21 although: 비록 ~이지만(= though, even though)

22 have[has] gone to ~: ~에 갔다(그래서 여기 없다) 결과를 나타내는 현재완료이다.

23 보기, ② 경험 ①, ④ 계속 ③ 완료 ⑤ 결과

24 ③ though를 이유를 나타내는 접속사 as나 because로 고쳐야 한다.

25 ① ~ ago라는 과거 시점이 있으므로 과거시제 went가 맞다.

26 though: 비록 ~이지만(= although, even though)

27 사물이 사람을 흥미 있게 하는 것이므로 현재분사형의 형용사를 써야 한다.

28 '많은'의 뜻이지만 뒤에 복수명사가 오므로 much는 쓸 수 없다.

29 문맥상 '~할 때'의 뜻인 when이 알맞다.

30 ② BMX의 가격은 언급되지 않았다.

31 for example: 예를 들면

32 it은 인칭대명사로 앞에 나온 단수명사를 받는다.

33 it looks like (that): ~처럼 보이다

34 Why don't you ~?: ~하지 그래요?

35 ③ 그림들에 손을 댈 수 있다고 언급되어 있다.

36 safe: 안전한 / safety: 안전

37 since와 as though는 양보를 나타내는 접속사가 아니다.

단원별 예상문제   p.150~153

01 ④	02 ②	03 arrival	04 ④
05 in mind	06 ④	07 ④	08 ④
09 bird watching	10 ③	11 ②	

12 새를 관찰할 때 아무 소리도 내지 않는 것   13 ⑤

14 ③	15 ⑤	16 has lived	17 I have

not seen him since I was eleven.   18 ②

| 19 ④ | 20 ⑤ | 21 ③ | 22 ④ |

23 과거 사람들이 셀피를 찍는 것   24 ⑤

25 Anastasia가 처음으로 셀피를 찍고 있었기 때문이라고 생각한다.   26 ④   27 excited → exciting

| 28 ②, ③ | 29 but | 30 ① | 31 careful |

01 ④는 유의어 관계이고 나머지는 남성명사 - 여성명사 관계이다.

02 be fond of: ~을 좋아하다 / in front of: ~ 앞에

03 동사 : 명사의 관계이다.

04 ④는 push(밀다)의 영영풀이다.

05 keep in mind: ~을 명심하다, ~을 잊지 않다

06 shouldn't는 '~해서는 안 된다'의 뜻으로 금지를 나타낼 때 쓰

는 표현이다.

07 No, I haven't.로 답했으므로 현재완료를 이용해서 경험을 묻는 질문이 와야 알맞다.

08 주어진 문장은 그밖에 또 무엇을 명심해야 하느냐고 묻는 질문이므로 새들을 관찰할 때 아무 소리도 내지 말아야 한다는 문장 앞에 와야 한다.

09 it은 앞에 나온 단수명사를 받는다.

10 for the first time: 처음으로

11 make noise: 떠들다

12 that은 앞에 나온 문장의 내용을 받는다.

13 ⑤ 소년은 처음으로 들새 관찰을 하는 것이므로 취미라고 말할 수 없다.

14 현재완료의 경험 용법이 사용된 문장에서 빈도부사 never는 have[has]와 been 사이에 위치해야 한다.

15 although: 비록 ~이지만

16 since 이하가 과거에서 현재에 이르는 기간을 말하므로 현재완료의 계속 용법이 필요하다.

17 since는 현재완료 시제와 함께 쓰이므로 didn't see는 have not seen이 되어야 한다.

18 though는 but을 써서 같은 의미로 바꿔 쓸 수 있다.

19 시계를 잃어버려 현재 가지고 있지 않다는 것을 나타낸다. 결과를 나타내는 현재완료이다.

20 ⑤ Because 대신에 Though 또는 Although를 써야 한다.

21 ③의 has gone은 '~에 가고 없다'는 의미의 현재완료 결과 용법이다. 나머지는 모두 현재완료 경험 용법으로 쓰였다.

22 이유를 묻는 문장이므로 그녀가 긴장하고 있는 것처럼 보인다는 문장 다음에 와야 한다.

23 it은 앞에 나온 문장의 내용을 받는다.

24 ⓑ, ⑤ 목적을 나타내는 부사적 용법 ①, ③ 명사적 용법 ②, ④ 형용사적 용법

26 주어진 문장은 헬멧과 장갑을 착용하라는 뜻이므로 주의하라는 문장 다음에 와야 한다.

27 사물이 사람을 흥분시키는 것이므로 현재분사형의 형용사를 써야 한다.

28 much는 양을 나타내는 명사에 쓰인다. a few는 '조금'이라는 뜻이다.

29 though와 but은 같은 뜻의 문장으로 바꿔 쓸 수 있다.

30 문맥상 '~할 때'의 뜻인 when이 알맞다.

31 be동사의 보어인 형용사형을 써야 한다.

서술형 실전문제
p.154~155

01 climber 02 seen 03 She will teach rock climbing at a camp. 04 (B) – (C) – (D) – (A)
05 (1) Peter has lived in Peking since 2010.

(2) Tom has been in hospital for a week.
(3) My mother has gone shopping.
06 (1) Though it was windy, it wasn't very cold.
(2) Although Tim often annoyed Anne, she was fond of him.
(3) You must do it though you don't like it.
07 (1) has gone → went (2) have you seen → did you see
(3) have often played → often played
08 heard 09 you → yourself 10 for
11 자기 자신의 사진을 직접 찍는 것이다. 12 to make
13 take 14 plants 15 joining

01 스포츠나 취미로 바위나 산을 오르는 사람: climber(등반가)
02 현재완료 구문이므로 see의 과거분사로 고쳐야 한다.
04 잠깐, 지민. - 왜? - 저 표지판 좀 봐. 여기서 사진 찍으면 안 돼. - 아, 알았어.
05 현재완료(have+p.p.)를 이용해 문장을 완성한다. (1) 현재완료의 계속 용법 (2) 현재완료의 계속 용법 (3) 현재완료의 결과 용법
07 (1) 과거 시점을 나타내는 last year가 있으므로 과거시제로 쓴다. (2) 의문사 when으로 시작하므로 과거시제로 쓴다. (3) when 이하의 부사절이 과거의 특정 시점을 나타내므로 과거시제로 쓴다.
08 현재완료이므로 hear의 과거분사를 쓴다.
09 전치사 of의 목적어가 주어 자신이므로 재귀대명사를 써야 한다.
10 search for: ~을 찾다 / for+수사가 붙은 기간
12 목적을 나타내는 부사적 용법의 to부정사가 알맞다.
13 take selfies: 셀피를 찍다
14 줄기, 잎, 뿌리를 가지고 있으며 땅에서 자라는 살아 있는 것, 특히 나무나 덤불보다 작은 것: plant(식물)
15 전치사 다음에는 동명사형을 써야 한다.

창의사고력 서술형 문제
p.156

|모범답안|
01 (1) I have just sent an e-mail to Jane.
(2) Kate has just cleaned her room.
(3) Mike has already finished his job.
(4) Have you taken your medicine yet?
(5) Mary hasn't sung yet.
(6) You haven't studied enough yet.
(7) Has Tom done his homework yet?
02 (1) Though my mother was sick, she tried to clean the house. / My mother tried to clean the house though she was sick.
(2) Although the food smelled delicious, I didn't feel like eating it. / I didn't feel like eating the food although it smelled delicious.

> (3) Even though I was sick, I didn't want to go to hospital. / I didn't want to go to hospital even though I was sick.

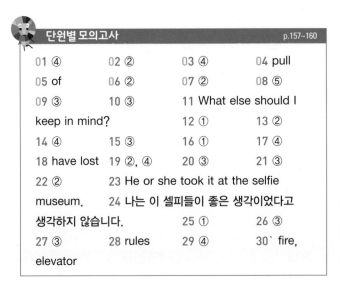

단원별 모의고사
p.157~160

01 ④	02 ②	03 ④	04 pull
05 of	06 ②	07 ②	08 ⑤
09 ③	10 ③	11 What else should I keep in mind?	12 ①	13 ②
14 ④	15 ③	16 ①	17 ④
18 have lost	19 ②, ④	20 ③	21 ③
22 ②	23 He or she took it at the selfie museum.	24 나는 이 셀피들이 좋은 생각이었다고 생각하지 않습니다.	25 ①	26 ③
27 ③	28 rules	29 ④	30 ` fire, elevator

01 be good for: ~에 좋다

02 다른 사람들이나 다른 것들보다 더 좋거나 더 중요한: 특별한 (special)

03 during: ~ 중에, ~ 동안 / else 또[그 밖의] 다른, 다른

04 반의어 관계이다. 안전한 : 위험한 = 밀다 : 끌다

05 hear of: ~에 대해 소식을 듣다 / lots of: 많은

06 너 말을 타본 적 있니? - 응, 있어. 너는 어때? - 아니, 난 없어. 말 타는 거 어땠어? - 재미있었지만, 조금 무섭기도 했어.

07 Have you ever+과거분사 ~?에 대한 응답은 Yes, I have. / No, I haven't.이다. 빈칸 다음의 말로 보아 부정의 대답이 와야 한다.

08 You'd better not+동사원형 ~은 '~하지 않는 게 좋겠다'는 뜻으로 금지하는 표현이므로 You shouldn't + 동사원형 ~.으로 바꿔 쓸 수 있다.

09 hear of: ~에 관해 듣다 / for the first time: 처음으로

10 ⓒ, ③ 형용사적 용법 ①, ④ 명사적 용법 ②, ⑤ 부사적 용법

11 else는 '또[그 밖의] 다른'의 뜻으로 의문대명사 what 뒤에 위치한다.

12 문맥상 '~할 때'의 뜻을 나타내는 when이 알맞다.

13 ② 소년이 들새 관찰을 좋아하는지는 언급되지 않았다.

14 완료를 나타내는 현재완료의 부정문이다.

15 even though: 비록 ~이지만(= though, although)

16 ① ~ ago라는 과거 시점이 있으므로 과거시제 went가 맞다.

17 though: 비록 ~이지만

18 열쇠를 잃어버린 결과가 현재까지 영향을 미치므로 현재완료의 결과 용법으로 나타낸다.

19 though: 비록 ~이지만 (= although, even though)

20 과거에서 지금까지의 경험을 나타내는 문장이므로 현재완료 (have+p.p.) 시제로 써야 한다.

21 hear of: ~에 관해 듣다 / in front of: ~ 앞에서

22 ⓑ, ② 경험 ①, ④ 계속 ③ 완료 ⑤ 결과

23 셀피를 박물관에서 찍었다고 언급되어 있다.

24 so는 지시대명사로 앞 문장의 they were a good idea를 받는다.

25 문맥상 '안전한'이 알맞다.

26 '아니면, 또는'의 뜻으로 선택을 나타내는 접속사 or가 알맞다.

27 ③ 원숭이가 사람을 잘 따르는지는 알 수 없다.

28 당신이 할 수 있는 일과 할 수 없는 일을 알려주는 지침: rule(규칙)

29 문맥상 '비록 ~이리도'의 뜻으로 양보를 나타내는 접속사기 알 맞다.

25

Memories in Your Heart

Conversation

핵심 Check   p.166~167

| 1 ② | 2 ① | 3 ③ | 4 think |

시험대비 실력평가   p.164

| 01 special | 02 secrets | 03 ④ | 04 ② |
| 05 ⑤ | 06 super | 07 ③ | 08 ④ |

01 둘은 반의어 관계다. 두꺼운 : 얇은 – 일반적인 : 특별한

02 숨겨져 있거나 극소수의 사람들에 의해 알려져 있는 것은 '비밀 (secret)'이다. 'all the+복수명사'이므로 secrets가 적절하다.

03 laughter는 명사로 '웃음'이다. '웃다'는 laugh이다.

04 눈에서 흐르는 짠 액체 방울: 눈물

05 희귀하거나 비싸거나 중요하기 때문에 매우 소중한: 귀중한

06 부사 hard를 수식하는 강조어로 '매우'의 의미를 가지는 super 가 적절하다.

07 '그녀는 그에게 축구공을 튀겼다'는 의미가 자연스럽다.

08 그의 축구공은 그에게 금만큼 소중하다(precious)는 의미가 자 연스럽고, 어린 '소년 덕분에'의 의미로 thanks to가 적절하다.

교과서 대화문 익히기

Check(√) True or False   p.168

1 T   2 T   3 T   4 F

서술형 시험대비   p.165

01 (1) one by one   (2) laughter   (3) lost
02 (1) remember, past   (2) under, hen   (3) hot air, looked like   03 (1) take   (2) remember
04 (1) whisper   (2) neighbor   (3) bounce   (4) special
05 (1) (c)ut   (2) (g)et married   (3) (t)hrow   (4) (s)ock puppet

01 (1) 그녀에게 물건을 하나씩 주었다. (2) '그의 양말 인형은 항 상 그의 부모님에게 큰 웃음을 안겨 드렸다.' 동사의 목적어 자 리에 사용되기 때문에 동사 laugh를 명사 형태로 바꾸어야 한 다. (3) '기억을 잃다'는 의미로 동사 lose를 사용해야 하고, she has[she's] 뒤에 사용되므로 과거분사 lost가 적절하다.

02 (1) remember: 기억하다, past: 과거 (2) from under: ~ 아 래에서, hen: 암탉 (3) hot air balloon: 열기구, look like: ~ 처럼 보이다

03 (1) bring '가져오다' ↔ take '가져가다' (2) forget '잊다' ↔ remember '기억하다'

04 (1) 매우 조용히 말하다 (2) 당신 근처에 사는 사람 (3) 표면을 치고 나서 위로 또는 멀리 이동하다 (4) 평범하거나 일반적이지 않은

교과서 확인학습   p.170~171

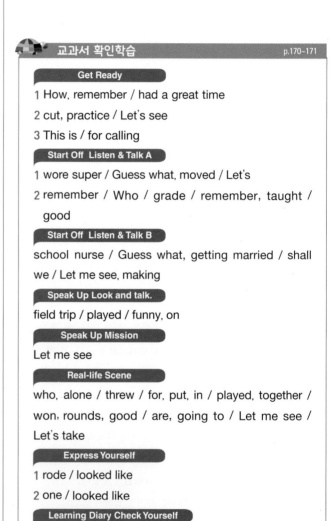

Get Ready
1 How, remember / had a great time
2 cut, practice / Let's see
3 This is / for calling

Start Off Listen & Talk A
1 wore super / Guess what, moved / Let's
2 remember / Who / grade / remember, taught / good

Start Off Listen & Talk B
school nurse / Guess what, getting married / shall we / Let me see, making

Speak Up Look and talk.
field trip / played / funny, on

Speak Up Mission
Let me see

Real-life Scene
who, alone / threw / for, put, in / played, together / won, rounds, good / are, going to / Let me see / Let's take

Express Yourself
1 rode / looked like
2 one / looked like

Learning Diary Check Yourself
singing competition / super / funny

시험대비 기본평가   p.172

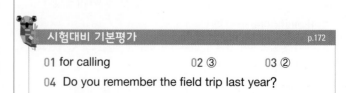

01 for calling   02 ③   03 ②
04 Do you remember the field trip last year?

01 'thank A for B: B 때문에 A에게 감사하다'는 뜻으로 전치사 for 뒤에 동명사 calling이 적절하다.

02 나머지는 생각할 시간을 달라는 표현이고, ③번은 생각할 시간 요청을 수락할 때 사용하는 표현이다.

03 빈칸 뒤의 내용으로 보아 G는 Ms. Lee를 기억하고 있다는 것을 알 수 있다.

04 일반동사 의문문으로 '조동사+주어+동사원형 ~?' 형태로 사용한다.

01 상대방의 기억 여부를 묻는 표현으로 remember가 일반 동사이므로 조동사 Do로 시작하는 의문문을 완성한다.

02 ④번 앞 문장에 그녀가 모든 판을 이겼다고 했기 때문에 bad를 good으로 바꾸어야 한다.

03 어떤 일에 대해 주의 깊게 생각하고 싶거나 기억하려고 애쓸 때 사용하는 표현

04 흥미롭거나 놀라운 일을 누군가에게 말하기 전에 사용하는 표현

05 What about + -ing?' 구문을 이용하여 영작한다.

01 ③　　02 making a special album　03 ③
04 ⑤　　05 ①　　06 looked like
07 ②　　08 ③　　09 ⑤　　10 ③
11 remember　　12 calling

01 대화를 시작할 때나 대화의 화제를 바꿀 때 사용하는 표현으로 '있잖아'라는 뜻의 'Guess what?'이 적절하다.

02 What about은 뒤에 명사나 동명사를 사용해야 한다.

03 밑줄 친 super는 부사로 '매우, 극도로'의 의미를 가진다. ③번은 부사로 사용이 되었고, 나머지는 형용사로 '멋진, 굉장한'의 의미를 가진다.

04 Ben과 Jenny는 함께 김 선생님을 방문하기로 했다.

05 글의 흐름상 상대방의 기억을 묻는 remember가 자연스럽다.

06 '~처럼 보이다'는 의미로 look이 명사와 함께 사용될 때는 전치사 like가 필요하다.

07 빈칸에는 선행사 the old lady(사람)를 수식하는 절을 이끌고, lives의 주어 역할을 하는 주격 관계대명사 who가 적절하다.

08 (B) '파티를 열다'는 의미로 동사 throw, have, give, hold를 사용한다. 과거형이 적절하다. (C) 동사 cook은 간접목적어 앞에 전치사 for를 사용한다.

09 Let me see.는 상대방에게 생각할 시간을 요청할 때 사용하는 표현으로 '언제 그녀를 방문할 거니?'라는 물음 다음인 (⑤)에 오는 것이 자연스럽다.

10 ③은 내 생일을 기억하느냐는 질문에 '그것은 틀렸어. 7월 26일이다'라고 대답하는 것은 어색하다.

11 어떤 정보를 생각해 내거나 또는 어떤 정보를 기억 속에 보존하다 : remember(기억하다)

12 전치사 for 뒤에는 명사나 동명사가 와야 한다. 동사 call을 동명사로 바꾸어야 한다.

서술형 시험대비 p.175

01 Do you remember Ms. Lee?　02 ④, bad
→ good　03 Let me see[think].　04 Guess what?　05 What about making a special album?

Grammar

핵심 Check p.176~177

1 (1) who/that　(2) which/that
2 (1) which[that]　(2) whom[that]

시험대비 기본평가 p.178

01 ⑤
02 (1) which → who[that]　(2) who → which[that]
(3) whom → which 또는 that　(4) that → whom
03 (1) that has a pretty garden　(2) that he wanted to have　04 (1) whom　(2) which was

01 선행사가 The girl로 사람이며 is singing의 주어 역할을 할 수 있는 주격 관계대명사 who나 that이 적절하다.

02 (1) 선행사가 사람이므로 which를 who나 that으로 고쳐야 한다. (2) 선행사가 사물이므로 who를 which나 that으로 고쳐야 한다. (3) wrote의 목적어 역할을 해야 하며 선행사가 사물이므로 whom을 which나 that으로 고쳐야 한다. (4) 전치사 with의 목적어 역할을 해야 하며 선행사가 사람이므로 that을 whom으로 고쳐야 한다. that은 전치사 다음에 사용할 수 없다.

03 (1) 선행사가 사물이고 주격이므로 which나 that을 쓴다. (2) 선행사가 사물이고 목적격이므로 which나 that을 쓴다.

04 (1) 목적격 관계대명사는 흔히 생략된다. (2) 주격 관계대명사는 생략할 수 없으나 뒤에 분사가 오는 경우 '주격 관계대명사+be동사'를 생략할 수 있다.

시험대비 실력평가 p.179~181

01 ②　　02 This is the book (which[that]) I am looking for.　03 ④　　04 (1) which　(2) who
(3) that　(4) which　(5) whom　(6) who　(7) that

27

05 ⑤　　　06 ②　　　07 (1) which　(2) who is
08 ①　　　09 ①, ②, ④　10 ③　　　11 ①
12 ⑤　　　13 (1) that looked like an elephant
(2) which I took a rest　(3) whom I can trust
14 ③　　　15 ②, ④
16 (1) This is the man who[whom/that] I met
　　 yesterday.
　(2) I don't know the girl who[that] is singing.
　(3) Julie bought a computer which[that] she likes
　　 very much yesterday.
　(4) He completed drawing two pictures
　　 which[that] look very similar.
　(5) Mary took a picture of a man and his dog that
　　 were crossing the road.
　(6) Mike needs a friend who[whom/that] he wants
　　 to play with. 또는 Mike needs a friend with
　　 whom he wants to play.
17 watched the movie that Steve talked about to her
　 last week

01 모두 주격이나 목적격으로 사용된 관계대명사 that이 들어갈 수
　 있지만 ②번은 소유격 관계대명사 whose가 들어가야 한다.
02 for의 목적어 역할을 해야 하며 선행사가 사물이므로 which나
　 that을 쓴다. 또한 목적격 관계대명사이므로 생략해도 좋다.
03 ④ 선행사가 사람인 a cousin이므로 which가 아니라 who가
　 되어야 한다.
04 (1) 선행사가 사물이므로 which (2) 선행사가 사람이므로
　 who (3) 선행사가 사물이므로 that (4) 전치사가 관계대명사
　 바로 앞에 있으므로 which (5) 선행사가 사람이므로 whom
　 (6) who를 목적격 whom 대신 쓸 수 있지만 whom을 who
　 대신 쓰지는 않는다. (7) 선행사가 '사람+동물[사물]'인 경우에
　 는 반드시 관계대명사 that을 써야 한다.
05 ⑤번은 접속사이지만 나머지는 모두 관계대명사이다.
06 주격 관계대명사의 선행사가 사람이면 who나 that을 쓰고 사물
　 이면 which나 that을 쓴다.
07 목적격 관계대명사와 '주격 관계대명사+be동사'는 생략할 수 있
　 다.
08 관계대명사는 접속사와 대명사의 역할을 하므로 목적격 관계대
　 명사가 생략된 ①번은 목적어로 쓰인 it이 없어야 한다.
09 사람을 선행사로 받는 목적격 관계대명사는 whom과 that이다.
　 또한 whom 대신 who를 쓸 수 있다.
10 선행사가 사물이므로 which나 that을 이용하고 목적격이므로
　 목적어로 쓰인 it은 쓰지 말아야 한다.
11 ③번에서는 who를 which나 that으로 바꿔야 하고, ②, ④,
　 ⑤에서는 관계대명사는 접속사와 대명사 역할을 하므로 it이 없
　 어야 한다.

12 관계대명사의 선행사가 사람이면 who, whom이나 that을 쓰
　 고 사물이면 which나 that을 쓴다. 전치사가 관계대명사 바로
　 앞에 있을 때는 that을 쓰지 않는다.
13 관계대명사의 선행사가 사람이면 who, whom이나 that을 쓰고
　 사물이면 which나 that을 쓴다. 전치사가 관계대명사 바로 앞에
　 있을 때는 that을 쓰지 않는다.
14 ③ 전치사가 관계대명사 바로 앞에 있으므로 that이 아니라
　 which를 써야 한다.
15 주어진 문장과 ②, ④번의 who는 주격 관계대명사이다. ①, ⑤
　 번은 목적격 관계대명사이고, ③번은 의문대명사이다.
16 관계대명사의 선행사가 사람이면 who, whom이나 that을 쓰고
　 사물이면 which나 that을 쓴다. 선행사가 '사람+동물'이면 that
　 을 쓴다. 전치사가 관계대명사 바로 앞에 있을 때는 that을 쓰지
　 않는다.
17 목적격 관계대명사 다음에는 '주어+동사'가 이어진다.

서술형 시험대비
p.182~183

01 (1) Sejong was a great King who[that] invented
　　 Hangeul.
　(2) An elephant is an animal which[that] has a
　　 long nose.
　(3) Sharon met a man who[whom, that] she loved
　　 very much.
　(4) Tony bought a nice bag which[that] he gave to
　　 Karen.
　(5) There are Ms. Han and her cats that are playing
　　 together.
02 (1) which Melanie works　(2) which Melanie works
　(3) that Melanie works　(4) Melanie works at
03 (1) who is sitting on a wheelchair
　(2) who is playing cards
　(3) that is sleeping on the chair
04 (1) who → which[that]　(2) which → who[that]
　(3) whom → who[that]　(4) were → was
　(5) it 삭제
05 (1) You can create a scene.
　(2) He bought them at the shop.
　(3) I took them yesterday.
　(4) It can be my friend.
06 (1) She has a son of whom she is very proud. /
　　 She has a son whom she is very proud of.
　(2) Do you like the dog which is jumping near the
　　 piano?
　(3) This is the hospital which I was born in. /
　　 This is the hospital in which I was born.

07 (1) There are a lot of active seniors who[that] share their knowledge and talents.

(2) What is the title of the film which[that] you saw yesterday?

(3) Emma bought a dress which[that] looked very expensive.

(4) The woman who is wearing nice glasses is talking on the phone.

(5) The computer which Mom bought for me last week is really cool.

08 (1) Adelene saves money to buy a computer that she wants.

(2) I have a friend who helps me a lot.

(3) Sam met a man that he worked with two years ago.

01 (1), (3) 선행사가 사람이므로 주격에는 관계대명사 who나 that을, 목적격에는 who나 whom 또는 that을 써야 한다. (2), (4) 선행사가 사물이므로 관계대명사 which나 that을 써야 한다. (5) 선행사가 '사람+동물'이므로 관계대명사 that을 써야 한다.

02 선행사가 사물이므로 which나 that을 쓴다. 전치사를 관계대명사 앞으로 옮길 수 있으나 관계대명사 that은 전치사 다음에 쓸 수 없다. 목적격 관계대명사는 생략 가능하다.

03 관계대명사를 이용하여 질문을 완성한다. 주격 관계대명사일 경우 선행사가 사람이면 who, 사물이면 which가 쓰이며 선행사에 상관없이 that을 쓸 수도 있다.

04 (1) 선행사가 사물이므로 관계대명사 which나 that (2) 선행사가 사람이므로 관계대명사 who나 that (3) 목적격 관계대명사 whom대신 who를 쓸 수 있지만 주격 관계대명사 who 대신에 whom을 쓸 수 없다. (4) a scarf가 선행사이므로 was가 되어야 한다. (5) 관계대명사가 접속사와 대명사의 역할을 하므로 it을 삭제해야 한다.

05 선행사가 사람이면 관계대명사는 who나 that, 사물이나 동물이면 which나 that을 쓴다. 목적격 관계대명사일 경우 whom[who]이나 that, which나 that을 쓴다.

06 (1) 선행사가 사람이고 목적격이므로 whom을 쓴다. (2) 선행사가 동물이고 주격이므로 which를 쓴다. (3) 선행사가 사물이고 목적격이므로 which를 쓴다.

07 (1) 선행사가 사람이고 주격이므로 who나 that을 써야 한다. (2) 선행사가 사물이고 목적격이므로 which나 that을 써야 한다. (3) 선행사가 사물이고 주격이므로 which나 that을 써야 한다. (4) 관계대명사절의 수식을 받는 선행사가 The woman이므로 단수가 적절하다. (5) 관계대명사는 접속사와 대명사의 역할을 하므로 목적어로 쓴 it을 삭제해야 한다.

08 (1) 원하는 컴퓨터: a computer that she wants (2) 나를 도와주는 친구: a friend who helps me (3) 관계대명사 that은 전치사 다음에 쓸 수 없다.

교과서

Reading

확인문제 p.184

1 T 2 F 3 F 4 T 5 F

확인문제 p.185

1 T 2 F 3 T 4 F 5 T 6 F 7 T

교과서 확인학습 A p.186~187

01 What's
02 who, next to
03 who lived there
04 his favorite person, the same as his
05 all his secrets
06 were talking about
07 Poor old lady
08 Why, asked
09 Because she's lost
10 What's
11 something you remember
12 to know more
13 was enjoying
14 he asked
15 Something warm
16 was reading
17 What's a memory
18 brings you laughter
19 cleaning his medal
20 as precious as gold
21 to look for memories
22 went into, from under
23 Next, looked for
24 brought, to
25 Finally
26 as precious as gold
27 one by one
28 all these wonderful things
29 to remember
30 held, whispered to
31 smiled at, performing, for
32 a lot
33 bounced the football
34 My friend
35 one by one
36 each other
37 got, back, with, as hers

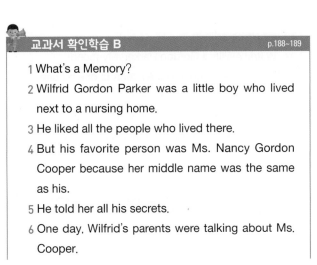

교과서 확인학습 B p.188~189

1 What's a Memory?

2 Wilfrid Gordon Parker was a little boy who lived next to a nursing home.

3 He liked all the people who lived there.

4 But his favorite person was Ms. Nancy Gordon Cooper because her middle name was the same as his.

5 He told her all his secrets.

6 One day, Wilfrid's parents were talking about Ms. Cooper.

7 "Poor old lady," said his mother.

8 "Why is she a poor old lady?" asked Wilfrid.

9 "Because she's lost her memory," said his father.

10 "What's a memory?" asked Wilfrid.

11 "It is something you remember," said his father.

12 Wilfrid wanted to know more, so he went to his neighbors.

13 Ms. Jordan was enjoying the sunlight.

14 "What's a memory?" he asked.

15 "Something warm, my child," she said.

16 Ms. Mitchell was reading a cartoon.

17 "What's a memory?" he asked.

18 "Something that brings you laughter," she said.

19 Mr. Hunter was cleaning his medal.

20 "It's something as precious as gold, young man," he said.

21 So Wilfrid went back home to look for memories for Ms. Cooper.

22 He went into the hen house and took a fresh, warm egg from under a hen.

23 Next, he looked for his sock puppet.

24 It always brought laughter to his parents.

25 Finally, he found his football in his toy box.

26 It was as precious as gold to him.

27 Wilfrid went to Ms. Cooper and gave her the things one by one.

28 "What a strange, sweet child!" thought Ms. Cooper, "He's brought all these wonderful things."

29 Then she started to remember her past.

30 She held the warm egg and whispered to Wilfrid, "Long ago, I found a small blue egg in my aunt's garden."

31 She smiled at the sock puppet and remembered performing a puppet show for her sister.

32 "My sister laughed a lot," said Ms. Cooper.

33 She bounced the football to Wilfrid and remembered him.

34 "Wilfrid? Wilfrid Gordon Parker! My friend!"

35 She also remembered their secrets one by one.

36 The two smiled at each other.

37 Ms. Cooper got her memory back thanks to the little boy with the same middle name as hers.

시험대비 실력평가
p.190~193

01 ①, ④   02 her middle name was the same as his   03 his middle name

04 knowing → to know   05 ②

06 Something that(또는 which) brings you laughter

07 ①, ③   08 ④   09 from under a hen

10 ⑤   11 very   12 this → these

13 middle   14 ⓑ she has   ⓒ What is

15 ③   16 ①, ④

17 Ms. Jordan → Ms. Mitchell   18 ③

19 thanks to 20 hers   21 ⑤

22 (A) 따뜻한 달걀   (B) 자신의 양말 인형   (C) 축구공

23 from under a hen   24 ④   25 ③

26 a fresh egg, a sock puppet, and his precious football   27 ⑤

01 선행사가 사람이므로 주격 관계대명사 that이나 who가 적절하다.

02 'Ms. Cooper의 가운데 이름이 자신의 이름과 같기' 때문이었다.

03 '그의 가운데 이름'을 가리킨다.

04 want는 목적어로 to부정사를 쓰는 것이 적절하다.

05 이 글은 '추억이란 무엇인가?'에 관해 Wilfrid가 알아보는 내용이므로, 제목으로는 ②번 '추억이란 무엇인가?'가 적절하다.

06 'that'이나 'which'를 보충하면 된다.

07 ⓐ와 ②, ④, ⑤는 부사적 용법, ① 명사적 용법, ③ 형용사적 용법

08 ⓑ Cooper 할머니께 드릴 기억이라고 해야 하므로 for가 적절하다. ⓒ '그에게는'이라고 해야 하므로 to가 적절하다.

09 암탉이 '품고 있던' 신선하고 따뜻한 달걀을 꺼냈다. from under: ~ 밑에서

10 give는 to를 사용하여 3형식으로 고친다. gave the things 'to' her one by one

11 감탄문을 평서문으로 고칠 때, very를 사용하는 것이 적절하다.

12 뒤에 복수 명사(things)가 나오므로 지시형용사도 복수로 쓰는 것이 적절하다.

13 Wilfrid Gordon Parker와 Ms. Nancy Gordon Cooper는 둘 다 '가운데' 이름이 Gordon으로 서로 같다.

14 ⓑ she's lost는 she has lost의 줄임말이며, '결과' 용법으로 쓰인 현재완료이다.

15 'Wilfrid'가 'Cooper 할머니'에게 자신의 모든 비밀을 말했다.

16 ⓐ와 ②, ③, ⑤번은 현재분사, ①, ④번은 동명사

17 만화책을 읽고 있으면서 기억이란 너에게 웃음을 가져다주는 것이라고 말한 사람은 'Mitchell 할머니'이다.

18 이 글은 기억에 관해 Wilfrid의 이웃들이 정의를 내리는 내용에 관한 글이므로, 주제는 '기억의 의미'가 적절하다.

19 thanks to: ~ 덕분에

20 '그녀의 것'과 같은 가운데 이름이라고 해야 하므로 소유대명사로 쓰는 것이 적절하다.

21 ⑤ 이 글은 Cooper 할머니가 자신의 이름과 같은 가운데 이름을 가진 어린 소년 덕분으로 기억을 다시 찾게 되었다는 내용의 글이다.

22 ⓐ 닭장에서 신선하고 '따뜻한 달걀'을 가져왔다. ⓑ '자신의 양말 인형'이 그의 부모님에게 언제나 웃음을 가져다주었다. ⓒ '축구공'은 그에게 금만큼 소중했다.

23 from under: ~ 밑에서

24 ④ 축구공이 Wilfrid에게 금만큼 소중한 이유는 알 수 없다. ① Wilfrid가 집으로 돌아간 이유는 Cooper 할머니께 드릴 기억들을 찾기 위해서이다. ② Wilfrid가 닭장에 간 이유는 따뜻한 달걀을 꺼내기 위해서이다. ③ Wilfrid의 부모님에게 항상 큰 웃음을 안겨 드리는 것은 Wilfrid의 양말 인형이다. ⑤ Cooper 할머니를 위해 찾은 따뜻한 달걀, 양말 인형, 축구공이다.

25 ③번 다음 문장의 내용은 주어진 문장으로 인해 Wilfrid가 하게 된 행동을 말하는 것이므로 ③번이 적절하다.

26 '신선한 달걀', '양말 인형', 그리고 '그의 소중한 축구공'을 가리킨다.

27 ⑤ 축구공이 왜 Wilfrid에게 소중한지는 대답할 수 없다. ① Yes. get along well with: ~와 잘 지내다, ② Ms. Nancy Gordon Cooper. ③ They say that Ms. Cooper has lost her memory. ④ No.

서술형 시험대비
p.194~195

01 ③ him → his

02 It is something that(또는 which) you remember

03 the same middle name

04 she's lost her memory   05 doesn't have

06 A memory

07 (a) warm egg   (b) laughter   (c) football
(d) precious   08 (A) home   (B) for   (C) brought

09 Wilfrid's[his] sock puppet

10 whispered   11 remembered
performing a puppet show for her sister

12 first → middle

01 'his middle name'을 가리키도록 소유대명사로 고치는 것이 적절하다.

02 목적격 관계대명사 'that 또는 which'가 생략되어 있다.

03 Wilfrid는 Cooper 할머니의 가운데 이름이 그의 것과 같았기 때문에 그녀를 가장 좋아했다.

04 '그녀가 기억을 잃었기' 때문이다.

05 has lost: 과거에 잃어버려서 그 결과 지금 가지고 있지 않다

06 '기억'을 가리킨다.

07 ⓐ 그는 달걀이 따뜻하기 때문에 닭장에 가서 신선하고 '따뜻한 달걀'을 가져왔다. ⓑ 그는 자신의 양말 인형이 그의 부모님에게

항상 '웃음'을 안겨 드렸기 때문에 자신의 양말 인형을 찾았다. ⓒ 그는 축구공이 그에게 금만큼 '소중'하기 때문에 자신의 장난감 상자 속에서 '축구공'을 찾았다.

08 (A) home이 부사로 쓰여 '집에[으로]'라는 뜻이므로 전치사 없이 바로 home을 쓰는 것이 적절하다. (B) 기억을 '찾기' 위해라고 해야 하므로 for가 적절하다. look at: ~을 보다, look for: ~을 찾다, (C) 웃음을 '안겨 드렸다'고 해야 하므로 brought가 적절하다. take: ~을 가지고 가다

09 Wilfrid의 부모들은 '그의 양말 인형'을 볼 때 항상 웃으셨다.

10 whisper: 속삭이다, 오직 한 사람만 당신의 말을 들을 수 있도록 하기 위하여 목 내신 숨을 사용하여 아주 조용하게 말하는 것. held와 시제를 일치시켜서 과거시제로 쓰면 된다.

11 'performing'을 보충하면 된다.

12 Cooper 할머니와 Wilfrid는 '가운데' 이름이 같다.

영역별 핵심문제
p.197~201

01 special   02 ⑤   03 ④   04 ③
05 next   06 ②   07 ④   08 ④
09 looked like 10 ⓐ the hot air balloon ⓑ the rock
11 the old lady who lives alone   12 ③
13 ①, ③, ⑤   14 ③   15 This is the bookmark.
She gave it to me on the last day.
16 (1) Jiwon is wearing the ribbon which[that] Mira
      bought for her.
   (2) Harry chats with the man who[whom, that] he
      made friends with on line.
   (3) Ginseng is a food which[that] can make you
      stay healthy.
   (4) We saw many children who[that] were playing
      soccer together.
17 ②   18 ①   19 ②   20 ③
21 ①, ③   22 ⑤
23 It's something as precious as gold   24 ②
25 ⑤   26 ③
27 (A) Next   (B) What   (C) past
28 His football   29 ②   30 ③

01 반의어 관계다. 함께 : 따로 ↔ 일반적인 : 특별한

02 ⓐ는 형용사 thick을 수식하는 '매우'의 의미를 가지는 부사 super가 적절하다. ⓑ는 '있잖아'라는 의미로 흥미롭거나 놀라운 일을 말하기 전에 화제를 전환할 때 사용하는 Guess what이 적절하다.

03 ④ look for는 '~을 찾다'는 뜻이다.

04 연기를 하거나 음악을 연주함으로써 사람을 즐겁게 하는 일을 하다

05 next to: ~ 바로 옆에

06 Nancy의 중간 이름이 Wilfrid의 중간 이름과 같았다. '~와 똑같은'의 의미로 the same as가 적절하다.

07 ④번은 생각할 시간을 요청하는 표현이 아니다.

08 (C) 작년의 노래 경연대회를 기억하는지 여부를 묻고 → (A) 물론이라는 긍정의 대답과 열심히 연습했다는 내용이 이어지고 → (B) 휴대 전화에 그때 찍은 재미있는 사진이 있다는 내용이 오고 → (D) 마지막으로 '멋지다!'라는 표현으로 대화를 마무리하는 것이 적절하다.

09 두 대화의 빈칸은 '~처럼 보이다'는 look like가 적절하다. 둘 다 과거의 기억에 대한 대화이므로 과거형을 사용한다.

10 it은 앞의 단수명사를 가리키는 인칭대명사로 ⓐ는 열기구를 ⓑ는 바위를 가리킨다.

11 the old lady를 수식하는 주격 관계대명사절을 뒤에 사용한다.

12 ⓒ put A in B 형태로 'A를 B에 넣다'는 의미로 전치사 in은 적절하지만 '닭고기를 잡채에 넣다'는 의미로 japchae를 가리키는 단수 대명사인 it이 적절하다.

13 동사 met의 목적어가 없으므로 목적격 관계대명사가 필요하다. 선행사가 사람이므로 who, whom, that을 쓸 수 있으며 생략할 수도 있다.

14 ③번은 목적격 관계대명사이지만 나머지는 모두 주격 관계대명사이다.

15 선행사가 사물이므로 관계대명사 that으로 연결한 문장이다.

16 (1) bought의 목적어로 쓰인 it을 관계대명사 which나 that으로 (2) with의 목적어로 쓰인 him을 who나 whom, that으로 (3) 주어로 쓰인 It을 which나 that으로 (4) 주어로 쓰인 They를 who나 that으로 연결한다.

17 모두 주격이나 목적격으로 사용된 관계대명사 that이 들어갈 수 있지만 ②번은 소유격 관계대명사 whose가 들어가야 한다.

18 ① 목적격 whom 대신 who를 쓸 수 있지만 who 대신 whom을 쓸 수는 없다.

19 ① I like Christine from whom I got a letter. ③ Dan has two dogs which have brown hair. ④ We saw a rock that looked like a queen's head. ⑤ A computer is a thing that we do many things with.

20 ③ Mom bought me a present that I liked very much.

21 ⓐ와 ①, ③은 명사적 용법, ②와 ⑤는 부사적 용법, ④는 형용사적 용법

22 ⑤는 Hunter 할아버지를 가리키고, 나머지는 다 Wilfrid를 가리킨다.

23 as ~ as 사이에 precious를 쓰면 된다.

24 ⓑ의 his는 '소유대명사'이고, 나머지는 다 '소유격'이다.

25 ⑤번 다음 문장의 It에 주목한다. 주어진 문장의 a memory를 가리키므로 ⑤번이 적절하다.

26 ⓐ와 ③번은 결과 용법, ① 경험 용법, ②와 ④ 계속 용법, ⑤

완료 용법

27 (A) 먼저 닭장에 갔고 '그 다음' 양말 인형을 찾았다고 해야 하므로 Next가 적절하다. to begin with: 우선, 먼저, (B) 명사가 있으므로 감탄문을 만들 때 What이 적절하다. What+a + 형용사+명사! / How+형용사[부사]! (C) '과거'를 기억해내기 시작했다고 해야 하므로 past가 적절하다.

28 '그의 축구공'을 가리킨다.

29 ② the same ... as ~: ~와 (똑)같은 ..., ① usual: 흔히 하는 [있는], 평상시의, 보통의, ⑤ similar: 비슷한

30 ③ 'Cooper 할머니'가 축구공을 바닥에 튀게 해서 'Wilfrid'에게 던져 주었다.

단원별 예상문제 p.202~205

01 special
02 (A) won (B) who[that], next to
03 ④
04 ③
05 ⑤
06 ④
07 ④
08 ②
09 ①
10 ①
11 ③
12 ④
13 ③
14 (1) Jieun is the girl whom[who, that] I like the best.
(2) These are the pictures which[that] were taken by my brother.
15 (A) Something warm (B) you (C) as
16 ②, ⑤
17 ⑤
18 ③
19 He found it in his toy box.
20 one by one 또는 one after another
21 How strange and sweet this[the] child is!
22 ①, ⑤
23 ②
24 ④
25 Ms. Cooper and Wilfrid's

01 유의어 관계이다. 맛있는 = 특별한

02 (A) 매달을 따다는 의미로 동사 win의 과거형 won이 적절하다. (B) 선행사가 사람인 a little boy를 수식하는 관계대명사절을 이끄는 who가 적절하고, '~ 옆에'는 next to가 적절하다.

03 활동적인 노후 생활에 관한 글이므로 (A)에는 그들의 지식과 재능을 나누는(share) 노인들이 많다가 적절하고, (B)는 이전에 과학 선생님이었기 때문에 아이들에게 식물과 새에 관해 가르치기(teach) 위해 공원에서 일한다가 적절하다. (C)에는 농사에 관해 가르치기 때문에 농부(farmer)가 적절하다.

04 물체의 빈 공간, 대개 물체의 표면에 있는 틈[구멍]

05 Ben은 Ms. Park과 함께 사진을 찍자고 Ariel에게 제안하고 있다.

06 주어진 문장은 '어디 보자.'라고 생각할 시간을 요구하는 B의 대답 앞에 오는 것이 적절하다.

07 ④ let은 목적어 뒤에 동사원형을 취하는 동사다.

08 '물론이지. 우리는 재미있는 게임을 했어.'라는 B의 대답으로 보아 ②가 가장 자연스럽다.

09 선생님이 새 학교로 옮기셨다는 말에 ①이 가장 어울리는 대답이다.

10 ⓐ B의 대답으로 보아 Mr. Kim을 기억하는지 묻는 말이 자연스럽다. ⓑ 동사원형 visit과 함께 사용할 수 있는 '~하자'는 제안의 표현으로 Let's가 자연스럽다.

11 ③번만 목적격 관계대명사이고 나머지는 다 주격 관계대명사이다.

12 선행사가 사람과 사물이므로 관계대명사는 that을 써야 한다.

13 선행사가 사람과 사물, 주격과 목적격일 경우에 모두 쓰이는 관계대명사는 that이 적절하다.

14 (1) like의 목적어가 없으므로 목적격 관계대명사를 써야 한다. (2) 선행사가 사물이므로 that이나 which를 써야 한다.

15 (A) -thing으로 끝나는 말은 형용사가 뒤에서 수식해야 하므로 Something warm이 적절하다. (B) '간접목적어+직접목적어'의 순서로 쓸 때는 전치사가 필요 없으므로 you가 적절하다. (C) 동등비교는 as ~ as 사이에 형용사의 원급을 써야 하므로 as가 적절하다. 부정문일 때는 not so ~ as도 가능하다.

16 ⓐ와 ②, ⑤번은 관계대명사, ① 지시대명사, ③ 접속사, ④ 지시형용사

17 Hunter 할아버지는 '기억은 금처럼 소중한 것'이라고 말했다.

18 ⓐ와 ③ 마침내, 마지막으로, ① 처음에는, ② 게다가, ④ 그러므로, ⑤ 무엇보다도, 특히

19 그의 장난감 상자 속에서 축구공을 찾았다.

20 one by one 또는 one after another: 하나하나씩[차례차례]

21 What+a+형용사+명사(+주어 + 동사)! How+형용사[부사](+주어+동사)!

22 ①과 ⑤는 ⓒ에 해당하는 물건들을 찾은 장소이다.

23 ②번 다음 문장의 내용은 주어진 문장 끝에서 Cooper 할머니가 Wilfrid를 기억한 다음에 하는 말이므로 ②번이 적절하다.

24 ⓐ smile at: ~을 보고 미소 짓다, ⓒ 가운데 이름이 자신의 것과 같은(자신의 이름과 같은 가운데 이름을 '가진') 어린 소년

25 Cooper 할머니와 Wilfrid가 공동으로 소유한 것을 나타낼 때는 끝에 's를 붙이는 것이 적절하다.

서술형 실전문제 p.206~207

01 Do you remember the singing competition

02 threw a part, cooked, delicious, card games / next Saturday, take pictures

03 (A) She's getting married next month.
    (B) What about making a special album?

04 (1) This is a picture which[that] we bought at the market.
    (2) That is the house which[that] Tom was born in.
    또는 That is the house in which Tom was born.

---

(3) Marilyn is talking with a man who[that] is wearing a thick coat.

05 As Wilfrid wanted to know more, he went to his neighbors.

06 something warm / something that brings you laughter / something as precious as gold

07 meaning   08 to perform → performing

09 Ms. Cooper and Wilfrid

10 thanks to the little boy with the same middle name as hers

01 과거의 일을 기억하는지 물을 때 'Do you remember ~?'를 이용한다.

03 (A) be동사와 일반동사 get을 함께 이용하여 현재진행형을 만든다. 현재진행형이 미래의 일을 나타낼 때 사용될 수 있다. 결혼하다는 표현은 get married이다. (B) what about은 뒤에 동명사(-ing)를 사용한다.

04 (1) 선행사가 사물이고 목적격이므로 which나 that을 이용한다. (2) 관계대명사가 전치사의 목적격일 경우 전치사는 관계사절의 끝이나 관계대명사 앞에 올 수 있다. that은 전치사 다음에 쓸 수 없으며 목적격 관계대명사는 흔히 생략된다. (3) 선행사가 사람이고 주격이므로 who나 that을 이용한다.

05 so를 없애고 As를 맨 앞에 쓰면 된다.

06 Jordan 할머니는 '따뜻한 것'이라고 말했다. Mitchell 할머니는 '너에게 웃음을 가져다주는 것'이라고 말했다. Hunter 할아버지는 '금처럼 소중한 것'이라고 말했다.

07 Wilfrid는 기억에 대해 더 알기를 원했기 때문에 그의 세 명의 이웃에게 기억의 '의미'에 대해 물었다.

08 remember+to부정사: '미래'에 해야 할 일을 기억하다, remember+동명사: '과거'에 했던 일을 기억하다

09 Cooper 할머니와 Wilfrid를 가리킨다.

10 thanks to: ~ 덕분으로, hers: 그녀의 것

창의사고력 서술형 문제 p.208

|모범답안|

01 (1) A: We rode a hot air balloon in Turkey. Do you remember that?
      B: Of course. It looked like an elephant.
   (2) A: We took pictures of Korean traditional dancers in Korea. Do you remember that?
      B: Sure. We saw them at the town festival.
   (3) A: We saw a rock in Taiwan. Do you remember that?
      B: Of course. It looked like a queen's head.

02 (1) that helps people in need

   (2) that I can be proud of

   (3) that I can look back on with pride

   (4) that can support a lot of people

   (5) that I like

03 (A) that (B) that[which] (C) stressed (D) at

단원별 모의고사

p.209~212

01 ③	02 enter	03 ①
04 the field trip	05 ⑤	06 ③
07 Let's see.	08 ③	09 ④	10 ③
11 ⑤	12 ③	13 ②, ④	14 ①, ⑤
15 ③	16 ②	17 bring → brings
18 ④	19 It always brought his parents
laughter.	20 remembering	21 ③
22 ③	23 her middle name	

01 ③번의 super는 'very, extremely'와 같은 뜻으로 '매우'라는 강조의 뜻을 가진다. 'a main meal eaten in the evening'은 supper(저녁식사)를 설명한 것이다.

02 유의어 관계이다. 대답하다 = 들어가다

03 일부 사람들이 이름과 성 사이에 가지고 있는 이름. ②와 ③은 '성'을 의미하고, ④는 '별명', ⑤는 '이름'을 의미한다.

04 it은 단수 명사를 가리키는 대명사이기 때문에 단수 명사인 the field trip을 가리킨다.

05 (A) smile at: ~을 보고 웃다 (B) remember+동명사(-ing): ~한 것을 기억하다

06 빈칸 뒤 G의 말로 보아 선생님을 기억하고 있다는 것을 알 수 있다.

07 상대방에게 생각할 시간을 요청할 때 사용하는 표현으로 Let's see.가 적절하다.

08 '그것 기억나니?'라는 물음은 사람에 대한 기억을 묻는 것이 아니라 어떤 일에 대한 기억을 묻는 것임을 알 수 있다.

10 ③ 긍정의 대답을 하고 나서 기억나지 않는다고 말하는 것은 어색하다.

11 언제 특별 앨범을 만들지는 대화에 언급되어 있지 않다.

12 (A)는 흥미롭거나 놀라운 일을 말하기 전에 '있잖아'의 의미로 사용이 되는 Guess what?이 자연스럽고, (B)는 생각할 시간을 요청하는 표현인 Let me see.가 적절하다.

13 ①, ③, ⑤는 접속사로 쓰인 that이고, ②와 ④는 관계대명사이다.

14 선행사가 사람이고 주격이므로 who나 that을 써야 한다.

15 ③ 선행사가 사람과 사물이므로 관계대명사는 that을 써야 한다.

16 ⓐ와 ②, ④번은 현재분사, 나머지는 다 동명사

17 선행사가 단수 Something이므로 'brings'로 고치는 것이 적절하다.

18 ④ Hunter 할아버지가 왜 메달을 받았는지는 대답할 수 없다. ① Because he wanted to know more about memory. ② Ms. Jordan did. ③ She was reading a cartoon. ⑤ He said that it is something as precious as gold.

19 to를 없애고 '간접목적어+직접목적어'의 순서로 쓰면 된다.

20 start는 목적어로 to부정사와 동명사를 둘 다 취할 수 있다.

21 ③ Wilfrid에게 축구공은 금만큼이나 소중했다.

22 ③ one by one = one after another: 하나하나씩[차례차례], ① 나란히, ② 서로서로, ④ 자주, 매번, ⑤ 점점, 더욱

23 '그녀의 가운데 이름'을 가리킨다.

Little Red Writing Hood

Reading

교과서

확인문제 p.216

1 T 2 F 3 T 4 F 5 T

확인문제 p.217

1 T 2 F 3 F 4 T 5 F 6 T

교과서 확인학습 A p.218~219

01 Little	02 Scene, In front of
03 comes in with	04 take a break
05 looks into	06 for lunch
07 is shaking	08 to stop, change the story
09 by that	10 Taking, writing
11 shouldn't do	12 come out of
13 Hey there	14 blew my nose
15 Go away	16 so sorry
17 go back into	18 this happened
19 for	20 Where
21 at the end of	22 To himself, for
23 to herself, works	24 Scene
25 happy, excited	26 it's me
27 happily, dance	28 for pleasing
29 that's	30 jumps over
31 dangerous	32 for
33 to	34 By the way
35 Would you like	36 No, thanks
37 Don't worry, What should I do	
38 tired	40 think
41 so glad	42 Who's
43 heard of	44 have
45 changed, got tired	46 change the story
47 you gave to me	48 No problem
49 That'll	50 dancing
51 stop dancing	52 enjoys cookies together

교과서 확인학습 B p.220~221

1 Little Red Writing Hood

2 Scene 1: In front of the three little piggies' house

3 (Red comes in with a basket of cakes and cookies.)

4 Red: Now I can see the three little piggies' house. I'll take a break here under the tree.

5 (Wolf walks in and looks into the house.)

6 Wolf: Baby piggies! They look delicious. I'll eat them for lunch.

7 (Wolf blows the house hard and it is shaking.)

8 Red: Oh, that bad Wolf! What can I do to stop him? Let me see. … That's it! (To Wolf) Hey, you! I'll change the story!

9 Wolf: What do you mean by that?

10 Red: (Taking out a pen and writing something) "There lived three big strong piggies in the house."

11 Wolf: You shouldn't do that!

12 (Wolf blows again, but the three big strong piggies come out of the house.)

13 Three Piggies: Hey there! Why did you blow our house?

14 Wolf: Um … I didn't. I just blew my nose.

15 Three Piggies: Don't do that again here. Go away!

16 Wolf: Okay. I'm so sorry.

17 (The piggies go back into the house.)

18 Wolf: I can't believe this happened. I'm so hungry! (Looking at Red's basket) What are those?

19 Red: These are cookies for Grandma.

20 Wolf: Where does she live?

21 Red: She lives at the end of this road.

22 Wolf: (To himself) Grandma is good for lunch, too. (To Red) See you later. (Wolf leaves.)

23 Red: Bye. (Talking to herself) Hmm …. He's going to Grandma's. I think I should change the story again. (Taking out the pen and writing something) Okay. If my story works, Grandma will be safe. I'll follow him. (Red leaves.)

24 Scene2: Grandma's house

25 (Wolf dances around Grandma. She looks very happy and excited.)

26 Red: (Knocking on the door) Grandma, it's me. Are you okay?

27 Grandma: (Laughing happily and opening the door) Sure, Red. Come on in. I was watching Wolf dance for me.

28 Red: Hey, Wolf. Thank you for pleasing my grandmother.

29 Wolf: Well, that's ….

30 Prince: (Opening the door and running in) Hey, you bad Wolf! (Prince jumps over Wolf.)

31 Red: No, no! Stop. He's not dangerous.

32 Grandma: Right. Look. He is dancing for us.

33 Prince: Really? Wolf, I'm sorry. I'm glad you're kind to Grandma.

34 Wolf: Well, … I'm glad, too. By the way, do you have anything to eat?

35 Red: (Taking some cookies out the basket) Would you like some cookies?

36 Wolf: No, thanks. I don't eat cookies. I like chicken.

37 Red: Don't worry. I'll change the story again. Then you will like eating cookies. (Checking the basket) Oh, I lost my pen. What should I do?

38 Wolf: (Dancing and crying) Oh, no! I'm so tired and hungry now.

39 (Andersen comes in.)

40 Andersen: I think you need my help, right?

41 Red: Oh, Mr. Andersen. I'm so glad you're here.

42 Grandma: (To Red) Who's that?

43 Red: He is Mr. Andersen, the famous writer. Have you ever heard of "The Red Shoes"?

44 Grandma: Yes, I have. Is he the one who wrote that story?

45 Red: Right. (To Andersen) I changed the story, and the poor Wolf got tired and hungry.

46 Andersen: You can change the story again.

47 Red: I'm sorry, but I lost the pen you gave to me. Please help me.

48 Andersen: No problem. I'll write a happy ending for everyone. Is that okay?

49 Red: That'll be great!

50 Andersen: All right. I'll use my pen here. "The kind Wolf stops dancing. He can enjoy cakes and cookies."

51 Wolf: (Stopping dancing) I can stop dancing! (Eating cookies) And I can eat cookies! Thank you very much.

52 (Everybody laughs and enjoys cookies together.)

🐺 서술형 실전문제
p.222~223

01 (d)angerous 02 Have
03 Let 04 for
05 (1) himself (2) under (3) (g)ets / (l)eave
06 (1) need (2) check (3) blew (4) knocked

---

07 (1) dance (또는 dancing) (2) since (3) to write on
   (4) that
08 (1) I like the pen (which/that) you gave (to) me.
   (2) Mary had dinner with Sam who[that] is her best friend.
   (3) Kate read the book which[that] was about global warming.
09 (A) Scene (B) delicious (C) hard
10 for 11 What do you mean by that?
12 ⑤ tiring → tired
13 If I change the story again
14 eating 또는 to eat 15 famous writer

01 주어진 단어는 반의어 관계이다. dangerous: 위험한 safe: 안전한

02 Have you ever heard of ~?: ~에 대해 들어 본 적 있니?

03 대화 중에 질문을 받았을 때, 생각할 시간이 필요하면 'Let me think.'나 'Let me see.'를 말할 수 있다 Let me see.: 어디 보자., 글쎄.

04 be good for: ~에 좋다 thank A for B: B에 대해 A에게 감사하다

05 (1) talk to oneself: 혼잣말하다 (2) under: ~ 아래에 (3) get+형용사: ~해지다 leave: 떠나다

06 (1) need: ~을 필요로 하다 (2) check: 점검하다 (3) blow: (입으로) 불다, (바람이) 불다 (4) knock: 두드리다

07 (1) 지각동사의 목적격보어로 동사원형이나 현재분사가 적절하다. (2) 현재완료의 계속적 용법으로 '~ 이래로'를 뜻하는 since가 적절하다. (3) 종이 위에 쓰는 것이므로 전치사 on을 빠뜨리면 안 된다. (4) believe의 목적어 역할을 하는 절을 이끄는 that이 적절하다.

08 (1) 선행사가 사물이고 gave의 목적어 역할을 해야 하므로 관계대명사 which나 that을 써야 한다. 목적격이므로 생략할 수도 있다. (2) 선행사가 사람이고 is의 주어 역할을 해야 하므로 관계대명사 who나 that을 써야 한다. (3) 선행사가 사물이고 was의 주어 역할을 해야 하므로 관계대명사 which나 that을 써야 한다.

09 (A) '장면 1'이라고 해야 하므로 Scene이 적절하다. scene: (영화·연극·책에 나오는) 장면, (연극·오페라의) 장(場), scenery: 경치, 풍경, (B) 감각동사 look의 보어이므로 형용사 delicious가 적절하다. (C) 집을 '세게' 불었다고 해야 하므로 hard가 적절하다. hardly: 거의 ~ 아니다

10 for lunch: 점심으로

11 by: [수단·방법·원인·작용·매개 따위] …에 의해서, …으로

12 너무 '피곤하다'고 해야 하므로 tired로 고치는 것이 적절하다. tiring: 피곤하게 하는

13 '내가 이야기를 다시 바꾸면'이라는 뜻이다. 조건의 부사절이므로 현재시제로 쓰는 것이 적절하다.

14 like는 목적어로 동명사와 to부정사를 둘 다 취할 수 있다.

15 Andersen은 "빨간 구두"를 쓴 '유명한 작가'이다.

01 ③   02 ⑤   03 ⑤
04 What, mean by
05 (1) By   (2) away   (3) to   (4) of   (5) of
06 (1) if   (2) though   (3) that
07 (1) if → though[although]
    (2) opened → open[opening]
    (3) has met → met   (4) will find → find   (5) it 삭제
08 ④, ⑤   09 to eat
10 practice singing 또는 practicing singing
11 (1) Though   (2) calling   (3) open   (4) been
    (5) which   12 ⑤   13 ①   14 ②, ⑤
15 blow your nose   16 (A) happened
(B) himself   (C) safe   17 ③   18 ⑤
19 ④   20 (A) happy   (B) excited   (C) happily
21 ①, ②   22 I'm glad you're kind to Grandma.
23 ④   24 chicken → cookies   25 ②
26 ②, ⑤   27 have   28 ④
29 to dance → dancing   30 ④
31 Mr. Andersen did.

01 blow one's nose: 코를 풀다

02 leave: 떠나다

03 ① Shake 병을 열기 전에 흔들어라. ② needs 그것은 새로운 배터리를 필요로 한다. ③ please 그녀는 그를 기쁘게 하기 위해 그것을 했다. ④ follow 나는 이번에는 그의 조언을 따를 것이라고 생각한다. ⑤ stop 너는 언제 일을 그만두니?

04 What do you mean by that?: 그게 무슨 말이야?

05 (1) by the way: 그런데, 그건 그렇고 (2) go away: 가 버리다, 사라지다 (3) talk to oneself: 혼잣말하다 (4) get out of: ~에서 나가다 (5) Have you ever heard of ~?: ~에 대해 들어 본 적 있니?

06 (1) 주절은 미래시제이고 종속절은 현재시제이므로 조건의 접속사 if가 적절하다. (2) 앞과 뒤에 나오는 절의 내용이 상반되므로 양보의 접속사 though가 적절하다. (3) 직접목적어를 이끄는 접속사 that이 적절하다.

07 (1) 앞과 뒤에 나오는 절의 내용이 상반되므로 양보의 접속사가 적절하다. (2) 지각동사의 목적격보어로 동사원형이나 현재분사가 적절하다. (3) 현재완료는 then과 같이 과거를 나타내는 부사와 함께 쓰이지 않는다. (4) 조건의 부사절에서는 현재시제로 미래를 나타낸다. (5) 관계대명사가 접속사와 대명사의 역할을 하므로 it을 삭제해야 한다.

08 목적격 관계대명사가 필요하며 선행사가 사물이므로 which나 that이 적절하다.

09 첫 번째 문장에서는 something을 수식하는 to부정사가 필요하고, 두 번째 문장에서는 부사적 용법의 to부정사가 필요하다. 의미상 to eat이 적절하다.(2) Unless는 접속사로 '~하지 않으면'이라는 의미로 사용된다.

10 지각동사 watch의 목적격보어로 동사원형이나 현재분사가 나와야 하고 practice는 동명사를 목적어로 받으므로 singing이 적절하다.

11 (1) 앞과 뒤에 나오는 절의 내용이 상반되므로 양보의 접속사

가 적절하다. (2) 지각동사 watch의 목적격보어로 동사원형이나 현재분사가 나와야 한다. (3) 조건의 부사절에서는 현재시제로 미래를 나타낸다. (4) have been to: ~에 가 본 적이 있다, have gone to: ~에 가고 없다 (5) 선행사가 사물이고 주어가 필요하므로 관계대명사 which가 적절하다.

12 ⑤는 change the story를 가리킨다.

13 ⓐ for lunch: 점심으로, ⓑ by: (수단·방법·원인·작용·매개 따위) …에 의해서(through), …으로(with)

14 ⓑ와 ①, ③, ④는 부사적 용법, ② 명사적 용법, ⑤ 형용사적 용법

15 '코를 푸는 것'을 가리킨다.

16 (A) happen은 자동사라서 수동태로 만들 수 없으므로 happened가 적절하다. (B) '혼잣말로'라고 해야 하므로 himself가 적절하다. (C) 내 이야기가 제대로 돌아가면 할머니는 '안전하실' 거라고 해야 하므로 safe가 적절하다.

17 ⓑ와 ③번은 (계획 등이) 잘되어 가다, (원하는) 효과가 나다[있다], ① (어떤 직장에서) 일하다, ② 직업, 일자리 ④ (예술 등의) 작품, 저작, 저술, ⑤ 일

18 ⑤ 할머니를 잡아먹으려는 늑대의 속셈을 눈치 채고 Red가 이야기를 다시 바꿔야겠다고 했으므로, '뛰는 놈 위에 나는 놈 있다.'가 적절하다. No matter how good you are, there's always someone better.도 같은 뜻을 나타낸다. ① 남의 떡이 더 커 보인다.(이웃집 잔디가 더 푸르다.) ② 불행한 일은 겹치기 마련이다.(비가 왔다 하면 억수로 퍼붓는다.) ③ 호랑이 굴에 가야 호랑이를 잡는다.(모험하지 않으면 얻는 것도 없다.) ④ 시장이 최고의 반찬이다.

19 ④ 늑대는 너무 배가 고파서 Red의 바구니를 보며 그건 뭐냐고 물었을 뿐이다.

20 (A) 감각동사 looks의 보어이므로 형용사 happy가 적절하다. (B) 감정을 나타내는 동사가 사람을 수식할 때는 과거분사를 쓰므로 excited가 적절하다. (C) Laughing을 수식하므로 부사 happily가 적절하다.

21 ⓐ와 ①, ②번은 동명사, 나머지는 다 현재분사이다.

22 'to'를 보충하면 된다.

23 대화에서 화제를 바꿀 때 쓰는 'By the way'가 적절하다. by the way: 그런데, ① 그러므로, ② 마침내, ③ 그 결과, ⑤ 즉, 다시 말해

24 Red가 이야기를 다시 바꾸면 과자를 먹지 않고 닭고기를 좋아하던 늑대가 '과자' 먹는 걸 좋아하게 될 것이라고 하는 것이 적절하다.

25 ② 당황한, ① 지루한, ③ 만족하는, ④ 우울한, ⑤ 흥분한

26 ⓒ와 ②, ⑤번은 경험 용법, ① 결과 용법, ③ 계속 용법, ④ 완료 용법

27 현재완료로 물었기 때문에 have로 대답하는 것이 적절하다.

28 문맥상 역접의 접속사 but이 알맞다.

29 늑대는 '춤추기를' 멈춘다고 해야 하므로 동명사로 고치는 것이 적절하다. stop+~ing: ~하기를 그만두다, stop+to부정사: ~하기 위해 멈추다

30 ④ Red가 Mr. Andersen이 그녀에게 준 펜을 어디에서 잃어버렸는지는 대답할 수 없다. ① He writes stories. ② Red did. ③ Because she lost the pen he gave to her and couldn't change the story again. ⑤ He wrote a happy ending for everyone.

37

교과서 파헤치기

Lesson 1

01 게시[공고]하다　02 깨닫다　03 계속하다
04 수첩, 일기　05 접시; 요리　06 표지
07 팬; 부채　08 결승전　09 바닥
10 정말　11 건강　12 풀다
13 믿다　14 표, 입장권　15 엄격한
16 종　17 신선한　18 맛있는
19 재미있는　20 구석　21 판단하다
22 친절한　23 활동　24 메모
25 수학　26 맞는, 알맞은　27 함께
28 말, 단어　29 어쨌든　30 외치다
31 기쁜　32 대답하다　33 기르다, 재배하다
34 연습하다　35 (말 · 대화에) 끼어들다
36 ~에 대해 생각하다　37 ~에 부딪히다
38 ~이 몹시 기다려지다　39 ~을 알게 되다
40 ~에 좋다　41 ~으로 가는 길에[도중에]
42 ~에게 신세를 갚다　43 마음속으로 생각하다

01 boring　02 problem　03 practice
04 hurry　05 take　06 excited
07 magic　08 cafeteria　09 busy
10 shout　11 present　12 remember
13 grow　14 always　15 serious
16 anyway　17 hard　18 cool
19 homeroom teacher　20 join
21 reply　22 serve　23 exciting
24 class　25 pleased　26 mean
27 saying　28 trick　29 health
30 floor　31 strict　32 continue
33 judge　34 cover　35 be good for
36 bump into　37 cut in　38 after school
39 think of　40 find out　41 look for
42 right now　43 think to oneself

1 grow, 재배하다　2 hurry, 서두르다, 서둘러 가다
3 cover, 표지　4 reply, 대답하다　5 strict, 엄격한
6 dish, 접시　7 final, 결승전　8 realize, 깨닫다
9 serve, 제공하다　10 judge, 판단하다　11 magic, 마술
12 post, 게시[공고]하다　13 trust, 믿다　14 saying, 속담
15 cafeteria, 구내식당　16 fan, 팬

Get Ready - 2

1 what, think of / looks, for / This year, going to study, with
2 Look at, going to, homeroom teacher / find out / excited, can't wait
3 everyone. your English teacher / Glad to meet / What, think of / interesting, a lot

Start Off - Listen & Talk A

1 looks good for, What, think of it / think, boring / which club, to join / join the soccer, plyaing
2 think of / think, right. to learn many interesting tricks / too. first meeting / can't wait for

Start Off - Listen & Talk B

Let's, What do you think of / growing vegetables / what, eating / Let's join, right now, with, every month / on April 30 / can't wait for

Step Up - Real-life Scene

what, think of / looks, strict, serious / Don't judge, by / What, mean / with, was great, exciting / During, class, math activities with / can't wait for, this year

Express Yourself A

1 What do you think / I think, on / can eat / can't wait for lunchtime
2 dishes, think of / not bad, vegetables / don't eat / Try, good for our health

Check Yourself - Listen & Speak

Let's join, What, of / playing the flute / like playing / right now, after school, Tuesday, Thursday / going to have, on / to play / too, can't wait for

Get Ready - 2

1 G: Hey, what do you think of this notebook?
　B: It looks great! Is it for science?
　G: Yes. This year I'm going to study science harder with this notebook.

2 B: Look at the teachers. Who's going to be our new homeroom teacher?

G: We'll find out in 10 minutes.

B: I'm very excited. I can't wait!

3 M: Hello, everyone! My name is Yun Kihun. I'm your English teacher.

G&B: Glad to meet you, Mr. Yun.

M: What do you think of English?

G: It's interesting. I like English a lot.

Start Off - Listen & Talk A

1 B: This club looks good for you. What do you think of it?

G: The health club? I think it's boring.

B: Then which club do you want to join?

G: I'll join the soccer club. I like playing soccer.

2 G: What do you think of the magic club?

B: I think it's the right club for me. I want to learn many interesting tricks.

G: I'll join it, too. When is the first meeting?

B: Next Wednesday. I can't wait for the first meeting!

Start Off - Listen & Talk B

B: Let's join the Green Garden club together. What do you think of it?

G: Okay. I like growing vegetables.

B: You know what? I like eating vegetables.

G: Let's join the club right now. We can have a party with fresh vegetables every month.

B: Great. The first party is on April 30.

G: I can't wait for the party.

Step Up - Real-life Scene

Seho: Miso, what do you think of Mr. Park?

Miso: The new math teacher? He looks very strict and serious.

Seho: Don't judge a book by its cover.

Miso: What do you mean, Seho?

Seho: My first class with Mr. Park was great. He was very kind, and his class was so exciting.

Miso: Really?

Seho: Yes. During the first class, we did interesting math activities with our cell phones.

Miso: Wow! I can't wait for his class tomorrow. It's my first math class this year.

Express Yourself A

1 B: What do you think of today's lunch?

G: I think it's okay. What's on tomorrow's menu?

B: Wow! We can eat spaghetti tomorrow.

G: I can't wait for lunchtime tomorrow

2 G: Look! Two dishes of vegetables! What do you think of today's menu?

B: It's not bad. I like vegetables.

G: I don't eat vegetables.

B: Try some. They are good for our health.

Check Yourself - Listen & Speak

B: Let's join the School Band club together. What do you think of it?

G: Okay. I like playing the flute.

B: I like playing the ukulele.

G: Let's join the club right now. They practice after school every Tuesday and Thursday.

B: They're going to have the first concert on July 15.

G: Great. I hope to play in the concert.

B: Me, too. I can't wait for the concert.

본문 TEST Step 1   p.09~10

01 talking, when, came

02 Happy, said to   03 from, my

04 two, tickets   05 going, take, asked

06 took, to, before   07 time, back

08 what, cut   09 isn't, fan, am

10 ask, anyway, replied

11 won't, with, Trust

12 thought, herself, wants   13 bell, See, later

14 hurried, class 15 on, started to

16 At, bumped into

17 said, continued to   18 then, saw, on

19 Wait, but, not

20 After, went, can't, find   21 happen, see

22 she, answered 23 Isn't, your   24 not, think, lost

25 On, way, saw 26 had, in

27 got angry, Why

28 saw, shouted, found   29 think, yours

30 looking for, said   31 not, thought

32 were, saying   33 something say, asked

34 about going to   35 It's, finals

36 looked, pleased, to

본문 TEST Step 2   p.11~12

01 were talking, when, came over

02 Happy birthday, said to   03 from my dad

04 two KBL tickets   05 going to take

06 took me to   07 time to pay him back

39

08 know what, cut in   09 isn't, fan, But

10 ask, anyway, replied

11 won't go with, Trust

12 thought to herself, wants, ticket

13 There's, See you later

14 hurried to class

15 on, started to run

16 At, bumped into someone

17 continued to run   18 Just then, on

19 but, was not

20 After class, went to, one of my tickets

21 happen to   22 answered

23 Isn't, in your bag   24 not, think, lost

25 On her way home

26 had, in his hand

27 got angry, Why

28 Just then, shouted, found a ticket in

29 think, yours   30 was looking for

31 not so bad, thought   32 were, saying

33 have, to say, asked

34 about going to, with me   35 finals

36 looked, pleased, love to

19 "기다려, 세호야!" 그가 말했지만 세호는 거기에 없었다.

20 수업이 끝난 후, 세호는 다미에게 가서 말했다, "내 입장권 한 장을 찾을 수 없어.

21 너 혹시 입장권을 봤니?"

22 "아니," 그녀가 대답했다.

23 "네 가방 안에 있지 않니?"

24 "아니, 거기에 없어. 내 생각에 그것을 잃어버린 것 같아." 세호가 말했다.

25 집으로 돌아오는 길에 다미는 지훈을 보았다.

26 그는 손에 입장권을 가지고 있었다.

27 다미는 화가 나서 "이봐! 너가 왜 ...?"라고 말했다.

28 바로 그때, 지훈이는 세호를 보고 소리쳤다, "세호야! 내가 복도에서 입장권을 찾았어.

29 네 것 같아."

30 "고마워! 나는 그것을 찾고 있었어!" 세호가 말했다.

31 "그는 그렇게 나쁘진 않아." 다미는 생각했다.

32 "그래서, 무슨 말을 하고 있었던 거야?

33 너 할 말이 있니, 다미야?" 지훈이가 물었다.

34 "음, 이번 금요일에 나랑 학교 농구 경기에 같이 가는 게 어때?

35 그것은 결승전이야."

36 지훈은 정말 기뻐 보였다. "가고 싶어!"

본문 TEST Step 3   p.13~14

1 세호와 지훈이는 다미가 왔을 때 복도에서 이야기를 나누고 있었다.

2 생일 축하해!" 다미가 세호에게 말했다.

3 "이거 받아. 우리 아빠가 주신 거야."

4 "와, KBL 입장권 두 장! 고마워!"

5 "넌 누구를 데려갈 거니?" 다미가 물었다.

6 "민준이. 그가 전에 나를 축구 경기에 데려갔어.

7 그래서 그에게 신세를 갚아야 할 때야."

8 "그거 알아?" 지훈이가 끼어들었다.

9 "민준이는 농구 팬이 아니야. 하지만 난 농구 팬이야!"

10 "음, 어쨌든 먼저 민준이에게 물어볼 거야." 세호가 대답했다.

11 "그는 너와 함께 가지 않을 거야. 날 믿어." 지훈이가 말했다.

12 "이 녀석은 누구지?" 다미는 "그는 민준이의 입장권을 원하는구나."라고 마음속으로 생각했다.

13 "아, 종이 울린다. 나중에 보자,"라고 다미가 말했다.

14 그녀는 서둘러 수업에 들어갔다.

15 "어서, 지훈아." 세호는 말하고 달리기 시작했다.

16 모퉁이에서, 세호는 누군가와 부딪혔다.

17 그는 "미안해!"라고 말하고는 계속 달렸다.

18 바로 그때, 지훈이가 바닥에 있는 무언가를 보았다.

본문 TEST Step 4~Step 5   p.15~18

1 Seho and Jihun were talking in the hallway when Dami came over.

2 "Happy birthday!" she said to Seho.

3 "Here. They're from my dad."

4 "Wow, two KBL tickets! Thanks!"

5 "Who are you going to take with you?" Dami asked.

6 "Minjun. He took me to a soccer game before.

7 So, it's time to pay him back."

8 "You know what?" Jihun cut in.

9 "Minjun isn't a fan of basketball. But I am!"

10 "Well, I'll ask him first anyway," replied Seho.

11 "He won't go with you. Trust me," said Jihun.

12 "Who is this guy?" Dami thought to herself, "He wants Minjun's ticket."

13 "Oh! There's the bell. See you later," said Dami.

14 She hurried to class.

15 "Come on, Jihun," said Seho, and he started to run.

16 At the corner, Seho bumped into someone.

17 "Sorry!" he said and continued to run.

18 Just then, Jihun saw something on the floor.

19 "Wait, Seho!" he said, but Seho was not there.

20 After class, Seho went to Dami and said, "I can't find one of my tickets.

21 Did you happen to see it?"

22 "No," she answered.

23 "Isn't it in your bag?"

24 "No, it's not there. I think I lost it," said Seho.

25 On her way home, Dami saw Jihun.

26 He had the ticket in his hand.

27 Dami got angry and said, "Hey! Why do you ...?"

28 Just then, Jihun saw Seho and shouted, "Seho! I found a ticket in the hallway.

29 I think it's yours."

30 "Thanks! I was looking for that!" said Seho.

31 "He's not so bad," Dami thought.

32 "So, what were you saying?

33 Do you have something to say, Dami?" asked Jihun.

34 "Um, how about going to the school basketball game with me this Friday?

35 It's the finals."

36 Jihun looked really pleased. "I'd love to!"

2. I will say nice words to others first.

3. Then they will say nice words to me, too.

4. I believe that I can make lots of good friends this way.

5. This year, I will always try to remember this saying and say nice words to others.

Check Yourself - Read & Write

1. Dami gave Seho two basketball tickets.

2. Jihun wanted to go to the basketball game with Seho.

3. Seho dropped one of the tickets on his way to go class.

4. Jihun found Seho's ticket in the hallway.

5. Dami saw Seho's ticket in Jihun's hand, and she thought, "He's a bad boy."

6. Jihun gave the ticket back to Seho, and Dami realized that she was wrong.

7. Dami wanted to go to the school basketball game with Jihun.

8. Jihun was really pleased.

구석구석지문 TEST Step 1   p.19

Project - Link to the World

1. means, words, in

2. will say, others

3. nice words, too

4. believe, make, friends

5. always try to, saying, others

Check Yourself - Read & Write

1. Seho two basketball tickets

2. wanted to go, with

3. dropped, on his way to

4. found, hallway

5. saw, thought

6. gave, back to, realized, was wrong

7. wanted to go to

8. pleased

구석구석지문 TEST Step 2   p.20

Project - Link to the World

1. This saying means "Nice words for nice words" in English.

11 cut, 상처   12 nod, (고개를) 끄덕이다   13 rest, 휴식
14 spot, 점, 반점   15 borrow, 빌리다
16 doorbell, 초인종

단어 TEST Step 1 — p.21

01 연세가 드신	02 자세히, 면밀히	03 구역, 블록
04 이웃	05 나비	06 주소
07 귀여운	08 감독	09 초인종
10 먹이를 주다	11 무료의, 한가한	12 살피다, 확인하다
13 문	14 초록색의	15 급히[서둘러] 가다
16 ~을 두고 오다[가다]		17 상처; 자르다, 베다
18 잃어버린	19 짓다, 건축하다	20 수다를 떨다
21 자원봉사자; 자원봉사하다		22 희망
23 갈색의	24 휴식	25 울다
26 이상한	27 씻다	28 빌리다
29 옷, 의복	30 외로운	31 완벽한
32 긴장되는	33 꼭, 정확히	34 밖에, 밖에서
35 ~을 쫓아다니다, ~을 뒤쫓다		36 휴식을 취하다
37 둘러보다	38 좋아지다, 호전되다	
39 A를 B로 데려가다		40 충분한 휴식을 취하다
41 ~을 붙이다	42 ~을 잘하다	43 ~을 돌보다

단어 TEST Step 2 — p.22

01 around	02 nod	03 shape
04 perfect	05 care	06 clothes
07 practice	08 special	09 enough
10 follow	11 spot	12 stage
13 exactly	14 hard	15 inside
16 return	17 lonely	18 miss
19 still	20 move	21 nervous
22 outside	23 pass	24 sell
25 guess	26 used	27 borrow
28 strange	29 chat	30 neighbor
31 feed	32 elderly	33 address
34 doorbell	35 be late for	36 prepare for
37 take A to B	38 in front of	39 look around
40 take a break	41 put up	42 clean up
43 thanks to		

단어 TEST Step 3 — p.23

1 perfect, 완벽한   2 build, 짓다   3 feed, 먹이를 주다
4 lonely, 외로운   5 return, 돌아오다[가다]
6 volunteer, 자원봉사자   7 address, 주소
8 block, 구역, 블록   9 neighbor, 이웃   10 butterfly, 나비

대화문 TEST Step 1 — p.24~25

Get Ready - 2

1 going to take, in front of / Sounds, over there
2 It's, think, get / Let's meet at, in front of
3 planning, for / selling, over there / Let's go, look around

Start Off - Listen & Talk A

1 any plans for / planning to, dancing / Sounds, Can, join / not
2 planning to go, to prepare for / mean, to study / make it at / See you then

Start Off - Listen & Talk B

are, going to do / to clean up, with / like, Can, join / make it, at / afraid not, How about / Fine with, bring a pair of / See, on Saturday

Start Off - Speak Up - Look and talk.

planning to Saturday / Can, come with you / Why not, can, make it / Let's meet in front of

Step Up - Real-life Scene

planning to volunteer, animal care center / mean, near / Will, come with, volunteers to take care of / love to, feeding, walking, good at washing / bring, with, too / ask my neighbor, too, shall, meet / make, at, at / see, on Sunday

Express Yourself A

1 I'm planning to go to, to watch / interesting, come with / Of course, Can you make it, at / No, See you then
2 planning to enter, nervous / Don't worry, If, practice, can win / Thank

Learning Diary - Listen & Speak

are you going to / planning to volunteer / great / Will, come with / When shall, meet / Can you make it / afraid not, How about / See you then

대화문 TEST Step 2 — p.26~27

Get Ready - 2

1 B: I'm going to take some pictures in front of the flower gate.
  G: Sounds good. It's over there.

2 B: Hello. It's me, Jamie. I think I'll get there in 20 minutes.

G: Okay. Let's meet at 2 p.m. in front of the clock tower.

3 B: I'm planning to buy some clothes for a school picnic.

G: Look. They're selling old books and clothes over there.

B: Great. Let's go and look around.

Start Off - Listen & Talk A

1 G: Do you have any plans for the weekend?

B: Yes. I'm planning to practice dancing at the youth center.

G: Sounds great. Can I join you?

B: Why not?

2 G: I'm planning to go to the library to prepare for the exam.

B: You mean City Library? I want to study with you.

G: Great. Can you make it at 3 p.m. tomorrow?

B: Sure. See you then.

Start Off - Listen & Talk B

B: What are you going to do this Saturday?

G: I'm planning to clean up the park with my dad.

B: Sounds like a wonderful plan. Can I join you?

G: Sure. Can you make it at the bus stop at 1 p.m.?

B: I'm afraid not. How about 2?

G: Fine with me. Please bring a pair of gloves and a big plastic bag.

B: Okay. See you on Saturday.

Start Off - Speak Up - Look and talk.

A: I'm planning to volunteer at the library this Tuseday.

B: Great. Can I come with you?

A: Why not? Can you make it at 3 p.m.?

B: Sure. Let's meet in front of the library.

Step Up - Real-life Scene

Jina: I'm planning to volunteer at the animal care center this Sunday morning.

Alex: You mean the one near Grand Park, Jina?

Jina: Right. Will you come with me, Alex? They need volunteers to take care of the animals.

Alex: I'd love to join. I like feeding and walking animals. I'm also good at washing them.

Jina: Great. You can bring other friends with you, too.

Alex: Okay. I'll ask my neighbor Nancy. She loves animals, too. What time shall we meet?

Jina: Can you make it at 8 a.m. at the Grand Park bus stop?

Alex: Sure. I'll see you on Sunday.

Express Yourself A

1 M: I'm planning to go to the town festival to watch a dance show.

W: Sounds interesting. Can I come with you?

M: Of course. Can you make it at the school gate at 6 p.m.?

W: No problem. See you then.

2 W: I'm planning to enter a singing contest in my town, but I'm nervous.

M: Don't worry. If you practice hard, you can win the contest.

W: Thank you.

Learning Diary - Listen & Speak

B: What are you going to do this Friday, Aria?

G: I'm planning to volunteer at the post office.

B: Sounds great!

G: Will you come with me, Eric?

B: Sure. When shall we meet ?

G: Can you make it at 3 p.m.?

B: I'm afraid not. How about 4 p.m.?

G: Good. See you then.

본문 TEST Step 1 · p.28~29

01 black, brown, with
02 lived with
03 perfect, because, spot, shape
04 outside, run after
05 always came, in
06 away, lived with
07 moved, last, lonely
08 had no
09 after, followed, became
10 One, saw, under
11 making, sound
12 wrong, asked
13 at, closely, found, cut
14 took, to, hospital
15 better, gets rest, Keep
16 at, was no
17 outside, couldn't find
18 made, put, up
19 third, passed, no
20 walking near, saw, lost
21 read, closely, got
22 looks, like, strange
23 hurried, home
24 on, Let's
25 took, to, on
26 heard, ring, ran, opened
27 back, cried
28 jumped, into, arms
29 Let, guess

43

30 comes, only, doesn't   31 Ryan nodded

32 lost, last, didn't   33 How, know

34 Because, too, only during   35 Our, has, said

36 if, in, have   37 Sure, said

38 Thank, thought   39 met, thanks to

---

01 with green eyes   02 lived with

03 always thought, perfect, because, spot, shape

04 liked to go outside, run after

05 always, in, for 06 away, lived with

07 When, moved to, last month, lonely

08 had no friends

09 after, followed her home, became

10 One day, saw, sitting

11 was making a strange sound   12 wrong, asked

13 looked at, closely, found a bad cut

14 took, to, animal hospital

15 get better, gets enough rest, Keep him inside

16 at, was no   17 checked outside, couldn't find

18 made, put, up 19 third, night passed, Still

20 When, was walking near, saw, the lost cat

21 read, closely, got big

22 looks, like, strange   23 hurried, home

24 on, Let's go 25 took, to

26 When, heard, ring, ran to, opened

27 back, cried   28 jumped, up, into

29 Let me guess 30 comes home, in, doesn't

31 nodded   32 lost, last, didn't you

33 How did, know

34 Because, too, usually comes, during the day

35 has two families

36 if you have time, come in, have

37 Sure   38 Thank, thought

39 met, thanks to you

---

1 Bear는 초록색 눈을 가진 검은색과 갈색의 고양이였다.

2 그는 소년 Ryan과 함께 살았다.

3 Ryan은 항상 "Bear"가 곰 모양의 검은 반점이 있기 때문에 그 고양이에게 딱 맞는 이름이라고 생각했다.

4 Bear는 매일 아침 밖으로 나가 나비를 쫓아다니는 것을 좋아했다.

5 그는 항상 저녁 식사 시간에 맞춰 집에 왔다.

6 다섯 블록 떨어진 곳에, 고양이 Max는 Sheila라는 소녀와 함께 살았다.

7 지난달에 Sheila가 이 마을로 이사 왔을 때, 그녀는 외로웠다.

8 그녀는 그곳에 친구가 없었다.

9 하지만 Max가 그녀를 따라 집으로 온 후, 그는 그녀에게 좋은 친구가 되었다.

10 어느 날, Sheila는 책상 밑에 앉아 있는 Max를 보았다.

11 그는 이상한 소리를 내고 있었다.

12 "무슨 일 있니?" Sheila가 물었다.

13 그녀는 그를 자세히 살펴보고 그의 다리에 심한 상처가 난 것을 발견했다.

14 그녀는 그를 동물 병원으로 데려갔다.

15 의사는 "충분한 휴식을 취하면 좋아질 거야. 그를 일주일 동안 안에 있도록 해라."라고 말했다.

16 그날 밤, Ryan의 집에는 Bear가 없었다.

17 Ryan은 바깥을 살폈지만 그는 그를 찾을 수 없었다.

18 그는 포스터를 만들어서 마을을 다니며 그것을 붙였다.

19 세 번째 밤이 지났다. 여전히 Bear는 나타나지 않았다.

20 Sheila가 그녀의 집 근처를 걷고 있었을 때, 그녀는 잃어버린 고양이에 대한 포스터를 보았다.

21 그녀는 그것을 자세히 읽고, 그녀의 눈은 커졌다.

22 "이 고양이는 꼭 Max 같아 보여. 너무 이상해."

23 그녀는 서둘러 집으로 돌아갔다.

24 "자, Max! 가자!"

25 그녀는 그를 포스터에 적힌 주소로 데려갔다.

26 "딩동." Ryan은 초인종이 울리는 소리를 듣고 문으로 달려가 문을 열었다.

27 "Bear야, 돌아왔구나!" Ryan이 외쳤다.

28 Max가 Ryan의 팔 안으로 뛰어올랐다.

29 "내가 맞춰 볼게," Sheila가 말했다.

30 "너의 고양이는 저녁에만 집에 오지, 그렇지?"

31 Ryan은 고개를 끄덕였다.

32 "그리고 너는 지난 금요일에 그를 잃어버렸지, 그렇지 않니?" Sheila가 말했다.

33 "응! "어떻게 알았니?"라고 Ryan은 말했다.

34 "이것은 또한 내 고양이이기 때문이야, 보통 낮에만 우리 집에 오거든."

35 "우리 고양이는 가족이 둘이야!" Ryan이 말했다.

36 이봐, 시간이 있으면 들어와서 쿠키 좀 먹어."

37 "그래," Sheila가 말했다.

38 "고마워, Max." 그녀는 생각했다.

39 "나는 네 덕분에 좋은 이웃을 만났어!"

---

1 Bear was a black and brown cat with green eyes.

2 He lived with a boy, Ryan.

3 Ryan always thought that "Bear" was a perfect name for the cat because he had a black spot in the shape of a bear.

4 Bear liked to go outside every morning and run after butterflies.

5 He always came home just in time for dinner.

6 Five blocks away, Max the cat lived with a girl, Sheila.

7 When Sheila moved to this town last month, she was lonely.

8 She had no friends there.

9 But, after Max followed her home, he became a good friend to her.

10 One day, Sheila saw Max sitting under the desk.

11 He was making a strange sound.

12 "What's wrong?" asked Sheila.

13 She looked at him closely and found a bad cut on his leg.

14 She took him to the animal hospital.

15 The doctor said, "He will get better if he gets enough rest. Keep him inside for a week."

16 That night, at Ryan's house, there was no Bear.

17 Ryan checked outside, but he couldn't find him.

18 He made posters and put them up around town.

19 A third night passed. Still no Bear.

20 When Sheila was walking near her house, she saw a poster about the lost cat.

21 She read it closely, and her eyes got big.

22 "This cat looks exactly like Max. It's so strange."

23 She hurried home.

24 "Come on, Max! Let's go!"

25 She took him to the address on the poster.

26 "Ding-Dong." When Ryan heard the doorbell ring, he ran to the door and opened it.

27 "Bear, you're back!" Ryan cried.

28 Max jumped up into Ryan's arms.

29 "Let me guess," said Sheila.

30 "Your cat comes home only in the evenings, doesn't he?"

31 Ryan nodded.

32 "And you lost him last Friday, didn't you?" Sheila said.

33 "Yes! How did you know?" said Ryan.

34 "Because this is my cat, too, and he usually comes to my home only during the day."

35 "Our cat has two families!" said Ryan.

36 "Hey, if you have time, please come in and have some cookies."

37 "Sure," said Sheila.

38 "Thank you, Max," she thought.

39 "I met a good neighbor thanks to you!"

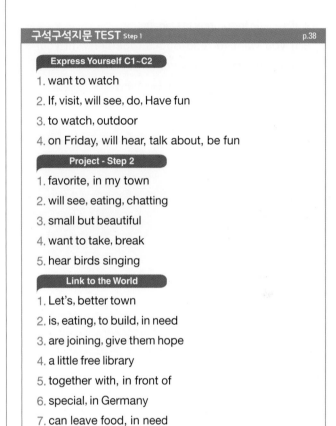

구석구석지문 TEST Step 1 p.38

Express Yourself C1~C2

1. want to watch
2. If, visit, will see, do, Have fun
3. to watch, outdoor
4. on Friday, will hear, talk about, be fun

Project - Step 2

1. favorite, in my town
2. will see, eating, chatting
3. small but beautiful
4. want to take, break
5. hear birds singing

Link to the World

1. Let's, better town
2. is, eating, to build, in need
3. are joining, give them hope
4. a little free library
5. together with, in front of
6. special, in Germany
7. can leave food, in need

구석구석지문 TEST Step 2 p.39

Express Yourself C1~C2

1. C1: Do you want to watch a magic show?
2. If you visit the town festival on Monday, you will see Harry do magic tricks. Have fun at the festival!
3. C2: Do you want to watch an outdoor movie?
4. If you visit the town festival on Friday, you will hear Mr. Jackson, a director talk about his new movie. It will be fun!

Project - Step 2

1. This is my favorite *tteokbokki* restaurant in my town.
2. If you go there, you will see many students eating *tteokbokki* and chatting.
3. This is a small but beautiful park near the school.
4. If you want to take a nice break, please visit it.
5. You can hear birds singing in the trees.

단어 TEST Step 1   p.40

01 혼자	02 (이빨로) 물다, 베어 물다
03 조심하는, 주의 깊은	04 위험한
05 방향, (주로 복수로) 지시	06 옷, 의복
07 ~에 있다, 존재하다	08 과거, 지난날

09 먼, 멀리	10 인물, 모습	11 등반가
12 실제로, 정말로	13 다음에 나오는, 그 다음의	
14 재미; 재미있는	15 안전, 안전성	16 진짜의, 현실적인
17 특별한, 특수한	18 기억하다	19 오르다, 올라가다
20 경치, 풍경	21 조화, 화합	22 ~ 뒤에, 뒤에
23 언젠가, 훗날	24 함께하다, 가입하다	
25 종류	26 창조하다, 만들다	27 균형, 평형
28 나중에, 후에	29 아마	30 규칙
31 찾다, 수색하다	32 만지다, 건드리다	33 기술, 기량
34 아직	35 전화를 끊다	

36 ~을 명심하다, ~을 잊지 않다	37 저쪽에, 저기에서
38 떠들다, 소란 피우다	39 ~에 좋다

40 ~에 대해 듣다	41 처음으로
42 예를 들면, 예를 들어	43 오르다

단어 TEST Step 2   p.41

01 active	02 sign	03 festival
04 figure	05 push	06 place
07 grass	08 practice	09 advice
10 close	11 safe	12 pose
13 information	14 street	15 rock
16 teenage	17 princess	18 loose
19 mirror	20 helmet	21 museum
22 chat	23 past	24 trick
25 without	26 beach	27 scenery
28 balance	29 harmony	30 clothes
31 careful	32 dangerous	33 safety
34 special	35 for example	
36 for the first time		37 keep ~ in mind
38 be good for	39 in front of	40 hang up
41 make noise	42 hear of	43 over there

단어 TEST Step 3   p.42

1 painter, 화가   2 dangerous, 위험한

3 active, 활동적인, 활발한   4 beach, 해변, 바닷가

5 ride, 타다   6 chat, 담소[이야기]하다   7 princess, 공주
8 street, 길, 도로   9 teenage, 십대의   10 clothes, 옷, 의복
11 rock, 바위, 암석   12 helmet, 헬멧
13 advice, 조언, 충고   14 climb, 오르다, 올라가다
15 push, 밀다   16 mirror, 거울

대화문 TEST Step 1   p.43~44

Get Ready - 2

1 at, great / riding, know about / What / special, for riding on

2 Don't, into, yet / Why not / shouldn't, without, Put, on

3 Look at, over there, like to take, in front of / shouldn't, over / okay

4 want to watch, in / shouldn't go up, birds / right

Start Off - Listen & Talk A

1 have, ever heard of, climber / seen, on TV / teaching rock climbing, camp, want to join / but, shouldn't climb up / right

2 Have, heard / No, I haven't / favorite, concert, Can I go / shouldn't come home / right

Start Off - Listen & Talk B

Have, heard of / tried, when / doing, for the first time / should bring, something to eat / should, keep in mind / shouldn't make, when / keep that in mind

Step Up - Real-life Scene

It's, Can, see me / hi, up / isn't it, chat, Have, heard of / Yes, I have, want / Guess what, going to go up / great / hang up, scenery / Be, shouldn't use, while you're walking / right, Thank, send, later

Express Yourself A

1 Have you heard of, No, I haven't. Who / famous American singer, actor, figure / Sounds, take pictures / Let's go.

2 shouldn't take, painting, behind / Don't worry, real, So, in front of / Can, selfies, not

---

대화문 TEST Step 2   p.45~46

Get Ready - 2

1 G: Look at that boy. He's great.
  B: He's riding an MTB. Do you know about it?
  G: No. What is it?
  B: It's a special bike for riding on a mountain.

2 G: Wait. Don't jump into the water yet.
  B: Why not?
  G: You shouldn't swim without a life jacket. Put it on.

3 G: Look at the beautiful flowers over there! I'd like to take a selfie in front of them.
  B: You shouldn't go over there.
  G: Oh, okay.

4 B: I want to watch the birds in the trees.
  G: You shouldn't go up too close to the birds.
  B: All right, thanks.

Start Off - Listen & Talk A

1 G: Dad, have you ever heard of Kim Soyun, the rock climber?
  M: Yes, I've seen her on TV.
  G: She's teaching rock climbing at a camp this Saturday. I want to join the camp.
  M: Okay, Miso, but you shouldn't climb up too high.
  G: All right. Thanks, Dad.

2 G: Have you heard of Rock Boys?
  M: No, I haven't.
  G: It's my favorite band. There's a concert this Saturday. Can I go?
  M: Okay, Minju, but you shouldn't come home too late.
  G: All right. Thanks, Dad.

Start Off - Listen & Talk B

B: Have you heard of bird watching?
M: Sure. I tried it when I was a child.
B: That's nice. Actually, I'm doing it for the first time this Saturday.
M: Are you? You should bring warm clothes and something to eat.
B: Okay. What else should I keep in mind?
M: You shouldn't make any noise when you watch the birds.
B: I'll keep that in mind. Thanks, Dad.

Step Up - Real-life Scene

A: Hello, Somin! It's me! Can you see me?
B: Oh, hi, Minjun! What's up?
A: This is so cool, isn't it? We can video chat on the phone! Have you heard of Jeju Olle?
B: Yes, I have. I really want to go there someday.
A: Guess what? I'm on it now. Actually, I'm going to go up Seongsan Ilchulbong now.
B: That's great!

A: Don't hang up. Enjoy the beautiful scenery with me.

B: Be careful! You shouldn't use your cell phone while you're walking.

A: Oh, right. Thank you. I'll send you photos later.

Express Yourself A

1 G: Have you heard of Elvis Presley?

B: No, I haven't. Who is he?

G: He was a famous American singer and actor. We can see a figure of Elvis here.

B: Sounds interesting. I want to take pictures with it.

G: Okay. Let's go.

2 W: You shouldn't take selfies here. Van Gogh's painting is behind you.

B: Don't worry, Mom. It's not his real painting. So I can take selfies in front of it.

W: Really? Sounds interesting. Can I take selfies here, too?

B: Why not?

본문 TEST Step 1   p.47~48

01 Have, ever heard
02 When, take, yourself
03 have, for, about
04 Here, presentations, selfies   05 people, take
06 Though, at, answer   07 Look at, of
08 used, take, herself   09 loos nervous
10 guess why   11 think, first
12 probably, teenage, ever   13 take, at, like
14 take, poses, tricks
15 also, special, fun
16 example, is, famous   17 spots, take
18 touch, even step   19 at, following
20 Though, riding, like
21 holding, brush, painting   22 exist, too
23 visited, before 24 don't, yourself 25 look, but were
26 don't, so   27 look safe
28 should, care, selfies, places
29 bite, time, could   30 are, safety
31 Don't, while, walking
32 Do, pose, near
33 Never, in, places
34 use, make, better
35 can, things, take
36 post, on, website

본문 TEST Step 2   p.49~50

01 Have, ever heard, of
02 take, of yourself
03 club, searched for information, for
04 Here, their presentations
05 people, take selfies
06 Though, wasn't, answer   07 Look at
08 used, to take, herself   09 loos nervous
10 Can, guess why
11 think, her first selfie
12 probably, teenage
13 can take selfies, like
14 To take, pictures, poses, use camera tricks
15 also, fun   16 example, famous
17 has special spots, take
18 touch, even step
19 Look at, following
20 Though, riding, looks like
21 just holding, brush, looks like, painting
22 exist, too   23 have visited, before
24 Why don't, yourself   25 look, but
26 don't think so 27 don't look safe
28 should take special care, places like
29 could bite, at any time, could fall
30 Here are, safety tips
31 take, while you're walking
32 not pose, wild 33 Never take selfies, places
34 use, better   35 things, take
36 can post, website
37 watered, school
38 also helped, at many times   39 Look at, those
40 How about, create

---

37 watered, plants, for   38 also, at, times
39 Look at, those 40 about joining, create

본문 TEST Step 3   p.51~52

1 여러분은 "셀피"에 대해 들어 본 적이 있나요? 여러분 자신의 사진을 찍을 때 그것이 셀피에요.
2 민지의 사진 동아리 학생들은 한 달 동안 셀피에 대한 정보를 찾았습니다.
3 여기 셀피에 대한 그들의 발표 내용이 있습니다.
4 과거의 사람들은 셀피를 찍었나요?

5 그 때는 셀피를 찍는 것이 쉽지는 않았지만, 답은 '그렇다' 입니다.

6 아나스타샤 공주의 이 사진을 보세요. 그녀는 거울을 사용하여 자신의 사진을 찍었습니다.

7 그녀는 긴장되어 보입니다. 왜인지 추측할 수 있나요?

8 글쎄, 나는 그것이 그녀의 첫 번째 셀피였다고 생각해요.

9 그리고 그것은 아마도 세계 최초의 10대 소녀의 셀피였을 거예요.

10 여러분은 빅벤과 피사의 사탑과 같은 세계적으로 유명한 장소에서 셀카를 찍을 수 있습니다.

11 멋진 사진을 찍기 위해서, 단지 재미있는 포즈를 취하고 카메라 기술을 이용하세요.

12 여러분은 또한 재미있는 셀피를 찍기 위해 특별한 박물관을 방문할 수 있습니다.

13 예를 들어, 필리핀에는 유명한 셀프 박물관이 있습니다.

14 그곳은 셀피를 찍기 위한 특별한 장소들이 있습니다.

15 여러분은 그림들을 만질 수 있고 심지어 그림들 안으로 들어갈 수도 있어요.

16 다음 사진들을 보세요.

17 비록 그 소년들은 말을 타고 있는 것이 아니지만, 말을 타고 있는 것처럼 보입니다.

18 비록 그 남자는 단지 커다란 붓을 잡고 있지만, 모나리자를 그리고 있는 것처럼 보입니다.

19 한국에도 셀피 박물관이 있습니다. 나는 전에 춘천에 있는 한 박물관을 방문한 적이 있습니다.

20 여러분도 직접 그곳에 가는 게 어때요? 이 셀피들은 멋져 보이지만,그것들은 좋은 생각이었나요?

21 난 그렇게 생각하지 않아요. 그것들은 안전해 보이지 않습니다.

22 여러분은 야생이나 이와 같이 높은 곳에서 셀피를 찍을 때 특별한 주의를 기울여야 합니다.

23 원숭이가 언제든지 당신을 물거나 또는 당신은 떨어질 수 있습니다.

24 여기 몇 가지 안전 수칙이 있습니다.

25 걸으면서 셀피를 찍지 마세요.

26 야생 동물들과 함께 또는 가까이에서 포즈를 취하지 마세요.

27 위험한 곳에서는 절대 셀피를 찍지 마세요.

28 나는 우리가 더 나은 학교생활을 만들기 위해 셀피를 이용할 수 있다고 생각해요.

29 우리는 학교에서 좋은 일을 할 수 있고 셀피를 찍을 수도 있습니다.

30 그리고 나서 우리는 학교 웹사이트에 사진을 올릴 수 있어요.

31 나는 한 달 동안 학교에서 식물과 꽃에 물을 주었습니다.

32 나는 또한 학교 도서관에서 선생님을 여러 번 도왔습니다.

33 그런 것들에 대한 내 셀피를 보세요.

34 저와 함께 더 나은 학교생활을 만들어 보는 건 어떨까요?

1 Have you ever heard of a "selfie"? When you take a photograph of yourself, it's a selfie.

2 The students from Minji's photo club have searched for information about selfies for one month.

3 Here are some of their presentations about selfies.

4 Did people in the past take selfies?

5 Though it wasn't easy at that time. the answer is yes.

6 Look at this photo of Princess Anastasia. She used a mirror to take a picture of herself.

7 She looks nervous. Can you guess why?

8 Well, I think it was her first selfie.

9 And it was probably the world's first teenage selfie ever.

10 You can take selfies at world-famous places like Big Ben and the Leaning Tower of Pisa.

11 To take great pictures, just do fun poses and use camera tricks.

12 You can also visit special museums to take fun selfies.

13 For example, there is a famous selfie museum in the Philippines.

14 It has special spots to take selfies.

15 You can touch the paintings and even step inside them.

16 Look at the following pictures.

17 Though the boys are not really riding horses, it looks like they are.

18 Though the man is just holding a big brush, it looks like he is painting the Mona Lisa.

19 Selfie museums exist in Korea, too. I have visited one in Chuncheon before.

20 Why don't you go there yourself? These selfies look great, but were they a good idea?

21 I don't think so. They don't look safe.

22 You should take special care when you take selfies in the wild or at high places like these.

23 A monkey could bite you at any time, or you could fall.

24 Here are some safety tips:

25 Don't take selfies while you're walking.

26 Do not pose with or near wild animals.

27 Never take selfies in dangerous places.

28 I think we can use selfies to make a better school life.

29 We can do good things at school and take selfies.

30 Then we can post the photos on our school website.

31 I've watered the plants and flowers at school for one month.

32 I've also helped the teacher at the school library many times.

33 Look at my selfies of those things.

34 How about joining me to create a better school life?

구석구석지문 TEST Step 1   p.57

Express Yourself-C

1. Have, heard

2. have, seen been to, in front of

3. took, museum

Project-Step 2

1. Safety Rules

2. Have, heard of

3. Though, be safe

4. shouldn't take

5. follow, directions

Link to the World

1. Riding

2. Riding, is, exciting

3. lots of skills

4. turn, freely, even jump

5. Though, easy, exciting

6. can start with

7. When, standing, balancing

8. be careful, should wear

9. shouldn't go, when, riding

구석구석지문 TEST Step 2   p.58

Express Yourself-C

1. Have you heard of the pyramids in Egypt?

2. Though I have never seen been to Egypt before, I'm standing in front of a pyramid in this picture.

3. I took it at the selfie museum.

Project-Step 2

1. Fire Safety Rules

2. Have you heard of fire safety rules?

3. Though there's a fire, you can be safe.

4. You shouldn't take the elevator.

5. You should follow the teacher's directions.

Link to the World

1. BMX Bike Riding

2. Riding a BMX bike is very exciting.

3. You can try lots of skills.

4. You can turn the bike freely and even jump with the bike.

5. Though it's not easy, it's very exciting.

6. You can start with standing skills.

7. When you try standing skills, balancing is very important.

8. But be careful. You should wear a helmet and gloves.

9. Also, you shouldn't go too fast when you're riding.

9 bounce, 튀기다　10 memory, 기억　11 grade, 학년

12 secret, 비밀　13 hole, 구멍　14 precious, 귀중한

15 perform, 공연하다　16 puppet, 인형, 꼭두각시

단어 TEST Step 1 　　　　p.59

01 기억하다　　02 연습하다　　03 학년, 성적

04 매우; 굉장히 좋은　05 옮기다, 이사[이동]하다

06 2월　　07 특별한　　08 현장 학습

09 우스운, 웃기는, 재미있는　　10 요리하다

11 멀리　　12 맛있는　　13 기억, 추억

14 메달　　15 양로원　　16 비밀

17 잃다　　18 햇빛

19 가져다 주다, 가지고 오다　　20 웃음

21 암탉　　22 속삭이다　　23 숙모, 이모

24 ~을 튀기다　　25 머리핀　　26 전통적인, 전통의

27 두꺼운　　28 대회, 시합, 경쟁　29 이웃 (사람)

30 공연하다　　31 혼자, 홀로　　32 꼭두각시, 인형

33 함께, 같이　　34 귀중한

35 B 때문에 A에게 감사하다　　36 ~하는 게 어때?

37 ~와 똑같은, 동종의, 동일한　　38 ~으로 들어가다

39 하나씩, 차례차례　40 ~한 것을 기억하다

41 구멍을 내다　　42 ~ 덕분에　　43 ~처럼 보이다

단어 TEST Step 2 　　　　p.60

01 together　　02 board　　03 again

04 wear　　05 thick　　06 school nurse

07 album　　08 fun　　09 competition

10 fly　　11 alone　　12 round

13 puppet　　14 science　　15 favorite

16 person　　17 neighbor　　18 cartoon

19 clean　　20 precious　　21 fresh

22 ago　　23 perform　　24 tear

25 hairpin　　26 grade　　27 whisper

28 memory　　29 sunlight　　30 bounce

31 laughter　　32 delicious　　33 practice

34 special　　35 remember+-ing

36 look like+명사　37 go into　　38 thanks to

39 the same as ~　40 get married　41 thank A for B

42 one by one　43 smile at

단어 TEST Step 3 　　　　p.61

1 whisper, 속삭이다　2 favorite, 가장 좋아하는

3 tear, 눈물　4 special, 특별한　5 hairpin, 머리핀

6 laughter, 웃음　7 neighbor, 이웃　8 hen, 암탉

대화문 TEST Step 1 　　　　p.62~63

Get Ready

1 How, watched, last weekend, Do, remember / had, with

2 learned to cut holes, last time, Let's practice / Let's see / remember everything

3 This is, remember me / for calling

Start Off Listen & Talk A

1 remember, our 6th grade / Of course, wore, thick glasses / Guess, moved to, this year / didn't know, Let's visit / Good idea

2 Do, remember / Who, she / our 4th grade / remember, taught a lot of / good dancer, too

Start Off Listen & Talk B

remember, school nurse / nice to everyone / Guess what, getting married / shall, do / Let me see, about making / good idea

Speak Up Look and talk.

last year / Of course / funny pictures, on / great

Speak Up Mission

remember my birthday / Let me see, June / right, not right, June 13

Real-life Scene

who lives alone / Of course, threw, last year / cooked, put, in / delicious, played, together, remember that / won, rounds, good at / are, going to / Let me see / Let's take, this time / Great idea

Express Yourself

1 Do you remember, rode / looked like

2 one in Taiwan / remember, looked like

Learning Diary Check Yourself

singing competition / Of course, practiced, hard / funny pictures, on / great

대화문 TEST Step 2 　　　　p.64~65

Get Ready

1 G: How are you, Ms. Hwang? We watched TV together last weekend. Do you remember that?

　W: Sure, Jieun. I had a great time with you.

2 M: Hi, Minjun. So, you learned to cut holes in the board last time. Let's practice again now.

B: Okay. Let's see. Is this right?

M: Yes. You remember everything.

3 G: Hello, Mr. Yang. This is Minji. Do you remember me?

M: Sure, Minji. Thank you for calling.

1 G: Do you remember Mr. Kim, our 6th grade teacher?

B: Of course. He wore super thick glasses.

G: Guess what? He moved to a new school in February this year.

B: I didn't know that. Let's visit him together.

G: Okay. Good idea.

2 B: Do you remember Ms. Lee?

G: Ms. Lee? Who is she?

B: She was our 4th grade English teacher.

G: Now I remember. She taught a lot of pop songs in her class.

B: She was a good dancer, too.

B: Do you remember Ms. Kang, the school nurse?

G: Sure. She was nice to everyone.

B: Guess what? She's getting married next month.

G: Wow! What shall we do for her?

B: Let me see. What about making a special album?

G: That's a good idea.

A: Do you remember the field trip last year?

B: Of course. We played fun games.

A: I have some funny pictures from it on my phone.

B: That's great!

A: Do you remember my birthday?

B: Let me see. It's June 3. Right?

A: That's right. / That's not right. It's June 13.

G: Do you remember Ms. Park, the old lady who lives alone?

B: Of course. We threw her a birthday party last year.

G: And she cooked japchae for us. She put some chicken in it.

B: Right. It was delicious. And we played card games together. Do you remember that?

G: Yes. She won all the rounds. She's really good at games.

B: When are we going to see her next, Mina?

G: Let me see. Next Saturday.

B: Let's take some pictures with her this time.

G: Great idea, Junsu.

1 G: Do you remember the hot air balloon? We rode it in Turkey.

M: Of course. It looked like an elephant.

2 G: Do you remember the rock?

M: Is it the one in Taiwan?

G: Right.

M: I remember it. It looked like a queen's head.

B: Do you remember the sing`ing competition last year?

G: Of course. We practiced super hard.

B: I have some funny pictures from it on my phone.

G: That's great!

01 What's, Memory　　　02 little, who, next

03 all, who, there 04 favorite, same, his

05 her all, secrets

06 One, talking about　　07 Poor, lady, his

08 Why, old, asked

09 Because, lost, memory　　10 What's, asked

11 something, remember

12 more, so, neighbors

13 enjoying, sunlight

14 memory, asked

15 Something warm, child

16 reading, cartoon　　17 memory, asked

18 Something, brings, laughter

19 was cleaning, medal

20 something, precious as

21 went back, look for

22 went into, took, from

23 Next, looked for

24 always brought, to

25 Finally, found, in

26 as precious, gold　　27 went, gave, by

28 What, brought, things

29 to remember, past

30 held, whispered to, ago

31 at, remembered performing, for 32 laughed a lot

33 bounced, to, remembered　　34 My friend

35 also remembered, one

36 at each other 37 got, back, with, as

01 What's   02 a little boy, lived next to

03 all, who lived

04 favorite person, because, the same as his

05 told her, secrets   06 talking about

07 Poor old lady, said

08 Why, poor, asked

09 Because, lost, said

10 memory, asked

11 something you remember

12 wanted to, went   13 was enjoying

14 he asked   15 Something warm

16 was reading   17 What's a memory

18 brings you laughter   19 was cleaning

20 as precious as

21 went back, to look for

22 went into, from under a hen   23 looked for

24 always brought laughter   25 found, in

26 as, as gold   27 went to, one by one

28 What, thought, brought

29 started to remember

30 held, whispered, found

31 smiled at, remembered performing

32 laughed a lot   33 bounced, to   34 My friend

35 remembered, secrets

36 at each other   37 thanks to, the same, as

1 추억이란 무엇일까?

2 Wilfrid Gordon Parker는 요양원 옆에 사는 어린 소년이었다.

3 그는 그곳에 사는 모든 사람들을 좋아했다.

4 하지만 그가 가장 좋아하는 사람은 Nancy Gordon Cooper 할머니였는데, 그 이유는 그녀의 가운데 이름이 그의 것과 같았기 때문이었다.

5 그는 자기의 모든 비밀을 그녀에게 말했다.

6 어느 날, Wilfrid의 부모님은 Cooper 할머니에 관해 이야기를 하고 있었다.

7 "불쌍한 분." 그의 어머니가 말했다.

8 "왜 불쌍한 분이세요?"라고 Wilfrid가 물었다.

9 "왜냐하면 그분은 기억을 잃으셨거든." 그의 아버지가 말했다.

10 "기억이 뭐예요?" Wilfrid가 물었다.

11 "그것은 네가 기억하는 것이란."라고 그의 아버지가 말했다.

12 Wilfrid는 더 알고 싶어서, 그의 이웃들에게 갔다.

13 Jordan 할머니는 햇볕을 즐기고 있었다.

14 "기억이 뭐예요?" 그가 물었다.

15 "따뜻한 거란다, 아가야." 그녀가 말했다.

16 Mitchell 할머니는 만화책을 읽고 있었다.

17 "기억이 뭐예요?" 그가 물었다.

18 "너에게 웃음을 가져다주는 것이란." 그녀가 말했다.

19 Hunter 할아버지는 자신의 메달을 닦고 있었다.

20 "그건 금처럼 소중한 거지, 어린 친구."라고 그가 말했다.

21 그래서 Wilfrid는 Cooper 할머니께 드릴 기억들을 찾으러 집으로 돌아갔다.

22 그는 닭장 안으로 들어가서 암탉이 품고 있던 신선하고 따뜻한 달걀을 꺼냈다.

23 다음으로, 그는 자신의 양말 인형을 찾았다

24 그것은 항상 그의 부모님께 큰 웃음을 안겨 드렸다.

25 마지막으로, 그는 자신의 장난감 상자 속에서 축구공을 찾아냈다.

26 그것은 그에게는 금만큼이나 소중했다.

27 Wilfrid는 Cooper 할머니께 가서 그녀에게 물건들을 하나씩 드렸다.

28 "이상하면서도 귀여운 아이구나! 이 멋진 물건들을 다 가져오다니 말이야."라고 Cooper 할머니는 생각했다.

29 그러다가 그녀는 자신의 과거를 기억해 내기 시작했다.

30 그녀는 따뜻한 달걀을 쥐고 Wilfrid에게, "오래 전에, 나는 나의 이모님 댁 정원에서 작고 푸른 알을 찾았단다."라고 속삭였다.

31 그녀는 양말 인형을 보며 미소를 짓다가 자기 여동생에게 인형극을 공연해 주었던 것을 기억해 냈다.

32 "내 여동생이 엄청나게 웃었지."라고 Cooper 할머니가 말했다.

33 그녀는 축구공을 바닥에 튀게 해서 Wilfrid에게 던져 주다가 그를 기억해 냈다.

34 "Wilfrid? Wilfrid Gordon Parker! 내 친구!"

35 그녀는 또한 그들만의 비밀을 하나씩 기억해 냈다.

36 두 사람은 서로 바라보며 미소 지었다.

37 Cooper 할머니는 가운데 이름이 자신의 것과 같은 어린 소년 덕분에 기억을 다시 찾게 되었다.

1 What's a Memory?

2 Wilfrid Gordon Parker was a little boy who lived next to a nursing home.

3 He liked all the people who lived there.

4 But his favorite person was Ms. Nancy Gordon Cooper because her middle name was the same as his.

5 He told her all his secrets.

6 One day, Wilfrid's parents were talking about Ms. Cooper.

7 "Poor old lady," said his mother.

8 "Why is she a poor old lady?" asked Wilfrid.

9 "Because she's lost her memory," said his father.

10 "What's a memory?" asked Wilfrid.

11 "It is something you remember," said his father.

12 Wilfrid wanted to know more, so he went to his neighbors.

13 Ms. Jordan was enjoying the sunlight.

14 "What's a memory?" he asked.

15 "Something warm, my child," she said.

16 Ms. Mitchell was reading a cartoon.

17 "What's a memory?" he asked.

18 "Something that brings you laughter," she said.

19 Mr. Hunter was cleaning his medal.

20 "It's something as precious as gold, young man," he said.

21 So Wilfrid went back home to look for memories for Ms. Cooper.

22 He went into the hen house and took a fresh, warm egg from under a hen.

23 Next, he looked for his sock puppet.

24 It always brought laughter to his parents.

25 Finally, he found his football in his toy box.

26 It was as precious as gold to him.

27 Wilfrid went to Ms. Cooper and gave her the things one by one.

28 "What a strange, sweet child!" thought Ms. Cooper, "He's brought all these wonderful things."

29 Then she started to remember her past.

30 She held the warm egg and whispered to Wilfrid, "Long ago, I found a small blue egg in my aunt's garden."

31 She smiled at the sock puppet and remembered performing a puppet show for her sister.

32 "My sister laughed a lot," said Ms. Cooper.

33 She bounced the football to Wilfrid and remembered him.

34 "Wilfrid? Wilfrid Gordon Parker! My friend!"

35 She also remembered their secrets one by one.

36 The two smiled at each other.

37 Ms. Cooper got her memory back thanks to the little boy with the same middle name as hers.

구석구석지문 TEST Step 1   p.76

Express Yourself

1. On, went to
2. painting that we bought
3. never forget
4. took pictures, traditional dancers

5. saw, town
6. On, arrived in
7. girl who was wearing
8. never forget, experience
9. saw, looked like

Do It Yourself

1. like to tell
2. That person
3. Don't forget that, Just go for it
4. on the last day
5. feel stressed, look at

Link to the World

1. active seniors, share their knowledge
2. teaches, about farming
3. in the past
4. works, to teach
5. cooking class, learn to make

구석구석지문 TEST Step 2   p.77

Express Yourself

1. On May 29, 2017, we went to India.
2. This is a painting that we bought in the market.
3. I'll never forget the experience.
4. We took pictures of Korean traditional dancers.
5. We saw them at the town festival.
6. On June 7, 2017, we arrived in Laos.
7. We met a girl who was wearing a beautiful dress.
8. I'll never forget the experience.
9. We saw a rock. It looked like a queen's head.

Do It Yourself

1. I'd like to tell you about a student teacher I can't forget.
2. That person is Ms. Jeon.
3. Don't forget that you're great, Miso! Just go for it.
4. This is the bookmark that she gave to me on the last day.
5. When I feel stressed, I always look at this.

Link to the World

1. There are a lot of active seniors who share their knowledge and talents.
2. Mr. Kim in Busan is a smart farmer and teaches people about farming.
3. Ms. Lee was a science teacher in the past.
4. Now she works in a park to teach children about plants and birds.
5. In Ms. Choi's cooking class, young people learn to make gimchi and Korean hot pepper sauce.

9 front, 앞, 정면   10 road, 도로, 길   11 lose, 잃어버리다

12 dangerous, 위험한

13 stop, (~하는 것을) 막다, 그만두게 하다   14 laugh, 웃다

15 hood, (외투 등에 달린) 모자   16 knock, 두드리다

단어 TEST Step 1 · p.78

01 잃어버리다, 지다   02 ~을 필요로 하다   03 ~을 기쁘게 하다

04 점검하다   05 따라가다, 뒤따르다

06 (~하는 것을) 막다, 그만두게 하다   07 위험한

08 끝, 마지막   09 장면, 광경   10 신난

11 정면, 앞   12 바구니   13 안전한

14 (외투 등에 달린) 모자   15 두드리다

16 웃다   17 (입으로) 불다, (바람이) 불다

18 떠나다   19 pig의 애칭   20 길, 도로

21 함께   22 ~ 아래에   23 작가

24 유명한   25 흔들리다   26 그런데, 그건 그렇고

27 ~해지다   28 코를 풀다   29 어디 보자.. 글쎄.

30 ~에 좋다   31 ~을 꺼내다

32 그럼요, 전혀 문제 되지 않아요.   33 ~의 밖으로

34 ~을 들여다보다   35 혼잣말하다   36 ~해선 안 된다

37 휴식을 취하다   38 ~을 보다

39 가 버리다, 사라지다

40 B에 대해 A에게 감사하다

단어 TEST Step 2 · p.79

01 laugh   02 together   03 under

04 writer   05 blow   06 follow

07 please   08 stop   09 road

10 front   11 famous   12 piggy

13 shake   14 lose   15 check

16 need   17 dangerous   18 basket

19 safe   20 hood   21 end

22 scene   23 knock   24 excited

25 leave   26 look into   27 out of

28 be good for   29 No problem.   30 look at

31 take out   32 go away

33 should not+동사원형   34 Let me see.

35 by the way   36 thank A for B   37 take a break

38 blow one's nose   39 talk to oneself

40 Have you ever heard of ~?

단어 TEST Step 3 · p.80

1 leave, 떠나다   2 blow, (입으로) 불다   3 end, 끝, 마지막

4 famous, 유명한   5 follow, 따라가다, 뒤따르다

6 please, ~을 기쁘게 하다   7 safe, 안전한   8 writer, 작가

본문 TEST Step 1 · p.81~83

01 Red, Hood   02 Scene, front, little

03 in with, basket   04 take, break, under

05 walks, looks into   06 look, for lunch

07 blows, hard, shaking   08 stop, Let, see, change

09 What, mean by   10 Taking, writing, lived

11 shouldn't do   12 blows, but, out of

13 there, Why, blow   14 didn't, blew, nose

15 Don't, Go away   16 so sorry

17 go back into   18 believe, happened, at

19 These, for   20 Where, live

21 lives at, end   22 himself, for, later

23 herself, works, safe, follow

24 Scene, house   25 around, happy, excited

26 Knocking on, it's

27 happily, opening, dance

28 Thank, for pleasing   29 Well, that's

30 running, jumps over   31 not dangerous

32 dancing for   33 glad, kind to

34 too, By, way, anything

35 out, Would, like   36 thanks, don't, like

37 Don't, eating, lost, should

38 crying, tired, hungry   39 comes in

40 think, need, right   41 so glad, here

42 To, that   43 famous, heard of

44 have, one, wrote   45 changed, got tired

46 can change, again   47 lost, gave, help

48 problem, ending, okay

49 That'll be   50 stops dancing, can enjoy

51 stop dancing, can eat

52 laughs, enjoys, together

본문 TEST Step 2 · p.84~86

01 Red, Hood   02 Scene, In front of, little

03 comes in with

04 can see, take a break, under

05 walks in, looks into   06 look delicious, for lunch

07 blows, hard, is shaking

08 to stop, Let me see, change the story

09 What, mean by

10 Taking out, writing something, There lived

11 shouldn't do   12 blows, come out of

13 there, Why did, blow 14 didn't, just blew, nose

15 Don't do, Go away   16 so sorry

17 go back into

18 can't believe, happened, Looking at 19 These, for

20 Where does, live   21 lives at the end

22 himself, for lunch, too, later

23 herself, going to, works, safe, follow

24 Scene, house

25 dances around, looks, happy, excited

26 Knocking on, it's, okay

27 happily, opening, watching, dance

28 Thank, for pleasing 29 Well, that's

30 running in, jumps over

31 not dangerous   32 is dancing for

33 glad, kind to

34 By the way, have anything to eat

35 Taking, out the basket, Would, like

36 No, thanks, don't, like

37 Don't worry, eating, lost, What should I do

38 crying, so tired, hungry   39 comes in

40 think, need, help, right

41 so glad, here   42 To, Who's that

43 famous, Have, ever heard of

44 have, one, wrote 45 changed, got tired, hungry

46 can change, again 47 lost, gave, help me

48 problem, a happy ending for, okay

49 That'll be great   50 stops dancing, can enjoy

51 stop dancing, can eat

52 laughs, enjoys, together

본문 TEST Step 3   p.87~89

1 빨간 모자

2 장면 1: 아기 돼지 삼 형제의 집 앞에서

3 (Red가 케이크와 과자가 든 바구니를 들고 등장한다.)

4 Red: 이제 아기 돼지 삼 형제의 집이 보인다. 여기 나무 아래에서 좀 쉬어야지.

5 (늑대가 걸어 들어와 집 안을 들여다본다.)

6 늑대: 새끼 돼지들이네! 맛있어 보인다. 점심으로 그들을 먹어야겠어.

7 (늑대가 집을 세게 불자 집이 흔들리고 있다.)

8 Red: 오, 저런 나쁜 늑대 같으니라고! 그를 멈추게 하려면 내가 뭘 할 수 있을까? 어디 보자.… 바로 그거야! (늑대에게) 이봐! 내가 이야기를 바꾸겠어!

9 늑대: 그게 무슨 말이야?

---

10 Red: (펜을 꺼내 뭔가를 쓰면서) "크고 힘센 아기 돼지 삼 형제가 그 집에 살고 있었다."

11 늑대: 그렇게 하면 안 돼!

12 (늑대가 다시 집을 분다. 그러나 크고 힘센 돼지 삼 형제가 집에서 나온다.)

13 돼지 삼 형제: 이봐, 거기! 왜 우리 집을 불고 있어?

14 늑대: 음… 그러지 않았어. 나는 그냥 코를 풀었을 뿐이야.

15 돼지 삼 형제: 여기서 다시는 그러지 마. 가 버려!

16 늑대: 알았어. 정말 미안해.

17 (돼지들은 집 안으로 다시 들어간다.)

18 늑대: 이런 일이 일어나다니 믿을 수가 없어. 나는 너무 배가 고파! (Red의 바구니를 보며) 그건 뭐야?

19 Red: 할머니께 드릴 과자들이야.

20 늑대: 어디 사시는데?

21 Red: 이 길의 끝에 사셔.

22 늑대: (혼잣말로) 할머니도 점심으로 좋지. (Red에게) 나중에 보자. (늑대가 떠난다.)

23 Red: 안녕. (혼잣말로) 흠…. 그는 할머니 댁으로 갈 거야. 이야기를 다시 바꿔야겠어. (펜을 꺼내서 뭔가를 쓰며) 좋아. 내 이야기가 제대로 돌아가면 할머니는 안전하실 거야. 그를 따라가 봐야지. (Red가 떠난다.)

24 장면 2: 할머니의 집

25 (늑대가 할머니 주변을 맴돌며 춤을 춘다. 할머니는 아주 행복하고 신나 보인다.)

26 Red: (문을 두드리며) 할머니, 저예요. 괜찮으세요?

27 할머니: (행복하게 웃으며 문을 열면서) 물론이지, Red야. 어서 들어와. 늑대가 나를 위해 춤추는 걸 보고 있었단다.

28 Red: 이봐, 늑대야. 우리 할머니를 기쁘게 해드려서 고마워.

29 늑대: 음, 그게 ….

30 왕자: (문을 열고 뛰어 들어오며) 이봐, 이 나쁜 늑대야! (왕자가 늑대에게 달려든다.)

31 Red: 아니, 아니에요! 멈춰요. 그는 위험하지 않아요.

32 할머니: 맞아. 보세요. 그가 우리를 위해 춤추고 있잖아요.

33 왕자: 정말요? 늑대야, 미안해. 네가 할머니께 잘해 드린다니 기쁘다.

34 늑대: 음 … 나도 기뻐. 그런데, 먹을 것 좀 있어?

35 Red: (바구니에서 과자를 좀 꺼내며) 과자 좀 먹을래?

36 늑대: 고맙지만 됐어. 난 과자를 먹지 않아. 나는 닭고기가 좋아.

37 Red: 걱정하지 마. 내가 이야기를 다시 바꿔야겠네. 그러면 넌 과자 먹는 걸 좋아하게 될 거야. (바구니를 뒤지며) 오, 펜을 잃어버렸어. 어떻게 하지?

38 늑대: (춤을 추며 울부짖으며) 오, 안 돼! 난 지금 너무 피곤하고 배고파.

39 (Andersen이 들어온다.)

40 Andersen: 내 도움이 필요한 것 같은데, 맞지?

41 Red: 오, Andersen 씨. 여기 오셔서 너무 기뻐요.

42 할머니: (Red에게) 저 사람이 누구니?

43 Red: 저분은 유명한 작가 Andersen 씨예요. "빨간 구두"에 대해 들어 보신 적이 있죠?

44 할머니: 그래, 들어 봤지. 그 이야기를 쓴 사람이란 말이지?

45 Red: 맞아요. (Andersen에게) 제가 이야기를 바꿔서 저

불쌍한 늑대가 피곤하고 배고파졌어요.

46 Andersen: 너는 다시 이야기를 바꿀 수 있잖아.

47 Red: 죄송하지만, 제가 작가님이 주신 펜을 잃어버렸어요. 저 좀 도와주세요.

48 Andersen: 문제없지. 내가 모두에게 행복한 결말을 쓸게. 괜찮지?

49 Red: 아주 좋아요!

50 Andersen: 좋아. 여기 내 펜을 써야지. "그 친절한 늑대는 춤추기를 멈춘다. 그는 케이크와 과자를 즐겨 먹을 수 있다."

51 늑대: (춤을 멈추며) 춤을 멈출 수가 있다! (과자를 먹으며) 그리고 과자를 먹을 수 있어! 정말 고마워요.

52 (모두 웃으며 한께 과자를 맛있게 먹는다.)

---

1 Little Red Writing Hood

2 Scene 1: In front of the three little piggies' house

3 (Red comes in with a basket of cakes and cookies.)

4 Red: Now I can see the three little piggies' house. I'll take a break here under the tree.

5 (Wolf walks in and looks into the house.)

6 Wolf: Baby piggies! They look delicious. I'll eat them for lunch.

7 (Wolf blows the house hard and it is shaking.)

8 Red: Oh, that bad Wolf! What can I do to stop him? Let me see. ... That's it! (To Wolf) Hey, you! I'll change the story!

9 Wolf: What do you mean by that?

10 Red: (Taking out a pen and writing something) "There lived three big strong piggies in the house."

11 Wolf: You shouldn't do that!

12 (Wolf blows again, but the three big strong piggies come out of the house.)

13 Three Piggies: Hey there! Why did you blow our house?

14 Wolf: Um ... I didn't. I just blew my nose.

15 Three Piggies: Don't do that again here. Go away!

16 Wolf: Okay. I'm so sorry.

17 (The piggies go back into the house.)

18 Wolf: I can't believe this happened. I'm so hungry! (Looking at Red's basket) What are those?

19 Red: These are cookies for Grandma.

20 Wolf: Where does she live?

21 Red: She lives at the end of this road.

22 Wolf: (To himself) Grandma is good for lunch, too. (To Red) See you later. (Wolf leaves.)

23 Red: Bye. (Talking to herself) Hmm .... He's going to Grandma's. I think I should change the story again. (Taking out the pen and writing something) Okay. If my story works, Grandma will be safe. I'll

follow him. (Red leaves.)

24 Scene 2: Grandma's house

25 (Wolf dances around Grandma. She looks very happy and excited.)

26 Red: (Knocking on the door) Grandma, it's me. Are you okay?

27 Grandma: (Laughing happily and opening the door) Sure, Red. Come on in. I was watching Wolf dance for me.

28 Red: Hey, Wolf. Thank you for pleasing my grandmother.

29 Wolf: Well, that's ....

30 Prince: (Opening the door and running in) Hey, you bad Wolf! (Prince jumps over Wolf.)

31 Red: No, no! Stop. He's not dangerous.

32 Grandma: Right. Look. He is dancing for us.

33 Prince: Really? Wolf, I'm sorry. I'm glad you're kind to Grandma.

34 Wolf: Well, ... I'm glad, too. By the way, do you have anything to eat?

35 Red: (Taking some cookies out the basket) Would you like some cookies?

36 Wolf: No, thanks. I don't eat cookies. I like chicken.

37 Red: Don't worry. I'll change the story again. Then you will like eating cookies. (Checking the basket) Oh, I lost my pen. What should I do?

38 Wolf: (Dancing and crying) Oh, no! I'm so tired and hungry now.

39 (Andersen comes in.)

40 Andersen: I think you need my help, right?

41 Red: Oh, Mr. Andersen. I'm so glad you're here.

42 Grandma: (To Red) Who's that?

43 Red: He is Mr. Andersen, the famous writer. Have you ever heard of "The Red Shoes"?

44 Grandma: Yes, I have. Is he the one who wrote that story?

45 Red: Right. (To Andersen) I changed the story, and the poor Wolf got tired and hungry.

46 Andersen: You can change the story again.

47 Red: I'm sorry, but I lost the pen you gave to me. Please help me.

48 Andersen: No problem. I'll write a happy ending for everyone. Is that okay?

49 Red: That'll be great!

50 Andersen: All right. I'll use my pen here. "The kind Wolf stops dancing. He can enjoy cakes and cookies."

51 Wolf: (Stopping dancing) I can stop dancing! (Eating cookies) And I can eat cookies! Thank you very much.

52 (Everybody laughs and enjoys cookies together.)

MEMO

MEMO

MEMO

적중 100 + 특별부록

Plan B

우리학교 최신기출

천재 · 정사열 교과서를 배우는

학교 시험문제 분석 · 모음 · 해설집

전국단위 학교 시험문제 수집 및 분석
출제 빈도가 높은 문제 위주로 선별
문제 풀이에 필요한 상세한 해설

중2-1
영어

천재 · 정사열

Lesson 1   **Time to Start Again**

Lesson 2   **I Love My Town!**

Lesson 3   **Be Active, Be Safe!**

Lesson 4   **Memories in Your Heart**

◎ 선택형 문항의 답안은 컴퓨터용 수정 싸인펜을 사용하여 OMR 답안지에 바르게 표기하시오.
◎ 서술형 문제는 답을 답안지에 반드시 검정 볼펜으로 쓰시오.
◎ 총 25문항 100점 만점입니다. 문항별 배점은 각 문항에 표시되어 있습니다.

[경기 ㅇㅇ중]

1. 다음 대화가 자연스럽도록 (A)~(D)를 바르게 배열한 것은? (4점)

(A) I'll join it, too. When is the fist meeting?
(B) Next Wednesday. I can't wait for the first meeting!
(C) I think it's the right club for me. I want to learn many interesting tricks.
(D) What do you think of the magic club?

① (A)-(B)-(D)-(C)
② (B)-(A)-(C)-(D)
③ (C)-(B)-(A)-(D)
④ (D)-(A)-(C)-(B)
⑤ (D)-(C)-(A)-(B)

[송파구 ㅇㅇ중]

2. 주어진 단어를 배열하여 문장을 완성하시오. (5점)

(1) We _____.
(bowls, to, wash, many, have)
(2) Dad _____.
(a list of, to, books, me, read, gave)

[충북 ㅇㅇ중]

3. 다음 중 that의 쓰임이 다른 하나는? (4점)

① I guess that he likes sports.
② I think that it's the boy's bag.
③ I believe that he is in the second grade.
④ I want to see that book on the desk.
⑤ I hope that he can find his schoolbag soon.

[송파구 ㅇㅇ중]

4. 대화가 이루어지는 장소는? (3점)

A: Look! Two dishes of vegetables. How do you like today's menu?
B: I think it's okay. I like vegetables.
A: I don't eat vegetables.
B: Try some. They are good for our health.

① library
② garden
③ cafeteria
④ kitchen
⑤ supermarket

[광주 ㅇㅇ중]

5. 다음 대화가 자연스럽게 이어지도록 문장의 순서를 바르게 배열한 것은? (4점)

Seho: Miso, what do you think of Mr. Park?
Miso: The new math teacher? He looks very strict and serious.
ⓐ What do you mean, Seho?
ⓑ Really?
ⓒ Yes. During the first class, we did interesting math activities with our cell phones.
ⓓ Don't judge a book by its cover.
ⓔ My first class with Mr. Park was great. He was very kind, and his class was so exciting.
Miso: Wow! I can't wait for his class tomorrow. It's my first math class this year.

① ⓓ-ⓐ-ⓒ-ⓑ-ⓔ
② ⓓ-ⓐ-ⓔ-ⓑ-ⓒ
③ ⓓ-ⓐ-ⓑ-ⓒ-ⓔ
④ ⓓ-ⓔ-ⓒ-ⓐ-ⓑ
⑤ ⓓ-ⓑ-ⓐ-ⓒ-ⓔ

6. 다음 중 영영풀이가 바르지 <u>않은</u> 것은? (4점)

① judge: the person in a court of law who decides how the law should be applied, for example how criminals should be punished

② continue: keep doing and do not stop

③ tidy: neat and arranged in an organized way

④ brush: an object which has a large number of bristles or hairs fixed to it for painting, for cleaning things, and for tidying your hair

⑤ hallway: a room with doors in a building

8. 위 대화의 ⓐ의 우리말에 해당하는 속담을 영어로 쓰시오. (5점)

답: ＿＿＿＿＿＿＿＿＿＿＿＿＿＿＿＿＿＿＿＿

9. 위 대화의 ⓑ가 의미하는 바로 적절한 것은? (4점)

① 내일 진행되는 그의 수업이 정말 기다려져.

② 내일 그의 수업을 듣고 싶지 않아.

③ 나는 내일까지 수업에 들어갈 수 없어.

④ 그는 내일까지 나를 기다려 주지 않을 거야.

⑤ 그의 수업은 내일로 연기되었어.

[7~9] 다음 대화를 읽고 물음에 답하시오.

> Seho: Miso, what do you think of Mr. Park?
> Miso: The new math teacher? He looks very (A)＿＿＿＿＿＿＿＿＿＿＿＿＿.
> Seho: ⓐ겉모습만 보고 판단하지 마.
> Miso: What do you mean, Seho?
> Seho: My first class with Mr. Park was great. He was very kind, and his class was so exciting.
> Miso: Really?
> Seho: Yes. During the first class, we did interesting math activities with our cell phones.
> Miso: Wow! ⓑI can't wait for his class tomorrow. It's my first math class this year.

7. 위 대화의 흐름상, 빈칸 (A)에 들어갈 말로 가장 알맞은 것은? (4점)

① funny and kind

② serious and strict

③ sweet and thoughtful

④ gentle and generous

⑤ rude and honest

[10~12] 다음 글을 읽고 물음에 답하시오.

> After class, Seho went to Dami and said, "I can't find one of my ⓐ<u>ticket</u>. Did you happen ⓑ<u>seeing</u> it?"
> "No," she answered.
> "Isn't it in your bag?"
> "No, it's not there. I think I lost it," said Seho.
> On ⓒ<u>his</u> way home, Dami saw Jihun. He had the ticket in his hand. (A)<u>Dami got angry</u> and said, "Hey! Why do you ...?"
> Just then, Jihun saw Seho and ⓓ<u>shout</u>, "Seho! I found a ticket in the hallway. I think it's yours."
> "Thanks! I was looking for that!" said Seho.
> 'He's not so bad,' Dami thought.
> "So, what were you saying? Do you have something (B)<u>to say</u>, Dami?" asked Jihun.
> "Um, how about going to the school basketball game with me this Friday? It's the finals."
> Jihun looked really ⓔ<u>pleased</u>. "I'd love to!"

10. 위 글의 ⓐ~ⓔ 중 어법상 옳은 것은? (4점)

① ⓐ   ② ⓑ   ③ ⓒ   ④ ⓓ   ⑤ ⓔ

11. 위 글의 흐름으로 보아 (A)에서 Dami가 화가 난
    이유는?   (4점)

She was angry because _____.

① she thought Jihun had taken Seho's ticket
② Jihun told Seho that he had found the ticket
③ she saw Jihun give the ticket back to Seho
④ Jihun asked Seho to go to the KBL game
   with him
⑤ she knew Seho lost the ticket and couldn't
   find it

12. 위 글의 (B)와 다음 문장의 밑줄 친 부분 중 쓰임
    이 다른 것은?   (3점)
① He has a large family to support.
② Dad gave me a list of books to read.
③ His next work was to sweep the floor.
④ I'm looking for a good movie to see with
   my parents.
⑤ She had no running shoes to wear for the
   marathon.

[경기 ○○중]

13. 다음 대화의 빈칸 (A)와 (B)에 들어갈 말로 가장
    적절한 것은?   (4점)

B: Shall we join the Green Garden club
   together?
G: Good idea. I like growing vegetables.
B: You (A)_____? I like eating
   vegetables.
G: Let's join the club right now. When do
   they meet?
B: They meet on the third Thursday of each
   month after school in the school garden.
G: That's fine with me.

B: Also, they have a party with fresh
   vegetables every month. The first party is
   on May 30th.
G: It's going to be awesome. (B)_____
   the party.

	(A)	(B)
①	guess that	I'll have fun at
②	guess what	I can't expect
③	know what	I am looking for
④	know that	I can't stand
⑤	know what	I can't wait for

[송파구 ○○중]

[14~15] 다음 대화를 읽고 물음에 답하시오.

A: I'll join it, too. When is the first meeting?
B: I think it's the right club for me. I want
   to learn many interesting tricks.
C: What do you think of this club?
D: Next Wednesday. I can't wait for the first
   meeting.

14. 자연스러운 대화가 되도록 A~D를 바르게 배열
    한 것은?   (4점)
① A-D-C-B   ② A-C-B-D
③ B-A-C-D   ④ C-A-D-B
⑤ C-B-A-D

15. 밑줄 친 this club에 해당되는 동아리는?   (4점)
① Movie Movie   ② Cartoon Club
③ Great Magic   ④ Health Club
⑤ Green Garden

[16~18] 다음 글을 읽고 물음에 답하시오.

Seho and Jihun were talking in the hallway when Dami came over. "Happy birthday!" she said to Seho. "Here. They're from my dad."

"Wow, two KBL tickets! Thanks!"

"Who are you going to take with you?" Dami asked.

"Minjun. ⓐHe took me to a soccer game before. So, it's time to pay ⓑhim back."

"You know what?" Jihun (A)_____.

"(B)Minjun isn't a fan of basketball. But I am!"

"Well, I'll ask ⓒhim first anyway," replied Seho.

"ⓓHe won't go with you. Trust me," said Jihun.

"Who is this guy?" Dami thought to herself, "ⓔHe wants Minjun's ticket."

16. 밑줄 친 ⓐ~ⓔ 중 가리키는 대상이 다른 하나는?

(4점)

① ⓐ   ② ⓑ   ③ ⓒ   ④ ⓓ   ⑤ ⓔ

17. 빈칸 (A)에 들어갈 표현으로 아래 보기와 공통으로 쓰인 것은? (4점)

<보기>
• Stand in line. You shouldn't _____ line.
• Don't _____ when I speak.

① cut in   ② speak of
③ get to   ④ throw away
⑤ bump into

18. (B)에서 Jihun이 말한 의도로 가장 알맞은 것은?

(5점)

① Jihun is a good basketball player.
② Jihun wants to talk about Seho's ticket.
③ Minjun isn't good at playing basketball.
④ Jihun wants to go to a KBL game with Seho.
⑤ Jihun thinks that Minjun will go to a KBL game.

19. 다음 중 어법상 옳은 것을 고르면? (4점)
① I expect seeing you again.
② They have no house to live.
③ She needs somebody to talk to.
④ I need a piece of paper to write.
⑤ He puts off to visit the teachers by the next day.

[20~21] 다음 글을 읽고 물음에 답하시오.

Do you want to say about the school cafeteria? Then post your notes here!
• I think the line is too long. Are there any ways to solve this problem?
• I think the chairs are too high. Do you have any plans to change them?
• I think the pasta was really delicious today. Do you have any plans to serve it more often?

20. 위 글을 쓴 목적으로 가장 알맞은 것은? (4점)
① To say hello
② To say sorry
③ To say thank you
④ To get volunteers
⑤ To get people's opinions

21. 위 글의 밑줄 친 부분과 쓰임이 <u>다른</u> 것은? (3점)

① They found a big house <u>to live in.</u>

② She has three children <u>to take care of.</u>

③ She got up early <u>to catch the first train.</u>

④ The baby has a lot of toys <u>to play with.</u>

⑤ He was the first man <u>to reach the South Pole.</u>

22. 위 글의 (A)와 (B)에 들어갈 말로 바르게 짝지어진 것은? (4점)

① (A) take   (B) take

② (A) take   (B) took

③ (A) took   (B) take

④ (A) took   (B) taking

⑤ (A) took   (B) took

23. 위 글의 빈칸 (C)에 들어갈 말로 가장 적절한 것은? (4점)

① myself   ② yourself   ③ himself

④ herself   ⑤ itself

[광주 ○○중]

[22~25] 다음 글을 읽고 물음에 답하시오.

Seho and Jihun were talking in the hallway when Dami came over. "Happy birthday!" she said to Seho. "Here. They're from my dad."

"Wow, two KBL tickets! Thanks!"

"Who are you going to (A)_____ with you?" Dami asked.

"Minjun. He (B)_____ me to a soccer game before.

So, 그에게 보답할 때야.

"You know what?" Jihun cut in. "Minjun isn't a fan of basketball. But I am!"

"Well, I'll ask him first anyway," replied Seho.

"He won't go with you. Trust me," said Jihun.

"Who is this guy?" Dami thought to (C)_____, "He wants Minjun's ticket."

"Oh! There's the bell. See you later," said Dami. She hurried to class.

"Come on, Jihun," said Seho, and he started to run. At the corner, Seho bumped into someone.

"Sorry!" he said and continued to run. Just then, Jihun saw something on the floor.

"Wait, Seho!" he said, but Seho was not there.

24. Choose one that you can't answer after you read the passage above. (4점)

① When is Jihun's birthday?

② What did Dami give Seho and why?

③ Who did Seho want to go with to the basketball game?

④ Did Jihun want to go to the game?

⑤ What did Jihun try to do when he saw something on the floor?

25. 위 글의 밑줄 친 우리말을 조건에 맞는 영어 문장으로 작성하시오. (5점)

[조건]
1. to부정사의 형용사적 용법을 사용.
2. 주어진 단어를 사용. (time, pay, back)
3. 철자 및 어법 오류는 1개당 1점 감점.

→ _____ _____ _____ _____

_____ _____

◎ 선택형 문항의 답안은 컴퓨터용 수정 싸인펜을 사용하여 OMR 답안지에 바르게 표기하시오.
◎ 서술형 문제는 답을 답안지에 반드시 검정 볼펜으로 쓰시오.
◎ 총 28문항 100점 만점입니다. 문항별 배점은 각 문항에 표시되어 있습니다.

[경기 ㅇㅇ중]

1. 다음 빈칸에 들어갈 말로 가장 적절한 것은?   (3점)

• She _____ to see the old man.

① allowed   ② replied   ③ reduced

④ happened   ⑤ continued

[인천 ㅇㅇ중]

2. 다음 중 어법상 옳은 것은?   (4점)

① I will go fishing if it will be sunny tomorrow.

② Nancy saw her grandmother make a soup.

③ I asked my science teacher let me work alone.

④ Though you are hungry, eat some cookies on the table.

⑤ Unless you don't study harder, you'll get bad grades.

[대전 ㅇㅇ중]

3. 다음 빈칸에 들어갈 말로 알맞은 것은?   (3점)

• Please give me a pen to write _____.

① on   ② at   ③ with

④ from   ⑤ inside

[대전 ㅇㅇ중]

4. 다음 〈보기〉의 밑줄 친 부분과 쓰임이 같은 것은?   (3점)

<보기>
• Do you have any plans to visit Seoul?

① We want to visit your house.

② They are planning to visit Hawaii.

③ I would love to visit your restaurant.

④ People started to visit her hometown.

⑤ There are famous places to visit in Paris.

[경기 ㅇㅇ중]

5. 다음 대화의 빈칸 (A), (B)에 들어갈 말로 가장 적절한 것은?   (4점)

A: Let's join the School Band club together. What do you think of it?
B: Okay. I (A)_____ playing the flute.
A: Oh, really? I can play the ukulele.
B: Let's join this school band right now. They practice after school every Tuesday.
B: They're going to have the first concert on July 15.
A: Great. I hope to play in the concert.
B: Me, too. I can't (B)_____ for the concert.

	(A)	(B)
①	enjoy	wait
②	love	wish
③	hate	look
④	like	stand
⑤	finish	work

[6~7] 다음 대화를 읽고 물음에 답하시오.

> Tom: Molly, what do you think of Mr. Park?
> Molly: The new math teacher? He looks very strict and serious.
> Tom: (A)Don't judge a book by its cover.
> Molly: What do you mean, Tom?
> Tom: My first class with Mr. Park was great. He was very kind, and his class was so exciting.
> Molly: Really?
> Tom: Yes. During the first class, we did interesting math activities with our cell phones.
> Molly: Wow! I'm looking forward to seeing him tomorrow. It's my first math class this year.

6. 위 대화의 내용과 일치하는 것은? (3점)

① Mr. Park taught Tom and Molly last year.

② Mr. Park lets students play with cell phones.

③ Mr. Park is the most famous teacher at school.

④ Tom already met Mr. Park before talking to Molly.

⑤ Molly doesn't take Mr. Park's math class this year.

7. 위 대화의 밑줄 친 (A)의 영영풀이로 가장 적절한 것은? (4점)

① The more you do something, the better you will become at it.

② Don't put all your hopes and resources into one goal or dream.

③ The more you know, the more powerful you can be in different areas of your life.

④ Don't try to do too many things at the same time; focus on one thing at a time.

⑤ You should not form an opinion about somebody/something from their appearance only.

8. 다음 밑줄 친 단어의 영영 풀이로 알맞은 것은? (4점)

> • She <u>realized</u> that she didn't bring her homework.

① to believe that someone is good

② to buy something in the end

③ to continue a series of games or competitions

④ to understand a situation, sometimes suddenly

⑤ to stop doing something because it is complete

9. 다음 짝지어진 대화 중 <u>어색한</u> 것은? (4점)

① A: I can't wait for the birthday party.
   B: Fine with me.

② A: He looks very strict and serious.
   B: Don't judge a book by its cover.

③ A: I'm nervous about the singing contest.
   B: Don't worry.

④ A: You look thirsty. Do you want something to drink?
   B: Thanks.

⑤ A: Are you busy now?
   B: Yes, I have lots of plants to water.

[10~12] 다음 글을 읽고 물음에 답하시오.

Seho and Jihun were talking in the hallway when Dami came over. "Happy birthday!" she said to Seho. "Here. ⓐThey're from my dad."

"Wow, two KBL tickets! Thanks!"

"Who are you going to take with you?" Dami asked.

"Minjun. He took me to a soccer game before. So, (A)_____."

"You know what?" Jihun cut in. "Minjun isn't a fan of basketball. But I am!"

"Well, I'll ask him first anyway," replied Seho.

"He won't go with you. Trust me," said Jihun.

"Who is this guy?" Dami thought to herself, "He wants Minjun's ticket."

"Oh! There's the bell. See you later," said Dami. She hurried to class.

"Come on, Jihun," said Seho, and he started to run.

At the corner, Seho bumped into someone. "Sorry!" he said and continued to run. Just then, Jihun saw something on the floor.

"Wait, Seho!" he said, but Seho was not there.

10. 위 글의 빈칸 (A)에 들어갈 말을 아래 단어들을 사용하여 배열하시오. (4점)

to	it	time	back
him	pay	is	

→ _____ _____ _____ _____

_____ _____

11. 위 글의 내용과 <u>다른</u> 대화는? (3점)

① Q: What was Seho doing when Dami saw him?
  A: He was talking with his friend Jihun.

② Q: Who did Seho want to go with to the basketball game?
  A: He wanted to take Jihun to the game.

③ Q: Did Jihun want to go to the game?
  A: Yes. He really wanted to go.

④ Q: What did Seho start to do when the bell rang?
  A: He started to run.

⑤ Q: What happened while Seho was running?
  A: He bumped into someone.

12. 위 글의 ⓐ<u>They</u>가 가리키는 것으로 알맞은 것은? (2점)

① Seho and Jihun
② Seho and Minjun
③ soccer games
④ basketball tickets
⑤ fans of basketball

13. <보기>를 활용하여 ⓐ, ⓑ의 뜻에 맞는 영어 문장을 쓰시오. (5점)

Sue: Hey, let's go bike riding this afternoon!
Jamie: Well ....
Sue: What's wrong? ⓐ할 말 있니?
Jamie: I'm too busy. ⓑ나 써야 할 편지가 많아.

<보 기>
something, lots, have, say

ⓐ _____

ⓑ _____

[14~15] 다음 글을 읽고 물음에 답하시오.

Seho and Jihun were talking in the hallway when Dami came over.

"Happy birthday!" she said to Seho.

"Here. They're from my dad."

"Wow, two KBL tickets! Thanks!"

"Who are you going to take with you?" Dami asked.

"Minjun. ⓐHe took me to a soccer game before.

So, it's time to pay ⓑhim back.

"You know what?" Jihun cut in.

"Minjun isn't a fan of basketball. But I am!"

"Well, I'll ask ⓒhim first anyway," replied Seho.

"ⓓHe won't go with you. Trust me," said Jihun.

"Who is this guy?" Dami thought to herself.

"ⓔHe wants Minjun's ticket."

14. 위 글을 읽고 대답할 수 <u>없는</u> 질문은? (3점)

① What was Seho doing when Dami saw him?

② What did Dami give Seho?

③ Who did Seho want to go with to the basketball game?

④ Did Jihun want to go to the game?

⑤ What did Jihun think of Dami?

15. 위 글의 밑줄 친 ⓐ~ⓔ 중 가리키는 대상이 나머지 넷과 <u>다른</u> 것은? (3점)

① ⓐ   ② ⓑ   ③ ⓒ   ④ ⓓ   ⑤ ⓔ

16. 밑줄 친 단어의 쓰임이 <u>어색한</u> 것은? (4점)

① Turn right at the <u>corner</u>.

② <u>Hurry</u> up, and you will arrive in time.

③ The teacher <u>replied</u> a sign on the wall.

④ The leaves on the trees <u>reduce</u> pollution.

⑤ They went to the <u>cafeteria</u> to have lunch.

[17~19] 다음 글을 읽고 물음에 답하시오.

After class, Seho went to Dami and said, "I can't find one of my tickets. Did you ⓐ<u>happen to</u> see it?"

"No," she answered.

"Isn't it in your bag?"

"No, it's not there. I think I lost it," said Seho.

(A)_____ her way home, Dami saw Jihun. He had the ticket in his hand. Dami got angry and said, "Hey! Why do you ...?"

Just then, Jihun saw Seho and ⓑ<u>shouted</u>, "Seho! I found a ticket in the ⓒ<u>hallway</u>. I think it's yours."

"Thanks! I was looking (B)_____ that!" said Seho.

(가)"He's not so bad," Dami thought.

"So, what were you saying? Do you have something to say, Dami?" asked Jihun.

"Um, how (C)_____ going to the school basketball game with me this Friday? It's the ⓓ<u>finals</u>."

Jihun ⓔ<u>looked</u> really pleased. "I'd love to!"

17. 위 글의 (A), (B), (C)에 들어갈 말로 바르게 짝지은 것은? (4점)

	(A)	(B)	(C)
①	In	at	about
②	In	for	on
③	On	for	about
④	On	into	about
⑤	Of	into	to

18. 위 글의 ⓐ~ⓔ 중, 해석이 바르지 <u>못한</u> 것은? (4점)

① ⓐ happen to: ~할 수 있다

② ⓑ shout: 소리치다

③ ⓒ hallway: 복도

④ ⓓ final: 결승전

⑤ ⓔ look: ~처럼 보이다

19. 위 글을 읽고, Dami가 (가)처럼 생각한 이유를 우리말로 쓰시오. (4점)

→ _____

21. 위 글의 빈칸 (A), (B), (C)에 들어갈 단어가 바르게 짝지어진 것은? (4점)

	(A)	(B)	(C)
①	realize	cut	Judge
②	shoot	reply	Trust
③	pay	cut	Bump
④	pay	cut	Trust
⑤	realize	reply	Believe

[서대문구 ○○중]

[20~21] 다음 글을 읽고 물음에 답하시오.

Seho and Jihun were talking in the hallway when Dami came over. "Happy birthday!" she said to Seho. "Here. They're from my dad."
"Wow, two KBL tickets! Thanks!"
"Who are you going to take with you?" Dami asked.
"Minjun. He took me to a soccer game before. So, it's time to (A)_____ him back."
"You know what?" Jihun (B)_____ in. "Minjun isn't a fan of basketball. But I am!"
"Well, I'll ask him first anyway," replied Seho.
"He won't go with you. (C)_____ me," said Jihun.
"Who is this guy?" Dami thought to herself, "He wants Minjun's ticket."

20. Which <u>cannot</u> be answered based on the given text? (3점)

① What did Dami think of Jihun?

② Who gave the KBL tickets to Dami's dad?

③ What was Seho doing when Dami saw him?

④ Did Jihun want to go to the basketball game?

⑤ Who did Seho want to go with to the basketball game?

[부산 ○○중]

22. 단어와 그 영영 뜻풀이가 바르게 연결된 것은? (3점)

① forgive: to stop being angry

② strict: an opportunity to do something

③ guess: using a lot of effort, energy, or attention

④ respect: to find the right answer to a question

⑤ reply: an organization for people who share a particular interest

[세종 ○○중]

23. <보기>를 활용하여 ⓐ, ⓑ의 뜻에 맞는 영어 문장을 쓰시오. (주어진 단어를 변형하여 사용할 수 있음.) (5점)

ⓐ 나는 그가 Sue의 남자친구인지 몰랐다.
ⓑ Jamie는 친구가 중요하다고 생각한다.

<보기> friends, important, that

ⓐ _____

ⓑ _____

[24~26] 다음 글을 읽고 물음에 답하시오.

Seho and Jihun were talking in the hallway when Dami came over. "Happy birthday!" she said to Seho. "Here. They're from my dad."
"Wow, two KBL tickets! Thanks!"
"Who are you going to take with you?" Dami asked.
"Minjun. He took me to a soccer game before. So, it's ⓐpay / to / time / back / him."
"You know what?" Jihun cut in. "Minjun isn't a fan of basketball. But I am!"
"Well, I'll ask him first anyway," replied Seho. "He won't go with you. Trust me," said Jihun.
"Who is this guy?" Dami thought to herself, "He wants Minjun's ticket."

24. 위 글의 밑줄 친 ⓐ부분을 어법에 맞게 배열하였을 때 (B)와 (D)에 들어갈 말이 알맞게 짝지어진 것은? (4점)

| it's (A)_____ (B)_____ (C)_____ |
| (D)_____ (E)_____. |

	(B)	(D)
①	to	him
②	to	back
③	pay	him
④	pay	time
⑤	time	to

25. 다음 물음에 적절한 답을 어법상 올바른 하나의 문장으로 답하시오. (3점)

Q: What did Dami give Seho and why?

A: _____

26. 위 글의 내용상 답할 수 없는 질문은? (3점)

① Is Jihun a fan of basketball?
② Is Dami's dad a basketball player?
③ What did Dami give Seho for his birthday?
④ Who took Seho to a soccer game before?
⑤ How many tickets did Dami give to Seho?

27. that의 쓰임이 같은 것끼리 묶은 것은? (4점)

ⓐ We all believe that we can touch the sky.
ⓑ Look at that elephant!
ⓒ I thought that you called my name.
ⓓ He hopes that you will enjoy this movie.
ⓔ That smart phone is so expensive.

① ⓐⓓ - ⓑⓒⓔ   ② ⓐⓒ - ⓑⓓⓔ
③ ⓐⓑⓒ - ⓓⓔ   ④ ⓐⓒⓓ - ⓑⓔ
⑤ ⓐⓓⓔ - ⓑⓒ

28. 다음 글의 세호의 심정으로 알맞은 것은? (3점)

After class, Seho went to Dami and said, "I can't find one of my tickets. Did you happen to see it?"
"No," she answered.
"Isn't it in your bag?"
"No, it's not there. I think I lost it," said Seho.

① 기쁘다   ② 걱정스럽다   ③ 외롭다
④ 심심하다   ⑤ 신난다

◎ 선택형 문항의 답안은 컴퓨터용 수정 싸인펜을 사용하여 OMR 답안지에 바르게 표기하시오.
◎ 서술형 문제는 답을 답안지에 반드시 검정 볼펜으로 쓰시오.
◎ 총 28문항 100점 만점입니다. 문항별 배점은 각 문항에 표시되어 있습니다.

[인천 ㅇㅇ중]

1. 다음 글의 ⓐ~ⓔ 중 그 쓰임이 가장 <u>어색한</u> 것은?

(4점)

That night, at Ryan's house, ⓐ<u>there was no</u> <u>Bear</u>. Ryan checked outside, ⓑ<u>but he could</u> <u>find him</u>. He made posters and ⓒ<u>put them</u> <u>up around town</u>. ⓓ<u>A third night passed</u>. ⓔ <u>Still no Bear</u>.

① ⓐ　　② ⓑ　　③ ⓒ　　④ ⓓ　　⑤ ⓔ

[광주 ㅇㅇ중]

2. Choose two grammatically correct ones.　(3점)

① There are many things to see in Seoul.
② If it will rain, I read a book.
③ The boy needed friends to play.
④ You can see the Eiffel Tower if you visit Paris.
⑤ I saw Brain to do a magic trick.

[송파구 ㅇㅇ중]

[3~4] 다음 글을 읽고 물음에 답하시오.

Bear was a black and brown cat with green eyes. He lived with a boy, Ryan. Ryan always thought that "Bear" was a perfect name for the cat because he had a black spot in the shape of a bear. Bear liked to go outside every morning and run after butterflies. He always came home just in time for dinner. Five blocks away, Max the cat lived with a girl, Sheila. When Sheila moved to this town last month, she was _____. She had no friends there. But, after Max followed her home, he became a good friend to her.

3. 위 글의 흐름상 빈칸에 가장 알맞은 것은?　(3점)

① kind　　② lonely　　③ busy
④ happy　　⑤ excited

4. 위 글을 읽고 답할 수 <u>없는</u> 것은?　(3점)

① What did Bear like to do?
② What color are Bear's eyes?
③ How far does Sheila live from Ryan?
④ Why did Sheila move to the town?
⑤ What did Ryan think about the name of his cat?

[세종 ㅇㅇ중]

5. 'Bear'에 대한 설명으로 옳은 것은?　(4점)

Bear was a black and brown cat with green eyes. He lived with a boy, Ryan. Ryan always thought that "Bear" was a perfect name for the cat because he had a black spot in the shape of a bear. Bear liked to go outside every morning and run after butterflies. He always came home just in time for dinner.

① Bear는 검정색과 녹색이 섞인 고양이었다.
② Ryan은 Bear의 이름을 싫어했다.
③ Bear는 몸에 고양이 모양의 검은 점이 있었다.
④ Bear는 아침에 나가서 나비를 쫓는 것을 좋아했다.
⑤ Bear는 항상 저녁 시간에 밖으로 나갔다.

6. 다음 빈칸에 들어갈 말로 알맞게 짝지어진 것은?

(3점)

> • It will be sunny. I will ride my bike.
> → If (A)_____ sunny, I (B)_____ my bike.

	(A)	(B)
①	it's	ride
②	it's	will ride
③	it's	will be ride
④	it will be	ride
⑤	it will be	will ride

[7~10] 다음 글을 읽고 물음에 답하시오.

> (A)
> One day, ⓐSheila는 Max가 책상 아래에 앉아 있는 것을 보았다. He was making a strange sound. "What's wrong?" asked Sheila. She looked at him closely and found a bad cut on his leg.
>
> (B)
> Five blocks away, Max the cat lived with a girl, Sheila. When Sheila moved to this town last month, she was lonely. She had no friends there. But, after Max followed her home, he became a good friend to her.
>
> (C)
> She took him to the animal hospital. The doctor said, "ⓑHe will get better if he will get enough rest. Keep him inside for a week."

7. 글의 순서로 가장 적절한 것은? (4점)

① (A)-(B)-(C)   ② (A)-(C)-(B)
③ (B)-(A)-(C)   ④ (B)-(C)-(A)
⑤ (C)-(B)-(A)

8. ⓐ의 해석에 맞게 〈보기〉의 단어를 활용하여 문장을 만드시오. (주어진 단어를 변형하여 사용할 수 있음.)

(5점)

> <보 기>
> see, the

답: _____

9. Why was Max making a strange sound? (4점)

① Because Sheila wanted to go to the hospital.
② Because Max had a bad cut on his leg.
③ Because Max liked to play with Sheila.
④ Because Sheila looked at him closely.
⑤ Because Max was a strange cat.

10. 밑줄 친 ⓑ를 바르게 고친 것은? (3점)

① will get better → gets better
② will get better → got better
③ will get better → will get sooner
④ will get enough → got enough
⑤ will get enough → gets enough

11. 밑줄 친 부분을 생략할 수 있는 것은? (4점)

① Who is that girl over there?
② I'd like to see that book on the shelf.
③ Jeniffer wanted to wear that purple dress.
④ Mr. Smith hopes he will buy that gray cat.
⑤ Ms. Kim guesses that the boy is an excellent rapper.

[12~13] 다음 대화를 읽고 물음에 답하시오.

Amy: What are your plans for this Sunday?

Jihun: My plan is to clean up the park with my mom.

Amy: Sounds like a wonderful plan. Can I join you?

Jihun: Certainly. Shall we meet at the subway station at 2 in the afternoon?

Amy: (A)_____ What about 3?

Jihun: Fine with me. Please bring a pair of gloves and a big plastic bag.

Amy: Alright. See you on Sunday.

12. 위 대화의 내용과 일치하는 것은? (4점)

① Amy will clean up the park alone.

② Jihun will bring his father to the park.

③ Amy and Jihun will clean up the park this Sunday.

④ Amy and Jihun will meet at the subway station at 3 this afternoon.

⑤ Amy and Jihun need to bring a pair of gloves and a small plastic bag.

13. 위 글의 빈칸 (A)에 들어갈 가장 알맞은 것은? (3점)

① Sure.

② No problem.

③ I'm afraid not.

④ That sounds wonderful.

⑤ I'm sorry, but you can't.

[14~15] 다음 대화를 읽고 물음에 답하시오.

Jina: I'm planning to volunteer at the animal care center this Sunday morning.

Alex: You mean the one near Grand Park, Jina?

Jina: Right. Will you come with me, Alex? They need volunteers to take care of the animals.

Alex: I'd love to join. I like to ⓐfeed and ⓑwalk animals. I'm also good at ⓒ wash them.

Jina: Great. You can bring other friends with you, too.

Alex: Okay. I'll ask my neighbor Nancy. She loves animals, too. What time shall we meet?

Jina: Can you make it at 8 a.m. at the Grand Park bus stop?

Alex: Sure. I'll see you on Sunday.

14. 위 대화의 밑줄 친 ⓐ, ⓑ, ⓒ를 어법에 맞게 바르게 고쳐 쓴 것은? (4점)

① ⓐ feeding　ⓑ walking　ⓒ to washing

② ⓐ feeding　ⓑ to walk　ⓒ wash

③ ⓐ feed　ⓑ walking　ⓒ to wash

④ ⓐ feed　ⓑ walk　ⓒ washing

⑤ ⓐ feeding　ⓑ walking　ⓒ washing

15. According to the conversation, which is incorrect? (3점)

① Jina will volunteer at the animal care center.

② Alex wants to take care of animals with Jina.

③ Alex wants to bring Nancy because she loves animals.

④ Jina and Alex are going to meet at 8 a.m.

⑤ Jina and Alex will meet in front of Grand Park.

[16~18] 다음을 읽고 물음에 답하시오.

ⓐWhen Sheila was walked near her house, she saw a poster about the lost cat. She read it closely, and her eyes got big. "This cat looks exactly like Max. It's so strange." She hurried home. "Come on, Max! Let's go!" She took him to the address on the poster. "Ding-Dong." ⓑWhen Ryan heard the doorbell ringing, he ran to the door and opened it. "Bear, you're back!" Ryan cried. Max jumped up into Ryan's arms. ⓒ"Let me guessing," said Sheila. ⓓ"Your cat comes home only in the evenings, does he?" Ryan nodded. "And you lost him last Friday, didn't you?" Sheila said. "Yes! How did you know?" said Ryan. ⓔ"Because this is my cat, too, and he comes usually to my home only during the day." "Our cat has two families!" said Ryan. "Hey, if you have time, please come in and have some cookies." "Sure," said Sheila. (A)"Thank you, Max," she thought. "I met a good neighbor thanks to you!"

16. 위 글의 내용과 순서가 일치하는 것은? (4점)

A. When Ryan opened the door, Max jumped into Ryan's arms.
B. Ryan invited Sheila into his house.
C. Sheila took Max to Ryan's house.
D. Sheila saw a poster about the lost cat.
E. Sheila and Ryan realized that their cat has two families.

① A – C – E – D – B
② B – C – A – E – D
③ B – E – C – D – A
④ D – B – A – C – E
⑤ D – C – A – E – B

17. 위 글의 ⓐ~ⓔ 중 어법에 맞는 문장은? (3점)

① When Sheila was walked near her house, she saw a poster about the lost cat.
② When Ryan heard the doorbell ringing, he ran to the door and opened it.
③ "Let me guessing," said Sheila.
④ "Your cat comes home only in the evenings, does he?"
⑤ "Because this is my cat, too, and he comes usually to my home only during the day."

18. 위 글의 Sheila가 (A)와 같이 생각한 이유로 알맞은 것은? (3점)

① Max가 쿠키를 권해서
② Max가 Ryan에게 돌아가서
③ Max가 Bear와 똑같이 생겨서
④ Max가 낮에만 Sheila에게 가서
⑤ Max 덕분에 좋은 이웃을 만나서

19. 다음 중 빈칸에 들어갈 말이 나머지와 다른 것은? (4점)

① _____ you have any questions, raise your hand.
② You will miss the bus _____ you don't hurry.
③ He said _____ he didn't do anything wrong.
④ What will happen _____ I don't pass the exam?
⑤ _____ you turn right, you will see the City Hall.

[20~21] 다음을 읽고 물음에 답하시오.

One day, Sheila saw Max ⓐsit under the desk. He was ⓑmaking a strange sound. "What's wrong?" asked Sheila. She looked at him closely and ⓒfound a bad cut on his leg. She took him to the animal hospital. The doctor said, "He will get better if he ⓓget enough rest. Keep him inside for a week."

That night, at Ryan's house, there was no Bear. Ryan checked outside, but he couldn't find him. He made posters and ⓔput them up around town. A third night passed. Still on Bear.

20. 위 글의 ⓐ~ⓔ 중 어법상 알맞은 형태가 <u>아닌</u> 것은? (4점)

① ⓐ   ② ⓑ   ③ ⓒ   ④ ⓓ   ⑤ ⓔ

21. What did Ryan do when he couldn't find Bear? (3점)

① He kept Bear inside for a week.

② He took him to the animal hospital.

③ He took some rest inside his house.

④ He made posters and put them up around town.

⑤ He sat under the desk and made a strange sound.

[22~24] 다음 글을 읽고 물음에 답하시오.

(A) Bear was a black and brown cat with green eyes. He lived with a boy, Ryan. Ryan always thought that "Bear" was a perfect name for the cat because he had a black spot in the shape of a bear. Bear liked to go outside every morning and run after butterflies. He always came home just in time for dinner.

(B) Five blocks away, Max the cat lived with a girl, Sheila. When Sheila moved to this town last month, she was ⓐ_____. She had no friends there. ⓑ_____, after Max followed her home, he became a good friend to her.

22. 위 글 (A)의 Bear에 대한 설명으로 옳지 <u>않은</u> 것은? (4점)

① Bear는 초록 눈동자에 검고 갈색 털을 갖고 있다.

② Bear의 주인은 Ryan이다.

③ Bear는 곰 모양의 검은 점을 갖고 있는 고양이이다.

④ Bear는 나비를 쫓아 달리는 것을 좋아한다.

⑤ Bear는 아침 일찍 나가서 저녁 식사 시간 후에 돌아온다.

23. 위 글 (A)의 제목으로 가장 적절한 것은? (4점)

① The Bear's Birth

② Who is Bear?

③ The Bear's Friend, Ryan

④ The Bear's Childhood

⑤ The Bear's Life

24. 위 글 (B)의 빈칸 ⓐ와 ⓑ에 들어갈 어휘가 바르게 연결된 것은? (3점)

	ⓐ	ⓑ
①	happy	And
②	lonely	But
③	nervous	And
④	pleased	But
⑤	bored	And

25. 다음 대화에서 알 수 <u>없는</u> 정보는?   (4점)

Jina: I'm planning to volunteer at the animal care center this Sunday morning.

Alex: You mean the one near Grand Park, Jina?

Jina: Right. Will you come with me, Alex? They need volunteers to take care of the animals.

Alex: I'd love to join. I like feeding and walking animals. I'm also good at washing them.

Jina: Great. You can bring other friends with you, too.

Alex: Okay. I'll ask my neighbor Nancy. She loves animals, too. What time shall we meet?

Jina: Can you make it at 8 a.m. at the Grand Park bus stop?

Alex: Sure. I'll see you on Sunday.

① Alex의 이웃 주민 이름

② 동물 보호 센터의 위치

③ Jina가 자원봉사를 할 장소

④ 동물 보호 센터의 직원 수

⑤ Alex와 Jina가 만날 시간과 장소

26. 빈칸에 들어갈 말이 순서대로 바르게 짝지어진 것은?   (3점)

• If I _____ Paris, I _____ the Eiffel Tower.

① visit - climb

② will visit - will climb

③ will visit - climb

④ visit - will climb

⑤ visiting - will climb

[27~28] 다음 글을 읽고 물음에 답하시오.

When Sheila was walking near her house, she saw a poster about the lost cat. She read it closely, and her eyes got big. "This cat looks exactly like Max. It's so strange." She hurried home. "Come on, Max! Let's go!" She took him to the address on the poster.

"Ding-Dong." When Ryan heard thc doorbell ring, he ran to the door and opened it. "Bear, you're back!" Ryan cried. Max jumped up into Ryan's arms.

"Let me guess," said Sheila. "Your cat comes home only in the evenings, (A)_____?" Ryan nodded. "And you lost him last Friday, (B)_____?" Sheila said. "Yes! How did you know?" said Ryan. "Because this is my cat, too, and he usually comes to my home (C)_____."

"Our cat has two families!" said Ryan. "Hey, if you have time, please come in and have some cookies." "Sure," said Sheila. "Thank you, Max," she thought. "I met a good neighbor thanks to you!"

27. 위 글의 빈칸 (A), (B)에 들어갈 표현으로 가장 적절한 것은?   (4점)

	(A)	(B)
①	don't he	didn't you
②	doesn't he	didn't you
③	didn't he	did you
④	doesn't he	did you
⑤	does he	don't you

28. 위 글의 흐름상 빈칸 (C)에 들어갈 어구로 가장 적절한 것은?   (3점)

① during the night

② only every Friday

③ whenever he wants

④ only during the day

⑤ during the weekend

◎ 선택형 문항의 답안은 컴퓨터용 수정 싸인펜을 사용하여 OMR 답안지에 바르게 표기하시오.
◎ 서술형 문제는 답을 답안지에 반드시 검정 볼펜으로 쓰시오.
◎ 총 28문항 100점 만점입니다. 문항별 배점은 각 문항에 표시되어 있습니다.

[서대문구 ○○중]

1. 다음 주어진 대화 중 자연스럽지 <u>않은</u> 것은? (3점)

① A: Can I join you?
　 B: Why not?
② A: Why don't we meet at 5 in the park?
　 B: I'm afraid not. See you then.
③ A: What time shall we meet?
　 B: How about 2 p.m.?
④ A: I'm planning to go shopping this Sunday.
　 B: Sounds great.
⑤ A: Let's meet at 3.
　 B: No problem. See you at the bus stop.

[관악구 ○○중]

2. Which is NOT true about this dialog? (4점)

Tom: What are you going to do this Saturday?
Mary: I'm planning to clean up the park with my dad.
Tom: Sounds like a wonderful plan. Can I join you?
Mary: Sure. Shall we meet at the bus stop at one o'clock?
Tom: I'm sorry, but I can't. How about two?
Mary: Fine with me. Please bring a pair of gloves and a big plastic bag.
Tom: Okay. See you then.

---

① Tom can meet Mary at two.
② Mary will meet Tom at the bus stop.
③ Tom thinks that Mary's plan is good.
④ Tom needs a big plastic bag this Sunday.
⑤ They are talking about the plan of this weekend.

[서대문구 ○○중]

3. 다음 중 어법상 올바르게 쓰인 문장은? (3점)

① I missed the bus if I am late.
② We will stay at home if it rained.
③ If I get there on time, I will catch the train.
④ I will not go outside if it will be cold tomorrow.
⑤ If you will visit Hawaii, you can swim in the sea.

[서대문구 ○○중]

4. 다음 중 어법상 올바르게 정확하게 쓰인 문장은? (4점)

① Ryan heard the doorbell to ring.
② Sheila saw Max sits under the desk.
③ I saw Amy read a book to the children.
④ I watched he play soccer with his friends.
⑤ She felt something to touch her shoulder.

[대전 ○○중]

5. 다음 중 어법상 알맞은 것을 〈보기〉에서 있는 대로 고른 것은? (3점)

<보기>
A. I saw Kate watering the plants.
B. Did you hear he play the piano?
C. Their parents listened the children sing.
D. Mom watched us clean our room.

---

① A, B　　② A, D　　③ C, D
④ A, B, D　　⑤ B, C, D

[6~8] 다음 글을 읽고 물음에 답하시오.

"Ding-Dong." When Ryan heard the doorbell ring, he ran to the door and opened it. "Bear, you're back!" Ryan cried. Max jumped up into Ryan's arms.

"Let me guess," said Sheila. "Your cat comes home only in the evenings. ___ⓐ___?" Ryan nodded.

"And you lost him last Friday, ___ⓑ___?" Sheila said.

"Yes! How did you know?" said Ryan. "Because this is my cat, too, and he usually comes to my home only during the day."

"Our cat has two families!" said Ryan. "Hey, ⓒ만약 시간이 있다면, 들어와서 쿠키 좀 먹어." "Sure," said Sheila. "Thank you, Max," she thought. "I met a good neighbor thanks to you!"

6. 빈칸 ⓐ와 ⓑ에 적절한 것은? (3점)

	ⓐ	ⓑ
①	doesn't he	don't you
②	doesn't he	didn't you
③	didn't he	don't you
④	didn't he	didn't you
⑤	didn't you	doesn't he

7. 위 글의 내용을 잘못 이해한 것은? (4점)

① Ryan은 Max를 Bear라고 불렀다.

② Ryan은 Max를 다시 만나서 반가워했다.

③ Ryan은 Sheila의 추측에 동의하지 않았다.

④ Ryan은 금요일에 고양이를 잃어버렸다.

⑤ Sheila는 새로운 이웃을 알게 되어 기뻐했다.

8. ⓒ의 해석에 맞게 〈보기〉의 단어를 활용하여 문장을 만드시오. (주어진 단어를 변형하여 사용할 수 있음.) (5점)

```
<보 기>
come in, cookies, please
```

답: _____

[9~10] 다음 글을 읽고 물음에 답하시오.

When Sheila was walking near her house, she saw a poster about the lost cat. She read it closely, and _____. "This cat looks exactly like Max, it's so strange." She hurried home and took him to the address on the poster. When she rang the doorbell, Ryan ran to the door and opened it. "Bear, you're back!" Ryan cried. Max jumped up into Ryan's arms.

9. 위 글의 빈칸에 들어갈 말로 가장 적절한 것은? (3점)

① got very surprised

② started to tear it down

③ looked everywhere to find it

④ pictured the house in her mind

⑤ changed the poster information

10. 위 글에 드러난 Ryan의 심경으로 가장 적절한 것은? (4점)

① sad　　② angry　　③ bored

④ joyful　　⑤ scared

[11~13] 다음 대화를 읽고 물음에 답하시오.

> Jina: I'm planning to volunteer at the animal care center this Sunday morning.
>
> Alex: You mean the one near Grand Park, Jina?
>
> Jina: Right. Will you come with me, Alex? They need volunteers to take care of the animals.
>
> Alex: I'd love to join. I like (ⓐ) and (ⓑ) animals. I'm also good at (ⓒ) them.
>
> Jina: Great. You can bring other friends with you, too.
>
> Alex: Okay. I'll ask my neighbor Nancy. She loves animals, too. What time shall we meet?
>
> Jina: (A)_____
>
> Alex: Sure. I'll see you on Sunday.

11. 대화의 내용과 일치하는 것은?　(3점)

① Nancy는 Jina의 이웃에 사는 친구이다.

② Alex는 동물보호센터의 위치를 알고 있다.

③ Alex와 Jina는 학교 숙제에 대해 의논 중이다.

④ Jina는 매주 일요일 자원봉사활동을 하고 있다.

⑤ Alex가 Jina에게 자원봉사활동 참여를 권유하고 있다.

12. 대화의 ⓐ~ⓒ에 들어가기에 적당하지 <u>않은</u> 것은?

(3점)

① bothering　　② helping

③ washing　　④ walking

⑤ exercising

13. 위 대화의 빈칸 (A)에 다음의 내용을 포함하되 주어진 단어를 반드시 이용하여 만나는 약속을 정하는 영어 문장을 쓰시오.　(5점)

> □ 만나는 시간: 오전 8시
> □ 만나는 장소: 대공원(Grand Park) 버스 정류장
> □ make를 반드시 이용할 것.

답: _____

14. 다음 대화에서 흐름상 <u>어색한</u> 것은?　(4점)

> Hajun: What are you going to do this Saturday?
>
> Miso: ⓐI'm planning to clean up the park with my dad.
>
> Hajun: Sounds like a wonderful plan. ⓑCan I join you?
>
> Miso: Yes. Can you make it at the bus stop at 1 p.m.?
>
> Hajun: ⓒSure. How about 2?
>
> Miso: Fine with me. ⓓPlease bring a pair of gloves and a big plastic bag.
>
> Hajun: Okay. ⓔI'm glad to join you. See you on Saturday.

① ⓐ　　② ⓑ　　③ ⓒ　　④ ⓓ　　⑤ ⓔ

15. 다음 빈칸에 들어갈 말로 알맞은 것은?　(4점)

> Minji: What are your plans for this semester?
>
> Yuna: I'm _____ join the art club net semester.

① planning to　　② planning on

③ plan to　　④ plan on

⑤ planning

[16~17] 다음 대화를 읽고 물음에 답하시오.

> A: I'm planning to volunteer at the animal care center this Sunday morning.
> B: You mean the ⓐone near Grand Park, Jina?
> A: Right. Will you come with me, Alex? They need volunteers to take care of the animals.
> B: I'd love to. I like feeding and walking animals. I'm also good at washing ⓑthem.
> A: Great. You can bring other friends with you, too.
> B: Okay. I'll ask my neighbor Nancy. ⓒShe loves animals, too. What time shall we meet?
> A: Can you ⓓmake it at 8 a.m. at the Grand Park bus stop?
> B: Sure. I'll see you on Sunday.

16. 위 대화의 ⓐ~ⓒ가 가리키는 것끼리 알맞게 짝지어진 것은? (3점)

	ⓐ	ⓑ	ⓒ

① the animal care center - animals - Nancy

② the animal care center - volunteers - Jina

③ the Grand Park - animals - Nancy

④ the Grand Park - volunteers - Jina

⑤ the Grand Park - bus stop - Alex and Nancy

17. 위 대화의 ⓓ와 같은 의미로 쓰인 것은? (4점)

① If you didn't buy this scarf, did you make it?

② Look at this cake. I tried to make it for you.

③ Let's hurry. I hope we can make it to the party on time.

④ She is preparing dinner. She will make it with fresh vegetables.

⑤ She wanted a dress just like yours, so I promised to make it.

18. 다음 중 우리말을 영어로 바르게 옮긴 것을 모두 고르면? (4점)

① 나는 Amy가 아이들에게 책을 읽어주는 걸 들었다.

→ I heard Amy read a book to the children.

② 그는 누군가가 자신의 손을 만지는 걸 느꼈다.

→ He felt somebody touching his hand.

③ 나는 그가 친구들과 농구하는 것을 보았다.

→ I saw he play basketball with friends.

④ 나는 Brian이 아이들에게 마술 묘기를 보여주는 것을 봤어.

→ I watched Brian did a magic trick for children.

⑤ 너는 네 남동생이 창문을 닫는 것을 봤니?

→ Did you see your brother to close the window?

19. 다음 주어진 문장의 밑줄 친 단어가 잘못 쓰인 것은? (3점)

① I feed my cat every day.

② I tried to shoot my weight.

③ Be careful not to bump your head.

④ Our soccer team moved up to the final.

⑤ She will volunteer as a doctor in the homeless center.

[20~22] 다음 글을 읽고 물음에 답하시오.

Bear was a black and brown cat ⓐ_____ green eyes. He lived with a boy, Michael. Michael always thought Bear was a perfect name for the cat because he had a black spot in the shape of a bear. Bear liked to go outside every morning and run ⓑ_____ butterflies. (A) He always came home just ⓒ_____ time for dinner. (B)

Five blocks away, Cooper the cat lived with a girl, Charlotte. (C) When Charlotte moved to this town last month, she was lonely. (D) She had no friends there. (E)

20. 위 글의 빈칸 ⓐ~ⓒ에 들어갈 말이 순서대로 알맞게 짝지어진 것은? (3점)

	ⓐ	ⓑ	ⓒ
①	by	to	on
②	in	after	in
③	in	away	on
④	with	after	in
⑤	with	away	on

21. 위 글에서 다음의 문장이 들어갈 위치로 가장 알맞은 것은? (4점)

But, after Cooper followed her home, he became a good friend to her.

① (A) ② (B) ③ (C) ④ (D) ⑤ (E)

22. 위 글을 읽고 답할 수 <u>없는</u> 질문은? (3점)

① What did Bear like to do?

② Why is the cat named "Bear"?

③ What made Charlotte move to this town?

④ How did Charlotte get to know Cooper?

⑤ How far did Charlotte live from Michael?

23. 다음 대화에서 ⓐ~ⓒ의 순서를 가장 바르게 나열한 것은? (4점)

G: Do you have any plans for the weekend?
B: Yes. I'm planning to practice dancing at the youth center.
ⓐ Why not? Can you make it at the bus stop at 1 p.m.?
ⓑ I'm afraid not. How about 2?
ⓒ Sounds great. Can I join you?
B: Okay. See you on Saturday.

① ⓐ-ⓒ-ⓑ   ② ⓑ-ⓐ-ⓒ
③ ⓑ-ⓒ-ⓐ   ④ ⓒ-ⓐ-ⓑ
⑤ ⓒ-ⓑ-ⓐ

24. 다음 중 어법상 <u>어색한</u> 문장을 고르시오. (3점)

① I heard Jake singing a song loudly.

② She watched me clean the classroom.

③ Mom felt someone touch her shoulder.

④ I saw Amy to read a book to the children.

⑤ Amy wanted me to send her some flowers.

25. 다음 두 사람의 대화에서 흐름상 어색한 것은? (4점)

Jina: I'm planning to volunteer at the animal care center this Sunday morning.

Alex: ⓐYou mean the one near Grand Park, Jina?

Jina: Right. Will you come with me, Alex? ⓑThey don't need volunteers to take care of the animals.

Alex: That sounds good. ⓒI like feeding and walking animals. I'm also good at washing them.

Jina: Great. You can bring other friends with you, too.

Alex: Okay, I'll ask my neighbor Nancy. ⓓShe love animals, too. What time shall we meet?

Jina: ⓔLet's meet at 8 a.m. at the Grand Park bus stop.

Alex: Sure. I'll see you on Sunday.

① ⓐ　　② ⓑ　　③ ⓒ　　④ ⓓ　　⑤ ⓔ

26. 다음 글의 내용과 일치하지 <u>않는</u> 것은? (4점)

"Let me guess," said Sheila. "Your cat Bear comes home only in the evenings, doesn't he?" Ryan nodded. "And you lost him last Friday, didn't you?" Sheila said. "Yes! How did you know?" said Ryan. "Because this is my cat, too, and Max usually comes to my home only during the day."

"Our cat has two families!" said Ryan. "Hey, if you have time, please come in and have some cookies." "Sure," said Sheila. 'Thank you, Max,' she thought. 'I met a good neighbor thanks to you!'

① Ryan의 고양이는 저녁에만 Ryan 집에 왔다.

② Ryan은 지난주 금요일에 고양이를 잃어버렸다.

③ Ryan과 Sheila는 같은 고양이를 공유하고 있었다.

④ Sheila의 고양이는 주로 낮에만 Sheila 집에 머물렀다.

⑤ Ryan과 Sheila는 이미 좋은 이웃 사이로 지내고 있었다.

27. 다음 글의 분위기로 가장 알맞은 것은? (3점)

That night, at Michael's house, there was no Bear. Michael checked outside, but he couldn't find him. He made posters and put them up around town. A third night passed. Still no Bear.

① nervous and worried

② fun and exciting

③ calm and peaceful

④ joyful and humorous

⑤ boring and monotonous

28. 다음 중 어법상 올바른 것은? (3점)

① If you turn right, you will see it.

② He will passes the exam if he study harder.

③ I stay at home if it will be cold this weekend.

④ If it is sunny tomorrow, I take a walk in the park.

⑤ If he won't come back by 10, I will call the police.

2학년 영어 1학기 기말고사(3과) 1회

문항수 : 선택형(24문항) 서술형(2문항)   20 . . .

◎ 선택형 문항의 답안은 컴퓨터용 수정 싸인펜을
  사용하여 OMR 답안지에 바르게 표기하시오.
◎ 서술형 문제는 답을 답안지에 반드시 검정
  볼펜으로 쓰시오.
◎ 총 26문항 100점 만점입니다. 문항별 배점
  은 각 문항에 표시되어 있습니다.

[경기 ㅇㅇ중]

1. 다음 글의 빈칸에 공통으로 들어갈 말로 가장 적절
   한 것은?   (4점)

> I think we can use _____ to make a
> better school life. We can do good things at
> school and take _____. Then we can post
> those photos on our school website. I've
> watered the plants and flowers at school for
> one month. I've also helped the teacher at
> the school library many times. Look at my
> _____ of those things. How about joining
> me to create a better school life?

① signs   ② selfies   ③ events
④ memories   ⑤ cell phones

[충북 ㅇㅇ중]

2. 다음 대화를 읽고, 내용이 올바르지 <u>않은</u> 것을 고
   르면?   (4점)

> Daughter: Dad, have you ever heard of Kim
>   Soyun, the rock climber?
> Dad: Yes. I've seen her on TV.
> Daughter: She's teaching rock climbing at the
>   camp this Saturday. I want to join
>   the camp.
> Dad: Okay. Miso, but you shouldn't climb up
>   too high.
> Daughter: All right. Thanks, Dad.

① Kim Soyun is a rock climber.
② Dad has seen Kim Soyun on TV.
③ A man asks a girl to climb up very high.
④ It is a conversation between a dad and a
   daughter.
⑤ The girl wants to join the camp to learn
   rock climbing.

[경기 ㅇㅇ중]

3. 다음 대화의 빈칸 (A)에 들어갈 말로 가장 적절한 것
   은?   (3점)

> Yunho: Have you heard of bird watching?
> Dad: Sure. I tried it when I was a child.
> Yunho: That's nice. Actually, I'm doing it for
>   the first time this Saturday.
> Dad: Are you? You should bring warm clothes
>   and something to eat.
> Yunho: Okay. (A)_____
> Dad: You shouldn't make any noise when you
>   watch the birds.
> Yunho: I'll keep that in mind. Thanks, Dad.

① How long should we watch the birds?
② What time should we meet on Saturday?
③ What should we bring for bird watching?
④ What should the birds eat for the first time?
⑤ What else should I keep in mind for bird
   watching?

[경기 ㅇㅇ중]

4. 다음 중 어법상 옳은 것을 고르면?   (4점)
① He have just come back home.
② When have you talked with him?
③ He has lived here since ten years.
④ She has never been to Paris before.
⑤ Does he have tried Italian food many times?

[5~7] 다음 글을 읽고 물음에 답하시오.

Minji - Selfies in the Past
Did people in the past take selfies? (A)_____ it wasn't easy at that time, the answer is yes. Look at this photo of Princess Anastasia. She used a mirror to take a picture of herself. She looks nervous. Can you guess why? Well, I think it was her first selfie. And it was probably the world's first teenage selfie ever.

Yunho - Fun Places for Selfies
You can take selfies at world-famous places like Big Ben and the Leaning Tower of Pisa. To take great pictures, just do fun poses and use camera tricks.
You can also visit special museums to take fun selfies. For example, there is a famous selfie museum in the Philippines. It has special spots ⓐto take selfies. You can touch the paintings and even step inside them. Look at the following pictures. Though the boys are not really riding horses, it looks like they are. Though the man is just holding a big brush, it looks like he is painting the Mona Lisa. Selfie museums exist in Korea, too. I have visited one in Chuncheon before. Why don't you go there yourself?

5. 위 글의 빈칸 (A)에 들어갈 말로 가장 적절한 것은?
(3점)

① If   ② When   ③ Since
④ Though   ⑤ Because

6. 위 글의 내용을 바탕으로 〈보기〉에서 Yunho와 관련된 표현만을 있는 대로 고른 것은?   (4점)

〈보기〉
ㄱ. the teenage selfie   ㄴ. special museums
ㄷ. fun selfies   ㄹ. used a mirror
ㅁ. Princess Anastasi   ㅂ. the first selfie
ㅅ. world-famous places

① ㄱ,ㄴ   ② ㄴ,ㄷ,ㅅ
③ ㄴ,ㅁ,ㅂ   ④ ㄷ,ㄹ,ㅅ
⑤ ㄴ,ㄷ,ㅂ,ㅅ

7. 위 글의 밑줄 친 ⓐ와 쓰임이 같은 것은?   (4점)

① Mike has a lot of homework to do.
② It is difficult to read English books.
③ I called my friend to ask a question.
④ I like to go shopping with my sister.
⑤ Tom went to a hospital to see a doctor.

8. 다음 글의 흐름으로 보아 주어진 문장이 들어갈 알맞은 곳은?   (4점)

Look at my selfies of those things.

I think we can use selfies to make a better school life. (A) We can do good things at school and take selfies. (B) Then we can post the photos on our school website. (C) I've watered the plants and flowers at school for one month. (D) I've also helped the teacher at the school library many times. (E) How about joining me to create a better school life?

① (A)   ② (B)   ③ (C)   ④ (D)   ⑤ (E)

[9~10] 다음 글을 읽고 물음에 답하시오.

You can take selfies at world-famous places like Big Ben and the Leaning Tower of Pisa. To take great pictures, just do fun poses and use camera tricks.

You can also visit special museums to take fun selfies. For example, there is a famous selfie museum in the Philippines. It has special spots ⓐto take selfies. You can touch the paintings and even step inside them. Look at the following pictures. Though the boys are not really riding horses, it looks like they are. Though the man is just holding a big brush, it looks like he is painting the Mona Lisa. Selfie museums exist in Korea, too. I have visited one in Chuncheon before. Why don't you go there yourself?

9. 위 글의 제목으로 가장 적절한 것은?　(4점)

① Selfies in the Past
② Good Poses for Selfies
③ Tips to Take Selfies Safely
④ Famous Places for Fun Selfies
⑤ Selfies for a Better School Life

10. 위 글의 내용과 일치하는 것은?　(3점)

① 세계적으로 유명한 장소에서는 셀피를 찍으면 안 된다.
② 카메라 기법을 이용해서 멋진 셀피를 찍을 수 있다.
③ 셀피 박물관에서는 그림을 만질 수 없다.
④ 사진 속 소년들은 실제로 말을 타고 있다.
⑤ 한국에는 춘천에만 한 군데 셀피 박물관이 있다.

11. 다음 글의 주제로 가장 적절한 것은?　(4점)

Soyun's presentation
I think we can use selfies to make a better school life. We can do good things at school and take selfies. Then we can post the photos on our school website. I've watered the plants and flowers at school for one month. I've also helped the teacher at the school library many times. Look at my selfies of those things. How about joining me to create a better school life?

① the roles of plants in our lives
② the importance of reading books
③ using selfies for a better school life
④ the increase in using the school website
⑤ the introduction of many kinds of flowers in our school

12. 다음 글의 흐름으로 보아 빈칸에 들어갈 말로 알맞지 않은 것은?　(4점)

These selfies look great, but were they a good idea? I don't think so. They don't look safe. You should take special care when you take selfies in the wild or at high places like these. A monkey could bite you at any time, or you could fall. Here are some other selfie safety tips: _____

① Avoid posing near wild animals.
② Stay away from dangerous places.
③ Take selfies when crossing the street.
④ You should not go too close to the river.
⑤ Do not take selfies with dangerous things.

[13~14] 다음 글을 읽고 물음에 답하시오.

Jihun - Selfie Safety

These selfies look great, but were they a good idea? I don't thinks so. They don't look safe. You should take special care when you take selfies in the wild or at high places like these. A monkey could bite you at any time, or you could fall. Here are some safety tips:

1. Don't take selfies while you're walking.
2. Do not pose with or near wild animals.
3. Never take selfies in dangerous places.

Soyun - Selfies for a Better School Life

I think we can use selfies to make a better school life. We can do good things at school and take selfies. Then we can post the photos on our school website. I've watered the plants and flowers at school for one month. I've also helped the teacher at the school library many times. Look at my selfies of those things. How about joining me to create a better school life?

13. 위 글의 내용과 일치하는 것으로 가장 적절한 것을 모두 고르시오.   (4점)

① 높은 곳에서 셀피를 찍어도 떨어질 확률은 적다.
② 지훈이는 멋있게 셀피를 찍는 방법을 소개하고 있다.
③ 소윤이는 학교에서 다친 친구를 한 번 도와준 적이 있다.
④ 야생에서 셀피를 찍을 때에는 특별히 조심할 필요가 있다.
⑤ 소윤이는 더 나은 학교생활을 만들기 위해 함께하자고 제안하고 있다.

14. 위 글에서 소윤이가 더 나은 학교생활을 위해 한 일로 가장 적절한 것은?   (3점)

① 걷는 동안 셀피를 찍기
② 위험한 장소에서 셀피를 찍기
③ 야생동물들과 함께 자세를 취하기
④ 한 달 동안 학교에 있는 식물들과 꽃에 물주기
⑤ 학교 웹사이트에 선생님들의 재미있는 사진들을 올리기

[15~16] 다음을 읽고 물음에 답하시오.

You can take selfies at world-famous places like Big Ben and the Leaning Tower of Pisa. To take great pictures, just do fun poses and use camera tricks.

You can also visit special museums to take fun selfies. For example, there is a famous selfie museum in the Philippines. It has special spots to take selfies. You can touch the paintings and even step inside them. Look at the following pictures.

(A)_____ the boys are not really riding horses, it looks like they are. (B)_____ the man is just holding a big brush, it looks like he is painting the Mona Lisa. Selfie museums exist in Korea, too. I have visited one in Chuncheon before. Why don't you go there yourself?

15. 위 글의 제목으로 가장 알맞은 것은?   (4점)

① Selfies in the Past
② Fun Places for Selfies
③ Selfie Safety
④ Selfies for a Better School Life
⑤ Posting Selfies on the School Website

16. 위 글의 빈칸 (A), (B)에 공통으로 들어갈 말을 쓰시오.   (5점)

→ _____

[17～19] 다음 글을 읽고 물음에 답하시오.

When you (A)_____ a photograph of yourself, it's a selfie. The students from Minji's photo club have searched for information about selfies for one month. Here are some of their presentations about selfies.

Did people in the past (B)_____ selfies? (C)_____ it wasn't easy at that time, the answer is yes. Look at this photo of Princess Anastasia. She used a mirror to take a picture of herself. She looks nervous. Can you guess why? Well. I think it was her first selfie. And it was probably the world's first teenage selfie ever.

17. 위 글의 내용과 일치하는 것은?   (4점)

① 과거에는 셀피를 찍지 않았다.

② Princess Anastasia는 셀피를 찍을 때 행복해 보였다.

③ Princess Anastasia는 이 사진 이전에도 셀피를 찍었다.

④ Princess Anastasia는 거울을 이용하여 셀피를 찍었다.

⑤ 사진 동아리 회원들은 한 달에 한 번 셀피에 대한 정보를 수집한다.

18. 위 글의 빈칸 (A), (B)에 공통으로 들어갈 말을 쓰시오.   (5점)

→ _____

19. 위 글의 빈칸 (C)에 들어갈 말로 문맥상 알맞은 것은?   (3점)

① If   ② When   ③ That

④ Though   ⑤ Because

[20～22] 다음 글을 읽고 물음에 답하시오.

(A) I think we can use selfies to make better school life. (B) We can do good things at school and take selfies. (C) I've watered the plants and lowers at school for one month. (D) I've also helped the teacher at the school library many times. (E) Look at my selfies of those things. _____ me to create a better school life?

20. 위 글의 (A)～(E) 중 〈보기〉의 문장이 들어갈 위치로 가장 알맞은 곳은?   (4점)

<보기>
Then we can post the photos on our school website.

① (A)   ② (B)   ③ (C)   ④ (D)   ⑤ (E)

21. 위 글의 빈칸에 들어갈 말로 문맥상 알맞은 것은?   (4점)

① How about using

② How about taking

③ How about joining

④ What about posting

⑤ Why don't you care

22. 위 글의 제목으로 가장 알맞은 것은?   (4점)

① Growing Plants and Flowers

② Doing Good Things for One Month

③ Using Selfies for a Better School Life

④ Looking at the Selfies of the Students

⑤ Posting School Life on the School Website

[23~24] 다음을 읽고 물음에 답하시오.

Have you ever ⓐ<u>hear</u> of a "selfie"? When you take a photograph of yourself, it's a selfie. The students from Minji's photo club ⓑ<u>has</u> searched for information about selfies for one month. Here ⓒ<u>are</u> some of their presentations about selfies.

Past Selfies
Did people in the past take selfies? ⓓ<u>Though</u> it wasn't easy at that time, the answer is yes. Look at this photo of Princess Anastasia. She used a mirror to take a picture of herself. She looks ⓔ<u>nervously</u>. Can you guess why? Well, I think it was her first selfie. And it was probably the world's first teenage selfie ever.

23. 위 글의 밑줄 친 ⓐ~ⓔ 중 어법상 <u>어색한</u> 것의 개수는? (4점)

① 1개 　　② 2개 　　③ 3개
④ 4개 　　⑤ 5개

24. 위 글의 내용과 일치하는 것은? (3점)
① 셀피는 당신이 당신 자신의 사진을 찍은 것입니다.
② 민지의 사진 동아리 학생들은 한 달 반 동안 셀피에 대한 정보를 조사해 왔다.
③ 과거 사람들은 셀피를 찍지 않았다.
④ 아나스타샤 공주는 셀피 사진을 찍기 위해 핸드폰을 사용했다.
⑤ 아나스타샤 공주의 셀피 사진은 아마 전 세계 두 번째 십대 셀피일 것이다.

[25~26] 다음 글을 읽고 물음에 답하시오.

The selfies look great, but were they a good idea? I don't think so. They don't look (A)_____ You should take special care when you take selfies in the wild or at high places like these. A monkey could bite you at any time, or you could fall. Here are some (B)_____ tips:
1. Don't take selfies while you are walking.
2. Do not pose with or near wild animals.
3. Never take selfies in dangerous places.

25. 위 글의 빈칸 (A), (B)에 알맞은 말이 순서대로 바르게 짝지어진 것은? (4점)

　　(A)　　　　　　(B)
① safe　　　　　safe
② safe　　　　　safety
③ safety　　　　safe
④ safely　　　　safety
⑤ safety　　　　safety

26. 위 글의 내용과 일치하지 <u>않는</u> 것은? (4점)
① 걸어가면서 셀피를 찍어서는 안 된다.
② 야생동물 근처에서 포즈를 취해서는 안 된다.
③ 야생에서는 위험 요소가 많지만 셀피 찍는 것은 괜찮다.
④ 높은 장소에서 셀피를 찍는 것은 좋은 생각이 아니다.
⑤ 높은 장소에서 셀피 사진을 찍을 때 특별히 주의를 기울여야 한다.

◎ 선택형 문항의 답안은 컴퓨터용 수정 싸인펜을 사용하여 OMR 답안지에 바르게 표기하시오.
◎ 서술형 문제는 답을 답안지에 반드시 검정 볼펜으로 쓰시오.
◎ 총 26문항 100점 만점입니다. 문항별 배점은 각 문항에 표시되어 있습니다.

[송파구 ○○중]

1. 다음 〈보기〉의 빈칸에 공통으로 들어갈 단어를 쓰시오. (5점)

<보기>
• She has _____ to Jeju Island.
• Have you ever _____ to the Alps?

[경기 ○○중]

2. 다음 두 사람의 대화 가운데 들어갈 순서로 가장 적절한 것은? (4점)

Minjun: Hello, Somin! It's me! Can you see me?
Somin: Oh, hi, Minjun! What's up?

(A) Don't hang up. I will show the beautiful scenery for you.
(B) Guess what? Actually, I'm on Jeju *Olle* now. Do you know Jeju *Olle*?
(C) Be careful! You shouldn't use your cell phone while you're walking.
(D) Yes, I do. I really want to go there someday.

Minun: Oh, right. Thank you. I'll send you photos later.

① (B) - (A) - (C) - (D)
② (B) - (D) - (A) - (C)
③ (C) - (A) - (B) - (D)
④ (C) - (A) - (D) - (B)
⑤ (D) - (B) - (A) - (C)

[경기 ○○중]

3. 다음 글의 밑줄 친 (A)와 어법의 쓰임이 같은 것만을 〈보기〉에서 있는 대로 고른 것은? (3점)

Today let's talk about "selfie". (A)Have you ever heard of a "selfie"? When you take a photograph of yourself, it's a selfie.
Did people in the past take selfies? Even if it wasn't easy at that time, the answer is yes. The photo of Princess Anastasia was probably the world's first teenage selfie ever.

<보기>
ⓐ I have seen the movie before.
ⓑ Minju has lived in this house since 2015.
ⓒ She has never learned to play the piano.
ⓓ Andy and I have been friends for three years.

① ⓐ, ⓑ
② ⓐ, ⓒ
③ ⓑ, ⓒ
④ ⓐ, ⓒ, ⓓ
⑤ ⓑ, ⓒ, ⓓ

[송파구 ○○중]

4. 다음 중 어법상 올바른 것은? (4점)

① She has went to France.
② Anthony has left the school 2 years ago.
③ Jenny never has lived in Sokcho until now.
④ Do you have eaten hamburger in that restaurant?
⑤ My homeroom teacher has taught English here for 3 years.

[5~6] 다음 대화를 읽고 물음에 답하시오.

M: Hello. Somin! It's me! Can you see me?

S: Oh, hi, Minjun! What's up?

M: This is so cool, isn't it? We can video chat on the phone! Have you heard of Jeju *Olle*?

S: Yes, I have. I really want to go there someday.

M: Guess what? I'm on it now. Actually, I'm going to go up Seongsan Ilchulbong now.

S: That's great!

M: Don't hang up. Enjoy the beautiful scenery with me.

S: Be careful! You shouldn't use your cell phone while you're walking.

M: Oh, right. Thank you. I'll send you photos later.

5. 위 대화의 내용과 일치하지 <u>않는</u> 것은? (4점)

① 민준이는 지금 성산 일출봉을 올라가고 있다.

② 소민이는 제주 '올레'에 대해서 들어 본 적이 있다.

③ 민준이와 소민이는 전화로 화상통화를 하고 있다.

④ 소민이는 언젠가는 제주 '올레'에 가보고 싶어 한다.

⑤ 민준이는 나중에 소민이에게 제주도 기념품을 보내줄 것이다.

6. 위 대화에서 소민이가 민준이에게 한 충고로 가장 적절한 것은? (4점)

① 감사함을 느껴야 한다.

② 전화를 끊으면 안 된다.

③ 아름다운 경치를 즐겨야 한다.

④ 걷는 동안 핸드폰을 사용해서는 안 된다.

⑤ 성산 일출봉에서 사진을 찍어서는 안 된다.

7. 다음 문장을 현재완료 시제를 사용하여 올바르게 표현한 것은? (4점)

• My family started to live in Cheong-ju 10 years ago. My family still lives in Cheong-ju.

① My family has lived in Cheong-ju for 10 years.

② My family had lived in Cheong-ju for 10 years.

③ My family started to live in Cheong-ju 10 years ago.

④ My family has lived in Cheong-ju for 10 years ago.

⑤ My family had lived in Cheong-ju for 10 years ago.

8. 다음 글의 빈칸에 들어갈 말로 가장 적절한 것은? (3점)

These selfies look great, but were they a good idea? I don't think so. They don't look safe. You should _____ when you take selfies in the wild or at high places like these. A monkey could bite you at any time, or you could fall. Here are some safety tips:

1. Don't take selfies while you're walking.
2. Do not pose with or near wild animals.
3. Never take selfies in dangerous places.

① take special care

② touch the animals

③ go near the wild animals

④ climb the mountain higher

⑤ take pictures with many animals

[9~10] 다음 글을 읽고 물음에 답하시오.

You can take selfies at world-famous places (A)[like / because of] Big Ben and the Leaning Tower of Pisa. To take great pictures, just do fun poses and use camera tricks.

You can also visit special museums to take fun selfies. (B)[For example / However], there is a famous selfie museum in the Philippines. It has special spots to take selfies. You can touch the paintings and even step inside them. Look at the following pictures.

The boys are not really riding horses, but is looks like they are. (C)[Unless / Though] the man is just holding a big brush, it looks like he is painting the Mona Lisa. Selfie museums exist in Korea, too. I visited one in Chuncheon last month. Why don't you go there yourself?

9. 위 글의 괄호 (A), (B), (C) 안에서 문맥에 맞는 어구로 가장 적절한 것은? (4점)

	(A)	(B)	(C)
①	like	For example	Unless
②	like	For example	Though
③	because of	For example	Unless
④	because of	However	Though
⑤	because of	However	Unless

10. 위 글의 내용과 일치하는 것은? (3점)

① You cannot take pictures in front of famous places.

② It is not good to use camera tricks to take great pictures.

③ The selfie museum in the Philippines has special spots to take selfies.

④ You don't need to use your camera in selfie museums.

⑤ There is not a selfie museum in Chuncheon.

11. 다음 중 짝지어진 대화가 <u>어색한</u> 것은? (4점)

① A: Has she met him before?
   B: Yes, she did.

② A: Who has had lunch already?
   B: I don't know.

③ A: I have never watched the movie.
   B: Really?

④ A: I have seen a rainbow once in Seoul.
   B: Wow, that is amazing. I have never seen it.

⑤ A: I have stayed in Los Angeles during the vacation.
   B: Then, have you visited the Disneyland?

12. 다음 글의 제목으로 가장 적절한 것은? (4점)

Have you ever heard of a "selfie"? When you take a photograph of yourself, it's a selfie. Did people in the past take selfies? Though it wasn't easy at that time, the answer is yes. Look at this photo of Princess Anastasia. She used a mirror to take a picture of herself. She looks nervous. Can you guess why? Well, I think it was her first selfie. And it was probably the world's first teenage selfie ever.

① Selfies in the Past

② A History of Mirrors

③ How to Take Good Pictures

④ Princess Anastasia: Who is She?

⑤ The World's First Teenage Model

[13~15] 다음 글을 읽고 물음에 답하시오.

Yunho's presentation
You can take selfies at world-famous places like Big Ben and the Leaning Tower of Pisa. To take great pictures, just do fun poses and use camera tricks.
You can also visit special museums to take fun selfies. ⓐ_____, there is a famous selfie museum in the Philippines. It has special spots to take selfies. You can touch the paintings and even step inside them. (A) Though the boys are not really riding horses, it looks like they are. (B) Though the man is just holding a big brush, it looks like he is painting the Mona Lisa. (C) Selfie museums exist in Korea, too. (D) I have visited one in Chuncheon before. (E) Why don't you go there yourself?

13. 위 글의 빈칸 ⓐ에 들어갈 말로 가장 적절한 것은? (4점)

① Yet
② Instead
③ However
④ In contrast
⑤ For example

14. 위 글의 흐름으로 보아 주어진 문장이 들어가기에 가장 적절한 곳은? (3점)

Look at the following two pictures.

① (A)　② (B)　③ (C)　④ (D)　⑤ (E)

15. 위 글의 내용을 한 문장으로 요약하고자 할 때, 빈칸 (a), (b)에 들어갈 말로 가장 적절한 것은? (4점)

Yunho introduced the (a)_____ to take great pictures and (b)_____ for selfies.

	(a)	(b)
①	tips	a famous camera
②	tips	fun places
③	prices	fun places
④	prices	good time
⑤	photographers	good time

[16~17] 다음 글을 읽고 물음에 답하시오.

I think we can use selfies to make a better school life. (A) We can do good things at school and take selfies. (B) You can see them when you visit our school website. I watered the plants and flowers at school. (C) I also helped the teacher at the school library in lunch time. Look at my selfies of those things. (D) How about joining me to create a better school life? (E)

16. 위 글의 흐름으로 보아, 주어진 문장이 들어가기에 가장 적절한 곳은? (4점)

Then we can post the photos on our school website.

① (A)　② (B)　③ (C)　④ (D)　⑤ (E)

17. 위 글의 제목으로 가장 적절한 것은? (4점)

① Selfies in Our Lives
② Tips for Selfie Safety
③ Good Places for Selfies
④ How to Take a Good Selfie
⑤ Selfies for a Better School Life

[18~19] 다음 글을 읽고 물음에 답하시오.

Fun Places for Selfies

Yunho

You can take selfies at world-famous places like Big Ben and the Leaning Tower of Pisa. To take great pictures, just do fun poses and use camera tricks.

You can also visit special museums to take fun selfies. For example, there is a famous selfie museum in the Philippines. It has special spots to take selfies. You can touch the paintings and even step inside them. Look at the following pictures. Though the boys are not really riding horses, it looks like they are (A)_____.

Though the man is just holding a big brush, it looks like he is paining the Mona Lisa. Selfie museums exist in Korea, too. I have visited one in Chuncheon before. Why don't you go there yourself?

18. 위 글의 내용과 일치하지 <u>않는</u> 것은? (4점)

① There are selfie museums in Korea.

② Yunho has never visited a selfie museum in Korea.

③ There is a famous place to take selfies in the Philippines.

④ Do fun poses and use camera tricks to take great pictures.

⑤ Big Ben and the Leaning Tower of Pisa are word-famous places.

19. 위 글의 빈칸 (A)에 들어갈 말로 가장 적절한 것은? (3점)

① riding horses

② taking pictures

③ fighting each other

④ holding a small brush

⑤ painting horses and people

[20~22] 다음 글을 읽고 물음에 답하시오.

Have you ever heard of a "selfie"? When you take a photograph of ⓐyourself, it's a selfie. The students from Minji's photo club ⓑhas searched for information about selfies for one month. Here ⓒare some of their presentations about selfies.

Minji: Did people in the past take selfies? _____ it wasn't easy at that time, the answer is yes. Look at this photo of Princess Anastasia. She used a mirror ⓓto take her selfie. She looks ⓔnervous. Can you guess why? Well, I think it was her first selfie. And it was probably the world's first teenage selfie ever.

20. 위 글의 밑줄 친 ⓐ~ⓔ 중 어법상 어색한 것을 올바르게 고치시오. (5점)

→ _____

21. 위 글의 빈칸에 들어갈 말로 가장 적절한 것은? (3점)

① When　　② Because　　③ Unless

④ Although　　⑤ As long as

22. 위 글의 내용과 일치하는 것은? (4점)

① 과거의 사람들에게는 셀피 찍는 기술이 없었다.

② Anastasia는 책상을 이용해서 셀피를 찍었다.

③ Anastasia는 셀피를 찍을 때 차분한 표정이었다.

④ Anastasia는 세계 최초로 카메라를 사용하였을 것이다.

⑤ 민지는 Anastasia의 사진이 그녀의 첫 번째 셀피 라고 생각한다.

23. 다음 빈칸 (A)에 들어갈 글의 제목으로 가장 알맞은 것은? (4점)

(A)_____
                                    Soyun

I think we can use selfies to make a better school life. We can do good things at school and take selfies. Then we can post the photos on our school website. I've watered the plants and flowers at school for one month. I've also helped the teacher at the school library many items. Look at my selfies of those things. How about joining me to create a better school life?

① A Good Tip to Take Selfies
② Rules of the School Library
③ Making a Worse School Life
④ Selfies for a Better School Life
⑤ The Plants and Flowers on the School Website

24. 다음 글을 Jihun이가 쓴 목적으로 가장 알맞은 것은? (4점)

Selfie Safety
                                    Jihun

These selfies look great, but were they a good idea? I don't think so. They don't look safe. You should take special care when you take selfies in the wild or at high places like these. A monkey could bite you at any time, or you could fall. Here are some safety tips:

1. Don't take selfies while you're walking.
2. Do not pose with or near wild animals.
3. Never take selfies in dangerous places.

① Selfie의 단점을 알려주기 위해
② 추락과 관련한 안전 수칙을 알려주기 위해
③ Selfie를 찍을 때 안전 수칙을 알려주기 위해
④ 원숭이가 언제든 사람을 깨물 수 있다는 것을 알려주기 위해
⑤ 야생 지역이나 높은 곳을 갈 때 지켜야 할 안전 수칙을 알려주기 위해

25. 다음 글을 읽고 질문에 답할 수 <u>없는</u> 것은? (4점)

Have you ever heard of a "selfie"? When you take a photograph of yourself, it's a selfie. The students from Minji's photo club have searched for information about selfies for one month. Here are some of their presentations about seflies.

Selfies in the Past
                                    Minji

Did people in the past take selfies? Though it wasn't easy at that time, the answer is yes. Look at this photo of Princess Anastasia. She used a mirror to take a picture of herself. She looks nervous. Can you guess why? Well, I think it was her first selfie. And it was probably the world's first teenage selfie ever.

① Selfie의 의미는 무엇인가요?
② Minji의 사진 동아리의 이름은 무엇인가요?
③ 사진 찍을 때 Anastasia 공주의 모습은 어땠나요?
④ Anastasia 공주가 그녀 사진을 찍을 때 사용한 물건은 무엇인가요?
⑤ Minji의 동아리에서 Selfie에 대한 정보를 찾기 위해 얼마의 시간이 걸렸나요?

26. 다음 문장에 쓰인 "mind" 중 나머지 넷과 <u>다른</u> 의미로 사용된 것은? (4점)

① John tries to change his <u>mind</u>.
② Please keep the promise in <u>mind</u>.
③ Do you <u>mind</u> if I open the window?
④ Her <u>mind</u> is closed because of stress.
⑤ They replayed the scene in their <u>mind</u>.

2학년 영어 1학기 기말고사(4과) 1회

문항수 : 선택형(24문항) 서술형(2문항) 　20 ． ． ．

◎ 선택형 문항의 답안은 컴퓨터용 수정 싸인펜을
사용하여 OMR 답안지에 바르게 표기하시오.
◎ 서술형 문제는 답을 답안지에 반드시 검정
볼펜으로 쓰시오.
◎ 총 26문항 100점 만점입니다. 문항별 배점
은 각 문항에 표시되어 있습니다.

[인천 ○○중]

1. 다음 대화의 빈칸에 들어갈 말로 가장 적절한 것은?

(4점)

A: Do you remember Ms. Park?
B: Of course. We threw her a birthday party last year.
A: And she cooked *japchae* for us. She put some chicken in it.
B: Right. It was delicious.
A: ＿＿＿＿＿＿＿＿＿＿＿＿＿＿
B: Yes, I do. She won all the rounds. She's really good at games.
A: When are we going to see her next?
B: Let me see. Next Saturday.
A: Let's take some pictures with her this time.
B: Great idea.

① What else did we do?
② Did we cook and eat *japchae* together?
③ Could you tell me how to play the game?
④ After eating together, we played card games.
⑤ And we played computer games. Do you remember that?

[송파구 ○○중]

2. 다음 〈보기〉 대화의 밑줄 친 말과 바꿔 쓰기에 어색한 것은?

(4점)

<보기>
A: Do you remember Mr. Kim, our 6th grade teacher?
B: <u>Well</u>, I can't remember him.

① Let's see.　　　② Of course.
③ Let me see.　　④ Let me think.
⑤ Just a moment.

[인천 ○○중]

3. 다음 중 어법상 올바른 것은?　　(4점)

① We've being to Paris once.
② I have studied never Japanese.
③ Have you ever heard of bird watching?
④ Kate and I has done volunteer work many times.
⑤ Amy has play the piano since she was five years old.

[송파구 ○○중]

4. 밑줄 친 부분을 생략할 수 <u>없는</u> 것은?　　(3점)

① Look at the girl <u>who</u> is playing the piano.
② This is the book <u>that</u> I bought yesterday.
③ You are the person <u>whom</u> I have been looking for.
④ Do you know the boy <u>who is</u> dancing on the stage?
⑤ The steak <u>which</u> I ate at this restaurant was great.

[송파구 ○○중]

5. 다음 〈보기〉의 우리말을 영작할 때, 빈칸에 알맞은 말을 쓰시오.　　(5점)

<보기>
• 이것이 네가 그토록 갖고 싶어 하는 자전거이구나.
→ This is the bike ＿＿＿ ＿＿＿ ＿＿＿
＿＿＿ ＿＿＿ so much.

6. 다음 중 어법상 <u>어색한</u> 것은? (4점)

① Daniel is the friend who I can trust the most.

② Do you like the dog that is running after a cat?

③ You are the person whom I have been looking for.

④ League of Legends is the game whom many students like.

⑤ You have a beautiful garden that everyone wants to have.

[7~9] 다음 글을 읽고 물음에 답하시오.

Wilfrid went back home to look for memories for Ms. Cooper. He went into the hen house and took a fresh, warm egg. Next, he looked for his sock puppet. It always brought laughter to his parents. Finally, he found his football in his toy box. It was as precious as gold to him.
ⓐWilfrid went to Ms. Cooper and gave her the things one by one. "What a strange, sweet child!" thought Ms. Cooper, "He's brought all these wonderful things." Then she started to remember her past.
She held the warm egg and whispered to Wilfrid, "Long ago, I found a small blue egg in my aunt's garden." She smiled at the sock puppet and remembered performing a puppet show for her sister. "My sister laughed a lot," said Ms. Cooper. She bounced the football to Wilfrid and remembered him. "Wilfrid? Wilfrid Gordon Parker! My friend!" She also remembered their secrets one by one.
The two smiled at each other. Ms. Cooper got her memory back thanks to the little boy with the same middle name as hers.

7. 위 글에서 Wilfrid가 밑줄 친 ⓐ처럼 행동한 이유는? (4점)

① to please Wilfrid's parents

② to sell what he gets to Ms. Cooper

③ to make Ms. Cooper remember her past

④ to play with Ms. Cooper using those items

⑤ to know which item Ms. Cooper wants to get

8. 위 글에서 Ms. Cooper가 겪은 심경 변화로 가장 적절한 것은? (3점)

① 외로운 → 화난

② 긴장한 → 겁먹은

③ 실망한 → 당황한

④ 어리둥절한 → 기쁜

⑤ 무관심한 → 질투 나는

9. 위 글의 내용과 일치하는 것은? (4점)

① Cooper 할머니는 Wilfrid Gordon Parker와 친구였다.

② Cooper 할머니는 오래전에 파란 달걀을 마트에서 샀다.

③ Cooper 할머니는 축구를 좋아했다.

④ Wilfrid는 Cooper 할머니와 실제로 나이가 같은 친구 사이다.

⑤ Wilfrid는 Cooper 할머니에게 웃음을 주기 위해 따뜻한 달걀을 가져갔다.

[10~11] 다음 글을 읽고 물음에 답하시오.

Wilfrid Gordon Parker was a little boy who lived next to a nursing home. ⓐ그는 그곳에 사는 모든 사람들을 좋아했다. But his favorite person was Ms. Nancy Gordon Cooper because her middle name was the same as his. He told her all his secrets.

One day, Wilfrid's parents were talking about Ms. Cooper. "Poor old lady," said his mother. "Why is she a poor old lady?" asked Wilfrid. "Because she's lost her memory," said his father. "What's a memory?" asked Wilfrid. "It is something you remember," said his father.

Wilfrid wanted to know more, so he went to his neighbors.

Ms. Jordan was enjoying the sunlight. "What's a memory?" he asked. "Something warm, my child," she said.

Ms. Mitchell was reading a cartoon. "What's a memory?" he asked. "Something that brings you laughter," she said.

Mr. Hunter was cleaning his medal. "It's something as precious as gold, young man," he said.

10. 위 글을 읽고 파악할 수 없는 정보는?   (4점)

① 기억을 잃어버린 사람
② 메달을 닦고 있는 사람의 이름
③ 만화를 읽고 있는 사람의 이름
④ 보육원 근처에 사는 소년의 이름
⑤ Wilfrid Gordon Parker가 가장 좋아하는 사람

11. 위 글의 밑줄 친 ⓐ를 다음과 같이 영작했을 때, 빈 칸 (A), (B)에 들어갈 단어로 알맞게 짝지어진 것은?

(4점)

He (A)_____ all the people (B)_____ lived there.

	(A)	(B)
①	hated	who
②	liked	which
③	liked	who
④	liked	whom
⑤	disliked	who

[12~15] 다음 글을 읽고 물음에 답하시오.

So Wilfrid went back home to ⓐlook for memories for Ms. Cooper. He went into the hen house and took a fresh, warm egg from under a ⓑhen. Next he looked for his sock ⓒpuppet. It always brought laughter to his parents. Finally, he found his football in his toy box. It was as ⓓprecious as gold to him. Wilfrid went to Ms. Cooper and gave her the things one by one. "What a strange, sweet child!" thought Ms. Cooper, "He's brought all these wonderful things." Then she started to remember her ⓔpast.

She held the warm egg and whispered to Wilfrid, "Long ago. I found a small blue egg in my aunt's garden." She smiled at the sock puppet and remembered performing a puppet show for her sister. "My sister laughed a lot," said Ms. Cooper. She bounced the football to Wilfrid and remembered him. "Wilfrid? Wilfrid Gordon Parker! My friend!" She also remembered their secrets one by one. The two smiled at each other. Ms. Cooper got her memory back thanks to the little boy with the same middle name as hers.

12. 위 글의 밑줄 친 ⓐ~ⓔ의 의미가 다른 것은? (3점)

① ⓐ - ~을 찾다   ② ⓑ - 수탉
③ ⓒ - 인형, 꼭두각시 ④ ⓓ - 귀중한
⑤ ⓔ - 과거

13. 위 글에서 Wilfrid가 Ms. Cooper에게 줬던 세 가지 물건은?　　　　　　　　　　(5점)

① football, hen, sock puppet

② gold, sock puppet, football

③ hen house, sock puppet, football

④ sock puppet, toy, and fresh, warm egg

⑤ sock puppet, football, and fresh, warm egg

14. 위 글의 내용과 일치하지 <u>않는</u> 것은?　　(4점)

① Ms. Cooper가 들고 있던 달걀은 따뜻했다.

② Ms. Cooper는 장난감 상자에서 축구공을 찾았다.

③ Ms. Cooper와 Wilfrid의 가운데 이름이 동일하다.

④ Ms. Cooper는 오래전에 그녀의 이모님 댁 정원에서 작고 푸른 알을 찾았다.

⑤ Ms. Cooper는 양말 인형을 보고 미소를 지우며 자기 여동생에게 인형극을 공연해 준 것을 기억하였다.

15. 위 글에서 축구공이 Ms. Cooper가 기억하게 해 준 것은?　　　　　　　　　　(3점)

① Wilfrid Gordon Parker가 자신의 친구라는 것

② Wilfrid Gordon Parker가 자신의 조카라는 것

③ Wilfrid Gordon Parker가 자신의 요양 봉사자라는 것

④ Wilfrid Gordon Parker가 자신의 조카 아들이라는 것

⑤ Wilfrid Gordon Parker가 자신의 축구공을 가져간 사람이라는 것

[16~17] 다음 글을 읽고 물음에 답하시오.

One day, Wilfrid's parents were talking about Ms. Cooper.

"Poor old lady," said his mother.

"Why is she a poor old lady?" asked Wilfrid.

"Because she's lost her memory," said his father.

"What's a memory?" asked Wilfrid.

"It is something you remember," said his father.

Wilfrid wanted to know more, so he went to his neighbors. Ms. Jordan was enjoying the sunlight.

"What's a memory?" he asked.

"Something warm, my child," she said. Ms. Mitchell was reading a cartoon.

"What's a memory?" he asked.

"Something that brings you laughter," she said.

Mr. Hunter was cleaning his medal.

"It's something as precious as gold, young man," he said.

16. 위 글의 제목으로 가장 적절한 것은?　　(4점)

① What Makes You Happy

② How to Keep in Good Memory

③ Various Meanings of a Memory

④ How People Enjoy the Daytime

⑤ The Most Precious Things in My Life

17. 위 글을 읽고 대답할 수 <u>없는</u> 질문으로 가장 알맞은 것은?　　　　　　　　　　(4점)

① Wilfrid는 무엇을 궁금해 하였는가?

② Ms. Mitchell는 어떤 종류의 책을 읽었는가?

③ Ms. Cooper는 언제 그녀의 기억을 잃었는가?

④ Mr. Hunter는 그의 메달을 가지고 무엇을 하였는가?

⑤ Wilfrid의 부모님은 왜 Ms. Cooper에 대하여 걱정하였는가?

[18~19] 다음 글을 읽고 물음에 답하시오.

Wilfrid Gordon Parker was a little boy (A)_____ lived next to a nursing home. He liked all the people (A)_____ lived there. But his favorite person was Ms. Nancy Gordon Cooper because her middle name was the same as ⓐhis. He told her all his secrets.

18. 위 글의 빈칸 (A)에 들어갈 말로 가장 알맞은 것은?

(3점)

① who ② when ③ what
④ which ⑤ where

19. 위 글의 밑줄 친 ⓐ와 같은 의미로 쓰인 것은? (3점)

① He should do his homework right now.
② He played soccer game with his friends.
③ His plan is to finish the project by Friday.
④ His sister comes to school to give him a ride.
⑤ I had a desk in my room which was bigger than his.

[20~22] 다음 글을 읽고 물음에 답하시오.

Wilfrid went to Ms. Cooper and gave her ⓐ the things one by one. "What a strange, sweet child!" thought Ms. Cooper, "He's brought all these wonderful things." Then she started to remember her past.
She held the warm egg and ⓑwhisper to Wilfrid, "Long ago, I found a small blue egg in my aunt's garden." She smiled at the sock puppet and remembered ⓒperform a puppet show for her sister. "My sister laughed a lot," said Ms. Cooper. She bounced the football to Wilfrid and remembered him. "Wilfrid? Wilfrid Gordon Parker! My friend!" She also remembered their secrets one by one.

20. 위 글의 밑줄 친 ⓐ에 해당하는 것을 영어로 쓰시오. (3개)   (5점)

→ _____

21. 위 글의 밑줄 친 ⓑ, ⓒ의 동사 형태가 순서대로 바르게 짝지어진 것은?   (4점)

	ⓑ	ⓒ
①	whisper	perform
②	whispered	performed
③	whispering	performed
④	whispered	performing
⑤	to whisper	to perform

22. 위 글의 내용과 일치하는 것은?   (4점)

① Cooper 할머니는 마침내 Wilfrid를 기억했다.
② Cooper 할머니는 처음부터 Wilfrid를 알아보았다.
③ Cooper 할머니는 Wilfrid와의 비밀을 한 번에 기억했다.
④ Cooper 할머니는 Wilfrid가 가져온 물건들을 좋아하지 않았다.
⑤ Wilfrid는 Cooper 할머니에게 가져온 물건들을 한꺼번에 드렸다.

[23~24] 다음 글을 읽고 물음에 답하시오.

Wilfrid Gordon Parker was a little boy ⓐwho lived next to a nursing home. He liked all the people ⓑwho lived there. But his favorite person was Ms. Nancy Gordon Cooper ⓒbecause her middle name was the same as his. He told ⓓthat her all his secrets.

One day, Wilfrid's parents were talking about Ms. Cooper.

"Poor old lady," said his mother.

"Why is she a poor old lady?" asked Wilfrid.

"Because she has lost her memory," said his father.

"What's a memory?" asked Wilfrid.

"It is something ⓔthat you remember," said his father.

23. 위 글의 ⓐ~ⓔ 중 쓰임이 어색한 것은? (4점)

① ⓐ　② ⓑ　③ ⓒ　④ ⓓ　⑤ ⓔ

24. 위 글을 읽고 답할 수 없는 질문은? (4점)

① Where did Wilfrid live?

② What was wrong with Ms. Cooper?

③ Who was Wilfrid's favorite person?

④ Why did Wilfrid's parents like Ms. Cooper?

⑤ Did Wilfrid like all the people who lived at the nursing home?

[25~26] 다음 글을 읽고 물음에 답하시오.

Wilfrid Gordon Parker is a little boy and he is friends with the old people at the nursing home.

(A) Wilfrid finds a fresh egg for warmth, a sock puppet for laughter, and his precious football.

(B) One day, Wilfrid hears from his parents that Ms. Cooper has lost her memory. He asks everyone he knows about the meaning of a memory.

(C) His favorite person is Ms. Nancy Gordon Cooper because she has the same middle name as Wilfrid. He even shares his secrets with her.

When he gives them to Ms. Cooper, she gets her memory back.

25. 위 글의 흐름에 맞게 단락 (A)~(C)의 순서를 바르게 배열한 것은? (3점)

① (A)-(C)-(B)　② (B)-(A)-(C)

③ (B)-(C)-(A)　④ (C)-(A)-(B)

⑤ (C)-(B)-(A)

26. 위 글에서 Wilfrid가 한 행동과 그 이유를 바르게 연결한 것은? (5점)

① 행동: told his secrets to her

　이유: It was precious to him.

② 행동: looked for his sock puppet

　이유: It had warmth.

③ 행동: found his football

　이유: It brought laughter.

④ 행동: took a fresh egg

　이유: He liked it most.

⑤ 행동: tried to know the meaning of memory

　이유: He wanted to get her memory back.

2학년 영어 1학기 기말고사(4과) 2회

문항수 : 선택형(23문항) 서술형(4문항)   20   .   .   .

◎ 선택형 문항의 답안은 컴퓨터용 수정 싸인펜을 사용하여 OMR 답안지에 바르게 표기하시오.
◎ 서술형 문제는 답을 답안지에 반드시 검정 볼펜으로 쓰시오.
◎ 총 27문항 100점 만점입니다. 문항별 배점은 각 문항에 표시되어 있습니다.

[관악구 ㅇㅇ중]

1. 다음 대화를 읽고 답할 수 <u>없는</u> 질문은?   (3점)

Billie: Do you remember Ms. Kang, the school nurse?
Lipa: Sure. She was nice to everyone.
Billie: Guess what? She's getting married next month.
Lipa: Wow! What shall we do for her?
Billie: Let me see. What about making a special album?
Lipa: That's a good idea.

① Who is Ms. Kang?
② How was Ms. Kang to everyone?
③ What will Ms. Kang do next month?
④ What are Lipa and Billie going to do for Ms. Kang?
⑤ What song will Lipa and Billie sing at Ms. Kang's wedding?

[관악구 ㅇㅇ중]

2. 다음 중 우리말을 바르게 영작한 것은?   (3점)

• 수질오염은 대기오염만큼 심각하다.

① Water pollution is so serious as air pollution.
② Water pollution is serious air pollution as.
③ Water pollution is as serious to air pollution.
④ Water pollution is as serious as air pollution.
⑤ Water pollution is as seriously as air pollution.

3. Choose the best answer for the underlined blank.   (3점)

Maddie: Do you remember the field trip last year?
Kevin: _____
Maddie: Me, too.

① Let me see. It's a trip. Right?
② Let me see. It's a field. Right?
③ Of course. I will take a lot of pictures.
④ Of course. I took a lot of pictures.
⑤ Of course. That's right.

[관악구 ㅇㅇ중]

4. 다음 중 어법상 옳은 것을 <u>모두</u> 고른 것은?   (4점)

ⓐ This is a gold medal which we won it at the race.
ⓑ We saw the monkey opening the car door.
ⓒ This is a painting that we bought it at the market.
ⓓ We met a girl who was wearing a beautiful dress.
ⓔ We took some pictures of Korean traditional dancers who saw at the town festival.
ⓕ It is something as precious as gold.
ⓖ Her idea is the same as his.

① ⓐ, ⓑ, ⓒ   ② ⓑ, ⓔ, ⓖ
③ ⓑ, ⓓ, ⓕ   ④ ⓑ, ⓓ, ⓕ, ⓖ
⑤ ⓒ, ⓓ, ⓔ, ⓖ

[5~6] 다음 대화를 읽고 물음에 답하시오.

Mina: Do you remember Ms. Park, the old lady who lives alone?

Junsu: ⓐOf course. We threw her a birthday party last year.

Mina: And she cooked *japchae* for us. She put some chicken in ⓑit.

Junsu: Right. It was delicious. And we played card games together. Do you remember that?

Mina: Yes. She won all the rounds. She's really good at games.

Junsu: When are we going to see her next, Mina?

Mina: Let me see. Next Saturday.

Junsu: Let's take some pictures with her this time.

Mina: Great idea, Junsu.

5. 위 대화의 ⓐ와 바꾸어 쓸 수 있는 것은? (3점)

① No, I don't.　　② That's good.

③ Unbelievable.　　④ Me too.

⑤ Sure.

6. 위 대화의 ⓑ가 가리키는 것은? (3점)

① a birthday party　② Ms. Park

③ chicken　　　④ *japchae*

⑤ last year

[7~8] 다음 글을 읽고 물음에 답하시오.

(A)Wilfrid Gordon Parker는 요양원 옆에 사는 어린 소년이었다. He liked all the people who lived there. However, his favorite person was Ms. Nancy Gordon Cooper because her middle name was the same as his. He told all his secrets to her.

One day, Wilfrid's parents were talking about Ms. Cooper.

"Poor old lady," said his mother.

"Why is she a poor old lady?" asked Wilfrid.

"Because she's lost her memory," said his father.

7. 위 글 (A)를 조건에 맞게 영작하시오. (5점)

<조건>
- 관계대명사 'that'을 사용할 것
- 14 단어의 완전한 문장으로 쓸 것

답: _____

8. Ms. Cooper에 대해 답할 수 없는 것은? (4점)

① Where did she live?

② What's wrong with her?

③ Why did Wilfrid like her most?

④ Why did she live at the nursing home?

⑤ What made Wilfrid's parents think she was poor?

9. Choose the best answer for the underlined blank. (4점)

Chris: Do you remember my favorite food?

Jamie: _____

Chris: That's not right. It's pizza.

① Let me see. It's pizza, right?

② Let me see. It's chicken, right?

③ Let me see. It's not right.

④ Of course. Let me eat chicken.

⑤ Of course. Let me eat pizza.

[10~13] 다음 글을 읽고 물음에 답하시오.

So Wilfrid went back home ⓐto look for memories for Ms. Cooper. He went into the hen house and took a fresh, warm egg ⓑfrom under a hen. Next, he looked for his sock puppet. It always brought laughter to his parents. Finally, he found his football in his toy box. It was as precious as gold to him. Wilfrid went to Ms. Cooper and gave her the things (A)(하나하나씩). "(B)(이상하면서도 귀여운 아이구나!)" thought Ms. Cooper, "He's brought all these wonderful things." Then she started ⓒto remember her past. She held the warm egg and whispered to Wilfrid, "Long ago, I found a small blue egg in my aunt's garden." She smiled at the sock puppet and remembered ⓓperformed a puppet show for her sister. "My sister laughed a lot," said Ms. Cooper. She bounced the football to Wilfrid and remembered him. "Wilfrid? Wilfrid Gordon Parker! My friend!" She also remembered their secrets. The two smiled at each other. Ms. Cooper got her memory back (C)_____ the little boy with the same middle name as ⓔhers.

10. 위 글의 밑줄 친 (B)의 우리말을 바르게 영작한 것은? (4점)

① What a child strange and sweet!

② What strange and sweet a child!

③ What a strange, sweet child!

④ How a strange, sweet child!

⑤ How a child strange and sweet!

11. 위 글의 빈칸 (C)에 들어갈 말로 가장 알맞은 것은? (2점)

① thanks from   ② thanks to

③ thanks for   ④ thank you

⑤ thankful

12. 위 글의 ⓐ~ⓔ 중 어법상 바르지 못한 것은? (3점)

① ⓐ   ② ⓑ   ③ ⓒ   ④ ⓓ   ⑤ ⓔ

13. 위 글의 (A)의 우리말을 영어로 쓰시오. (3 단어) (5점)

답: _____ _____ _____

14. 다음을 관계대명사를 이용하여 다음 두 문장을 한 문장으로 쓰시오. (5점)

- I watched a movie.
- It was very interesting.

답: _____

15. 다음 글의 밑줄 친 부분 중 어법상 올바르지 않은 것은? (2개) (4점)

Ms. Cooper ⓐhold the warm egg ⓑwhich Wilfrid gave her and whispered to Wilfrid, "Long ago, I found a small blue egg in my aunt's garden." She smiled at the sock puppet and remembered ⓒto perform a puppet show for her sister. "My sister laughed ⓓa lot," said Ms. Cooper. She bounced the football to Wilfrid and remembered him. "Wilfrid? Wilfrid Gordon Parker! My friend!" She also remembered their secrets one by one. The two smiled at each other. Ms. Cooper ⓔgot her memory back thanks to the little boy with the same middle name as hers.

① ⓐ   ② ⓑ   ③ ⓒ   ④ ⓓ   ⑤ ⓔ

[16~18] 다음 글을 읽고 물음에 답하시오.

Wilfrid went back home to look for memories for Ms. Cooper. He went into the hen house and took a fresh, warm egg ⓐfrom under a hen. Next, he looked for his sock puppet. It always brought laughter to his parents. Finally, he found his football in his toy box. It was as precious as gold to him.

Wilfrid went to Ms. Cooper and gave ⓑthe things her ⓒone by one. "What a strange, sweet child!" thought Ms. Cooper, "He's brought all these wonderful things." Then she started ⓓremembering her past.

She held the warm egg and whispered to Wilfrid, "Long ago, I found a small blue egg in my aunt's garden." She smiled at the sock puppet and remembered ⓔperforming a puppet show for her sister. "My sister laughed a lot," said Ms. Cooper. She bounced the football to Wilfrid and remembered him. "Wilfrid? Wilfrid Gordon Parker! My friend!" She also remembered their secrets one by one.

The two smiled at each other. Ms. Cooper got her memory back thanks to the little boy with the same middle name as (A)_____.

16. 위 글의 밑줄 친 ⓐ~ⓔ 중 표현이 바르지 않은 것은? (3점)

① ⓐ   ② ⓑ   ③ ⓒ   ④ ⓓ   ⑤ ⓔ

17. Choose the best two answers for the underlined blank. (4점)

① hers   ② his

③ her middle name   ④ their given name

⑤ theirs

18. Which is correct according to the passage above? (3점)

① The first thing that Wilfrid looked for was his sock puppet.

② A fresh, warm egg was as precious as gold to Wilfrid.

③ Wilfrid looked for his sock puppet because it brought laughter to his parents.

④ Ms. Cooper remembered a small blue egg when she bounced the football to Wilfrid.

⑤ Ms. Cooper couldn't remember the secrets between Wilfrid and her.

[19~20] 다음 글을 읽고 물음에 답하시오.

So Wilfrid went back home to look for memories for Ms. Cooper. He went into the hen house and took a fresh, warm egg from under a hen. (A)_____ he looked for his sock puppet. It brought his parents laughter all the time. In the end, he found his football in his toy box. It was as precious as gold to him.

Wilfrid went to Ms. Cooper and gave her the things one by one. "(B)_____ a strange, sweet child" thought Ms. Cooper, "He's brought all these wonderful things." Then she started to remember her (C)_____.

She held the warm egg and whispered to Wilfrid, "Long time ago, I found 2 small blue egg in my aunt's garden." She smiled at the sock puppet and remembered performing a puppet show for her sister. "My sister laughed a lot," said Ms. Cooper. She bounced the football to Wilfrid and remembered him. "Wilfrid? Wilfrid Gordon Parker! My friend!" She also remembered their secrets one by one. The two smiled at each other. Ms. Cooper got her memory back thanks to the little boy with the same middle name as hers.

19. 위 글의 빈칸 (A)~(C)에 들어갈 말이 순서대로 알맞게 짝지어진 것은? (4점)

	(A)	(B)	(C)
①	Then	What	future
②	Next	What	past
③	Next	How	future
④	Above all	How	past
⑤	To begin with	What	past

20. 위 글의 내용과 일치하는 것은? (4점)

① Ms. Cooper has seen blue eggs before.

② Wilfrid gave the things to Ms. Cooper at a time.

③ Ms. Cooper gave the football to Wilfrid by kicking it.

④ Ms. Cooper's sister performed a puppet show for Ms. Cooper.

⑤ Ms. Cooper didn't recall the secrets between her and Wilfrid.

[인천 ○○중]

[21~22] 다음 대화를 읽고 물음에 답하시오.

Sujin: Do you remember Ms. Lee, the old lady who lives by herself?

Junsu: Of course. We gave her a birthday party last year.

Sujin: And she made *japchae* for us. She put some chicken in it.

Junsu: Right. It was delicious. And we played card games together. Do you remember that?

Sujin: Yes. She won every round. She's really good at games.

Junsu: When are we going to see her next, Sujin?

Sujin: Let me see. Next Sunday.

Junsu: Shall we take some pictures with her this time?

Sujin: Sounds great, Junsu.

21. 위 대화의 분위기로 가장 알맞은 것은? (3점)

① urgent   ② pleasant   ③ gloomy

④ frustrated   ⑤ desperate

22. 위 대화의 내용과 일치하는 문장의 개수는? (4점)

ⓐ They threw Ms. Lee a birthday party.

ⓑ Ms. Lee lives alone.

ⓒ Next Sunday is Ms. Lee's birthday.

ⓓ Ms. Lee played card games very well.

ⓔ Sujin will take pictures with the old lady.

ⓕ Ms. Lee has grandchildren who held a party for her.

ⓖ Sujin and Junsu are going to meet to prepare for the party.

ⓗ Sujin won all the rounds when they played games.

① 2개   ② 3개   ③ 4개   ④ 5개   ⑤ 6개

[광주 ○○중]

[23~26] 다음 글을 읽고 물음에 답하시오.

Wilfrid Gordon Parker was a little boy ⓐwho lived next to a nursing home. He liked all the people ⓑwho lived there. But his favorite person was Ms. Nancy Gordon Cooper because her middle name was the same as his. He told her all his secrets.

One day, Wilfrid's parents were talking about Ms. Cooper.

"Poor old lady," said his mother.

"Why is she a poor old lady?" asked Wilfrid.

"Because 그녀는 기억을 잃었다." said his father.

"What's a memory?" asked Wilfrid.

"It is something ⓒthat you remember," said this father.

Wilfrid wanted to know more, so he went to his neighbors.

Ms. Jordan was enjoying the sunlight.

"What's a memory?" he asked.

"Something warm, my child," she said.

Ms. Mitchell was reading a cartoon.

"What's a memory?" he asked.

"Something ⓓthat brings you laughter," she said.

Mr. Hunter was cleaning his medal. "It's something ⓔthat is as (A)precious as gold, young man," he said.

23. 밑줄 친 (A)의 영영풀이로 바른 것은? (4점)

① back in the past

② valuable or important

③ the act or sound of laughing

④ to use something at the same time as someone else

⑤ to act, dance, sing, or play music in front of an audience

24. 밑줄 친 ⓐ~ⓔ 중 생략할 수 있는 것은? (3점)

① ⓐ ② ⓑ ③ ⓒ ④ ⓓ ⑤ ⓔ

25. Choose one that you can't answer according to the passage above. (4점)

① Where did Wilfrid live?

② Why did Wilfrid like Ms. Cooper?

③ What did Wilfrid do to learn more about a memory?

④ What is a memory to Wilfrid's mother?

⑤ What is a memory to Mr. Hunter?

26. 위 글의 밑줄 친 우리말을 조건에 맞는 영어 문장으로 작성하시오. (5점)

<조건>

1. 주어진 우리말 뜻과 일치할 것.

2. 그녀는 과거에 기억을 잃고 현재 기억을 하지 못하는 상태로 표현할 것.

3. 철자 및 어법 오류는 1개당 1점 감점.

징답: _____

27. 다음 대화의 내용과 일치하는 것은? (4점)

Jasmin: Do you remember Ms. Park, the old lady who lives alone?

Genie: Of course. We threw her a birthday party last year.

Jasmin: And she cooked *japchae* for us. She put some chicken in it.

Genie: Right. It was delicious. And we played card games together. Do you remember that?

Jasmin: Yes. She won all the rounds. She's really good at games.

Genie: When are we going to see her next, Jasmin?

Jasmin: Let me see. Next Saturday.

Genie: Let's take some pictures with her this time.

Jasmin: Great idea, Genie.

① Ms. Park invited Jasmin and Genie to her birthday party.

② Jasmin made some food for Ms. Park.

③ Ms. Park really loves to eat *japche* and chicken.

④ Ms. Park is the one who won at card games.

⑤ Jasmin and Genie will take some pictures this Saturday.

MEMO

정답 및 해설

Lesson 1 (중간) 1회

01 ⑤
02 (1) have many bowls to wash
    (2) gave me a list of books to read
03 ④ **04** ③ **05** ② **06** ⑤ **07** ②
08 Don't judge a book by its cover. **09** ① **10** ⑤
11 ① **12** ③ **13** ⑤ **14** ⑤ **15** ③ **16** ⑤ **17** ①
18 ④ **19** ③ **20** ⑤ **21** ③ **22** ② **23** ④ **24** ①
25 It's time to pay him back.

01 (D) 마술 동아리 어떻게 생각하니? (의견 묻기) → (C) 그건 나에게 적절한 동아리라고 생각해. 나는 많은 재미있는 기술을 배우고 싶어. (의견 말하기) → (A) 나도 가입할 거야. 첫 번째 모임이 언제이니? (모임 질문) → (B) 다음 주 수요일이야. 첫 번째 모임이 너무 기다려진다. (모임 대답)

02 to부정사의 형용사적 용법은 '~할, ~하기 위한'의 뜻으로 명사를 뒤에서 꾸며준다. (1) 우리는 씻어야 할 많은 그릇을 가지고 있다. (2) 아버지는 나에게 읽을 책의 목록을 주셨다.

03 ①, ②, ③, ⑤는 명사절의 접속사 that이고, ④는 명사 book을 꾸며주는 지시형용사이다.

04 두 가지의 채소 요리가 있고 A가 메뉴에 대하여 물어보는 것으로 보아, 구내식당이 적절하다. ① 도서관 ② 정원 ③ 구내식당 ④ 부엌 ⑤ 슈퍼마켓

05 미소가 선생님이 매우 엄격하고 진지해 보인다고 말한 것에 ⓓ에서 "책을 표지로 판단하지 말아라."라고 말한 후에 ⓐ에서 그 속담의 의미를 물은 다음 ⓔ에서 박 선생님과의 수업 경험으로부터 얻은 의견을 말하고 ⓑ에서 사실인지 물은 후 ⓒ에서 Yes.로 대답 후 자세하게 설명하는 순서가 적절하다.

06 hallway(복도): a passage with doors in a building

07 (A)를 듣고 세호가 겉모습만 보고 판단하지 말라고 하였으므로 부정적인 외모에 관련된 ②번이 적절하다. ① 재미있고 친절한 ② 진지하고 엄격한 ③ 상냥하고 사려 깊은 ④ 상냥하고 관대한 ⑤ 무례하고 정직한

08 직역: 책의 표지로 책을 판단하지 마.

09 'can't wait for 명사'는 '~가 몹시 기다려진다'라는 뜻

10 ① one of 복수명사로 one of my tickets로 쓴다.
② '우연히 ~하다'는 'happen to부정사'이므로 happen to see로 쓴다.
③ on one's way에서 Dami는 여학생이므로 on her ways로 쓴다.
④ 연결된 동사 saw처럼 과거시제 shouted로 쓴다.

11 ① 그녀는 지훈이가 세호의 표를 가져갔다고 생각했기 때문에 ② 지훈이는 세호에게 그가 표를 찾았다고 말했기 때문에 ③ 그녀는 지훈이가 그 표를 세호에게 돌려주는 것을 보았기 때문에 ④ 지훈이는 세호에게 KBL경기를 같이 보러 가자고 했기 때문에 ⑤ 그녀는 세호가 표를 잃어버렸고 찾지 못했다는 것을 알았기 때문에

12 (B)는 대명사 something을 꾸며주는 형용사적 용법의 to부정사이다. ③은 보어로 쓰인 명사적 용법이다.

13 (A)에서 "너 그거 아니?"라고 묻는 것은 "You know what?"이 적절하다. (B)에서 매우 기다려진다는 의미로 "I can't wait for ~"를 쓰는 것이 적절하다.

14 이 클럽에 관해 의견을 묻는 C가 가장 먼저 온 후 그에 대한 대답인 B가 온 다음, 첫 번째 모임을 묻는 A가 오고 그에 대한 대답인 D가 오는 것이 적절하다.

15 B 문장에서 재미있는 마술을 배우고 싶다고 하였으므로 마술 동아리가 적절하다.

16 ⓐ~ⓓ는 Minjun이고, ⓔ는 Jihun이다.

17 빈칸 (A)에 지훈이 끼어들었다고 하는 것이 적절하다. ① 끼어들다 ② ~에 대해 말하다 ③ 도착하다 ④ 버리다 ⑤ 우연히 마주치다

18 (B)의 "민준이는 농구팬이 아니야."는 민준이 대신 지훈이가 가고 싶다는 뜻이 가장 적절하다. ④ 지훈이는 세호와 KBL 경기에 가고 싶다. ① 지훈이는 훌륭한 농구선수이다. ② 지훈이는 세호의 표에 관해 이야기하고 싶다. ③ 민준이는 농구를 잘하지 않는다. ⑤ 지훈이는 민준이가 KBL 경기에 갈 것이라고 생각한다.

19 ① I expect to see you again. ② They have no house to live in. ④ I need a piece of paper to write on. ⑤ He puts off visiting the teachers by the next day.

20 ⑤ 사람들의 의견을 얻으려고 ① 안부 인사를 하려고 ② 사과하려고 ③ 고맙다고 말하려고 ④ 자원봉사자를 모으려고

21 밑줄 친 to부정사구는 명사 ways를 꾸며주는 형용사적 용법으로 쓰였다. ③ 그녀는 첫 번째 기차를 잡기 위하여 일찍 일어났다.(목적을 나타내는 부사적 용법)

22 (A)는 'be going to 동사원형'이므로 take를 쓴다. (B)는 전에 데려갔다고 하였으므로 과거형인 took이 적절하다.

23 다미가 혼자 생각한 것이므로 'herself'를 쓰는 것이 가장 적절하다.

24 지훈이의 생일은 알 수 없다. ① 지훈이의 생일은 언제인가? ② 다미는 세호에게 무엇을 주었고 왜 주었는가? ③ 세호는 누구와 농구경기에 가기를 원했는가? ④ 지훈이는 경기에 가고 싶어했는가? ⑤ 바닥에 떨어진 무엇인가를 보았을 때 지훈이는 무엇을 하려고 노력했는가?

25 '~할 시간이야,'는 'it's time to부정사'를 쓰고, pay back의 목적어가 대명사이면 두 단어 사이에 들어가야 하므로 정답은 It's time to pay him back이다.

Lesson 1 (중간)

```
01 ④  02 ②  03 ③  04 ⑤  05 ①  06 ④  07 ⑤
08 ④  09 ①  10 it is time to pay him back
11 ②  12 ④
13 ⓐ Do you have something to say?
    ⓑ I have lots of letters to write.
14 ⑤  15 ⑤  16 ③  17 ③  18 ①
19 세호에게 티켓을 찾아 주었기 때문에
20 ②  21 ④  22 ①
23 ⓐ I didn't know that he is Sue's boyfriend.
    ⓑ Jamie thinks that friends are important.
24 ①
25 She gave him two KBL tickets for his birthday.
26 ②  27 ④  28 ②
```

01 ① 허용했다 ② 응답했다 ③ 줄였다 ④ 우연히 ~했다 ⑤ 계속했다
그녀는 우연히 그 노인을 만났다.

02 ① 조건의 if절에서는 현재시제로 미래를 나타낸다. I will go fishing if it is sunny tomorrow. ③ 5형식 동사 ask의 목적보어는 to부정사를 쓴다. I asked my science teacher to let me work alone. ④ 접속사 If를 쓰는 것이 문맥상 자연스럽다. If you are hungry, eat some cookies on the table. ⑤ 접속사 Unless는 'if … not'의 뜻으로 이어지는 절을 부정문으로 쓰지 않는다. Unless you study harder, you'll get bad grades.

03 '(가지고) 쓸 펜을 주세요.'라는 문장에서 명사 a pen을

꾸며줄 to부정사에 전치사 with를 쓰는 것이 적절하다.

04 보기에 쓰인 부정사는 명사 plans를 꾸며주는 형용사적 용법으로 사용되었다. ⑤는 명사 places를 꾸며주는 형용사적 용법이다. ①~④는 일반동사의 목적어로 사용된 명사적 용법이다.

05 the School Band에 함께 가입하자고 하는 것으로 미루어 보아, flute을 연주할 수 있다고 해야 자연스럽고, 또한 A가 콘서트에서 연주하기를 바란다는 말에 '나도 그래.'라고 대답한 것으로 보아 콘서트가 매우 기다려진다고 해야 문맥상 어울린다. 'can't wait for 명사'는 '~가 매우 기다려진다'라는 뜻이다.

06 ① Mr. Park은 작년에 Tom과 Molly를 가르치셨다. ② Mr. Park은 학생들이 휴대전화를 가지고 놀게 허락하신다. ③ Mr. Park은 교내에서 가장 유명한 선생님이시다. ⑤ Molly는 올해 Mr. Park의 수학수업을 받지 않는다.

07 (A)는 '책을 표지로 판단하지 말라'는 속담이다. ⑤ 너는 어떤 사람이나 사물에 대한 의견을 오직 그들의 외모로만 판단해서는 안 된다.

08 realize: 깨닫다 (to understand a situation, sometimes suddenly: 어떤 상황을 가끔은 갑자기 이해하게 되다)

09 A: 나는 그 생일파티가 정말 기다려져. B: 괜찮아.

10 '~할 시간이야,'는 'It's time to부정사'를 쓰고, pay back의 목적어가 인칭대명사이면 두 단어 사이에 들어가야 한다.

11 Q : 세호는 누구와 농구경기에 가고 싶어 했나요? A: 그는 지훈이를(→민준이를) 데리고 가고 싶어했다.

12 '그것들은 아버지가 주신 거야.'라고 다미가 말한 것으로 미루어 보아 농구표임을 알 수 있다.

13 to부정사의 형용사적 용법을 사용하여 앞의 명사를 뒤에서 꾸민다.

14 지훈이가 다미에 관해 어떻게 생각하는지는 언급되어 있지 않다. ⑤ 지훈이는 다미를 어떻게 생각했나요? ① 다미가 세호를 보았을 때 세호는 무엇을 하는 중이었나요? ② 다미는 세호에게 무엇을 주었나요? ③ 세호는 누구와 농구경기에 가기를 원했나요? ④ 지훈이는 경기에 가고 싶었나요?

15 ⓔ는 지훈이를 지칭한다. ⓐ~ⓓ는 민준이를 가리킨다.

16 ③의 replied는 '응답했다'의 뜻으로 이 문장에서 쓰임이 어색하다.

17 (A) on one's way: ~에 가는 길에
(B) look for: ~를 찾다
(C) how about -ing ~?: ~하는 것이 어때?

18 happen to : 우연히 ~하다

19 Just then, Jihun saw Seho and shouted, "Seho! I found a ticket in the hallway. I think it's yours."에서 미루어 보아 Dami가 오해를 했다는 것을 알 수 있다.

20 누가 다미의 아버지에게 표를 주었는지는 알 수 없다. ② 누가 다미의 아버지에게 KBL 표를 주었나요? ① 다미는 지훈이를 어떻게 생각했나요? ③ 다미가 세호를 보았을 때 세호는 무엇을 하는 중이었나요? ④ 지훈이는 농구경기에 가고 싶었나요? ⑤ 세호는 누구와 농구경기에 가고 싶었나요?

21 (A) 갚다: pay back (B) 끼어들다: cut in (C) 믿다: Trust

22 forgive(용서하다) - 화내는 것을 멈추다

23 명사절의 접속사 that을 사용하여 문장의 목적어로 쓴다.

24 '~할 시간이야,'는 'it's time to부정사'를 쓰고, pay back의 목적어가 인칭대명사이면 두 단어 사이에 들어가야 하므로 ⓐ의 문장은 'it's (A)time (B)to (C)pay (D)him (E)back.'이다.

25 Q: 다미는 세호에게 무엇을 왜 주고 싶었나요?

26 ② 다미의 아버지는 농수선수인가? ① 지훈이는 농구 팬입니까? ③ 다미는 세호의 생일날 그에게 무엇을 주었나요? ④ 누가 세호를 전에 축구 경기에 데리고 갔었나요? ⑤ 몇 장의 표를 다미는 세호에게 주었나요?

27 ⓐ, ⓒ, ⓓ (명사절의 접속사) - ⓑ, ⓔ (지시형용사)

28 세호가 다미에게 표를 찾을 수 없다고 했고, 잃어버린 것 같다고 한 것으로 미루어 보아, ②의 '걱정스럽다'가 세호의 심경으로 가장 적절하다.

Lesson 2 (중간) 1회

01 ②	02 ①, ④	03 ②	04 ④	05 ④	06 ②
07 ③	08 Sheila saw Max sitting under the desk				
09 ②	10 ⑤	11 ⑤	12 ③	13 ③	14 ④	15 ⑤
16 ⑤	17 ②	18 ⑤	19 ③	20 ④	21 ④	22 ⑤
23 ②	24 ②	25 ④	26 ④	27 ②	28 ④	

01 'Ryan이 밖을 확인했지만, 그는 그를(Bear) 찾을 수 없었다.'라고 해야 자연스럽다. 'but he could not find him'으로 쓴다.

02 ② 조건의 if에서는 현재시제로 미래를 대신한다. (If it rains, I will read a book.) ③ 명사 friends를 부정사 'to play'가 꾸며 줄 때 적절한 전치사가 필요하다.(The boy needed friends to play with.) ⑤ 지각동사의 목적격보어는 원형부정사 또는 현재분사를 쓴다.(I saw Brain do(ing) a magic trick.)

03 빈칸 다음에 그녀는 친구가 없다고 한 것으로 미루어 보아 정답은 '외로운'이 적절하다. ① 친절한 ③ 바쁜 ④ 행복한 ⑤ 신난

04 Sheila가 왜 이사했는지는 알 수 없다.
① Bear는 무엇 하기를 좋아했는가?
② Bear의 눈은 무슨 색인가?
③ Sheila는 Ryan과 얼마나 멀리 떨어져 사는가?
④ 왜 Sheila가 이사했는가?
⑤ Ryan은 자기 고양이의 이름을 어떻게 생각하는가?

05 ① 검정색과 갈색이다.
② Ryan은 Bear의 이름이 완벽하다고 생각했다.
③ 곰 모양의 점이 있었다.
⑤ 매일 아침 밖으로 나갔다.

06 조건의 접속사 if가 쓰인 절에서는 미래시제를 현재시제로 나타내고, 주절은 그대로 미래로 쓴다. 그러므로 정답은 ②가 적절하다.

07 Sheila가 처음 소개되는 (B)가 처음에 오고 그 다음 Max가 다리를 다친 내용이 나오는 (A), 마지막으로 Sheila가 Max를 병원에 데리고 가는 (C) 순서가 적절하다.

08 지각동사를 이용한 5형식 문장으로 쓴다. 이때 목적보어는 원형부정사 또는 현재분사를 쓴다.

09 본문의 'She looked at him closely and found a bad cut on his leg.' 문장으로 미루어 보아 정답은 ② 'Max가 다리에 심한 베인 상처가 있었기 때문에'가 적절하다.

10 조건의 접속사 if가 쓰인 절에서는 미래시제를 현재시제로 쓴다. 그러므로 정답은 ⑤가 적절하다.

11 목적어 역할을 하는 명사절의 접속사 that은 생략이 가능하다. ①, ②, ③, ④: 지시형용사

12 ① 지훈이는 Amy와 함께 공원을 청소할 예정이다. ② 지훈이는 장갑과 비닐 봉투를 공원에 가지고 올 것이다. ④ 오늘 오후가 아닌 이번 주 일요일에 만난다. ⑤ 큰 비닐 봉지가 필요하다.

13 2시에 만나자는 제안을 3시로 변경하는 것으로 미루어 보아, 제안을 거절하는 내용이 적절하다.

14 ⓐ, ⓑ 일반동사 like의 목적어로 to부정사(to+동사원형)나 동명사를 쓴다. ⓒ 전치사 at의 목적어로 동명사를 쓴다.

15 Jina와 Alex는 Grand Park 정류장에서 만날 예정이다.

16 D: Sheila가 잃어버린 고양이에 관한 포스터를 보았다. C: Sheila는 Max를 Ryan의 집으로 데리고 갔다. A: Ryan이 문을 열었을 때, Max는 Ryan의 팔에 뛰어들었

다. E: Sheila와 Ryan은 그들의 고양이가 두 가족을 갖고 있는 것을 깨달았다. B: Ryan은 Sheila를 자신의 집으로 초대했다.

17 ① walked → walking

③ guessing → guess

④ does → doesn't

⑤ comes usually → usually comes

18 마지막에 "I met a good neighbor thanks to you!"의 문장으로 미루어 보아 정답은 ⑤가 적절하다.

19 ③은 일반동사 said의 목적어절이 필요하므로 접속사 that이 적절하다. ①, ②, ④, ⑤는 모두 부사절이고 의미상으로도 조건의 접속사 If[if]가 적절하다.

20 주어가 he이므로 'gets'로 쓰는 것이 적절하다.

21 Ryan checked outside, but he couldn't find him.(Ryan은 밖을 확인했지만, 그를 찾을 수 없었다.) 이 문장 다음에 He made posters and put them up around town.이 이어지므로 정답은 ④이다.

22 Bear는 아침에 나가서 저녁 먹는 시간에 맞추어 집에 돌아온다.

23 Bear를 소개하는 글이다. ② Bear는 누구인가? ① Bear의 탄생 ③ Bear의 친구, Ryan ④ Bear의 어린 시절 ⑤ Bear의 삶

24 ⓐ는 다음 문장에서 친구가 없다고 하였으므로 'lonely(외로운)' 또는 'bored(지루한)'가 적절하고, ⓑ는 Max가 친구가 되었다고 하였기에 'But(그러나)'이 적절하다.

25 동물 보호 센터에 관한 정보는 센터의 위치와 동물을 돌볼 자원봉사자가 필요하다는 내용만 알 수 있다.

26 조건의 접속사 if가 쓰인 절에서는 미래시제를 현재시제로 나타내고, 주절은 그대로 미래로 쓴다. 그러므로 정답은 ④가 가장 적절하다.

27 부가의문문은 동사와 주어로 이루어져 있고, 문장이 긍정문이면 부가의문문은 부정문을 사용하고, 부가의문문의 주어는 문장의 주어를 인칭대명사로 바꾸어 쓴다. Your cat comes → doesn't he, You lost → didn't you

28 Sheila가 Ryan 집에 Max가 저녁에만 온 것으로 추측하고 Ryan도 동의하는 것으로 보아, 반대로 Sheila의 집에는 낮에 왔다는 것을 알 수 있다.

Lesson 2 (중간) 2회

> **01** ② **02** ④ **03** ③ **04** ③ **05** ② **06** ② **07** ③
> **08** if you have time, please come in and have some cookies
> **09** ① **10** ④ **11** ② **12** ①
> **13** Can you make it at 8 a.m. at the Grand Park bus stop?
> **14** ③ **15** ① **16** ① **17** ③ **18** ①, ② **19** ②
> **20** ④ **21** ⑤ **22** ③ **23** ④ **24** ④ **25** ② **26** ⑤
> **27** ① **28** ①

01 ② I'm afraid not.은 거절의 표현이다. 이어지는 See you then.과 어울리지 않는다. I'm afraid not.을 No problem. 또는 Why not? 정도로 바꾸는 것이 적절하다.

02 Tom needs a big plastic bag this Saturday.

03 ① I will miss the bus if I am late.

② We will stay at home if it rains.

④ I will not go outside if it is cold tomorrow.

⑤ If you visit Hawaii, you can swim in the sea.

04 ① Ryan heard the doorbell ring(ing).

② Sheila saw Max sit(ting) under the desk.

④ I watched him play soccer with his friends.

⑤ She felt something touch(ing) her shoulder.

05 B. Did you hear him play the piano?

C. Parents listened to the children sing.

06 부가의문문은 동사와 주어로 이루어져 있고, 문장이 긍정문이면 부가의문문은 부정문을 사용하고, 부가의문문의 주어는 문장의 주어를 인칭대명사로 바꾸어 쓴다. Your cat comes → doesn't he, You lost → didn't you

07 Sheila의 추측에 "Yes! How did you know?"로 대답한 것으로 보아, Ryan은 그녀의 추측에 동의하였다는 것을 알 수 있다.

08 조건의 if절을 사용하여 문장을 완성한다.

09 빈칸 다음에 "This cat looks exactly like Max, it's so strange.(이것은 Max와 똑같아 보여, 그것은 정말 이상해.)"라고 한 것으로 미루어 보아, ① got very surprised(매우 놀랐다)가 가장 적절하다.

10 잃어버린 Bear를 찾았기 때문에 ④ joyful(기쁜)이 가장 적절하다. ① 슬픈 ② 화난 ③ 지루한 ⑤ 겁먹은

11 ① Nancy는 Alext의 이웃이다. ③ Alex와 Jina는 자원봉사에 대해 의논 중이다. ④ Jina는 이번 주 일요일 자원봉사활동을 할 예정이다. ⑤ Jina가 Alex에게 봉사활동을 권유했다.

12 동사 like와 전치사 at의 목적어로 쓰일 동명사 중에서, 자원봉사에 관련된 내용이므로 ① bothering(괴롭히기)은 어울리지 않는다.

13 약속을 정할 때 'make it (만나다, 약속을 정하다)'를 사용할 수 있다.

14 Miso가 1시에 버스 정류장에서 만날 것을 제안하였고, Hajun은 "How about 2?"라고 한 것으로 보아, Hajun이는 1시 제안을 거절해야 내용상 자연스럽다. ⓒ를 "I am afraid I can't." 정도로 바꾸어 쓰는 것이 적절하다.

15 계획을 나타낼 때 'plan to 동사원형', 'be planning to 동사원형', 'have a plan to 동사원형' 등을 사용한다. 빈칸 앞에 be동사가 있으므로 'planning to'가 오는 것이 적절하다.

16 ⓐ의 one은 앞서 나온 the animal care center를 의미하고, ⓑ는 동물들 씻기기를 잘한다는 내용이다. 바로 앞 문장에서 이웃 Nancy에게 물어보다고 하였으므로 ⓒ는 Nancy를 가리킨다.

17 ⓓ에 쓰인 'make it'은 '만나다, 시간을 정하다'의 뜻이다. ①, ②, ④, ⑤ 모두 '그것을 만들다'의 의미이다.

18 ③ I saw him play basketball with friends.
④ I watched Brian do(ing) a magic trick for children.
⑤ Did you see your brother close(closing) the window?

19 동사 'shoot'은 '쏘다, 촬영하다'는 뜻으로 문장과 어울리지 않는다. I tried to lose my weight.(나는 살을 빼려고 노력했다.)로 쓰는 것이 자연스럽다.

20 ⓐ는 '녹색 눈을 가진'의 의미로 전치사 with가 적절하고, ⓑ는 '뒤쫓아 다닌다'의 '(run) after'가 적절하다. ⓒ는 시간에 늦지 않게 온다는 'in (time)'이 적절하다.

21 주어진 문장은 '그러나, Cooper가 그녀의 집에 따라온 후, 그는 그녀에게 좋은 친구가 되어 주었다'라는 뜻이므로 "She had no friends there."라는 문장 다음에 오는 것이 가장 적절하다.

22 ③의 내용은 이 글에 나타나 있지 않다. ① Bear는 무엇을 하기 좋아했는가? ③ 왜 Charlotte은 이 마을에 이사를 왔는가? ② 왜 그 고양이는 Bear라는 이름을 갖게 되었는가? ④ 어떻게 Charlotte은 Cooper를 알게 되었는가? ⑤ Charlotte는 Michael과 얼마나 멀리 떨어져 살았는가?

23 B가 주말에 청소년 센터에서 춤 연습을 할 계획이라고 하였고, 그 다음에 같이 하자는 내용의 ⓒ와 그에 대한 대답인 ⓐ가 온다. ⓐ 문장에서 만나는 시간 약속을 1시에 제

안하였고, 2시로 변경을 청하는 ⓑ가 오는 것이 적절하다.

24 지각동사의 목적격보어는 원형부사 또는 현재분사를 쓴다. (I saw Amy read(ing) a book to the children.)

25 Jina는 이번 주 일요일에 animal care center에서 자원봉사를 할 예정이고, Alex에게 다른 친구와 함께 오라고 이야기한 것으로 보아, ⓑ는 'They need volunteers to take care of the animals.'로 쓰는 것이 적절하다.

26 Ryan과 Sheila는 이미 좋은 이웃 사이로 지내고 있는 것이 아니고, 이번에 서로 알게 되었다.

27 Bear가 사라져서 돌아오지 않는다는 내용이므로, ① '초조하고 걱정하는'이 가장 적절하다. ② 재밌고 신나는 ③ 고요하고 평화로운 ④ 즐겁고 유머러스한 ⑤ 지루하고 단조로운

28 ② He will pass the exam if he studies harder.
③ I will stay at home if it is cold this weekend.
④ If it is sunny tomorrow, I will take a walk in the park.
⑤ If he doesn't come back by 10, I will call the police.

Lesson 3 (기말)

1회

01 ②	02 ③	03 ⑤	04 ④	05 ④	06 ②	07 ①
08 ⑤	09 ④	10 ②	11 ③	12 ③	13 ④, ⑤	
14 ④	15 ②	16 Though[Although]		17 ④		
18 take		19 ④	20 ③	21 ③	22 ③	23 ③
24 ①	25 ②	26 ③				

01 본문에서 'those photos'라고 하였으므로 사진을 나타내는 ②가 정답이다. ② 셀피 ① 표지판 ③ 사건들 ④ 기억들 ⑤ 휴대전화

02 아버지가 딸에게 'you shouldn't climb up too high.'라고 하였으므로 ③은 대화의 내용과 맞지 않는다.

03 (A) 질문에 대한 대답인 'You shouldn't make any noise when you watch the birds.'로 미루어 보아 지켜야 할 것을 물어보는 ⑤가 적절하다. ① 얼마나 오래 우리는 새를 지켜보아야 하나요? ② 우리는 토요일에 몇 시에 만나야 하나요? ③ Bird watching을 위해 무엇을 가져와야 하나요? ④ 처음에 새들은 무엇을 먹어야 하나요?

04 ① He has just come back home.
② When did you talk with him?
③ He has lived here for ten years.
⑤ Has he tried Italian food many times?

05 '비록 그 당시에는 쉽지 않았지만'이 자연스러우므로, 정답은 ④가 가장 적절하다.

06 윤호의 글은 셀피를 위한 재밌는 장소에 관한 것이므로, ㄴ(특별한 박물관), ㄷ(재미있는 셀피들), ㅅ(세계적으로 유명한 장소들)이 관련된 표현으로 적절하다.

07 ⓐ는 명사 spots를 꾸며주는 형용사적 용법의 to부정사이다. ①은 명사 homework를 꾸며주는 형용사적 용법 ② 진주어로 쓰인 명사적 용법 ③, ⑤ 목적을 나타내는 부사적 용법 ④ 목적어로 쓰인 명사적 용법

08 주어진 문장의 those things는 글의 흐름상 글쓴이가 더 나은 학교생활을 위해 한 일들이다. 그러므로 학교생활을 위해 한 일의 열거가 끝나는 (E)가 주어진 문장의 위치로 가장 적절하다.

09 ④ 재미있는 셀피를 위한 유명 장소들 ① 과거의 셀피 ② 셀피를 위한 좋은 포즈들 ③ 셀피를 안전하게 찍기 위한 조언들 ⑤ 더 나은 학교생활을 위한 셀피들

10 ① 세계적으로 유명한 장소에서는 셀피를 찍을 수 있다. ③ 셀피 박물관에서는 그림을 만질 수 있다. ④ 사진 속 소년들은 실제로는 말을 타고 있지 않다. ⑤ 한국에는 여러 군데 셀피 박물관이 있다.

11 ③ 더 나은 학교생활을 위해 셀피 사용하기 ① 우리 생활에서 식물의 역할들 ② 독서의 중요성 ④ 학교 웹사이트 사용의 증가 ⑤ 학교에서 많은 종류의 꽃의 도입

12 셀피를 찍을 때 조심해야 한다는 내용이므로 ③의 '길을 건널 때 셀피를 찍어라.'는 빈칸에 적절하지 않다. ① 야생 동물 근처에서 포즈 잡기를 피해라. ② 위험한 장소에서 떨어져라. ④ 강으로 너무 가까이 가지 마라. ⑤ 위험한 물건들을 가지고 셀피를 찍지 마라.

13 ① 높은 곳에서 특별히 주의해야 한다.
② 지훈이는 셀피 안전에 관해 소개하고 있다.
③ 선생님을 도와드렸다.

14 'I've watered the plants and flowers at school for one month.'의 문장으로 미루어 보아 ④가 정답이다.

15 ② 셀피를 위한 재미있는 장소들 ① 과거의 셀피 ③ 셀피 안전 ④ 더 나은 학교생활을 위한 셀피들 ⑤ 학교 웹사이트에 셀피 게시하기

16 (A) 소년들은 정말로 말을 타고 있고 있지 않지만, 그렇게 보인다. (B) 남자가 단지 큰 붓을 들고 서 있지만, 그는 모나리자를 그리고 있는 것처럼 보인다. 내용상 '비록 ~일지라도'의 though나 although가 빈칸에 가장 적절하다.

17 ① 과거에도 셀피를 찍었다. ② 긴장돼 보였다. ③ 아마 처음일 것이다. ⑤ 한 달 동안 셀피에 관한 정보를 찾았다.

18 take a photograph[selfies] 사진을[셀피를] 찍다

19 '비록 그 당시에는 쉽지 않았지만'의 뜻이 가장 적절하다.

20 주어진 보기에서 그 사진을 학교 웹사이트에 올린다고 하였으므로, 'We can do good things at school and take selfies.' 문장의 다음 위치인 (C)가 보기의 위치로 가장 적절하다.

21 더 나은 학교생활을 위해 셀피를 이용하자는 내용이고 빈칸 뒤 목적어 'me'로 미루어 보아, 참여를 권유하는 ③이 정답이다.

22 ③ 더 나은 학교생활을 위해 셀피들을 이용하기 ① 식물과 꽃 기르기 ② 한 달 동안 좋은 일들을 하기 ④ 그 학생들의 셀피를 보기 ⑤ 학교 웹사이트에 학교생활을 게시하기

23 ⓐ 현재완료 시제의 문장이므로 과거분사가 필요하다.(heard) ⓑ 주어가 The students이므로 has가 아니라 have가 올바르다. ⓔ 2형식 동사 look의 보어로 형용사 nervous가 올바르다.

24 ② 한 달 반이 아닌 한 달이다.
③ 과거 사람들도 셀피를 찍었다.
④ 핸드폰이 아닌 거울을 사용했다.
⑤ 첫 번째 십대 셀피일 것이다.

25 (A)에는 2형식 동사의 보어의 위치이므로 형용사 'safe'가 적절하고, (B)는 '안전 팁'의 의미로 명사 'safety'가 적절하다.

26 'You should take special care when you take selfies in the wild or at high places like these.'의 문장으로 보아 야생에서는 특별히 조심해야 한다.

Lesson 3 (기말) [2회]

01 been	**02** ②	**03** ②	**04** ⑤	**05** ⑤	**06** ④
07 ①	**08** ①	**09** ②	**10** ①	**11** ①	**12** ①	**13** ⑤
14 ①	**15** ②	**16** ②	**17** ⑤	**18** ②	**19** ①	
20 ⓑ have	**21** ④	**22** ②	**23** ④	**24** ③	**25** ②	
26 ③						

01 현재완료의 문장이므로 빈칸에 과거분사가 필요하고, 두 번째 문장에서 '알프스에 가 본 적 있니?'라는 내용이 적절하므로 공통으로 들어갈 단어는 'been'이 가장 적절하다.

02 무슨 일이냐고 묻는 질문에 대한 대답으로 제주에 왔다고 설명하는 (B)가 온 다음, 올레를 아느냐고 질문한 것에 대한 대답인 (D) 문장이 오고, 가보고 싶다는 말에 사진을 보여주겠다고 한 (A)가 온 후, 걸으면서 사진을 찍는 것은 위험하다고 충고하는 (C)가 마지막으로 온다.

03 (A)는 현재완료시제로 '경험'을 묻는 문장이다.

ⓐ 나는 그 영화를 전에 본 적이 있다.(경험)

ⓑ 민주는 2015년 이후로 이 집에 살고 있다.(계속)

ⓒ 그녀는 전에 피아노 연주를 배워 본 적이 없다. (경험)

ⓓ Andy와 나는 3년간 친구로 지내고 있다.(계속)

04 ① She has gone to France.

② Anthony left the school 2 years ago.

③ Jenny has never lived in Sokcho until now.

④ Have you eaten hamburger in that restaurant?

05 민준이는 나중에 소민이에게 사진을 보내줄 것이다.

06 'Be careful! You shouldn't use your cell phone while you're walking.'이라고 한 것으로 미루어 보아 ④가 가장 적절하다.

07 10년 전부터 지금까지는 'for 10 years'로 표현하고 동사는 현재완료의 형태 'has+과거분사'를 쓴다.

08 빈칸 이후로 안전에 관한 조언이 이어지는 것으로 보아 ① '특별히 조심하다'가 빈칸에 가장 적절하다. ② 동물을 만진다 ③ 야생동물 근처로 간다 ④ 산을 더 높이 오른다 ⑤ 많은 동물들과 사진을 찍는다

09 (A)는 world-famous places의 예시를 열거하고 있으므로 like가 적절하고, (B)는 special museums의 예시를 설명하므로 For example이 적절하다. (C)는 '비록 그 남자는 단지 큰 붓을 들고 있지만'의 의미가 자연스러우므로 Though를 쓴다.

10 ① 유명한 장소에서 사진을 찍을 수 있다.

② 좋은 사진을 찍기 위해 카메라 트릭을 이용한다.

④ 셀피 박물관에서 카메라가 필요하다.

⑤ 춘천에 셀피 박물관이 있다.

11 현재완료로 질문한 경우 조동사 'have[has]'로 답해야 한다. Yes, she did. → Yes, she has.

12 ① 과거의 셀피들 ② 거울의 역사 ③ 좋은 사진을 찍는 방법 ④ 아나스타샤 공주: 그녀는 누구인가? ⑤ 세계 최초의 십대 모델

13 빈칸 ⓐ 앞에 재미있는 셀피를 위한 특별한 박물관에 방문할 수 있다고 했고, 그 다음에 필리핀에 있는 셀피 박물관을 소개한 것으로 보아 ⑤ '예를 들어'가 가장 적절하다. ① 그러나 ② 대신에 ③ 그러나 ④ 대조적으로

14 주어진 문장이 '두 개의 사진을 보라.'는 내용이므로 소년들과 남자의 사진을 설명하기 전인 (A) 위치로 가장 적절하다.

15 윤호는 훌륭한 사진을 찍기 위한 (a) '조언'과 셀피를 위한 (b) '재미있는 장소'를 소개했다.

16 주어진 보기에서 '그 사진들'을 학교 웹사이트에 올린다고 하였으므로, 'We can do good things at school and

take selfies.' 문장의 다음 위치인 (B)가 가장 적절하다.

17 ⑤ 더 나은 학교생활을 위한 셀피들

① 우리 생활에서의 셀피들

② 셀피 안전을 위한 조언

③ 셀피를 위한 좋은 장소

④ 좋은 셀피를 찍는 방법

18 윤호는 춘천에 있는 셀피 박물관에 가 본 적이 있다.

19 'Though the boys are not really riding horses'라는 앞 문장으로 미루어 보아, ①이 적절하다.

20 동사 has의 주어는 The students라는 복수 명사이므로 have로 쓰는 것이 올바르다.

21 글의 흐름상 '비록 그 당시에는 쉽지 않았겠지만'의 의미이므로, ④가 가장 적절하다.

22 ① 과거에도 셀피를 찍었다.

② 거울을 이용하여 셀피를 찍었다.

③ 긴장한 표정이었다.

④ 세계 최초인 것은 10대 셀피에 관한 내용이다.

23 글의 첫줄 'I think we can use selfies to make a better school life.'로 보아 '더 나은 학교생활을 위한 셀피'가 적절하다. ① 셀피를 찍는 훌륭한 팁 ② 학교 도서관의 규칙 ③ 더 악화된 학교생활을 만들기 ⑤ 학교 웹사이트에 있는 식물과 꽃들

24 'Here are some safety tips'로 미루어 보아 안전 수칙을 알려주기 위해 글을 썼다는 것을 알 수 있다.

25 사진 동아리의 이름은 글에 나타나 있지 않다.

26 ①, ②, ④, ⑤ 마음 ③ 꺼리다

Lesson 4 (기말) ^{1회}

```
01 ⑤   02 ②   03 ③   04 ①
05 which[that] you want to have      06 ④   07 ③
08 ④   09 ①   10 ④   11 ③   12 ②   13 ⑤   14 ②
15 ①   16 ③   17 ③   18 ①   19 ⑤
20 the warm egg, the sock puppet, the football
21 ④   22 ①   23 ④   24 ④   25 ⑤   26 ⑤
```

01 빈칸의 질문에 대한 답으로 'Yes, I do.'로 대답한 것으로 보아, ⑤가 가장 적절하다.

02 보기의 'Well'은 '글쎄요'라는 뜻으로 할 말을 생각할 때 쓰는 표현이다. ①. ③, ④, ⑤는 같은 상황에서 쓰는 표현이다.

03 ① We've been to Paris once. ② I have never studied Japanese. ④ Kate and I have done volunteer work many times. ⑤ Amy has played the piano since she was five years old.

04 ①은 주격 관계대명사이므로 생략할 수 없다. ②, ③, ⑤는 목적격 관계대명사로, ④는 '주격 관계대명사+be동사'로 생략이 가능하다.

05 This is the bike which[that] you want to have so much.

06 관계대명사 whom의 선행사는 사람이어야 한다. 선행사가 사물이므로 which 또는 that을 쓴다. ④ League of Legends is the game which[that] many students like.

07 ③ Ms. Cooper가 그녀의 과거를 기억하게 만들기 위해
① Wilfrid의 부모님을 기쁘게 하기 위해
② 그가 가진 것을 Ms. Cooper에게 팔기 위해
④ Ms. Cooper와 그 물건들을 사용해서 놀기 위해
⑤ 어느 물건을 Ms. Cooper가 갖기 원하는지 알기 위해

08 이 글의 초반에 Ms. Cooper가 'What a strange, sweet child!'라고 한 것으로 보아 어리둥절한 심정에서 후반부에 'The two smiled at each other. ~'라는 부분으로 미루어 보아 기뻐했음을 알 수 있다.

09 ② 마트가 아니라 이모의 정원에서 파란 달걀을 찾았다. ③ Cooper 할머니가 축구를 좋아하는지는 알 수 없다. ④ Wilfrid는 어린 소년이다. ⑤ 기억을 되살리기 위해 달걀을 가져갔다.

10 Wildfrid는 보육원이 아닌 요양원 근처에 사는 소년이다.

11 (A)는 좋아했다는 의미의 liked가 적절하고, (B)는 people이라는 선행사를 꾸며주는 주격 관계대명사 who가 적절하다.

12 hen: 암탉

13 He went into the hen house and took a fresh, warm egg from under a hen. Next he looked for his sock puppet. Finally, he found his football in his toy box.

14 장난감 상자에서 축구공을 찾은 사람은 Wilfrid이다.

15 'She bounced the football to Wilfrid and remembered him. "Wilfrid? Wilfrid Gordon Parker! My friend!'라고 한 부분으로 미루어 보아 정답은 ①이다.

16 ③ 기억의 다양한 의미
① 너를 행복하게 만드는 것
② 좋은 기억력을 유지하는 방법
④ 어떻게 사람들이 낮 시간을 즐기는가
⑤ 나의 삶에서 가장 중요한 것들

17 Ms. Cooper가 언제 그녀의 기억을 잃었는지는 이 글에 나타나 있지 않다.

18 선행사 a little boy와 all the people을 꾸며줄 관계대명사로 who가 적절하다.

19 ⓐ와 ⑤는 소유대명사이고, ①, ②, ③, ④는 대명사 he의 소유격이다.

20 ⓐ의 the things는 할머니의 과거를 찾기 위한 물건들이고, the warm egg, the sock puppet, the football이다.

21 ⓑ는 동사 held와 연결된 과거동사 whispered가 적절하고, ⓒ는 '~했던 것을 기억하다'로 해야 문맥상 자연스러우므로, remember의 목적어로 동명사가 오는 것이 올바르다.

22 Cooper 할머니는 Wilfrid가 가져온 물건을 하나씩 보면서 과거의 기억을 떠올리다가 마지막에 축구공을 보았을 때 Wilfrid를 기억해냈다. 그 물건들을 wonderful things라고 한 것으로 미루어 보아 좋아하지 않았다고 할 수 없다.

23 동사 told의 간접목적어(her)와 직접목적어(all his secrets)가 있으므로 that은 불필요하다.

24 ④ '왜 Wilfrid의 부모님은 Ms. Cooper를 좋아했는가?'는 이 글에서 알 수 없다. ① Wilfrid는 어디서 살았는가? ② Ms. Cooper에게 무슨 문제가 있었는가? ③ 누가 Wilfrid의 가장 좋아하는 사람이었는가? ⑤ Wilfrid는 요양원에 사는 사람들을 좋아했는가?

25 첫 번째 문장에서 Wilfrid가 요양원의 노인분들과 친구라는 내용 이후에 그 중 Ms. Cooper가 가장 좋아하는 사람이라는 내용의 (C)가 이어지고, 부모님에게 Ms. Cooper가 기억을 잃어버려서 Wilfrid가 기억의 의미를 묻는 (B)가 온 후 Wilfrid가 Ms. Cooper의 기억을 찾아 줄 물건을 찾는 (A)가 이어진다.

26 ⑤ 기억의 의미를 찾으려고 노력했다./그는 그녀의 기억을 되돌려주고 싶었다.
① 그의 비밀을 그녀에게 말했다./그것이 그에게 소중했다.
② 그의 양말 인형을 찾았다./그것은 온기를 가지고 있었다.
③ 그의 축구공을 찾았다./그것이 웃음을 가져다주었다.
④ 신선한 달걀을 가져왔다./그가 그것을 가장 좋아했다.

01 ⑤ 02 ④ 03 ④ 04 ④ 05 ⑤ 06 ④
07 Wilfred Gorden Parker was a little boy that lived next to the nursing home.
08 ④ 09 ② 10 ③ 11 ② 12 ④ 13 one by one
14 I watched a movie which[that] was very interesting.
15 ①, ③ 16 ② 17 ①, ③ 18 ③ 19 ②
20 ① 21 ② 22 ③ 23 ② 24 ③ 25 ④
26 she has lost her memory. 27 ④

01 ⑤ 'Lipa와 Billie가 Ms. Kang의 결혼식에서 무슨 노래를 부를 것인가?'는 이 글에서 알 수 없다.
  ① Ms. Kang은 누구인가?
  ② Ms. Kang은 모두에게 어떠했는가?
  ③ Ms. Kang은 다음 달에 무엇을 할 것인가?
  ④ Lipa와 Billie는 Ms. Kang을 위해 무엇을 할 예정인가?

02 '~만큼 …하다'는 동등비교 'as 원급 as'를 쓰고, 문장의 동사가 is이므로 형용사의 원급 serious를 쓴다.

03 작년의 현장학습에 관해 기억을 묻는 질문이고 빈칸에 대해 'Me, too.'로 대답한 것으로 보아 ④가 가장 적절하다.

04 목적격 관계대명사는 접속사와 목적어를 결합한 것으로, 목적어를 이중으로 쓰지 않도록 주의해야 한다. 또한, 목적어로 관계사를 만들었기에 바로 뒤에 주어와 동사가 이어진다. ⓐ This is a gold medal which we won at the race. ⓒ This is a painting that we bought at the market. ⓔ We took some pictures of Korean traditional dancers who[whom] we saw at the town festival.

05 ⓐ는 '물론이야.'의 뜻을 갖고 있고 바꾸어 쓸 수 있는 말은 'Sure.'이다.

06 그 안에 닭고기를 넣었다고 했으므로 대명사 it은 앞서 언급된 잡채를 지칭한다.

07 관계대명사 that이 선행사 a little boy를 뒤에서 꾸며주도록 문장을 완성한다.

08 ④ 그녀는 왜 요양원에서 살았는가? ① 그녀는 어디에 살았는가? ② 그녀에게 무슨 문제가 있었는가? ③ 왜 Wilfrid는 그녀를 가장 좋아했는가? ⑤ 무엇이 Wilfrid의 부모가 그녀가 불쌍하다고 생각하게 만들었는가?

09 마지막 대답에 'That's not right. It's pizza.'라고 말한 것으로 보아, 틀린 대답을 했고 동의를 구한 ②가 가장 적절하다.

10 a strange, sweet child처럼 형용사와 명사로 이루어진 경우 what으로 감탄문을 만든다.

11 글의 흐름상 '~ 덕분에'라는 thanks to를 쓰는 것이 적절하다.

12 '~했던 것을 기억하다'로 해야 문맥상 자연스러우므로, remember의 목적어로 동명사(performing)가 오는 것이 올바르다.

13 하나하나씩은 one by one으로 쓴다.

14 두 문장을 접속사로 연결했을 때 명사 a movie와 대명사 It이 같은 단어이므로, 접속사와 대명사 it을 합친 관계대명사 that이나 which를 사용하여 두 문장을 하나로 연결한다.

15 ⓐ는 과거에 있었던 일이므로 과거동사가 필요하고, ⓒ는 '~했던 것을 기억하다'로 해야 문맥상 자연스러우므로, remembered의 목적어로 동명사가 오는 것이 올바르다.
  ⓐ hold → held ⓒ to perform → performing

16 동사 'gave'는 4형식 동사로 간접목적어(~에게)와 직접목적어(~를) 2개의 목적어를 순서대로 취한다. 이를 3형식으로 바꿀 경우 '직접목적어 to 간접목적어'의 형태로 써야 한다. 그러므로 ⓑ는 'her the things' 또는 'the things to her'로 쓰는 것이 적절하다.

17 그녀의 미들 네임과 같은 미들 네임을 가진 소녀라는 의미로 써야 하므로 her middle name 또는 소유대명사 hers를 쓴다.

18 ① his sock puppet → a fresh, warm egg
  ② A fresh, warm egg → His football
  ④ she bounced the football to Wilfrid → she held the warm egg
  ⑤ couldn't → was able to

19 ① 그 뒤에/What 감탄문/미래 ② 그 다음/What 감탄문/과거 ③ 그 다음/ How 감탄문/미래 ④ 우선/How 감탄문/과거 ⑤ 우선/What 감탄문/과거

20 파란 달걀을 본 적이 있다.
  ② Wilfrid는 Ms. Cooper에게 한 번에 물건을 주었다.
  ③ Ms. Cooper는 Wilfrid에게 공을 차서 주었다.
  ④ Ms. Cooper의 여동생이 Ms. Cooper를 위해 인형극을 해주었다.
  ⑤ Ms. cooper는 그녀와 Wilfrid 사이의 비밀을 회상하지 못했다

21 ① 긴급한 ② 유쾌한 ③ 우울한 ④ 좌절한 ⑤ 절박한

22 이 글의 내용과 일치하는 문장은 4개이다.
  ⓐ 그들은 Ms. Lee의 생일파티를 열어주었다.
  ⓑ Ms. Lee는 혼자 살고 계신다.

ⓓ Ms. Lee는 카드 게임을 매우 잘하신다.

ⓔ 수진이는 할머니와 사진을 찍을 것이다.

23 'precious'는 '매우 귀중한'이라는 뜻이다. ② 귀중하거나 중요한

24 목적격 관계대명사는 생략이 가능하다. ⓐ, ⓑ, ⓓ, ⓔ는 모두 주격 관계대명사이고, 생략할 수 없다.

25 Wilfrid의 어머니가 생각하는 기억에 관한 내용은 글에 나타나 있지 않다. ④ Wilfrid의 어머니에게 기억이란 무엇인가? ① Wilfrid는 어디에 살았는가? ② 왜 Wilfrid는 Ms. Cooper를 좋아했는가? ③ Wilfrid는 기억에 관해 더 배우기 위해 무엇을 했는가? ⑤ Mr. Hunter에게 기억이란 무엇인가?

26 과거에 기억을 잃고 현재까지 기억을 하지 못하는 상태는 동사 'lose'를 현재완료 시제로 써서 표현한다.

27 ④ Ms. Park은 카드 게임에서 이긴 사람이다.

① Ms. Park은 Jasmin과 Genie를 그녀의 생일파티에 초대했다.

② Jasmin은 Ms. Park을 위해 약간의 음식을 만들었다.

③ Ms. Park은 잡채와 치킨 먹는 것을 좋아한다.

⑤ Jasmin과 Genie는 이번 주 토요일에 사진을 찍을 것이다.

MEMO